Chrysler Mini Pick-ups Automotive Repair Manual

by Curt Choate and John H Haynes Member of the Guild of Motoring Writers

Models covered:

1979 thru 1988 Dodge D-50/Ram Pick-up and D-50/Ram Sport Pick-up
Plymouth Arrow Pick-up and Arrow Sport Pick-up
Mitsubishi Pick-up
2.0 liter and 2.6 engines with 4-speed, 5-speed and automatic transmissions, two and four wheel drive

Does not include diesel engine information

ISBN 1 85010 536 7

ABCDE
FGHI

Printed in England *(11P2–556)*

Haynes Publishing Group
Sparkford Nr Yeovil
Somerset BA22 7JJ England

Haynes Publications, Inc
861 Lawrence Drive
Newbury Park
California 91320 USA

Library of Congress
Catalog card number
88–82111

Acknowledgements

We are grateful for the help and cooperation of Chrysler Motors Corporation, USA, who supplied technical information, certain illustrations and the vehicle photos and the Champion Spark Plug Company, who supplied the illustrations showing the various spark plug conditions.

About this manual

Its purpose

The purpose of this manual is to help you get the best value from your vehicle. It can do so in several ways. It can help you decide what work must be done even if you choose to get it done by a dealer service department or a repair shop; it provides information and procedures for routine maintenance and servicing; and it offers diagnostic and repair procedures to follow when trouble occurs.

It is hoped that you will use the manual to tackle the work yourself. For many simpler jobs, doing it yourself may be quicker than arranging an appointment to get the vehicle into a shop and making the trips to leave it and pick it up. More importantly, a lot of money can be saved by avoiding the expense the shop must pass on to you to cover its labor and overheads costs. An added benefit is the sense of satisfaction and accomplishment that you feel after having done the job yourself.

Using the manual

The manual is divided into Chapters. Each Chapter is divided into numbered Sections, which are headed in bold type between horizontal lines. Each Section consists of consecutively numbered paragraphs.

The two types of illustrations used (figures and photographs) are referenced by a number preceding their captions. Figure reference numbers denote Chapter and numerical sequence in the Chapter; i.e. Fig. 12.4 means Chapter 12, figure number 4. Figure captions are followed by a Section number which ties the figure to a specific portion of the text. All photographs apply to the Chapter in which they appear, and the reference number pinpoints the pertinent Section and paragraph.

Procedures, once described in the text, are not normally repeated. When it is necessary to refer to another Chapter, the reference will be given as Chapter and Section number; i.e. Chapter 1/16. Cross reference given without use of the word 'Chapter' apply to Sections and/or paragraphs in the same Chapter. For example, 'see Section 8' means in the same Chapter.

Reference to the left or right of the vehicle is based on the assumption that one is sitting in the driver's seat facing forward.

Even though extreme care has been taken during the preparation of this manual, neither the publisher nor the author can accept responsibility for any errors in, or omissions from, the information given.

Introduction to the
Dodge D-50/Plymouth Arrow mini-truck

Imported by Chrysler Corporation, the D-50 and Arrow are built by Mitsubishi Motors Corporation in Japan, and were first introduced to the fast-growing light truck market in the United States during the 1979 model year.

For 1979-80 there are two versions of the small truck, differentiated by engine displacement, transmission choice and trim. The lower-priced version features modest trim and a 1995 cc overhead cam, 4-cylinder engine with Silent Shaft, and either a 4-speed manual or automatic transmission. The more expensive version, the Sport, has fancier trim, a 2555 cc Silent Shaft engine, a choice of 5-speed manual or automatic transmission, radial tires, styled wheels and

bucket seats. In addition, the models built for the U.S.A. are equipped with the MCA Jet Valve, a pollution control system designed to help meet exhaust emissions standards.

For 1981, the vehicle is offered in three versions. The Dodge is available as the Ram 50 Custom, the Ram 50 Royal and the Ram 50 Sport. The Plymouth is available as the Arrow, Arrow Custom and Arrow Sport. The engine/transmission packages are identical to those offered in 1979-80, but the trim levels have been changed. In addition, a new 18-gallon gas tank comes as standard equipment on the Ram 50 Sport and Ram 50 Royal, Arrow Sport and Arrow Custom models and is available as an option on the Ram 50 Custom and the Arrow.

Contents

A   Chrysler mini-truck

General dimensions and capacities

Refer to Chapter 13 for specifications and information related to 1981 thru 1988 models

	Engines	
Dimensions	**9JL4U 0JI4U**	**9JP4W 0JP4W**
Overall length	184.6 in (4690 mm)	184.6 in (4690 mm)
Overall width	65.0 in (1650 mm)	65.0 in (1650 mm)
Overall height	58.5 in (1485 mm)	57.7 in (1465 mm)
Wheelbase	109.4 in (2780 mm)	109.4 in (2780 mm)
Gross weight		
With manual transmission	4045 lb (1835 kg)	4120 lb (1869 kg)
With automatic transmission	4085 lb (1853 kg)	4136 lb (1876 kg)
Payload	1400 lb (635 kg)	1400 lb (635 kg)
Capacities		
Fuel tank	15.1 US gal (12.6 Imp gal, 57.2 liters)	
Coolant		
U-engine	9.5 US qt (7.9 Imp qt, 9.0 liters)	
W-engine	9.7 US qt (8.1 Imp qt, 9.2 liters)	
Engine oil	3.97 US qt (3.25 Imp qt, 3.8 liters)	
with filter change	4.5 US qt (3.7 Imp qt, 4.3 liters)	
Manual transmission oil		
4-speed	2.2 US qt (1.9 Imp qt, 2.1 liters)	
5-speed	2.4 US qt (2.0 Imp qt, 2.3 liters)	
Automatic transmission fluid		
1979 models	6.8 US qt (5.6 Imp qt, 6.4 liters)	
1980 models	7.2 US qt (6.0 Imp qt, 6.8 liters)	
Rear axle/differential lubricant	1.4 US qt (1.1 Imp qt, 1.3 liters)	
Manual steering gearbox oil	0.27 US qt (0.23 Imp qt, 260 cc)	
Power steering system fluid		
separate reservoir	1.15 US qt (1060 cc)	
unit reservoir	1.0 US qt (930 cc)	

Buying spare parts and vehicle identification numbers

Buying spare parts

Spare parts are available from many sources, which generally fall into one of two categories – authorized dealer parts departments and independant retail auto parts stores. Our advice concerning spare parts is as follows:

Authorized dealer parts department: This is the best source for parts which are peculiar to your vehicle and not generally available elswhere (i.e. major engine parts, transmission parts, trim pieces, etc.). It is also the only place you should buy parts if your vehicle is still under warranty, as non-factory parts may invalidate the warranty. To be sure of obtaining the correct parts, have your vehicle's engine and chassis numbers available and, if possible, take the old parts along for positive identification.

Retail auto parts stores; Good auto parts stores will stock frequently needed components which wear out relatively fast (i.e.

clutch components, exhaust systems, brake parts, tune-up parts, etc.). These stores often supply new or reconditioned parts on an exchange basis, which can save a considerable amount of money. Discount auto parts stores are often very good places to buy materials and parts needed for general vehicle maintenance (i.e. oil, grease, filters, spark plugs, belts, touch-up paint, bulbs, etc.). They also usually sell tools and general accessories, have convenient hours, charge lower prices, and can often be found not far from your home.

Vehicle identification numbers

Regardless from which source parts are obtained, it is essential to provide correct information concerning the vehicle model and year of manufacture plus the engine serial number and the vehicle identification number (VIN). The accompanying illustrations show where these important numbers can be found.

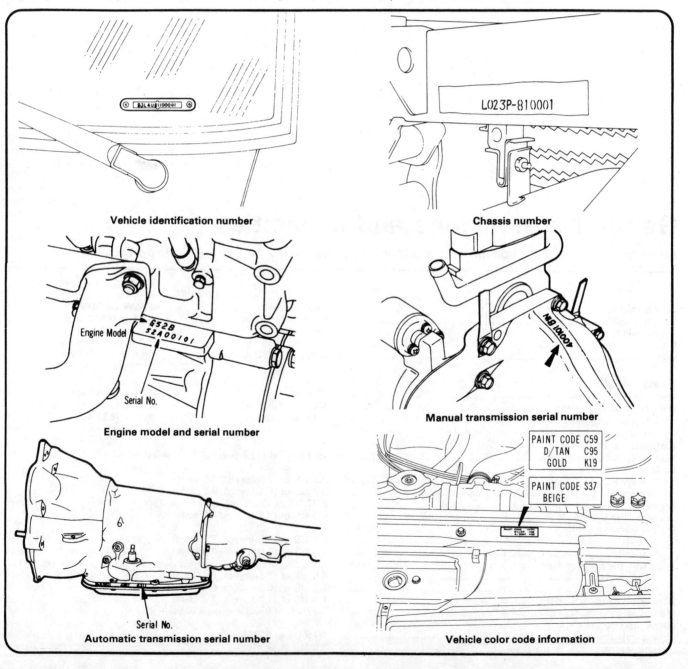

Vehicle identification number

Chassis number

Engine model and serial number

Manual transmission serial number

Automatic transmission serial number

Vehicle color code information

Maintenance techniques, tools and working facilities

Basic maintenance techniques

There are a number of techniques involved in maintenance and repair that will be referred to throughout this manual. Application of these techniques will enable the home mechanic to be more efficient, better organized and capable of performing the various tasks properly, which will ensure that the repair job is thorough and complete.

Fastening systems

Fasteners, basically, are nuts, bolts, pins or clamps used to hold two or more parts together. There are a few things to keep in mind when working with fasteners. Almost all of them use a locking device of some type; either a lock washer, lock nut, a key or thread adhesive. All threaded fasteners should be clean, straight, have undamaged threads and undamaged corners on the hex head where the wrench fits. Develop the habit of replacing all damaged nuts and bolts with new ones.

Rusted nuts and bolts should be treated with a rust penetrating fluid. Some mechanics use turpentine in a spout type oil can, a procedure which works quite well. After applying the rust penetrant, let it "work" for a few minutes before trying to loosen the nut or bolt. Badly rusted fasteners may have to be chiseled off or removed with a special nut breaker, available at tool stores.

Flat washers and lock washers, when removed from an assembly, should always be replaced exactly as removed. Replace any damaged washers with new ones. Always use a flat washer between a lock washer and any soft metal surface (such as aluminium) or thin sheet metal. Special lock nuts can only be used once or twice before they lose their locking ability and must be replaced.

If a bolt or stud breaks off in an assembly, it can be drilled out and removed with a special tool called an E-Z out. Most automotive machine shops can perform this task, as well as others (such as the repair of threaded holes that have been stripped out).

Torqueing sequences and procedures

When threaded fasteners are tightened down, they are tightened to a specific torque value (torque is basically a twisting force). Over tightening the fastener can weaken it and cause it to break, while under tightening can cause it to eventually come loose. Each bolt, depending on the material it's made of and the diameter of its shank, has a specified torque value. The size and strength of a bolt is determined by the job it must do. Small bolts are generally used in light duty applications, while larger ones are used for heavy duty requirements.

Throughout this manual, references are made to specific torque values for fasteners in various components or assemblies. Be sure to follow the torque recommendations closely. For fasteners not requiring a specific torque, a general torque value chart is presented as a guide.

Fasteners laid out in a pattern on an assembly (i.e. cylinder head bolts, oil pan bolts, differential cover bolts, etc.) must be loosened and torqued in a sequence to avoid warping the assembly. Initially, the bolts/nuts should go on finger tight only. Next, they should be tightened one full turn each, in a criss-cross or diagonal pattern. After each one has been tightened one full turn, return to the first one tightened and tighten them all one half turn, following the same pattern. Then tighten each of them one quarter turn at a time until each fastener has been torqued to the proper value. To loosen and remove as assembly, the procedure would be reversed.

Disassembly sequence

Component disassembly should be done with care and purpose to help ensure that the parts go back together properly with nothing left over. Always keep track of the sequence in which parts are removed. Make note of special characteristics or markings on parts than can be installed more than one way (such as a grooved thrust washer on a shaft). Its a good idea to lay the disassembled parts out on a clean surface in the order that they were removed.

When removing fasteners from an assembly, keep track of which ones belong in which location. Sometimes threading a bolt back in a part, or putting the washers and nut back on a stud, can prevent mixups later. If nuts and bolts cannot be returned to their original

locations, they should be kept in a compartmented box or a series of small boxes. A cupcake or muffin tin is ideal for this purpose, since each cavity can hold the bolts and nuts from a particular area (i.e. oil pan bolts, valve cover bolts, engine mount bolts, etc.). A pan of this type is especially helpful when working on assemblies with very small parts (such as the carburetor, alternator, valve train or interior dash and trim pieces). The cavities can be marked with paint or tape to identify the contents.

Whenever wiring looms, harnesses or connectors are separated, it's a good idea to identify them with numbered pieces of masking tape so that they can be easily reconnected.

Gasket sealing surfaces

Throughout any vehicle, gaskets are used to seal the mating surfaces between two parts and keep lubricants, fluids, vacuum or pressure contained in an assembly.

Many times these gaskets are coated with a liquid or paste type gasket sealing compound before assembly. Age, heat and pressure can sometimes cause the two parts to stick together so tightly that they are very difficult to separate. Often the assembly can be loosened by striking it with a soft-faced hammer near the mating surfaces. A regular hammer can be used if a block of wood is placed between the hammer and the part. Do not hammer on cast parts or parts that could be easily damaged. With any particularly stubborn part, always recheck to see that every fastener has been removed.

Avoid using a screwdriver or bar to pry apart an assembly, as they can easily mar the gasket sealing surfaces of the parts (which must remain smooth). If prying is absolutely necessary, use an old broom handle, but keep in mind that extra clean-up will be necessary if the wood splinters.

After the parts are separated, the old gasket must be carefully scraped off and the gasket surfaces cleaned. Stubborn gasket material can be soaked with rust penetrant or treated with a special chemical to soften it so that it can be easily scraped off. A scraper can be fashioned from a piece of copper tubing by flattening and sharpening one end. Copper is recommended because it is usually softer than the surfaces to be scraped, which reduces the chance of gouging the part. Some gaskets can be removed with a wire brush, but regardless of the method used, the mating surfaces must be left clean and smooth. If for some reason the gasket surface is gouged, then a gasket sealer thick enough to fill scratches will have to be used upon reassembly of the components. For most applications, a non-drying (or semi-drying) gasket sealer should be used.

Hose removal tips

Hose removal precautions closely parallel gasket removal precautions. Avoid scratching or gouging the surface that the hose mates against or the connection may leak. Because of various chemical reactions, the rubber in hoses can bond itself to the metal spigot that the hose fits over. To remove a hose, first loosen the hose clamps that secure it to the spigot. Then, with slip joint pliers, grab the hose at the clamp and rotate it around the spigot. Work it back and forth until it is completely free, then pull it off (silicone or other lubricants will ease removal if they can be applied between the hose and the spigot). Apply the same lubricant to the inside of the hose and the outside of the spigot to simplify installation.

If a hose clamp is broken or damaged, do not reuse it. Do not reuse hoses that are cracked, split or torn.

Tools

A selection of good tools is a basic requirement for anyone who plans to maintain and repair his or her own vehicle. For the owner who has few tools, if any, the initial investment might seem high, but when compared to the spiraling costs of routine maintenance and repair, it is a wise one.

To help the owner decide which tools are needed to perform the tasks detailed in this manual, the following tool lists are offered: *Maintenance and minor repair, Repair and overhaul* and *Special*. The newcomer to practical mechanics should start off with the *Mainten-*

ance and minor repair tool kit, which is adequate for the simpler jobs performed on a vehicle. Then, as his confidence and experience grow, he can tackle more difficult tasks, buying additional tools as they are needed. Eventually the basic kit will be built into the *Repair and overhaul* tool set. Over a period of time, the experienced do-it-yourselfer will assemble a tool set complete enough for most repair and overhaul procedures and will add tools from the *Special* category when he feels the expense is justified by the frequency of use.

Maintenance and minor repair tool kit

The tools in this list should be considered the minimum required for performance of routine maintenance, servicing and minor repair work. We recommend the purchase of combination wrenches (box end and open end combined in one wrench); while more expensive than open-ended ones, they offer the advantages of both types of wrench.

> Combination wrench set ($\frac{1}{4}$ in to 1 in or 6 mm to 19 mm)
> Adjustable wrench – 8 in
> Spark plug wrench (with rubber insert)
> Spark plug gap adjusting tool
> Feeler gauge set
> Brake bleeder wrench
> Standard screwdriver ($\frac{5}{16}$ in x 6 in)
> Phillips screwdriver (No 2 x 6 in)
> Combination pliers – 6 in
> Hacksaw and assortment of blades
> Tire pressure gauge
> Grease gun
> Oil can
> Fine emery cloth
> Wire brush
> Battery post and cable cleaning tool
> Funnel (medium size)
> Safety goggles
> Jack stands (2)
> Drain pan

If basic tune-ups are going to be a part of routine maintenance, it will be necessary to purchase a good quality stroboscopic timing light and a combination tachometer/dwell meter. Although they are included in the list of *Special* tools, they are mentioned here because they are absolutely necessary for tuning most vehicles properly.

Repair and overhaul tool set:

These tools are essential for anyone who plans to perform major repairs and are in addition to those in the *Maintenance and minor repair* tool kit. Included is a comprehensive set of sockets which, though expensive, will be found to be invaluable because of their versatility (especially when various extensions and drives are available). We recommend the $\frac{1}{2}$ in drive over the $\frac{3}{8}$ in drive. Although the larger drive is bulky and more expensive, it has the capability of accepting a very wide range of large sockets (ideally, the mechanic would have a $\frac{3}{8}$ in drive set and a $\frac{1}{2}$ in drive set).

> Socket set(s)
> Reversible ratchet
> Extension – 10 in
> Universal joint
> Torque wrench (same size drive as sockets)
> Ball pein hammer – 8 oz
> Soft-faced hammer (plastic/rubber)
> Standard screwdriver ($\frac{1}{4}$ in x 6 in)
> Standard screwdriver (stubby – $\frac{5}{16}$ in)
> Phillips screwdriver (No 3 x 8 in)
> Phillips screwdriver (stubby – No 2)
> Pliers – vise grip
> Pliers – lineman's
> Pliers – needle nose
> Pliers – circlip (internal and external)
> Cold chisel – $\frac{1}{2}$ in
> Scriber
> Scraper (made from flattened copper tubing)
> Center punch
> Pin punches ($\frac{1}{16}$, $\frac{1}{8}$, $\frac{3}{16}$ in)
> Steel rule/straight edge – 12 in
> Allen wrench set ($\frac{1}{8}$ to $\frac{3}{8}$ in or 4 mm to 10 mm)

> A selection of files
> Wire brush (large)
> Jack stands (second set)
> Jack (scissor or hydraulic type)

Another tool which is often useful is an electric drill motor with a chuck capacity of $\frac{3}{8}$ in (and a set of good quality drill bits).

Special tools

The tools in this list include those which are not used regularly, are expensive to buy, or which need to be used in accordance with their manufacturer's instructions. Unless these tools will be used frequently, it is not very economical to purchase many of them. A consideration would be to split the cost between yourself and a friend or friends. In addition, most of these tools can be obtained from a tool rental shop on a temporary basis.

This list contains only those tools and instruments widely available to the public, and not those special tools produced by vehicle manufacturers for distribution to dealer service departments. Occasionally, references to the manufacturer's special tools are included in the text of this manual. Generally, an alternative method of doing the job without special tool is offered. However, sometimes there is no alternative to their use. Where this is the case, and the tool cannot be purchased or borrowed, the work should be turned over to the dealer, a repair shop or an automotive machine shop.

> Valve spring compressor
> Piston ring compressor
> Cylinder ridge reamer
> Cylinder surfacing hone
> Balljoint separator
> Universal hub/bearing puller
> Impact screwdriver
> Micrometer(s) and/or dial calipers
> Dial indicator set
> Stroboscopic timing light
> Tachometer/dwell meter
> Universal electrical multi-meter
> Cylinder compression gauge
> Cable hoist
> Floor jack

Buying tools

For the do-it-yourselfer who is just starting to get involved in vehicle maintenance and repair, there are a couple of options available when purchasing tools. If maintenance and minor repair is the extent of the work to be done, the purchase of individual tools is satisfactory. If, on the other hand, extensive work is planned, it would be a good idea to purchase a modest tool set from one of the large retail chain stores. A set can usally be bought at a substantial savings over the individual tool prices (and they often come with a tool box). As additional tools are needed, add-on sets, individual tools and a larger tool box can be purchased to expand the tool selection. Building a tool set gradually allows the cost of the tools to be spread over a longer period of time and gives the mechanic the freedom to choose only those tools that will actually be used.

Tool stores will often be the only source of some of the special tools that are needed, but regardless of where tools are brought, try to avoid cheap ones (especially when buying screwdrivers and sockets) because they won't last very long. The expense involved in replacing cheap tools will eventually be greater than the initial cost of quality tools.

Care and maintenance of tools

Good tools are expensive, so it makes sense to treat them with respect. Keep them in a clean and usable condition and store them properly when not in use. Always wipe off any dirt, grease or metal chips before putting them away. Never leave tools lying around in the work area. Upon completion of a job, always check closely under the hood for tools that may have been left there (so they don't get lost during a test drive).

Some tools, such as screwdrivers, pliers, wrenches and sockets, can be hung on a panel mounted on the garage or workshop wall, while others should be kept in a tool box or tray. Measuring instruments, gauges, meters, etc. must be carefully stored where they cannot be damaged by weather or impact from other tools.

When tools are used with care and stored properly, they will last a very long time. Even with the best of care, tools will wear out if used frequently. When a tool is damaged or worn out, replace it; subsequent jobs will be safer and more enjoyable if you do.

For those who desire to learn more about tools and their uses, a book entitled *How to Choose and Use Car Tools* is available from the publishers of this manual.

Working facilities

Not to be overlooked when discussing tools is the workshop. If anything more than routine maintenance is to be carried out, some sort of suitable work area is essential.

It is understood and appreciated, that many home mechanics do not have a good workshop or garage available, and end up removing an engine or doing major repairs outside (it is recommended that the overhaul or repair be completed under the cover of a roof).

A clean, flat workbench or table of suitable working height is an absolute necessity. The workbench should be equipped with a vise that has a jaw opening of at least 4 inches.

As mentioned previously, some clean, dry storage space is also required for tools, as well as the lubricants, fluids, cleaning solvents, etc. which soon become necessary.

Sometimes waste oil and fluids, drained from the engine or transmission during normal maintenance or repairs, present a disposal problem. To avoid pouring oil on the ground or into the sewage system, simply pour the used fluids into large containers, seal them with caps and place them in a normal trash receptacle. Plastic jugs (such as old antifreeze containers) are ideal for this purpose.

Always keep a supply of old newspapers and clean rags available. Old towels are excellent for mopping up spills. Many mechanics use rolls of paper towels for most work because they are readily available and disposable. To help keep the area under the vehicle clean, a large cardboard box can be cut open and flattened to protect the garage or shop floor.

Whenever working over a painted surface (such as when leaning over a fender to service something under the hood), always cover it with an old blanket or bedspread to protect the finish. Vinyl covered pads, made especially for this purpose, are available at auto parts stores.

Jacking and Towing

The jack, jack handle and wheel wrench are stored under the seat. To gain access to them, slide the seat all the way forward and fold down the seat back. Keep in mind that the jack supplied with the vehicle is intended for use only in changing tires, not for repair work. If it is necessary to get under the vehicle for any reason, raise it and support it on jack stands.

The spare tire is stored under the rear portion of the pick-up bed.

To remove the spare tire from its storage location

Fit the jack handle into the lowering screw by inserting the end of the handle into the hole in the license plate bracket and pushing the handle all the way in until it engages the lowering screw.

Slip the wheel wrench through the end of the jack handle and turn the jack handle counterclockwise until the tire is lowered completely to the ground and the supporting chain is slack.

Disengage the holding bracket clip free the tire.

Reverse the procedure to return the spare tire to its stored position. Be sure that the valve stem is facing up and the lowering screw is tightened securely.

There are two jacking points on each side of the vehicle. Use the jack only at these locations.

To change a tire

Park on a level surface, set the parking brake and turn on the hazard warning lights.

Block the wheels on the side of the vehicle opposite the flat (to prevent rolling).

Automatic transmissions should be set in 'Park'; manual transmissions in 'Reverse'.

Pry off the center cap or wheel cover with the flat end of the wheel wrench.

Loosen the wheel nuts with the wrench, but do not remove them.

Using the jack handle, tighten the relief valve on the jack.

Fit the jack handle into the pressure piston by lining up the groove on the handle with the notch in the holder.

Place the jack under the jacking point nearest to the flat tire and raise the vehicle, by moving the jack handle up and down, until the flat tire just clears the ground.

Make sure the vehicle is stable and will not move or slip before continuing.

Remove the wheel nuts and the wheel.

Mount the spare tire in position and install the wheel nuts. The tampered side of the nut should be facing in.

Slowly loosen the relief valve on the jack and lower the vehicle to the ground.

Securely tighten the wheel nuts with the wrench, using a crisscross pattern. Reinstall the wheel cover or center cap.

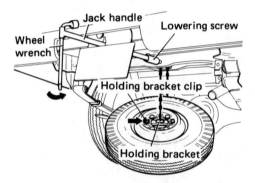

Removal of spare tire from storage location

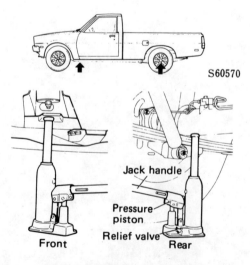

Jacking points/proper use of jack

Towing

Proper procedures must be followed to prevent damage to the vehicle during any towing operation. State and local laws applicable to vehicle towing must be followed.

Vehicles with manual transmission may be towed on all 4 wheels if there is no damage to the transmission, rear axle or steering system. If these components are damaged, a towing dolly must be used.

If the vehicle is equipped with an automatic transmission it can be towed with all 4 wheels on the ground for distances up to 15 miles, provided that there is no damage to the transmission, rear end or steering components. Vehicle speed must not exceed 30 mph (50 km/h). If there is no damage to the transmission or rear axle, the vehicle should be towed with the rear wheels off the ground or the driveshaft disconnected.

When towing, the gearshift lever or selector lever must be in the 'Neutral' position and the ignition key in the 'Acc' position. The power steering and power brake assist will not be available when the engine is not running.

Towing hooks have been provided at each side of the vehicle, just under the front bumper. A tow chain or strap can be attached at these points for vehicle towing. Make sure that the towing line is strong enough for the job, as serious injury can result when a chain or strap breaks or becomes disconnected while under load.

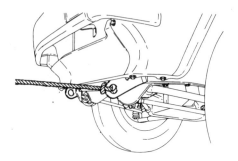

Location of towing points at the front of the vehicle

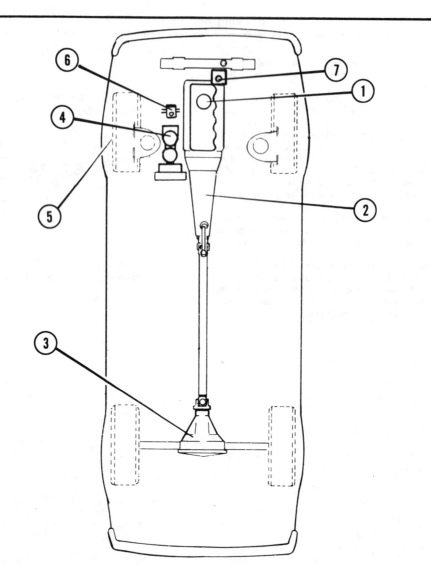

Recommended lubricants and fluids

Component or system	Grade or type
Engine (1)	
Above 32°F (0°C)	20W20
	20W40
	20W50
	10W30
	10W40
May be used as low as 10°F (−12°C)	10W30
	10W40
	10W50
	5W40
Consistently below 10°F (−12°C)	5W20
	5W30
	5W40
Manual transmission (2)	API Classification GL-4, GL-5
	SAE 80W or 75W-85W
Automatic transmission (2)	DEXRON II
Rear axle/differential (3)	API Classification GL-4, GL-5
Above −10°F (−23°C)	SAE 90W, 80W-90, 85W-90
−10° to −30°F (−23° to −34°C)	SAE 80W, 80W-90
Below −30°F (−34°C)	SAE 75W
Manual steering gearbox (6)	API Classification GL-5, SAE 90
Power steering reservoir (7)	DEXRON II
Brake fluid reservoir (4)	DOT 3 (SAE J1703)
Wheel bearings, etc. (5)	NLGI Grade 2 Multipurpose grease

Automotive chemicals and lubricants

A number of automotive chemicals and lubricants are available for use in vehicle maintenance and repair. They represent a wide variety of products ranging from cleaning solvents and degreasers to lubricants and protective sprays for rubber, plastic and vinyl.

Contact point/spark plug cleaner is a solvent used to clean oily film and dirt from points, grime from electrical connectors and oil deposits from spark plugs. It is oil free and leaves no residue. It can also be used to remove gum and varnish from carburetor jets and other orifices.

Carburetor cleaner is similar to contact point/spark plug cleaner but it is usually has a stronger solvent and may leave a slight oily residue. It is not recommended for cleaning electrical components or connections.

Brake system cleaner is used to remove grease or brake fluid from brake system components (where clean surfaces are absolutely necessary and petroleum-based solvents cannot be used); it also leaves no residue.

Silicone based lubricants are used to protect rubber parts such as hoses, weatherstripping and grommets, and are used as lubricants for hinges and locks.

Multi-purpose grease is an all purpose lubricant used wherever grease is more practical than a liquid lubricant such as oil. Some multi-purpose grease is colored white and specially formulated to be more resistant to water than ordinary grease.

Bearing grease/wheel bearing grease is a heavy grease used where increased loads and friction are encountered (i.e. wheel bearings, universal joints, etc.).

High temperature wheel bearing grease is designed to withstand the extreme temperatures encountered by wheel bearings in disc brake equipped vehicles. It usally contains molybdenum disulfide, which is a 'dry' type lubricant.

Gear oil (sometimes called gear lube) is a specially designed oil used in differentials, manual transmissions and manual gearboxes, as well as other areas where high friction, high temperature lubrication is required. It is available in a number of viscosities (weights) for various applications.

Motor oil, of course, is the lubricant specially formulated for use in the engine. It normally contains a wide variety of additives to prevent corrosion and reduce foaming and wear. Motor oil comes in various weights (viscosity ratings) of from 5 to 80. The recommended weight of the oil depends on the seasonal temperature and the demands on the engine. Light oil is used in cold climates and under light load conditions; heavy oil is used in hot climates and where high loads are encountered. Multi-viscosity oils are designed to have characteristics of both light and heavy oils and are available in a number of weights from 5W-20 to 20W-50.

Oil additives range from viscosity index improvers to slick chemical treatments that purportedly reduce friction. It should be noted that most oil manufacturers caution against using additives with their oils.

Gas additives perform several functions, depending on their chemical makeup. They usally contain solvents that help dissolve gum and varnish that build up on carburetor and intake parts. They also serve to break down carbon deposits that form on the inside surfaces of the combustion chambers. Some additives contain upper cylinder lubricants for valves and piston rings.

Brake fluid is a specially formulated hydraulic fluid that can withstand the heat and pressure encountered in brake systems. Care must be taken that this fluid does not come in contact with painted surfaces or plastics. An opened container should always be resealed to prevent contamination by water or dirt.

Undercoating is a petroleum-based tar-like substance that is designed to protect metal surfaces on the under-side of a vehicle from corrosion. It also acts as a sound deadening agent by insulating the bottom of the vehicle.

Weatherstrip cement is used to bond weatherstripping around doors, windows and trunk lids. It is sometimes used to attach trim pieces as well.

Degreasers are heavy duty solvents used to remove grease and grime that accumulates on engine and chassis components. They can be sprayed or brushed on and, depending on the type, are rinsed with either water or solvent.

Solvents are used alone or in combination with degreasers to clean parts and assemblies during repair and overhaul. The home mechanic should use only solvents that are non-flammable and that do not produce irritating fumes.

Gasket sealing compounds may be used in conjunction with gaskets, to improve their sealing capabilities, or alone, to seal metal-to-metal joints. Many gaskets can withstand extreme heat, some are impervious to gasoline and lubricants, while others are capable of filling and sealing large cavities. Depending on the intended use, gasket sealers either dry hard or stay relatively soft and pliable. They are usually applied by hand, with a brush, or are sprayed on the gasket sealing surfaces.

Thread cement is an adhesive locking compound that prevents threaded fasteners from loosening because of vibration. It is available in a variety of types for different applications.

Moisture dispersants are usually sprays that can be used to dry out electrical components such as the distributor, fuse block and wiring connectors. Some types can also be used as treatment for rubber and as a lubricant for hinges, cables and locks.

Waxes and polishes are used to help protect painted and plated surfaces from the weather. Different types of paint may require the use of different types of wax or polish. Some polishes utilize a chemical or abrasive cleaner to help remove the top layer of oxidized (dull) paint in older vehicles. In recent years, many non-wax polishes (that contain a wide variety of chemicals such as polymers and silicones) have been introduced. These non-wax polishes are usually easier to apply and last longer than conventional waxes and polishes.

Safety first!

Regardless of how enthusiastic you may be about getting on with the job at hand, take the time to ensure that your safety is not jeopardized. A moment's lack of attention can result in an accident, as can failure to observe certain simple safety precautions. The possibility of an accident will always exist, and the following points should not be considered a comprehensive list of all dangers. Rather, they are intended to make you aware of the risks and to encourage a safety conscious approach to all work you carry out on your vehicle.

Essential DOs and DON'Ts

DON'T rely on a jack when working under the vehicle. Always use approved jackstands to support the weight of the vehicle and place them under the recommended lift or support points.

DON'T attempt to loosen extremely tight fasteners (i.e. wheel lug nuts) while the vehicle is on a jack — it may fall.

DON'T start the engine without first making sure that the transmission is in Neutral (or Park where applicable) and the parking brake is set.

DON'T remove the radiator cap from a hot cooling system — let it cool or cover it with a cloth and release the pressure gradually.

DON'T attempt to drain the engine oil until you are sure it has cooled to the point that it will not burn you.

DON'T touch any part of the engine or exhaust system until it has cooled sufficiently to avoid burns.

DON'T siphon toxic liquids such as gasoline, antifreeze and brake fluid by mouth, or allow them to remain on your skin.

DON'T inhale brake lining dust — it is potentially hazardous (see *Asbestos* below)

DON'T allow spilled oil or grease to remain on the floor — wipe it up before someone slips on it.

DON'T use loose fitting wrenches or other tools which may slip and cause injury.

DON'T push on wrenches when loosening or tightening nuts or bolts. Always try to pull the wrench toward you. If the situation calls for pushing the wrench away, push with an open hand to avoid scraped knuckles if the wrench should slip.

DON'T attempt to lift a heavy component alone — get someone to help you.

DON'T rush or take unsafe shortcuts to finish a job.

DON'T allow children or animals in or around the vehicle while you are working on it.

DO wear eye protection when using power tools such as a drill, sander, bench grinder, etc. and when working under a vehicle.

DO keep loose clothing and long hair well out of the way of moving parts.

DO make sure that any hoist used has a safe working load rating adequate for the job.

DO get someone to check on you periodically when working alone on a vehicle.

DO carry out work in a logical sequence and make sure that everything is correctly assembled and tightened.

DO keep chemicals and fluids tightly capped and out of the reach of children and pets.

DO remember that your vehicle's safety affects that of yourself and others. If in doubt on any point, get professional advice.

Asbestos

Certain friction, insulating, sealing, and other products — such as brake linings, brake bands, clutch linings, torque converters, gaskets, etc. — contain asbestos. *Extreme care must be taken to avoid inhalation of dust from such products since it is hazardous to health.* If in doubt, assume that they *do* contain asbestos.

Fire

Remember at all times that gasoline is highly flammable. Never smoke or have any kind of open flame around when working on a vehicle. But the risk does not end there. A spark caused by an electrical short circuit, by two metal surfaces contacting each other, or even by static electricity built up in your body under certain conditions, can ignite gasoline vapors, which in a confined space are highly explosive. Do not, under any circumstances, use gasoline for cleaning parts. Use an approved safety solvent.

Always disconnect the battery ground (–) cable *at the battery* before working on any part of the fuel system or electrical system. Never risk spilling fuel on a hot engine or exhaust component.

It is strongly recommended that a fire extinguisher suitable for use on fuel and electrical fires be kept handy in the garage or workshop at all times. Never try to extinguish a fuel or electrical fire with water.

Fumes

Certain fumes are highly toxic and can quickly cause unconsciousness and even death if inhaled to any extent. Gasoline vapor falls into this category, as do the vapors from some cleaning solvents. Any draining or pouring of such volatile fluids should be done in a well ventilated area.

When using cleaning fluids and solvents, read the instructions on the container carefully. Never use materials from unmarked containers.

Never run the engine in an enclosed space, such as a garage. Exhaust fumes contain carbon monoxide, which is extremely poisonous. If you need to run the engine, always do so in the open air, or at least have the rear of the vehicle outside the work area.

If you are fortunate enough to have the use of an inspection pit, never drain or pour gasoline and never run the engine while the vehicle is over the pit. The fumes, being heavier than air, will concentrate in the pit with possibly lethal results.

The battery

Never create a spark or allow a bare light bulb near the battery. The battery normally gives off a certain amount of hydrogen gas, which is highly explosive.

Always disconnect the battery ground (–) cable *at the battery* before working on the fuel or electrical systems.

If possible, loosen the filler caps or cover when charging the battery from an external source. Do not charge at an excessive rate or the battery may burst.

Take care when adding water and when carrying a battery. The electrolyte, even when diluted, is very corrosive and should not be allowed to contact clothing or skin.

Always wear eye protection when cleaning the battery to prevent the caustic deposits from entering your eyes.

Household current

When using an electric power tool, inspection light, etc., which operates on household current, always make sure that the tool is correctly connected to its plug and that, where necessary, it is properly grounded. Do not use such items in damp conditions and, again, do not create a spark or apply excessive heat in the vicinity of fuel or fuel vapor.

Secondary ignition system voltage

A severe electric shock can result from touching certain parts of the ignition system (such as the spark plug wires) when the engine is running or being cranked, particularly if components are damp or the insulation is defective. In the case of an electronic ignition system, the secondary system voltage is much higher and could prove fatal.

Troubleshooting

Contents

---

1 Engine will not rotate when attempting to start

1   Battery terminal connections loose or corroded. Check the cable terminals at the battery; tighten or clean corrosion as necessary.
2   Battery discharged or faulty. If the cable connectors are clean and tight on the battery posts, turn the key to the 'On' position and switch on the headlights and/or windshield wipers. If these fail to function, the battery is discharged.
3   Automatic transmission not fully engaged in 'Park' or manual transmission clutch not fully depressed.

4   Broken, loose or disconnected wiring in the starting circuit. Inspect all wiring and connectors at the battery, starter solenoid and ignition switch (on steering column).
5   Starter motor pinion jammed on flywheel ring gear. If manual transmission, place gearshift in gear and rock the car to manually turn the engine. Remove starter (Chapter 5) and inspect pinion and flywheel (Chapter 2) at earliest convenience.
6   Starter solenoid faulty (Chapter 5).
7   Starter motor faulty (Chapter 5).
8   Ignition switch faulty (Chapter 10).

2 Engine rotates but will not start

1   Fuel tank empty.
2   Battery discharged (engine rotates slowly). Check the operation of electrical components as described in previous Section (see Chapter 1).
3   Battery terminal connections loose or corroded. See previous Section.
4   Carburetor flooded and/or fuel level in carburetor incorrect. This will usually be accompanied by a strong fuel odor from under the hood. Wait a few minutes, depress the accelerator pedal all the way to the floor and attempt to start the engine.
5   Choke control inoperative (Chapters 1 and 4).
6   Fuel not reaching carburetor. With ignition switch in 'Off' position, open hood, remove the top plate of air cleaner assembly and observe the top of the carburetor (manually move choke plate back if necessary). Have an assistant depress accelerator pedal fully and check that fuel spurts into carburetor. If not, check fuel filter (Chapters 1 and 4), fuel lines and fuel pump (Chapter 4).
7   Excessive moisture on, or damage to, ignition components (Chapter 1).
8   Worn, faulty or incorrectly adjusted spark plugs (Chapter 1).
9   Broken, loose or disconnected wiring in the starting circuit (see previous Section).
10 Distributor loose, affecting ignition timing. Turn the distributor body as necessary to start the engine, then set ignition timing as soon as possible (Chapter 1).
11 Broken, loose or disconnected wires at the ignition coil, or faulty coil (Chapter 5).

3 Starter motor operates without rotating engine

1   Starter pinion sticking. Remove the starter (Chapter 5) and inspect.
2   Starter pinion or engine flywheel teeth worn or broken. Remove the inspection cover at the rear of the engine and inspect.

4 Engine hard to start when cold

1   Battery discharged or low. Check as described in Section 1.
2   Choke control inoperative or out of adjustment (Chapters 1 and 4).
3   Carburetor flooded (see Section 2).
4   Fuel supply not reaching the carburetor (see Section 2).
5   Carburetor dirty or worn and in need of overhauling (Chapter 4).

5 Engine hard to start when hot

1   Choke sticking in the closed position (Chapter 1).
2   Carburetor flooded (see Section 2).
3   Air filter in need of replacement (Chapter 1).
4   Fuel not reaching the carburetor (see Section 2).

6 Starter motor noisy or excessively rough in engagement

1   Pinion or flywheel gear teeth worn or broken. Remove the inspection cover at the rear of the engine and inspect.
2   Starter motor retaining bolts loose or missing.

7 Engine starts but stops immediately

1   Loose or faulty electrical connections at distributor, coil or alternator.
2   Insufficient fuel reaching the carburetor. Disconnect the fuel line at the carburetor and remove the filter (Chapter 1). Place a container under the disconnected fuel line. Ground the wire coming out of the coil tower. Have an assistant crank the engine several revolutions by turning the ignition key. Observe the flow of fuel from the line. If little or none at all, check for blockage in the lines and/or replace the fuel pump (Chapter 4).
3   Vacuum leak at the gasket surfaces or the intake manifold and/or carburetor. Check that all mounting bolts (nuts) are tightened to specifications and all vacuum hoses connected to the carburetor and manifold are positioned properly and are in good condition.

8 Engine 'lopes' while idling or idles erratically

1   Vacuum leakage. Check mounting bolts (nuts) at the carburetor and intake manifold for tightness. Check that all vacuum hoses are connected and are in good condition. Use a docter's stethoscope or a length of fuel line hose held against your ear to listen for vacuum leaks while the engine is running. A hissing sound will be heard. A soapy water solution will also detect leaks. Check the carburetor and intake manifold gasket surfaces.
2   Leaking EGR valve or plugged PCV valve (see Chapter 6).
3   Air cleaner clogged and in need of replacement (Chapter 1).
4   Fuel pump not delivering sufficient fuel to the carburetor (see Section 7).
5   Carburetor out of adjustment (Chapter 4).
6   Leaking head gasket. Perform a compression check.
7   Timing chain or gears worn and in need of replacement (Chapter 2).
8   Camshaft lobes worn, necessitating the removal of the camshaft for inspection (Chapter 2).

9 Engine misses at idle speed

1   Spark plugs faulty or not gapped properly (Chapter 1).
2   Faulty spark plug wires (Chapter 1).
3   Carburetor choke not operating properly (Chapter 1).
4   Sticking or faulty emissions systems (see Chapter 6).
5   Clogged fuel filter and/or foreign matter in fuel. Remove the fuel filter (Chapter 1) and inspect.
6   Vacuum leaks at carburetor, intake manifold or at hose connections. Check as described in Section 8.
7   Incorrect idle speed (Chapter 1) or idle mixture (Chapter 4).
8   Incorrect ignition timing (Chapter 1).
9   Uneven or low cylinder compression. Remove plugs and use compression tester as per manufacturer's instructions.

10 Engine misses throughout speed range

1   Carburetor fuel filter clogged and/or impurities in the fuel system (Chapter 1). Also check fuel output at the carburetor (see Section 7).
2   Faulty or incorrectly gapped spark plugs (Chapter 1).
3   Incorrectly set ignition timing (Chapter 1).
4   Cracked distributor cap, disconnect distributor wires, or damage to the distributor components (Chapter 1).
5   Leaking spark plug wires (Chapter 1).
6   Emissions system components faulty (see Chapter 6).
7   Low or uneven cylinder compression pressures. Remove spark plugs and test compression with gauge.
8   Weak or faulty ignition coil.
9   Weak or faulty electronic ignition system (EIS) (see Chapter 5).
10 Vacuum leaks at carburetor, intake manifold or vacuum hoses (see Section 8).

11 Engine stalls

1   Carburetor idle speed incorrectly set (Chapter 1).
2   Carburetor fuel filter clogged and/or water and impurities in the fuel system (Chapter 1).
3   Choke improperly adjusted or sticking (Chapter 1).
4   Distributor components damp, damage to distributor cap, rotor, etc. (Chapter 1).
5   Emissions system components faulty (see Chapter 6).
6   Faulty or incorrectly gapped spark plugs (Chapter 1). Also check spark plug wires (Chapter 1).
7   Vacuum leak at the carburetor, intake manifold or vacuum hoses. Check as described in Section 8.
8   Valve lash incorrectly set (Chapter 2).

12 Engine lacks power

1 Incorrect ignition timing (Chapter 1).
2 Excessive play in distributor shaft. Check for faulty distributor cap, wires, etc. (Chapter 1).
3 Faulty or incorrectly gapped spark plugs (Chapter 1).
4 Carburetor not adjusted properly or excessively worn (Chapter 4).
5 Weak coil (Chapter 5).
6 Faulty EIS system coil (Chapter 5).
7 Brakes binding (Chapters 1 and 9).
8 Automatic transmission fluid level incorrect, causing slippage (Chapter 1).
9 Manual transmission clutch slipping (Chapter 1).
10 Fuel filter clogged and/or impurities in the fuel system (Chapter 1).
11 Emissions control systems not functioning properly (see Chapter 6).
12 Use of sub-standard fuel. Fill tank with proper octane fuel.
13 Low or uneven cylinder compression pressures. Test with compression tester, which will also detect leaking valves and/or blown head gasket.

13 Engine backfires

1 Emissions systems not functioning properly (see Chapter 6).
2 Ignition timing incorrect (Section 1).
3 Carburetor in need of adjustment or worn excessively (Chapter 4).
4 Vacuum leak at carburetor, intake manifold or vacuum hoses. Check as described in Section 8.
5 Valve lash incorrectly set, and/or valves sticking (Chapter 2).

14 Pinging or knocking engine sounds on hard acceleration or uphill

1 Incorrect grade of fuel. Fill tank with fuel of the proper octane rating.
2 Ignition timing incorrect (Chapter 1).
3 Carburetor in need of adjustment (Chapter 4).
4 Improper spark plugs. Check plug type with that specified on tune-up decal located inside engine compartment. Also check plugs and wires for damage (Chapter 1).
5 Worn or damaged distributor components (Chapter 1).
6 Faulty emissions systems (see Chapter 6).
7 Vacuum leak. (Check as described in Section 8).

15 Engine diesels (continues to run) after switching off

1 Idle speed too fast (Chapter 1).
2 Ignition timing incorrectly adjusted (Chapter 1).
3 Excessive engine operating temperatures. Probable causes of this are: malfunctioning thermostat, clogged radiator, faulty water pump (Chapter 3).

Engine electrical

16 Battery will not hold a charge

1 Alternator drive belt defective or not adjusted properly (Chapter 1).
2 Electrolyte level too low or too weak (Chapter 1).
3 Battery terminals loose or corroded (Chapter 1).
4 Alternator not charging properly (Chapter 5).
5 Loose, broken or faulty wiring in the charging circuit (Chapter 5).
6 Short in vehicle circuitry causing a continual drain on battery.
7 Battery defective internally.

17 Ignition light fails to go out

1 Fault in alternator or charging circuit (Chapter 5).
2 Alternator drive belt defective or not properly adjusted (Chapter 1).

18 Ignition light fails to come on when key is turned

1 Ignition light bulb faulty (Chapter 10).
2 Alternator faulty (Chapter 5).
3 Fault in the printed circuit, dash wiring or bulb holder (Chapter 10).

Engine fuel system

19 Excessive fuel consumption

1 Dirty or choked air filter element (Chapter 1).
2 Incorrectly set ignition timing (Chapter 1).
3 Choke sticking or improperly adjusted (Chapter 1).
4 Emissions systems not functioning properly
5 Carburetor idle speed and/or mixture not adjusted properly (Chapters 1 and 4).
6 Carburetor internal parts excessively worn or damaged (Chapter 4).
7 Low tire pressure or incorrect tire size (Chapter 1).

20 Fuel leakage and/or fuel odor

1 Leak in a fuel feed or vent line (Chapter 6).
2 Tank overfilled. Fill only to automatic shut-off.
3 EECS emissions system filter in need of replacement (Chapter 6).
4 Vapor leaks from EECS system lines (Chapter 6).
5 Carburetor internal parts excessively worn or out of adjustment (Chapter 4).

Engine cooling system

21 Overheating

1 Insufficient coolant in system (Chapter 1).
2 Fan belt defective or not adjusted properly (Chapter 1).
3 Radiator core blocked or radiator grille dirty and restricted (Chapter 3).
4 Thermostat faulty (Chapter 3).
5 Freewheeling clutch fan not functioning properly. Check for oil leakage at the rear of the cooling fan, indicating the need for replacement (Chapter 3).
6 Radiator cap not maintaining proper pressure. Have cap pressure tested by gas station or repair shop.
7 Ignition timing incorrect (Chapter 1).
8 Inaccurate temperature gauge (Chapter 10).

22 Overcooling

1 Thermostat faulty (Chapter 3).
2 Inaccurate temperature gauge (Chapter 10).

23 External water leakage

1 Deteriorated or damaged hoses. Loose clamps at hose connections (Chapter 1).
2 Water pump seals defective. If this is the case, water will drip from the 'weep' hole in the water pump body (Chapter 3).
3 Leakage from radiator core or header tank. This will require the radiator to be professionally repaired (see Chapter 3 for removal procedures).
4 Engine drain plugs or water jacket freeze plugs leaking (see Chapters 2 and 3).

24 Internal water leakage

Note: *Internal coolant leaks can usually be detected by examining the oil. Check the dipstick and inside of valve cover for water deposits and an oil consistency like that of a milkshake.*
1 Faulty cylinder head gasket. Have the system pressure-tested professionally or remove the cylinder heads (Chapter 2) and inspect.

2   Cracked cylinder bore or cylinder head. Dismantle engine and inspect (Chapter 2).

25 Water loss

1   Overfilling system (Chapter 1).
2   Coolant boiling away due to overheating (see causes in Section 15).
3   Internal or external leakage (see Sections 22 and 23).
4   Faulty radiator cap. Have the cap pressure-tested.

26 Poor coolant circulation

1   Inoperative water pump. A quick test is to pinch the top radiator hose closed with your hand while the engine is idling, then let loose. You should feel a surge of water if the pump is working properly (Chapter 3).
2   Restriction in cooling system. Drain, flush and refill the system (Chapter 1). If it appears necessary, remove the radiator (Chapter 3) and have it reverse-flushed or professionally cleaned.
3   Fan drive belt defective or not adjusted properly (Chapter 1).
4   Thermostat sticking (Chapter 3).

Clutch

27 Fails to release (pedal pressed to the floor – shift lever does not move freely in and out of reverse)

1   Improper linkage adjustment (Chapter 8).
2   Clutch disc hub spline worn.
3   Clutch disc warped, bent or excessively damaged (Chapter 8).

28 Clutch slips (engine speed increases with no increase in road speed)

1   Linkage in need of adjustment (Chapter 8).
2   Clutch disc oil-soaked or facing worn. Remove disc (Chapter 8) and inspect.
3   Clutch disc not seated in. It may take 30 or 40 normal starts for a new disc to seat.

29 Grabbing (shuddering) on engagement

1   Oil on clutch disc facings. Remove disc (Chapter 8) and inspect. Correct any leakage source.
2   Worn or loose engine or transmission mounts. These units may move slightly when clutch is released. Inspect mounts and bolts.
3   Worn splines on clutch gear. Remove clutch components (Chapter 8) and inspect.
4   Warped pressure plate or flywheel. Remove clutch components and inspect.

30 Squeal or rumble with clutch fully engaged (pedal released)

1   Improper adjustment; no lash (Chapter 8).
2   Release bearing binding on transmission bearing retainer. Remove clutch components (Chapter 8) and check bearing. Remove any burrs or nicks, clean and relubricate before reinstallation.
3   Weak linkage return spring. Replace the spring.

31 Squeal or rumble with clutch fully disengaged (pedal depressed)

1   Worn, faulty or broken release bearing (Chapter 8).
2   Worn or broken pressure plate springs (or diaphragm fingers) (Chapter 8).

32 Clutch pedal stays on floor when disengaged

1   Bind in linkage or release bearing. Inspect linkage or remove clutch components as necessary.
2   Linkage springs being over-traveled. Adjust linkage for proper lash. Make sure proper pedal stop (bumper) is installed.

Manual transmisssion

Note: *All the following section references contained within Chapter 7.*

33 Noisy in neutral with engine running

1   Input shaft bearing worn (Sections 11 – 14).
2   Damaged main drive gear bearing (Sections 11 – 14).
3   Worn countergear bearings (Sections 11 – 14).
4   Worn or damaged countergear anti-lash plate (Sections 11 – 14).

34 Noisy in all gears

1   Any of the above causes, and/or:
2   Insufficient lubricant (see checking procedure in Chapter 1).

35 Noisy in one particular gear

1   Worn, damaged or chipped gear teeth for that particular gear (Section1 11 – 14).
2   Worn or damaged synchronizer for that particular gear (Sections 11 – 14).

36 Slips out of high gear

1   Transmission loose on clutch housing. (Section 3).
2   Damaged mainshaft pilot bearing (Section 10).
3   Dirt between transmission case and clutch housing, or misalignment of transmission (Section 10).
4   Worn or improperly adjusted linkage (Section 2).

37 Difficulty in engaging gears

1   Clutch not releasing fully. (see clutch adjustment, Chapter 8).
2   Synchronizers worn/damaged.

38 Fluid leakage

1   Excessive amount of lubricant in transaxle (see Chapter 1 for correct checking procedures. Drain lubricant as required).
2   Pan loose or gasket damaged (Sections 7 – 9).
3   Rear oil seal or speedometer oil seal in need of replacement (Section 6).

Automatic transmission

Note: *Due to the complexity of the automatic transmission, it is difficult for the home mechanic to properly diagnose and service this component. For problems other than the following, the vehicle should be taken to a reputable mechanic.*

39 Fluid leakage

1   Automatic transmission fluid is a deep red color, and fluid leaks should not be confused with engine oil which can easily be blown by airflow to the transmission.
2   To pinpoint a leak, first remove all built-up dirt and grime from around the transmission. Degreasing agents and/or steam cleaning will achieve this. With the underside clean, drive the car at low speeds

so the airflow will not blow the leak far from its source. Raise the car and determine where the leak is coming from. Common areas of leakage are:

a) Fluid pan: tighten mounting bolts and/or replace pan gasket as necessary (see Chapter 1).

b) Rear extension: tighten bolts and/or replace oil seal as necessary (Chapter 8).

c) Filler pipe: replace the rubber oil seal where pipe enters transmission case.

d) Transmission oil lines: tighten connectors where lines enter transmission case and/or replace lines.

e) Vent pipe: transaxle over-filled and/or water in fluid (see checking procedures, Chapter 1).

f) Speedometer connector: replace the O-ring where speedometer cable enters transmission case.

40 Hard or rough selector lever operation

1 Selector lever improperly adjusted
2 Control rod and control arm improperly connected.
3 Detent plate worn.
4 Selector lever rod end pin worn.
5 Control arm shaft overtightened.

41 Transmission will not downshift with accelerator pedal pressed to the floor

1 Throttle valve body not working properly or leaking fluid.
2 Incorrect throttle linkage adjustment.
3 Kickdown servo valve or linkage malfunction.
4 Governor malfunction.

42 Engine will start in gears other than 'P' (Park) or 'N' (Neutral)

1 Inhibitor switch improperly adjusted.
2 Defective inhibitor switch.

43 Transmission slips, shifts rough, is noisy or has no drive in forward or reverse gears

1 There are many probable causes for the above problems, but the home mechanic should concern himself only with one possibility: fluid level.
2 Before taking the vehicle to a specialist, the level and condition of the fluid should be checked as described in Chapter 1. Correct the fluid level as necessary or change the fluid and filter if needed. If the problems persist, have a specialist diagnose the probable cause.

Driveshaft

44 Leakage of fluid at front of driveshaft

1 Defective transmission rear oil seal. See Chapter 7 for replacing procedures. While this is done, check the splined yoke for burrs or a rough condition which may be damaging the seal. If found, these can be dressed with crocus cloth or a fine dressing stone.

45 Knock or clonk when transmission is under initial load (just after transmission is put into gear)

1 Loose or disconnected rear suspension components. Check all mounting bolts and bushings (Chapter 1).
2 Loose driveshaft bolts. Inspect all bolts and nuts and tighten to torque specifications (Chapter 8).
3 Worn or damaged universal joint bearings. Test for wear (Chapter 8).

46 Metallic grating sound consistent with road speed

1 Pronounced wear in the universal joint bearings. Test for wear (Chapter 8).

47 Vibration

Note: *Before it can be assumed that the driveshaft is at fault, make sure the tires are perfectly balanced and perform the following test.*

1 Install a tachometer inside the car to monitor engine speed as the car is driven. Drive the car and note the engine speed at which the vibration (roughness) is most pronounced. Now shift the transmission to a different gear and bring the engine speed to the same point.
2 If the vibration occurs at the same engine speed (rpm) regardless of which gear the transmission is in, the driveshaft is NOT at fault, since the driveshaft speed varies.
3 If the vibration decreases or is eliminated when the transmission is in a different gear at the same engine speed, refer to the following probable causes.
4 Bent or dented driveshaft. Inspect and replace as necessary (Chapter 8).
5 Undercoating or built-up dirt, etc, on the driveshaft. Clean the shaft thoroughly and test.
6 Worn universal joint bearings. Remove and inspect (Chapter 8).
7 Driveshaft and/or companion flange out of balance. Check for missing weights on the shaft. Remove driveshaft (Chapter 8) and reinstall 180 from original position. Retest. Have driveshaft professionally balanced if problem persists.

Rear axle

48 Noise – same when in drive as when vehicle is coasting

1 Road noise. No corrective procedures available.
2 Tire noise. Inspect tires and tire pressures (Chapter 1).
3 Front wheel bearings loose, worn or damaged (Chapter 1).

49 Vibration

1 See probable causes under 'Driveshaft'. Proceed under the guidelines listed for the driveshaft. If the problem persists, check the rear wheel bearings by raising the rear of the car and spinning the wheels by hand. Listen for evidence of rough (noisy) bearings. Remove and inspect (Chapter 8).

50 Oil leakage

1 Pinion oil seal damaged (Chapter 8).
2 Axle shaft oil seals damaged (Chapter 8).
3 Differential inspection cover leaking. Tighten mounting bolts or replace the gasket as required (Chapter 1).

Brakes
Note: *Before assuming a brake problem exists, check: that the tires are in good condition and are inflated properly (see Chapter 1); that front end alignment is correct; and that the vehicle is not loaded with weight in an unequal manner.*

51 Vehicle pulls to one side under braking

1 Defective, damaged or oil-contaminated disc pad on one side. Inspect as described in Chapter 1. Refer to Chapter 9 if replacement is required.
2 Excessive wear of brake pad material or disc on one side. Inspect and correct as necessary.
3 Loose or disconnected front suspension components. Inspect and tighten all bolts to specifications (Chapter 1).
4 Defective caliper assembly. Remove caliper and inspect for stuck piston or damage (Chapter 9).

52 Noise (high pitched squeak without brake applied)

1 Front brake pads worn out. This noise comes from the wear sensor rubbing against the disc. Replace pads with new ones immediately (Chapter 9).

53 Excessive brake pedal travel

1   Partial brake system failure. Inspect entire system (Chapter 1) and correct as required.
2   Insufficient fluid in master cylinder. Check (Chapter 1) and add fluid and bleed system if necessary.
3   Rear brakes not adjusting properly. Make a series of starts and stops while the vehicle is in 'R' (Reverse). If this does not correct the situation remove drums and inspect self-adjusters (Chapter 1).

54 Brake pedal appears spongy when depressed

1   Air in hydraulic lines. Bleed the brake system (Chapter 9).
2   Faulty flexible hoses. Inspect all system hoses and lines. Replace parts as necessary.
3   Master cylinder mountings insecure. Inspect master cylinder bolts (nuts) and torque tighten to specifications.
4   Master cylinder faulty (Chapter 9).

55 Excessive effort required to stop vehicle

1   Power brake servo not operating properly (Chapter 9).
2   Excessively worn linings or pads. Inspect and replace if necessary (Chapter 1).
3   One or more caliper pistons (front wheels) or wheel cylinders (rear wheels) seized or sticking. Inspect and rebuild as required (Chapter 9).
4   Brake linings or pads contaminated with oil or grease. Inspect and replace as required (Chapter 1).
5   New pads or linings fitted and not yet 'bedded in'. It will take some time for the new material to seat against the drum (or rotor).

56 Pedal travels to floor with little resistance

1   Little or no fluid in the master cylinder caused by: leaking wheel cylinder(s); leaking caliper piston(s); loose or damaged or disconnected brake lines. Inspect entire system and correct as necessary.

57 Brake pedal pulsates during brake application

1   Wheel bearings not adjusted properly or in need of replacement (Chapter 1).
2   Caliper not sliding properly due to improper installation or obstructions. Remove and inspect (Chapter 9).
3   Rotor not within specifications. Remove the rotor (Chapter 9) and check for excessive lateral run-out and parallelism. Have the rotor professionally machined or replace it with a new one.

Suspension and steering

58 Vehicle pulls to one side

1   Tire pressures uneven (Chapter 1).
2   Defective tire (Chapter 1).
3   Excessive wear in suspension or steering components (Chapter 1).
4   Front end in need of alignment. Take vehicle to a qualified specialist.
5   Front brakes dragging. Inspect braking system as described in Chapter 1.

59 Shimmy, shake or vibration

1   Tire or wheel out of balance or out of round. Have professionally balanced.

2   Loose, worn or out-of-adjustment wheel bearings (Chapter 1).
3   Shock absorbers and/or suspension components worn or damaged (Chapter 11).

60 Excessive pitching and/or rolling around corners or during braking

1   Defective shock absorbers. Replace as a set (Chapter 11).
2   Broken or weak coil springs and/or suspension components. Inspect as described in Chapter 11.

61 Excessively stiff steering

1   Lack of lubricant in steering box (manual) or power steering fluid reservoir (Chapter 1).
2   Incorrect tire pressures (Chapter 1).
3   Lack of lubrication at steering joints (Chapter 1).
4   Front end out of alignment.
5   See also Section 62: Lack of power assistance.

62 Excessive play in steering

1   Loose wheel (Chapter 1).
2   Excessive wear in suspension or steering components (Chapter 1).
3   Steering gear out of adjustment (Chapter 11).

63 Lack of power assistance

1   Steering pump drive belt faulty or not adjusted properly (Chapter 1).
2   Fluid level low (Chapter 1).
3   Hoses or pipes restricting the flow. Inspect and replace parts as necessary.
4   Air in power steering system. Bleed system (Chapter 11).

64 Excessive tire wear (not specific to one area)

1   Incorrect tire pressures (Chapter 1).
2   Tires out of balance. Have professionally balanced.
3   Wheels damaged. Inspect and replace as necessary.
4   Suspension or steering components excessively worn (Chapter 1).

65 Excessive tire wear on outside edge

1   Inflation pressures not correct (Chapter 1).
2   Excessive speed on turns.
3   Front end alignment incorrect (excessive toe-in). Have professionally aligned.
4   Suspension arm bent or twisted.

66 Excessive tire wear on inside edge

1   Inflation pressures incorrect (Chapter 1).
2   Front end alignment incorrect (toe-out). Have professionally aligned.
3   Loose or damaged steering components (Chapter 1).

67 Tire tread worn in one place

1   Tires out of balance. Balance tires professionally.
2   Damaged or buckled wheel. Inspect and replace if necessary.
3   Defective tire.

Chapter 1 Tune-up and routine maintenance

Refer to Chapter 13 for specifications and information related to 1981 thru 1988 models

Contents

Specifications

Note: *Additional specifications and torque figures can be found in each individual Chapter.*

Engine oil capacity .... 4.5 US qt (4.3 liters) with new filter

Coolant system capacity
U-engine .... 9.5 US qt (9.0 liters)
W-engine .... 9.7 US qt (9.2 liters)

Firing order .... 1 – 3 – 4 – 2

Spark plug type and gap .... See Chapter 5

Ignition timing .... See Tune-up decal on underside of hood or Chapter 5

Clutch pedal free play
1979 models .... 0.8 to 1.0 in (20 to 25 mm)
1980 models .... 0.8 to 1.4 in (20 to 35 mm)

Valve clearances (engine hot)
Intake and Jet Valve .... 0.006 in (0.15 mm)
Exhaust valve .... 0.010 in (0.25 mm)

Compression pressure .... 149 psi

Alternator and power steering pump belt tension (deflection) .... $\frac{1}{4}$ to $\frac{3}{8}$ in (7 to 10 mm)

Torque specifications

	ft-lb	Nm
Oil pan drain plug	44 to 57	(59 to 78)
Spark plugs	18 to 21	(25 to 28)
Manual transmission		
Drain plug	43	(59)
Fill plug	22 to 25	(30 to 34)
Automatic transmission pan bolts	12.5	(16.9)
Rear axle		
Inspection/fill plug	29 to 43	(39 to 59)
Drain plug	43 to 50	(59 to 68)
Wheel nuts	51 to 58	(69 to 78)
Valve cover bolts	4 to 5	(5 to 6)

1 Introduction

This Chapter was designed to help the home mechanic maintain his (or her) vehicle for peak performance, economy, safety and longevity.

On the following pages you will find a maintenance schedule along with Sections which deal specifically with each item on the schedule. Included are visual checks, adjustments and item replacements.

Servicing your vehicle using the time/mileage maintenance schedule and the sequenced sections will give you a planned program of maintenance. Keep in mind that it is a full plan, and maintaining only a few items at the specified intervals will not give you the same results.

You will find as you service your vehicle that many of the procedures can, and should, be grouped together due to the nature of the job at hand. Examples of this are as follow:

If the vehicle is fully raised for a chassis lubrication, for example, this is the ideal time for the following checks: manual transaxle fluid, exhaust system, suspension, steering and the fuel system.

If the tires and wheels are removed, as during a routine tire rotation, go ahead and check the brakes and wheel bearings at the same time.

If you must borrow or rent a torque wrench, it would be advisable to service the spark plugs and repack (or replace) the wheel bearings all in the same day to save time and money.

The first step of this or any maintenance plan is to prepare yourself before the actual work begins. Read through the appropriate sections for all work that is to be performed before you begin. Gather together all necessary parts and tools. If it appears you could have a problem during a particular job, don't hesitate to ask advice from your local parts man or dealer service department.

Routine maintenance intervals

The following recommendations are given with the assumption that the vehicle owner will be doing the maintenance or service work (as opposed to a dealer service department). They are based on factory service/maintenance recommendations, but the time and/or mileage intervals have been shortened, in most cases, to ensure that the service is thorough and complete.

When the vehicle is new, it should be serviced initially by a factory authorized dealer service department to protect the factory warranty. In most cases the initial maintenance check is done at no cost to the owner.

Every 250 miles or weekly – whichever comes first

Check the engine oil level (Section 2).
Check the engine coolant level (Section 2).
Check the windshield washer fluid level (Section 2).
Check the battery water level (if equipped with removable vent caps) (Section 2).
Check the tires and tire pressures (Section 3).
Check the automatic transmission fluid level (Section 2).
Check the power steering fluid level (Section 2).

Every 3750 miles or 6 months – whichever comes first

Change engine oil and filter (Section 4).
Lubricate the chassis components (Section 5).
Check the cooling system (Section 6).
Check the exhaust system (Section 7).
Check the suspension and steering components (Section 8).
Check and adjust (if necessary) the engine drive belts (Section 9).
Check the fuel system components (Section 10).
Check the brake master cylinder fluid level (Section 2).
Check the manual transmission fluid level (Section 2).
Check the rear axle fluid level (Section 2).
Replace the air filter (Section 11).

Every 7500 miles or 12 months – whichever comes first

Check the clutch pedal free-play (manual transmission only) (Section 12).
Rotate the tires (Section 13).
Check and adjust (if necessary) the engine idle speed (Section 14).
Replace the fuel filter (Section 15).
Check and adjust (if necessary) the engine ignition timing (Section 16).
Check the operation of the choke (Section 17).
Change rear axle fluid (if vehicle is used to pull a trailer) (Section 18).
Check disc brake pads for wear.

Every 15 000 miles or 12 months – whichever comes first

Replace the spark plugs (Section 19).
Check and repack the front wheel bearings (perform this procedure whenever brakes are relined, regardless of maintenance interval) (Section 21).
Change the automatic transmission fluid and filter (if mainly driven under following conditions: heavy city traffic in hot-climate regions; in hill or mountain areas; frequent trailer pulling (Section 22).
Check the braking system (Section 23).
Check the spark plug wires (Section 24).
Drain, flush and refill the cooling system (Section 25).
Check and adjust valve clearances (Section 20).
Check and adjust Jet Valve clearances (Section 20).

Every 30 000 miles or 24 months – whichever comes first

Change the rear axle fluid (if vehicle is used to pull a trailer, change at 7500 miles) (Section 18).
Change the automatic transmission fluid and filter (if driven under abnormal conditions, see 15 000 miles servicing) (Section 22).
Check the EECS emissions system and replace the charcoal canister (Section 26).
NOTE: *Maintenance procedures and intervals for most emission control system components are covered in Chapter 6.*
Change the brake fluid in the entire brake system (Chapter 9).

2 Fluid levels check

1 There are a number of components on a vehicle which rely on the use of fluids to perform their job. Through the normal operation of the vehicle, these fluids are used up and must be replenished before damage occurs. See the Recommended Lubricants Section for the specific fluid to be used when adding is required. When checking fluid levels, it is important that the vehicle is on a level surface.

Engine oil

2 The engine oil level is checked with a dipstick which is located at the side of the engine block. This dipstick travels through a tube and into the oil pan at the bottom of the engine.

3 The oil level should be checked preferably before the vehicle has been driven, or about 15 minutes after the engine has been shut off. If the oil is checked immediately after driving the vehicle, some of the oil will remain in the upper engine components, thus giving an inaccurate reading on the dipstick.

4 Pull the dipstick from its tube (photo) and wipe all the oil from the end with a clean rag. Insert the clean dipstick all the way back into the oil pan and pull it out again. Observe the oil at the end of the dipstick. At its highest point, the level should be between the 'Add' and 'Full' marks.

5 It takes approximately 1 quart of oil to raise the level from the 'Add' mark to the 'Full' mark on the dipstick. Do not allow the level to drop below the 'Add' mark, as this may cause engine damage due to oil starvation. On the other hand, do not overfill the engine by adding oil above the 'Full' mark, as this may result in oil-fouled spark plugs, oil leaks or oil seal failures.

6 Oil is added to the engine after removing a twist-off cap located on the rocker arm cover. An oil can spout or funnel will reduce spills as the oil is poured in.

7 Checking the oil level can also be an important preventative maintenance step. If you find the oil level dropping abnormally, it is an indication of oil leakage or internal engine wear which should be corrected. If there are water droplets in the oil, or if it is milky-looking, this also indicates component failure and the engine should be checked immediately. The condition of the oil can also be checked along with the level. With the dipstick removed from the engine, take your thumb and index finger and wipe the oil up the dipstick, looking for small dirt particles or engine filings which will cling to the dipstick (photo). This is an indication that the oil should be drained and fresh oil added (Section 4).

Engine coolant

8 Most vehicles are equipped with a pressurized coolant recovery system which makes coolant level checks very easy. A clear or white coolant reservoir, attached to the inner fender panel, is connected by a hose to the radiator cap. As the engine heats up during operation, coolant is forced from the radiator, through the connecting tube and into the reservoir. As the engine cools, this coolant is automatically drawn back into the radiator to keep the level correct.

9 The coolant level should be checked when the engine is cold. Merely observe the level of fluid in the reservoir, which should be between the 'Low' and the 'Full' marks on the side of the reservoir (photo). If the system is completely cooled, also check the level in the radiator by removing the cap.

10 If your particular vehicle is not equipped with a coolant recovery system, the level should be checked by removing the radiator cap. However, the cap should not under any circumstances be removed while the system is hot, as escaping steam could cause serious injury. Wait until the engine has completely cooled, then wrap a thick cloth around the cap and turn it to its first stop. If any steam escapes from the cap, allow the engine to cool further. Then remove the cap and check the level in the radiator. It should be about 1 in below the bottom of the filler neck.

11 If only a small amount of coolant is required to bring the system up to the proper level, regular water can be used. However, to maintain the proper antifreeze/water mixture in the system, both should be mixed together to replenish a low level. High-quality antifreeze offering protection to -20° should be mixed with water in the proportion specified on the container. Do not allow antifreeze to come in contact with your skin or painted surfaces of the car. Flush contacted areas immediately with plenty of water.

12 On systems with a recovery tank, coolant should be added to the

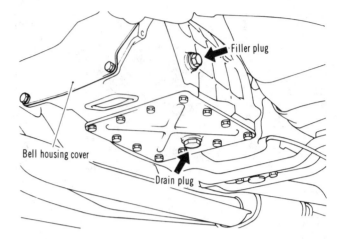

Fig. 1.1 The oil level in the manual transmission should be even with the bottom of the filler plug hole (Sec 2)

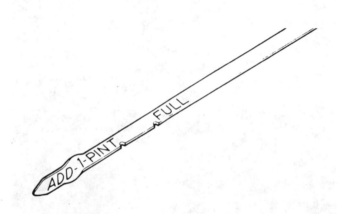

Fig. 1.2 The automatic transmission fluid level should be between the 'Full' and 'Add 1 pint' marks on the dipstick (Sec 2)

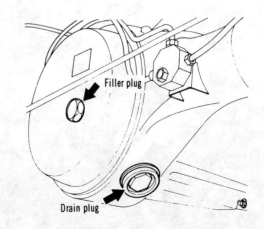

Fig. 1.3 The oil level in the rear axle should be even with the bottom of the filler plug hole (Sec 2)

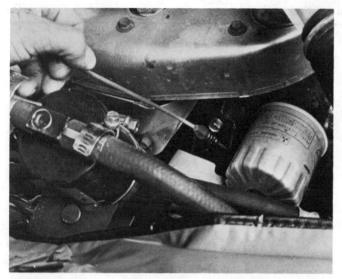

2.4 The oil dipstick is located on the right side of the engine, just to the rear of the oil filter

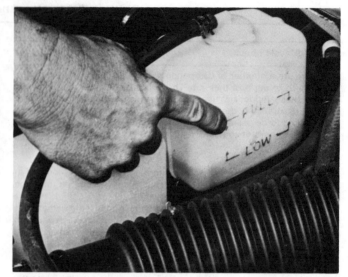

2.9 The coolant level in the reservoir tank should be between the 'Low' and 'Full' marks

2.18 The battery electrolyte level should be checked periodically (add only distilled water if the level is low)

2.22 Make sure the brake fluid level is between the maximum and minimum lines on the reservoir at all times

2.51 Correct power steering fluid level is vital for proper steering system operation

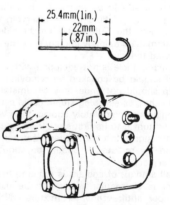

Fig. 1.4 A dipstick must be fabricated from a piece of wire to check the manual steering gearbox oil level (Sec 2)

resevoir after removing the cap at the top of the reservoir. Coolant should be added directly into the radiator on systems without a coolant recovery check.

13 As the coolant level is checked, observe the condition of the coolant. It should be relatively clear. If the fluid is brown or a rust color, this is an indication that the system should be drained, flushed and refilled (Section 29).

14 If the cooling system requires repeated additions to keep the proper level, have the radiator pressure cap checked for proper sealing ability. Also check for leaks in the system (cracked hoses, loose hose connections, leaking gaskets, etc.).

Windshield washer

15 The fluid for the windshield washer system is located in a plastic reservoir. The level inside the reservoir should be maintained at the 'Full' mark.

16 A good quality washer solvent should be added through the plastic cap whenever replenishing is required. Do not use plain water alone in this system, especially in cold climates where the water could freeze.

Battery

17 There are certain precautions to be taken when working on or near the battery: a) Never expose a battery to open flame or sparks which could ignite the hydrogen gas given off by the battery; b) Wear protective clothing clothing and eye protection to reduce the possibility of the corrosive surface acid solution inside the battery harming you; if the fluid is splashed or spilled, flush the contacted area immediately with plenty of water); c) Remove all metal jewelry which could contact the positive terminal and another grounded metal source, thus causing a short circuit; d) Always keep batteries and battery acid out of the reach of chidren.

18 The caps on the top of the battery should be removed periodically to check for a low water level. This check will be more critical during the warm summer months.

19 Remove each of the caps and add distilled water to bring the level of each cell to the split ring in the filler opening.

20 At the same time the battery water level is checked, the overall condition of the battery and its related components should be inspected. If corrosion is found on the cable ends or battery terminals, remove the cables and clean away all corrosion using a baking soda/water solution or a wire brush cleaning tool designed for this purpose. See Chapter 5 for complete battery care and servicing.

Brake fluid reservoir

21 The brake fluid reservoir is located on the left side on the engine compartment, just above the fender well.

22 Check that the brake fluid level is between the upper and lower level markings on the reservoir (photo). If it is low, you will have to add brake fluid to bring it up to the proper level.

23 Before removing the cap on the reservoir, use rag to clean all dirt and grease from around the cap area. If any foreign matter enters the reservoir with the cap removed, blockage in the brake system lines can occur. Also, make sure all painted surfaces around the resevoir are covered, as brake fluid will ruin paintwork.

24 Carefully lift the cap off the cylinder and set it aside, taking care not to set it on a painted surface.

25 Carefully pour the specified brake fluid into the reservoir to bring it up to the proper level. Be careful not to spill the fluid on painted surfaces. Be sure the specified fluid is used, as mixing different types of brake fluid can cause damage to the system (see Recommended Lucricants and Fluids or your owner's manual). Note: Change the brake fluid every 2 years (30 000 miles) as described in Chapter 9.

26 At this time the fluid and reservoir can be inspected for contamination. Normally, the braking system will not need periodic draining and refilling, but if rust deposits, dirt particles or water droplets are seen in the fluid, the system should be dismantled, drained and refilled with fresh fluid.

27 Reinstall the reservoir cap. Make sure the lid is properly seated to prevent fluid leakage and/or system pressure loss.

28 The brake fluid in the reservoir will drop slightly as the brake shoes or pads at each wheel wear down during normal operation. If it requires repeated replenishing to keep it at the proper level, this is an indication of leakage in the brake system which should be corrected immediately. Check all brake lines and their connections, along with the wheel cylinders and booster (see Chapter 9 for more information).

29 If upon checking the reservoir fluid level you discover that one or both reservoirs is empty or nearly empty, the braking system should be bled (Chapter 9). When the fluid level gets low, air can enter the system and should be removed by bleeding the brakes.

Manual transmission

30 Manual transmissions do not have a dipstick. The fluid level is checked by removing a plug in the left side of the transmission case. Locate this plug and use a rag to clean the plug and the area around it.

31 With the vehicle components cold, remove the plug. If fluid immediately starts leaking out, thread the plug back into the transmission because the fluid level is all right. If there is no fluid leakage, completely remove the plug and place your little finger inside the hole. The fluid level should be just at the bottom of the plug hole.

32 If the transmission needs more fluid, use a syringe to squeeze the appropriate lubricant into the plug hole to bring the fluid up to the proper level.

33 Thread the plug back into the transmission and tighten it securely. Drive the vehicle and check for leaks around the plug.

Automatic transmission

34 The fluid inside the transmission must be at normal operating temperature to get an accurate reading on the dipstick. This is done by driving the vehicle for several miles, making frequent starts and stops to allow the transmission to shift through all gears.

35 Park the vehicle on a level surface. With the parking brake engaged and the engine idling, select each gear momentarily, ending with the selector lever in the 'N' (neutral) position.

36 Remove the transmission dipstick (located on the right side, near the rear of the engine) and wipe all the fluid from the end of the dipstick with a clean rag.

37 Push the dipstick back into the transmission until the cap seats firmly on the dipstick tube. Now remove the dipstick again and observe the fluid on the end. The highest point of fluid should be between the 'Full' mark and $\frac{1}{4}$ inch below the 'Full' mark.

38 If the fluid is at or below the 'Add' mark, add sufficient fluid to raise the level to the 'Full' mark. One pint of fluid will raise the level from 'Add' to 'Full'. Fluid should be added directly into the dipstick guide tube, using a funnel to prevent spills (photo).

39 It is important that the transmission must not be overfilled. Under no circumstances should the fluid level be above the 'Full' mark on the dipstick, as this could cause internal damage to the transmission. The best way to prevent overfilling is to add fluid a little at a time, driving the vehicle and checking the level between additions.

40 Use only transmission fluid specified by the manufacturer. This information can be found in the Recommended Lubricants and Fluids Sectionc.

41 The condition of the fluid should also be checked along with the level. If the fluid at the end of the dipstick is a dark reddish-brown color, or cif the fluid has a 'burnt' smell, the transmission fluid should be changed with fresh. If you are in doubt about the condition of the fluid, purchase some new fluid and compare the two for color and smell.

Rear axle

42 Like the manual transmission, the rear axle has an inspection and fill plug which must be removed to check the fluid level.

43 Remove the plug which is located at the rear of the differential. Use your little finger to reach inside the differential housing to feel the level of the fluid. It should be at the bottom of the plug hole.

44 If this is not the case, add the proper lubricant through the plug hole. A syringe or a small funnel can be used for this.

45 Make certain the correct lucbricant is used.

46 Tighten the plug securely and check for leaks after the first few miles of driving.

Power steering

47 Unlike manual steering, the power steering system relies on fluid which may, over a period of time, r[equire replenishing.

48 The reservoir for the power steer[ing pump is located near the front of the engine, on the right side.

49 The power steering fluid level should be checked only after the vehicle has been driven, with the fluid at operating temperature. The front wheels should be pointed straight ahead.

50 With the engine shut off, use a rag to clean the reservoir cap and the areas around the cap. This will help to prevent foreign material from falling into the reservoir when the cap is removed.

51 Twist off the reservoir cap which has a built-in dipstick attached to it. Pull off the cap and clean off the fluid at the bottom of the dipstick with a clean rag. Now reinstall the dipstick/cap assembly to get a fluid level reading. Remove the dipstick/cap and observe the fluid level. It should be at the 'Full hot' mark on the dipstick (photo).
52 If additional fluid is required, pour the specified lubricant directly into the reservoir using a funnel to prevent spills.
53 If the reservoir requires frequent fluid additions, all power steering hoses, hose connections, the power steering pump and the steering box should be carefully checked for leaks.

Manual steering

54 It is unlikely that the manual steering gearbox oil would ever need replenishing, but it should be checked occasionally.
55 With the vehicle on a level surface, remove the bolt from the lower right corner of the gearbox upper cover.
56 Insert a thin screwdriver into the hole. The oil level should be 0.8 in (20 mm) below the hole.
57 Add oil of the recommended type and grade if necessary, but do not overfill. Replace the bolt and tighten it securely.
58 If the gearbox requires oil, check for leaks and have them repaired if any are found.

3 Tire and tire pressure checks

1 Periodically inspected the tires can not only prevent you from being stranded with a flat tire, but can also give you clues as to possible problems with the steering and suspension systems before major damage occurs.
2 Proper tire inflation add miles to the life of the tires, allows the vehicle to achieve maximum gas mileage and contributes to overall riding comfort.
3 When inspecting the tire, first check the wear on the tread. Irregularities in the tread pattern (cupping, flat spots, more wear on one side than the other) are indications of front end alignment and/or balance problems. If any of these conditions are found you should take the vehicle to a wheel alignment shop to correct the problem.
4 Also check the tread area for cuts or punctures. Many times a nail or tack will imbed itself into the tire tread and yet the tire will hold its air pressure for a short time. In most cases, a repair shop or gas station can repair the punctured tire.
5 It is also important to check the sidewalls of the tire, both inside and outside. Check for the rubber being deteriorated, cut or punctured. Also inspect the inboard side of the tire for signs of brake fluid leakage, indicating a thorough brake inspection is needed immediately (Section 23).
6 Incorrect tire pressure cannot be determined merely by looking at the tire. This is especially true for radial tires. A tire pressure gauge must be used. If you do not already have a reliable gauge, it is a good idea to purchase one and keep it in the glove box. Built-in pressure gauges at gas stations are often unreliable. If you are in doubt as to the accuracy of your gauge, many repair shops have 'master' pressure gauges which you can use for comparison purposes.
7 Always check tire inflation when the tires are cold. Cold, in this case, means that the vehicle has not been driven more than one mile after sitting for three hours or more. It is normal for the pressure to increase 4 to 8 pounds or more when the tires are hot.
8 Unscrew the valve cap protruding from the wheel and firmly press the gauge onto the valve stem. Observe the reading on the gauge and check this figure against the recommended tire pressure for your vehicle.
9 Check all tires and add air as necessary to bring all tires up to the recommended pressure levels. Do not forget the spare tire. Be sure to reinstall the valve caps, which will keep dirt and moisture out of the valve stem mechanism.

4 Engine oil and filter change

1 Frequent oil changes may be the best form of preventative maintenance available for the home mechanic. When engine oil get old, it gets diluted and contaminated, which ultimately leads to premature engine wear.
2 Although some sources recommended oil filter changes every other oil change, we feel that the minimal cost of an oil filter and the relative ease with which it is installed dictate that a new filter be used whenever the oil is changed.
3 The tools necessary for a normal oil and filter change are: a wrench to fit the drain plug at the bottom of the oil pan; an oil filter wrench to remove the old filter; a container with at least a six-quart capacity to drain the old oil into; and a funnel or oil can spout to help pour fresh oil into the engine.
4 In addition, you should have plenty of clean rags and newspapers handy to mop up any spills. Access to the underside of the car is greatly improved if it can be lifted on a hoist, driven onto ramps or supported by jack stands. Do not work under a vehicle which is supported only by a bumper, hydraulic or scissors-type jack.
5 If this is your first change on the vehicle, it is a good idea to crawl underneath and familiarize yourself with the locations of the oil drain plug and the oil filter. Since the engine and exhaust components will be warm during the actual work, it is best to figure out any potential problems before the vehicle and its accessories are hot.
6 Allow the engine to warm up to normal operating temperature. If the new oil or any tools are needed, use this warm-up time to gather everything necessary for the job. The correct type of oil to buy for your application can be found in *Recommended Lubricants* in the front of this manual.
7 With the engine oil warm (warm engine oil will drain better and more built-up sludge will be removed with the oil), raise the vehicle for access beneath. Make sure it is firmly supported. If jack stands are used they should be placed towards the front of the frame rails which run the length of the vehicle.
8 Move all necessary tools, rags and newspapers under the vehicle. Position the drain pan under the drain plug. Keep in mind that the oil will initially flow from the pan with some force, so place the pan accordingly.
9 Being careful not to touch any of the hot exhaust pipe components, use the wrench to remove the drain plug near the bottom of the oil pan. Depending on how hot the oil has become, you may want to wear gloves while unscrewing the plug the final few turns.
10 Allow the old oil to drain into the pan. It may be necessary to remove the pan farther under the engine as the oil flow reduces to a trickle.
11 After all the oil has drained, clean the drain plug thoroughly with a clean rag. Small metal filings may cling to this plug, which could immediately contaminate your new oil.
12 Clean the area around the drain plug opening and reinstall the drain plug. Tighten the plug securely with your wrench. If a torque wrench is available, the torque setting is 44 to 57 ft-lbs.
13 Move the drain pan into position under the oil filter.
14 Now use the filter wrench to loosen the oil filter. Chain or metal band-type filter wrenches may distort the filter canister, but don't worry too much about this as the filter will be discarded anyway.
15 Sometimes the oil filter is on so tight it cannot be loosened, or is inaccessible with a filter wrench. As a last resort you can punch a metal bar or long screwdriver directly through the bottom of the canister and use this as a T-bar to turn the filter. If this must be done, be prepared for oil to spurt out of the canister as it is punctured.
16 Completely unscrew the old filter. Be careful, it is full of oil. Empty the old oil inside the filter into the drain pan.
17 Compare the old filter with the new one to make sure they are of the same type.
18 Use a clean rag to remove all oil, dirt and sludge from the area where the oil filter mounts to the engine. Check the old filter to make sure the rubber gasket is not stuck to the engine mounting surface. If this gasket is stuck to the engine (use a flashlight if necessary), remove it.
19 Smear a light coat of fresh oil onto the rubber gasket of the new oil filter.
20 Screw the new filter to the engine following the tightening directions printed on the filter canister or packing box. Most filter manufacturers recommend against using a filter wrench due to possible overtightening or damage to the canister.
21 Remove all tools, rags, etc., from under the vehicle, being careful not to spill the oil in the drain pan. Lower the vehicle off its support stands.
22 Move to the engine compartment and locate the oil filler cap on the valve cover, near the front of the engine.
23 If an oil can spout is used, push the spout into the top of the oil can and pour the fresh oil through the filler opening. A funnel placed into the opening may also be used.

24 Pour about 3 qts. of fresh oil into the engine. Wait a few minutes to allow the oil to drain to the pan, then check the level on the oil dipstick (see Section 2 if necessary). If the oil level is at or near the lower 'Add' mark, start the engine and allow the new oil to circulate.

25 Run the engine for only about a minute and then shut it off. Immediately look under the vehicle and check for leaks at the oil pan drain plug and around the oil filter. If either is leaking, retighten and recheck them.

26 With the new oil circulated and the filter now completely full, recheck the level on the dipstick and add enough oil to bring the level to the 'Full' mark on the dipstick.

27 During the first few trips after an oil change, make it a point to check for leaks, and proper oil level.

28 The old oil drained from the engine cannot be reused in its present state and should be disposed of. Oil reclamation centers, auto repair shops and gas stations will normally accept the oil which can be refined and used again. After the oil has cooled, it can be drained into a suitable container (capped plastic jugs, topped bottles, milk cartons, etc.) for transport to one of these disposal sites.

5 Chassis lubricant

1 A grease gun and a cartridge filled with the proper grease (see *Recommended Lubricants)* are usually the only equipment necessary to lubricate the chassis components. Occasionally on later model vehicles, plugs will be installed rather than grease fittings, in which case grease fittings will have to be purchased and installed.

2 Look under the vehicle see if grease fittings or solid plugs are installed. If there are plugs, remove them with the correct wrench and buy grease fittings which will thread into the component. A Chrysler dealer or auto parts store will be able to find replacement fittings. Straight, as well as angled, fittings are available for easy greasing.

3 For easier access under the vehicle, raise the vehicle with a jack and place jack stands under the frame. Make sure it is firmly supported by the stands.

4 Before you do any greasing, force a little of the grease out the nozzle to remove any dirt from the end of the gun. Wipe the nozzle clean with a rag.

5 With the grease gun, plenty of clean rags and the location diagram, go under the vehicle to begin lubricating the components.

6 Wipe the grease fitting nipple clean and push the nozzle firmly over the fitting nipples. Squeeze the trigger on the grease gun to force grease into the component. The balljoints (one upper and one lower for each wheel) should be lubricated until the rubber reservoir is firm to the touch. Do not pump too much grease into these fittings as this could rupture the reservoir. For all other suspension and steering fittings, continue pumping grease into the nipple until grease seeps out of the joint between the two components. If the grease seeps out around the grease gun nozzle, the nipple is clogged or the nozzle is not fully seated around the fitting nipple. Re-secure the gun nozzle to the fitting and try again. If necessary, replace the fitting.

7 Wipe the excess grease from the components and the grease fitting. Follow these procedures for the remaining fittings.

8 Check the universal joints on the driveshaft; some have fittings, some are factory sealed. About two pumps is all that is required for grease type universal joints. While you are under the vehicle, clean and lubricate the parking brake cable along with its cable guides and levers. This can be done by smearing some of the chassis grease onto the cable and its related parts with your fingers.

9 Lower the vehicle to the ground for the remaining body lubrication process.

10 Open the hood and smear a little chassis grease on the hood latch mechanism. If the hood has an inside release, have an assistant pull the release knob from inside the car as you lubricate the cable at the latch.

11 Lubricate all the hinges (door, hood, etc.) with a few drops of light engine oil to keep them in proper working order.

12 Finally, the key lock cylinders can be lubricated with spray-on graphite which is available at auto parts stores.

6 Cooling system check

1 Many major engine failures can be attributed to a faulty cooling system. If equipped with an automatic transmission, the cooling system also plays an important role in transmission life.

2 The cooling system should be checked with the engine cold. Do this before the vehicle is driven for the day or after it has been shut off for one or two hours.

3 Remove the radiator cap and thoroughly clean the cap (inside and out) with clean water. Also clean the filler neck on the radiator. All traces of corrosion should be removed.

4 Carefully check the upper and lower radiator hoses along with the smaller diameter heater hoses. Inspect their entire length, replacing any hose which is cracked, swollen or show signs of deterioration. Cracks may become more apparent if the hose is squeezed (photos).

5 Also check that all hose connections are tight. A leak in the cooling system will usually show up as white or rust colored deposits on the areas adjoining the leak.

6 Use compressed air or a soft brush to remove bugs, leaves, etc., from the front of the radiator or air conditioning condensor. Be careful not to damage the delicate cooling fins, or cut yourself on the sharp fins.

7 Finally, have the cap and system tested for proper pressure. If you do not have a pressure tester, most gas stations and repair shops will do this for a minimal charge.

7 Exhaust system check

1 With the exhaust system cold (at least three hours after being driven), check the complete exhaust systen from its starting point at the engine to the end of the tailpipe. This is best done on a hoist where full access is available.

2 Check the pipes and their connections for signs of leakage and/or corrosion indicating a potential failure. Check that all brackets and hangers are in good condition and are tight (photo).

3 At the same time, inspect the underside of the body for holes, corrosion, open seams, etc. which may allow exhaust gases to enter the passenger compartment. Seal all body openings with silicone or body putty.

4 Rattles and other driving noises can often be traced to the exhaust system, especially the mounts and hangers. Try to move the pipes and muffler. If the components can come into contact with the body or driveline parts, secure the exhaust system with new mountings.

5 This is also an ideal time to check the running condition of the engine by inspecting the very end of the tailpipe. The exhaust deposits here are an indication of engine tune. If the pipe is black and sooty (photo), or bright white deposits are found here, the engine is in need of a tune-up including a thorough carburetor inspection and adjustment.

8 Suspension and steering check

1 Whenever the front of the vehicle is raised for service it is a good idea to visually check the suspension and steering components for wear.

2 Indications of a fault in these systems are: excessive play in the steering wheel before the front wheels react; excessive sway around corners or body movement over rough roads; binding at some point as the steering wheel is turned.

3 Before the vehicle is raised for inspection, test the shock absorbers by pushing downward to rock the vehicle at each corner. If you push the vehicle down and it does not come back to a level position without one or two bounces, the shocks are worn and need to be replaced. As this is done, check for squeaks and strange noises from the suspension components. Information on shock absorber and suspension components can be found in Chapter 11.

4 Now raise the front end of the vehicle and support it firmly on jack stands placed under the frame rails. Because of the work to be done, make sure the vehicle cannot fall from the stands.

5 Grab the top and bottom of the front tire with your hands and rock the tire/wheel on its spindle. If there is movement of more than .059 in, the wheel bearings should be serviced (see Section 21).

6 Crawl under the vehicle and check for loose bolts, broken or disconnected parts and deteriorated rubber bushings on all suspension and steering components. Look for grease or fluid leaking from around the steering box. Check the power steering hoses and their connections for leaks. Check the ball joints for wear.

7   Have an assistant turn the steering wheel from side to side and check the steering components for free movement, chafing or binding. If the steering does not react with the movement of the steering wheel, try to determine where the slack is located.

9   Engine drive belt check and adjustment

1   The drive belts, or V-belts as they are sometimes called, at the front of the engine play an important role in the overall operation of the vehicle and its components. Due to their function and material make-up, the belts are prone to failure after a period of time and should be inspected and adjusted periodically to prevent major engine damage.
2   The number of belts used on a particular vehicle depends on the accessories installed. Drive belts are used to turn: the alternator; power steering pump; water pump; fan; and air conditioning compressor. Depending on the pulley arrangement, a single belt may be used for more than one of these components.
3   With the engine off, open the hood and locate the various belts at the front of the engine. Using your fingers (and a flashlight if necessary), move along the belts checking for cracks or separation. Also check for fraying and glazing which gives the belt a shiny appearance. Both sides of the belts should be inspected, which means you will have to twist the belt to check the underside.
4   The tension of each belt is checked by pushing on the belt at a distance halfway between the pulleys. Push firmly with your thumb and see how much the belt moves downward (deflects). A rule of thumb, so to speak, is that if the distance (pulley center to pulley center) is between 7 inches and 11 inches the belt should deflect $\frac{1}{4}$ inch. If the belt is longer and travels between pulleys spaced 12 inches to 16 inches apart, the belt should deflect $\frac{1}{2}$ in.
5   If it is found necessary to adjust the belt tension, either to make the belt tighter or looser, this is done by moving the belt-driven accessory on its bracket.
6   For each component there will be an adjustment or strap bolt and a pivot bolt. Both bolts must be loosened slightly to enable you to move the component (photo).
7   After the two bolts have been loosened, move the component away from the engine (to tighten the belt) or forward the engine (to loosen the belt) (photo). Hold the accessory in this position and check the belt tension. If it is correct, tighten the two bolts until snug, then recheck the tension. If it is all right, fully tighten the two bolts.
8   It will often be necessary to use some sort of pry bar to move the accessory while the belt is adjusted. If this must be done to gain the proper leverage, be very careful not to damage the component being moved, or the part being pried against.

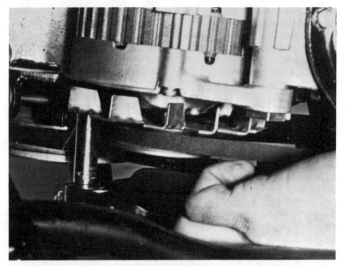

9.6b On air conditioner-equipped vehicles, the upper alternator mount bolt must be loosened to adjust the alternator drive belt tension

9.6c The power steering pump pivot bolt must be loosened slightly before adjusting the drive belt tension

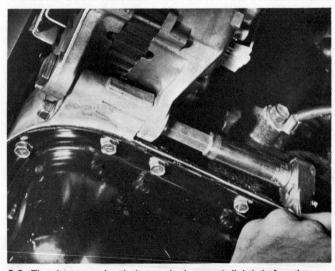

9.6a The alternator pivot bolt must be loosened slightly before the drive belt tension is adjusted

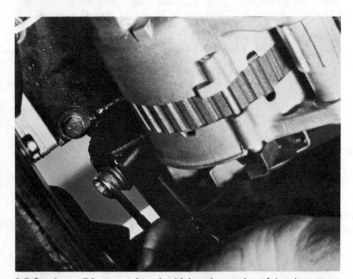

9.7 On air conditioner-equipped vehicles, the tension of the alternator drive belt can be adjusted by turning the tensioner bolt in or out, as necessary

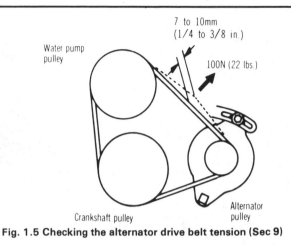

Fig. 1.5 Checking the alternator drive belt tension (Sec 9)

Labels: Water pump pulley; 7 to 10mm (1/4 to 3/8 in.); 100N (22 lbs.); Crankshaft pulley; Alternator pulley

10 Fuel system check

1   There are certain precautions to taken when inspecting or servicing the fuel system components. Work in a well ventilated area and do not allow open flames (cigarettes, appliance pilot lights, etc.) to get near the work area. Mop up spills immediately and do not store fuel-soaked rags where they could ignite.
2   The fuel system is under some amount of pressure, so if any fuel lines are disconnected for servicing, be prepared to catch the fuel as it spurts out. Plug all disconnected fuel lines immediately after disconnection to prevent the tank from emptying itself.
3   The fuel system is most easily checked with the vehicle raised on a hoist where the components under the vehicle are readily visible and accessible.
4   If the smell of gasoline is noticed while driving, or after the vehicle has sat in the sun, the system should be thoroughly inspected immediately.
5   Remove the gas filler cap and check for damage, corrosion and a proper sealing imprint on the gaskcet. Replace the cap with a new one if necessary.
6   With the vehicle raised, inspect the gas tank and fillcer neck for punctures, cracks or any damage. The connection between the filler neck and the tank is especially critical. Sometimes a rubber filler neck will leak due to loose clamps or deteriorated rubber; problecms a home mechanic can usually rectify.
7   Do not under any circumstances try to repair a fuel tank yourself (except rubber components) unless you have considerable experience. A welding torch or any open flame can easily cause the fuel vapors to explode if the proper precautions are not taken.
8   Carefully check all rubber hoses and metal lines leading away from the fuel tank. Check for loose connections, deteriorated hose, crimped lines or damage of any kind. Follow these lines up to the front of the vehicle, carefully inspecting them all the way. Repair or replace damaged sections as necessary.
9   If a fuel odor is still evident after the inspection, refer to Section 26 on the evaporative emissions system.

11 Air filter replacement

1   At the specified intervals, the air filter should be replaced with a new one. A thorough program of preventative maintenance would call for the filter to be inspected periodically between changes.
2   The air filter is located inside the air cleaner housing on the top of the engine. To remove the filter, unscrew the wing nut at the top of the air cleaner, unsnap the four spring-type clamps, and lift off the top plate (photo).
3   While the top plate is off, be careful not to drop anything down into the carburetor.
4   Lift the air filter out of the housing (photo).
5   To check the filter, hold it up to strong sunlight, or place a flashlight or droplight on the inside of the ring-shaped filter. If you can see light coming through the paper element, the filter is all right. Check all the way around the filter.
6   Wipe the inside of the air cleaner clean with a rag.
7   Place the old filter (if in good condition) or the new filter (if

specified interval has elapsed) back into the air cleaner housing. Make sure it seats properly in the bottom of the housing.
8   Reinstall the top plate with the four clamps and wing nut. Be sure to align the arrow stamped on the plate with the arrow stamped on the snorkel tube (photo).

12 Clutch pedal free play check

1   Proper clutch pedal free play is very important for clutch operation and to ensure normal clutch service life.
2   Clutch pedal free play is the distance the clutch pedal moves before the mechanical linkage actually begins to disengage the clutch disc from the flywheel and pressure plate.
3   To check the free play, slowly depress the clutch pedal until the resistance offered by the clutch release mechanism is felt. (The pedal will suddenly become much more difficult to move).
4   Measure the distance the clutch pedal has travelled and compare it to the specifications. If adjustment is required, refer to Chapter 8 for the step-by-step procedure to follow.

13 Tire rotation

1   The tires should be rotated at the specified intervals and whenever uneven wear is noticed. Since the vehicle will be raised and the tires removed anyway, this is a good time to check the brakes (Section 23) and/or repack the wheel bearings (Section 21). Read over these sections if this is to be done at the same time.
2   The location for each tire in the rotation sequence depends on the type of tire used on your vehicle. Tire type can be determined by reading the raised printing on the sidewall of the tire.
3   See the information in *Jacking and Towing* at the front of this manual for the proper procedures to follow in raising the vehicle and changing a tire; however, if the brakes are to be checked do not apply the parking brake as stated. Make sure the tires are blocked to prevent the vehicle from rolling.
4   Preferably, the entire vehicle should be raised at the same time. This can be done on a hoist or by jacking up each corner of the vehicle and then lowering it onto jack stands placed under the frame rails. Always use four jack stands and make sure the vehicle is firmly supported all around.
5   After rotation, check and adjust the tire pressures as necessary and be sure to check wheel nut tightness.

14 Engine idle speed adjustment

1   Engine idle speed is the speed at which the engine operates when no accelerator pedal pressure is applied. This speed is critical to the performance of the engine itself, as well as many engine sub-systems.
2   A hand-held tachometer must be used when adjusting idle speed to get an accurate reading. The exact hook-up for these meters varies with the manufacturer, so follow the particular directions included.
3   Basically, for most applications, the idle speed is set by turning an adjustment screw located at the side of the carburetor. This screw changes the linkage, in essence, depressing or letting up on your accelerator pedal. Refer to the decal on the underside of the hood (upper right corner).
4   Once you have found the idle screw, experiment with different length screwdrivers until the adjustments can be easily made, without coming into contact with hot or moving engine components.
5   Refer to the decal on the underside of the hood (upper left corner), or to Chapter 4 for the proper procedure to follow when adjusting idle speed.
6   Make sure the parking brake is firmly set and the wheels blocked to prevent the vehicle from rolling. This is especially true if the transmission is to be in 'Drive'. An assistant inside the vehicle pushing on the brake pedal is the safest method.
7   For all applications, the engine must be completely warmed-up to operating temperature, which will automatically render the choke fast idle inoperative.

11.2a Pull up on the spring clamp handles to release the air cleaner top plate.

11.2b After the wing nut has been removed, the top can be lifted off of the air cleaner

11.4 The air filter should be replaced with a new one at the specified intervals

11.8 Line up the arrows on the plate and the snorkel tube when the plate is installed

15 Fuel filter replacement

1   The fuel filter is located on the left side of the fuel tank and is accessible from under the vehicle. When changing the fuel filter, the fuel tank must be empty or you must somehow clamp the lower fuel hose leading to the fuel filter off in order to prevent fuel from leaking out when the hoses are disconnected.

2   Jack up the rear of the vehicle and support it on jack stands. Be sure to block the front wheel to prevent rolling. Gather up all necessary tools and some rags, as well as the fuel filter, before getting under the vehicle. Since you will be working around gasoline, make sure that there are no bare lightbulbs or open flames nearby.

3   Release and slide back the hose clamps at the fuel filter inlet and outlet. Pull the fuel filter out of the spring-type mounting bracket and disconnect both hoses. Be prepared to catch some gasoline in a rag when the hoses are disconnected and take care not to get any gasoline in your eyes. Pull the hose clamps off the hoses and discard them.

4   Slide new hose clamps onto both hoses. Connect the hoses to the new filter, taking care that the fuel inlet and outlet spigots are in the proper position. Install the hose clamps on both hoses approximately $\frac{1}{4}$ in back from the hose ends.

5   Push the fuel filter back into the mounting bracket. Check to make sure that it is held securely and that the hoses are not kinked.

6   Start the vehicle and check for leaks.

16 Ignition timing – adjustment

1   All vehicles are equipped with a tune-up decal on the underside of the hood. This decal lists important ignition timing settings and procedures to be followed which are specific to that vehicle. Information on the tune-up decal supersedes the information given in this Section. The decal should be followed if information on it is different from that given here.

2   At the specified intervals, when the distributor has been removed or a change made in the fuel type, the ignition timing must be checked and adjusted if necessary.

3   Before attempting to check the timing, make sure that the transmission is in 'neutral' (or 'park') with the parking brake set. Turn off the air conditioner and lights. Make sure the idle speed is as specified.

4   Connect a timing light in accordance with the manufacturer's instructions. Generally, the light will be connected to power and ground terminals and to the number one spark plug in some fashion. The number one spark plug is the one closest to the front of the engine.

5   Locate the numbered timing tag on the front of the engine. It is just behind and above the pulley on the crankshaft. If necessary, clean it off with solvent so that the printing and small raised lines are clearly visible.

21.5a Removing the dust cap from the end of the hub

21.5b Pulling out the cotter key

21.5c Once the nut and special washer are removed, the outer bearing is exposed

21.5d Pull out on the hub to dislodge the bearing

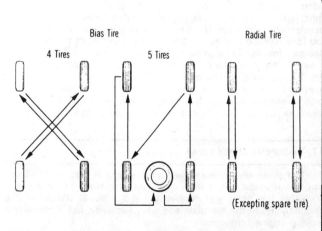

Fig. 1.6 Checking the power steering pump drive belt tension (Sec 9)

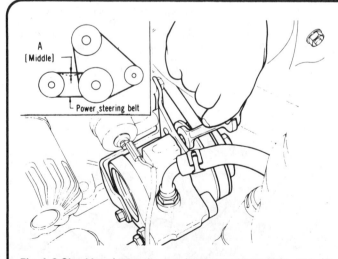

Fig. 1.7 Tire rotation diagram (Sec 13)

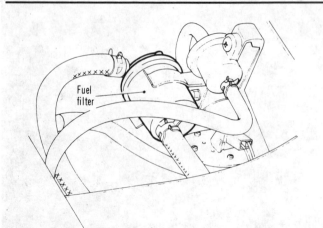

Fig. 1.8 The fuel filter is mounted in a spring-type clamp (Sec 15)

6   Locate the notch on the rear flange of the crankshaft pulley. It may be necessary to have an assistant turn the starter on and off (in short bursts), without starting the engine, to bring this notch into a position where it can be easily cleaned and marked. Stay clear off all moving engine parts if the engine is turned over in this manner.
7   Use white soap-stone, chalk or paint to mark the notch in the crankshaft pulley. Also mark the timing tab line which represents the number of degrees of ignition advance required in the Specifications (Chapter 5) or the tune-up decal on the underside of the hood. Each line on the timing tab represents 5°. The letters BTDC stand for 'before top dead center' (advance) and the letter 'T' indicates top dead center (TDC). Thus, is your vehicle specifications call for 5° BTDC, you will mark the timing tab line just before the 'T'.
8   Check that the wiring for the timing light is clear of all moving engine parts, then start the engine.
9   Point the flashing timing light at the timing marks. Again, be careful not to come in contact with moving parts of the engine. The marks you made should appear stationary and be lined up opposite each other. If the marks are in alignment, the timing is correct. If the marks are not aligned, turn off the engine.
10 Loosen the locknut at the base of the distributor just enough to enable you to turn the distributor (see Chapter 5 for further details if necessary).
11 Restart the engine and slowly turn the distributor until the timing marks are aligned.
12 Shut off the engine and tighten the locknut. Be careful not to disturb the distributor.
13 Start the engine and recheck the timing to make sure the marks did not shift when you tightened the distributor locknut.
14 Disconnect the timing light and remove any tools from under the hood. Drive the vehicle and listen for 'pinging' noises. These will be most noticeable when the engine is hot and under load (climbing a hill, accelerating from stop). If the engine is 'pinging', the ignition timing is too far advanced (before top dead center). Reconnect the timing light and turn the distributor to move the mark on the pulley 1 or 2 degrees closer to the 'T' on the timing tab. Road test the vehicle again.
15 To keep 'pinging' at a minimum and allow vehicle operation at the specified timing setting, it is a good idea to use gasoline of the same octane rating at all times. Switching fuel brands and octane levels can decrease performance and economy and possibly damage the engine.

17 Carburetor choke check

1   The choke only operates when the engine is cold, so this check can be performed before the vehicle has been started for the day.
2   Open the hood and remove the top plate of the air cleaner assembly. Place the top plate and wing nut aside, out of the way of moving engine components.
3   Look at the top of the carburetor at the center of the air cleaner housing. You will notice a flat plate at the carburetor opening (photo).
4   Have an assistant press the accelerator pedal to the floor. The plate should close fully. Start the engine while you observe the plate at the carburetor. Do not position your face directly over the

carburetor, as the engine could backfire, causing serious burns. When the engine starts, the choke plate should open slightly.
5   Allow the engine to continue running at an idle speed. As the engine warms up to operating temperature, the plate should slowly open, allowing more air to enter through the top of the carburetor.
6   After a few minutes, the choke plate should be fully open to the vertical position.
7   You will notice that the engine speed corresponds with the plate opening. With the plate fully closed, the engine should run at a fast idle speed. As the plate opens, the engine speed will decrease.
8   If during the above checks a fault is detected, refer to Chapter 4 for specific information on adjusting and servicing the choke components.

18 Rear axle fluid change

1   The vehicle should be driven for a few minutes before draining the rear axle fluid. This practice will tend to warm up the fluid and ensure complete drainage.
2   Move a drain pan, rags, newspapers, and tools under the rear of the vehicle. With the drain pan under the differential, remove the drain plug from the bottom of the housing. While the fluid is draining, remove the inspection plug.
3   After the fluid has completely drained, wipe the area around the drain hole with a clean rag and install the drain plug.
4   Fill the housing (through the inspection hole) with the recommended lubricant until the level is even with the bottom of the inspection hole. Install the inspection plug.
5   After driving the vehicle, check for leaks at the drain and inspection plugs.
6   When the job is complete, check for metal filings or chips in the drained fluid, which indicate that the differential should be thoroughly inspected and repaired (see Chapter 8 for more information).

19 Spark plug replacement

1   The spark plugs are located on the right side of the engine and are easily accessible for servicing.
2   In most cases the tools necessary for a spark plug replacement job are: a plug wrench or spark plug socket which fits onto a ratchet wrench (this special socket will be insulated inside to protect the procelain insulator) and a feeler gauge to check and adjust the spark plug gap.
3   The best policy to follow when replacing the spark plugs is to purchase the new spark plugs beforehand, adjust them to the proper gap and then replace each plug one at a time. When buying the new spark plugs it is important that the correct plug is purchased for your specific engine. This information can be found in the Specifications Section of Chapter 5, but should be checked against the information found on the tune-up decal located under the hood of your vehicle or in the factory owner's manual. If differences exist between these sources, purchase the spark plug type specified on the tune-up decal as this information was printed for your specific engine.

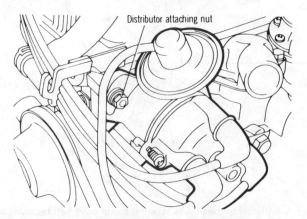

Fig. 1.9 Loosen the distributor nut and turn the distributor to change the ignition timing (Sec 16)

4 With the new spark plugs at hand, allow the engine to thoroughly cool before attempting the removal. During this cooling time, each of the new spark plugs can be inspected for defects and the gap can be checked.

5 The gap is checked by inserting the proper thickness gauge between the electrodes at the tip of the plug. The gap between these electrodes should be the same as that given in the Specifications or on the tune-up decal. The wire should just touch each of the electrodes. If the gap is incorrect, use the notched adjuster on the feeler gauge body to bend the curved side electrode slightly until the proper gap is achieved. Also, at this time check for cracks in the spark plug body, indicating the spark plug should be replaced with a new one. If the side electrode is not exactly over the center one, use the notched adjuster to align the two.

6 Cover the fenders of the vehicle to prevent damage to exterior paint.

7 With the engine cool, remove the spark plug wire from one spark plug. Do this by grabbing the boot at the end of the wire, not the wire itself. Sometimes it is necessary to use a twisting motion while the boot and plug wire is pulled free. Using a plug wire removal tool is the easiest and safest method.

8 If compressed air is available, use this to blow any dirt or foreign material away from the spark plug area. A common bicycle pump will also work. The idea here is to eliminate the possibility of material falling into the engine cylinder as the spark plug is removed.

9 Now place the spark plug wrench or socket over the plug and remove it from the engine by turning in a counter-clockwise motion.

10 Compare the spark plug with those shown on page 107 to get an indication of the overall running condition of the engine (photo).

11 Carefully insert one of the new plugs into the spark plug hole and tighten it by hand. Since the cylinder head on your engine is aluminum, you must be especially careful not to cross-thread the spark plug in the hole. If resistance is felt as you thread the spark plug in by hand, back it out and start again. *Do not, under any circumstances, force the spark plug into the hole with a wrench or socket.*

12 Finally tighten the spark plug with the wrench or socket. It is best to use a torque wrench for this to ensure the plug is seated correctly. The correct torque figure is given in Specifications.

13 Before pushing the spark plug wire onto the end of the plug, inspect it following the procedures outlined in Section 24.

14 Install the plug wire to the new spark plug, again using a twisting motion on the boot until it is firmly seated on the spark plug. Make sure the wire is routed away from the hot exhaust manifold.

15 Follow the above procedures for the remaining spark plugs, replacing each one at a time to prevent mixing up the spark plug wires.

20 Valve clearance adjustment

1 The intake, exhaust and Jet Valve clearances must be periodically checked and adjusted to ensure efficient and trouble-free engine operation. Always adjust the Jet Valve clearance before adjusting the intake valve clearance. Also, whenever the cylinder head is removed, or the bolts are re-torqued, the valve clearances must be readjusted.

2 The engine must be at normal operating temperature when the valve clearances are adjusted.

3 With the engine stopped, remove the air cleaner assembly. Detach the throttle cable, the carburetor vent tube, and the CECS hoses from the top of the valve cover. Remove the spark plug leads from the spark plugs. Pull the wire lead out of the center terminal of the distributor cap and ground it to the engine block. Also, remove the spark plugs so that each piston can easily be positioned at Top Dead Center (TDC) on the compression stroke.

4 Unfasten the distributor cap, remove the two bolts attaching the valve cover and lift off the valve cover with the distributor cap and spark plug wire harness attached to it.

5 While watching the rocker arms for the number one cylinder, rotate the engine in a clockwise direction (with a wrench on the large bolt at the front of the crankshaft) until the exhaust valve is closing and the intake valve has just started to open. (The intake valve is on the carburetor side of the engine, the exhaust valve is on the exhaust manifold side of the engine). Line up the notch in the pulley (on the front of the crankshaft) with the 'T' on the timing mark tab (on the timing chain case). At this point, the number 4 piston will be at TDC on the compression stroke and the number 4 cylinder valve clearances can be adjusted. Remember, the Jet Valve clearance is always

adjusted before the intake and exhaust valve clearances.

6 The intake valve and Jet Valve adjusting screws are located on a common rocker arm. Loosen the locknut on the intake valve adjusting screw and back off the adjusting screw at least two full turns.

7 Loosen the locknut on the Jet Valve adjusting screw. Turn the Jet Valve adjusting screw counter-clockwise and insert a .006 in (0.15 mm) feeler gauge between the Jet Valve stem and the adjusting screw.

8 Carefully tighten the adjusting screw until you can feel a slight drag on the feeler gauge as it is withdrawn from between the stem and adjusting screw. **Note:** *Since the Jet Valve spring is relatively weak, use special care not to force the Jet Valve open. Be particularly careful if the adjusting screw is hard to turn.*

9 Hold the adjusting screw with a screwdriver to keep it from turning and tighten the locknut. Recheck the clearance to make sure it hasn't changed.

10 Next, adjust the intake valve clearance. Insert a .006 in (0.15 mm) feeler gauge between the intake valve stem and the adjusting screw.

11 Carefully tighten the adjusting screw until you can feel a slight drag on the feeler gauge as it is withdrawn from between the stem and adjusting screw.

12 Hold the adjusting screw with a screwdriver, to keep it from turning, and tighten the locknut. Recheck the clearance to make sure it hasn't changed.

13 Loosen the locknut on the exhaust valve adjusting screw. Turn the adjusting screw counter-clockwise and insert a .010 in (0.25 mm) feeler gauge between the valve stem and the adjusting screw.

14 Carefully tighten the adjusting screw until you can feel a slight drag on the feeler gauge as it is withdrawn from between the stem and adjusting screw.

15 Hold the adjusting screw with a screwdriver to keep it from turning and tighten the locknut. Recheck the clearance to make sure it hasn't changed.

16 Repeat the procedure to adjust the valve clearances for cylinders 1, 2 and 3. Use the following table for determining when the pistons are at TDC.

Exhaust valve closing, intake valve just opening	Adjust valve clearances at
No. 1 cylinder	No. 4 cylinder
No. 2 cylinder	No. 3 cylinder
No. 3 cylinder	No. 2 cylinder
No. 4 cylinder	No. 1 cylinder

17 Install the valve cover (using a new gasket), distributor cap, spark plugs, throttle cable, carburetor vent tube, CECS hoses and air cleaner assembly. Push the lead wire into the center terminal of the distributor cap, and attach the spark plug wires to the spark plugs.

18 Start and run the engine. Check for oil leakage between the valve cover and the cylinder head.

21 Wheel bearings check and repack

1 In most cases, the front wheel bearings will not need servicing until the brake pads are changed. However, these bearings should be checked whenever the front wheels are raised for any reason.

2 With the vehicle securely supported on jack stands, spin the wheel and check for noise, rolling resistance or free play. Now grab the top of the wheel with one hand and the bottom of the wheel with the other. Move the tire in and out on the spindle. If there is noticeable movement, the bearings should be checked, then repacked with grease or replaced, if necessary.

3 Remove the wheel/tire from the hub.

4 Refer to Chapter 9 and remove the brake caliper assembly and bracket.

5 Remove the dust cap from the hub with a screwdriver (photo) or pry bar. Remove the cotter pin, the nut and the special washer from the end of the spindle (photo). Pull the hub assembly out slightly, then push it back to its original position. This should slide the outer bearing off the spindle enough so that it can be removed by hand. As you slide it off, note how the bearing is installed. Next, pull off the hub, which will contain the inner bearing and the seal.

6 Use a screwdriver or pry bar to pry out the seal on the rear of the hub. Note how it is installed. The inner bearing can now be removed from the hub. Again, note how it is installed.

7 Use clean parts solvent to remove all traces of the old grease from

the bearings and spindle. Do not wash the hub in solvent unless the brake disc is separated from the hub first. A small brush may prove useful; however, make sure no bristles from the brush are left inside the bearing cage. Allow the parts to air dry.

8   Carefully inspect the bearings for cracks, heat discoloration, bent rollers, etc. Check the bearing races inside the hub for cracks, scoring or uneven surfaces. If the bearing races are in need of replacement, the job is best left to a repair shop which can press the new races into position.

9   Use an approved high temperature wheel bearing grease to pack the bearings. Work the grease fully into the bearings, forcing the grease between the rollers, cone and cage.

10 Apply a thin coat of grease to the spindle at the outer bearing seat, inner bearing seat, shoulder and seal seat.

11 Put a small quantity of grease inboard at each bearing race inside the hub. Using your finger, form a dam at these points to provide extra grease availability and to keep thinned grease from flowing out of the bearing.

12 Place the grease-packed inner bearing into the rear of the hub and put a little more grease outboard of the bearing. Do not get any grease on the brake disc.

13 Place a new seal over the inner bearing and tap the seal into place with a flat piece of wood and hammer until it is flush with the hub.

14 Carefully place the hub assembly onto the spindle and push the grease-packed outer bearing into position.

15 Install the washer and spindle nut. While rotating the hub in a forward direction, tighten the nut to 21.7 ft-lbs (using a torque wrench) to seat the bearings. Completely loosen the nut and then retighten it to 5.8 ft-lbs. Install the cotter pin. If the slot on the nut does not line up with the cotter pin hole, loosen the nut (30° maximum) to align them.

16 Bend the ends of the new cotter pin until they are flat against the nut. Cut off any extra length which could interfere with the dust cap.

17 Install the dust cap, tapping it into place with a rubber mallet.

18 Install the bake caliper support bracket and caliper assembly.

19 Slip the tire/wheel into place and tighten the mounting nuts.

20 Grab the top and bottom of the tire and check the bearings in the same manner as described at the beginning of this section.

21 Lower the vehicle to the ground and fully tighten the wheel nuts.

22 Automatic transmission fluid changes

1   At the specified time intervals, the transmission fluid should be changed and the filter replaced with a new one. Since there is no drain plug, the transmission oil pan must be removed from the bottom of the transmission to drain the fluid.

2   Before any draining, purchase the specified transmission fluid (see *Recommended Lubricants*) and a new filter. The necessary gaskets should be included with the filter; if not, purchase an oil pan gasket and a strainer-to-valve body gasket.

3   Other tools necessary for this job include: jack stands to support the vehicle in a raised position; wrench to remove the oil pan bolts; standard screwdriver; drain pan capable of holding at least 8 pints; newspapers and clean rags.

4   The fluid should be drained immediately after the vehicle has been driven. This will remove any built-up sediment better than if the fluid were cold. Because of this, it may be wise to wear protective gloves (fluid temperature can exceed 350° in a hot transmission).

5   After the vehicle has been driven to warm up the fluid, raise it and place it on jack stands for access underneath. Make sure it is firmly supported by the four stands placed on the frame rails.

6   Move the necessary equipment under the vehicle, being careful not to touch any of the hot exhaust components.

7   Place the drain pan under the transmission oil pan and remove the oil pan bolts along the rear and sides of the pan. Loosen, but do not remove, the bolts at the front of the pan.

8   Carefully pry the pan downward at the rear, allowing the hot fluid to drain into the drain pan. If necessary, use a screwdriver to break the gasket seal at the rear of the pan; however, do not damage the pan or transmission in the process.

9   Support the pan and remove the remaining bolts at the front of the pan. Lower the pan and drain the remaining fluid into the drain receptacle. As this is done, check the fluid for metal particles which may be an indication of internal failure.

10 Now visible on the bottom of the transmission is the filter/strainer held in place by three screws.

11 Remove the screws, the filter and its gasket.

12 Thoroughly clean the transmission oil pan with solvent. Inspect for metal particles or foreign matter. Dry with compressed air, if available. It is important that all remaining gasket material be removed from the oil pan mounting flange. Use a gasket scraper or putty knife for this.

13 Clean the filter mounting surface on the valve body. Again, this surface should be smooth and free of any leftover gasket material.

14 Place the new filter into position, with a new gasket between it and the transmission valve body. Install the mounting screws and tighten securely.

15 Apply a bead of gasket sealant around the oil pan mounting surface, with the sealant to the inside of the bolt holes. Press the new gasket into place on the pan, making sure all bolt holes line up.

16 Lift the pan up to the bottom of the transmission and install the mounting bolts. Tighten the bolts in a diagonal fashion, working around the pan. Using a torque wrench, tighten the bolts to the specified torque.

17 Lower the vehicle off the jack stands.

18 Open the hood and remove the transmission fluid dipstick from its guide tube.

19 Add 4 quarts of the specified transmission fluid through the tube, (use a funnel to prevent spills).

20 With the selector lever in 'Park', apply the parking brake and start the engine without depressing the accelerator pedal (if possible). Do not race the engine at a high speed; run at slow idle only, for at least two minutes.

21 Depress the brake pedal and shift the transmission through each gear. Place the selector in the 'Neutral' position and check the level on the dipstick (with the engine still idling). Look under the vehicle for leaks around the transmission oil pan mating surface.

22 Add more fluid through the dipstick tube until the level on the dipstick is at the 'Add' mark on the dipstick. Do not allow the fluid level to go above this point, as the transmission would then be overfilled, necessitating the removal of the pan to drain the excess fluid.

23 Push the dipstick firmly back into its tube and drive the vehicle to reach normal operating temperature (15 miles of highway driving or its equivalent in the city). Park on a level surface and check the fluid level on the dipstick with the engine idling and the transmission in 'Neutral'. The level should now be at the 'Full' mark on the dipstick. If not, add more fluid as necessary to bring the level up to this point. Again, do not overfill.

23 Brakes check

1   The brakes should be inspected every time the wheels are removed or whenever a fault is suspected. Indications of a potential braking system fault are: the vehicle pulls to one side when brake pedal is depressed; noises coming from the brakes when they are applied; excessive brake pedal travel; pulsating pedal; and leakage of fluid, usually seen on the inside of the tire or wheel.

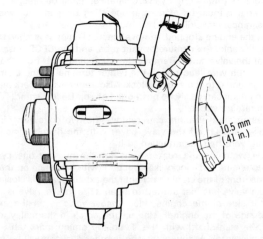

Fig. 1.10 Front brake pad lining thickness can be checked through the window in the caliper body (Sec 23)

Disc brakes

2 Disc brakes can be visually checked without the need to remove any parts except the wheels.

3 Raise the vehicle and place securely on jack stands. Remove the front wheel (see *Jacking and Towing* at the front of this manual if necessary).

4 Now visible is the disc brake caliper which contains the pads. There is an outer brake pad and an inner pad. Both should be inspected.

5 Inspect the pad thickness by looking through the cut-out inspection hole in the caliper body. If the lining material is .41 in or less in thickness, the pads should be replaced. Keep in mind that the lining material is riveted or bonded to a metal backing shoe and the metal portion is not included in this measuring.

6 Since it will be difficult, if not impossible, to measure the exact thickness of the remaining lining material, if you are in doubt as to the pad quality, remove the pads for further inspection or replacement. See Chapter 9 for disc brake pad replacement.

7 Before installing the wheels, check for any leakage around the brake hose connections leading to the caliper or damage (cracking, splitting, etc) to the brake hose. Replace the hose or fittings as necessary, referring to Chapter 9.

8 Also check the condition of the disc for scoring, gouging or burnt spots. If these conditions exist, the hub/rotor assembly should be removed for servicing (Chapter 9).

Drum brakes (rear)

9 Raise the vehicle and support it firmly on jack stands. Block the front tires to prevent rolling; however, do not apply the parking brake as this will lock the drums into place.

10 Remove the wheels, referring to *Jacking and Towing* at the front of this manual if necessary.

11 Mark the hub so it can be reinstalled in the same place. Use a scribe, chalk, etc. on drum and center hub and backing plate.

12 Pull the brake drum off the axle and brake assembly. If this proves difficult, make sure the parking brake is released, then squirt some penetrating oil around the center hub area. Allow the oil to soak in and try again to pull the drum off. Then, if the drum cannot be pulled off, the brake shoes will have to be adjusted inward. This is done by first removing the rubber plug in the backing plate with a screwdriver. Use a screwdriver or brake adjusting tool to rotate the adjuster wheel, which will move the brake shoes away from the drum.

13 With the drum removed, carefully brush away any accumulations of dirt and dust. Do not blow this dust out with compressed air. Also, do not inhale this dust, as it contains asbestos and is harmful to your health.

14 Observe the thickness of the lining material on both the front and rear brake shoes. If the material has worn away to within $\frac{1}{32}$ in of the recessed rivets or metal backing, the shoes should be replaced. If the linings look worn, but you are unable to determine their exact thickness, compare them with a new set at an auto parts store. The shoes should also be replaced if they are cracked, glazed (shiny surface), or wet with brake fluid.

15 Check that all the brake assembly springs are connected and in good condition.

16 Check the brake components for any signs of fluid leakage. With your finger, carefully pry back the rubber cups on the wheel cylinder located at the top of the brake shoes. Any leakage is an indication that the wheel cylinders should be overhauled immediately (Chapter 9). Also check fluid hoses and connections for signs of leakage.

17 Wipe the inside of the drum with a clean rag, and denatured alcohol. Again, be careful not to breathe the asbestos dust.

18 Check the inside of the drum for cracks, scores, deep scratches or 'hard spots' which will appear as small discolorations. If these imperfections cannot be removed with fine emery cloth, the drum must be taken to a machine shop equipped to turn the drums.

19 If after the inspection process all parts are in good working conditions, reinstall the brake drum. Install the wheel and lower the vehicle to the ground.

Parking brake

20 The easiest way to check the operation of the parking brake is to park the vehicle on a steep hill, with the parking brake set and the transmission in 'Neutral'. If the parking brake cannot prevent the car from rolling it is in need of adjustment (see Chapter 9).

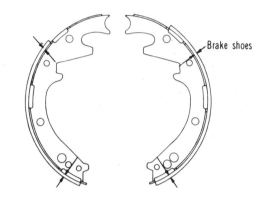

Fig. 1.11 Measure the lining thickness on both brake shoes to determine if new shoes are needed (Sec 23)

24 Spark plug wires check

1 The spark plug wires should be checked at the recommended intervals or whenever new spark plugs are installed.

2 The wires should be inspected one at a time to prevent mixing up the order which is essential for proper engine operation.

3 Disconnect the plug wire from the spark plug. A removal tool can be used for this, or you can grab the rubber boot, twist slightly and then pull the wire free. Do not pull on the wire itself, only on the rubber boot.

4 Inspect inside the boot for corrosion, which will look like a white, crusty powder (photo). Some vehicles use a conductive white grease which should not be mistaken for corrosion.

5 Now push the wire and boot back onto the end of the spark plug. It should be a tight fit on the plug end. If not, remove the wires and use a pair of pliers to carefully crimp the metal connector inside the wire boot until the fit is secure.

6 Now using a clean rag, clean the wire its entire length. Remove all built-up dirt and grease. As this is done, inspect for burns, cracks or any other form of damage.

7 Disconnect the wire at the distributor (again, pulling and twisting only on the rubber boot). Check for corrosion and a tight fit in the same manner as the spark plug end.

8 Check the remaining spark plug wires in the same way, making sure they are securely fastened at the distributor and spark plug.

9 A visual check of the spark plug wires can also be made. In a darkened garage (make sure there is ventilation), start the engine and observe each plug wire. Be careful not to come into contact with any moving engine parts. If there is a break or fault in the wire, you will be able to see arcing or a small spark at the damaged area.

10 If it is decided the spark plug wires are in need of replacement, purchase a new set for your specific engine model. Wire sets can be purchased which are pre-cut to the proper size and with the rubber boots already installed. Remove and replace each wire individually to prevent mix-ups in the firing sequence.

25 Cooling system servicing (draining, flushing and refilling)

1 Periodically, the cooling system should be drained, flushed and refilled to replenish the antifreeze mixture and prevent the formation of rust and corrosion which can impair the performance of the cooling system and ultimately cause engine damage.

2 At the same time the cooling system is serviced, all hoses and the radiator pressure cap should be inspected and replaced if faulty (see Section 6).

3 As antifreeze is a poisonous solution, take care not to spill any of the cooling mixture on the vehicle's paint or your own skin. If this happens, rinse immediately with plenty of clear water. Also, it is advisable to consult your local authorities about the dumping of antifreeze before draining the cooling system. In many areas reclamation centers have been set up to collect automobile oil and drain antifreeze/water mixtures rather than allowing these liquids to be added to the sewage and water facilities.

4 With the engine cold, remove the radiator pressure cap.

26.3 Removing the snorkel tube hose clamp

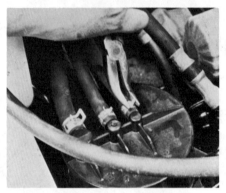

26.4 Removing the hose clamps from the canister hoses

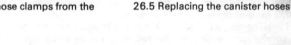

26.5 Replacing the canister hoses

5   Move a large container under the radiator to catch the water/antifreeze mixture as it is drained.
6   Drain the radiator by opening the drain petcock at the bottom of the radiator.
7   Remove the engine drain plug (photo) from the right side of the engine. This will allow the coolant to drain from the engine itself.
8   Disconnect the overflow tube and remove the coolant reserve system reservoir. Flush it out with clean water.
9   Place a cold water hose (a common garden hose is fine) in the radiator filler neck at the top of the radiator and flush the system until the water runs clear at all drain points.
10   In severe cases of contamination or clogging of the radiator, remove it (see Chapter 3) and reverse flush it. This involves simply inserting the cold pressure hose in the bottom radiator outlet to allow the clear water to run against the normal flow, draining through the top. A radiator repair shop should be consulted if further cleaning or repair is necessary.
11   Where the coolant is regularly drained and the system refilled with the correct antifreeze/inhibitor mixture there should be no need to employ chemical cleaners or descalers.
12   To refill the system, install the drain plug securely in the engine. Special thread sealing tape (available at auto parts stores) should be used on the drain plug in the engine block. Install the reserve system reservoir and the overflow hose.
13   Fill the radiator to the base of the filler neck and then add more coolant to the coolant reserve system reservoir until it reaches the 'FULL' mark.
14   Run the engine until normal operating temperature is reached and with the engine idling, add coolant up to the correct level (see Section 2). Install the reservoir cap.
15   Always refill the system with a mixture of high quality ethylene glycol-based antifreeze and water in the proportion called for on the antifreeze container or in your owner's manual. Chapter 3 also contains information on antifreeze mixtures.
16   Keep a close watch on the coolant level and the various cooling hoses during the first few miles of driving. Tighten the hose clamps and/or add more coolant mixture as necessary.

26 Evaporation control system (ECS) canister replacement

1   The function of the ECS emissions system is to draw fuel vapors from the tank and carburetor, store them in a charcoal-filled canister, and then burn them during normal engine operation.
2   The charcoal canister should be replaced at the specified intervals. If, however, a fuel odor is detected, the canister and system hoses should be inspected immediately.
3   The canister is located at the front right side of the engine compartment. It has three hoses attached to the top side. In order to facilitate removal of the canister, release the flexible rubber snorkel

tube from the air cleaner housing and the front grill support (photo).
4   Loosen and slide back the hose clamps on the three hoses and pull the hoses off the canister (photo). Loosen the spring type clamp at the rear of the canister and lift the canister out of its holder.
5   Place a new canister into position in the holder, tighten the spring-type clamp and replace the hoses (photo) (they are all different sizes, so they cannot be mixed up) and hose clamps. Install the flexible rubber snorkel tube between the air cleaner housing and the front grill support.
6   The ECS system is explained in more detail in Chapter 6.

27 Compression check

1   A compression check will tell you what mechanical condition the engine is in. Specifically, it can tell you if the compression is down due to leakage caused by worn piston rings, defective valves and seats or a blown head gasket.
2   Begin by cleaning the area around the spark plugs before you remove them. This will keep dirt from falling into the cylinders while you are performing the compression test.
3   Remove the coil high-tension lead from the distributor and ground it on the engine block. Block the throttle and choke valves wide open.
4   With the compression gauge in the number one cylinder's spark plug hole, crank the engine over at least 4 compression strokes and observe the gauge (the compression should build up quickly in a healthy engine). Low compression on the first stroke, followed by gradually increasing pressure on successive strokes, indicates worn piston rings. A low compression reading on the first stroke, which does not build up during successive strokes, indicates leaking valves or a defective head gasket. Record the highest gauge reading obtained.
5   Repeat the procedure for the remaining cylinders and compare the results to the specifications. Compression readings 10% above or below the specified amount can be considered normal.
6   Pour a couple of teaspoons of engine oil (a squirt can works great for this) into each cylinder, through the spark plug hole, and repeat the test.
7   If the compression increases after the oil is added, the piston rings are definitely worn. If the compression does not increase significantly, the leakage is occurring at the valves or head gasket.
8   If two adjacent cylinders have equally low compression, there is a strong possibility that the head gasket between them is blown. The appearance of coolant in the combustion chambers of the crankcase would verify this condition.
9   If the compression is higher than normal, the combustion chambers are probably coated with carbon deposits. If that is the case, the cylinder head (or heads) should be removed and decarbonized.
10   If compression is way down, or varies greatly between cylinders, it would be a good idea to have a 'leak-down' test performed by a reputable automotive repair shop. This test will pinpoint exactly where the leakage is occurring and how severe it is.

Chapter 2 Engine

Refer to Chapter 13 for specifications and information related to 1981 thru 1988 models

Contents

Specifications

Engine designations
USA
   U G52B
   W G54B
Canada
   U 4G52
   W 4G54

Displacement
U-engine .... 1995 cc (121.75 ci)
W-engine .... 2555 cc (155.92 ci)

Bore/stroke
U-engine .... 3.31 x 3.54 in (84.0 x 90.0 mm)
W-engine .... 3.59 x 3.86 in (91.1 x 98 mm)

Compression ratio
U-engine 8.5:1
W-engine 8.2:1

Firing order 1-3-4-2

Cylinder head
Warpage of cylinder head gasket surface .... Less then 0.004 in (0.1 mm)

Valve seat insert oversizes
Intake
  0.012 in (0.3 mm) O.S.
    Size mark 30
    Insert height .... 0.3110 to 0.3189 in (7.9 to 8.1 mm)
    Insert bore size .... 1.7441 to 1.7451 in (44.30 to 44.33 mm)
  0.024 in (0.6 mm) O.S.
    Size mark 60
    Insert height .... 0.3228 to 0.3307 in (8.2 to 8.4 mm)
    Insert bore size .... 1.7559 to 1.7569 in (44.60 to 44.63 mm)

Exhaust
    0.012 in (0.3 mm) O.S.
        Size mark 30
        Insert height .... 0.3110 to 0.3189 in (7.9 to 8.1 mm)
        Insert bore size .... 1.5079 to 1.5089 in (38.30 to 38.33 mm)
    0.024 in (0.6 mm) O.S.
        Size mark 60
        Insert height .... 0.3228 to 0.3307 in (8.2 to 8.4 mm)
        Insert bore size .... 1.5197 to 1.5207 in (38.60 to 38.63 mm)
Valve seat angles
    Intake .... 45°
    Exhaust .... 45°
    Valve seat width .... 0.035 to 0.051 in (0.9 to 1.3 mm)
Valve guide oversizes
    0.002 in (0.05 mm) O.S.
        Size mark 5
        Guide bore size .... 0.5138 to 0.5145 in (13.05 to 13.068 mm)
    0.010 in (0.25 mm) O.S.
        Size mark 25
        Guide bore size .... 0.5216 to 0.5224 in (13.25 to 13.268 mm)
    0.020 in (0.50 mm) O.S.
        Size mark 50
        Guide bore size .... 0.5315 to 0.5323 in (13.5 to 13.518 mm)

Camshaft
Minimum lobe height (intake and exhaust) .... 1.6414 in (41.7 mm)
End play .... 0.004 to 0.008 in (0.1 to 0.2 mm)

Valve train
Valve margin width
    Intake .... 0.028 to 0.047 in (0.7 to 1.2 mm)
    Exhaust .... 0.039 to 0.079 in (1 to 2 mm)
Valve stem-to-guide clearance
    Intake .... 0.0012 to 0.0024 in (0.03 to 0.06 mm)
    Exhaust .... 0.002 to 0.0035 in (0.05 to 0.09 mm)
Valve guide
    Installed dimension .... 0.5394 to 0.5630 in (13.7 to 14.3 mm)
    Oversizes .... 0.002, 0.010, 0.020 in (0.05, 0.25, 0.50 mm)
Valve spring
    Free length .... 1.830 to 1.869 in (46.5 to 47.5 mm)
    Under load .... 1.590 in/61 lbs (40.4 mm/270 N)
    Squareness .... 1.5° or less
    Installed height .... 1.590 to 1.629 in (40.4 to 41.4 mm)
Jet valve
    Stem O.D. .... 0.1693 in (4.300 mm)
    Seat angle .... 45°
Jet valve spring
    Free length .... 1.1654 in (29.60 mm)
    Under load .... 0.846 in/5.5 lbs (21.5 mm/34.3 N)
Valve clearances (cold engine)
    Intake valve .... 0.003 in (0.07 mm)
    Exhaust valve .... 0.007 in (0.17 mm)
    Jet valve .... 0.003 in (0.07 mm)

Engine block
Std. bore
    U-engine .... 3.3071 in (84 mm)
    W-engine .... 3.5866 in (91.1 mm)
Out-of-round/taper of cylinder bore .... Within 0.0008 in (0.02 mm)
Piston-to-bore clearance .... 0.0008 to 0.0016 in (0.02 to 0.04 mm)
Timing chain tensioner
    Spring free length .... 2.587 in (65.7 mm)
    Length under load .... 1.453 in/4.4 lbs (36.9 mm/19.6 N)
Oil pump
    Relief valve opening pressure .... 49.8 to 64.0 psi (343 to 441 kPa)
    Tip clearance .... 0.0043 to 0.0059 in (0.11 to 0.15 mm)
    Gear/bearing clearance (drive gear rear end) .... 0.0016 to 0.0028 in (0.04 to 0.07 mm)
    Gear end play .... 0.0024 to 0.0047 in (0.06 to 0.12 mm)
    Gear/bearing clearance .... 0.0008 to 0.0020 in (0.02 to 0.05 mm)
    Relief spring free length .... 1.850 in (47 mm)
    Under load .... 1.575 in/9.5 lbs (40 mm/42.2 N)

Silent Shaft
Silent shaft chain slack .... 0.040 to 0.140 in (1 to 3.5 mm)
Front journal OD .... 0.906 in (23 mm)
Rear journal OD .... 1.693 in (43 mm)
    Oil clearance
        Front bearing .... 0.0008 to 0.0024 in (0.02 to 0.06 mm)
        Rear bearing .... 0.0020 to 0.0035 in (0.05 to 0.09 mm)

Piston assembly

Piston identification
    U-engine (U.S.A.) 52J
    U-engine (Canada) 52
    W-engine (U.S.A.) 54J
    W-engine (Canada) 54

Oversize pistons
0.010 in (0.25 mm) oversize
    Size mark 0.25
    Diameter
        U-engine .... 3.3163 in (84.25 mm)
        W-engine .... 3.5964 in (91.35 mm)
0.020 in (0.50 mm) oversize
    Size mark 0.50
    Diameter
        U-engine .... 3.3262 in (84.50 mm)
        W-engine .... 3.6063 in (91.60 mm)
0.030 in (0.75 mm) oversize
    Size mark 0.75
    Diameter
        U-engine .... 3.3360 in (84.75 mm)
        W-engine .... 3.6161 in (91.85 mm)
0.039 in (1.00 mm) oversize
    Size mark 1.00
    Diameter
        U-engine .... 3.3464 in (85.00 mm)
        W-engine .... 3.6260 in (92.10 mm)

Piston ring identification
  Number 1 ring
    U-engine N1
    W-engine .... T
  Number 2 ring
    U-engine .... N
    W-engine 2T
  Oil ring .... No marking

Piston ring side clearance
  Number 1 ring .... 0.0024 to 0.0039 in (0.06 to 0.10 mm)
  Number 2 ring .... 0.0008 to 0.0024 in (0.02 to 0.06 mm)

Piston ring end gap
  Number 1 and 2 rings .... 0.010 to 0.018 in (0.25 to 0.45 mm)
  Oil ring side rail .... 0.008 to 0.035 in (0.2 to 0.9 mm)

Piston ring oversizes
  0.010 in (0.25 mm) O.S. .... Stamped 25
  0.020 in (0.50 mm) O.S. .... Stamped 50
  0.030 in (0.75 mm) O.S. .... Stamped 75
  0.039 in (1.00 mm) O.S. .... Stamped 100

Connecting rod

Bend .... 0.002/3.937 in (0.05/100 mm)
Twist .... 0.0039/3.937 in (0.1/100 mm)
Big-end side clearance .... 0.004 to 0.010 in (0.1 to 0.25 mm)
Piston pin installation pressure .... 1654 to 3859 lbs (7350 to 17100 N)

Crankshaft

Connecting rod bearing
  Oil clearance .... 0.0008 to 0.0028 in (0.02 to 0.07 mm)
  Undersizes .... 0.010, 0.020, 0.030 in (0.25, 0.50, 0.75 mm)
Main bearing
  Oil clearance .... 0.0008 to 0.0028 in (0.02 to 0.07 mm)
  Undersizes .... 0.010, 0.020, 0.030 in (0.25, 0.50, 0.75 mm)
Connecting rod journal OD .... 2.08666 in (53 mm)
Main bearing journal OD .... 2.3622 in (60 mm)
Out of round/taper of journals .... 0.0004 in (0.01 mm) or less
Crankshaft end play .... 0.002 to 0.007 in (0.05 to 0.18 mm)
Undersize rework dimensions of rod and main bearing journals .... Contact your dealer or a reputable automotive machine shop

Flywheel out-of-roundness .... 0.005 in (0.13 mm) or less

Torque specifications

	ft-lb	(Nm)
Front insulator-to-crossmember bolts	22 to 29	(29 to 39)
Front insulator-to-engine mount nuts	10 to 14	(13 to 19)
Rear insulator-to-engine support bracket bolts	10 to 14	(13 to 19)
Rear insulator-to-transmission nuts		
1979 models	14 to 17	(20 to 23.5)
1980 model	11 to 14	(15 to 20)
Engine support bracket-to-vehicle body bolts	7	(9.5)
Engine mount-to-engine block bolts	29 to 36	(39 to 49)
Cylinder head-to-timing chaincase bolt	11 to 15	(15 to 21)

Cylinder head bolt (cold engine)	65 to 72	(89 to 98)
Cylinder head bolt (hot engine)	72 to 80	(98 to 107)
Camshaft bearing cap bolt	14 to 15	(17 to 20)
Camshaft sprocket bolt	37 to 43	(49 to 58)
Spark plug	15 to 21	(20 to 29)
Valve cover bolts	4 to 5	(5 to 6)
Heater joint	15 to 28	(20 to 39)
Main bearing cap bolts	55 to 61	(74 to 83)
Connecting rod cap bolts	33 to 34	(45 to 47)
Flywheel bolts (M/T only)	94 to 101	(128 to 137)
Driveplate bolts (A/T only)	83 to 90	(112.7 to 121.5)
Crankshaft pulley bolt	80 to 94	(108 to 127)
Oil pump sprocket bolt	22 to 28	(29 to 39)
Oil pan bolts	4.5 to 5.5	(6 to 7)
Oil pan drain plug	44 to 57	(59 to 78)
Oil pump bolts	6 to 7	(8 to 9)
Intake/exhaust manifold nuts	11 to 14	(15 to 19)
Exhaust pipe-to-manifold nuts	11 to 18	(15 to 24)
Silent chamber cover bolts	3 to 4	(4 to 5)
Silent Shaft sprocket bolts	22 to 28	(29 to 39)
Silent Shaft-to-oil pump gear bolt	22 to 28	(29 to 39)
Oil pressure sending unit	11 to 15	(15 to 21)
Jet valve	13 to 15	(18 to 21)

1 General information

Two variations of the same basic engine are used in the Chrysler Mini Truck. They are designated 'U' and 'W', the only difference being displacement, which results from different bore/stroke combinations.

The engine is an inline vertical four, with a chain-driven overhead camshaft and a Silent Shaft counterbalancing system which cancels the engine's power pulses and produces relatively vibration-free operation. The crankshaft rides in 5 renewable insert-type main bearings, with the center bearing assigned the additional task of controlling crankshaft end thrust.

The pistons have 2 compression rings and 1 oil control ring. The piston pins are the semi-floating type, being a press fit in the small end of the connecting rod. The connecting rod big ends are also fitted with renewable insert-type plain bearings.

Trucks sold in the USA are equipped with a Jet Valve assembly, which reduces certain exhaust emissions.

The engine is liquid-cooled, utilizing a centrifugal impeller-type pump driven by a belt from the crankshaft to circulate coolant around the cylinders and combustion chambers and through the intake manifold.

Lubrication is handled by a gear-type oil pump mounted on the front of the engine under the timing chain cover. It is driven by the Silent Shaft chain. The oil is filtered continuously by a cartridge-type filter mounted on the right side of the engine.

2 Repair operations possible with the engine in the vehicle

1 Many major repair operations can be accomplished without removing the engine from the vehicle.
2 It is a very good idea to clean the engine compartment and the exterior of the engine with some type of pressure washer before any work is begun. A clean engine will make the job easier and will prevent the possibility of getting dirt into internal areas of the engine.
3 Remove the hood and cover the fenders to provide as much working room as possible and to prevent damage to the painted surfaces.
4 If oil or coolant leaks develop, indicating a need for gasket or seal replacement, the repairs can generally be made with the engine in the vehicle. The oil pan gasket, the cylinder head gasket, intake and exhaust manifold gaskets, timing chain case gaskets and the front and rear crankshaft oil seals are accessible with the engine in place, In the case of the rear crankshaft oil seal, the transmission, the clutch components and the flywheel must be removed first.
5 Exterior engine components, such as the starter motor, the alternator, the distributor, the fuel pump and the carburetor, as well as the intake and exhaust manifolds, are quite easily removed for repair with the engine in place.

6 Since the cylinder head can be removed without pulling the engine, valve servicing can also be accomplished with the engine in the vehicle.
7 Repairs to or inspection of the camshaft, the timing chain assembly, the Silent Shafts and chain assembly and the oil pump are all possible with the engine in place.
8 In extreme cases caused by a lack of necessary equipment, repair or replacement of piston rings, pistons, connecting rods and rod bearings and reconditioning of the cylinder bores is possible with the engine in the vehicle. This practice is not recommended because of the cleaning and preparation work that must be done to the components involved.

3 Engine overhaul – general note

1 It is not always easy to determine when, or if, an engine should be completely overhauled, as a number of factors must be considered.
2 High mileage is not necessarily an indication that an overhaul is needed while low mileage, on the other hand, does not preclude the need for an overhaul. Frequency of servicing is probably the single most important consideration. An engine that has regular (and frequent) oil and filter changes, as well as other required maintenance, will most likely give many thousands of miles of reliable service. Conversely, a neglected engine may require an overhaul very early in its life.
3 Excessive oil consumption is an indication that piston rings and/or valve guides are in need of attention. (Make sure that oil leaks are not responsible before deciding that the rings and guides are bad). Have a cylinder compression or leak-down test performed by an experienced tune-up mechanic to determine for certain the extent of the work required.
4 If the engine is making obvious 'knocking' or rumbling noises, the connecting rod and/or main bearings are probably at fault. Check the oil pressure with a gauge (installed in place of the oil pressure sending unit) and compare it to the specifications. If it is extremely low, the bearings and/or oil pump are probably worn out.
5 Loss of power, rough running, excessive valve train noise and high fuel consumption rates may also point to the need for an overhaul (especially if they are all present at the same time). If a complete tune-up does not remedy the situation, major mechanical work is the only solution.
6 An engine overhaul generally involves restoring the internal parts to the specifications of a new engine. During an overhaul, the piston rings are replaced and the cylinder walls are reconditioned (rebored and/or honed). If a rebore is done, then new pistons are also required. The main and connecting rod bearings are replaced with new ones and, if necessary, the crankshaft may be reground to restore the journals. Generally, the valves are serviced as well, since they are usually in less-than-perfect condition at this point. While the engine is

being overhauled, other components such as the carburetor, the distributor, the starter and the alternator can be rebuilt also. The end result should be a like-new engine that will give as many trouble-free miles as the original.

7 Before beginning the engine overhaul, read through the entire procedure to familiarize yourself with the scope and requirements of the job. Overhauling an engine is not that difficult, but it is time-consuming. Plan on the vehicle being tied up for a minimum of two weeks, especially if parts must be taken to an automotive machine shop for repair or reconditioning. Check on availability of parts and make sure that any necessary special tools and equipment are obtained in advance. Most work can be done with typical shop hand tools, although a number of precision measuring tools are required for inspecting parts to determine if they must be replaced. Often a reputable automotive machine shop will handle the inspection of parts and offer advice concerning reconditioning and replacement. As a general rule, time is the primary cost of an overhaul, so it doesn't pay to install worn or sub-standard parts.

8 As a final note, to ensure maximum life and minimum trouble from a rebuilt engine, everything must be assembled with care in a spotlessly clean environment.

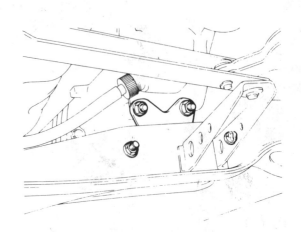

Fig. 2.1 Remove the 2 rear transmission mount nuts (Sec 4)

4 Engine – removal

1 The engine can be removed from the vehicle in either of two ways. One would be with the engine and transmission intact, as a unit. The other would be with the engine separated from the transmission before being removed from the vehicle. The procedure outlined here is for removing the engine and trransmission as a unit. If you choose to remove only the engine, leaving the transmission in place in the vehicle, refer to Chapter 7 for the procedure to follow for separating the transmission from the engine.

2 Whichever engine removal method is used, a suitable means of lifting the engine must be available. Ideally, a small crane mounted on wheels should be rented or borrowed. These are readily available, and easy to use. An alternative would be to suspend a chain fall or cable hoist from the garage ceiling beams, or a framework fabricated from large timbers. Regardless of which type of hoist support is utilized, it must be strong enough to support the full weight of the engine and transmission. Do not take chances or cut corners here, as serious injury and damage to the engine and vehicle could result.

3 The following sequence of operations does not necessarily need to be performed in the order given. It is, rather, a checklist of everything that must be disconnected or removed before the engine and transmission can be lifted out of the vehicle. If your vehicle is equipped with an automatic transmission the engine removal procedure will be slightly different. It is very important that all linkages, electrical wiring, hoses and cables are removed or disconnected before attempting to lift the engine clear of the vehicle, so double-check everything thoroughly.

4 Scribe or mark with paint the location of the hood hinge brackets on the hood (to ensure proper alignment of the hood upper reinstallation). Loosen and remove the 4 bolts attaching the hood to the brackets and lift the hood carefully away from the vehicle (with the help of an assistant).

5 Raise the vehicle and set it on jack stands.

6 Disconnect both battery cables from the battery (negative first, then positive), remove the battery hold-down and lift the battery out of the vehicle.

7 Drain the engine oil and the transmission lubricant.

8 Remove the radiator pressure cap, then drain the coolant from the radiator and the engine block. The radiator drain petcock is located on the lower left side of the radiator. The engine block drain is located on the lower right side of the engine, underneath the exhaust manifold. Once the coolant has been drained, remove the radiator hoses by loosening and sliding back the hose clamps (photo) and pulling the hoses off the radiator and engine. If your vehicle is equipped with an automatic transmission, disconnect and plug the transmission fluid cooling lines at the bottom of the radiator. Do not allow any dirt to enter the lines or fittings.

9 If your vehicle is equipped with a fan shroud, remove both the upper and lower sections. Each section is held in place by 2 bolts and a sheetmetal screw.

10 Remove the 4 bolts attaching the fan clutch to the water pump flange and lift the fan and clutch assembly away from the engine.

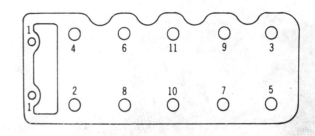

Fig. 2.2 Cylinder head bolt-loosening sequence (Sec 10)

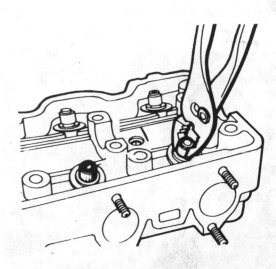

Fig. 2.3 Removing the valve stem seals with a pliers (Sec 11)

4.8 Loosening the radiator hose clamps

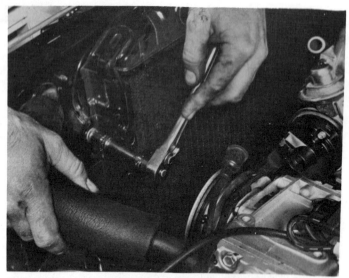

4.11a Removing the radiator mounting bolts

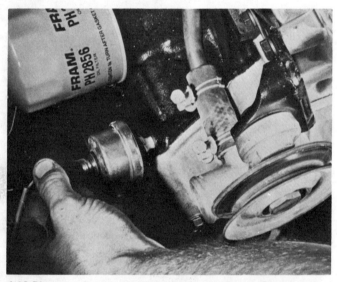

4.13 Disconnecting the wire from the oil pressure sending unit

4.14 Removing the power steering pump drive pulley

4.15 Removing the heat shield from the right motor mount

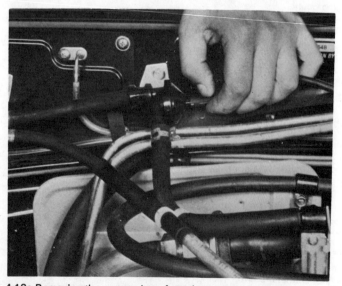

4.18a Removing the vacuum hose from the purge control valve

4.18b Removing the carburetor float bowl vent hose

4.18c Removing the purge hose bracket

4.19 Removing the throttle cable housing bracket from the valve cover

4.20 Removing the heater hose from the intake manifold fitting

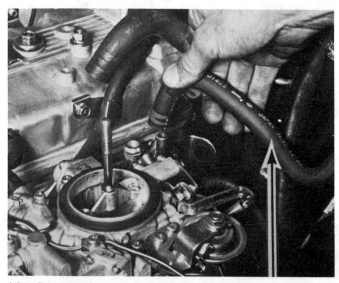

4.21a Removing the power brake vacuum hose from the intake manifold fitting

4.21b Removing the vacuum hoses from the throttle positioner and the air switching valve

4.22 Disconnecting the electrical lead from the carburetor

4.24 Disconnecting the fuel hoses from the carburetor

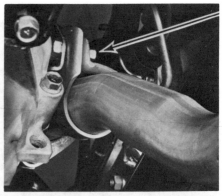

4.25 Remove the exhaust pipe bracket bolt

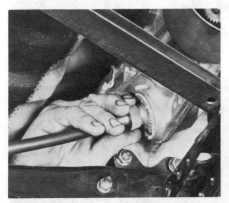

4.26 Disconnecting the speedometer cable from the transmission

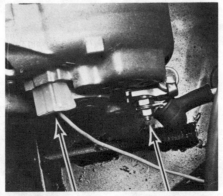

4.29 Disconnect the bayonet-type connector and the battery lead from the alternator

4.32 Loosening the transmission support crossmember bolts

4.34 Lifting off the rubber boot retaining plate on the gearshift lever

4.35 Removing the gearshift control lever assembly

5.2 Removing the exhaust pipe bracket from the bellhousing

5.3 Removing the starter motor

11 Remove the 4 bolts attaching the radiator to the vehicle (photo), and remove the overflow tube where it attaches at the radiator filler neck. Lift the radiator out of the vehicle and store it where it will not be damaged.
12 Remove the rubber snorkel connecting the air cleaner housing to the headlight support channel.
13 Disconnect the wire from the oil pressure sending unit on the right side of the engine (photo).
14 If the vehicle is equipped with power steering, remove the nut and the washer attaching the pulley to the power steering pump shaft (photo). Loosen the 2 power steering pump pivot bolts and the 1 adjusting bolt. Remove the drive belt from the pulley and slide the pulley off the front of the power steering pump shaft. Remove the 2 pivot bolts and the adjustment bolt and pull the power steering pump, with the hoses still attached, out of the mounting bracket. Tie the pump out of the way, making sure that the hoses are not kinked or twisted.
15 On trucks sold in the USA only, remove the nut attaching the heat shield to the right front engine mount (photo) and lift the heat shield away from the engine.
16 Remove the electrical ground strap connecting the firewall heat shield to the exhaust manifold.
17 Remove the top cover from the air cleaner. It is held in place by 4 spring clips and a wing nut. Lift out the filter element. Disconnect the various hoses leading to the air cleaner housing and remove the air cleaner housing from the engine. It is held in place by 2 nuts.
18 Pull the vacuum hose off of the purge control valve (photo), then remove the carburetor float bowl vent hose (at the valve cover) (photo) and the bracket that supports the purge hose (photo).
19 Remove the throttle cable housing brackets at the carburetor and the valve cover (photo), and disconnect the throttle cable from the carburetor.
20 Disconnect the heater hoses from the intake manifold fitting (photo) and the water pump transfer tube fitting at the rear of the engine.
21 Disconnect the power brake vacuum hose from the intake manifold fitting (photo). Disconnect the vacuum hose from the diaphragm at the left rear corner of the carburetor (a/c only). Disconnect the vacuum hose (color-coded yellow) from the air switching valve on the front left corner of the carburetor (photo).
22 Disconnect the electrical connector just below and to the left of the carburetor (photo). Remove the wire from the coolant temperature sending unit just behind the distributor. Remove the coil wire from the center tower of the distributor and unplug the primary circuit connector on the distributor body.
23 If your vehicle is equipped with air conditioning, disconnect the air conditioning compressor electrical lead. Remove the compressor and tie it out of the way.
24 Disconnect and plug the 2 fuel hoses at the fuel pump, and the 3 fuel hoses at the carburetor (photo). Disconnect the plastic tie-wraps, as necessary, to separate the fuel hoses, vacuum lines and electrical wiring. Slip all the belts off their pulleys and lift off the water pump pulley.
25 Remove the 2 nuts and washers holding the exhaust pipe to the exhaust manifold and remove the bolt ataching the exhaust pipe bracket to the transmission bellhousing (photo). Remove the 2 bolts at the exhaust pipe-to-muffler flange and the bolt at the rear exhaust pipe mounting bracket, immediately in front of the muffler. Lift the exhaust pipe out from under the vehicle.
26 Disconnect the speedometer cable where it enters the transmission (photo). Bend back the retaining strap that holds the speedometer cable housing to the frame crossmember and pull the speedometer cable away from the engine and transmission. Lay it on top of the left frame rail to keep it out of the way. Push forward on the parking brake lever and disengage the cable from the lever. Loosen the parking brake cable housing clamp in front of the frame crossmember and slide the cable housing forward to free the cable from the support bracket on the crossmember. Lay the cable on top of the left frame rail to keep it out of the way. Remove the pin attaching the rear parking brake cable balancer to the parking brake lever.
27 Disconnect the wiring harness from the back-up light switch, just behind the steering box. Disconnect the clutch cable from the clutch control lever at the transmission bellhousing. Back off the clutch cable adjuster and put as much free play as possible in the cable. Pull the rubber dust cover from the end of the clutch cable and slip the clutch cable through the mounting boss on the transmission bellhousing. Lay

the clutch cable on top of the left frame rail to keep it out of the way.
28 Disconnect the bayonet-type connector from the starter solenoid on the lower left side of the engine. Disconnect the battery lead from the solenoid.
29 Disconnect the bayonet-type connector and the battery lead from the alternator (photo). Tie the electrical harness out of the way, so that it will not interfere with the engine removal Separate the battery ground cable from the engine block (immediately behind the alternator). Remove the alternator pivot and adjusting bolts and lift the alternator away from the engine.
30 Remove the fuel line retaining strap from the left motor mount. At this point, double-check all around the engine to make sure that all electrical harnesses, vacuum lines, fuel lines, hoses, cables, and so forth, have been disconnected or removed.
31 Next, remove the drive shaft as described in Chapter 8.
32 Loosen the 2 bolts holding each of the motor mounts to the frame and loosen, but do not remove, the 6 bolts on each side of the crossmember that supports the rear of the transmission (where it connects to the frame rails) (photo). Also, remove the 2 nuts on the transmission mount at the top of the crossmember.
33 If your vehicle is equipped with a center console, remove the 4 screws that attach it to the vehicle. Loosen the jam nuts on the shift lever and unscrew the shift knob. Lift the console away from the shift lever and unplug the electrical connector behind the console.
34 Remove the 3 screws that attach the shifter boot retainer plate to the tunnel. Lift off the retainer plate and pull back the rubber boot (photo). It has a lip that fits over the sheetmetal of the tunnel; take care not to tear it as you pull the boot back.
35 Remove the 3 bolts attaching the control lever assembly to the transmission (photo) and slip the control lever assembly off. (If your vehicle is equipped with a 5 speed transmission, place the shift lever in first gear before removing the control lever assembly; if it is equipped with a 4-speed transmission, place the shift lever in second gear).
36 Support the transmission with a jack, or some other suitable support, and remove the twelve bolts and 2 nuts on the transmission support crossmember.
37 Secure a short length of heavy chain between the hoisting brackets on the engine. Attach the engine hoist lifting hook to the chain and raise the hoist slightly to take the weight off the front motor mounts. Remove the 2 bolts from each of the motor mounts and carefully hoist the engine while the jack supporting the transmission is removed. Gradually move the engine up and forward (by moving the hoist) and lower the transmission. Continue hoisting the engine until it clears the front of the vehicle, then pull forward on the hoist (do not allow the engine to swing freely) and lower the engine to the floor.

5 Separating the engine and transmission

1   Remove the splash shield from the bottom of the transmission bellhousing and block the engine and transmission securely in an upright position.
2   Remove the exhaust pipe bracket from the right side of the bellhousing (photo).
3   Remove the starter motor from the left side of the bellhousing (photo). It is held in place by 2 bolts.
4   Remove the 4 bolts attaching the transmission to the engine block.
5   Support the transmission near the front and pull straight back until it is completely free from the engine. If it is allowed to fall, damage to the input shaft could result.

6 Clutch and flywheel – removal and installation

1   Remove the clutch disc and clutch cover assembly by referring to Chapter 8.
2   Remove the 6 attaching bolts and separate the flywheel from the crankshaft. Lift the dust cover away from the engine.
3   When installing the flywheel, be sure to slip the dust cover into place first (the 2 bushings at the bottom of the engine block will locate it properly).
4   Hold the flywheel in position and install the 6 attaching bolts into place in the end of the crankshaft.

5   While holding the flywheel so that it doesn't turn, tighten the bolts (using a crisscross pattern) to the specified torque.
6   Install the clutch disc and clutch cover assembly as described in Chapter 8.

7   Engine – disassembly and reassembly

1   To completely disassemble the engine, remove the following items in the order given:

Engine external components	(Section 8)
Oil pan	(Section 9)
Cylinder head/valve train components	(Section 10)
Timing chain case/Silent Shaft chain and sprockets	(Section 12)
Timing chain and sprockets	(Section 13)
Piston/connecting rod assemblies	(Section 16)
Crankshaft	(Section 17)
Left Silent Shaft	(Section 14)
Oil pump/right Silent Shaft	(Section 15)

2   Engine reassembly is basically the reverse of disassembly. Install the following components in the order given:

Oil pump/right Silent Shaft	(Section 28)
Left Silent Shaft	(Section 14)
Crankshaft	(Section 25)
Piston/connecting rod assemblies	(Section 27)
Timing chain and sprockets	(Section 13)
Silent Shaft chain and sprockets/timing chain case	(Section 29)
Cylinder head/valve train components	(Section 31)
Oil pan	(Section 9)
Engine external components	(Section 32)

8   External engine components – removal

Note: *When removing the external components from the engine, pay close attention to details that may be helpful or important during installation. Look for the correct positioning of gaskets, seals, spacers, pins, washers, bolts and other small items. If necessary, refer to the illustrations in Section 32 and use them as guide during disassembly.*

1   It is much easier to dismantle and repair the engine if it is mounted on a portable-type engine stand. These stands can often be rented, for a reasonable fee, from an equipment rental yard.
2   If a stand is not available, it is possible to dismantle the engine with it blocked up on a sturdy workbench or on the floor. Be extra-careful not to tip or drop the engine when working without a stand.
3   Before the engine can be mounted on a stand, the flywheel, the dust shield and the rear seal housing must be removed. Remove the flywheel and dust shield by referring to Section 6, then loosen and remove the 7 bolts attaching the seal housing to the rear of the engine block and the oil pan. Carefully remove the housing (try not to let the oil separator inside the seal housing fall out of place). Note how the oil separator is installed, to prevent confusion during reassembly. You may have to tap the seal housing lightly with a soft-faced hammer to break it loose. Do not pry between the seal housing and engine block, as damage to the gasket sealing surfaces may result. At this point, the engine is ready to mount on the stand.
4   Remove the left engine mount insulator and metal roll restrictor. They are attached by 1 nut. Remove the 2 bolts attaching the left engine mount bracket to the engine block and remove the engine mount bracket. Next, remove the insulator, the roll restrictor and the motor mount bracket from the right side of the engine. Store the right and left motor mount bracket components separately, to avoid confusion during reassembly. Be sure to inspect the metal parts for cracks and the rubber parts for deterioration and delamination from the metal. If any defects are found, replace the parts with new ones.
5   If your vehicle is equipped with air-conditioning, remove the upper and lower compressor brackets from the engine block. There are a total of 7 bolts attaching the brackets to the engine. Remove the air-conditioning idler pulley bracket from the upper right side of the engine.
6   Remove the 3 bolts and lift the power steering pump bracket away from the lower right side of the engine.
7   Pull the crankcase emissions control system hose off the fitting at the rear of the valve cover and release it from the clamp on the valve cover. Remove the bowl vent tube from the metal pipe attached to the valve cover. Remove the rubber hose connecting the fitting at the rear of the intake manifold to the coolant transfer tube.
8   Remove the 9 nuts and 1 bolt attaching the intake manifold to the engine cylinder head and lift the manifold and the carburetor, as an assembly, from the head. Note the position of the engine hoisting bracket attached to the rear intake manifold studs.
9   Remove the 2 nuts attaching the fuel pump to the cylinder head, and slip off the fuel pump and the insulator.
10   Remove the distributor cap by depressing and turning the spring-loaded screws on the cap. Remove the distributor mounting nut and slip the distributor out of the engine by pulling straight out on it.
11   Loosen and slide back the hose clamp on the rubber hose connecting the water pump to the coolant transfer tube. Remove the 5 bolts attaching the water pump to the front of the engine and pull the water pump off. You may have to tap lightly on the pump body with a soft-faced hammer to break the gasket seal.
12   Remove the coolant transfer tube. It is held in place by a bracket on the right side of the engine and a bracket at the rear of the engine.
13   Unscrew and remove the oil pressure sending unit at the right front side of the engine.
14   Take off the secondary air supply system air pipe by removing the bracket bolts, and the fitting on top of the exhaust manifold. Separate the 2 heat shields attached to the exhaust manifold, remove the 8 nuts attaching the manifold to the head and lift the exhaust manifold away from the engine. Note the position of the engine hoisting bracket attached to the front exhaust manifold stud.
15   Remove the 4 bolts attaching the spark plug lead brackets to the valve cover and lift the distributor cap and spark plug leads away from the engine as an assembly.
16   Unscrew and remove the oil filter and take out the oil dipstick.

9   Oil pan – removal and installation

1   Remove the bolts securing the oil pan to the engine block.
2   Tap on the pan with a soft-faced hammer, to break the gasket seal, and lift the oil pan off the engine.
3   Using a gasket scraper, scrape off all traces of the old gasket from the engine block, the timing chain cover and the oil pan. Be especially careful not to nick or gouge the gasket sealing surface of the timing chain cover (it is made of aluminum and is quite soft).
4   Clean the oil pan with solvent and dry it thoroughly. Check the gasket sealing surfaces for distortion.
5   Before installing the oil pan, apply a thin coat of silicone-type gasket sealer to the engine block gasket sealing surfaces. Lay a new oil pan gasket in place and carefully apply a coat of gasket sealer to the exposed side of the gasket.
6   Gently lay the oil pan in place (photo); (do not disturb the gasket) and install the bolts. Start with the bolts closest to the center of the pan and tighten them to the specified torque using a crisscross pattern. Do not overtighten them or leakage may occur.

9.6 Installing the oil pan

10 Cylinder head – removal

1   Remove the 2 bolts, washers and rubber seals attaching the valve cover to the cylinder head and lift off the cover. Remove the breather grommet from the front of the cylinder head and the circular seal from the rear of the cylinder head.
2   Rotate the engine (with a wrench on the large bolt at the front of the crankshaft) until the number 1 piston is at top dead center on the compression stroke. To do this, watch the rocker arms for the number 1 cylinder valves while slowly rotating the crankshaft in a clockwise direction (viewed from the front). When the intake valve closes, continue rotating the crankshaft until the mark on the pulley is aligned with the 'T' on the timing tab (photo).
3   Locate the timing mark on the camshaft sprocket and make sure the plated link of the cam chain is opposite the mark.
4   Remove the camshaft sprocket bolt and oil shield from the front of the camshaft (photo). Hold the large bolt on the end of the crankshaft (to keep the engine from turning) while loosening the bolt. Remove the distributor drive gear from the front of the camshaft by tapping it with a soft-faced hammer. Pull the camshaft sprocket (with the chain in place) off the camshaft, and allow it to rest on the sprocket holder.
5   Loosen the 10 camshaft bearing cap bolts, $\frac{1}{2}$ turn each, in sequence, until all pressure from the valve springs has been released. Then remove the 6 inner bolts and lift the rocker arm shaft assembly away from the cylinder head with the 4 end bolts in place. Do not disassemble the components any further, unless new parts are required. Carefully lift the camshaft out of the cylinder head and store it where it will not be damaged.
6   Remove the 2 bolts attaching the cylinder head to the timing chain cover (at the very front of the cylinder head). Remove the 10 bolts attaching the cylinder head to the engine block. Turn them $\frac{1}{4}$ of a turn each, in the sequence shown, until they are all loose enough to remove by hand.
7   Remove the cylinder head by lifting it straight up and off the engine block. Do not pry between the cylinder head and the engine block, as damage to the gasket sealing surfaces may result. Instead use a soft-faced hammer to tap the cylinder head and break the gasket seal.
8   Lift off the old head gasket.

11 Cylinder head – disassembly

1   Cylinder head disassembly involves removal and disassembly of the jet valves and removal of the intake and exhaust valves and their related components.
2   Using a 6-point deep socket and a breaker bar, carefully remove the jet valve assemblies from the cylinder head. Do not tilt the socket, as the jet valve stems can be bent very easily by the force exerted on the valve spring retainer (which will cause defective jet valve operation). Label each jet valve assembly so it can be reinstalled in the same hole it was removed from.
3   Disassemble each jet valve by carefully compressing the spring and removing the keepers, the valve spring retainer and the valve spring. Slide the valve out of the body and pull off the seal with a pliers. (Discard the oil seals, as they should not be reused). Keep the parts for each jet valve assembly separate (photo) so that they are not acidentally interchanged with parts from other jet valve assemblies.
4   Before the valves are removed, arrange to label and store them, along with their related components, so that they can be kept separate and reinstalled in the same valve guides they were removed from. Also, measure the valve spring installed height (for each valve) and compare it to the specifications (photo). If it is greater than specified, the valve seats and valve faces need attention.
5   Compress the valve spring on the first valve with a spring compressor (photo) then remove the keepers and the retainer from the valve assembly. Carefully release the valve spring compressor and remove the spring, the spring seat and the valve from the head. If the valve binds in the guide (won't pull through), push it back into the head and deburr the area around the keeper groove with a fine file.
6   Repeat the procedure for the remaining valves. Remember to keep all the parts for each valve in order so that they can be reinstalled in the same position (photo).
7   Once the valves have been removed and safely stored, pull off the valve stem seals with a pliers and discard them; the old seals should never be reused.

8   Refer to Section 23 for cylinder head cleaning and inspection procedures.

12 Silent Shaft chain/sprockets – removal and inspection

1   Before attempting to remove the Silent Shaft chain and sprockets, remove the cylinder head and the oil pan by referring to the appropriate sections.
2   Remove the large bolt at the front of the crankshaft and slide the pulley off.
3   Remove the bolts attaching the timing chain case to the engine block. Draw a simple diagram showing the location of each of the bolts (so they can be returned to the same holes they were removed from).
4   Tap the timing chain case with a soft-faced hammer, to break the gasket seal, and remove the case from the engine block. Do not pry between the case and the engine block, as damage to the gasket sealing surfaces will result.
5   Remove the chain guides labeled A, B and C. They are held in place with 2 bolts each. Again, draw a simple diagram showing the location of each of the bolts (so they can be returned to the same holes they were removed from).
6   Reinstall the large bolt in the end of the crankshaft and hold it with a wrench (to keep the engine from turning) while loosening the bolt in the end of the right (lower) Silent Shaft, the bolt attaching the right Silent Shaft drive sprocket to the oil pump shaft and the bolt in the end of the left (upper) Silent Shaft. If the bolt in the end of the right Silent Shaft is difficult to loosen, remove the oil pump and Silent Shaft as an assembly (see Section 15), then remove the bolt with the Silent Shaft securely clamped in a vise.
7   Slide the crankshaft sprocket, the Silent Shaft sprockets and the chain off the engine as an assembly. Leave the bolt in the end of the right (lower) Silent Shaft in place. Do not lose the keys that index the sprockets to the shafts.
8   Check the sprocket teeth for wear and damage. Check the sprocket cushion rings and ring guides (Silent Shaft sprockets only) for wear and damage. Rotate the cushion rings and check for smooth operation. Inspect the chain for cracked side plates and pitted or worn rollers. Replace any defective or worn parts with new ones.

13 Timing chain/sprockets – removal, inspection and installation

1   Since the Silent Shaft chain and sprockets must be dismantled to gain access to the timing chain assembly, refer to Section 12 and remove the Silent Shaft chain and sprockets.
2   Depress the timing chain tensioner plunger (on the oil pump) and slide the camshaft sprocket, the crankshaft sprocket and the timing chain off the engine as an assembly. Do not lose the key that indexes the crankshaft sprocket in the proper place. Remove the timing chain tensioner plunger and spring from the oil pump.
3   Remove the camshaft sprocket holder and the right and left timing chain guides from the front of the engine block.
4   Inspect the sprocket teeth for wear and damage. Check the chain for cracked plates and pitted or worn rollers. Check the chain tensioner rubber shoe for wear and the tensioner spring for cracks or deterioration. Measure the tensioner spring free length and compare it to the specifications. Check the chain guides for wear and damage. Replace any defective parts with new ones.
5   Install the sprocket holder (photo) and the right and left timing chain guides onto the engine block. Tighten the attaching bolts securely, (the upper bolt in the left timing chain guide should be installed finger-tight only), then coat the entire length of the chain contact surfaces of the guides with clean, high-quality multi-purpose grease.
6   Turn the crankshaft, with a wrench on the large bolt at the front, until the number 1 piston is at top dead center. (When it is flush with the top of the engine block, it is at top dead center.) Apply a layer of clean multi-purpose grease (or engine assembly lube) to the timing chain tensioner plunger and install the tensioner spring and plunger loosely into the oil pump body (photo).
7   Position the timing chain sprocket on the end of the crankshaft, with the wide shoulder facing out (photo). Line up the key-way in the sprocket with the key on the crankshaft.
8   Install the camshaft sprocket onto the chain, lining up the plated link on the chain with the marked tooth on the sprocket (photo).

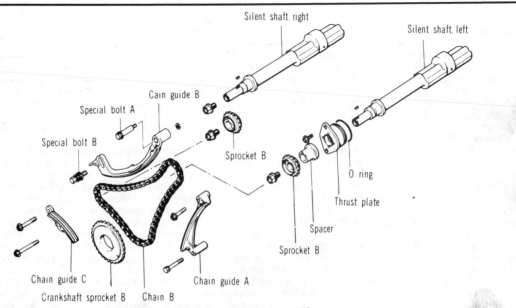

Fig. 2.4 Silent Shaft components (Sec 12)

9   Slip the chain over the crankshaft sprocket, lining up the plated link on the chain with the marked tooth on the sprocket (photo). Slide the crankshaft sprocket all the way onto the crankshaft while depressing the chain tensioner so that the chain fits into place in the guides. Rest the camshaft sprocket on the sprocket holder. Do not rotate the crankshaft for any reason until the cylinder head and camshaft have been properly installed.

14 Silent Shafts – removal, inspection and installation

1   During engine disassembly, the Silent Shaft chain and sprockets, the timing chain and sprockets and the oil pump should be removed before the Silent Shafts.
2   Remove the left Silent Shaft chamber cover plate from the engine block. It is held in place with two bolts. You may have to tap the cover with a soft-faced hammer to break the gasket seal.
3   Remove the 2 bolts attaching the left Silent Shaft thrust plate to the engine block, then carefully pull out the thrust plate and the Silent Shaft as an assembly. Support the rear of the shaft (by reaching through the access hole) to prevent damage to the rear bearing as the shaft is withdrawn from the engine (photo). If the thrust plate proves to be difficult to pull out, screw the appropriate size bolt into each of the threaded holes in the thrust plate flange until they bottom on the engine block. Continue turning them with a wrench, one turn at a time, alternating between the two, until the thrust plate is backed out of the engine block. Remove the bolts from the thrust plate flange.
4   The right Silent Shaft is removed with the oil pump (refer to Section 15).
5   To disassemble the left Silent Shaft, slip off the spacer and the thrust plate/bearing assembly. Do not lose the key in the end of the shaft. Remove the O-ring from the thrust plate.
6   Clean the components with solvent and dry them thoroughly. Make sure that the oil holes in the shafts and thrust plate are clean and clear.
7   Check both Silent Shafts and the thrust plate for cracks and other damage. Check the bearings in the engine block and the thrust plate (photo) for scratches, scoring and excessive wear. Check the bearing journals on the Silent Shafts for excessive wear and scoring.
8   Measure the outside diameter of each bearing journal (photo) and the inside diameter of each bearing. Subtract the journal diameter from the bearing diameter to obtain the bearing oil clearance. Compare the measured clearance to the specifications. If it is excessive, have an automotive machine shop or dealer service department replace the bearings with new ones. If new bearings do not restore the oil clearance, or if the bearing journals on the shafts are damaged or worn, replace the shafts also. If the bearing in the left Silent Shaft thrust plate is bad, replace the bearing and thrust plate as an assembly.

9   Apply a thin layer of clean multi-purpose grease (or engine assembly lube) to the bearing journals on the left Silent Shaft, then carefully insert it into the engine block. Support the rear of the shaft so that the rear bearing is not scratched or gouged as the shaft passes through it.
10 Install a new O-ring onto the outside of the thrust plate and lubricate it with clean multi-purpose grease. Also, apply a layer of grease to the thrust plate Silent Shaft bearing.
11 Cut the heads off two 6 x 50 mm bolts and install the bolts in the thrust place mounting bolt holes. Using the bolts as a guide, carefully slide the thrust plate into position in the engine block. The guides are necessary to keep the bolt holes in the thrust plate aligned with the holes in the engine block. If the thrust plate is turned to align the holes, the O-ring could be twisted or damaged.
12 Remove the guide bolts, install the mounting bolts and tighten them securely.
13 Slip the spacer onto the end of the Silent Shaft. (Make sure that the key is in place).
14 Turn the shaft by hand and check for smooth operation.
15 Using a new rubber gasket and silicone-type gasket sealer, as well as new O-rings on the bolts, install the left Silent Shaft chamber cover plate and tighten the bolts to the specified torque.
16 The right Silent Shaft is installed with the oil pump.

15 Oil pump – removal, disassembly and inspection

1   The oil pump and right Silent Shaft are removed from the engine as an assembly.
2   Remove the bolt attaching the oil pump to the engine block. Some of the Silent Shaft chain guide mounting bolts also serve as oil pump mounting bolts; they have already been removed. Leave the Phillips head screw in the left side of the pump in place.
3   Carefully pull straight ahead on the oil pump and remove it, along with the right Silent Shaft, from the engine block. You may have to tap gently on the oil pump body with a soft-faced hammer to break the gasket seal. Do not pry between the oil pump and engine block, as damage to the pump body could result.
4   Remove the bolt from the end of the right Silent Shaft and pull the shaft out of the oil pump from the rear. (Do not lose the key in the end of the shaft.) Refer to Section 14 for Silent Shaft inspection procedures.
5   Remove the plug from the upper side of the pump body and withdraw the relief spring and plunger. You may have to mount the pump body in a vise equipped with soft jaws to loosen the plug. If so, do not apply excessive pressure to the pump body.
6   Remove the Phillips head screw from the left side of the pump. Separate the oil pump cover from the body and lift out the 2 pump gears. Do not lose the key in the lower gear shaft. Do not pry between the cover and body, as damage to the pump may result.

10.2 Aligning the mark on the pulley with the 'T' on the timing tab

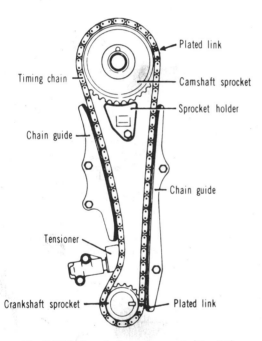

Timing chain
Plated link
Camshaft sprocket
Sprocket holder
Chain guide
Chain guide
Tensioner
Crankshaft sprocket
Plated link

Fig. 2.5 Timing chain components (Sec 13)

7   Clean the parts with solvent and dry them thoroughly. Use compressed air to blow out all of the oil holes and passages.
8   Check the entire pump body and cover for cracks and excessive wear. Look closely for a ridge where the gears contact the body and cover.
9   Insert the relief plunger into the pump body and check to see if it slides smoothly. Look for cracks in the relief spring and measure its free length. Inspect the timing chain tensioner plunger sleeve for noticeable wear and the rubber pad for cracks and excessive wear. Measure the tensioner spring free length and compare it to the specifications.
10 Refer to Figure 2.8. With the gears in place in the pump body, measure the top clearance (A) between the gears and the pump body with a feeler gauge. Measure the inside diameter of the bearing surfaces and the outside diameter of the gear shaft at (C) and (D). Subtract the gear shaft diameters from their matching bearing surface diameters to obtain the gear-to-bearing clearance. With the pump assembled, check the gear end play (B) using a dial indicator set. Compare the measured clearances to the specifications.
11 If the oil pump clearances are excessive or if excessive wear is evident, replace the oil pump as a unit.

16 Piston/connecting rod assembly – removal

1   Prior to removing the piston/connecting rod assemblies remove the cylinder head, the oil pan, the timing chain case, the Silent Shaft chain and sprockets and the timing chain and sprockets by referring to the appropriate sections.
2   Using a ridge reamer, completely remove the ridge at the top of each cylinder (follow the manufacturer's instructions provided with the ridge reaming tool). Failure to remove the ridge before attempting to remove the piston/connecting rod assemblies will result in piston breakage.
3   With the engine in the upside-down position, remove the oil pick-up tube and screen assembly from the bottom of the engine block (photo). It is held in place with 2 bolts.
4   Mark each of the connecting rods and connecting rod bearing caps to ensure that they are properly mated during reassembly.
5   Loosen each of the connecting rod cap nuts approximately $\frac{1}{2}$ turn each. Remove the number 1 connecting rod cap and bearing insert. Do not drop the bearing insert out of the cap. Slip a short length of plastic or rubber hose over each connecting rod cap bolt (to protect the crankshaft journal when the piston is removed) (photo) and push the connecting rod/piston assembly out through the top of the engine. Use a wooden tool to push on the upper bearing insert in the connecting rod. If resistance is felt, double-check to make sure that all of the ridge was removed from the cylinder.
6   Repeat the procedure for cylinders 2, 3 and 4. After removal, reassemble the connecting rod caps and bearing inserts to their respective connecting rods and install the cap nuts finger-tight. Leaving the old bearing inserts in place until reassembly will help prevent the connecting rod bearing surfaces from being accidentally nicked or gouged.

17 Crankshaft – removal

1   Before removing the crankshaft, you must remove the flywheel, the rear oil seal housing, the cylinder head, the oil pan, the timing chain case, the Silent Shaft chain and sprockets and the timing chain and sprockets, by referring to the appropriate sections.
2   With the engine upside-down, remove the oil pick-up tube and screen assembly from the bottom of the engine block. It is held in place with 2 bolts.
3   Remove the piston assemblies from the engine block, as described in Section 16. Be sure to mark each connecting rod and bearing cap so that they will be properly mated during reassembly.
4   Loosen each of the main bearing cap bolts $\frac{1}{4}$ of a turn at a time, in sequence, starting at the center of the engine, until they can be removed by hand.
5   Gently tap the main bearing caps with a soft-faced hammer, then remove them from the engine block. If necessary, use the main bearing cap bolts as levers to remove the caps. Try not to drop the bearing shell, if it comes out with the cap. The main bearing caps are marked at the factory with a number (1 through 5, starting at the front of the engine) and an arrow (indicating the front of the engine) so you do not have to mark them.
6   Carefully lift the crankshaft out of the engine. It is a good idea to have an assistant available, as the crankshaft is quite heavy. With the bearing inserts in place in the engine block and the main bearing caps, return the caps to their respective location on the engine block and tighten the bolts finger-tight.

18 Engine block – cleaning

1   Remove the 10 soft plugs from the engine block. To do this, knock the plugs into the block (using a hammer and punch), then grasp them with a large pliers and pull them back through the hole.
2   Using a gasket scraper, remove all traces of gasket material from the engine block. Be very careful not to nick or gouge the gasket sealing surfaces.
3   Remove the main bearing caps and separate the bearing shells from the caps and the engine block. Tag the bearing shells according to which cylinder they were removed from (and whether they were in the cap or the block) and set them aside.

4   Using a hex wrench of the appropriate size, remove the threaded oil gallery plugs from the front and back of the block.

5   If the engine is extremely dirty, it should be taken to an automotive machine shop to be steam cleaned or hot tanked. Any bearings left in the block (such as the Silent Shaft bearings) may be damaged by the cleaning process, so plan on replacing them.

6   After the block is reurned, clean all oil holes and oil galleries one more time (brushes for cleaning oil holes and galleries are available at most auto parts stores). Flushing the passages with warm water (until the water runs clear), dry the block thoroughly and wipe all machined surfaces with a light rust-preventative oil. If you have access to compressed air, use it to speed the drying process and to blow out all of the oil holes and galleries.

7   If the block is not extremely dirty or sludged up, you can do an adequate cleaning job with warm soapy water and a stiff brush. Take plenty of time and do a thorough job. Regardless of the cleaning method used, be very sure to thoroughly clean all oil holes and galleries, dry the block completely and coat all machined surfaces with light oil.

8   The threaded holes in the block must be clean to ensure accurate torque readings during reassembly. Run the proper size tap into each of the holes to remove any rust, corrosion, thread sealant or sludge and to restore any damaged threads. If possible, use compressed air to clear the holes of debris produced by this operation. Now is a good time to thoroughly clean the threads on the head bolts and the main bearing cap bolts as well.

9   Reinstall the main bearing caps and tighten the bolts finger tight.

10   After coating the sealing surfaces of the new soft plugs with a good quality gasket sealer, install them in the engine block (photo). Make sure they are driven in straight and seated properly, or leakage could result. Special tools are available for this purpose, but equally good results can be obtained using a large socket (with an outside diameter slightly larger than the outside diameter of the soft plug) and a large hammer.

11   If the engine is not going to be reassembled right away, cover it with a large plastic trash bag to keep it clean.

19 Engine block – inspection

1   Thoroughly clean the engine block as described in Section 19 and double-check to make sure that the ridge at the top of the cylinders has been completely removed.

2   Visually check the block for cracks, rust and corrosion. Look for stripped threads in the threaded holes. It is also a good idea to have the block checked for hidden cracks by an automotive machine shop

that has the special equipment to do this type of work. If defects are found, have the block repaired, if possible, or replaced.

3   Check the cylinder bores for scuffing and scoring.

4   Using the appropriate precision measuring tools, measure each cylinder's diameter at the top (just under the ridge), center and bottom of the cylinder bore, parallel to the crankshaft axis (photo). Next, measure each cylinder's diameter at the same 3 locations across the crankshaft axis. Compare the results to the specifications. If the cylinder walls are badly scuffed or scored, or if they are out-of-round or tapered beyond the limits given in the specifications, have the engine block rebored and honed at an automotive machine shop. If a rebore is done, oversized pistons and rings will be required as well.

5   If the cylinders are in reasonably good condition and not worn to the outside of the limits, and if the piston-to-cylinder clearances can be maintained properly, then they do not have to be rebored; honing is all that is necessary.

6   Before honing the cylinders, install the main bearing caps (without the bearings) and tighten the bolts to the specified torque.

7   To perform the honing operation, you will need the proper size flexible hone (with fine stones), plenty of light oil or honing oil, some rags and an electric drill motor. Mount the hone in the drill motor, compress the stones and slip the hone into the first cylinder. Lubricate the cylinder thoroughly, turn on the drill and move the hone up and down in the cylinder at a pace which will produce a fine cross-hatch pattern on the cylinder walls (with the cross-hatch lines intersecting at

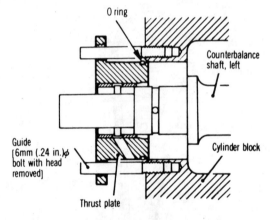

Fig. 2.6 Installing the left Silent Shaft thrust plate using 6 mm bolts as guides (Sec 14)

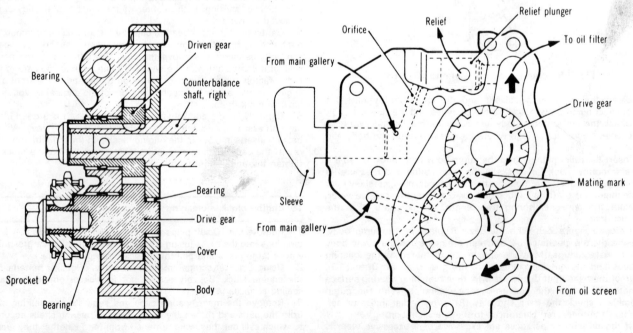

Fig. 2.7 Oil pump components (Sec 15)

approximately a 60° angle). Be sure to use plenty of lubricant, and do not take off any more material than is absolutely necessary to produce the desired finish. Do not withdraw the hone from the cylinder while it is running. Instead, shut off the drill and continue moving the hone up and down in the cylinder until it comes to a complete stop, then compress the stones and withdraw the hone. Wipe the oil out of the cylinder and repeat the procedure on the remaining cylinders. Remember, do not remove too much material from the cylinder wall. If you do not have the tools or do not desire to perform the honing operation, most automotive machine shops will do it for a reasonable fee (photo).

8   After the honing job is complete, chamfer the top edges of the cylinder bores with a small file so that the rings will not catch when the pistons are installed.

9   Next, the entire engine block must be thoroughly washed again with warm soapy water to remove all traces of the abrasive grit produced during the honing operation. Be sure to run a brush through all oil holes and galleries and flush them with running water. After rinsing, dry the block and apply a coat of light rust preventative oil to all machined surfaces. Wrap the block in a plastic trash bag to keep it clean and set it aside until reassembly.

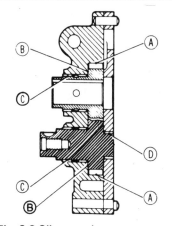

Fig. 2.8 Oil pump clearance measurement points (see text, Sec 15)

20 Crankshaft – inspection

1   Clean the crankshaft with solvent (be sure to clean the oil holes with a stiff brush and flush them with solvent) and dry it thoroughly. Check the main and connecting rod bearing journals for uneven wear, scoring, pitting and cracks. Check the remainder of the crankshaft for cracks and damage.

2   Using an appropriate size micrometer, measure the diameter of the main and connecting rod journals (photo) and compare the results to the specifications. By measuring the diameter at a number of points around the journal's circumference, you will be able to determine whether or not the journal is worn out-of-round. Take the measurement at each end of the journal, near the crank throw, to determine whether the journal is tapered.

3   If the crankshaft journals are damaged, tapered, out-of-round or worn beyond the limits given in the specifications, have the crankshaft reground by a reputable automotive machine shop. Be sure to use the correct undersize bearing inserts if the crankshaft is reconditioned.

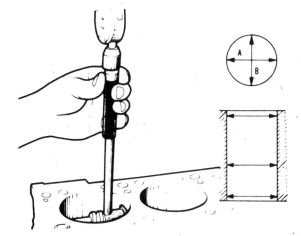

Fig. 2.9 Cylinder bore measurement locations (Sec 19)

21 Piston/connecting rod assembly – inspection

1   Before the inspection process can be carried out, the piston/connecting rod assemblies must be cleaned and the oil piston rings removed from the pistons.

2   Using a piston ring installation tool, carefully remove the rings from the pistons. Do not nick or gouge the pistons in the process.

3   Scrape all traces of carbon from the top (or crown) of the piston. A hand-held wire brush or a piece of fine emery cloth can be used once the majority of the deposits have been scraped away. Do not, under any circumstances, use a wire brush mounted in a drill motor to remove deposits from the pistons. The piston material is soft and will be eroded away by the wire brush.

4   Use a piston ring groove cleaning tool to remove any carbon deposits from the ring grooves (photo). If a tool is not available, a piece broken off the old ring will do the job. Be very careful to remove only the carbon deposits. Do not remove any metal and do not nick or scratch the sides of the ring grooves.

5   Once the deposits have been removed, clean the piston/rod assemblies with solvent and dry them thoroughly. Make sure that the oil hole in the big end of the connecting rod and the oil return holes in the back side of the ring groove are clear.

6   If the pistons are not damaged or worn excessively, and if the engine block is not rebored, new pistons will not be necessary. Normal piston wear appears as even vertical wear on the piston thrust surfaces and slight looseness of the top ring in its groove. New piston rings, on the other hand, should always be used when an engine is rebuilt.

7   Carefully inspect each piston for cracks around the skirt, at the pin bosses and at the ring lands.

8   Look for scoring and scuffing (on the thrust faces of the skirt), holes (in the piston crown) and burned areas (at the edge of the crown). If the skirt is scored or scuffed, the engine may have been suffering from overheating and/or abnormal combustion, which caused

excessively high operating temperatures. The cooling and lubrication systems should be checked thoroughly. A hole in the piston crown, an extreme to be sure, is an indication that abnormal combustion (preignition) was occurring. Burned areas at the edge of the piston crown are usually evidence of spark knock (detonation). If any of the above problems exist, the causes must be corrected or the damage will occur again.

9   Corrosion of the piston (evidenced by pitting) indicates that coolant is leaking into the combustion chamber and/or the crankcase. Again, the cause must be corrected or the problem may persist in the rebuilt engine.

10   Measure the piston ring side clearance by laying a new piston ring in the ring groove and slipping a feeler gauge in beside it (photo). Check the clearance at 3 or 4 locations around the groove. Be sure to use the correct ring for each groove; they are different. If the side clearance is greater than specified, new pistons will have to be used and the block rebored to accept them.

11   Check the piston-to-bore clearance by measuring the bore (see Section 19) and the piston diameter (photo). Make sure that the pistons and bores are correctly matched. Measure the piston across the skirt, on the thrust faces (at a 90° angle to the piston pin), about 0.100 in (2 mm) up from the bottom of the skirt. Subtract the piston diameter from the bore diameter to obtain the clearance. If it is greater than specified, the block will have to be rebored and new pistons and rings installed. Check the piston pin-to-rod clearance by twisting the piston and rod in opposite directions. Any noticeable play indicates that there is excessive wear, which must be corrected. The piston/connecting rod assemblies should be taken to an automotive machine shop to have new piston pins installed and the pistons and connecting rods rebored.

12   If the pistons must be removed from the connecting rods, such as when new pistons must be installed, or if the piston pins have too much play in them, they should be taken to an automotive machine

10.4 Removing the bolt and oil shield from the front of the camshaft

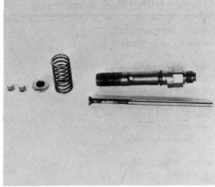
11.3 Jet valve assembly components

11.4 Measuring the installed height of the valve spring

11.5 Compressing the valve spring with a valve spring compressor

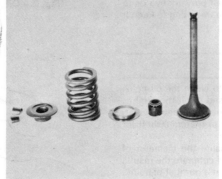
11.6 Intake/exhaust valve components

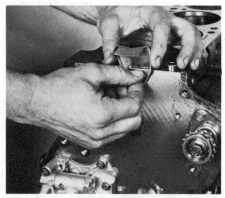
13.5 Installing the camshaft sprocket holder on the engine block

13.6 Installing the timing chain tensioner plunger in the oil pump bore

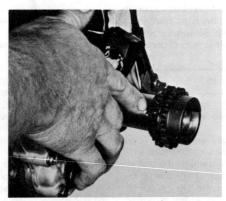
13.7 Installing the timing chain sprocket in the end of the crankshaft (note that the wide shoulder is facing out)

13.8 Meshing the camshaft sprocket with the timing chain (note that the mark on the sprocket is directly opposite the plated link on the chain)

13.9 Installing the timing chain on the camshaft sprocket (note that the mark on the sprocket is directly opposite the plated link on the chain)

14.3 Removing the left Silent Shaft/thrust plate assembly

14.7 Checking the bearing in the left Silent Shaft thrust plate

shop. While they are there, it would be convenient to have the connecting rods checked for bend and twist, as automotive machine shops have special equipment for this purpose.

13 Check the connecting rods for cracks and other damage. Temporarily remove the rod cap, lift out the old bearing inserts, wipe the rod and cap bearing surfaces clean and inspect them for nicks, gouges and scratches. After checking the rods, replace the old bearings, slip the caps in place and tighten the nuts finger-tight. Unless new pistons or connecting rods must be installed, do not disassemble the pistons from the connecting rods.

22 Main and connecting rod bearings – inspection

1 Even though the main and connecting rod bearings should be replaced with new ones during the engine overhaul, the old bearings should be retained for close examination, as they may reveal valuable information about the condition of the engine.

2 Bearing failure occurs mainly because of lack of lubrication, the presence of dirt or other foreign particles, overloading the engine and/or corrosion. Regardless of the cause of bearing failure, it must be corrected before the engine is reassembled to prevent it from happening again.

3 When examining the bearings, remove them from the engine block, the main bearing caps, the connecting rods and the rod caps and lay them out on a clean surface in the same general position as their location in the engine. This will enable you to match any noted bearing problems with the corresponding crankshaft journal.

4 Dirt and other foreign particles get into the engine in a variety of ways. It may be left in the engine during assembly, or it may pass through filters or breathers. It may get into the oil, and from there into the bearings. Metal chips from machining operations and normal engine wear are often present. Abrasives are sometimes left in engine components after reconditioning, especially when parts are not thoroughly cleaned using the proper cleaning methods. Whatever the source, these foreign objects often end up embedded in the soft bearing material and are easily recognized. Large particles will not embed in the bearing and will score or gouge the bearing and shaft. The best prevention for this cause of bearing failure is to clean all parts thoroughly and keep everything spotlessly clean during engine assembly. Frequent and regular changes of engine oil, and oil filters, is also recommended.

5 Lack of lubrication (or lubrication breakdown) has a number of interrelated causes. Excessive heat (which thins the oil), overloading (which squeezes the oil from the bearing face) and oil leakage or throw-off (from excessive bearing clearances, worn oil pump or high engine speeds) all contribute to lubrication breakdown. Blocked oil passages, which usually are the result of misaligned oil holes in a bearing shell, will also oil-starve a bearing and destroy it. When lack of lubrication is the cause of bearing failure, the bearing material is wiped or extruded from the steel backing of the bearing. Temperatures may increase to the point where the steel backing turns blue from overheating.

6 Driving habits can have a definite effect on bearing life. Full-throttle low-speed operation (or 'lugging' the engine) puts very high loads on bearings, which tends to squeeze out the oil film. These loads cause the bearings to flex, which produces fine cracks in the bearing face (fatigue failure). Eventually the bearing material will loosen in pieces and tear away from the steel backing. Short-trip driving leads to corrosion of bearings, as insufficient engine heat is produced to drive off the condensed water and corrosive gases produced. These products collect in the engine oil, forming acid and sludge. As the oil is carried to the engine bearings the acid attacks and corrodes the bearing material.

7 Incorrect bearing installation during engine assembly will lead to bearing failure as well. Tight-fitting bearings, which leave insufficient bearing oil clearance, result in oil starvation. Dirt or foreign particles trapped behind a bearing insert result in high spots on the bearing which lead to failure.

23 Cylinder head – cleaning and inspection

1 Thorough cleaning of the cylinder head and related valve train components, followed by a detailed inspection, will enable you to decide how much valve service work must be done during the engine overhaul.

Cleaning

2 Scrape away any traces of old gasket material and sealing compound from the head gasket, the intake manifold and the exhaust manifold sealing surfaces. Work slowly and do not nick or gouge the soft aluminum of the head.

3 Carefully scrape all carbon deposits out of the combustion chamber areas. A hand-held wire brush or a piece of fine emery cloth can be used once the majority of deposits have been scraped away. Do not use a wire brush mounted in a drill motor, as the head material is soft and can be eroded away by the wire brush.

4 Remove any scale that may be built up around the coolant passages.

5 Run a stiff wire brush through the oil holes, the EGR gas ports and the jet air passages to remove any deposits that may have formed in those areas (photo).

6 It is a good idea to run an appropriate size tap into each of the threaded holes to remove any corrosion of thread sealant that may be present. Be very careful when cleaning aluminum threads; they can be damaged easily with a tap. If compressed air is available, use it to clear the holes of debris produced by this operation. Clean the exhaust and intake manifold stud threads in a similar manner with an appropriate size die. Clean the camshaft bearing cap bolt threads with a wire brush.

7 Next, clean the cylinder head with solvent and dry it thoroughly. Compressed air will speed the drying process and ensure that all holes and recessed areas are clean. **Note:** *Decarbonizing chemicals are available and may prove very useful when cleaning cylinder heads and valve train components. They are very caustic and should be used with caution. Be sure to follow the directions on the container.*

8 Clean the camshaft with solvent and dry it thoroughly.

9 Without dismantling the rocker arm assembly, clean it with solvent (make sure all oil holes are clear) and dry it thoroughly. Compressed air, if it is available, will speed up the drying process and make it much easier.

10 Clean all the valve springs, keepers, retainers and spring seats with solvent and dry them thoroughly. Do the parts from one valve at a time, so that no mixing of parts between valves occurs.

11 Scrape off any heavy deposits that may have formed on the valves, then use a motorized wire brush to remove deposits from the valve heads and stems. Again, make sure the valves do not get mixed up.

12 Clean the jet valve components with solvent. Do one jet valve at a time so parts are not accidentally interchanged. Carefully remove any deposits from the jet valve stem and head with a fine wire brush. (Do not bend the valve stem in the process).

Inspection

Cylinder head

13 Inspect the head very carefully for cracks, evidence of coolant leakage and other damage. If cracks are found, a new head is in order.

14 Check the camshaft bearing surfaces in the head and the bearing caps (photo). If there is evidence of excessive wear, scoring or seizure, the cylinder head will have to be replaced with a new one to restore the camshaft bearing surfaces and proper oil clearance.

15 Using a straight edge and feeler gauge, check the head gasket mating surfaces for warpage at the points shown in Figure 2.10. If the head is warped beyond the limits given in the specifications, it can be resurfaced at an automotive machine shop.

16 Examine the valve seats in each of the combustion chambers. If they are pitted, cracked or burned, the head will require valve service that is beyond the scope of the home mechanic.

17 Measure the inside diameters of the valve guides (at both ends and the center of the guide) with a small hole gauge and a 0 to 1 in micrometer. Record the measurements for future reference. These measurements, along with the valve stem diameter measurements, will enable you to compute the valve stem-to-guide clearance. This clearance, when compared to the specifications, will be one factor that will determine the extent of the valve service work required. The guides are measured at the ends and at the center to determine if they are worn in a bell-mouth pattern (more wear at the ends). If they are, guide reconditioning or replacement is an absolute must.

Rocker arm assembly

18 Check the rocker arm faces (that contact the camshaft lobes) and the ends of the adjusting screws (that contact the valve stems) for pitting, excessive wear and roughness.

19 Check the adjusting screw threads for damage. Make sure they can be threaded in and out of the rocker arms.
20 Slide each rocker arm along its shaft, against the locating spring pressure, and check the rocker arm shafts for excessive wear and evidence of scoring in the areas that normally contact the rocker arms (photo).
21 Any damaged or excessively worn parts must be replaced with new ones. Refer to the exploded view of the rocker arm assembly components, which will enable you to correctly disassemble and reassemble them.

Camshaft

22 Inspect the camshaft bearing journals for excessive wear and evidence of seizure (photo). If the journals are damaged, the bearing surfaces in the head and bearing caps are probably damaged as well. Both the camshaft and cylinder head will have to be replaced with new ones.
23 Check the cam lobes for pitting, grooves, scoring or flaking. Measure the cam lobe height and compare it to the specifications (photo). If the lobe height is less than the minimum specified, and/or the lobes are damaged, a new camshaft must be obtained.

Valves

24 Carefully inspect each valve face for cracks, pitting and burned spots. Check the valve stem and neck for cracks. Rotate the valve and check for any obvious indication that it is bent. Check the end of the stem for pitting and excessive wear. The presence of any of the above conditions indicates a need for valve service by a professional.
25 Measure the width of the valve margin (on each valve) and compare it to the specifications (photo). Any valve with a margin narrower than specified will have to be replaced with a new one.
26 Measure the valve stem diameter (photo). By subtracting the stem diameter from the valve guide diameter, the valve stem-to-guide clearance is obtained. Compare the results to the Specifications. If the stem-to-guide clearance is greater than specified, the guides will have to be reconditioned or replaced and new valves may have to be installed, depending on the condition of the old ones.

Valve components

27 Check each valve spring for wear (on the ends) and pitting. Measure the free length (photo) and compare it to the specifications. Any springs that are shorter than specified have sagged and should not be reused. Stand the spring on a flat surface and check it for squareness.
28 Check the spring retainers and keepers for obvious wear and cracks. Any questionable parts should not be reused, as extensive damage will occur in the event of failure during engine operation.

Jet valve assemblies

29 Make sure the jet valve slides freely in the jet valve body. It should have no detectable side play. Check the valve head and seat for cracks and pitting. Check the spring for wear (on the ends) and cracks. Measure the valve spring free length and diameter of the valve stem. Compare the results to the specifications.
30 If defects are found in any of the jet valve components, the entire valve assembly should be replaced with a new one.
31 Be sure to check the remaining jet valve assemblies.
32 If the inspection process indicates that the valve components are in generally poor condition and worn beyond the limits specified, which is usually the case in an engine that is being overhauled, reassemble the valves in the cylinder head and refer to Section 24 for valve servicing recommendations.
33 If the inspection process turns up no excessively worn parts, and if the valve faces and seats are in good condition, the valve train components can be reinstalled in the cylinder head without major servicing. Refer to Section 30 for cylinder head reassembly procedures.

24 Valves – servicing

1 Because of the complex nature of the job and the special tools and equipment required, servicing of the valves, the valve seats and the valve guides (commonly known as a 'valve job') is best left to a professional.
2 The home mechanic can remove and disassemble the head, do the

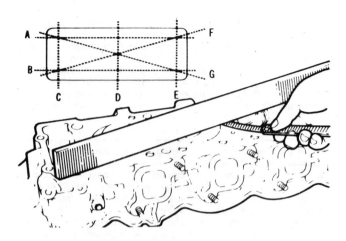

Fig. 2.10 Checking the cylinder head for warpage with a feeler gauge and straight edge (Sec 23)

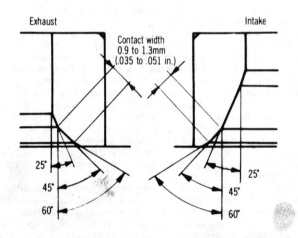

Fig. 2.11 Valve seat reconditioning dimensions (Sec 23)

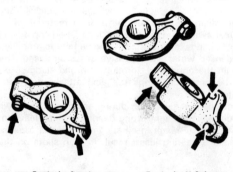

Fig. 2.12 Rocker arm wear check points (Sec 23)

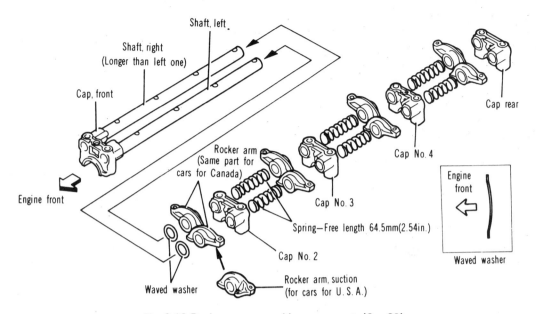

Fig. 2.13 Rocker arm assembly components (Sec 23)

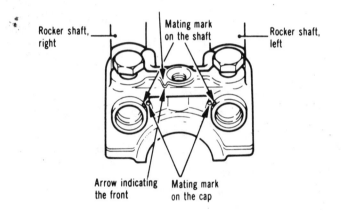

Fig. 2.14 Camshaft bearing cap details (Sec 23)

Fig. 2.15 Valve inspection points (Sec 23)

initial cleaning and inspection, then reassemble and deliver the head to a dealer service department or a reputable automotive machine shop for the actual valve servicing.

3   The dealer service department, or automotive machine shop, will remove the valves and springs, recondition or replace the valves and valve seats, recondition or replace the valve guides, check and replace the valve springs, spring retainers and keepers (as necessary), replace the valve seals with new ones, reassemble the valve components and make sure the installed spring height is correct. The cylinder head gasket surface will also be resurfaced if it is warped.

4   After the valve job has been performed by a professional, the head will be in like-new condition. When the head is returned, be sure to clean it again, very thoroughly (before installation on the engine), to remove any metal particles and abrasive grit that may still be present from the valve service or head resurfacing operations. Use compressed air, if available, to blow out all the oil holes and passages.

25   Crankshaft – installation

1   Crankshaft installation is generally one of the first steps in engine reassembly; it is assumed at this point that the engine block and crankshaft have been cleaned and inspected and repaired or reconditioned.

2   Position the engine so that the bottom is facing up.

3   Remove the main bearing cap bolts and lift out the caps. Lay them out in the proper order to help ensure they are installed correctly.

4   If they are still in place, remove the old bearing inserts from the block and the main bearing caps. Wipe the main bearing surfaces of the block and caps with a clean, lint-free cloth (they must be kept spotlessly clean).

5   Clean the back side of the new main bearing inserts and lay one bearing half in each main bearing saddle (in the block) and the other bearing half from each bearing set in the corresponding main bearing cap. Make sure the tab on the bearing insert fits into the recess in the block or cap. Also, the oil holes in the block and cap must line up with the oil holes in the bearing insert. Do not hammer the bearing into place and do not nick or gouge the bearing faces. No lubrication should be used at this time.

6   The flanged thrust bearing must be installed in the number 3 (center) cup and saddle.

7   Clean the faces of the bearings in the block and the crankshaft main bearing journal with a clean, lint-free cloth. Check or clean the oil holes in the crankshaft, as any dirt here can only go one way – straight through the new bearings.

8   Once you are certain that the crankshaft is clean, carefully lay it in position (an assistant would be very helpful here) in the main bearings with the counterweights lying sideways.

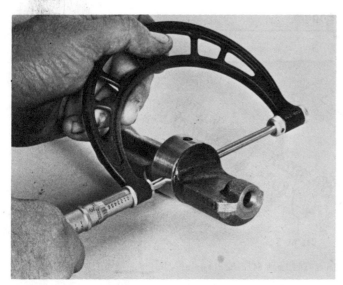

14.8 Measuring the Silent Shaft bearing journal outside diameter

16.3 Removing the oil pickup tube mounting bolts

16.5 Short lengths of rubber hose slipped over the connecting rod cap bolts will prevent damage to the crankshaft journal during removal of the piston/connecting rod assembly

18.10 Installing the soft plugs in the engine block

19.4 Measuring the cylinder diameter with a bore gauge

19.7 Honing the cylinder with a surfacing hone

20.2 Measuring a main bearing journal diameter

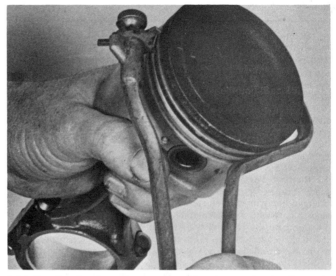
21.4 Cleaning the piston ring grooves with a ring groove cleaning tool

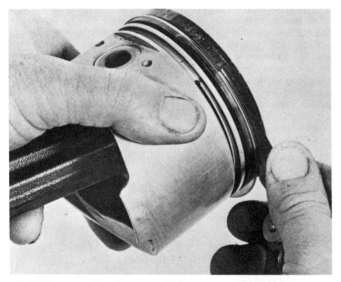
21.10 Measuring the piston ring side clearance with a feeler gauge

21.11 Measuring the piston diameter with an outside micrometer to determine the piston-to-bore clearance

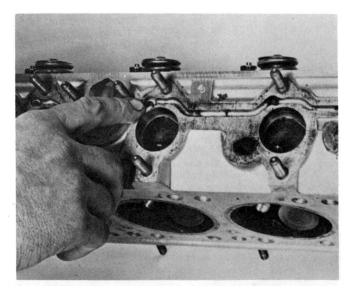
23.5 Make sure the Jet air passages, the EGR gas ports and the oil holes are thoroughly cleaned

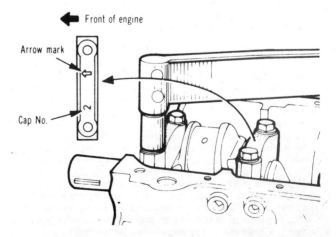

Front of engine

Arrow mark

Cap No.

Fig. 2.16 Correct main bearing cap installation (Sec 25)

9   Before the crankshaft can be permanently installed, the main bearing oil clearance must be checked.

10 Trim 5 pieces of the appropriate type of Plasti-gage (so that they are slightly shorter than the width of the main bearings) and place one piece on each crankshaft main bearing journal, parallel with the journal axis. Do not lay them across any oil holes.

11 Clean the faces of the bearings in the caps and install the caps in their respective positions (do not mix them up) with the arrows pointing toward the front of the engine. Do not disturb the Plasti-gage.

12 Starting with the center main and working out toward the ends, tighten the main bearing cap bolts, in 3 steps, to the specified torque. Do not rotate the crankshaft at any time during this operation.

13 Remove the bolts and carefully lift off the main bearing caps. Keep them in order. Do not disturb the Plasti-gage or rotate the crankshaft. If any of the main bearing caps are difficult to remove, tap gently from side to side with a soft-faced hammer to loosen them.

14 Compare the width of the crushed Plasti-gage on each journal to the scale printed on the Plasti-gage container (photo) to obtain the main bearing oil clearance. Check the specifications to make sure it is correct.

15 If the clearance is not correct, double-check to make sure that you have the right size bearing inserts. Also, recheck the crankshaft main bearing journal diameters and make sure that no dirt or oil was between the bearing inserts and the main bearing caps or the block when the clearance was measured.

16 Carefully scrape all traces of the Plasti-gage material off the main bearing journals and/or the bearing faces. Do not nick or scratch the bearing faces.

17 Carefully lift the crankshaft out of the engine. Clean the bearing faces in the block, then apply a thin, uniform layer of clean, high-quality multi-purpose grease (or engine assembly lube) to each of the bearing faces. Be sure to coat the thrust flange faces as well as the journal face of the thrust bearing in the number 3 (center) main. Make sure the crankshaft journals are clean, then carefully lay it back in place in the block. Clean the faces of the bearings in the caps, then apply a thin, uniform layer of clean, high-quality multi-purpose grease to each of the bearing faces and install the caps in their respective positions with the arrows pointing toward the front of the engine. Install the bolts and tighten them to the specified torque, starting with the center main and working out toward the ends. Work up to the final torque in 3 steps.

18 Rotate the crankshaft a number of times by hand and check for any obvious binding.

19 The final step is to check the crankshaft end play. This can be done with a feeler gauge or a dial indicator set (photo).

20 If a feeler gauge is used, gently pry the crankshaft all the way toward the back of the engine with a large screwdriver. Slip a feeler gauge between the crankshaft thrust face and the bearing thrust face at the rear side of the number 3 (center) main bearing. Compare the measured end play to the specifications.

21 If a dial indicator is used, mount it at the rear of the engine with the indicator stem touching the end of the flange on the crankshaft. Gently pry the crankshaft all the way to the back of the engine, then zero the dial indicator. Carefully pry the crankshaft as far as possible in the opposite direction and observe the needle movement on the dial indicator, which will indicate the amount of end play. Compare it to the specifications.

26 Piston rings – installation

1   Before installing the new piston rings, the ring end gaps must be checked.

2   Lay out the piston/connecting rod assemblies and the new ring sets so that the rings will be matched with the same piston and cylinder during the end gap measurement and engine assembly.

3   Insert the top (number 1) ring into the first cylinder and square it up with the cylinder walls by pushing it in with the top of the piston (photo). The ring should be at least 2 inches below the top edge of the cylinder. To measure the end gap, slip a feeler gauge between the ends of the ring (photo). Compare the measurement to the specifications.

4   If the gap is larger or smaller than specified, double-check to make sure that you have the correct rings before proceeding.

5   If the gap is too small, it must be enlarged or the ring ends may come in contact with each other during engine operation, which can cause serious damage to the engine. The end gap can be increased by

filing the ring ends very carefully with a fine file. Mount the ring in a vise equipped with soft jaws, holding it as close to the gap as possible. When performing this operation, file only from the outside in.

6   Excess end gap is not critical unless it is greater than 0.040 in (1 mm). Again, double-check to make sure you have the correct rings for your engine.

7   Repeat the procedure for each ring that will be installed in the first cylinder and for each ring in the remaining cylinders. Remember to keep rings, pistons and cylinders matched up.

8   Once the ring end-gaps have been checked/corrected, the rings can be installed on the pistons.

9   The oil control ring (lowest one on the piston) is installed first. It is composed of 3 separate components. Slip the spacer expander into the groove (photo) then install the upper side rail (photo) with the size mark and manufacturer's stamp facing up (photo). Do not use a piston ring installation tool on the oil ring side rails, as they may be damaged. Instead, place one end of the side rail into the groove between the spacer expander and the ring land, hold it firmly in place and slide a finger around the piston while pushing the rail into the groove (photo). Next, install the lower side rail (again, the size mark and manufacturer's stamp must face up) in the same manner.

10 After the 3 oil ring components have been installed, check to make sure that both the upper and lower side rails can be turned smoothly in the ring groove.

11 The number 2 (middle) ring is installed next. It is stamped with a '2' so that it can be readily distinguished from the top ring. Do not mix the top and middle rings up, as they have different cross sections.

12 Use a piston ring installation tool and make sure that the identification mark is facing up, then fit the ring into the middle groove on the piston (photo). Do not expand the ring any more than is necessary to slide it over the piston.

13 Finally, install the number 1 (top) ring in the same manner. Make sure the identifying mark is facing up.

14 Repeat the procedure for the remaining pistons and rings. Be careful not to confuse the number 1 and number 2 rings.

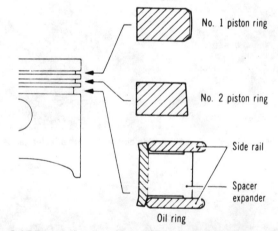

Fig. 2.17 The piston rings have different cross-sections and must be installed in the correct groove (Sec 26)

27 Piston/connecting rod assembly – installation

1   Before installing the piston/connecting rod assemblies, the cylinder walls must be perfectly clean, the top edge of each cylinder must be chamfered, and the crankshaft must be in place.

2   Remove the connecting rod cap from the end of the number 1 connecting rod. Remove the old bearing inserts and wipe the bearing surfaces of the connecting rod and cap with a clean, lint-free cloth (they must be spotlessly clean).

3   Clean the back side of the new upper bearing half, then lay it in place in the connecting rod. Make sure that the tab on the bearing fits into the recess in the rod. Also, the oil holes in the rod and bearing insert must line up. Do not hammer the bearing insert into place, and be very careful not to nick or gouge the bearing face. Do not lubricate the bearing at this time.

4   Clean the back side of the other bearing insert half and install it in the rod cap. Again, make sure the tab on the bearing fits into the

recess in the cap, and do not apply any lubricant. It is critically important to ensure that the mating surfaces of the bearing and connecting rod are perfectly clean and oil-free when they are assembled together.

5   Position the piston ring gaps as shown, then slip a section of plastic or rubber hose over the connecting rod cap bolts.

6   Lubricate the piston and rings with clean engine oil and install a piston ringcompressor on the piston. Leave the skirt protruding about $\frac{1}{4}$ in to guide the piston into the cylinder. The rings must be compressed as far as possible.

7   Rotate the crankshaft so that the number 1 connecting rod journal is as far from the number 1 cylinder as possible (bottom dead center), and apply a uniform coat of engine oil to the number 1 cylinder walls.

8   With the arrow on top of the piston pointing to the front of the engine, gently place the piston/connecting rod assembly into the number 1 cylinder bore (photo) and rest the bottom edge of the ring compressor on the engine block. Tap the top edge of the ring compressor to make sure it is contacting the block around its entire circumference.

9   Clean the number 1 connecting rod journal on the crankshaft and the bearing faces in the rod.

10   Carefully tap on the top of the piston with the end of a wooden hammer handle whilst guiding the end of the connecting rod into place on the crankshaft journal. The piston rings may try to pop out of the ring compressor just before entering the cylinder bore, so keep some downward pressure on the ring compressor. Work slowly, and if any resistance is felt as the piston enters the cylinder, stop immediately, find out what is hanging up and fix it before proceeding. Do not, for any reason, force the piston into the cylinder, as you will break a ring and/or the piston.

11   Once the piston/connecting rod assembly is installed, the connecting rod bearing oil clearance must be checked before the rod cap is permanently bolted in place.

12   Trim a piece of the appropriate type Plasti-gage so that it is slightly shorter than the width of the connecting rod bearing and lay it in place on number 1 connecting rod journal, parallel with the journal axis (it must not cross the oil hole in the journal).

13   Clean the connecting rod cap bearing face, remove the protective hoses from the connecting rod bolts and gently install the rod cap in place. Make sure the mating mark on the cap is on the same side as the mark on the connecting rod. Install the nuts and tighten them to the specified torque, working up to it in 3 steps. Do not rotate the crankshaft at any time during this operation.

14   Remove the rod cap, being very careful not to disturb the Plasti-gage. Compare the width of the crushed Plasti-gage to the scale printed on the Plasti-gage container (photo) to obtain the oil clearance. Compare it to the specifications to make sure the clearance is correct. If the clearance is not correct, double-check to make sure that you have the correct size bearing inserts. Also, recheck the crankshaft connecting rod journal diameter and make sure that no dirt or oil was between the bearing inserts and the connecting rod or cap when the clearance was measured.

15   Carefully scrape all traces of the Plasti-gage material off the rod journal and/or bearing face (be very careful not to scratch the bearing). Make sure the bearing faces are perfectly clean, then apply a uniform layer of clean, high quality multi-purpose grease (or engine assembly lube) to both of them. You will have to push the piston into the cylinder to expose the face of the bearing insert in the connecting rod; be sure to slip the protective hoses over the rod bolts first.

16   Slide the connecting rod back into place on the journal, remove the protective hoses from the rod cap bolts, install the rod cap and tighten the nuts to the specified torque. Again, work up to the torque in 3 steps.

17   Without turning the crankshaft, repeat the entire procedure for the number 4 piston/connecting rod assembly. Keep the back sides of the bearing inserts and the inside of the connecting rod and cap perfectly clean when assembling them. Make sure you have the correct piston for the cylinder and that the arrow on the piston points to the front of the engine when the piston is installed. Remember, use plenty of oil to lubricate the piston before installing the ring compressor, and be sure to match up the mating marks on the connecting rod and rod cap. Also, when installing the rod caps for the final time, be sure to lubricate the bearing faces adequately.

18   After completing the procedure for piston number 4, turn the crankshaft 180° and repeat the entire operation for pistons number 2 and 3.

19   After all the piston/connecting rod assemblies have been properly installed, rotate the crankshaft a number of times by hand and check for any obvious binding.

20   As a final step, the connecting rod big end side clearances must be checked. Slide the number 1 connecting rod all the way to one end of its journal and slip a feeler gauge between the side of the connecting rod and the crankshaft throw (photo). Be sure to compare the measured clearance to the specifications to make sure it is correct. Repeat the procedure for the other 3 connecting rods.

28 Oil pump – reassembly and installation

1   The oil pump and right Silent Shaft are installed as a unit.

2   Coat the oil pump relief plunger with clean multi-purpose grease and insert the plunger and spring into the oil pump body. Install the cap and tighten it securely.

3   Apply a layer of multi-purpose grease to the gear teeth, the sides of the gears and the bearing surfaces in the pump body and cover. Lay the gears in place in the body with the mating marks lined up as shown (photo). If the mating marks are not properly aligned, the right Silent Shaft will be out of phase and engine vibration will result.

4   Lay the cover in place using the dowel pins to align it properly. Install the Phillips head screw in the left side of the pump, but do not tighten it completely at this time. Make sure the gears rotate smoothly without binding.

5   Lay a new gasket in place on the cover (no sealer is required). The dowel pins should align it properly and hold it in place.

6   Make sure the key is in place in the front of the shaft, then slip the right Silent Shaft through the oil pump driven gear as you line up the key in the shaft with the key-way in the gear. Once the shaft and gear are properly mated, clamp the counterweight end of the shaft in a vise equipped with soft jaws, install the bolt in the front end of the shaft and tighten it to the specified torque.

7   Apply a thin layer of clean multi-purpose grease (or engine assembly lube) to the rear bearing journal of the right Silent Shaft.

8   Hold the pump upright and fill it with a minimum of 10 cubic centimeters of engine oil (photo). Insert the Silent Shaft into the engine block and through the rear bearing. Be careful not to scratch or gouge the bearing as the shaft is installed.

9   Make sure the pump is seated on the engine block, then install the mounting bolts and tighten them evenly and securely. Do not forget to tighten the Phillips head screw. The remaining pump mounting bolts will be installed with the chain guides.

10   Temporarily slip the Silent Shaft drive sprocket onto the lower pump gear shaft and use it to rotate the pump gears/Silent Shaft. Check for any obvious binding.

29 Silent Shaft chain/sprockets – installation

1   Before installing the Silent Shaft chain and sprockets, the timing chain must be properly installed and the number 1 piston must be at TDC on the compression stroke. It is assumed that both Silent Shafts and the oil pump are also in place.

2   Slide the crankshaft sprocket part-way onto the front of the crankshaft (by lining up the key-way in the sprocket with the key on the shaft).

3   Install the Silent Shaft chain onto the crankshaft sprocket and the left Silent Shaft sprocket. The dished or recessed side of the left Silent Shaft sprocket must face out. Line up the plated links on the chain with the mating marks stamped into the sprockets (see Figure 2.18).

4   With the dished or recessed side facing in, install the right Silent Shaft sprocket onto the chain. Line up the plated link on the chain with the mating mark on the sprocket. Slide the Silent Shaft sprockets onto their respective shafts, lining up the key-ways in the sprockets with the keys on the shafts. Simultaneously, push the crankshaft sprocket back until it bottoms on the crankshaft timing chain sprocket. Recheck the position of the mating marks on the chain and sprockets, then install the Silent Shaft sprocket attaching bolts and tighten them to the specified torque.

5   Install the chain guides labeled 'A', 'B' and 'C' (photo) and tighten the mounting bolts for chain guides 'A' and 'C' securely (leave the mounting bolts for chain guide 'B' finger-tight). Note the difference between the upper and lower chain guide 'B' mounting bolts. Make sure they are installed in the proper location.

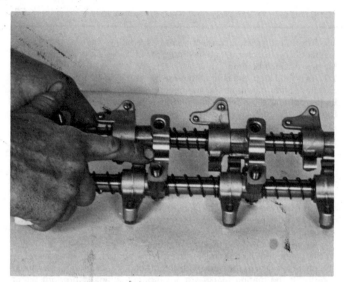

23.14 Inspecting the camshaft bearing cap bearing surfaces

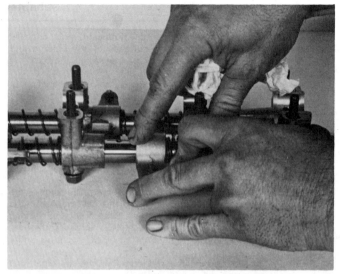

23.20 Checking the rocker arm shafts for wear

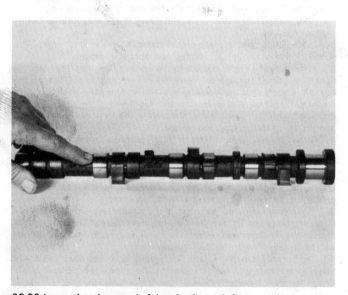

23.22 Inspecting the camshaft bearing journals for excessive wear or evidence of seizure

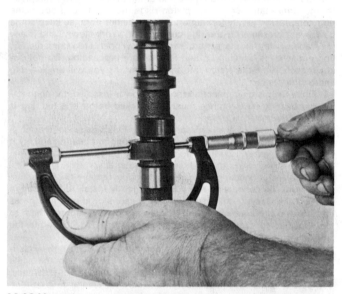

23.23 Measuring the cam lobe height

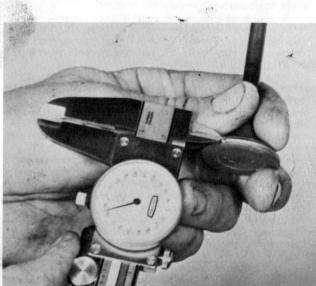

23.25 Measuring the valve margin width

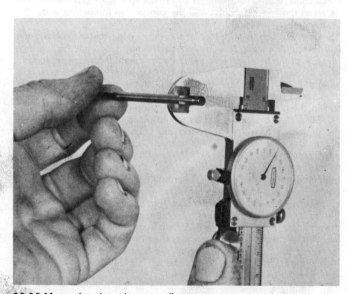

23.26 Measuring the valve stem diameter

23.27 Measuring the valve spring free length

6   Adjust the chain slack as follows: rotate the right Silent Shaft clockwise and the left silent shaft counterclockwise so that the chain slack is collected at point 'P' (refer to Fig.). Pull the chain with your finger tips in the direction of arrow 'F', then move the lower end of the chain guide 'B' up or down, as required, until the clearance between the chain and the guide (chain slack) is as specified (photo). Tighten the chain guide 'B' mounting bolts securely, then recheck the slack to make sure it has not changed. If the chain is not tensioned properly, engine noise will result.
7   Apply a coat of clean multi-purpose grease to the chain and chain guides.
8   Using a hammer and punch, drive the old seal out of the timing chain case (photo).
9   Lay a new seal in place (with the lip facing in) and tap around its entire circumference, with a block of wood and a hammer, until it is properly seated.
10   Using a new gasket and silicone-type gasket sealer, fit the timing chain case onto the front of the engine. Install the bolts and tighten them securely, using a criss-cross pattern. If the gasket protrudes beyond the top or bottom of the case and engine block, trim off the excess with a razor blade.
11   Apply a thin layer of clean multi-purpose grease to the seal contact surface of the crankshaft pulley (photo), then slide it onto the crankshaft. Install the bolt and tighten it finger-tight only. The bolt should be tightened to the specified torque only after the cylinder head and camshaft have been installed.

30 Cylinder head – reassembly

1   Regardless of whether or not the head was sent to an automotive machine shop for valve servicing, make sure it is clean before beginning reassembly.
2   If the head was sent out for valve servicing, the valves and related components will already be in place. Begin the reassembly procedure with step 6.
3   Lay all the spring seats in position, then install new seals on each of the valve guides. Using a hammer and an appropriate size deep socket, gently tap each seal into place until it is properly seated on its guide (photo). Do not twist or cock the seals during installation, as they will not seal properly on the valve stems.
4   Next, install the valves (taking care not to damage the new seals), the springs, the retainers and the keepers. Coat the valve stems with clean multi-purpose grease (or engine assembly lube) before slipping them into the guides, and install the springs with the painted side next to the retainer. When compressing the springs with the valve spring compressor, do not let the retainers contact the valve guide seals. Make certain that the keepers are securely locked in their retaining grooves.
5   Double-check the installed valve spring height. If it was correct before disassembly, it should still be within the specified limits.
6   Install new seals on each of the jet valve bodies. Gently tap them

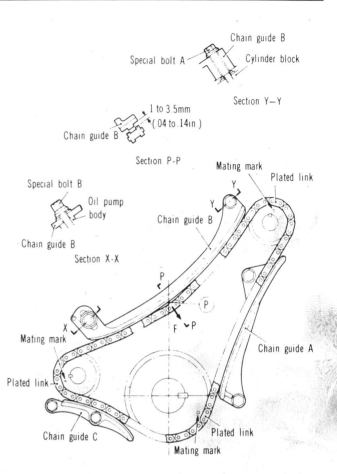

Fig. 2.18 Silent Shaft chain installation and adjustment details (Sec 29)

into place with a hammer and the appropriate size deep socket. Lubricate and install the valves and make sure the stems slide smoothly in the valve bodies. Install the springs, the retainers and the keepers. When compressing the springs, be careful not to damage the valve stems or the new seals.
7   Install a new O-ring on each jet valve body and apply a thin coat of clean engine oil or multi-purpose grease to each O-ring, the jet valve threads and the jet valve seating surfaces.
8   Carefully thread the jet valve assemblies into the cylinder head and tighten them to the specified torque. Be careful not to tilt the socket, as the valve stems can be bent very easily.

31 Cylinder head – installation

1   Before installing the cylinder head, the timing chain and sprockets, the Silent Shaft chain and sprockets and the timing chain case must be in place on the engine.
2   Make sure the gasket sealing surfaces of the engine block and cylinder head are clean and oil-free, then lay the new head gasket in place on the block (do not use any sealant) with the manufacturer's stamped mark facing up (photo). Use the dowel pins in the top of the block to properly locate the gasket.
3   Carefully set the cylinder head in place on the block. Use the dowel pins to properly align it.
4   Install the 10 head bolts and tighten them, in the sequence shown, to 1/3 of the specified torque. Repeat the procedure, using the same sequence, tightening them to 2/3 of the specified torque. Repeat the procedure one last time, tightening them to the final specified torque.
5   Install the 2 small head bolts (with washers) in the very front of the head and tighten them to the specified torque.
6   Wipe the camshaft bearing surfaces in the cylinder head clean and apply a coat of clean multi-purpose grease (or engine assembly lube) to each of them.

7   Make sure the bearing journals on the camshaft are clean, then carefully lay it in place in the head. Do not lubricate the camshaft lobes at this time. Rotate the camshaft until the dowel pin on the front is positioned at the top.

8   Loosen the jam nuts on the valve clearance adjusting bolts and back the adjusting bolts out a minimum of 2 full turns.

9   Wipe the camshaft bearing cap bearing surfaces clean and apply a coat of clean multi-purpose grease (or engine assembly lube) to each of them. Also, apply a very small amount of grease to the end of each valve stem. Lay the rocker arm shaft assembly in place with the number 1 bearing cap at the front of the engine. Install the camshaft bearing cap bolts and tighten them to 7 ft-lb in the following order: center, number 2, number 4, front, rear. Repeat the procedure, tightening them to the final specified torque.

10   Next, lift up on the camshaft sprocket (with the chain attached) and slip it into place on the end of the camshaft. The dowel pin on the cam should slip into the hole in the sprocket.

11   Install the distributor drive gear (again, line up the dowel pin and hole) the oil shield and the bolt. Tighten the bolt to the specified torque (photo). To keep the camshaft and crankshaft from turning, install 2 of the flywheel mounting bolts in the rear flange of the crankshaft (180° apart), then wedge a large screwdriver between the bolts. Also, tighten the large bolt on the front of the crankshaft to the specified torque at this time.

12   The camshaft end play can be checked with a dial indicator set or a feeler gauge.

13   If a feeler gauge is used, gently pry the camshaft all the way toward the front of the engine. Slip a feeler gauge between the flange at the front of the camshaft and the number 1 front cam bearing cap. Compare the measured end play to the specifications.

14   If a dial indicator is used, mount it at the front of the engine with the indicator stem touching the head of the bolt that attaches the sprocket to the camshaft. Carefully pry the camshaft all the way toward the front of the engine, then zero the dial indicator. Gently pry

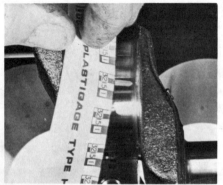
25.14 Comparing the width of the crushed Plastigage to the scale on the container to obtain the main bearing oil clearance

25.19 Checking the crankshaft end play with a dial indicator setup

26.3a Using the piston to square up the piston ring in the cylinder prior to measuring the end gap

26.3b Measuring the piston ring end gap with a feeler gauge

26.9a Installing the spacer expander in the oil control ring groove

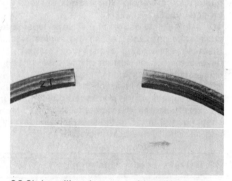
26.9b Installing the upper side rail in the oil control ring groove

26.9c The piston rings must be installed with the marked side up

26.12 Installing the piston ring with a piston ring installation tool

27.8 Placing the piston/connecting rod assembly (with the ring compressor installed) into the cylinder bore

the camshaft as far as possible in the opposite direction and observe the needle movement on the dial indicator, which will indicate the amount of end play. Compare it to the specifications.

15 Next, adjust the valve clearances using the 'cold engine' specifications.

16 While watching the rocker arms for the number one cylinder, rotate the engine in a clockwise direction (with a wrench on the large bolt at the front of the crankshaft) until the exhaust valve is closing and the intake valve has just started to open (the intake valve is on the carburetor side of the engine, the exhaust valve is on the exhaust manifold side of the engine). Line up the notch in the pulley on the front of the crankshaft with the 'T' on the timing mark tab on the timing chain case. At this point, the number 4 piston will be at TDC on the compression stroke and the number 4 cylinder valve clearances can be adjusted. The jet valve clearance is always adjusted before the intake and exhaust valve clearances.

17 The intake valve and jet valve adjusting screws are located on a common rocker arm. Make sure the intake valve adjusting screw has been backed off at least 2 full turns, then loosen the locknut on the jet valve adjusting screw. Turn the jet valve adjusting screw counterclockwise and insert the appropriate size feeler gauge between the jet valve stem and the adjusting screw. Carefully tighten the adjusting screw until you can feel a slight drag on the feeler gauge as it is withdrawn from between the stem and adjusting screw. Since the jet valve spring is relatively weak, use special care not to force the jet valve open. Be particularly careful if the adjusting screw is hard to turn. Hold the adjusting screw with a screwdriver (to keep it from turning) and tighten the locknut. Recheck the clearance to make sure it hasn't changed.

18 Next, adjust the intake valve clearance. Insert the appropriate size feeler gauge between the intake valve stem and the adjusting screw. Carefully tighten the adjusting screw until you can feel a slight drag on the feeler gauge as it is withdrawn from between the stem and adjusting screw. Hold the screw with a screwdriver (to keep it from

27.14 Comparing the width of the crushed Plastigage to the scale printed on the container to obtain the connecting rod bearing oil clearance

27.20 Checking the connecting rod big end side clearance with a feeler gauge

28.3 Lining up the mating marks on the oil pump gears

28.8 Filling the oil pump with 10 cc's of oil prior to installation

29.5 Installing the Silent Shaft chain guides

29.6 Adjusting the Silent Shaft chain slack

29.8 Driving the old oil seal out of the timing chain case

29.11 Applying grease to the seal contact surface of the crankshaft pulley

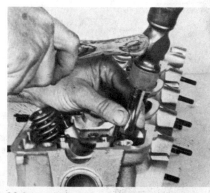
30.3 Installing new valve guide seals with a hammer and a deep socket

31.2 Installing the new head gasket

31.11 Tightening the camshaft sprocket mounting bolt

32.5 Tapping the rear oil seal housing with a soft-faced hammer to seat it on the engine block and oil pan

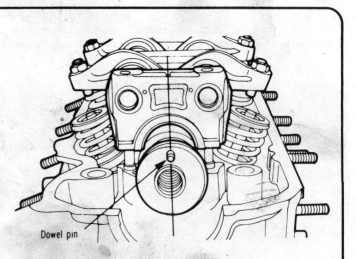

32.7 Installing the oil pressure sending unit

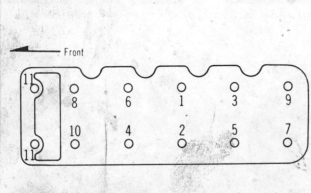

Fig. 2.19 Head bolt-tightening sequence (Sec 31)

Dowel pin

Fig. 2.20 Position the camshaft so that the dowel pin is on top (Sec 31)

turning) and tighten the locknut, then recheck the clearance to make sure it hasn't changed.

19 Loosen the locknut on the exhaust valve adjusting screw. Turn the adjusting screw counterclockwise and insert the appropriate size feeler gauge between the valve stem and the adjusting screw. Carefully tighten the adjusting screw until you can feel a slight drag on the feeler gauge, as it is withdrawn from between the stem and adjusting screw. Hold the adjusting screw with a screwdriver and tighten the locknut. Recheck the clearance to make sure it hasn't changed.

20 Repeat the procedure to adjust the valve clearances for cylinders 1, 2 and 3. Use the following table for determining when the pistons are at TDC:

Exhaust valve closing – intake valve just opening:	Adjust valve clearances at:
No. 1 cylinder	No. 4 cylinder
No. 2 cylinder	No. 3 cylinder
No. 3 cylinder	No. 2 cylinder
No. 4 cylinder	No. 1 cylinder

Remember to align the notch in the crankshaft pulley with the 'T' on the timing mark tab before making the adjustments.

21 It is a good idea to temporarily install the valve cover to keep dirt and other foreign objects out of the cylinder head.

---

32 External engine components – installation

1 Once the engine has been assembled to the point where all internal parts, the timing chain cover, the oil pan and the cylinder head are in place, the exterior components can be installed. At this point, if the engine is mounted on a stand, it should be removed from the stand so that the rear oil seal housing can be installed.

2 Lubricate the seal contact surface of the flange at the rear of the crankshaft with multi-purpose grease.

3 After noting which side is facing out, use a hammer and punch to drive the oil seal out of the housing. Lay a new seal in place (with the correct side out) and seat it in the housing with a hammer and a block of wood. Tap the seal around its entire circumference to seat it squarely in the housing.

4 Place the oil separator into the housing with the oil hole facing down (toward the bottom of the case) and the tabs pointing out. One or two strategically placed dabs of heavy grease will help keep the separator positioned properly.

5 Apply a thin, even coat of silicone-type gasket sealer to both sides of the new gasket and to the exposed portion of the oil pan gasket, then install the oil seal housing. Make sure the oil separator does not fall out of place. Tap the seal housing very gently with a soft-faced hammer (photo) to seat it properly. Install the attaching bolts and tighten them to the specified torque.

6 Install the dust shield and the flywheel by referring to Section 6 and slip the oil dipstick into its tube.

7 After coating its threads with a thread sealant, or sealing tape, screw the oil pressure sending unit into the block and tighten it securely (photo).

8 Lubricate the rubber gasket on the new oil filter and install it on the engine.

9 Install the motor mount brackets (photo) the insulator and the roll restrictors into place on the block (photo). The insulators have alignment pins (photo) which must fit into the holes in the brackets. Tighten the bolts/nuts to the specified torque.

10 Attach the air conditioner compressor brackets (photo) to the block and tighten the bolts securely (if so equipped).

11 Install the water pump and tighten the mounting bolts securely (photo). Be sure to coat both sides of the gasket with silicone-type gasket sealer. Install the rubber hose and the coolant transfer tube.

12 Install the hose clamps and tighten the transfer tube mounting bolts.

13 Install the air conditioner idler pulley and the power steering pump bracket (if so equipped).

14 Next, install the fuel pump. Use a new gasket and coat both sides with silicone-type gasket sealer. Tighten the mounting nuts securely.

15 Coat both sides of the areas immediately around the coolant passages in the intake manifold gasket with a silicone-type gasket sealer, then install the intake manifold/carburetor assembly in place on the engine. Do not allow any gasket sealer to get in the jet air passages in the manifold and head.

16 Slip the engine hoisting bracket into place on the rear studs

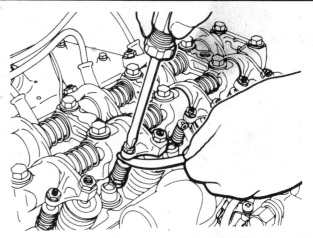

Fig. 2.21 Adjusting the Jet Valve clearance (Sec 31)

(photo) then install the nuts (and the 1 bolt) and tighten them to the specified torque. When tightening, start at the center of the manifold and work out toward the ends. Tighten each fastener in sequence, a little at a time, until they are all at the specified torque.

17 Slip the rubber coolant hose onto the intake manifold spigot (photo) and tighten the hose clamps securely.

18 Using a new gasket, install the exhaust manifold and tighten the nuts to the specified torque. Be sure to install the engine hoist bracket to the front (photo) and the SAS pipe bracket and electrical group strap to the rear of the manifold (photo) before tightening the nuts. When tightening, start at the center of the manifold and work out toward the ends. Tighten each nut in sequence, a little at a time, until they are all at the specified torque.

19 Attach the 2 heat shields to the exhaust manifold (photo). The 4 bolts that hold the upper shield in place must have the large washers on them.

20 Coat the Secondary Air Supply System air pipe fitting threads with an anti-seize compound, then thread the fitting into the top of the exhaust manifold and tighten it finger tight. Install the air pipe bracket bolt, then tighten the fitting and the bolt securely.

21 Make sure the number 1 piston is at top dead center on the compression stroke, then install the distributor. Line up the mating marks on the distributor housing (a line) and the driven gear (a punch mark). Slide the distributor into place in the cylinder head while lining up the mark on the distributor hold-down flange with the center of the stud. Make sure the distributor is completely seated, then install the mounting nut and tighten it securely.

22 Remove the valve cover. Coat the sealing surfaces of the cylinder head with silicone-type gasket sealer, then install the breather at the front and the semi-circular seal at the rear of the head.

23 Add the specified amount of the recommended type of oil to the engine. Pour it directly over the camshaft so that the lobes are thoroughly lubricated.

24 Coat the valve cover gasket sealing surface of the breather at the front of the head with silicone-type gasket sealer. Lay a new rubber seal in place in the valve cover (photo) and install the cover in place on the engine. Install the attaching bolts, using new rubber seals (photo), and tighten them securely.

25 Slip the rubber carburetor bowl vent tube onto the metal tube mounted on the valve cover (photo), then slide the hose clamp into place. Attach the crankcase breather hose to the spigot at the rear of the valve cover (photo).

26 Attach the clutch, the starter motor and the transmission to the engine.

---

33 Engine – Installation

1 Once the clutch components, the transmission and the starter are in place on the engine, it is ready to be reinstalled in the vehicle.

2 Raise the vehicle and set it securely on jack stands.

3 Install a short length of heavy chain between the hoisting brackets on the engine. Attach the engine hoist lifting hook to the chain and raise the engine until it clears the front of the vehicle. Do not let the engine swing freely.

32.9a Installing the motor mount brackets

32.9b Assembling the roll restrictor and insulator

32.9c Installing the insulator (note the alignment pin)

32.11 Installing the water pump

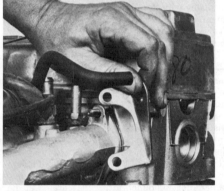

32.16 Be sure to install the engine hoisting bracket before tightening the intake manifold nuts

32.17 Installing the coolant hose on the intake manifold fitting

32.18a Install the engine hoisting bracket on the front exhaust manifold mounting studs

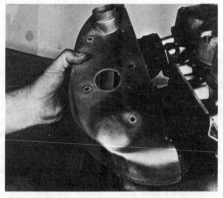

32.18b Attach the SAS pipe bracket and the electrical ground strap to the rear exhaust manifold studs

32.19 Installing the upper heat shield to the exhaust manifold

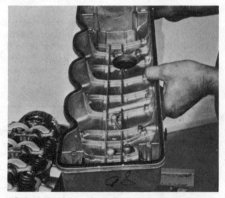

32.24a Installing the new valve cover seal. (It is molded to a definite shape and only fits into the valve cover recess 1 way)

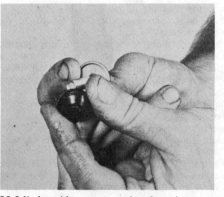

32.24b Attaching a new seal to the valve cover mounting bolt

4 Angle the transmission steeply toward the back of the vehicle and carefully lower the engine into place. Work slowly and use the transmission and hoist to direct the engine to its proper location on the motor mounts.

5 With the engine in place (still attached to the hoist), support the transmission with a jack and install the front motor mount bolts through the roll restrictors and insulators and into the frame holes. Tighten them finger-tight only.

6 Remove the chains and move the hoist out of the way.

7 Install the transmission support crossmember by raising or lowering the supporting jack as necessary. Tighten the 2 nuts attaching the transmission to the crossmember and the twelve bolts holding the crossmember to the frame.

8 Tighten the motor mount bolts securely.

9 Install the speedometer cable and housing at the drive unit and tighten the fittings. Bend the retaining strap that holds the speedometer cable to the crossmember back into position.

10 Slip the emergency brake cable housing end into the frame bracket and attach the cable end to the brake pull arm.

11 Attach the emergency brake cable balancer to the brake pull arm and slip a new cotter pin through the hole in the balancer pivot pin.

12 Install the driveshaft by referring to Chapter 8.

13 Slip the clutch cable housing into place on the transmission. Push the rubber dust cover over the end of the clutch cable and hook the cable end to the clutch control lever. Refer to Chapter 8 and adjust the clutch.

14 Plug in the back-up light switch wiring connector.

15 Install the exhaust pipe and tighten the rear mounting nuts first, followed by the front mounting nuts. Don't forget to tighten the bracket and hanger bolts also.

16 Attach the fuel hose isolator strap to the left engine mount with the concave side of the washer facing out. Install the metal insulator on the right engine mount (photo).

17 Hook the battery lead to the starter motor and plug in the bayonet-type connector at the starter solenoid. The starter motor wiring bracket is attached to the engine by the rear bolt on the lower air conditioner bracket (if so equipped).

18 If your vehicle is equipped with air conditioning, position the compressor in its mounts and install the 3 mounting bolts through the rear bracket and into the compressor. Tighten all mounting bolts securely.

19 Attach the battery ground wire (lower left) to the engine block.

20 Install the alternator and hook up the wiring. Do not tighten the mounting or pivot bolts at this time.

21 If your vehicle is equipped with power steering, position the pump in its mount and install, but do not tighten, the bolts. Install the pulley on the pump shaft with the concave side to the front. Hold the pulley carefully with a large pliers and tighten the nut securely.

22 Attach the wires to the water temperature and oil pressure sending units.

23 Insert the coil wire into the center terminal of the distributor cap and plug in the primary circuit connector on the distributor body (photo).

24 Plug in the air conditioner compressor electrical lead (if so equipped) and the 3-wire emission system electrical connector just below the carburetor.

25 Hook up the fuel hoses to the fuel pump and the carburetor. They are color-coded to decrease the possibility of mixing them up. Be sure to tighten the hose clamps securely.

26 Install the radiator and the lower fan shroud only. Tighten the shroud bolts finger-tight. Hook up the overflow tube to the spigot at the radiator filler neck.

27 Install the water pump pulley and the fan clutch, then position the power steering pump drive belt and adjust its tension. Be sure to tighten the pivot and adjusting bolts securely.

28 Install the alternator/water pump drive belt and adjust its tension. Be sure to tighten the alternator pivot and adjusting bolts securely.

29 If your vehicle is equipped with air conditioning, install and adjust the drive belt.

30 Install the upper fan shroud and fasten the shrouds together with the sheetmetal screws. Center the shroud on the fan and tighten the bolts attaching the shroud to the radiator. Rotate the fan to make sure it clears the shroud on all sides.

31 Install the upper and lower radiator hoses and tighten the hose clamps.

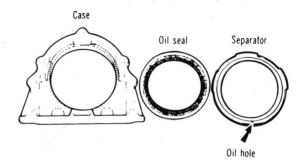

Fig. 2.22 When installing the rear oil seal housing, make sure the separator oil hole is at the bottom (Sec 32)

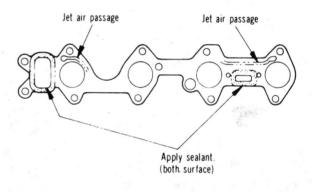

Fig. 2.23 Before installing the intake manifold, coat the areas around the coolant passages in the gasket with silicone-type gasket sealer (Sec 32)

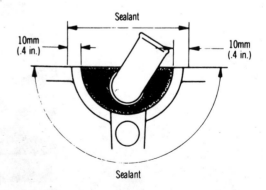

Fig. 2.24 To guard against oil leakage, apply a thin coat of silicone-type gasket sealer to the sealing surfaces of the semi-circular seal and the breather before installing them in the cylinder head (Sec 32)

32 Attach the heater hose to the metal coolant transfer tube at the rear of the engine and tighten the hose clamp.

33 Attach the brake vacuum booster hose to the intake manifold and slide the hose clamp into place.

34 Attach the electrical ground strap on the exhaust manifold to the firewall heat shield.

35 Attach the purge control valve hose bracket to the valve cover.

36 Hook up the throttle linkage at the carburetor and valve cover.

37 Attach the carburetor vent hose to the metal tube on the valve cover.

38 Attach the vacuum hoses to the distributor vacuum advance unit, the CAV on the carburetor, the throttle opener (if so equipped) on the carburetor and the air cleaning housing. Install the air cleaner housing and the rubber snorkel connecting the air cleaner housing to the headlight support channel.

39 Install the shift lever assembly and the center console (if so equipped).

40 Install the hood and the battery. Attach the battery cables (positive first, then negative). If sparking occurs when the battery cables are being hooked up, make sure all switches are off and the doors closed.

41 Fill the radiator with coolant (a 50/50 mixture of water and ethylene glycol-based antifreeze). You will have to add additional coolant after the engine is started, so keep a close eye on the level.

42 Add the proper amount of the recommended lubricant to the transmission and double-check the engine oil level.

43 Double-check all nuts and bolts for tightness and make sure all hoses, electrical wiring and other connections are properly installed, then lower the vehicle to the ground.

---

34 Initial start-up and break-in after overhaul

1 Once the engine has been properly installed in the vehicle, double-check the engine oil and coolant levels.

2 With the spark plugs out of the engine and the coil high-tension lead grounded to the engine block, crank the engine over until oil pressure registers on the gauge.

3 Install the spark plugs, hook up the plug wires and the coil high-tension lead.

4 Make sure the carburetor choke plate is closed, then start the engine. It may take a few moments for gasoline to reach the carburetor, but the engine should start without a great deal of effort.

5 As soon as the engine starts, it should be set at a fast idle (to ensure proper oil circulation) and allowed to warm up to normal operating temperature. While the engine is warming up, make a thorough check for oil and coolant leaks.

6 After the engine reaches normal operating temperature, shut it off, remove the valve cover, retorque the head bolts and recheck the valve clearances (using the hot engine specifications).

7 Install the valve cover and recheck the engine oil and coolant levels. Also, check the ignition timing and the engine idle speed (refer to Chapter 1) and make any necessary adjustment.

8 Drive the vehicle to an area with minimum traffic, accelerate at full throttle from 30 to 50 mph, then allow the vehicle to slow to 30 mph with the throttle closed. Repeat the procedure 10 or 12 times. This will load the piston rings and cause them to seal properly against the cylinder walls. Check again for oil and coolant leaks.

9 Drive the vehicle gently for the first 500 miles (no sustained high speeds) and keep a constant check on the oil level. It is not unusual for an engine to use oil during the break-in period.

10 At approximately 500 to 600 miles, change the oil and filter, retorque the cylinder head bolts and recheck the valve clearances.

11 For the next few hundred miles, drive the vehicle normally. Do not pamper it or abuse it.

12 After 2000 miles, change the oil and filter again and consider the engine fully broken in.

32.25a Attaching the carburetor bowl vent tube to the valve cover fitting

32.25b Attaching the crankcase breather hose to the valve cover spigot

33.16 Attach the metal insulator to the right motor mount (US only)

33.23 Plugging in the distributor primary circuit connector

Chapter 3 Cooling, heating and air conditioning

Refer to Chapter 13 for specifications and information related to 1981 thru 1988 models

Contents

Specifications

Cooling system type .... Liquid cooled, pressurized

Radiator
Type .... Vertical flow wth expansion tank
Pressure cap opens
    Pressure .... 11.3 to 14.2 psi (78.4 to 98.1 kPa)
    Vacuum .... -0.7 to -1.4 psi (-4.9 to -9.8 kPa)

Water pump type .... Centrifugal type impeller

Coolant capacity
U-engine .... 9.5 US qts (9.0 liters)
W-engine .... 9.7 US qts (9.2 liters)

Thermostat
Type .... Wax pellet
Starts to open at
    USA .... 180°F (82°C)
    Canada .... 190°F (88°C)
Fully open at
    USA .... 203°F (95°C)
    Canada .... 212°F (100°C)

Drive belt
Tension .... Deflection of $\frac{1}{4}$ to $\frac{3}{8}$ in (7 to 10 mm) is required when a 22 lb force is applied between alternator and water pump pulley
Circumference .... 37.4 in (949 mm)
I.D. number MD027458

Coolant temperature sending unit resistance
At 176°F (80°) .... 69.4 Ω
At 212°F (100°C) .... 36.4 Ω

Torque specifications
Coolant temperature sending unit .... 22 to 28 ft-lbs (30 to 39 Nm)

1 General information

The cooling system used on the Chrysler mini-truck is very conventional in design, utilizing a vertical-flow radiator, an engine driven water pump, and thermostat controlled coolant flow. The fan is equipped with a clutch, which allows it to draw air through the radiator at lower speeds. At higher speeds, where the fan is not needed for cooling, the clutch automatically lowers the fan speed and reduces the engine power required for fan operation.

The water pump is located on the right front side of the engine and is driven by a belt from the pulley mounted on the front of the crankshaft. This belt is also used to drive the alternator.

The heater utilizes the heat produced by the engine and contained in the coolant to warm the interior of the vehicle. It is manually controlled from inside by the driver or passenger.

Air conditioning is available as an option. All components of the system are mounted in the engine compartment and the system is driven by a belt from the pulley mounted on the front of the crankshaft. Output of the system is controlled from inside the vehicle.

2 Cooling system – draining, flushing and refilling

1   As part of regular routine maintenance, the coolant should be drained and the system completely flushed. Refer to Chapter 1 for the procedure to follow.
2   Always use a mixture of 50% soft water and 50% ethylene glycol based antifreeze when refilling the cooling system. Many of the engine parts are made of aluminum, which requires the corrosion protection offered by this type of antifreeze.

3 Thermostat – removal, testing and installation

1   The thermostat is located at the front of the engine inside a housing just to the rear of the distributor (photo). The thermostat allows for quick warmups and governs the normal operating temperature of the engine.
2   If the thermostat is functioning properly, the temperature gauge should rise to the normal operating temperature quickly and then stay there, only rising above the normal position occasionally when the engine gets unusually hot. If the engine does not rise to normal operating temperatures quickly, or if it overheats, the thermostat should be removed and checked or replaced.
3   The engine must be cool when this operation is performed.
4   Place a suitable container under the radiator and drain some of the coolant into the container by opening the radiator drain valve.
5   Loosen and slide back the hose clamp, then pull the upper radiator hose off the thermostat housing cover.
6   Remove the two bolts (photo) and lift off the housing cover (photo). you may have to tap the cover with a soft-faced hammer to break the gasket seal.
7   After the cover has been removed, note how the thermostat is installed then lift it out. If it is open when it is removed it is defective and must be replaced with a new one.
8   To check the thermostat, submerge it in a container of water along with a thermometer. The thermostat should be suspended so it does not touch the container.
9   Gradually heat the water in the container with a hotplate or stove and check the temperature when the thermostat first starts to open.
10 Continue heating the water and check the temperature when the thermostat is fully open.
11 Lift the fully open thermostat out of the water and allow it to cool.
12 Compare the opening temperature and the fully open temperature to the specifications.
13 If these specifications are not met, or if the thermostat does not open while the water is heated, replace it with a new one.
14 Scrape all traces of the old gasket from the thermostat housing and cover. Do not nick or gouge the gasket sealing surfaces.
15 To install the thermostat, lay it in place in the housing with the proper end facing up. Each thermostat is marked as to which end should face into the engine so examine yours carefully before installing it (photo). (Make sure that the thermostat flange is properly seated in the recessed area of the housing).
16 Apply a thin even layer of silicone-type gasket sealer to both sides

Fig. 3.1 Testing thermostat operation (Sec 3)

of a new gasket and lay it in place on the housing.
17 Next, carefully position the housing cover, install the two bolts and tighten them securely.
18 Slip the upper radiator hose onto the housing cover spigot, install the hose clamp and tighten it securely.
19 Pour the drained coolant back into the radiator then start the engine and check for leaks around the thermostat housing and the upper radiator hose.

4 Coolant reserve system – testing

1   Make sure the coolant level in the reserve system reservoir is at the 'FULL' mark.
2   With the radiator cap in place, open the radiator drain pet cock (place a suitable container under the radiator to catch the coolant).
3   Coolant should be drawn from the reserve system reservoir into the radiator. Close the radiator drain petcock before the reserve system reservoir is completely drained.
4   If coolant is not drawn from the reservoir, check for leaks in the hose from the reservoir to the radiator filler neck, the radiator cap, and the radiator top tank.
5   It may be necessary to have the cap and system pressure checked to locate any leaks.
6   Be sure to remove the radiator pressure cap and replenish the coolant in the radiator and the reserve system reservoir.

5 Coolant reserve system reservoir – removal and installation

1   The coolant reserve system reservoir located on the right fender well should be removed periodically, checked for cracks and other damage, and flushed with clean water.
2   To remove the reservoir, carefully pry off the cap with the hose attached and lay the cap and hose aside.
3   Pull out on the reservoir bottom and simultaneously pull up and slide the reservoir off its mount.
4   To install the reservoir, line it up with the mount and push down until it is properly seated. Don't forget to install the cap.

6 Fan/fan clutch – removal, inspection and installation

1   The fan clutch can fail in one of two ways: it can either slip excessively, which would prevent the fan from cooling the engine sufficiently at low speeds, or the drive can seize, causing noise and wasting engine power because the fan is turning with the engine no matter what the engine speed.
2   If your vehicle is equipped with a fan shroud, it must be removed first. The air conditioner belt should also be removed (loosen the idler pulley).
3   Loosen the alternator pivot and adjusting bolts and slip the drive belt off the water pump pulley.
4   Remove the four nuts attaching the fan clutch/pulley to the water pump flange (photo). Pull the fan clutch assembly forward and out of

3.1 Thermostat housing

3.6a Remove the thermostat housing bolts

3.6b Lift off the housing cover and note how the thermostat is installed

3.15 This end of the thermostat should face into the engine

the engine compartment. Be very careful not to gouge the radiator with the fan blades or clutch.

5   The fan is attached to the clutch assembly with four bolts.

6   Check the fan blades for cracks and evidence of damage.

7   Check for evidence of leaks where the two halves of the fan clutch are joined and where the input shaft enters the clutch case. If leaks are present, replace the clutch assembly.

8   Rotate the input shaft and check for obvious binding and noise. Also, check for side-to-side play between the shaft and case. If the shaft will not rotate, the drive mechanism is seized and a new clutch assembly should be obtained.

9   If it was removed, attach the fan to the clutch assembly and tighten the bolts securely. Install the water pump pulley and the fan clutch in place on the water pump flange. Install the four lock washers and nuts and tighten them evenly and securely.

10 Replace the drive belt and adjust the tension to the specified amount by turning the alternator adjusting bolt. Be sure to tighten the alternator pivot and mount bolts securely.

11 Reinstall the fan shroud (if so equipped).

7   Water pump – removal and installation

1   The water pump is mounted on the front of the engine and is driven by a belt from the crank shaft. Water pump problems can

generally be narrowed down to failed bearings or leaking seals.

2   The most common problem with water pumps is a leaking seal, evidenced by coolant leakage from behind the drive pulley. Bearing failure may appear as a squealing noise or too much free movement. Noises can be pin pointed with a length of hose held to the ear while moving the other end around the water pump itself. If this is done, be very careful of the fan and other moving parts of the engine, which can cause serious injury. Free play can be felt by moving the drive pulley back and forth.

3   To gain access to the water pump, disconnect the battery ground cable and remove the fan shroud (if so equipped), the fan/fan clutch assembly (see Section 6) and the water pump drive pulley. Place a suitable container under the vehicle to catch the coolant (it can be reused) and remove the radiator pressure cap. Drain the coolant from the radiator and the engine by opening the radiator drain petcock and removing the block drain plug on the right side of the engine. After the coolant has drained, close the radiator petcock and install the block drain plug. Use silicone type gasket sealer or thread tape on the drain plug threads.

4   Loosen and slide back the hose clamp, then remove the lower radiator hose from the radiator and water pump. Loosen and slide back the hose clamp attaching the rubber heater hose to the water pump.

5   Remove the bolts attaching the pump to the front of the engine and lift out the pump. You may have to tap gently on the pump with a soft-faced hammer to break the gasket seal. Be careful not to gouge the radiator when removing the bolts or the pump.

6   Scrape all traces of the old gasket and gasket sealer off of the engine. Do not nick or gouge the gasket sealing surfaces.
7   Coat both sides of a new gasket with silicone type gasket sealer, then install the new pump. Be sure to line up the bolt holes in the pump body and the gasket before placing the pump in position on the engine. Slip the rubber heater hose over the pump's spigot as the pump is installed (photo).
8   Install the pump mounting bolts and tighten them evenly and securely. Slip the heater hose clamp into place and tighten it securely.
9   Install the lower radiator hose and tighten the hose clamps. Install the drive pulley, the fan/fan clutch assembly and the fan shroud. Install and adjust the drive belt and hook up the battery ground cable.
10 Fill the radiator with a 50/50 mixture of soft water and ethylene glycol based antifreeze.
11 Start the engine and check for leaks around the water pump mounting area, the heater hose and the lower radiator hose. Keep an eye on the coolant level, as it will drop. More coolant should be added as required.

8   Radiator – removal and installation

1   Remove the radiator pressure cap and drain the coolant from the radiator and the engine block. The radiator drain petcock is located on the lower left side of the radiator. The engine block drain is located on the lower right side of the engine underneath the exhaust manifold.
2   Once the coolant has been drained, remove the radiator hoses by loosening and sliding back the hose clamps and pulling the hoses off the radiator and engine.
3   If your vehicle is equipped with an automatic transmission, disconnect and plug the transmission oil cooling lines at the bottom of the radiator. Do not allow any dirt to enter the lines or fittings.

4   If your vehicle is equipped with a fan shroud, remove both the upper and lower sections. Each section is held in place by two bolts and the two sections are fastened together with a sheet metal screw on each side.
5   Pull the overflow tube off of the spigot at the radiator filler neck. Remove the four bolts attaching the radiator to the vehicle and carefully lift the radiator out of the engine compartment. Do not gouge the radiator coolant tubes or cooling fins with the fan blades.
6   Carefully examine the radiator for evidence of leaks and damage. It is recommended that any necessary repairs be performed by a reputable radiator repair shop.
7   If the radiator is clogged, or if large amounts of rust or scale have formed, the repair shop will also do a thorough cleaning job.
8   Make sure the spaces between the cooling tubes and fins are clear. If necessary, use compressed air or running water to remove anything that may be clogging them.
9   Carefully lower the radiator into place in the engine compartment. Again, be very careful not to gouge the cooling fins and coolant tubes with the fan blades.
10 Install the four bolts attaching the radiator to the vehicle and tighten them securely. Slip the overflow tube over the spigot on the radiator filler neck.
11 Attach the fan shrouds to the radiator and center the shroud on the fan. Tighten the mounting bolts securely. Rotate the fan and check for adequate clearance around the entire shroud hole.
12 Unplug and hook up the automatic transmission fluid cooling lines at the bottom of the radiator. Tighten the fittings securely.
13 Install both radiator hoses and tighten the hose clamps securely. Make sure the radiator drain petcock is closed and the engine block drain is in place, then add coolant until the radiator is full.
14 Install the radiator cap. Start and run the engine and check for leaks. You will have to add additional coolant as the engine is running.

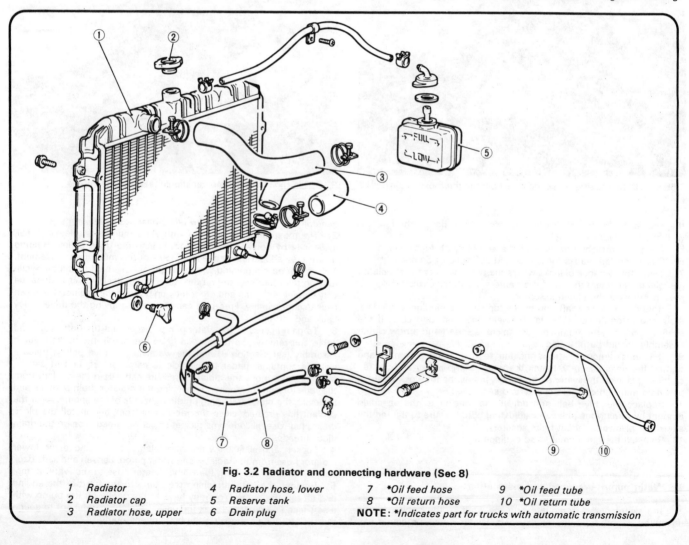

Fig. 3.2 Radiator and connecting hardware (Sec 8)

1	Radiator	4	Radiator hose, lower	7	*Oil feed hose	9	*Oil feed tube
2	Radiator cap	5	Reserve tank	8	*Oil return hose	10	*Oil return tube
3	Radiator hose, upper	6	Drain plug				

NOTE: *Indicates part for trucks with automatic transmission

9 Heater controls – adjustment

1   The heater controls should be periodically checked and adjusted to inside optimum heater performance.

2   The INSIDE/OUTSIDE air control is adjusted first. Place the control lever in the INSIDE position and check to make sure that the damper lever is down and the outside air intake is closed.

3   If it is not, move the cable housing in its securing clip until the intake is closed.

4   Move the control lever to the OUTSIDE position and make sure the air intake is open.

5   The heater temperature control is adjusted next. With the control lever in the OFF position, check to see if the control valve is fully closed. The lever on the valve should be in the "up" position.

6   If it is not, move the cable housing in its securing clip until the valve is fully closed with the control lever in the OFF position. Move the control lever to the HOT position and check for smooth and complete operation of the control valve. With the engine running at normal operating temperature, check for proper operation of the temperature control.

7   If the heater control valve binds and does not operate properly, it should be replaced with a new one.

8   The last control to be adjusted is the DEF-HEAT-VENT selector lever. Place the control lever in the DEF position. The damper lever should be in the up position.

9   With the engine running at normal operating temperature, turn on the heater fan switch and feel for air being forced out of the defroster duct at the base of the windshield. Move the control lever to the HEAT position. The air should no longer flow from the defroster duct or the vent ducts. If air movement is felt, move the cable housing in its clip to adjust the damper.

10 Heater control assembly – removal and installation

1   Pull off the radio knob and remove the nuts from the control shaft. Lift off the radio trim panel.

2   Pull off the heater fan control knob and the heater control lever end. Remove the nut from the fan control knob shaft.

3   Remove the ashtray.

4   Remove the four screws from the cluster rim and lift it out of place by carefully prying out on the lower left corner.

5   Disconnect the wiring harness and the wire lead at the lower right corner of the rim.

6   Disconnect the heater control cable from the heater (not from the control assembly).

7   Remove the four screws attaching the control assembly and withdraw it from the dashboard (photo).

8   Minor repairs, such as cleaning and lubrication of the pivots and cables, can be performed on the heater control assembly. But generally speaking, it would be a good idea to replace it with a new one if it is not operating properly.

9   Installation is basically the reverse of removal. Remember to plug in the electrical connector before installing the instrument cluster rim.

10   Refer to Section 9 for heater control adjustment procedures.

11 Heater assembly – removal and installation

1   In order to gain access to the heater core (in case of leaks or other damage) the heater assembly should be removed from the vehicle.

2   Disconnect the negative battery cable from the battery.

3   Place the heater controlled lever in the OFF position, then drain the coolant from the engine and radiator (see Section 8).

4   Remove the center console, if so equipped.

5   Remove the center panel, the center ventilator grill and duct, and the defroster ducts.

6   Disconnect the heater control cables at the heater (not at the control assembly). Hold a shallow container or some rags near the hoses, then disconnect the heater hoses from the inlet and outlet spigots of the heater core. Catch any coolant that may run out of the hoses and plug the hoses and the heater core spigot.

7   Unplug the heater fan motor wiring connectors.

8   Remove the two mounting bolts from the top and the two mounting nuts from the center of the heater assembly.

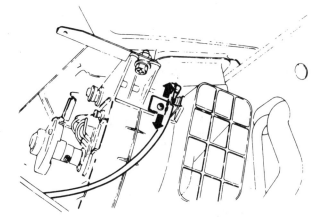

Fig. 3.3 To adjust the INSIDE/OUTSIDE air control, move the cable housing in the securing clip (Sec 9)

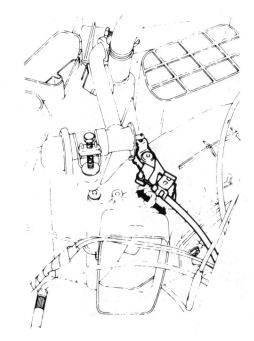

Fig. 3.4 The control valve should be fully closed (lever "up") with the heater control lever in the OFF position (move the cable housing in the securing clip to adjust it) (Sec 9)

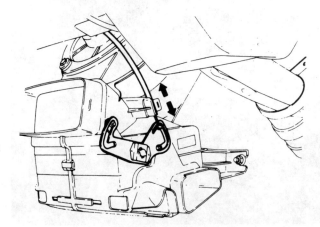

Fig. 3.5 To adjust the DEF-HEAT-VENT damper, move the cable housing in the securing clip

6.4 The fan/clutch and pulley are attached to the water pump flange with 4 nuts

6.7 As the pump is installed, slip the rubber heater hose over the spigot

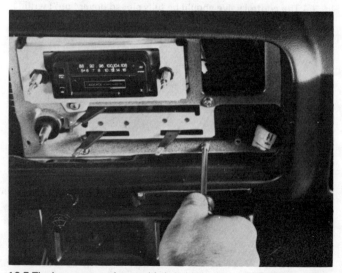

10.7 The heater control assembly is held in place with 4 screws

9   Carefully lift the heater assembly out of its mounting position.
10   Check for evidence of leaks and other damage. Make sure the heater control valve operates smoothly. Repair and cleaning of the core is best left to a radiator repair shop. If the heater core is in questionable condition, replace it with a new one.
11   Installation is the reverse of removal. Be sure the heater hoses are properly seated on the heater core inlet and outlet spigots, then tighten the hose clamps securely.
12   Adjust the heater control cables by referring to Section 9.
13   After the heater assembly is in place, fill the radiator with a 50/50 mixture of soft water and ethylene glycol based antifreeze. Place the heater control in the HOT position. Start the engine and allow it to run for a while to circulate the coolant and eliminate any air from the heater assembly and cooling system.
14   Keep an eye on the coolant level and add more coolant as the level drops. Once the level has stabilized, shut off the engine and install the radiator pressure cap.

12 Heater motor/fan – removal, testing and installation

1   The heater motor is attached to the heater assembly so it is automatically removed when the heater assembly is removed. It can also be taken out as a separate unit.
2   Remove the center console (if so equipped), the center panel and the center ventilator grill and duct.
3   Unplug the two motor electrical connectors.
4   Remove the three bolts attaching the motor and fan assembly to the heater, then lift out the motor and fan separately.
5   Refer to Chapter 10 for heater motor testing procedures.
6   Position the fan and motor in place in the heater assembly, install the mounting bolts and tighten them evenly and securely.
7   Plug in the two motor electrical connectors.
8   Install the center ventilator grill and duct, the center panel and the console.

13 Heater fan switch – testing

Refer to Chapter 10 for heater fan switch testing procedures.

14 Air conditioning system – servicing

1   Because of the special tools, equipment and skills required to service air conditioning systems, and the differences between the various systems that may be installed on vehicles, air conditioner servicing cannot be covered in this manual.
2   We will cover component removal, as the home mechanic may realize a substantial savings in repair costs if he removes components himself, takes them to a professional for repair, and/or replaces them with new ones.
3   Problems in the air conditioning system should be diagnosed, and the system refrigerant evacuated, by an air conditioning technician before component removal/replacement is attempted.
4   Once the new or reconditioned components has been installed, the system should then be charged and checked by an air conditioning technician.
5   Before indiscriminately removing air conditioning system components, get more than one estimate or repair costs from reputable air conditioning service centers. You may find it to be cheaper and less trouble to let the entire operation be performed by someone else.

15 Air conditioner condenser – removal and installation

1   The air conditioner condenser is mounted in front of the radiator.
2   Before removing the condenser, the system must be evacuated by an air conditioning technician. *Do not attempt to do this yourself; the refrigerant used in the system can cause serious injuries and respiratory irritation.*
3   Loosen the hose clamps and remove the hoses leading from the compresser and receiver/dryer to the condenser. Do not remove the hoses from the condenser.

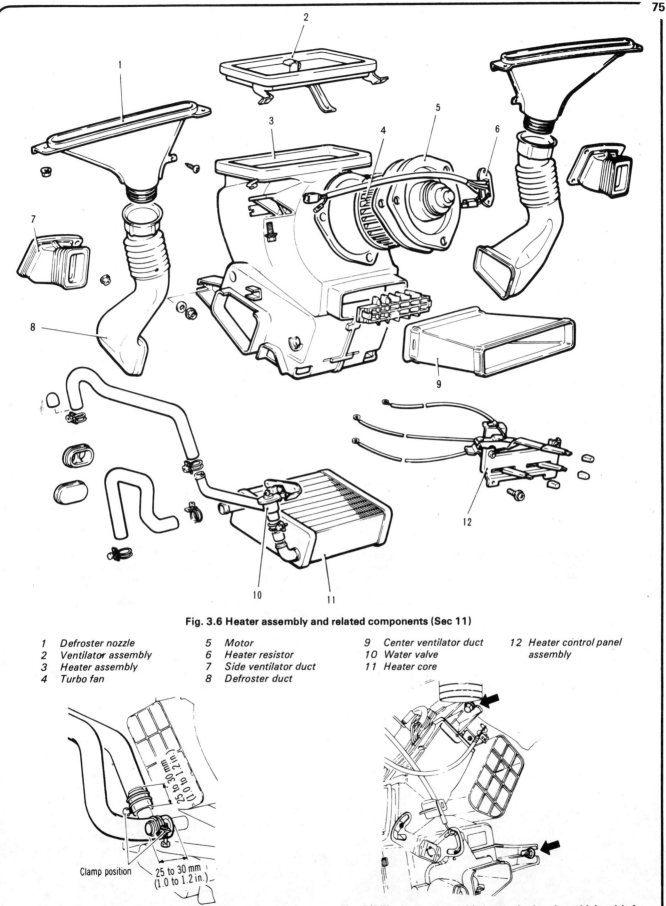

Fig. 3.6 Heater assembly and related components (Sec 11)

1   Defroster nozzle   5   Motor   9   Center ventilator duct   12 Heater control panel
2   Ventilator assembly   6   Heater resistor   10 Water valve   assembly
3   Heater assembly   7   Side ventilator duct   11 Heater core
4   Turbo fan   8   Defroster duct

Clamp position   25 to 30 mm
(1.0 to 1.2 in.)

Fig. 3.7 Heater hose clamp locations (Sec 11)

Fig. 3.8 The heater assembly is attached to the vehicle with 4 bolts; 2 at the top and 2 at the center of the assembly (Sec 11)

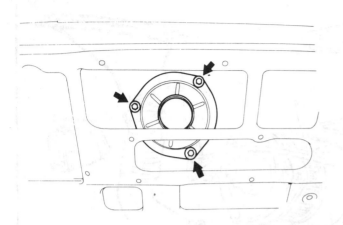

Fig. 3.9 The heater motor/fan assembly is held in place on the heater with 3 bolts (Sec 12)

4   Remove the grill (by referring to Chapter 12) and the verticle hood latch support.
5   Remove the four bolts attaching the condenser to the front panel. Carefully lift the condenser out of the vehicle; do not bend the cooling fins or coil.
6   Loosen the hose clamps and remove the hoses from the condenser.
7   Installation is basically the reverse of removal. When installing the hoses, lubricate the inside surfaces of the hoses and the outside of the fittings with refrigerant oil. Be sure to install the hoses onto the condenser before mounting the condenser in the vehicle. Support the hose fittings against a solid surface, such as a work bench, when pushing the hoses onto them. This will prevent bending of the fittings or the coils, which could cause leaks. Be sure to locate the clamps properly with the clamp finders and tighten them securely.

16 Air conditioner evaporator – removal and installation

1   The air conditioner evaporator is combined with the heater assembly and is mounted under the right side of the vehicle dash board.
2   Before removing the evaporator, the system must be evacuated by an air conditioning technician. *Do not attempt to do this yourself; the refrigerant used in the system can cause serious injuries and respiratory irritation.*
3   Loosen the hose clamps and remove the hoses from the evaporator fittings inside the engine compartment.
4   Disconnect the control cable from the damper control lever at the right side of the evaporator.
5   Slide back the hose clamp and remove the drain hose from the spigot at the rear of the evaporator.
6   Peel off the sealing compound around the evaporator inlet and outlet tubes at the vehicle fire wall.

7   Remove the bolts attaching the evaporator to the dashboard and fire wall and carefully move it down and out from under the fashboard. Do not misplace the plastic duct that fits between the heater assembly and the evaporator.
8   Installation is basically the reverse of removal. Be sure to position the plastic ducts before slipping the evaporator into place. When installing the hoses, lubricate their inside surfaces and the outside of the fittings with refrigerant oil. The hose clamps must be positioned properly with the clamp finders and tightened securely. Do not forget to install the drain hose and the sealing compound.

17 Air conditioner compresser – removal and installation

1   The air conditioner compresser is mounted at the front of the engine, at the upper left side, and is driven by a belt from the crank shaft.
2   Before removing the compresser, the system must be evacuated by an air conditioning technician. *Do not attempt to do this yourself; the refrigerant used in the system can cause serious injuries and respiratory irritation.*
3   Loosen the drive belt idler pulley and slip the drive belt off the compressor clutch pulley.
4   Loosen the hose clamps and remove the two hoses from the compressor.
5   Unplug the air conditioner compressor clutch electrical connector.
6   Remove the bolts attaching the compressor to the mounts and the compressor can be lifted out of the vehicle. The bolts on the bottom are accessible only from under the vehicle.
7   Installation is basically the reverse of removal. Lubricate the inside of the hoses and the outside of the fittings with refrigerant oil before installing the hoses. Be sure to carefully seat the hoses on the compressor fittings and install the hose clamps securely. Locate the hose clamps the correct distance from the hose end with the hose clamp finder. The belt must be correctly tensioned for proper air conditioner operation.

18 Air conditioner receiver/dryer – removal and installation

1   The receiver/dryer, which acts as a reservoir for the refrigerant, is the cannister-shaped object mounted on the right fender well in the engine compartment.
2   Before removing the receiver/dryer, the system must be evacuated by an air conditioning technician. *Do not attempt to do this yourself; the refrigerant used in the system can cause serious injuries and respiratory irritation.*
3   Loosen the hose clamps and remove both hoses from the receiver/dryer.
4   Loosen the clamp and pull up on the receiver/dryer to remove it from its mount.
5   When installing the receiver/dryer, lubricate the inside surfaces of the hoses and the outside of the fittings with refrigerant oil. Be sure the hose clamps are properly located by the clamp finders and securely tightened.

Chapter 4 Fuel and exhaust systems

Refer to Chapter 13 for specifications and information related to 1981 thru 1988 models

Contents

Specifications

Fuel tank capacity .... 15.1 US gal

Fuel pump
Type .... Mechanical diaphragm
Discharge pressure .... 4.6 to 6 psi (32 to 42 kPa)

Fuel filter .... Replaceable cartridge type

Carburetor
Type .... Downdraft, 2 barrel
Throttle bore size
  Primary .... 1.181 in (30 mm)
  Secondary .... 1.260 in (32 mm)

1979 models

		U-engine			W-engine	
	Calif.	49-states	Canada	Calif.	49-states	Canada
Main jet						
Primary	103.8	105	106.3	106.3	107.5	107.5
Secondary	190	190	190	185	185	185
Pilot jet						
Primary	52.5	52.5	60	60	60	55
Secondary	60	60	60	60	60	60
Enrichment jet	40	40	40	45	45	55

Carburetor application
O Applicable   X Not applicable

Requirement	Engine model	Transmission	Sub-EGR valve	CAV	Fuel cut-off solenoid	ASV	Dash pot	Carburetor model
49-states	U	M/T	O	X	X	O	X	30-32DIDTA-85
	U	A/T	O	X	X	O	X	30-32DIDTA-86
	W	M/T	O	X	O	O	X	30-32DIDTA-185
	W	A/T	O	X	O	O	X	30-32DIDTA-186
California	U	M/T	O	O	X	O	X	30-32DIDTA-83
	U	A/T	O	X	X	O	X	30-32DIDTA-84
	W	M/T	O	O	O	O	X	30-32DIDTA-183
	W	A/T	O	X	O	O	X	30-32DIDTA-184
Canada	U	M/T	X	X	O	X	O	30-32DIDTA-132
	U	A/T	X	X	O	X	X	30-32DIDTA-133
	W	M/T	X	X	O	X	O	30-32DIDTA-136
	W	A/T	X	X	O	X	X	30-32DIDTA-137

U:2.0 liter (121.7 CID), W:2.6 liter (155.9 CID) engine, M/T:Manual Transmission, A/T: Automatic Transmission.

Idle speed/mixture settings – USA
'U'-engine (manual transmission)
Curb idle speed .... 650 ± 50 rpm
Curb idle CO (%) .... Below 0.1
Enriched idle speed .... 730 ± 10 rpm
Enriched idle CO (%) .... 1.0 ± 0.1
'U'-engine (automatic transmission)
Curb idle speed .... 700 ± 50 rpm
Curb idle CO (%) .... Below 0.1
Enriched idle speed .... 780 ± 10 rpm
Enriched idle CO (%) .... 1.0 ± 0.1
'W'-engine (manual and automatic transmissions)
Curb idle speed .... 850 ± 50 rpm
Curb idle CO (%) .... Below 0.1
Enriched idle speed .... 930 ± 10 rpm
Enriched idle CO (%) .... 1.0 ± 0.1

Idle speed/mixture settings – Canada
'U'-engine (manual and automatic transmissions)
Idle speed .... 850 ± 50 rpm
Idle CO (%) .... Adjust idle CO to leanest possible without misfiring within 0.5 to 2.0% range

'W'-engine
Idle speed .... 850 ± 50 rpm
Idle CO (%) .... Adjust idle CO to leanest possible without misfiring within 1.0 to 2.5 range

1980 models

| | | U-engine | | | W-engine | |
	Calif.	49-states	Canada	Calif.	49-states	Canada
Main jet						
Primary	106.3 – M/T	106.3	106.3	108.8	108.8	107.5
Secondary	107.5 – A/T	190	190	185	185	185
Pilot jet						
Primary	52.5	52.5	60	60	60	55
Secondary	60	60	60	60	60	60
Enrichment jet	40	40	40	45	45	55

Carburetor application
O Applicable   X Not applicable

Requirement	Engine model	Transmission	Sub-EGR valve	CAV	Fuel cut off solenoid	ASV	Dash pot	Carburetor model
49-states	U	M/T	O	O	X	O	X	30-32DIDTA-85
	U	A/T	O	O	X	O	X	30-32DIDTA-86
	W	M/T	O	O	O	O	X	30-32DIDTA-185
	W	A/T	O	O	O	O	X	30-32DIDTA-186
California	U	M/T	O	O	X	O	X	30-32DIDTA-83
	U	A/T	O	O	X	O	X	30-32DIDTA-84
	W	M/T	O	O	O	O	X	30-32DIDTA-183
	W	A/T	O	O	O	O	X	30-32DIDTA-184
Canada	U	M/T	X	X	O	X	O	30-32DIDTA-132
	U	A/T	X	X	O	X	X	30-32DIDTA-133
	W	M/T	X	X	O	X	O	30-32DIDTA-136
	W	A/T	X	X	O	X	X	30-32DIDTA-137

U:2.0 liter (121.7 CID), W:2.6 liter (155.9 CID) engine, M/T:Manual Transmission, A/T: Automatic Transmission.
CAV: Coasting Air Valve, ASV: Air switching valve

Idle speed/mixture settings – California only
'U'-engine (manual transmission)
Curb idle speed .... 650 ± 50 rpm
Curb idle CO (%) .... 1.0 ± 0.5 (with Secondary Air Supply system disconnected)
'U'-engine (automatic transmission)
Curb idle speed .... 700 ± 50 rpm
Curb idle CO (%) .... Same as for manual transmission

'W'-engine (manual and automatic transmissions)
Curb idle speed .... 750 ± 50 rpm
Curb idle CO (%) .... Same as for 'U'-engine

All others
'U'-engine (manual transmission)
Curb idle speed .... 650 ± 50 rpm
Curb idle CO (%) .... Below 0.1
Enriched idle speed .... 730 ± 10 rpm
Enriched idle CO (%) .... 1.0 ± 0.1
'U'-engine (automatic transmission)
Curb idle speed .... 700 ± 50 rpm
Curb idle CO (%) .... Below 0.1
Enriched idle speed .... 780 ± 10 rpm
Enriched idle CO (%) 1.0
'W'-engine (manual and automatic transmissions)
Curb idle speed .... 750 ± 50 rpm
Curb idle CO (%) .... 1.0 ± 0.5 (with Secondary Air Supply System disconnected)

Air conditioner-equipped models only:
Engine idle speed (throttle opener activated)
   'U' – engine .... 1150 ± 50 rpm
   'W' – engine .... 1050 ± 50 rpm

Accelerator pedal free play .... 0.040 in (1 mm)

Torque specifications

	ft-lbs	Nm
Exhaust pipe-to-manifold nuts	11 to 18	(15 to 24)
Exhaust pipe-to-main muffler bolts	14 to 22	(20 to 30)

1 General information

The fuel system on the Chrysler mini-truck is very conventional, utilizing a rear mounted fuel tank, a mechanical diaphragm-type fuel pump which is driven off the engine camshaft, and a 2 barrel down draft carburetor. The fuel is routed through a cartridge-type filter, mounted on the fuel tank, before entering the fuel line and pump.

Since many of the emission control systems' components and parts of the fuel system are interrelated, the material covered in this Chapter should be used in conjunction with the material in Chapter 6.

The extra system consists of a front exhaust pipe, a main muffler assembly and the various brackets and hangers that support them.

2 Fuel filter – replacement

Refer to Chapter 1 for the fuel filter replacement procedure.

3 Air cleaner assembly – removal and installation

1 The air cleaner assembly must be removed in order to perform many maintenance repair and adjustment procedures. It is very important to remove and install it carefully and correctly to ensure proper engine operation.
2 Remove the snorkel tube (connected between the air cleaner and the headlight brace) from the air cleaner (photo).
3 Pull off the crankcase breather hose from the front of the air cleaner housing (photo).
4 Remove the large hose leading to the secondary air supply system valve (photo).
5 Slide back the hose clamp and remove the hose that leads to the purge control valve from the air cleaner housing (photo).
6 Remove the top cover (it is held in place with 4 spring clips and a wing nut) and lift out the filter element.
7 Remove the 2 nuts, lock washers and flat washers attaching the air cleaner housing to the valve cover (photo).
8 Carefully lift up on the housing and disconnect the hot-air duct between the exhaust manifold and air cleaner housing (photo) and the vacuum hose leading to the air bleed valve in the housing. (The hose is color coded white) (photo).
9 Install the air cleaner by reversing the removal procedure. Be sure

to line up the arrows on the top cover and the housing before setting the cover in place.

4 Throttle cable – adjustment

1 The throttle cable must be adjusted after it is installed to ensure proper accelerator pedal free play and complete opening of the throttle valve.
2 The adjustment is made by loosening the cable housing clamps on the valve cover and carburetor and moving the housing toward or away from the carburetor, as necessary.
3 The free play of the accelerator should be within the limits specified. If it is not, change it by moving the cable housing. Remember to tighten the clamps if adjustments are made.
4 The accelerator pedal must operate smoothly and the throttle valve must be fully open when the accelerator pedal is depressed as far as possible.
5 Periodically apply a thin coat of multi-purpose grease to the accelerator pedal pivot points.

5 Vapor separator – general note

1 The vapor separator is the small canister mounted high on the left front fender well. It is mounted in the fuel system between the fuel pump and the carburetor and is designed to prevent vapor lock caused by high underhood temperatures.
2 The main fuel line from the fuel pump is connected to the middle fitting (color-coded green) on the separator. The hose connected at the top fitting (color-coded red) leads to the carburetor accelerator pump housing (which is also color-coded red). The hose connected to the bottom fitting (color-coded yellow) leads to the carburetor fuel inlet (also color-coded yellow).
3 The color-coded lines and fittings reduce the possibility of incorrect hose installation during carburetor servicing.
4 If the vapor separator is somehow damaged or begins to leak, it must be replaced with a new one. When installing a new vapor separator, position it so that the red fitting is at the top.

6 Automatic choke – general note

1 The choke valve is automatically operated by a wax element that

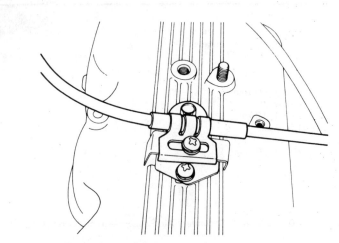

Fig. 4.1 Throttle cable housing valve cover clamp screw (Sec 4)

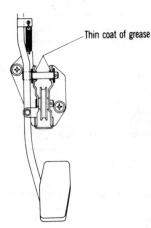

Thin coat of grease

Fig. 4.2 Apply a thin coat of grease to the accelerator pedal pivot bushings (Sec 4)

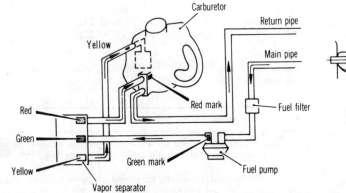

Fig. 4.3 Vapor separator hose routing (Sec 5)

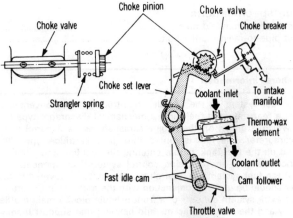

Fig. 4.4 Automatic choke (Sec 6)

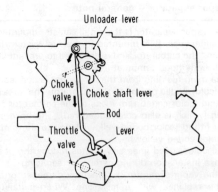

Fig. 4.5 Choke unloader mechanism (Sec 6)

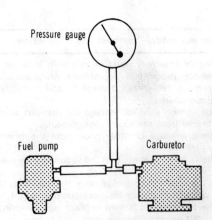

Fig. 4.6 Pressure testing the fuel pump (Sec 8)

3.2 Slide back the hose clamp and remove the snorkel tube

3.3 Pull off the crankcase breather hose

3.4 Remove the large hose leading to the secondary air supply system reed valve

3.5 Remove the hose that leads to the purge control valve

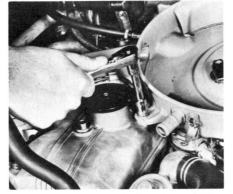

3.7 Remove the 2 nuts, lock washers and flat washers

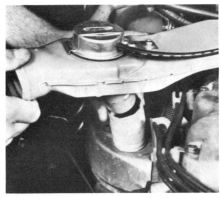

3.8a Disconnect the hot-air duct

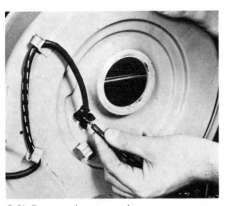

3.8b Remove the vacuum hose

11.4 Remove the float bowl vent tube from the carburetor

11.5 Remove the coolant hose from the rear of the carburetor

11.6 Disconnect the electrical lead

11.8a Removing the vacuum hose from the carburetor body

11.8b Removing the vacuum hose from the ASV

11.8c Removing the vacuum hose from the throttle opener (air conditioner-equipped vehicles only)

11.9 Remove and plug the 3 fuel hoses

12.1a Remove the air cleaner hold down stud

12.1b Slide back the hose clamps and remove the coolant hose

12.2a Remove the spring clip, then pry the throttle opener rod out of the throttle lever (air conditioner-equipped vehicles only)

12.2b The throttle opener is held in place with 2 screws

12.3a Remove the fuel cut-off solenoid ground wire

12.3b Remove the solenoid retaining screw

12.3c Carefully lift the solenoid away from the carburetor

12.4a Remove the idle mixture screw

12.4b Idle mixture screw, spring, washer and rubber seal

12.5a Pry the spring clip off the sub EGR valve linkage pin

senses the coolant temperature. This element allows the choke valve to close under spring pressure at low coolant temperatures and opens it through a set lever and a rack and pinion gear setup as the coolant temperature increases.

2   The wax element plunger pushes against an adjustable screw on the choke set lever. This screw is pre-set at the factory to provide for proper choke closing and opening and sealed with white paint. Do not tamper with it, as choke operation will be adversely affected.

3   The choke should not require any adjustment as long as the rack and pinion gears are properly oriented and the choke pinion gear assembly is adjusted so that the choke plate is lightly seated in the closed position when the choke linkage is installed.

7   Automatic choke — check

Refer to Chapter 1 for the procedure to follow when checking the choke for proper operation.

8   Fuel pump — testing

1   Before deciding that the fuel pump is defective, it should be tested for correct pressure while still in the vehicle.

2   To check the fuel pump pressure, you will need a 'T' fitting, a length of hose (with the same inside diameter as the fuel hoses), a fuel pressure gauge and a tachometer.

3   Loosen the hose clamp and pull the fuel hose off the fuel pump outlet fitting. Insert one end of the 'T' fitting into the hose that was disconnected from the pump and tighten the hose clamp. Cut a short length of hose, slip one end over the 'T' fitting and the other end onto the fuel pump outlet fitting.

4   Connect another length of hose (approximately 6 inches long) between the fuel pressure gauge and the remaining end of the 'T' fitting. Install hose clamps on all the connections.

5   Loosen the hose clamp and disconnect the fuel return hose, which returns fuel to the fuel tank from the carburetor. Slip a short length of hose, which has been plugged, onto the fitting and install the hose clamp.

6   Connect the tachometer according to the instructions provided by the manufacturer.

7   Start the engine and allow it to run for a few moments before taking the pressure reading. This will allow any air in the pump to be vented, which will ensure an accurate reading.

8   Make sure that the engine idle speed is correct, then note the pressure reading on the gauge and compare it to the specifications.

9   Stop the engine and observe the gauge. The pressure should remain constant or return to zero slowly.

10   If the pressure was higher or lower than specified, or if it dropped to zero instantly when the engine was shut off, the fuel pump is defective and should be replaced with a new one.

9   Fuel pump — removal and installation

1   The fuel pump is mounted on the cylinder head immediately in front of the carburetor. It is held in place with 2 nuts.

2   Pull the coil high-tension lead out of the distributor and ground it on the engine block. Remove the spark plugs and place your thumb over the number one cylinder spark plug hole.

3   Rotate the crankshaft in a clock-wise direction (with a wrench on the large bolt attaching the pulley to the front of the crankshaft) until you can feel the compression pressure rising in the number one cylinder.

4   Continue rotating the crankshaft until the notch on the crankshaft pulley lines up with the 'T' on the timing mark tab on the timing chain case. At this point, the lift of the fuel pump drive cam is reduced to a minimum, which will make the pump easier to remove.

5   Install the spark plugs and hook up the wires. Do not forget the coil high-tension lead.

6   Loosen the hose clamps and remove the fuel hoses from the pump fittings. Plug the ends of the hoses.

7   Remove the fuel pump mounting nuts and pull the pump off the engine. You may have to tap the pump body with a soft-faced hammer to break the gasket seal.

8   If the pump is difficult to remove, take off the valve cover (see Chapter 1, *Valve clearance adjustment*) and guide the pump rocker arm out of the head from the inside.

12.5b Sub EGR linkage pin

12.5c Unsnap the accelerator pump linkage from the throttle shaft arm

12.5d Remove the accelerator pump from the carburetor body

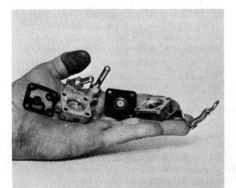
12.5e Accelerator pump components

12.6a Remove the ASV housing screws

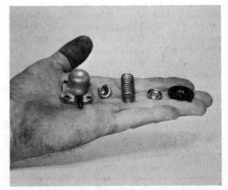
12.6b ASV components

9   Remove the insulator block and scrape off all traces of the old gaskets and sealer.

10   Before installing the new pump ensure that the rocker arm moves up and down without binding or sticking.

11   Coat both sides of the new gaskets with silicone-type gasket sealer before installation.

12   Slip the first gasket, the insulator block and the second gasket (in that order) onto the fuel pump mounting studs.

13   Install the fuel pump. It may be necessary to guide the rocker arm into place from inside the head. Work slowly; there is not much clearance between the rocker arm and the valve gear.

14   Once the fuel pump is properly seated, install the mounting nuts and tighten them evenly. Do not overtighten them or the insulator block may be cracked.

15   Install the valve cover if it was removed.

16   Install the hoses (after inspecting them for cracks) and the hose clamps.

17   Start the engine and check for fuel leaks at the hose fittings. Check for oil leaks where the fuel pump mounts on the cylinder head.

10   Carburetor – servicing

1   A thorough road test annd check of carburetor adjustments should be done before any major carburetor service. Specifications for some adjustments are listed on the vehicle emission control information label found in the engine compartment.

2   Some performance complaints directed at the carburetor are actually a result of loose, misadjusted or malfunctioning engine or electrical components. Others develop when vacuum hoses leak, are disconnected or are incorrectly routed. The proper approach to analyzing carburetor problems should include a routine check of the following areas:

3   Inspect all vacuum hoses and actuators for leaks and proper installation (see Chapter 6, *Emission control systems).

4   Tighten the intake manifold nuts and carburetor mounting nuts evenly and securely.

5   Perform a cylinder compression test.

6   Clean or replace the spark plugs as necessary.

7   Test the resistance of the spark plug wires (refer to Chapter 5).

8   Inspect the ignition primary wires and check the vacuum advance operation. Replace any defective parts.

9   Check the ignition timing with the vacuum advance line disconnected and plugged.

10   Set the carburetor idle mixture as described in Section 14.

11   Check the fuel pump pressure as described in Section 8.

12   Inspect the heat control valve in the air cleaner for proper operation (refer to Chapter 6).

13   Remove the carburetor air filter element and blow out any dirt with compressed air. If the filter is extremely dirty, replace it with a new one.

14   Inspect the crankcase ventilation system (see Chapter 6).

15   Carburetor problems usually show up as flooding, hard starting, stalling, severe backfiring, poor acceleration and lack of response to idle mixture screw adjustments. A carburetor that is leaking fuel and/or covered with wet-looking deposits definitely needs attention.

16   Diagnosing carburetor problems may require that the engine be started and run with the air cleaner removed. While running the engine without the air cleaner it is possible that it could backfire. A backfiring situation is likely to occur if the carburetor is malfunctioning, but removal of the air cleaner alone can lean the air/fuel mixture enough to produce an engine backfire.

17   Once it is determined that the carburetor is indeed at fault, it should be disassembled, cleaned and reassembled using new parts where necessary. Before dismantling the carburetor, make sure you have a carburetor rebuild kit, which will include all necessary gaskets and internal parts, carburetor cleaning solvent and some means of blowing out all the internal passages of the carburetor. To do the job properly, you will also need a clean place to work and plenty of time and patience.

11   Carburetor – removal

1   Remove the negative battery cable from the battery.

2   Remove the air cleaner assembly by referring to Section 3.

3   Remove the throttle cable clamps from the carburetor and the valve cover, then disconnect the cable from the throttle shaft.

4   Remove the float bowl vent tube from the carburetor (photo).

5   Remove the coolant hose from the rear of the carburetor (photo).

6   Disconnect the electrical lead at the left side of the carburetor (photo).

7   Note the color-code on the various vacuum hoses connected to the carburetor and to avoid confusion later, draw a simple diagram showing how they are connected.

8   Remove the vacuum hoses from the carburetor body (photo), the ASV (photo) and the throttle opener (air conditioner equipped vehicles only) (photo).

9   Remove the 3 fuel hoses from the carburetor and plug them (photo).

10   Remove the 5 nuts and lock washers attaching the carburetor to the intake manifold. Removal of the idle speed adjusting screws (SAS) from the carburetor body will make access to the left rear mounting nut less restricted.

11   Carefully lift the carburetor off the intake manifold. You may have to tap gently on the carburetor body with a soft-faced hammer to break the gasket seal. Do not pry between the carburetor and intake manifold, as damage to the gasket sealing surfaces may result. Remove the insulator block and all traces of gasket material or gasket sealer from the manifold.

12   Cover or plug the intake ports with clean rags to keep out dirt and foreign objects. Also, plug the coolant passage in the intake manifold so coolant does not get into the intake ports.

12   Carburetor – disassembly, inspection and reassembly

Disassembly

1   Remove the air cleaner hold down stud (photo) and the air cleaner gasket from the top of the carburetor. Pull back the hose clamp and remove the coolant hose from the back of the carburetor (photo).

2   Remove the spring clip and carefully pry the throttle opener actuating rod out of the primary throttle shaft lever (air conditioner-equipped model only) (photo). Remove the throttle opener from the carburetor body; it is held in place with two screws (photo).

3   Disconnect the fuel cut-off solenoid ground wires from the carburetor body (photo). Remove the solenoid retaining screw (photo) and lift the solenoid away from the carburetor (photo). Do not lose the O-ring on the solenoid body.

4   Unscrew and remove the idle mixture screw, the spring, the washer and rubber seal (photo).

5   Disconnect the linkage at the sub EGR valve by prying off the spring clip (photo) and removing the pin (photo). Slide the linkage out of position and remove the spring and ball from the end of the sub EGR plunger. Using a screwdriver, unsnap the accelerator pump linkage from the throttle shaft arm (photo) and remove the accelerator pump from the carburetor body. It is held in place with four screws (photo).

6   Remove the four screws holding the ASV housing in place (photo) and lift off the housing. Remove the spring, the spring cap, the spring guide and the diaphragm. Lay the parts out on a clean surface in the order of disassembly (photo).

7   Remove the screw attaching the ASV body to the carburetor (photo) and carefully lift off the ASV body (photo).

8   Remove the vent system ground wire (photo) and the three screws holding the solenoid to the carburetor body (photo). Carefully lift the solenoid and the spring inside it away from the carburetor (photo).

9   Remove the one remaining screw holding the vent system body to the carburetor (photo) and lift it off (don't forget to remove the rubber gasket from the carburetor body).

10   To disassemble the vent valve, remove the spring clip, the washer, and the valve seal from the end of the plunger. Slip the O-ring off the body. The diaphragm and plunger (one piece) can now be withdrawn from the valve body. Lay the parts out on a clean surface in the order of disassembly (photo).

11   Remove the enrichment system diaphragm housing. It is held in place by three screws. Remove the gasket, separate the two halves of the housing, and lift out the spring and the diaphragm (photo).

12   Remove the CAV housing. It is held in place by three screws (photo). Lift out the spring guide, the springs, the spring cap and the diaphragm. Lay the parts out on a clean surface in the order of disassembly (photo). Remove the three screws holding the choke

unloader diaphragm plate to the carburetor body (photo). Lift off the plate and remove the spring (photo).

13   Carefully pry the secondary diaphragm link out of the secondary throttle lever (photo) and pull the hose off the carburetor body (photo). Remove the two mounting screws and lift off the diaphragm assembly (photo).

14   Disconnect the throttle return spring from the primary throttle lever (photo). The upper choke pinion gear assembly mount has a series of lines scribed on it. Note which one is lined up with the dot on the body (photo).

15   Remove the two screws holding the choke pinion gear assembly to the carburetor body and carefully pull it free (photo).

16   Separate the choke plate from the choke shaft. It is held in place with two small screws (photo).

17   Remove the spring clip and carefully pry the manual choke unloader linkage rod out of the choke lever (photo).

18   Using small pliers, pull out the pin holding the choke unloader diaphragm in alignment (photo).

19   Remove the throttle return spring mount. It is held in place with one bolt (photo).

20   Pull out the choke unloader diaphragm and linkage (photo), then withdraw the choke shaft from the carburetor body (photo).

21   Unhook the secondary return spring from the choke mechanism housing (photo). Remove the two screws (photo) and lift the choke mechanism housing away from the carburetor body (photo). Separate the spacer and small O-ring from the housing (photo).

22   Remove the four remaining screws (photo) and lift the top cover off the carburetor. Be careful not to bend or otherwise damage the float mechanism (photo).

23   Before removing the float, invert the top cover and measure the distance from the float seam to the gasket surface of the top cover (see Fig. 4.7). Record the measurement for future reference.

24   Carefully slide out the pivot pin and separate the float and inlet needle from the top cover (photo). Slip the needle out of its mount on the float. Unscrew and remove the inlet needle seat and washer (photo).

25   Remove the top cover gasket from the carburetor body.

26   Hold your finger over the accelerator pump discharge plunger bore (photo). Tip the carburetor upside down and let the steel ball from the anti-overflow mechanism in the bottom of the float bowl fall out (photo). Next, remove the accelerator pump steel check ball and weight. Draw a simple diagram showing the sizes (stamped on the jets) and the locations of the primary and secondary main jets and the primary and secondary idle jets, then unscrew and remove them from the carburetor body (photos).

27   Remove the two attaching screws (photo) and separate the throttle body from the carburetor body (photo). *Do not remove any plugs or fittings from the carburetor body that have been sealed with white paint.*

28   Slip off the rubber boot and slide the sub-EGR valve plunger out of the throttle body (photo).

Inspection

29   Once the carburetor has been completely disassembled, the parts should be thoroughly cleaned and inspected. There are many commercial carburetor cleaning solvents available which can be used with good results.

30   The diaphragms and some plastic parts of the carburetor can be damaged by solvents; avoid placing these parts in any liquid. Clean the external surfaces of these parts with a clean cloth or soft brush. Shake or wipe dirt and other foreign material from the stem plunger side of the diaphragm. Compressed air can be used to remove loose dirt, but should not be connected to the vacuum diaphragm fitting.

31   If the commercial solvent or cleaner recommends the use of water as a rinse, hot water will produce the best results. After rinsing, all traces of water must be blown from the passages using compressed air. Never clean jets with a wire, drill bit or other objects. The orifices may be enlarged, making the mixture too rich for proper performance.

32   When checking parts removed from the carburetor, it is often difficult to be sure they are serviceable. It is therefore recommended that new parts be installed, if available, when the carburetor is disassembled. The required parts should be included in the carburetor rebuild kit.

33   After all the parts have been cleaned and dried, check the throttle valve shaft and choke shaft for proper operation. If sticking or binding occurs, clean the shafts with solvent and lubricate them with engine oil.

34   Check the jets for damage or clogging. Replace them if damage is evident.

35   Inspect the idle mixture adjusting screw. The tapered portion of the screw must be straight and smooth. If the tapered portion is grooved or ridged replace the screw with a new one.

36   Check the strainer screen for clogging and damage.

37   Check the vacuum chamber. Push the vacuum chamber rod in, seal off the nipple and release the rod. If the rod does not return, the vacuum chamber is most likely in good condition. If the rod returns when released, the diaphragm is defective. The vacuum chamber should be replaced with a new one if this condition exists.

38   To check the fuel cut-off solenoid, connect a jumper lead to the positive (+) terminal of a 12 volt battery and the wire lead of the solenoid. Connect a second jumper lead to the negative (-) terminal of the battery and the solenoid ground wire. The needle should move in toward the solenoid when the battery is connected and out when the battery is disconnected. If it does, the fuel cut-off solenoid is good.

Reassembly

Note: *The reassembly process will be easier if the sequenced photos in the disassembly section are followed in reverse.*

39   Using a new gasket, assemble the throttle body to the carburetor body and tighten the mounting screws securely.

40   Install the main and pilot jets in the carburetor body. The primary main jet, the secondary main jet, the primary pilot jet and the secondary pilot jet are each stamped with a different number that denotes their size. Consult the specifications to ensure proper installation of the jets.

41   Place the anti-overflow ball in place in the bottom of the float bowl and insert the accelerator pump steel check ball and weight into the accelerator pump bore.

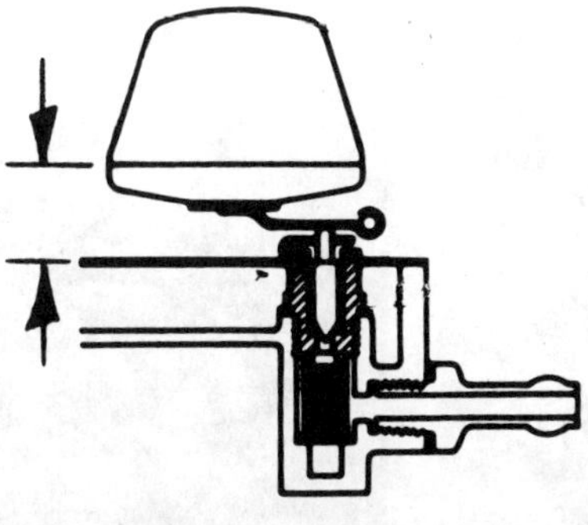

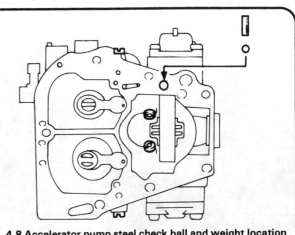

Fig. 4.7 Measure the distance from the float seam to the gasket surface of the top cover (Sec 12)

Fig. 4.8 Accelerator pump steel check ball and weight location (Sec 12)

12.7a Remove the ASV body attaching screw

12.7b The ASV body

12.8a Remove the vent system ground wire

12.8b Remove the screws attaching the solenoid to the carburetor body

12.8c The solenoid and spring

12.9 Remove the screw holding the vent system body to the carburetor

12.10 Vent system components

12.11 Enrichment system components

12.12a Remove the CAV housing screws

12.12b CAV components

12.12c Remove the choke unloader diaphragm plate screws

12.12d Choke unloader diaphragm plate and spring

12.13a Pry the secondary diaphragm link out of the secondary throttle lever

12.13b Pull the hose off the carburetor body

12.13c Remove the secondary diaphragm mounting screws

12.14a Disconnect the throttle return spring from the primary throttle lever

12.14b Note the reference lines on the upper choke pinion gear assembly mount

12.15 Remove the 2 screws holding the choke pinion gear assembly to the carburetor

12.16 Remove the screws attaching the choke plate to the choke shaft

12.17 Remove the spring clip from the manual choke unloader linkage rod

12.18 Pull out the pin holding the choke unloader diaphragm in alignment

12.19 Remove the throttle return spring mount

12.20a Pull out the choke unloader diaphragm and linkage

12.20b Withdraw the choke shaft

12.21a Unhook the secondary return spring

12.21b Remove the 2 choke mechanism housing screws

12.21c Lift the choke mechanism housing away from the carburetor body

12.21d Separate the spacer and O-ring from the housing

12.22a Remove the top cover screws

12.22b Lift the top cover off; do not bend the float arm

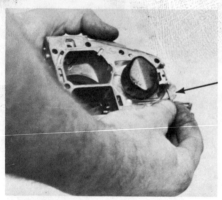
12.24a Slide out the pivot pin

12.24b Separate the float and needle from the top cover

12.24c Remove the inlet needle seat

12.25 Remove the top cover gasket

12.26a Accelerator pump discharge plunger bore

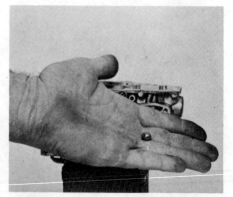
12.26b Anti-overflow mechanism steel ball

12.26c Remove the primary main jet

12.26d Remove the secondary main jet

12.26e Remove the idle jets

42 Install the new inlet needle seat in place in the carburetor top cover; (don't forget to include a new washer). Assemble the new inlet needle to the float and attach the float to the top cover.

43 Invert the top cover and measure the distance from the float seam to the gasket surface of the top cover (see Figure 4.7). If the measured distance is more or less than it was during disassembly, remove the float from the top cover, unscrew the inlet needle seat and add or remove washers (as necessary) to change the float height. Reassemble the inlet needle and float and recheck the measurement. Repeat the procedure as required until the distance is the same as it was during disassembly.

44 Gently lay the top cover in place using a new gasket and install the mounting screws. Tighten them evenly and securely.

45 Install the choke mechanism housing and tighten the screws securely. Make sure the manual choke unloader rod is facing in the proper direction.

46 Slide the choke shaft into place and install the choke plate. It is a very good idea to use a thread locking compound on the choke plate attaching screws.

47 Insert the manual choke unloader rod into the choke lever.

48 Install the choke unloader/diaphragm and push the pin into place.

49 Install the throttle return spring mount and tighten the screw securely.

50 Engage the spring loop on the choke pinion gear assembly, hold the choke plate closed and engage the plastic gear teeth of the choke pinion gear with the gear teeth on the choke set lever. Install the screws, move the pinion gear assembly to line up the marks exactly as they were before disassembly, then tighten the screws securely.

51 Install the secondary diaphragm assembly and hook up the hose. Slip the diaphragm link into the secondary throttle lever.

52 Install the choke unloader diaphragm plate and tighten the screws.

53 Install the CAV internal parts and housing then tighten the mounting screws evenly and securely.

54 Assemble the enrichment system components and install the housing in place on the carburetor body. (The wire clamp fits over the upper left mounting screw). Tighten the mounting screws securely.

55 Assemble the vent valve. Lubricate the O-ring on the valve body and slide the valve into place in the carburetor body. Tighten the mounting screws securely.

56 Install the vent valve solenoid and tighten the mounting screws. Attach the ground wire to the carburetor body.

57 Install the ASV housing (with the wire clamp on the longest screw) and tighten the mounting screws finger tight. Assemble the ASV internal parts, install the housing and tighten the mounting screws.

58 Install the accelerator pump and hook the linkage to the throttle shaft arm.

59 Slip the small steel ball and the spring into place in the end of the sub-EGR valve plunger. Install the rubber boot and push the plunger into place in the throttle body. Hold the linkage in place, install the pin and snap the spring clip into place on the end of the pin.

60 Make sure the O-ring is in place on the fuel cut-off solenoid body, then install the solenoid and tighten the mounting screws. Remove the short screw on the ASV body. Install the fuel cut-off solenoid ground wire and tighten both ASV body mounting screws securely.

61 Insert the throttle opener actuating rod into the primary throttle shaft lever. Install the spring clip and mount the throttle opener on the carburetor (air conditioner-equipped models only).

62 Install the coolant hose and slide the hose clamps into place.

63 Double check all screws to make sure they are tight and the carburetor reassembly is complete.

13 Carburetor – installation

1 Inspect the mating surfaces of the carburetor and intake manifold. They must be clean and free of nicks, burrs and other damage.

2 Hold the new carburetor base gasket in place on the carburetor to make sure that all the holes match up. It is possible to install the gasket upside down or backward so make sure it is properly oriented before laying it in place on the intake manifold.

3 Lay the new gasket in place then carefully set the carburetor on top of it.

4 Install the five mounting nuts and tighten them evenly and securely. Work slowly and make sure that each nut is tightened the same amount or vacuum leaks may occur between the carburetor and manifold. Removal of the idle-speed adjusting screw will make access to the left rear mounting nut easier. Attach the vacuum hoses to the ASV, the throttle opener (if so equipped) and the carburetor body. Refer to the diagram that you drew during carburetor removal (or the vacuum hose routing diagram on the underside of the hood) to ensure proper installation of the vacuum hoses.

5 Unplug and slip the fuel hoses into place on the carburetor. Tighten the hose clamps securely; the hoses and fittings are color-coded so installation is quite simple.

6 Plug in the electrical lead on the left side of the carburetor.

7 Slip the coolant hose onto the spigot at the rear of the carburetor and tighten the hose clamp securely.

8 Install the float bowl vent tube and slip the hose clamp into place.

9 Hook the end of the throttle cable to the throttle shaft and install the cable clamps on the carburetor and valve cover. Adjust the cable as described in Section 4. Make sure the throttle plate opens completely when the accelerator is depressed. The choke plate must also be free to close and open completely.

10 Connect the battery cable to the battery.

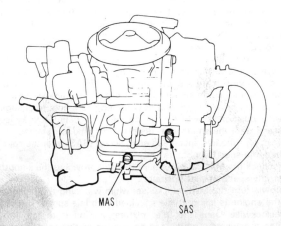

MAS   SAS

Fig. 4.9 Idle mixture and speed adjusting screw locations (Sec 14)

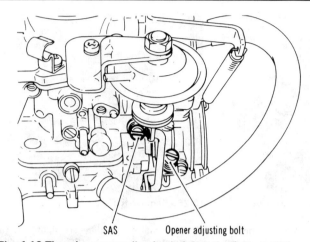

Fig. 4.10 Throttle opener adjusting bolt location (air conditioner-equipped vehicles only) (Sec 14)

11 *The practice of priming an engine by pouring gasoline into the carburetor air horn should be strictly avoided.* Cranking the engine and depressing the accelerator pedal several times should provide enough fuel for the engine to start.

12 Start the engine and adjust the idle-speed and mixture as described in Section 14.

14 Idle speed and mixture – adjustment

1   To properly set the idle mixture an exhaust gas analyzer must be used. Since the average home mechanic does not have access to such equipment, it is recommended that a dealer service department or a suitably-equipped automotive tune-up facility perform the idle speed and mixture adjustments.

2   Basic adjustment of the idle speed and mixture can be performed without an exhaust gas analyzer by following the steps outlined here. Final adjustment, as mentioned before, must be done with the proper equipment to ensure compliance with emission standards.

3   Before the idle speed and mixture adjustments are made, check the ignition system, including the ignition timing. Look for cracked or disconnected vacuum lines. Make sure the intake manifold and carburetor mounting nuts are tightened evenly and securely; any intake leaks must be fixed before proceeding. Also, the engine must be at normal operating temperature so the choke is completely open. Place the transmission in neutral and set the parking brake. The air conditioner, lights and all accessories must be off.

4   Hook up the tachometer according to the instructions supplied by the manufacturer.

U-engine (49 states only)

5   With the engine running, carefully turn the idle mixture adjusting screw (MAS) clockwise, preferably by hand, until the engine starts to slow down or misfire. When this happens, slowly turn the MAS in the opposite direction (counterclockwise). The engine should start to speed up again. Then, as the MAS is turned farther, the engine should begin to slow down or misfire.

6   These two points are sometimes difficult to discern, so keep a close eye on the tachometer. The idle mixture adjusting screw should be turned approximately $\frac{1}{16}$ of a turn each time, allowing about 10 seconds for the engine speed to stabilize between adjustments.

7   Once you have determined how the engine reacts to changes of the MAS position, slowly turn it clockwise or counterclockwise, as necessary, until the smoothest, fastest idle speed is obtained.

8   Next, turn the idle speed adjusting screw (SAS) until the specified enriched idle speed is obtained.

9   Recheck the MAS to make sure it is still providing the smoothest, fastest idle speed at that position.

10 Slowly turn the MAS clockwise, while watching the tachometer, until the engine is idling at the specified curb idle speed. Turning the MAS clockwise leans the idle mixture, forcing it to fall into the emission specification range, and causes the engine to slow down. If the engine misfires badly, repeat the procedure, turning the MAS further counterclockwise initially.

U-engine (California only) and W-engine (all)

11 Remove the air hose from the inlet of the secondary air supply system reed valve and plug the reed valve inlet.

12 With the engine running, carefully turn the idle mixture adjusting screw (MAS) clockwise, preferably by hand, until the engine starts to slow down or misfire. When this happens, slowly turn the MAS in the opposite direction (counterclockwise). The engine should start to speed up again. Then, as the MAS is turned further, it should begin to slow down or misfire.

13 These two points are sometimes difficult to discern, so keep a close eye on the tachometer. The MAS should be turned approximately $\frac{1}{16}$ of a turn each time, allowing about ten seconds for the engine speed to stabilize between adjustments.

14 Once you have determined how the engine reacts to changes of the MAS position, slowly turn it clockwise or counterclockwise, as necessary, until the smoothest, fastest idle speed is obtained. Next, turn the idle speed adjusting screw (SAS) until the specified curb idle speed is obtained. Recheck the MAS to make sure it is still providing the smoothest, fastest idle speed at that position.

15 Unplug the reed valve inlet and hook up the air hose.

16 If the idle speed changes, return it to the specified rpm by turning the SAS in or out as necessary.

17 If the engine misfires badly, repeat the procedure, turning the MAS further counterclockwise initially.

Vehicles equipped with air conditioning

18 Regardless of the engine type in the vehicle, an additional adjustment must be made if it is equipped with an air conditioning system.

19 After the idle mixture and speed have been adjusted as previously described, turn the air conditioner control switch to 'ON'. This will activate the throttle opener on the carburetor. Turn the throttle opener adjusting bolt clockwise or counterclockwise, as necessary, until the engine idle speed (throttle opener activated) is as specified.

20 When the air conditioner control switch is turned to 'OFF', the engine should return to the specified curb idle speed.

15 Fuel tank – removal and installation

1   *Before doing any work around the fuel tank, make sure that the ignition switch is off and remove the key from the ignition lock.* Block the front wheels to keep the vehicle from rolling, then raise the rear of the vehicle and set it on jack stands.

2   Remove the tank filler cap so any pressure in the tank can escape.

3   Position a suitable container (large enough to hold the fuel that it in the tank) under the tank. Remove the drain plug (photo) and allow the fuel to drain into the container. *Be very careful when working around gasoline; it is highly explosive.* After the fuel has drained completely, reinstall the drain plug.

4   Loosen the hose clamps on the main, return and vapor fuel hoses then pull the hoses off the tank (see Figure 4.11).

5   Unplug the electrical wire from the fuel level sending unit.

6   Remove the filler neck mud shield from the inside of the left rear wheel well. It is held in place with 3 bolts (photo).

7   Loosen the hose clamps on the filler connecting hose (large) and the breather hose (small) where they attach to the tank (photos). Pull the hoses off the tank. (Be careful not to damage them in the process).

8   Support the fuel tank, preferably with a portable jack and a block of wood. Remove the 4 mounting bolts (photo), lower the tank carefully and move it out from under the vehicle.

9   Check the tank interior for rust and corrosion. If the tank is not extremely corroded, it can be cleaned and reused. Special solvents made especially for cleaning fuel tanks are available. If you use one, be sure to follow the directions on the container. The inside of the tank is plated with zinc so be sure to use a cleaner that will not harm it in any way.

10 If the tank is severely corroded, replace it with a new one or a clean used one.

11 Look for evidence of leaks and cracks. If any are found, take the tank to a repair shop to have it fixed.

12 Inspect all fuel and breather hoses for cracks and deterioration. Check all hose clamps for damage and proper operation.

13 Installation of the tank is basically the reverse of removal. Be sure to double check all hoses for proper routing. Also, if you have not already done so, be sure to tighten the drain plug securely.

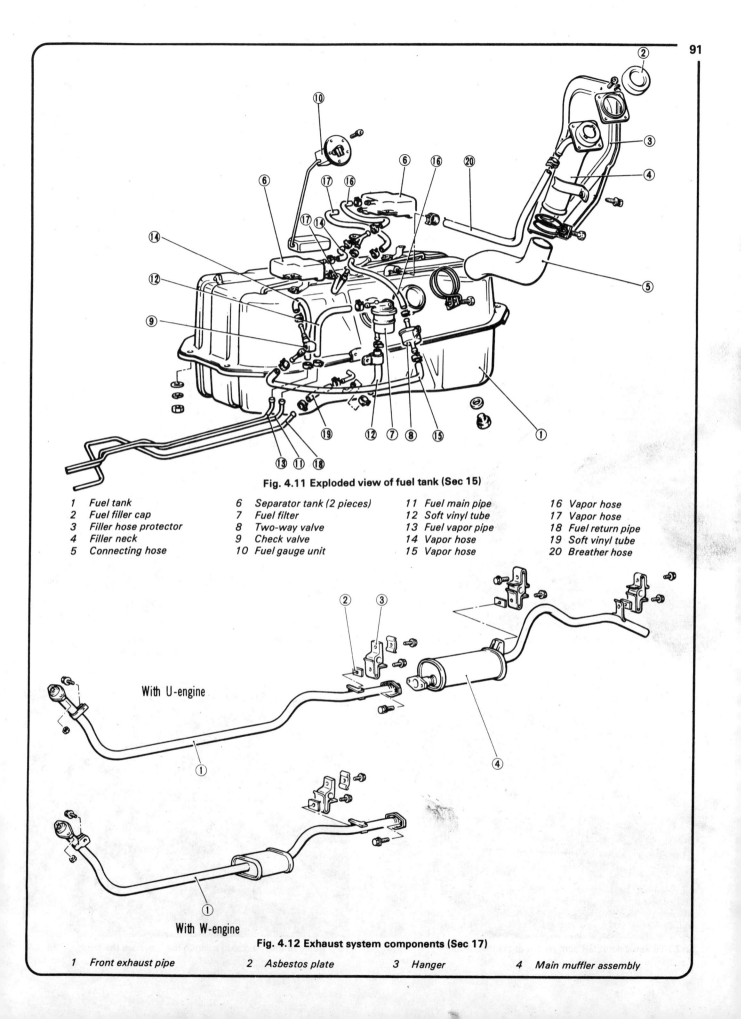

Fig. 4.11 Exploded view of fuel tank (Sec 15)

1 Fuel tank	6 Separator tank (2 pieces)	11 Fuel main pipe	16 Vapor hose
2 Fuel filler cap	7 Fuel filter	12 Soft vinyl tube	17 Vapor hose
3 Filler hose protector	8 Two-way valve	13 Fuel vapor pipe	18 Fuel return pipe
4 Filler neck	9 Check valve	14 Vapor hose	19 Soft vinyl tube
5 Connecting hose	10 Fuel gauge unit	15 Vapor hose	20 Breather hose

With U-engine

With W-engine

Fig. 4.12 Exhaust system components (Sec 17)

1 Front exhaust pipe	2 Asbestos plate	3 Hanger	4 Main muffler assembly

14 Fill the tank with fuel and check for leaks. After the engine has been run, make a second check for leaks, particularly at the hose fittings that were removed.

16 Exhaust system check

Refer to Chapter 1 for exhaust system checking procedures.

17 Front exhaust pipe – removal and installation

1 Raise the vehicle and set it on jack stands.
2 Remove the bolt attaching the front exhaust pipe to the main muffler assembly.
3 Remove the nuts attaching the front exhaust pipe to the exhaust manifold. It may be necessary to spray the threads extending beyond the nut with a penetrating oil to make removal of the nuts easier. If a penetrating oil is used, let the threads 'soak' for a few minutes before attempting to remove the nuts.
4 Remove the front exhaust pipe-to-bell housing clamp bolt.
5 Support the pipe, then remove the rear hanger bracket bolt. The pipe can now be pulled free from the muffler assembly and exhaust manifold and removed from under the vehicle.

6 If the exhaust pipe hanger is cracked or otherwise deteriorated, replace it with a new one.
7 Lubricate all bolt and stud threads with a small amount of oil.
8 Position the front exhaust pipe under the vehicle. Slip the front end into place on the exhaust manifold and the rear end into place on the main muffler assembly. The main muffler assembly can be pushed slightly to the rear to provide clearance for installation of the front exhaust pipe. Install the rear hanger bracket bolt and the exhaust pipe-to-bell clamp bolt. Do not tighten them completely
9 Install the pipe-to-exhaust manifold nuts and the pipe-to-main muffler bolts. Tighten them evenly, in steps, to the specified torque.
10 Check the clearance between the pipe and the other parts of the vehicle. If the clearance is adequate, tighten the exhaust pipe-to-bell housing clamp bolt and the hanger bracket bolt securely.
11 Start the engine and check for exhaust gas leaks where the front exhaust pipe attaches to the exhaust manifold and the main muffler assembly.
12 Test drive the vehicle. If the clearances between the exhaust system components and the other parts of the vehicle are inadequate, noise and vibration may occur during vehicle operation.

18 Main muffler assembly – removal and installation

1 Raise the vehicle and set it on jack stands.

12.27a Remove the 2 screws attaching the throttle body to the carburetor body

12.27b Separate the throttle body from the carburetor body. (Do not disassemble the throttle shafts and linkages at this time))

12.28 Slide the sub-EGR plunger out of the throttle body

15.3 Remove the drain plug to drain the fuel from the tank

15.6 Remove the filler neck mud shield

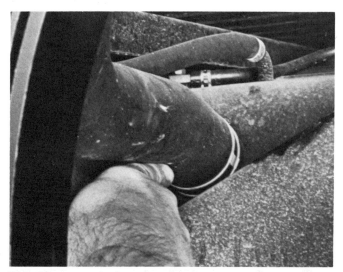

15.7a Filler connecting hose clamp location

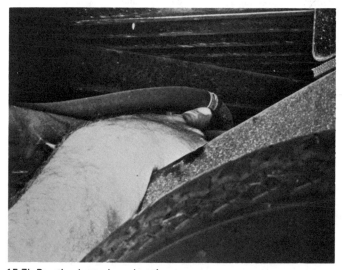

15.7b Breather hose clamp location

15.8 Remove the 4 fuel tank mounting bolts while supporting the tank securely

2   Remove the bolts attaching the main muffler assembly to the front exhaust pipe.
3   Support the muffler and remove the two hanger bracket bolts.
4   Lower the muffler and remove it from under the vehicle.
5   If the hanger brackets are cracked or otherwise deteriorated, replace them with new ones.
6   Lubricate all bolt threads with a small amount of oil.
7   To install the muffler, hold it in place and install the hanger bracket bolts. Do not tighten them completely.
8   Install the exhaust pipe-to-main muffler assembly attaching bolts and tighten them evenly, in steps, to the specified torque.
9   Check the clearance between the main muffler assembly and the other parts of the vehicle. If the clearance is adequate, tighten the hanger bracket bolts.
10 Lower the vehicle to the ground, start the engine and check for exhaust gas leaks where the front exhaust pipe attaches to the main muffler assembly.
11 Test drive the vehicle. If the clearances between the exhaust system components and the other parts of the vehicle are inadequate, noise and vibration may occur during vehicle operation.

Chapter 5 Ignition and starting systems

Refer to Chapter 13 for specifications and information related to 1981 thru 1988 models

Contents

Specifications

Distributor

Type
    1979 models T4T60171
    1980 models
    'U'-engine with manual transmission (49-state) T4T60174
    'U'-engine (all others) T4T60175
    'W'-engine T4T60171
Turning direction .... clockwise
Centrifugal advance (crankshaft°) .... 0°/1200 rpm
    12°/2800 rpm
    20°/6000 rpm

Vacuum advance (crankshaft°)
    1979 models .... 0°/1.51 in Hg
    7°/2.32 in Hg
    15°/3.48 in Hg

    1980 models
    'U'-engine with manual transmission (49-state) .... 0°/10.7 in Hg
    6°/20.0 in Hg
    12°/37.3 in Hg

    'U'-engine (all others) .... 0°/10.7 in Hg
    8°/20.0 in Hg
    20°/50.0 in Hg

    'W'-engine .... 0°/17.3 in Hg
    7°/26.7 in Hg
    15°/40.0 in Hg

Pickup coil resistance .... 1050 ± 50 Ω

Ignition timing
USA
    'U'-engine
    Manual transmission .... 5° BTDC at 650 rpm
    Automatic transmission .... 5° BTDC at 700 rpm
    'W'-engine (manual and automatic transmissions)
    1979 models .... 7° BTDC at 850 rpm
    1980 models .... 7° BTDC at 750 rpm
Canada
    'U'-engine (manual and automatic transmissions) .... 5° BTDC at 850 rpm
    'W'-engine (manual and automatic transmissions) .... 7° BTDC at 850 rpm

Ignition coil

Type	LB-119
Resistance	
Primary	0.7 to 0.85 Ω
Secondary	9 to 11 KΩ
Insulation (at 500 v)	Over 50 MΩ

Spark plug type

USA	
'U'-engine	NGK BPR6ES-11
	BP6ES-11
	BUR6EA
'W'-engine	NGK BPR5ES-11
	BP6ES-11
	BUR6EA
Canada	
'U'-engine	NGK BPR6ES
'W'-engine	NGK BPR5ES
Spark plug gap	
USA	0.039 to 0.043 in (1.0 to 1.1 mm)
Canada	0.028 to 0.031 in (0.7 to 0.8 mm)
Spark plug wire resistance	Less than 22 KΩ

Starter motor

Type	
1979 models	
Manual transmission	M3T25781
Automatic transmission	M4T14771
1980 models	
Manual transmission	M3T25781
Automatic transmission	M2T53081
No load characteristics	
Terminal voltage	
Automatic transmission	
1979 models	11 v
1980 models	11.5 v
Manual transmission	11.5 v
Current	
Automatic transmission	
1979 models	Less than 62 A
1980 models	Less than 90 A
Manual transmission	Less than 60 A
Speed	
Automatic transmission	
1979 models	More than 4500 rpm
1980 models	More than 3300 rpm
Manual transmission	More than 6600 rpm
Armature-to-bearing clearance	
Front and rear bearing	0.0028 to 0.008 in (0.07 to 0.2 mm)
Center bearing	0.0118 in (0.3 mm)
Commutator (direct drive motor)	
Runout	0.012 in (0.3 mm) or less
Outside diameter	No less than 1.4842 in (37.7 mm)
Depth of undercut	0.008 to 0.024 in (0.2 to 0.6 mm)
Commutator (reduction drive motor)	
Runout	0.012 in (0.3 mm) or less
Outside diameter	No less than 1.220 in (31 mm)
Depth of undercut	0.008 to 0.020 in (0.2 to 0.5 mm)
Brush length	
Standard	0.669 in (17 mm)
Service limit	0.453 in (11.5 mm)
Brush spring installed load	
Standard	2.9 to 3.7 lb (13 to 17 N)
Service limit	1.5 lb (7 N)
Pinion gap	0.020 to 0.079 in (0.5 to 2 mm)
Pinion shaft end-play (reduction drive motor)	Less than 0.020 in (0.5 mm)

Torque specifications

	ft-lb	(Nm)
Starter motor attaching bolts	16 to 23	(22 to 31)
Spark plugs	18 to 21	(25 to 28)

1   General information

The ignition system is designed to ignite the fuel/air charge entering the cylinder at just the right moment. It does so by producing a high-voltage electrical spark between the electrodes of the spark plug. The timing of the spark (when it occurs in the engine cycle) is automatically varied to meet the requirements of engine load and speed.

The system consists of a switch, the ignition coil, the distributor, an electronic control unit, spark plugs and wires and the battery.

Since the Dodge D-50/Plymouth Arrow is equipped with an electronic ignition system, its operation is very trouble and maintenance free.

The starting system consists of a switch, solenoid, starter motor, battery cables and wiring and the battery. Two different types of starter motors are in use on this vehicle. Models with manual transmissions are equipped with a 0.9 kW motor, while those with automatic transmissions are equipped with a 1.2 kW motor. They can be identified by a model number which is stamped on the nameplate attached to the front bracket.

2   Spark plugs – removal and installation

Spark plug removal and installation procedures are covered in detail in Chapter 1.

3   Spark plug wires – checking

1   The spark plug wires should be checked at the recommended intervals and whenever new spark plugs are installed in the engine.
2   The wires should be inspected one at a time to prevent mixing up the order, which is essential for proper engine operation.
3   Disconnect the plug wire from the spark plug. A removal tool can be used for this purpose or you can grab the rubber boot, twist slightly and pull the wire free. Do not pull on the wire itself, only on the rubber boot.
4   Inspect inside the boot for corrosion, which will look like a white crusty powder. Push the wire and boot back onto the end of the spark plug. It should be a tight fit on the plug end. If it is not, remove the wire and use a pair of pliers to carefully crimp the metal connector inside the wire boot until it fits securely on the end of the spark plug.
5   Using a clean rag, wipe the entire length of the wire to remove any built up dirt and grease. Once the wire is clean, check for burns, cracks and other damage. Do not bend the wire, since the conductor might break.
6   Disconnect the wire from the distributor. Again, pull only on the rubber boot. Check for corrosion and a tight fit in the same manner as the spark plug end.
7   Check the electrical resistance of each spark plug wire and compare it to the specifications. If the resistance is greater than specified, the spark plug wires should be replaced.
8   Check the remaining spark plug wires, making sure they are securely fastened at the distributor and spark plug when the check is complete.

4   Ignition timing – adjustment

Ignition timing adjustment procedures are covered in detail in Chapter 1.

5   Secondary ignition test

1   If ignition problems occur, perform the following test to determine whether the pickup coil and electronic ignition control unit are operating properly.
2   Check the ignition switch, wiring harness, spark plug wires and all ignition system connectors. Correct any problems found or replace any defective parts before proceeding.
3   Remove the distributor cap and lift out the rotor. Turn the ignition switch to 'On'.

4   Disconnect the coil high tension lead from the center terminal of the distributor cap and hold it about $\frac{1}{4}$ in away from the engine block or cylinder head.
5   Insert a flat blade screwdriver between the reluctor and stator of the distributor and see if a spark is produced between the coil lead and the engine. If a spark is not produced, a defective control unit, pickup coil, ignition coil or high-tension lead is at fault. Check all these parts thoroughly.

6   Ignition coil – checking

1   Mark the wires and terminals with pieces of numbered tape, then remove the primary wires and the high-tension lead from the coil.
2   Remove the coil from its mount, clean the outer case and check it for cracks and other damage.
3   Clean the primary coil terminals and check the coil tower terminal for corrosion. Check it with a wire brush if any corrosion is found.
4   Check the primary coil resistance by attaching the leads of an ohmmeter to the positive and negative primary terminals. Compare the measured resistance to the specifications.
5   Check the secondary coil resistance by hooking one of the ohmmeter leads to one of the primary terminals and the other ohmmeter lead to the high-tension coil tower terminal. Compare the measured resistance to the specifications.
6   If the measured resistances are not as specified, the coil is probably defective and should be replaced with a new one.
7   It is essential for proper ignition system operation that all coil terminals and wire leads be kept clean and dry.
8   Install the coil in the vehicle and hook up the wires.

7   Centrifugal advance – checking

1   Refer to Chapter 1, *Ignition Timing-Adjustment,* and hook up a timing light as if you were adjusting the ignition timing.
2   With the engine running at idle speed and the timing light properly connected, remove the vacuum hose from the vacuum advance control unit on the distributor.
3   Observe the timing marks on the front of the engine and slowly accelerate the engine. The timing mark on the crankshaft pulley should appear to move smoothly in a direction away from the stationary mark on the timing tab. Then when the engine is slowed down, the mark should return to its original position.
4   If the above conditions are not met, the advance mechanism inside the distributor should be checked for broken governor springs and other problems.

8   Vacuum advance – checking

1   Refer to Chapter 1, *Ignition Timing-Adjustment,* and hook up a timing light as if you were adjusting the ignition timing.
2   Start the engine and set it at approximately 2500 rpm.
3   Observe the timing marks at the front of the engine and remove the vacuum hose from the vacuum advance control unit on the distributor. When the hose is removed, the timing mark on the crankshaft pulley should appear to move closer to the stationary mark on the timing tab. When the hose is reconnected, the mark should move away again.
4   If re-connecting the vacuum hose produces an abrupt increase in advance, or none at all, the vacuum advance control unit is probably defective.

9   Distributor – removal and installation

1   Disconnect the negative battery cable from the battery. Unplug the wiring harness from the distributor control unit and remove the distributor cap by depressing and turning the spring-loaded screws.
2   Disconnect the vacuum hose from the vacuum advance control unit on the distributor.
3   Pull the spark plug wires off the spark plugs. Pull only on the rubber boot or damage to the spark plug wire could result.
4   Remove the spark plugs, then place your thumb over the No. 1

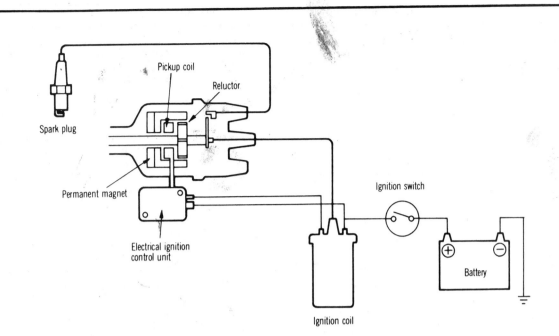

Fig. 5.1 Electronic ignition system wiring diagram (Sec 5)

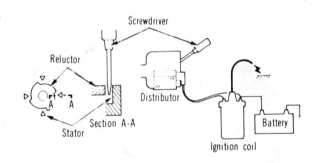

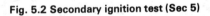

Fig. 5.2 Secondary ignition test (Sec 5)

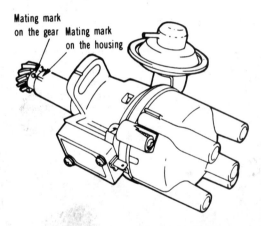

Fig. 5.3 Lining up the mating marks on the distributor and the gear
prior to installing the distributor (Sec 9)

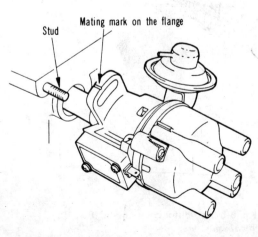

Fig. 5.4 Lining up the mating mark on the distributor flange with
the center of the stud during distributor installation (Sec 9)

spark plug hole and turn the crankshaft in a clockwise direction (looking at it from the front) until you can feel the compression pressure in the No. 1 cylinder. Continue to slowly turn the crankshaft until the notch in the crankshaft pulley lines up with the 'T' on the timing mark tab. At this point, the No. 1 piston is at TDC on the compression stroke.

5   Remove the distributor attaching nut and pull straight out on the distributor.

6   Do not allow the engine to be cranked until the distributor has been reinstalled.

7   To install the distributor, line up the mating marks on the distributor housing (line) and the distributor-driven gear (punch marks). Slide the distributor into place in the cylinder head while lining up the mark on the distributor hold-down flange with the center of the stud. Make sure the distributor is completely seated, then install the nut and tighten it finger tight.

8   Replace the spark plugs and install the plug wires.

9   Install the distributor cap, plug in the control unit wiring harness and connect the vacuum hose to the vacuum control unit.

10   Connect the negative battery cable to the battery and check the ignition timing as described in Chapter 1. Don't forget to tighten the distributor attaching nut securely when finished.

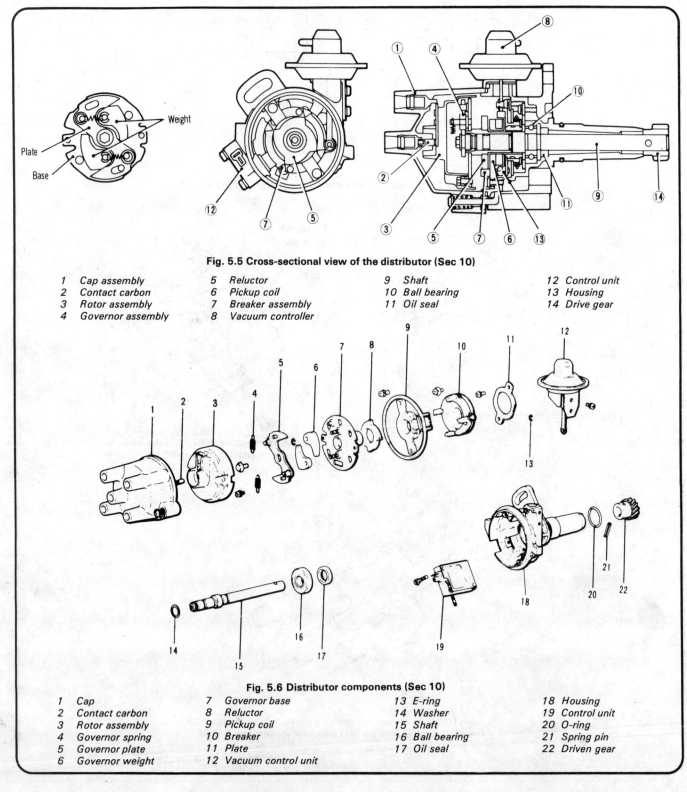

Fig. 5.5 Cross-sectional view of the distributor (Sec 10)

1 Cap assembly	5 Reluctor	9 Shaft	12 Control unit
2 Contact carbon	6 Pickup coil	10 Ball bearing	13 Housing
3 Rotor assembly	7 Breaker assembly	11 Oil seal	14 Drive gear
4 Governor assembly	8 Vacuum controller		

Fig. 5.6 Distributor components (Sec 10)

1 Cap	7 Governor base	13 E-ring	18 Housing
2 Contact carbon	8 Reluctor	14 Washer	19 Control unit
3 Rotor assembly	9 Pickup coil	15 Shaft	20 O-ring
4 Governor spring	10 Breaker	16 Ball bearing	21 Spring pin
5 Governor plate	11 Plate	17 Oil seal	22 Driven gear
6 Governor weight	12 Vacuum control unit		

10 Distributor – disassembly, inspection and reassembly

1   Remove the two mounting screws (photo) and lift the rotor off the governor assembly.
2   Remove the two screws attaching the control unit to the distributor (photo) and pull straight out on the control unit to separate it from the distributor. The mating surfaces of the control unit and the distributor are coated with silicone grease; do not wipe it off (photo).
3   Remove the bolt from the shaft (photo) and pull off the governor/reluctor assembly (photo).
4   Remove the two screws attaching the pickup coil to the distributor. The coil and cap gasket can now be lifted out (photo).
5   Remove the retaining clip that holds the vacuum link to the breaker assembly (photo). Remove the two screws attaching the vacuum advance control unit to the distributor (photo) and lift it off.
6   Remove the breaker assembly which is held in place with 2 screws (photo) and the bearing retainer plate (photo).
7   Support the distributor shaft and gear, then drive out the pin that attaches the gear to the shaft (photo).
8   Slide the gear off the shaft and withdraw the shaft from the distributor (photo).
9   Do not remove the bearing and seal from the shaft unless they require replacement.
10 Using an ohmmeter, measure the resistance of the pickup coil. Compare the measured resistance to the specifications.
11 Check for continuity between terminal 'C' and the back side (bare metal) of the control unit. Reverse the lead and repeat the test. If there is continuity or an open circuit in both test lead positions, the control unit is defective and should be replaced with a new one.
Note: *This test evaluates only the transistors in the control unit. Even if the results of the test are positive, the control unit could still be defective.*
12 Check the distributor gear for excessive wear and damage.
13 Check the shaft and bearing for end-to-end and side play. If excessive play is noted, replace the bearing, the seal and the shaft with new parts.
14 Check the governor springs for cracks and damage. Make sure the governor weights can move freely on their pivots.
15 Check the vacuum advance control unit by applying a vacuum at the fitting. The linkage should move in and remain in as long as a vacuum is applied to the fitting.
16 Check the distributor cap and rotor for cracks, carbon tracks and deposits on the metal terminals. If any of these conditions exist, replace them with new parts. The cost is minimal.
17 Lubricate the shaft with a small amount of multi-purpose grease, then insert the shaft into the distributor.
18 Slide the gear onto the end of the shaft and install the pin. Be sure to support the gear and shaft when tapping the pin into place.
19 Install the breaker assembly. Connect the vacuum advance link, (don't forget the retaining clip) and fasten the vacuum advance control unit in place.
20 Install the pickup coil and cap gasket. Tighten the screws securely but do not overtighten them.

21 Slip the governor/reluctor assembly onto the shaft, install the bolt and tighten it securely.
22 Install the control unit ensuring that the silicone grease is in place and tighten the screws securely.
23 Install the rotor by matching the pegs on the governor assembly with the holes in the rotor and tighten the screws securely.
24 Check to make sure the distributor shaft rotates smoothly and easily.

11 Starter motor – removal and installation

1   Before attempting to remove the starter motor, disconnect the negative battery cable from the battery.
2   Raise the vehicle and set it securely on jack stands.
3   Label the wires and terminals with pieces of numbered tape, then disconnect the starter motor wiring harness from the two terminals on the starter motor magnetic switch.
4   Remove the two starter motor mounting bolts and separate the motor from the transmission bellhousing. Work carefully, as the starter motor is quite heavy.
5   Before installing the motor, clean the mounting surfaces thoroughly. Slip the motor into place, install the mounting bolts and tighten them evenly and securely. If there is enough room to use a torque wrench, tighten the bolts to the specified torque.
6   Hook up the starter motor wiring leads (don't mix them up) and the negative battery cable.

12 Direct drive starter motor – overhaul and testing

1   When faced with starter motor problems, you must decide whether to disassemble and repair the motor or simply replace it with a new or rebuilt unit. The costs involved, in terms of time and money, and the availability of parts needed for repairs are the main factors to consider.
2   Remove the connector from Terminal 'M', the two magnetic switch mounting screws and the magnetic switch.
3   Remove the two through-bolts and the motor can be separated into the armature and yoke.
4   Carefully remove the armature and lever from the front bracket. Note how the lever is installed and keep in mind the order in which the spring and the spring holder are inserted.
5   Loosen the two screws and remove the rear bracket.
6   The brush holder assembly can be removed by pulling out the brushes and slipping the holder off.
7   Using a piece of tubing that will just fit over the shaft, push the stopper toward the pinion gear. Remove the snap-ring and pull off the stopper and over-running clutch from the armature shaft.
8   Measure the inside diameter of the bearings in the front and rear brackets. Measure the corresponding outside diameter of the armature shaft ends. Subtract the shaft diameter from the bearing diameter to obtain the armature-to-bearing clearance. Compare the measured

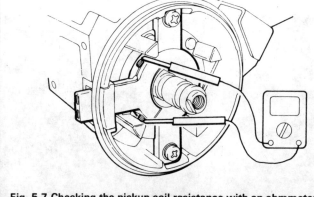

Fig. 5.7 Checking the pickup coil resistance with an ohmmeter (Sec 10)

Terminal "B"   Terminal "C"

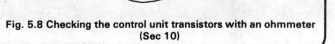

Fig. 5.8 Checking the control unit transistors with an ohmmeter (Sec 10)

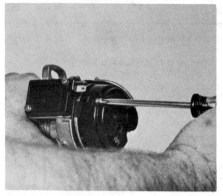

10.1 Removing the rotor mounting screws

10.2a Removing the control unit mounting screws

10.2b The mating surfaces of the control unit and distributor are coated with silicone grease

10.3a Removing the governor/reluctor assembly mounting bolt

10.3b Removing the governor/reluctor assembly

10.4 Lifting out the pickup coil and cap gasket

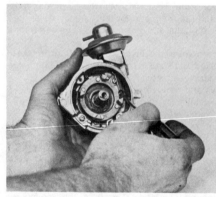

10.5a Removing the vacuum link circlip

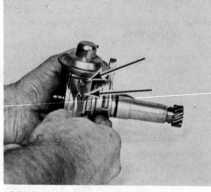

10.5b Removing the vacuum advance control unit mounting screws

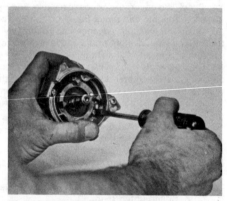

10.6a Removing the breaker assembly mounting screws

10.6b Removing the bearing retaining plate

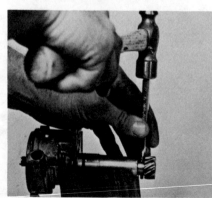

10.7 Removing the distributor drive gear retaining pin

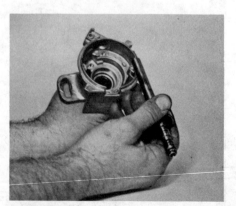

10.8 Withdrawing the shaft from the distributor body

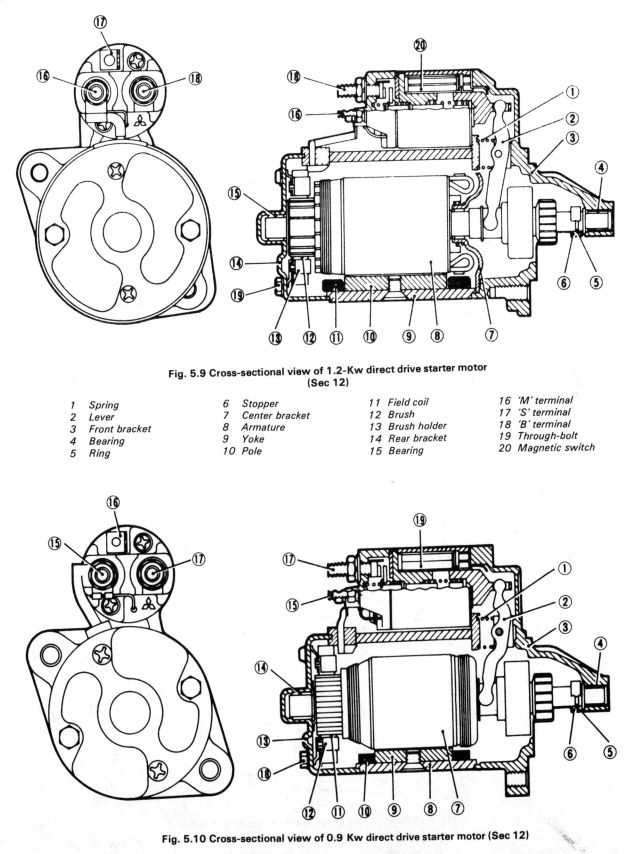

Fig. 5.9 Cross-sectional view of 1.2-Kw direct drive starter motor (Sec 12)

1	Spring	6	Stopper	11	Field coil	16	'M' terminal
2	Lever	7	Center bracket	12	Brush	17	'S' terminal
3	Front bracket	8	Armature	13	Brush holder	18	'B' terminal
4	Bearing	9	Yoke	14	Rear bracket	19	Through-bolt
5	Ring	10	Pole	15	Bearing	20	Magnetic switch

Fig. 5.10 Cross-sectional view of 0.9 Kw direct drive starter motor (Sec 12)

1	Spring	6	Stopper	11	Brush	16	Terminal 'S'
2	Lever	7	Armature	12	Brush holder	17	Terminal 'B'
3	Front bracket	8	Yoke	13	Rear bracket	18	Through-bolt
4	Bearing	9	Pole	14	Bearing	19	Magnetic switch
5	Ring	10	Field coil	15	Terminal 'M'		

values to the specifications. If they are greater than specified, the bearings must be replaced with new ones.

9 Check the commutator for scratches, dirt, and evidence of extreme heat. It can be cleaned up with a strip of fine emery cloth.

10 Measure the outside diameter of the commutator and compare it to the specifications. If it is less than the minimum specified, the armature will have to be replaced with a new one.

11 If the commutator is extremely dirty or scratched, it can be resurfaced by an automotive repair shop.

12 Using an ohmmeter or continuity tester, check for continuity between the commutator segments and the armature core. If continuity exists, the armature is faulty and must be replaced.

13 Check for continuity between the commutator's segments. If there is no continuity, the commutator has an open circuit and the armature must be replaced.

14 Check for continuity between the field coil connections. If no continuity exists, the field coil is faulty and should be replaced.

15 Check for continuity between the field coil and the yoke. If continuity exists, the field coil is faulty and should be replaced.

16 Push the magnetic switch plunger in and release it. The plunger should return quickly to its original position.

17 Push the plunger all the way in, hold it and check for continuity between the terminal labeled 'M' and the terminal labeled 'B'. If there is no continuity, the magnetic switch is faulty.

18 Measure the brush length and compare it to the specifications. If the brushes are shorter than specified, replace them with new ones.

19 Check for continuity between the positive side of the brush holder and the brush holder base. Continuity indicates that the brush holder assembly must be replaced.

20 Inspect the pinion, spline, and teeth of the over-running clutch for wear and damage. If they are damaged, also inspect the flywheel ring gear for wear and damage.

21 Rotate the pinion. It should turn freely in a clockwise direction and lock when turned counterclockwise.

22 Apply a thin coat of multi-purpose grease to the armature shaft, then install the over-running clutch onto the shaft.

23 Install the stopper onto the front end of the armature shaft, fit the snap-ring and push the stopper forward and over the snap-ring.

24 Slip the small washer onto the front end of the armature shaft, then lubricate the end of the shaft with multi-purpose grease.

25 Place the lever into the groove in the over-running clutch and install the armature and lever assembly into the front housing.

26 Install the lever, spring, and spring retainer and then clip the yoke assembly into place.

27 Install the brush holder, then fit the four brushes into the holder. (Make sure that the lead wires are not grounded). Measure the brush spring installed load with a pull scale and compare it to the specifications.

28 Install the washer on the rear end of the armature shaft, lubricate the shaft end, then slip the rear bracket into place and insert and tighten the two through-bolts.

29 Place the lever into the front end of the magnetic switch plunger and tighten the two magnetic switch mounting screws.

30 *The following test must be completed in less than 10 seconds to prevent damage to the magnetic switch.*

31 Connect a heavy jumper lead between the positive post of a 12-volt battery and terminal 'S' on the magnetic switch. Connect a second heavy jumper lead between the negative post of the battery and the starter motor body. When the connection is made, the pinion gear will move out on the armature shaft.

32 Check the pinion-to-stopper clearance (pinion gap) and compare it to the specifications. The pinion gap can be increased or decreased by adding or removing washers where the magnetic switch mounts to the front bracket.

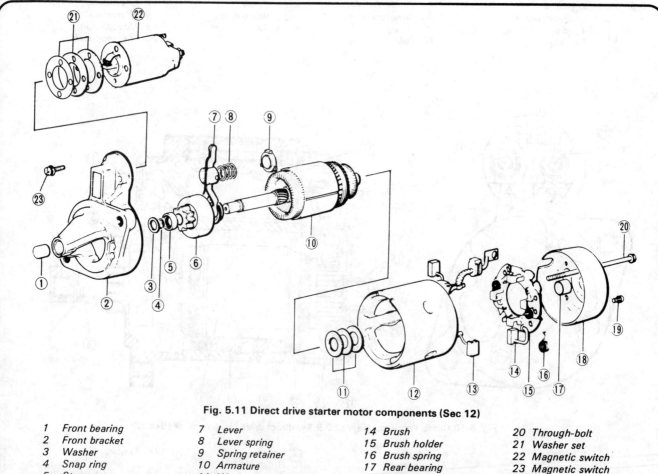

Fig. 5.11 Direct drive starter motor components (Sec 12)

1 Front bearing	7 Lever	14 Brush	20 Through-bolt
2 Front bracket	8 Lever spring	15 Brush holder	21 Washer set
3 Washer	9 Spring retainer	16 Brush spring	22 Magnetic switch
4 Snap ring	10 Armature	17 Rear bearing	23 Magnetic switch
5 Stopper	11 Washer set	18 Rear bracket	tightening screw
6 Over-running clutch	12 Yoke	19 Brush holder tightening	
and pinion	13 Brush	screw	

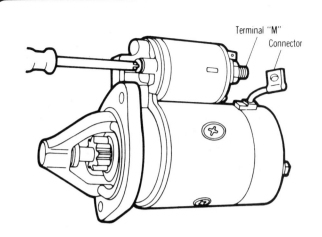

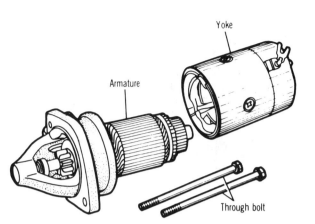

Fig. 5.12 Removing the magnetic switch from the starter motor (Sec 12)

Fig. 5.13 Separating the armature from the yoke (Sec 12)

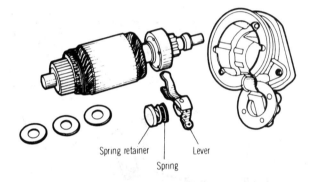

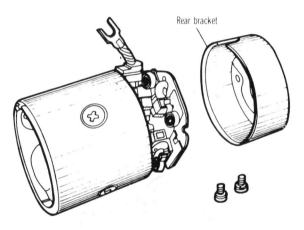

Fig. 5.14 Removing the armature and lever (and related components) from the front bracket (Sec 12)

Fig. 5.15 Removing the rear bracket (Sec 12)

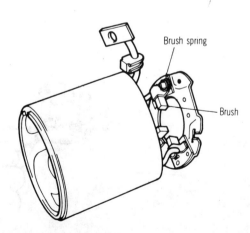

Fig. 5.16 Removing the brush holder assembly (Sec 12)

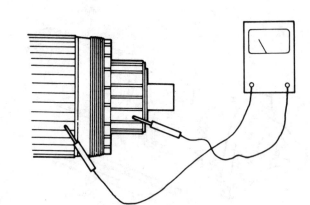

Fig. 5.17 Checking for continuity between the commutator segments and the armature core (Sec 12)

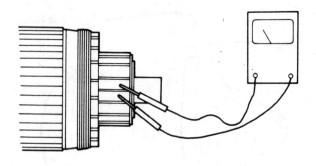

Fig. 5.18 Checking for continuity between the commutator segments (Sec 12)

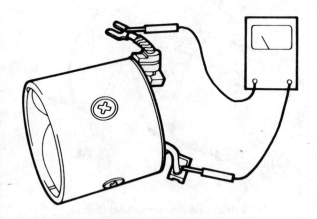

Fig. 5.19 Checking for continuity between the field coil connections (Sec 12)

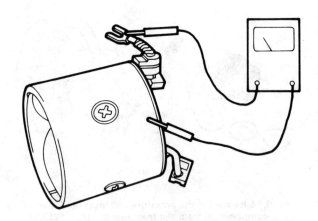

Fig. 5.20 Checking for continuity between the field coil and yoke (Sec 12)

Wear limit line

Fig. 5.21 If the brushes are worn beyond the wear limit line, they must be replaced with new ones (Sec 12)

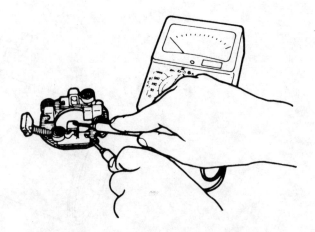

Fig. 5.22 Checking for continuity between the brush holder and the base (Sec 12)

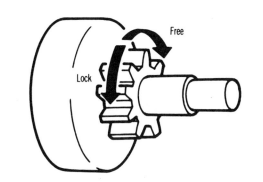

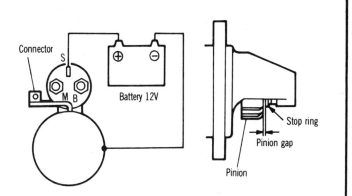

Fig. 5.23 Checking the operation of the over-running clutch (Sec 12)

Fig. 5.24 Checking the pinion gap (Sec 12)

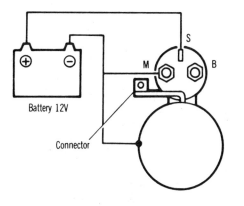

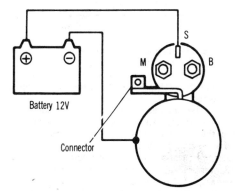

Fig. 5.25 Checking the pull-in coil of the magnetic switch (Sec 12)

Fig. 5.26 Checking the hold-in coil of the magnetic switch (Sec 12)

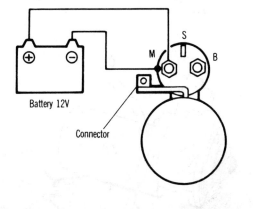

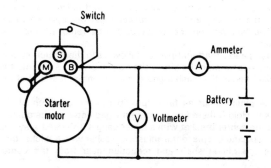

Fig. 5.27 Checking the magnetic switch for proper pinion return (Sec 12)

Fig. 5.28 Performing the starter motor no-load test (Sec 12)

33 *This test must also be performed in less than 10 seconds.*
34 Connect terminal 'S' to the positive post of the battery and
connect Terminal 'M' to the negative post of the battery. Connect
another jumper lead between Terminal 'M' and the magnetic switch
body. If the pinion gear moves out on the armature shaft, the pull-in
coil is good. If the pinion gear does not move, replace the magnetic
switch with a new one.
35 Disconnect the wire from Terminal 'M' only. If the pinion stays out,
the hold-in coil is working properly. If the pinion moves in when the
wire is disconnected, the magnetic switch must be replaced with a
new one.
36 Connect Terminal 'M' to the positive post of the battery and touch
the lead from the negative post of the battery to the magnetic switch
body. Pull the pinion out, then release it. If it quickly returns to its
original position, everything is working properly. If it doesn't return,
replace the magnetic switch with a new one.
37 Connect the battery to the starter motor as shown in Fig. 5.28. A
voltmeter and an ammeter must be included in the circuit as well. Hold
the starter motor securely while conducting this test.
38 If the motor rotates smoothly and steadily (and if the pinion gear
moves out on the armature shaft) and draws less than the specified
amount of current, the motor is working properly.

13 Reduction drive starter motor – overhaul and testing

1   Remove the 'M' Terminal nut from the magnetic switch and slip
off the connector.
2   Remove the two magnetic switch mounting screws and separate
the magnetic switch from the motor.
3   Remove the two through-bolts and the two brush holder screws,
then pull off the rear bracket. When the bracket is removed, do not lose
the spring washer.
4   Pull out on the brushes, then remove the yoke and brush holder
assembly. The armature can now be pulled out of the center bracket.
5   Remove the cover over the rear of the pinion gearshaft, then
remove the snap-ring and washer from the shaft.
6   Remove the bolt attaching the center bracket to the front bracket.
When the center bracket is separated from the front bracket, don't lose
the end play adjusting washers.
7   Remove the reduction gear from the pinion shaft and the lever and
lever spring from the front bracket.
8   Push the stopper off the snap-ring on the front of the pinion shaft,
then remove the ring, the stopper and the pinion gear from the shaft.
Withdraw the shaft from the front bracket.
9   The inspection procedures for the armature, the yoke and the field
coil assembly, the magnetic switch, the brushes, the over-running
clutch, and the pinion gear are the same as the procedures for the
direct-drive starter motor.
10 Visually check the armature shaft gear and the reduction gear for
cracks, excessive wear and other damage. Replace any defective parts
with new ones.
11 Check all ball bearings for smooth operation. If noise and binding
are evident, the bearing and front bracket must be replaced as an
assembly. The bearings on the armature can be removed and new
ones installed.
12 Adjust the pinion shaft end-play as follows: slip the reduction gear
and adjusting washer onto the pinion shaft and insert the shaft into the
center bracket. Install the washer and snap-ring on the rear end of the
pinion shaft.
13 Push the pinion shaft as far as possible in the direction of the
center bracket. Hold it there and measure the gap between the outside
washer and the center bracket with a feeler gauge. If the end-play gap
is more than specified, replace the adjusting washer with a thicker one.
14 Remove the pinion shaft and reduction gear from the center
bracket.
15 Install the pinion shaft, the reduction gear, the lever, and the lever
spring in the front bracket. Lubricate the reduction gear and the sliding
portion of the lever with multi-purpose grease. Slip the proper size
adjusting washer onto the pinion shaft.
16 Lubricate the pinion shaft, then install the center bracket and
tighten the mounting bolt securely.
17 Install the pinion gear, the snap-ring and the stopper on the front
of the pinion shaft. Lubricate the stopper and the pinion shaft with
multi-purpose grease.
18 Install the washer and the snap-ring on the rear of the pinion shaft,

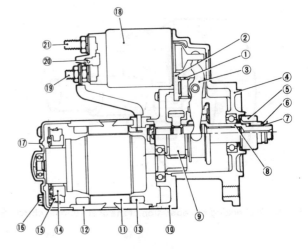

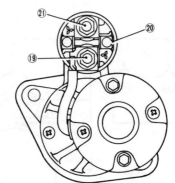

**Fig. 5.29 Cross-sectional view of reduction gear starter motor
(Sec 13)**

1	*Lever spring*	*12*	*Yoke*
2	*Packing*	*13*	*Field coil*
3	*Lever*	*14*	*Brush*
4	*Front bracket*	*15*	*Brush holder*
5	*Pinion*	*16*	*Through Bolt*
6	*Stopper*	*17*	*Rear bracket*
7	*Ring*	*18*	*Magnetic switch*
8	*Pinion shaft ass'y*	*19*	*Terminal 'M'*
9	*Gear*	*20*	*Terminal 'S'*
10	*Center bracket*	*21*	*Terminal 'B'*
11	*Pole*		

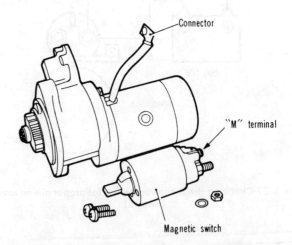

Fig. 5.30 Removing the magnetic switch (Sec 13)

Measuring plug gap. A feeler gauge of the correct size (see ignition system specifications) should have a slight 'drag' when slid between the electrodes. Adjust gap if necessary

Adjusting plug gap. The plug gap is adjusted by bending the ground electrode inwards, or outwards, as necessary until the correct clearance is obtained. Note the use of the correct tool

Normal. Gray brown deposits, lightly coated core nose. Gap increasing by around 0.001 in (0.025 mm) per 1000 miles (1600 km). Plugs ideally suited to engine, and engine in good condition

Carbon fouling. Dry, black, sooty deposits. Will cause weak spark and eventually misfire. Fault: over-rich fuel mixture. Check: carburetor mixture settings, float level and jet sizes; choke operation and cleanliness of air filter. Plugs can be re-used after cleaning

Oil fouling. Wet, oily deposits. Will cause weak spark and eventually misfire. Fault: worn bores/piston rings or valve guides; sometimes occurs (temporarily) during running-in period. Plugs can be re-used after thorough cleaning

Overheating. Electrodes have glazed appearance, core nose very white – few deposits. Fault: plug overheating. Check: plug value, ignition timing, fuel octane rating (too low) and fuel mixture (too weak). Discard plugs and cure fault immediately

Electrode damage. Electrodes burned away; core nose has burned, glazed appearance. Fault: pre-ignition. Check: as for 'Overheating' but may be more severe. Discard plugs and remedy fault before piston or valve damage occurs

Split core nose (may appear initially as a crack). Damage is self-evident, but cracks will only show after cleaning. Fault: pre-ignition or wrong gap-setting technique. Check: ignition timing, cooling system, fuel octane rating (too low) and fuel mixture (too weak). Discard plugs, rectify fault immediately

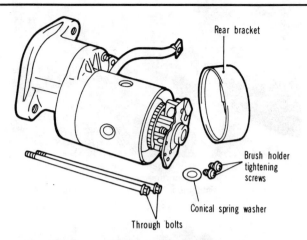

Fig. 5.31 Removing the rear bracket (Sec 13)

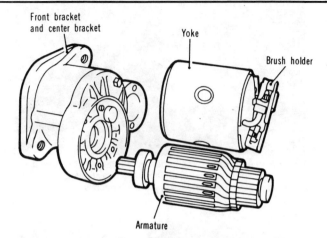

Fig. 5.32 Removing the brush holder assembly, the yoke and the armature from the front bracket (Sec 13)

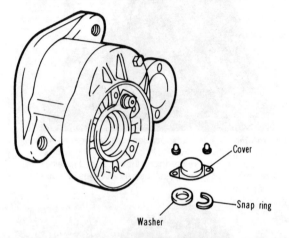

Fig. 5.33 Removing the cover, the snap-ring and the washer from the pinion gearshaft (Sec 13)

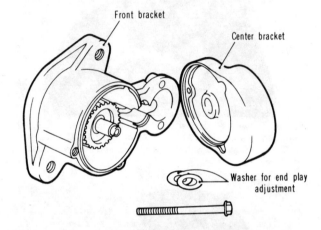

Fig. 5.34 Removing the center bracket from the front bracket (Sec 13)

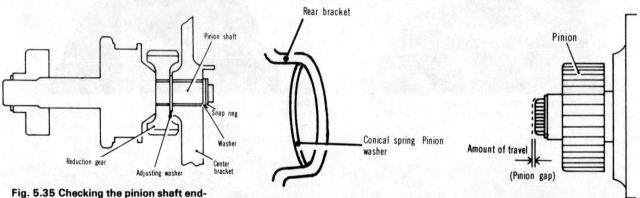

Fig. 5.35 Checking the pinion shaft end-play (Sec 13)

Fig. 5.36 Laying the spring washer in place in the rear bracket cavity (Sec 13)

Fig. 5.37 Checking the pinion gap (Sec 13)

then lay the cover in place and tighten the screws securely.

19 Lubricate the armature gear and the ball bearings with multi-purpose grease, then slip the armature through the center bracket and mesh the gear teeth on the armature with the reduction gear teeth.

20 Slide the yoke into place and position the brush holder assembly.

21 Place a dab of multi-purpose grease in the rear bracket cavity, then lay the spring washer in place.

22 Carefully attach the rear bracket to the yoke. Ensure that the bearing fits into the cavity and install the through-bolts and the brush holder screws. Tighten them securely.

23 Install the magnetic switch and tighten the screws securely.

24 Connect the large wire to terminal 'M' and tighten the nut securely.

25 Check the pinion gap as follows. *This test must be completed in less than 10 seconds to prevent damage to the magnetic switch:* Connect a heavy jumper lead between the positive post of a 12-volt battery and terminal 'S' on the magnetic switch. Connect another heavy jumper lead between the negative post of the battery and the starter motor body. When the connection is made, the pinion shaft and gears will move out.

26 Gently push the pinion gear back until it stops. The distance moved is the pinion gap. Compare it to the specifications. If the gap is more or less than specified, add or remove washers from between the magnetic switch and the front bracket. Increasing the washers will reduce the pinion gap.

27 The remaining performance tests are the same as those for the direct-drive starter motor.

Chapter 6 Emissions control systems

Refer to Chapter 13 for specifications and information related to 1981 thru 1988 models

Contents

Specifications

Dash pot adjustment (trucks for Canada only)

Engine set speed
U-engine	2200 ± 100 rpm
W-engine	1700 ± 100 rpm
Dash pot drop time	3 to 6 seconds

Torque specifications

	ft-lb	Nm
Exhaust manifold-to-catalyst case bolts	22 to 25	(29 to 34)
Exhaust manifold mounting nuts	11 to 14	(15 to 19)

1 General information

The Chrysler mini-truck is equipped with the Chrysler cleaner air system for controlling crankcase, evaporative, and exhaust emissions. It is a highly effective method of removing automotive air pollutants, eliminating more than 90% of hydrocarbons, 90% of carbon monoxide and 50% of oxides of nitrogen emissions as compared to a vehicle not equipped with the system.

It is composed of a catalytic converter, an evaporation control system (ECS), a jet air system, a secondary air supply system (SAS), a deceleration device, a heated air intake system, an exhaust gas recirculation system (EGR) and a crankcase emission control system.

2 Emission control systems – maintenance intervals

In order to ensure control of emissions and proper vehicle performance, the emission control system components should be maintained according to the following schedule.

Every 12 months or 12 000 miles
Check and clean the crankcase emission control system.
Check or replace the engine compartment rubber hoses.
Check the evaporative emission control system.
Check the EGR valve operation (trucks for Canada only).

Every 5 years or 50 000 miles
Check the heated air intake control valve operation.
Check the air switching valve operation.
Check the coasting air valve operation.
Check the thermo valve operation.
Check the purge control valve operation.

3 Evaporation control system (ECS) – general description

1   To prevent fuel vapors from escaping into the atmosphere from the fuel tank (due to normal vaporization) the Chrysler mini-truck is equipped with an evaporation control system (ECS).
2   The ECS is composed of a separator tank, a two-way valve, a fuel check valve, a purge control valve, a charcoal-filled cannister, and various connecting lines and hoses.
3   The charcoal filled-cannister is installed between the fuel tank and the air cleaner. Gasoline vapors are routed to this cannister for temporary storage. While the engine is running, outside air is drawn through the cannister, purging the vapors from the charcoal. This air/vapor mixture is then routed to the engine combustion chambers (through the air cleaner) and burned.
4   The purge control valve is kept closed at idle speeds to prevent vaporized fuel from entering the air cleaner and causing high-idle carbon monoxide emissions.
5   The carburetor itself is vented internally or through the charcoal cannister, depending on the temperature, which prevents the escape of gasoline vapors into the atmosphere from the carburetor.
6   When the engine is not running, gasoline vapors produced in the fuel tank (by an increase in atmospheric temperatures) are routed to the separator tank in which liquid gasoline formed by condensation of the vapors is separated. The remaining fuel vapor is led into a two-way valve. The two-way pressure valve is designed to open at a predetermined pressure, admitting the fuel vapors into the charcoal filled cannister. In the cannister, the vapors are trapped by the charcoal, preventing the discharge of raw hydrocarbons into the atmosphere.
7   While the engine is running, a vacuum is built above the cannister (on the carburetor side) causing outside air to be drawn into the cannister through the inlet holes in the case, passing through the filter and the charcoal. As the outside air flows through, the vapors trapped by the charcoal are carried away, passing through the passage at the center of the cannister into the air cleaner, the carburetor and ultimately the engine cylinders where they are burned.
8   During engine operation, vapors originating in the fuel tank are also routed directly into the cannister (through the passage in the center of the cannister) and fed into the engine for combustion.
9   As the fuel is used, a vacuum is produced inside the fuel tank. The two-way valve vacuum valve opens momentarily, drawing outside air through the air inlet hose of the cannister into the fuel tank, thus maintaining normal pressure in the tank.
10   During filling of the fuel tank, the air in the tank flows through the leveling pipe and out into the atmosphere, venting the tank. When the fuel entering the tank has sealed off the leveling pipe opening in the tank, further filling cannot be done because of the air pressure inside the tank. If filling is continued, overflow of fuel will result.

4 ECS cannister – removal and installation

1   Because of the fact that the cannister inlet air hose and filter can become clogged over a long period of time, it is recommended that the cannister be replaced according to the mileage intervals listed in Chapter 1.

2   Also, carefully inspect the rubber hoses attached to the cannister. If they are cracked or otherwise deteriorated, replace them with new ones when the cannister is replaced.
3   Refer to Chapter 1 for cannister removal and installation procedures.

5 Purge control valve – checking

1   The purge control valve is connected by hoses to the top of the ECS cannister, the air cleaner and the carburetor.
2   It is a simple spring-loaded closed valve, and its operation is controlled by negative pressure, generated at a port provided slightly above the carburetor throttle valve, which acts on a diaphragm in the valve. While the engine is idling, the valve and evaporated gas passage are closed. When the engine is running at 1500 rpm or more, the valve is opened and the fuel vapors stored in the cannister are drawn into the carburetor.
3   When inspecting the valve, the engine must be at normal operating temperature.
4   Disconnect the purge hose from the air cleaner (photo) and blow into it. If the valve is not open, it is in good condition. Next, start the engine and increase the engine speed to 1500 or 2000 rpm and blow into the purge hose again. If the valve is open, it is operating properly.
5   If the valve does not check out as described, replace it with a new one.

6 Fuel check valve – removal and installation

1   The fuel check valve, located just to the left of the fuel tank, is designed to prevent fuel leaks should the vehicle roll over during an accident. The check valve contains two balls. Under normal conditions the gasoline vapor passage in the valve is open, but if a roll over occurs, either of the two balls will close the fuel passage and prevent fuel leaks.
2   Remove the hose clamps and disconnect the hoses from the check valve.
3   Remove the bolt attaching the fuel check valve to the rear body mounting bracket.
4   Check the hoses for cracks and replace them if they are deteriorated. Installation of the valve is the reverse of removal.

7 Two-way valve – removal, checking and installation

1   The two-way valve, located just to the left of the fuel tank, is composed of a pressure valve and a vacuum valve. The pressure valve is designed to open when the fuel tank internal pressure has increased over the normal pressure, which allows the fuel vapors to enter the charcoal cannister for storage, and the vacuum valve opens when a vacuum has been produced in the tank.
2   Removal of the valve is quite simple. Loosen the hose clamps and pull off the two hoses, then remove the valve mounting bolt.
3   Blow lightly into the valve inlet. If there is an initial resistance followed by the passage of air, the valve is in good condition. Repeat the check by blowing into the outlet.
4   Installation is the reverse of removal. The valve must tilt approximately 7 degrees in relation to the fuel tank when it is installed.

8 Separator tank – removal and installation

1   The separator tank's function is to temporarily accommodate an increased volume of gasoline caused by expansion at high outside air temperatures. It also prevents liquid fuel from entering the vapor line during hard cornering.
2   Mark each fuel/vapor hose and its corresponding fitting with numbered pieces of tape.
3   Refer to Chapter 4 and remove the fuel tank.
4   The separator tank is attached to the top of the fuel tank. It can be removed very easily once the fuel tank has been separated from the vehicle.
5   Replace any cracked or deteriorated fuel/vapor hoses.
6   Installation is basically the reverse of removal. Chapter 4 contains detailed fuel tank installation procedures.

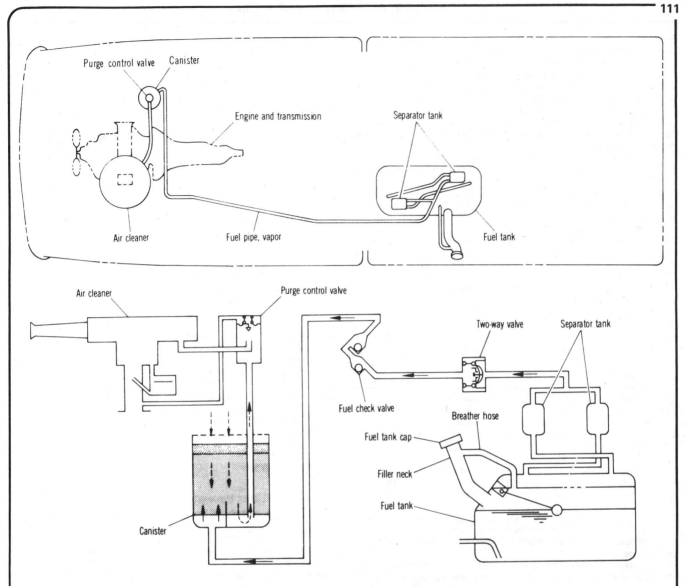

Fig. 6.1 Evaporation Control System (Sec 3)

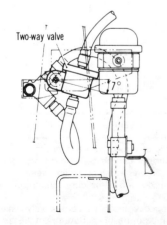

Fig. 6.2 The two-way valve must be installed at a 7 degree angle in relation to the tank (Sec 7)

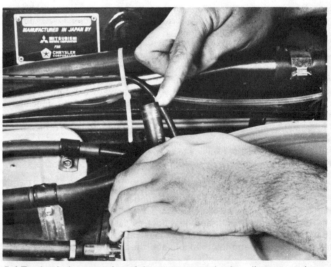

5.4 To check the operation of the purge control valve, disconnect the hose from the air cleaner housing and blow into it

9 Catalytic converter – general description

1   The catalytic converter provides for the oxidizing of hydrocarbons and carbon monoxide in the exhaust system, which reduces the levels of these pollutants in the exhaust.

2   Its ceramic monolithic element, coated with a catalytic agent, is pressed into the engine lower exhaust manifold. The catalyst cannot be replaced independently, as the catalyst and lower exhaust manifold are an assembly.

3   The catalytic converter requires the use of unleaded fuel only. Leaded gasoline will destroy the effectiveness of the catalyst as an emission control device.

4   Under normal operating conditions, the catalytic converter will not require maintenance. However, it is important to keep the engine properly tuned. If the engine is not properly tuned, engine misfiring may cause overheating of the catalyst, which may damage the converter or other vehicle components. Heat damage can also occur during diagnostic testing if spark plug wires are removed and the engine is allowed to idle for a prolonged period of time.

5   *Caution: Vehicle operation, including idling, should be avoided if engine misfiring occurs. Under these conditions the exhaust system will operate at an abnormally high temperature and may cause damage to the catalyst or other underbody parts of the vehicle. Alteration or deterioration of the ignition or fuel systems, or any type of operating condition which results in engine misfiring, must be corrected to avoid overheating the catalytic converter.*

10 Catalytic converter – removal and installation

1   Before working on the exhaust system, allow it to cool completely.

2   Remove the air cleaner and heat duct by referring to Chapter 4.

3   Remove the secondary air supply system air pipe from the top of the exhaust manifold.

4   Remove the heat shields from the exhaust manifold.

5   Disconnect the front exhaust pipe from the exhaust manifold. It may be necessary to soak the attaching nuts with penetrating oil if they are difficult to remove.

6   Remove the nuts attaching the exhaust manifold to the cylinder head, then carefully lift the manifold out of place.

7   Separate the exhaust manifold from the catalyst case/lower exhaust manifold.

8   The lower manifold and catalyst case must be replaced as a unit. The catalyst case/lower exhaust manifold is available in two different sizes; make sure you obtain the correct one for your particular vehicle.

9   Place a new cushion on the catalyst and a new steel gasket on the case. Be sure that the gasket fits in the inside diameter of the cushion.

10 Fasten the exhaust manifold/catalyst case together and tighten the bolts to the specified torque.

11 Using a new gasket, install the exhaust manifold and tighten the nuts to the specified torque. Be sure to install the engine hoist brackets to the front and the SAS pipe bracket and electrical ground strap to the rear of the manifold before tightening the nuts. When tightening, start at the center of the manifold and work out toward the end. Tighten each nut in sequence, a little at a time, until they are all at the specified torque.

12 Attach the front exhaust pipe to the manifold and tighten the nuts securely.

13 Attach the two heat shields to the exhaust manifold. The four bolts that hold the upper shield in place must have the large washers on them.

14 Coat the secondary air supply system pipe fitting threads with an anti-seize compound, then thread the fitting into the top of the exhaust manifold and tighten it securely.

15 Install the air cleaner and heat duct as described in Chapter 4.

16 Start the engine and check for exhaust leaks between the manifold and catalyst case and the manifold and the front exhaust pipe.

11 Secondary air supply system (SAS) – general description

1   The SAS is composed of a reed valve and an air pipe. The reed valve supplies secondary air into the exhaust manifold for the purpose

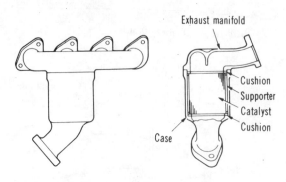

Fig. 6.3 Catalytic converter (Sec 9)

of promoting oxidation (or complete burning) of any remaining unburned fuel.

2   It is actuated by exhaust vacuum generated from pulsations in the exhaust manifold. Air is drawn through the air cleaner and directed into the manifold by the valve motion corresponding to the exhaust pulses.

12 Secondary air supply system (SAS) – checking

1   Check the air hose and air pipe for damage and cracks. Check the air pipe connections for leakage.

2   Start and run the engine at idle. Disconnect the rubber air hose from the reed valve and place your hand over the intake part of the valve (photo). If suction is felt, the reed valve is operating properly. If no suction is felt, or if pressure is felt, replace the reed valve with a new one.

13 Secondary air supply system reed valve – removal and installation

1   Removal of the reed valve is very simple. Pull the rubber hose off the inlet and unscrew the valve from the air pipe.

2   Installation is the reverse of removal.

14 Crankcase emission control system – general description

1   A closed-type crankcase ventilation system is utilized to prevent blow-by gases from escaping into the atmosphere. This system has a small orifice fixed at the intake manifold or at the rocker arm cover.

2   The blow-by gas is led through a rubber hose from the front of the rocker arm cover into the air cleaner and through another hose from the rear of the cover into the intake manifold through the orifice. At narrow throttle openings, the blow-by gas is drawn from the rear of the cover into the intake manifold with fresh air entering from the air cleaner through the front of the rocker arm cover. At wide open throttle, the blow-by gas is drawn through both passages.

3   Very little maintenance is required for the crankcase emission control system. Check the hoses for cracks and kinks. Replace them with new ones if they are deteriorated. Make sure that the orifice is not clogged or poor crankcase ventilation will result.

15 Heated air intake system – general description

1   The Chrysler mini-truck is equipped with a temperature-regulated air cleaner so that the carburetor can be calibrated leaner to reduce carbon monoxide and hydrocarbon emissions. Improved engine warm-up characteristics and minimized carburetor icing can also be attained with this system.

2   The air cleaner is equipped with an air control valve inside the snorkel to modulate the temperature of carburetor intake air which flows through the intake. The air control valve is controlled by a vacuum motor/temperature sensor combination system which responds to the intake manifold vacuum and temperature inside the air cleaner.

3   When the bi-metal senses a temperature inside the air cleaner

below about 84°F, the air bleed valve of the temperature sensor assembly remains closed, causing intake manifold vacuum to be applied to the diaphragm of the vacuum motor. This in turn opens the air control valve and allows the preheated intake air to flow through the heat cowl and air duct into the air cleaner.

4   When the bi-metal senses that the temperature inside the air cleaner is above about 113°F, the air bleed valve is fully open. As a result, the intake air to the carburetor comes directly through the fresh air duct, since the air control valve is positioned at 'B', as shown in Fig. 6.7, regardless of the intake manifold vacuum.

5   At intermediate temperatures, the air entering the carburetor is a blend of fresh and preheated air as regulated by the thermostatically-actuated air control valve.

16 Heated air intake system – checking

1   Make sure all vacuum hoses and the heat cowl-to-air cleaner air duct are properly attached and in good condition.

2   With the engine completely cold, and the outside air temperature less than 84°F, remove the rubber tube from the end of the air cleaner snorkel. Start the engine and look into the snorkel. *(Be careful when working around moving engine parts).* The air control valve should be in the 'Up' (Heat on) position.

3   With the engine running at normal operating temperatures, check the temperature of the air entering the end of the air cleaner snorkel. If the temperature is 113°F or higher, the air control valve should be

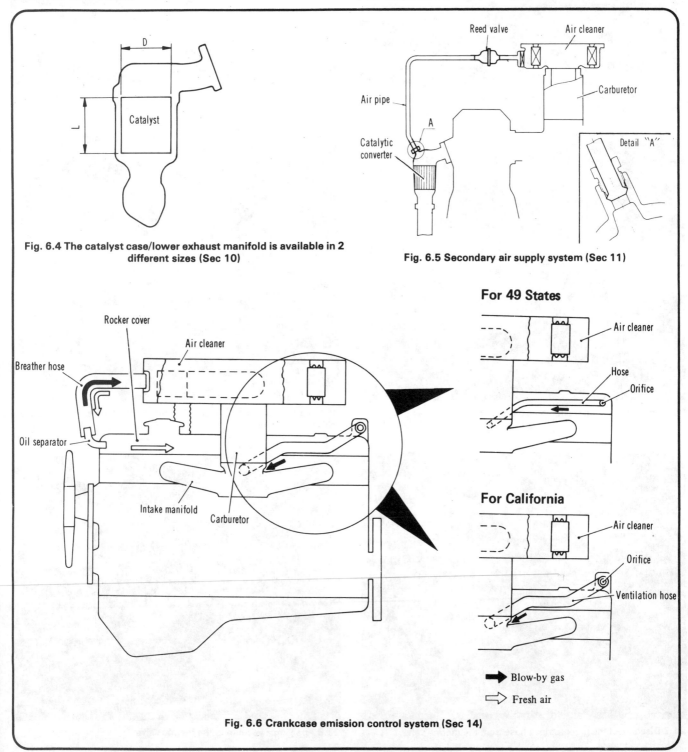

Fig. 6.4 The catalyst case/lower exhaust manifold is available in 2 different sizes (Sec 10)

Fig. 6.5 Secondary air supply system (Sec 11)

For 49 States

For California

➤ Blow-by gas

⇨ Fresh air

Fig. 6.6 Crankcase emission control system (Sec 14)

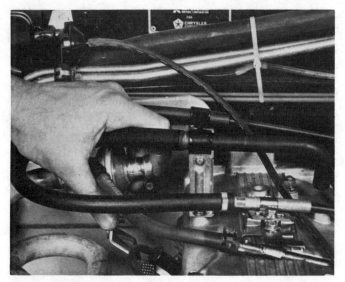

12.2 To check the operation of the SAS reed valve, place your finger over the valve inlet with the engine running

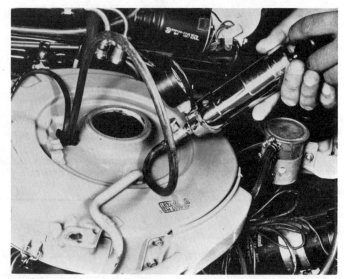

16.5 Applying a vacuum to the Heated Air Intake System temperature sensor

16.6 Applying a vacuum directly to the vacuum motor

18.2 The solenoid valve is located on the left fender well, immediately behind the battery

21.7 Disconnect the green-striped hose from the thermo valve

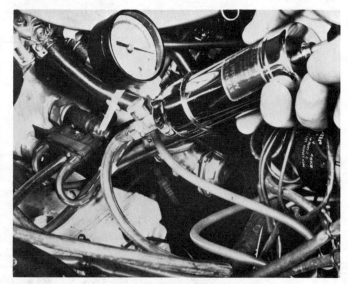

21.8 Applying a vacuum to the thermo valve

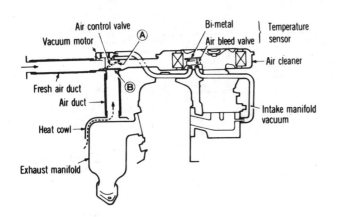

Fig. 6.7 Heated air intake system (Sec 15)

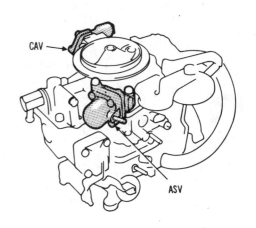

Fig. 6.8 Deceleration device components (Sec 17)

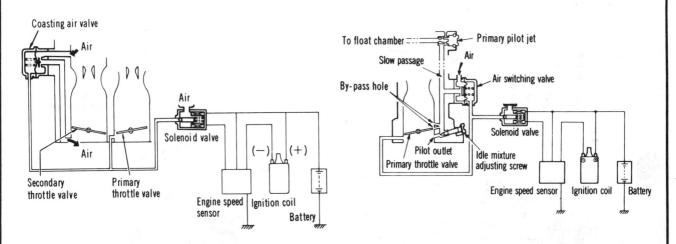

Fig. 6.9 Coasting air valve operation (Sec 17)

Fig. 6.10 Air switching valve operation (Sec 17)

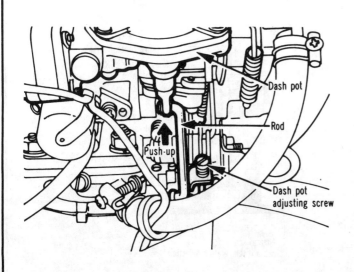

Fig. 6.11 Dash pot adjustment (trucks for Canada only) (Sec 19)

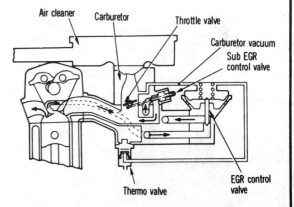

Fig. 6.12 EGR system (trucks for 49 states only) (Sec 20)

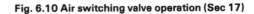

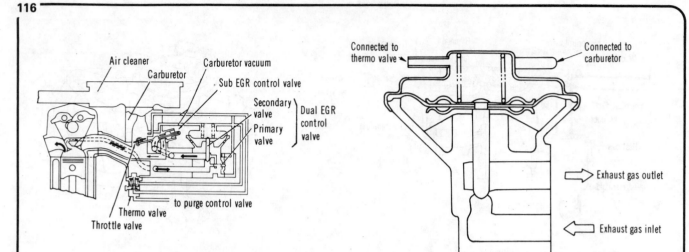

Air cleaner
Carburetor
Carburetor vacuum
Sub EGR control valve
Secondary valve
Primary valve
Dual EGR control valve
to purge control valve
Thermo valve
Throttle valve

Fig. 6.13 EGR system (trucks for California only) (Sec 20)

Connected to thermo valve
Connected to carburetor
Exhaust gas outlet
Exhaust gas inlet

Fig. 6.14 EGR control valve (trucks for 49 states only) (Sec 20)

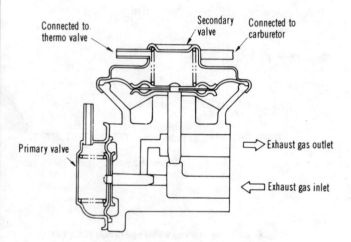

Connected to thermo valve
Secondary valve
Connected to carburetor
Primary valve
Exhaust gas outlet
Exhaust gas inlet

Fig. 6.15 Dual EGR control valve (trucks for California only) (Sec 20)

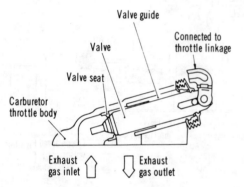

Valve guide
Valve
Valve seat
Connected to throttle linkage
Carburetor throttle body
Exhaust gas inlet
Exhaust gas outlet

Fig. 6.16 Sub-EGR control valve (Sec 20)

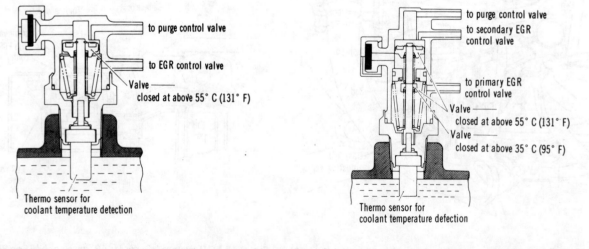

to purge control valve
to EGR control valve
Valve — closed at above 55° C (131° F)
Thermo sensor for coolant temperature detection

Fig. 6.17 Thermo valve (trucks for 49 states only) (Sec 20)

to purge control valve
to secondary EGR control valve
to primary EGR control valve
Valve — closed at above 55° C (131° F)
Valve — closed at above 35° C (95° F)
Thermo sensor for coolant temperature defection

Fig. 6.18 Thermo valve (trucks for California only) (Sec 20)

in the 'Down' (Heat off) position.

4   To check the operation of the sensor and vacuum motor, you will need a hand-type vacuum pump.

5   Remove the air cleaner from the engine (see Chapter 4) and allow it to cool to below 84°F. Hook the vacuum pump to the sensor hose and apply a vacuum to the sensor (photo). The air control valve should be in the 'Up' (Heat on) position. If it is not, check the vacuum motor for proper operation.

6   To check the vacuum motor, apply a vacuum directly to the motor inlet fitting (photo). The air control valve should be in the 'Up' (Heat on) position. If it is not, check to be sure it is not sticking. If the valve moves freely but will not operate properly when a vacuum is applied, the air cleaner housing will have to be replaced.

7   If the vacuum motor operates properly but the valve does not operate when vacuum is applied to the sensor, the sensor should be removed and replaced with a new one.

17 Deceleration device – general description

1   The deceleration device decreases hydrocarbon emissions during vehicle deceleration. It includes the coasting air valve (CAV), the air switching valve (ASV) and the fuel cut-off solenoid, which are built into the carburetor (some 1979 models are not equipped with a CAV).

2   The CAV, which is activated by carburetor ported vacuum, supplies additional air into the intake manifold, leaning the fuel/air mixture.

3   The ASV, which is also activated by carburetor ported vacuum, improves fuel economy by supplying additional air into the idle circuit slow passage.

4   In order to maintain smooth vehicle deceleration, and to prevent stalling, operation of the CAV and ASV is suspended by opening the solenoid valve (when the engine speed sensor detects engine speed at or below a specified value).

18 Deceleration device – checking

1   Start and run the engine at idle speed. It must be at normal operating temperature.

2   Disconnect the solenoid valve connector (photo) to deactivate the solenoid valve. Manifold vacuum will act on the air switching valve, causing the valve to open. If the idle speed falls excessively, or if the engine stalls, the air switching valve and solenoid valve are operating properly. If the idle speed does not change, check the vacuum passages for clogging and check the condition of the air switching valve and solenoid valve.

3   With the engine at idle, battery voltage should be present at the solenoid connector.

4   Increase the engine speed to 1500 rpm. Battery voltage should again be present at the solenoid valve connector. If there is no voltage present, the engine speed sensor is defective.

5   Increase the engine speed to 2500 rpm. Battery voltage should no longer be present at the solenoid valve connector. If voltage is present, the engine speed sensor is defective.

19 Dash pot (trucks for Canada only) – adjustment

1   Carburetors on some Canadian model trucks (automatic transmission only) are equipped with a dash pot, which delays the closing of the throttle valve during vehicle deceleration and reduces the hydrocarbon emissions.

2   Before adjusting the dash pot, make sure the idle speed is set correctly. Use a tachometer connected according to the manufacturer's instructions.

3   Push the dash pot rod up through its entire stroke until it comes to a stop as shown in Fig. 6.11.

4   Check the engine speed (set speed) at this point and compare it to the specifications. If it is not correct, turn the dash pot adjusting screw, as necessary, until the set speed is as specified.

5   Release the dash pot rod and count the number of seconds it takes for the engine speed to drop to 900 rpm. Compare the results to the specifications.

6   If the engine speed drops too quickly, the dash pot should be replaced with a new one.

20 Exhaust gas recirculation system (EGR) – general description

1   The Chrysler mini-truck utilizes an exhaust gas recirculation system (EGR) to reduce oxides of nitrogen in the exhaust.

2   The stringent oxides of nitrogen emission standards require high rates of EGR flow, which adversely affects driveability of the vehicle. To solve this problem, it is necessary to increase EGR flow during high load vehicle operation and decrease EGR flow to improve driveability during low load operation.

3   To accomplish this, two different systems are in use; one for vehicles sold in California and one for vehicles sold in the remaining 49 states. Both systems utilize an EGR control valve, a sub-EGR control valve and a thermal valve.

4   The California system has a dual EGR control valve (primary and secondary), which is controlled by different carburetor vacuums in response to throttle valve openings. The primary EGR valve controls EGR flow during relatively narrow throttle valve openings, while the secondary EGR valve takes over as the throttle valve is opened wider. EGR flow is suspended completely at idle and wide open throttle conditions. The thermal valve, which senses coolant temperature, controls the vacuum applied to the EGR control valve.

5   The 49-state EGR system utilizes a conventional-type EGR valve that is controlled by carburetor vacuum in response to various throttle valve openings. Again, EGR flow is suspended at idle and wide open throttle conditions. The thermal valve controls the vacuum applied to the EGR valve.

6   In both systems, the sub EGR control valve is opened and closed by a linkage connected to the throttle valve. This enables the sub-EGR valve to closely modulate the EGR flow according to the size of the throttle valve opening.

Green stripe hose
connected to thermo valve

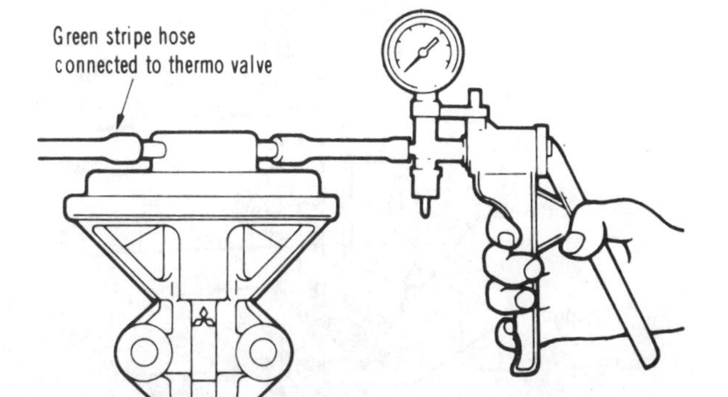

Fig. 6.19 To check for proper operation of the EGR control valve, hook a vacuum pump to the carburetor side of the valve (Sec 21)

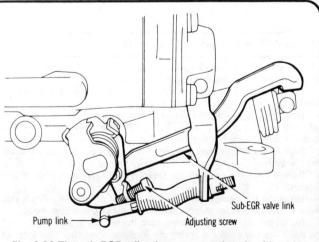

Pump link
Sub-EGR valve link
Adjusting screw

Fig. 6.20 The sub-EGR adjusting screw setting should not be changed (Sec 23)

21 Exhaust gas recirculation system (EGR) – checking

1   To check the EGR system properly, you will need a hand-held vacuum pump.
2   Check all vacuum hoses for cracks and correct installation.
3   Start the engine (it must be completely cool) and run it at idle speed.
4   Touch the underside of the secondary EGR valve diaphragm and increase the engine speed from idle to approximately 2500 rpm. No movement of the secondary EGR diaphragm should be felt. If it does move, which means the secondary EGR valve is opening, replace the thermo valve with a new one.
5   Allow the engine to warm up until the coolant temperature exceeds 131°F.
6   Again, touch the underside of the secondary EGR valve diaphragm and increase the engine speed from idle to approximately 2500 rpm. This time, the secondary EGR diaphragm should move. If it does not move, which means the secondary EGR valve is not opening, inspect the EGR control valve and the thermo valve.
7   To check the thermo valve, disconnect the green-striped hose from the valve (photo).
8   Connect the hand-held vacuum pump to the thermo valve and apply a vacuum (photo). If no vacuum can be held, the thermo valve is good.
9   To check the EGR control valve, disconnect the green-striped hose from the nipple on the carburetor and connect it to the hand-held vacuum pump.
10 Open the sub-EGR valve (by pulling on it by hand) and apply a vacuum to the EGR control valve with the pump.
11 If the idle speed becomes unstable, the EGR valve is operating properly. If the idle speeds remain the same, the valve is not operating properly and it should be replaced with a new one.
12 Pull on the sub-EGR valve and check for smooth operation. If the valve binds, it should be removed from its bore, cleaned thoroughly, lubricated with a small amount of light oil and reinstalled. If it still does not operate smoothly, replace it with a new one.

22 EGR control valve – removal and installation

1   The EGR valve is attached to the lower part of the intake manifold, directly under the carburetor.
2   Mark the vacuum hose and fittings with pieces of numbered tape, then disconnect the vacuum hoses from the EGR valve.
3   Remove the bolts attaching the EGR valve to the intake manifold and the valve can be lifted away. You may have to tap gently on the EGR body with a soft-faced hammer to break the gasket seal.
4   When installing the EGR valve, use a new gasket and tighten the mounting bolts evenly and securely. Also, be sure to install the vacuum hoses properly.

23 Sub-EGR valve – removal and installation

1   The sub-EGR valve is located on the base of the carburetor and is connected by a linkage to the throttle valve.
2   Carefully pry off the spring clip and remove the pin attaching the sub-EGR valve plunger to the linkage.
3   Hold the end of the linkage up and remove the spring and the steel ball from the end of the plunger. These parts are small and easily lost, so don't drop them.
4   Slip off the rubber boot and slide the plunger out of the carburetor throttle body.
5   Before installing the plunger, clean it with solvent to remove any deposits.
6   Lubricate the plunger with a small amount of light oil, slide it into place in the carburetor throttle body and install the rubber boot.
7   Install the steel ball and spring, hold the linkage in place and insert the pin. Carefully slide the spring clip in place, then check for smooth operation of the valve plunger.
8   The sub-EGR adjusting screw (located on the valve linkage) has been preset at the factory and should not be disturbed.

24 Thermal valve – removal and installation

1   The thermal valve is located just in front of the carburetor and is threaded into the coolant passage in the intake manifold.
2   Removal of the thermal valve is quite simple. Pull off the vacuum hoses that are connected to the thermal valve fittings, then unscrew the valve from the manifold.
3   When installing the thermal valve, be sure to use thread-sealing tape on the threads.

25 Exhaust gas recirculation system (trucks for Canada only) – general description

1   All engines built for use in Canada utilize an exhaust gas recirculation system to reduce oxides of nitrogen in the vehicle exhaust.
2   With this system, the exhaust gas is partially recirculated from an exhaust port in the cylinder head, through the EGR control valve, to a port located in the intake manifold below the carburetor.
3   EGR flow is controlled by the EGR control valve and is varied according to engine load. The flow is increased during high load vehicle operation and decreased to preserve driveability of the vehicle during low load operation.
4   With this arrangement, the EGR control valve is activated by carburetor vacuum, drawn from slightly above the throttle valve, so that EGR flow is modulated to attain effective oxides of nitrogen reduction and is suspended at idle and wide-open throttle conditions.
5   The vacuum to be applied on the EGR control valve is controlled by a thermal valve, which senses the coolant temperature and cuts off the vacuum when the engine is cold, and a vacuum valve which responds to vehicle load by detecting engine manifold vacuum.

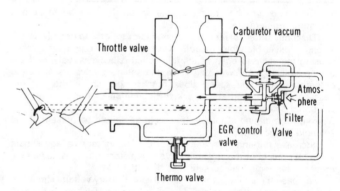

Fig. 6.21 EGR system (trucks for Canada only) (Sec 25)

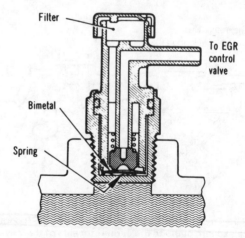

Fig. 6.22 Thermo valve (trucks tor Canada only) (Sec 25)

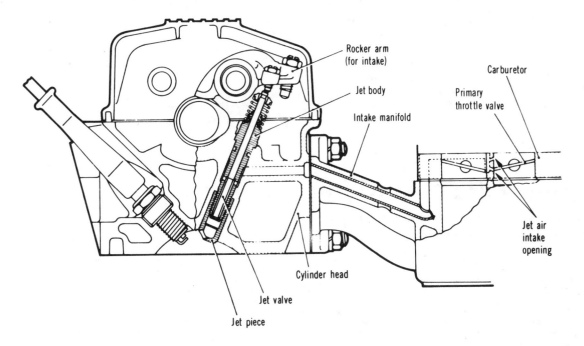

Rocker arm (for intake)

Carburetor

Jet body

Primary throttle valve

Intake manifold

Jet air intake opening

Cylinder head

Jet valve

Jet piece

Fig. 6.23 Jet air system (Sec 27)

26 Exhaust gas recirculation system (trucks for Canada only) – checking

1   Check all vacuum hoses for cracks and proper installation.
2   Start the engine (it must be completely cool) and run it at idle speed. Touch the underside of the EGR control valve diaphragm and increase the engine speed from idle to 2500 rpm. No movement of the diaphragm should be felt. If movement is felt, which means that the EGR valve is opening, check the green-striped vacuum hose to make sure it isn't clogged. If the hose is clear, the thermal valve is most likely defective and should be replaced with a new one.
3   If no movement was felt, allow the engine to warm up until the coolant temperature exceeds 104°F.
4   Repeat the test outlined in Step 2. This time movement of the diaphragm should occur. If no movement is felt, the EGR control valve, the thermal valve and the vacuum hoses should be checked for leaks and other defects.

27 Jet air system – general description

1   The jet air system utilizes an additional inlet valve (jet valve) which provides for air, or a super lean mixture, to be drawn from the air intake into the cylinder. The jet valve is operated by the same cam as the inlet valve. They use a common rocker arm so that the jet valve and the inlet valve open and close simultaneously.
2   On the intake stroke of the engine, fuel/air mixture flows through the intake ports into the combustion chamber. At the same time, jet air is forced into the combustion chamber because of the pressure difference between the jet intake in the throttle bore and the jet valve in the cylinder as the piston moves down. At small throttle openings, there is a large pressure difference, giving the jet air a high velocity. This scavenges the residual gases around the spark plug and creates good ignition conditions. It also produces a strong swirl in the combustion chamber, which lasts throughout the compression stoke and improves flame propagation after ignition, assuring high combustion efficiency and lowering exhaust emissions. As the throttle opening is increased, less jet air is forced in and jet swirl diminishes but the increased flow through the intake valve ensures satisfactory combustion.

28 Jet valve clearance – adjustment

1   Incorrect jet valve clearances will affect the emission levels and could also cause engine troubles.
2   Refer to Chapter 1 for jet valve clearance adjustment procedures.

29 Jet valve – removal, inspection and installation

Jet valve removal, inspection and installation procedures are covered in detail in Chapter 2, *Cylinder head-disassembly/cleaning and inspection/reassembly.*

Chapter 7 Part A Manual transmission

Refer to Chapter 13 for specifications and information related to 1981 thru 1988 models

Contents

Specifications

Shift fork-to-sleeve clearance
1-2 and 3-4 speed .... 0.004 to 0.012 in (0.1 to 0.3 mm)
Overdrive and reverse .... 0.006 to 0.014 in (0.15 to 0.35 mm)

Change lever-to-selector clearance .... 0.004 to 0.012 in (0.1 to 0.3 mm)

Poppet spring free length .... 0.744 in (18.9 mm)

Neutral return spring free length (5-speed only) .... 1.638 in (41.6 mm)

Resistance spring free length (5-speed only) .... 1.091 in (27.7 mm)

Snap-ring-to-main drive pinion bearing clearance .... 0 to .002 in (0 to 0.06 mm)

Main drive pinion bearing snap-ring thicknesses
White .... 0.091 in (2.3 mm)
No color-code .... 0.092 in (2.35 mm)
Red .... 0.094 in (2.4 mm)
Blue .... 0.096 in (2.45 mm)
Yellow .... 0.098 in (2.5 mm)

3-4 speed synchronizer hub end play .... 0 to 0.003 in (0 to 0.08 mm)

3-4 speed synchronizer hub snap-ring thicknesses
No color-code .... 0.085 (2.15 mm)
Yellow .... 0.087 in (2.22 mm)
Green .... 0.090 in (2.29 mm)
White .... 0.093 in (2.36 mm)

Third-speed gear end play .... 0.002 to 0.008 in (0.04 to 0.20 mm)

First- and second-speed gear end play .... 0.002 to 0.008 in (0.04 to 0.20 mm)

Front bearing retainer-to-bearing clearance .... 0 to 0.004 in (0 to 0.1 mm)

Bearing spacer thicknesses
Black .... 0.033 in (0.84 mm)
No color-code .... 0.037 in (0.93 mm)
Red .... 0.040 in (1.02 mm)
White .... 0.044 in (1.11 mm)
Yellow .... 0.047 in (1.2 mm)
Blue .... 0.051 in (1.29 mm)
Green .... 0.054 in (1.38 mm)

Counter reverse gear end play
(4-speed only) .... 0 to 0.003 in (0 to 0.07 mm)

Counter reverse gear snap-ring thicknesses
No color-code .... 0.059 in (1.5 mm)
Red .... 0.063 in (1.6 mm)
Blue .... 0.067 in (1.7 mm)
Green .... 0.073 in (1.85 mm)
Yellow .... 0.079 in (2.0 mm)

Reverse idler gear end play (5-speed only) .... 0.005 to 0.011 in (0.12 to 0.28 mm)

Overdrive gear end play (5-speed only) .... 0.004 to 0.010 in (0.1 to 0.25 mm)

Torque specifications

	ft-lb	(Nm)
Transmission-to-crossmember nuts	15 to 17	(20 to 24)
Crossmember-to-frame bolts	30 to 37	(40 to 50)
Transmission mounting bolts	22 to 30	(30 to 41)
Mainshaft locknut	73 to 94	(98 to 127)
Countershaft gear locknut (5-speed only)	50 to 72	(68.6 to 98.0)
Idler shaft locknut (5-speed only)	14.5 to 43	(19.6 to 58.8)
Idler shaft set screw (4-speed only)	4 to 5	(4.9 to 6.9)
Bottom cover plate bolts	6 to 7	(7.8 to 9.8)
Control lever housing bolts	4 to 5	(4.9 to 6.9)
Drain plug	43	(58.8)
Filler plug	22 to 25	(29.4 to 34.3)

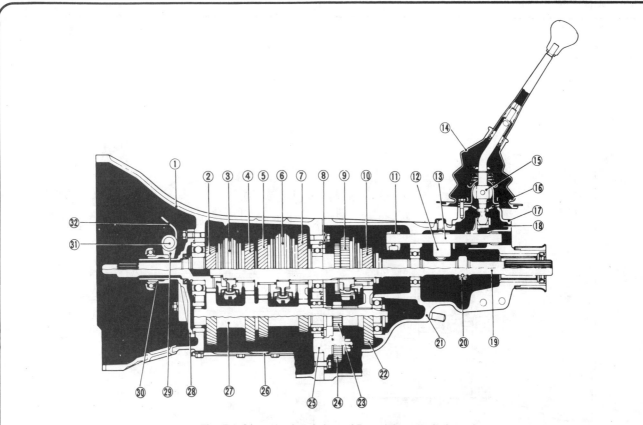

Fig. 7.1 Cross sectional view of 5-speed transmission

1   Transmission case
2   Main drive pinion
3   Synchronizer assy (3-4 speed)
4   3rd speed gear
5   2nd speed gear
6   Synchronizer assy (1-2 speed)
7   1st speed gear
8   Rear bearing retainer
9   Synchronizer assy (overdrive)
10 Overdrive gear
11 Control finger
12 Neutral return finger
13 Control shaft
14 Control lever cover
15 Control lever assy
16 Stopper plate
17 Control housing
18 Change shifter
19 Mainshaft
20 Speedometer drive gear
21 Extension housing
22 Counter overdrive gear
23 Counter reverse gear
24 Reverse idler gear
25 Reverse idler gear shaft
26 Under cover
27 Counter gear
28 Front bearing retainer
29 Clutch shift arm
30 Release bearing carrier
31 Clutch control shaft
32 Return spring

1 General information

1   Chrysler mini-truck is available with either 4-speed or 5-speed manual transmission. Both are conventional in design.
2   Since the two types of transmissions are nearly identical, the various repair procedures are combined in this Chapter. Where differences between the two exist, they are noted in the text.

2 Planning major transmission work

1   Before beginning the transmission disassembly, read through the entire procedure to familiarize yourself with the scope and requirements of the job.
2   One of the biggest problems a beginner will face when dismantling an assembly as complex as a transmission is trying to remember exactly where each part came from. To help alleviate this problem, it may be helpful to draw your own simple diagram or take instant photos during the disassembly process. Laying each part out in the order in which it was removed and tagging parts may also be useful.
3   Try to anticipate which parts may have to be replaced and have them available before beginning. Regardless of broken or badly worn components, there are certain items which must be replaced as a matter of course when the transmission is reassembled. These include gaskets, snap rings, oil seals and sometimes bearings. You will also need some multi-purpose grease and a silicone-type gasket sealer to properly reassemble the transmission.

4   Cleanliness is extremely important when working on a precision piece of equipment such as a transmission. The work area should be kept as clean and free of dirt and dust as possible. Also, adequate space should be available to lay out the various parts as they are removed.

3 Removal and installation

1   Disconnect tthe negative battery cable from the battery.
2   Remove the air cleaner assembly by referring to Chapter 4, then disconnect the starter motor wiring and remove the starter. It is held in place by 2 bolts.
3   Raise the vehicle and set it on jack stands. Place a drain pan under the transmission, remove the drain plug and allow the transmission oil to drain.
4   Remove the driveshaft as described in Chapter 8.
5   If your vehicle is equipped with a center console, remove the 4 screws that attach it to the vehicle. Loosen the jam nuts on the shift lever and unscrew the shift knob. Lift the console away from the lever and unplug the electrical connector behind the console.
6   Remove the 3 screws that attach the shifter boot retainer plate to the tunnel. Lift off the retainer plate and pull back the rubber boot. It has a lip that fits over the sheetmetal of the tunnel; take care not to tear it as you pull the boot back.
7   At this point, if the transmission is a 5-speed, place the shift lever in the first gear position. If it is a 4-speed, place it in the second gear position.

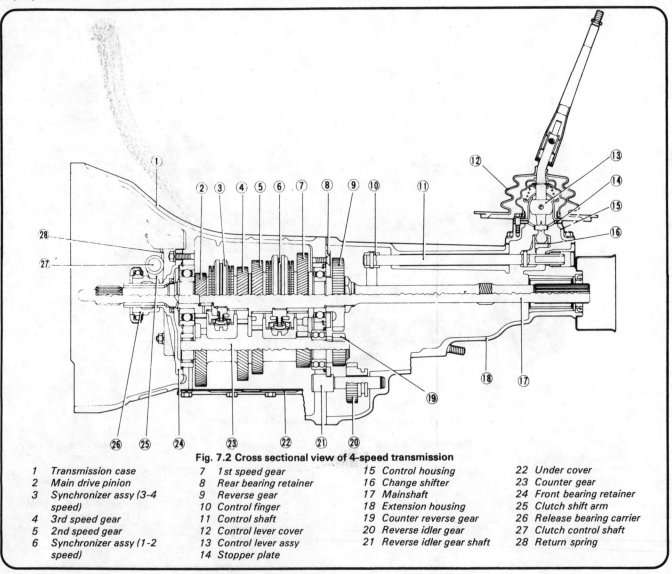

Fig. 7.2 Cross sectional view of 4-speed transmission

1 Transmission case	7 1st speed gear	15 Control housing	22 Under cover
2 Main drive pinion	8 Rear bearing retainer	16 Change shifter	23 Counter gear
3 Synchronizer assy (3-4 speed)	9 Reverse gear	17 Mainshaft	24 Front bearing retainer
4 3rd speed gear	10 Control finger	18 Extension housing	25 Clutch shift arm
5 2nd speed gear	11 Control shaft	19 Counter reverse gear	26 Release bearing carrier
6 Synchronizer assy (1-2 speed)	12 Control lever cover	20 Reverse idler gear	27 Clutch control shaft
	13 Control lever assy	21 Reverse idler gear shaft	28 Return spring
	14 Stopper plate		

4.3a Carefully unscrew the back-up light switch from the extension housing

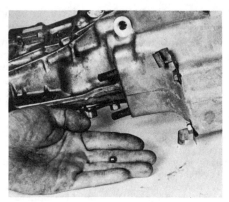

4.3b Don't forget to remove the steel ball from the back-up light switch hole

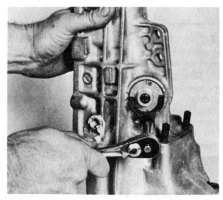

4.4 Note the position of the marks, then remove the speedometer-driven gear

4.5a Remove the 8 bolts attaching the intermediate shifter cover to the extension housing

4.5b Remove the sealant covering the 2 neutral-return plunger plugs (5-speed only)

4.6a Remove the 8 bolts attaching the extension housing to the main transmission body

4.6b Pull straight back on the extension housing to separate it from the transmission. (Don't forget to pull the change shifter back and to the left first)

4.10a Remove the snap-ring from the backside of the rear bearing on the mainshaft (5-speed only)

4.10b Slip the rear bearing off the mainshaft

4.11a Peel off the sealant covering the 3 poppet-spring plug holes on the right side of the case

4.11b Remove the plug, spring and steel ball from each hole

4.12 Remove the 12 bolts attaching the bottom cover plate to the transmission

8   Remove the 3 bolts attaching the shift lever assembly to the transmission and carefully lift out the lever. Plug or cover the hole with a clean rag.

9   Disconnect the speedometer cable where it enters the transmission. Bend back the retaining strap that holds the speedometer cable housing to the frame crossmember and pull the speedometer cable away from the engine and transmission. Lay it on top of the left frame rail to keep it out of the way.

10 Push forward on the parking brake lever and disengage the cable from the lever. Loosen the parking brake cable housing clamp in front of the frame crossmember and slide the cable housing forward to free it from the support bracket on the crossmember. Lay the cable on top of the left frame rail to keep it out of the way. Remove the pin attaching the rear parking brake cable balancer to the parking brake lever.

11 Unplug the back-up light switch wiring harness (just behind the steering box). Disconnect the clutch cable from the clutch control lever at the transmission bellhousing. Back off the clutch cable adjustor and put as much free play as possible in the cable. Pull the rubber dust cover from the end of the clutch cable and slip the cable through the mounting boss on the transmission bellhousing. Lay the clutch cable on top of the left frame rail to keep it out of the way.

12 Remove the splash shield from the front of the transmission. It is attached to the engine with 2 bolts and to the transmission with 2 bolts.

13 Remove the bolt attaching the exhaust pipe bracket to the transmission.

14 Securely support the rear of the engine and then remove the bolts that attach the transmission bellhousing to the engine block.

15 Remove the 2 nuts that attach the transmission to the transmission support crossmember.

16 Support the transmission with a sturdy jack (preferably one equipped with wheels or castors). Remove the 12 bolts that attach the transmission support crossmember to the frame and lift the crossmember out from under the vehicle.

17 Carefully withdraw the transmission straight back and away from the engine by moving the transmission supporting jack toward the rear of the vehicle. It would be very helpful to have an assistant at this point. You must pull the transmission straight back until it is completely free from the engine or damage to the input shaft may result.

18 Slowly lower the jack and move the transmission out from under the vehicle.

19 Installation would basically be the reverse of removal. Be sure to check the clutch disc to make sure it is centered (see Chapter 8) before sliding the transmission into place. Also, before installlation, apply a coat of lithium-based grease to the end of the transmission input shaft and the splines.

20 With the help of an assistant, line up the clutch with the transmission input shaft. Make sure the engine and transmission are in a straight line, not angled in relation to each other. Carefully slide the transmission forward until the bellhousing contacts the engine block. To properly engage the clutch disc and the transmission input shaft, you may have to rotate the crankshaft slightly (with a wrench on the bolt holding the pulley to the front of the crankshaft). Do not force the input shaft into the clutch. If the transmission does not move forward smoothly, either the clutch disc/input shaft splines are not lined up, or the transmission is cocked at an angle.

21 Once the transmission is in place, support it securely and tighten all of the mounting bolts to the specified torque.

22 Don't forget to fill the transmission to the proper level with the recommended lubricant.

23 When installing the shift lever assembly, if the transmission is a 5-speed, the lever must be in the first gear position. If it is a 4-speed, the lever must be in the second gear position.

24 Be sure to adjust the clutch as described in Chapter 8.

4.14a Release the locking tabs before attempting to remove the nuts

4.14b Remove the large nuts from the ends of the main and countershafts

4.15 Remove the counter overdrive gear and the ball bearing from the countershaft with a gear puller (5-speed only)

4.17a Using a ⅜ in pin punch, drive out the 1-2 and 3-4 speed shift fork roll pins

4.17b Pull out the 1-2 and 3-4 speed shift rails

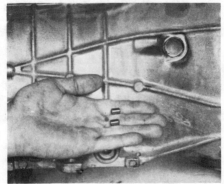

4.17c An interlock plunger is installed between each shift rail in the wall of the transmission case

4 Disassembly

1 Before starting to disassemble the transmission, clean the exterior with a water-soluble degreaser. This will make it easier to handle and will reduce the possibility of getting dirt and other contaminants inside the transmission.

2 Remove the clutch release mechanism from the transmission bellhousing by referring to Chapter 8.

3 Release the back-up light switch wiring loom from the 2 retaining clips and unscrew the back-up light switch from the extension housing (photo). When turning the switch, take care that the wiring harness is not twisted or damaged. There is a metal crush-type seal between the switch and the extension housing that should also be removed. There is a steel ball in the switch hole; if it does not fall out, remove it with a pencil-type magnet or other suitable tool (photo).

4 Scribe a line across the speedometer drive gear case and the extension housing (or record the position of the factory-supplied marks), then remove the locking plate and the speedometer-driven gear from the housing (photo).

5 Remove the 8 bolts attaching the intermediate shifter cover to the extension housing (photo) and lift off the cover. You may have to tap it gently with a soft-faced hammer to break the gasket seal. Remove the sealant covering the 2 neutral return plunger plugs (5-speed only) (photo). Back out the plugs (by turning them in a counterclockwise direction) to release the neutral return plungers. Withdraw the spring protruding from the top right side of the extension housing. Beneath the spring is a small steel ball, which may fall into the extension housing when the right-side neutral return plunger is removed from the case.

6 Remove the 8 bolts attaching the extension housing to the main transmission body (photo). Pull the change shifter back, and to the left, and remove the extension housing from the main transmission body (photo). You may have to tap gently with a soft-faced hammer to break the gasket seal.

7 Major differences between the 4-speed and the 5-speed transmissions involve the components installed at the rear ends of the main and countershafts. These components are exposed when the extension housing is removed.

8 The 4-speed has fewer components, whose removal and re-installation is quite straightforward, so it is not covered separately. It may be helpful to take a close look and draw a simple sketch before disassembly, to prevent difficulties later.

9 The 5-speed is equipped with a number of parts not installed on the 4-speed. Their removal and installation is covered in detail in the text.

10 Remove the snap-ring (photo) from the back side of the rear bearing on the transmission mainshaft (5-speed only). Remove the bearing, slip it off the mainshaft (photo) and remove the snap-ring from the front of the bearing.

11 Peel off the sealant covering the 3 poppet spring plug holes on the right rear side of the main transmission case (photo) and remove the poppet spring plugs. Withdraw the springs and the steel balls from the poppet spring holes.

12 Turn the transmission upside down, remove the 12 bolts attaching the bottom cover plate to the main transmission housing (photo) and lift off the plate.

13 Place the 1-2 speed shift rail in the neutral position, then pull out the reverse shift rail/fork assembly along with the reverse idler gear (4-speed only).

14 Remove the large nuts at the rear ends of the main and countershafts (photo). You will have to release the locking tab from the keyways in the slots before these nuts can be turned. The countershaft on the 4-speed transmission does not have a nut. In order to keep the shafts from turning while the nuts are loosened, you must simultaneously engage second gear and reverse gear (by pushing forward on the upper and lower shift rails) in the 5-speed transmission, and first gear and third gear in the 4-speed transmission.

15 Using an approved puller, simultaneously remove the counter overdrive gear and the ball-bearing from the countershaft (5-speed only) (photo). Then remove the spacer and the counter reverse gear.

16 Remove the snap-ring, the counter reverse gear and the spacer from the rear of the countershaft (4-speed only).

17 Using a $\frac{3}{16}$ in pin punch, drive out the 1-2 and 3-4 speed shift fork roll pins (photo). Pull out the 1-2 and 3-4 speed shift rails through the rear of the transmission case (photo). An interlock plunger is installed between each shift rail in the wall of the transmission case; do not forget to remove them (photo).

18 Noting their position to ease reassembly, remove the 1-2 and 3-4 shift forks from the main transmission case.

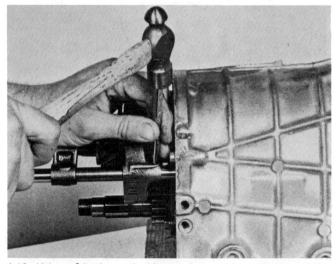

4.19a Using a $\frac{3}{16}$ in pin punch, drive out the overdrive and reverse shift fork roll pins (5-speed only)

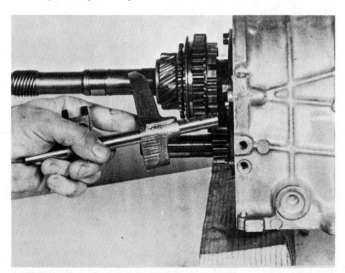

4.19b Pull out the shift rail with the fork attached

Fig. 7.3 Remove the plugs holding the neutral-return plungers and springs in place (5-speed only) (Sec 4)

Change shifter

Plug

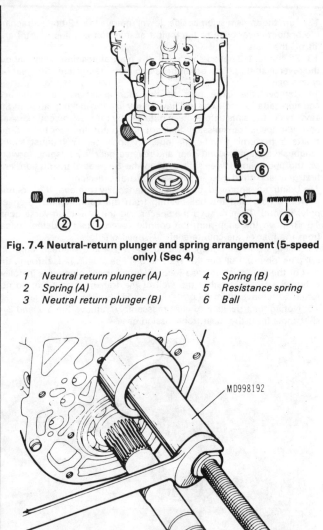

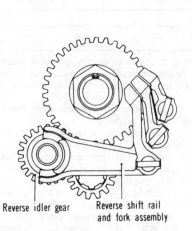

Fig. 7.4 Neutral-return plunger and spring arrangement (5-speed only) (Sec 4)

1	Neutral return plunger (A)	4	Spring (B)
2	Spring (A)	5	Resistance spring
3	Neutral return plunger (B)	6	Ball

Reverse idler gear   Reverse shift rail and fork assembly

Fig. 7.5 Place the 1-2 speed shift rail in the neutral position, then pull out the reverse shift rail/fork assembly along with the reverse idler gear (4-speed only) (Sec 4)

MD998192

Fig. 7.6 Removing the counter rear bearing (Sec 4)

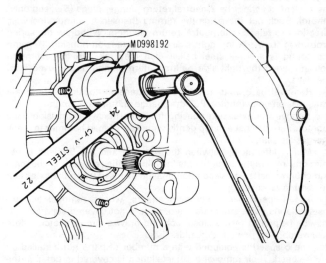

MD998192

Fig. 7.7 Removing the counter front bearing (Sec 4)

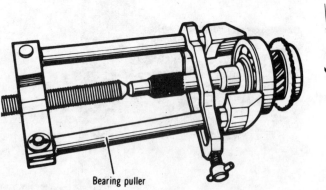

Bearing puller

Fig. 7.8 Removing the bearing from the main drive pinion (Sec 4)

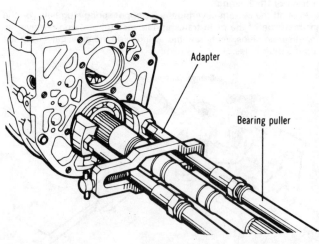

Adapter

Bearing puller

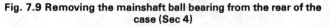

Fig. 7.9 Removing the mainshaft ball bearing from the rear of the case (Sec 4)

19 Using a $\frac{3}{16}$ in pin punch, drive out the overdrive and reverse shift fork roll pin (5-speed only) (photo). Pull out the overdrive and reverse shift rail with the shift fork attached (photo).
20 Remove the overdrive gear bearing and sleeve assembly from the mainshaft (5-speed only). You will have to use a hammer and punch to tap gently on the outer circumference of the sleeve, as you rotate the shaft, until the sleeve bearing and gear assembly can be slipped off (photos). Remove the overdrive gear synchronizer ring and slide the overdrive synchronizer assembly, the large washer and the spacer off the splines on the mainshaft (5-speed only) (photos).
21 Slide the reverse gear off of the mainshaft (4-speed only).
22 Remove the cotter key and nut from the end of the reverse idler gear shaft (photo) and slip the washer, the gear and the roller bearing off of the shaft (5-speed only).
23 Remove the rear bearing retainer and the reverse idler gear plate from the main transmission case (photos). Using a suitable punch, and working from inside the car, carefully drive the reverse idler gear shaft out of the main transmission case (5-speed only) (photo).
24 Remove the 6 nuts attaching the front bearing retainer to the main transmission case (photo). Remove the retainer and slip the spacer off of the shaft (photo).
25 With the counter gear pressed to the rear, remove the rear bearing snap-ring (photo). Using the bearing puller (special tool No MD-998192), or other suitable bearing puller, remove the counter rear bearing. Remove the snap-ring from the countershaft front bearing. Using the same bearing puller, pull out the front countershaft bearing (photo) and slip the counter gear out of the main transmission case toward the front (photo).
26 Remove the main drive pinion and bearing assembly through the front of the main transmission case (photo). To separate the bearing from the main drive pinion, remove the 2 snap-rings and pull the bearing using special tool No MD-998056, or another suitable puller. Pull off the main drive pinion-to-mainshaft bearing (photo). Remove the synchronizer ring from the mainshaft (photo). Using special tools numbered MD-998056 and MD-998056-10, remove the mainshaft ball-bearing from the rear of the main transmission cases. Remove the mainshaft assembly from the case, toward the front (photo).
27 Disassemble the mainshaft gears and bearings in the following order: using the previously mentioned puller, remove the first-speed gear. This will also remove the inner row of ball-bearings and their race from the rear of the mainshaft. Slip off the 1-2 speed synchronizer, the second speed gear and the roller bearing from the rear of the mainshaft. Remove the snap-ring from the forward end of the mainshaft, then remove the 3-4 speed synchronizer, the third speed gear, the roller bearing and the sleeve.
28 From the top of the extension housing (using a $\frac{3}{16}$ in pin punch) drive the roll pins out of the control shaft stabilizer tabs and the control shaft shifter receiver (photo). Pull the control shaft forward and out of the extension housing.

---

5 Inspection

1 Inspect the disassembled parts after cleaning them with solvent and drying them thoroughly. Repair or replace any parts that are found to be defective.

Transmission case and extension housing
2 Check the transmission case and extension housing for cracks and damage, especially at the bearing outer race bosses. Small nicks and burrs can be removed with a fine file.

Mainshaft
3 Check the mainshaft for worn or damaged gear mounting areas and worn or damaged splines. Check the first speed gear and overdrive gear spacer bushing for damage and wear.

Main drive gear
4 On the main drive gear assembly, check the front end outer diameter and the inner diameter of the needle bearing contact areas for damage and wear. Check the synchronizer cone surfaces for wear and damage. Check the splines for wear and damage and check the fit of the clutch disc on the shaft. It should move freely on the splines, but must not be excessively loose.

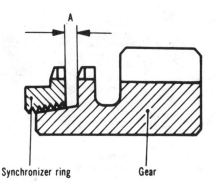

Fig. 7.10 Checking the synchronizer ring-to-gear clearance (A) (Sec 5)

Gears
5 Check all gears for worn and damaged teeth. Check the inner diameter and both ends of the each gear for wear and damage. Also, check the contact surface of the synchronizer cone for wear and damage.

Synchronizer rings
6 Check the gear teeth and cone inside diameter for wear and damage (photo). With the synchronizer rings assembled to their mating gears, check the synchronizer ring-to-gear clearance. If the clearance is greater than specified, replace the synchronizer ring.

Synchronizer sleeve and hub
7 With the hub and sleeve assembled, see if the sleeve slides smoothly. Also, check for excessive looseness in the direction of rotation. If either part is defective, both the hub and sleeve must be replaced as an assembly.

Synchronizer piece and spring
8 Check the synchronizer piece for wear and damage, especially at the projection. Check the springs for deterioration and cracks (photo).

Reverse idler gear and shaft
9 Inspect the teeth and both sides of the gear for wear and damage. Check the shaft for cracks, evidence of seizure and wear.

Shift forks, rails and selectors
10 Check the clearance between the shift fork and the groove in the synchronizer and compare it to the specifications. Inspect the poppet ball slots in the rails for wear. Check the change lever-to-selector clearance and compare it to the specifications.

Needle and ball bearings
11 Check the needle bearings for roller surface damage such as pitting, cracks and scoring. Assemble the needle bearings and gears on their respective shafts and check to see if they rotate smoothly and quietly. Inspect all ball-bearings for wear and damage. See if they rotate smoothly and quietly. If there is any doubt as to the condition of a bearing, replace it.

Poppet springs and plungers
12 Inspect the interlock plungers for wear and damage. Check the forward end of the neutral return plunger for wear. Also, check the resistance ball slot for wear. Check the poppet and neutral return springs for cracks. Measure the springs and compare the results to the specifications.

Control lever
13 Check the upper and lower levers for chatter marks and the stop plate for wear. Inspect the plastic bushing in the lower end of the lever. If it is deformed or worn, replace it. Check the rubber boot for damage and make sure the lever operates smoothly.

4.20a Remove the overdrive gear bearing and sleeve assembly from the mainshaft (5-speed only) by tapping gently on the outer circumference of the sleeve

4.20b The overdrive gear assembly

4.20c The overdrive bearing

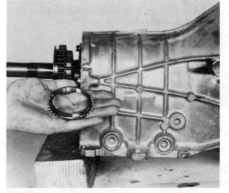

4.20d The overdrive gear synchronizer ring

4.20e The overdrive synchronizer assembly

4.22 Remove the cotter key and nut from the end of the reverse idler gear shaft (5-speed only)

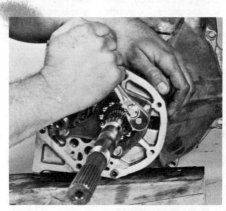

4.23a Remove the rear bearing retainer

4.23b Remove the reverse idler gear plate (5-speed only)

4.23c Using a large punch, and working from inside the case, carefully drive out the reverse idler gear shaft (5-speed only)

4.24a Remove the 6 nuts attaching the front bearing retainer to the case

4.24b Remove the retainer and the spacer

6 Reassembly

1 As was previously mentioned, be sure to wash all parts in solvent and dry them thoroughly before beginning reassembly. Be sure to use new gaskets, seals and roll pins. It is not advisable to reuse snap-rings. When an old snap-ring must be reused, make certain it is not bent. Straighten it, if necessary, so that it can be installed securely. Lubricate all bearings and any other sliding and rotating parts with multi-purpose grease before reassembly. Also, apply a layer of grease to all oil seal lips.

2 Install the ball-bearings onto the main drive pinion using the main drive gear bearing installer (special tool No. MD-998029) or other suitable bearing driver. Do not hammer on the outer bearing race, as damage to the bearing will result.

3 After installing the bearing, select a snap-ring that will provide the specified clearance between the snap-ring and the bearing (a list of available snap-ring thicknesses is included in the Specifications Section) and install it into place on the main drive pinion. Measure the clearance by slipping a feeler gauge between the snap-ring and the inner race of the bearing (photo).

4 Install the mainshaft components in the following order: assemble the 3-4 speed and 1-2 speed synchronizers. The front and rear ends of the synchronizer sleeve and hub can be identified as shown in Figure 11. The synchronizer spring can also be installed as shown in Figure 11. Slip the needle bearing, the third speed gear, the synchronizer ring and the 3-4 speed synchronizer assembly onto the mainshaft from the front end. Be careful not to confuse the front and rear ends of the synchronizer assembly. Install a snap-ring of the proper size, so that the 3-4 speed synchronizer hub end play will be within the specified tolerance (photo). A list of available snap-ring thicknesses is included in the Specifications Section. Check the third speed gear end play with a feeler gauge. Install the needle bearing, the second speed gear, the synchronizer assembly, the bearing sleeve, the needle bearing, the first speed gear and the bearing spacer onto the mainshaft from the rear end. With the bearing spacer pushed forward, check the second and first speed gear end play with a feeler gauge (photo).

5 Slide the mainshaft assembly into the transmission case and insert the mainshaft center bearing outer race into place in the case. Assemble the rear ball-bearings and inner race onto the mainshaft.

6 Install the needle bearing assembly and the synchronizer ring into place on the front of the mainshaft (make sure that the synchronizer pieces line up with the slots in the synchronizer ring).

7 Install the main drive pinion into place in the front of the main transmission case.

8 Install the countershaft into the transmission case. It may be necessary to slide the rear part of the mainshaft to the back of the case to provide enough clearance to install the countershafts.

9 Place the snap-ring in the groove of the countershaft front bearing outer race.

10 Slip the needle bearing into the countershaft front bearing outer race, then install the outer race into the transmission case. Drive it into place by tapping carefully with a soft-faced hammer.

11 Install the snap-ring on the countershaft rear bearing outer race, then seat the countershaft rear bearing in place in the transmission case using the bearing installer (special tool No MD-998199) or other suitable tool. Push the countershaft to the rear of the case as the bearing is installed.

12 Remove the lip seal from the front bearing retainer housing and install a new seal using special tool No MD-998200, or other suitable seal driver.

13 The front bearing retainer must be installed temporarily to check the retainer-to-front bearing clearance.

14 Lay a small piece of type PB-1 Plastigage across the outer race of the bearing. Install the spacer and the retainer, using a new gasket (a small amount of grease should hold the spacer in place in the retainer). Tighten the retainer mounting nuts to the specified torque, then remove the retainer and compare the width of the Plastigage material to the chart on the Plastigage package to obtain the clearance.

15 Compare the measured clearance to the specifications. If the clearance is greater than specified, replace the spacer with a thicker one (a list of available spacer thicknesses is included in the Specifications Section).

16 Once the bearing-to-retainer clearance has been checked and properly adjusted, coat both sides of the gasket with a silicone-type gasket sealer, lubricate the lip seal and install the retainer. Use new lock washers and tighten the mounting nuts to the specified torque.

17 Install the rear bearing retainer in place on the main transmission case and tighten the attaching bolts securely. The rear bearing retainer on the 4-speed transmission is held in place by flathead screws. Stake the screw heads to keep the screws from backing out.

18 Slide the reverse idler gear shaft, using the bolts as a guide, into the main transmission case and tighten the bolts securely (5-speed only). Slip the reverse idler gear needle bearing, the reverse idler gear and the thrust washer (with the ground side toward the gear) onto the reverse idler gear shaft. Thread on the locknut and tighten it to the specified torque. Line up the hole in the shaft with one of the slots in the nut and install a new cotter pin (photo).

19 Check the reverse idler gear end play with a feeler gauge and compare it to the specification (5-speed only) (photo).

20 Install the reverse gear onto the mainshaft (4-speed only). Tighten the locknut to the specified torque, then stake the locking collar on the nut into the keyway on the mainshaft with a centerpunch. Remember, the transmission must be simultaneously engaged in first and third gear to tighten or loosen the mainshaft nut.

21 Assemble the over drive synchronizer (5-speed only). The long flat on the synchronizer piece must be facing forward. Make sure that the synchronizer piece engages the slot in the synchronizer ring. The spring can be installed in a manner similar to the installation of the 3-4 and 1-2 speed synchronizer spring.

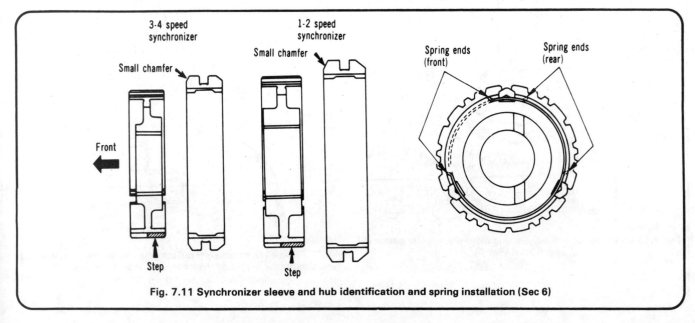

Fig. 7.11 Synchronizer sleeve and hub identification and spring installation (Sec 6)

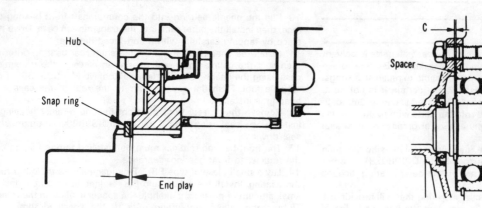

Fig. 7.12 Synchronizer hub end play (Sec 6)

Fig. 7.13 Front bearing retainer-to-bearing clearance (C) (Sec 6)

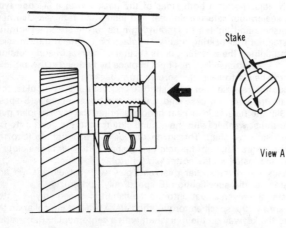

Fig. 7.14 The rear bearing retainer on the 4-speed transmission is held in place with flat head screws. Stake the screw heads with a center punch to keep the screws from backing out (Sec 6)

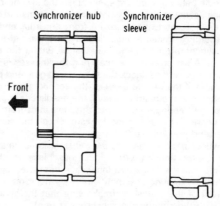

Fig. 7.15 Synchronizer hub and sleeve identification (5-speed only) (Sec 6)

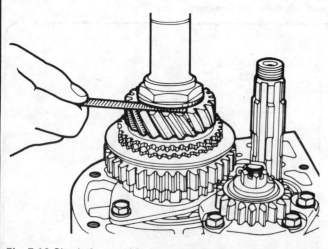

Fig. 7.16 Check the overdrive gear end play with a feeler gauge (5-speed only) (Sec 6)

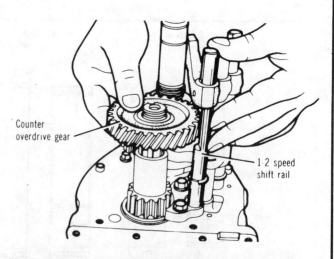

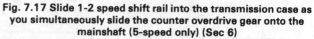

Fig. 7.17 Slide 1-2 speed shift rail into the transmission case as you simultaneously slide the counter overdrive gear onto the mainshaft (5-speed only) (Sec 6)

22 Install the spacer, the stop plate, the overdrive synchronizer assembly, the overdrive gear bearing sleeve, the needle bearing, the synchronizer ring and the overdrive gear onto the mainshaft from the rear end (5-speed only). Thread the locknut onto the mainshaft and tighten it to the specified torque.

23 Check the overdrive gear end play with a feeler gauge and compare it to the specifications. Stake the locking collar on the locknut into the keyway on the mainshaft with a centerpunch.

24 Install the first spacer, the counter reverse gear and the second spacer onto the countershaft. Slip the 1-2 speed and the 3-4 speed shift forks into their respective synchronizer sleeves inside the main transmission case (5-speed only).

25 Slip the spacer and the counter reverse gear onto the rear end of the countershaft (4-speed only). Install a snap-ring that will provide the specified amount of counter reverse gear end play onto the countershaft (a list of available snap-ring thicknesses is included in the Specifications Section). Measure the end play by slipping a feeler gauge between the counter reverse gear and the snap-ring.

26 Slide the 1-2 shift rail into the main transmission case from the rear as you simultaneously slide the counter overdrive gear onto the countershaft from the rear (5-speed only). The counter overdrive gear must fit into the notch ground into the shift rail.

27 Slip the 1-2 shift rail through the holes in the shift fork and into the recess in the front of the transmission case (5-speed only). Install the roll pin through the 1-2 speed shift fork and the 1-2 shift rail. Make sure that the slot in the roll pin is installed axially to the shift rail.

28 Slip the reverse/overdrive shift fork into place on its synchronizer sleeve. Slide the reverse/overdrive shift rail through the shift fork and into the hole in the transmission case. Install the roll pin into the shift fork and reverse/overdrive shift rail. Again, make sure that the slot in the roll pin is installed axially to the shift rail.

29 Slide the interlock plungers into position in the transmission case end (between the shift rails). You may have to use some light grease to hold them in position.

30 Slip the 3-4 shift rail through the reverse/overdrive shift fork, the rear of the transmission case, the two inside shift forks and into the recess in the front of the transmission case (5-speed only). Install the roll pin into the 3-4 speed shift fork and the 3-4 shift rail.

31 Install the 1-2 and 3-4 speed shift forks into their respective synchronizer sleeves inside the main transmission case (4-speed only). Insert the 1-2 and 3-4 speed shift rails into the transmission case and through the shift forks. Install the roll pins in the shift forks and rails (make sure that the slots in the roll pins are installed axially to the shift rails).

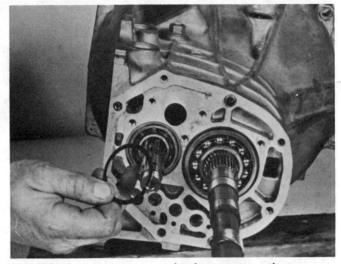

4.25a With the counter gear pressed to the rear, remove the rear bearing snap-ring

4.25b The countershaft front bearing

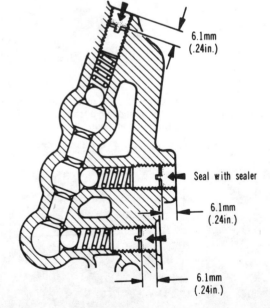

Fig. 7.18 The poppet-spring plugs must be threaded into the case until the distance from the plug head to the top of the hole is exactly as specified (threading the plugs in incorrectly will result in improper gearshift operation) (Sec 6)

6.1mm (.24in.)

Seal with sealer

6.1mm (.24in.)

6.1mm (.24in.)

4.25c Slip the counter gear out of the case toward the front

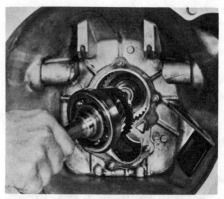

4.26a Remove the main drive pinion and bearing assembly through the front of the case

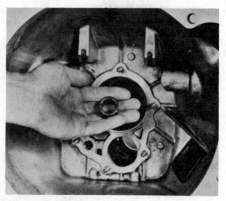

4.26b Pull off the main drive pinion-to-mainshaft bearing

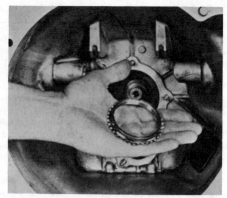

4.26c Remove the synchronizer ring from the mainshaft

4.26d Remove the mainshaft assembly from the case toward the front

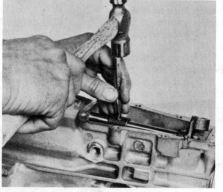

4.28 Drive the roll pins out of the control shaft stabilizer tabs and the shifter receiver

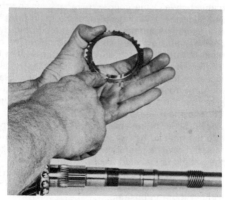

5.6 Check the inside diameter of the synchronizer rings for evidence of wear

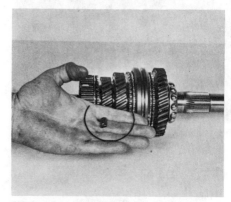

5.8 Synchronizer piece and spring

6.3 Measure the clearance between the snap-ring and inner race when installing the bearing on the main drive pinion

6.4a Check the 3-4 speed synchronizer hub end play by slipping a feeler gauge between the snap-ring and hub

6.4b With the bearing spacer pushed forward, check the second and first speed gear end play with a feeler gauge

6.18 Install a new cotter pin in the reverse idler gear locknut and shaft (5-speed only)

6.19 Check the reverse idler gear end play with a feeler gauge (5-speed only)

32 Install the counter rear bearing on the end of the countershaft (5-speed only). Thread on the retaining nut and tighten it to the specified torque. Remember that the transmission must be in reverse and second gear simultaneously in order to tighten the nut on the end of the countershaft.

33 Using a centerpunch, stake the locking collar on the locknut intto the keyway on the countershaft.

34 Simultaneously slide the reverse shift rail/fork assembly and the reverse idler gear into place (4-speed only).

35 Insert the 3 balls and the 3 poppet springs into each shift rail. (The small end of the spring must be against the steel ball). Thread the plugs into the transmission case and tighten them until the head of the plug is at the specified distance below the end of the hole in the transmission case (see Fig. 7.18). After installation, seal the plug head with silicone-type gasket sealer.

36 Install the inner snap-ring, the ball-bearings and the outer snap-rings onto the rear end of the mainshaft. Use special tool No MD-998199, or a similar type bearing installer.

37 Using a new gasket and gasket sealant, install the extension housing onto the rear of the main transmission case. When installing the housing, turn the change shifter down and to the left. Apply a thread sealant to each bolt, then install and tighten them to the specified torque.

38 Apply a thin coat of silicone-type gasket sealer to the outside of the speedometer drive gear sleeve. Install the speedometer drive gear assembly into the extension housing. (Be sure to line up the mating marks). Make sure the gears are properly meshed before installing the lock plate and tightening the bolts.

39 Install the neutral-return plungers, the springs and the plugs in each side of the extension housing. (The short plunger must be installed on the left side). Tighten the plugs until the ends are flush with the surface of the extension housing, then seal the plug heads with a silicone-type gasket sealer.

40 Install the resistance spring and ball into position from the top of the extension housing. **Caution**: *The spring and the ball are held in place by the top cover and will fall out if the transmission is turned upside down before the cover is installed.*

41 Using a new gasket and gasket sealant, install the top cover onto the extension housing. Tighten the 8 attaching bolts securely.

42 Insert the steel ball into the back-up light switch hole (use grease to hold it in place). Apply sealant to its threads, then install the back-up light switch into the bottom of the extension housing. Take care not to damage the wiring as you thread the switch into the case and tighten it in position.

43 Place the back-up light switch wiring harness into the 2 retaining clips on the bottom of the transmission case.

44 At this point, it is recommended that you temporarily install the transmission shift lever assembly and check to make sure that the transmission shifts and operates in all forward gears and reverse. Remove the shift lever assembly before proceeding.

45 Plug the hole that the transmission shift lever assembly fits into with a clean rag or paper towel to guard against dropping anything into the transmission.

46 Using a new gasket and gasket sealant, install the transmission bottom cover plate. Tighten the attaching bolts to the specified torque, using a crisscross pattern. Be very careful not to over-tighten the bolts or the gasket will be crushed out and oil leaks will result.

47 Install the clutch release mechanism and release bearing by referring to Chapter 8.

48 Don't forget to fill the transmission to the proper level with the recommended lubricant.

Chapter 7 Part B Automatic transmission

Refer to Chapter 13 for specifications and information related to 1981 thru 1988 models

Contents

Specifications

Pump clearances

Outer rotor-to-case bore .... 0.004 to 0.008 in (0.10 to 0.20 mm)
Outer-to-inner tip .... 0.005 to 0.010 in (0.13 to 0.25 mm)
Rotor end clearance .... 0.001 to 0.003 in (0.026 to 0.076 mm)

Gear train end play .... 0.006 to 0.033 in (0.16 to 0.83 mm)

Input shaft end play .... 0.022 to 0.091 in (0.56 to 2.3 mm)

Rear clutch snap-ring thicknesses
0.060 to 0.062 in (1.53 to 1.57 mm)
0.068 to 0.070 in (1.73 to 1.77 mm)
0.076 to 0.078 in (1.93 to 1.98 mm)

Output shaft (forward end) snap-ring thicknesses
0.040 to 0.044 in (1.02 to 1.11 mm)
0.048 to 0.052 in (1.22 to 1.32 mm)
0.059 to 0.065 in (1.50 to 1.65 mm)

Clutch plate clearances

Front clutch .... 0.077 to 0.122 in (1.96 to 3.09 mm)
Rear clutch .... 0.032 to 0.055 in (0.82 to 1.39 mm)

Band adjustments — Number of turns

Kickdown (front) 3*
Low/reverse (internal) 7.5**

*Backed off from 6.0 ft-lbs (8.1 Nm)
**Backed off from 3.5 ft-lbs (4.6 Nm)

Thrust-washer thicknesses

Reaction shaft support-to-front clutch retainer (1) .... 0.061 to 0.063 in (1.55 to 1.60 mm)
Front clutch-to-rear clutch (2) .... 0.061 to 0.063 in (1.55 to 1.60 mm)
Input shaft-to-output shaft (3)
    No color-code .... 0.052 to 0.054 in (1.32 to 1.37 mm)
    Red .... 0.068 to 0.070 in (1.73 to 1.77 mm)
    Black .... 0.083 to 0.085 in (2.11 to 2.15 mm)
Front annulus support-to-front carrier (4) .... 0.121 to 0.125 in (3.08 to 3.17 mm)
Front carrier-to-driving shell thrust plate (5) .... 0.048 to 0.050 in (1.22 to 1.27 mm)
Driving shell thrust plate (6 and 7) .... 0.034 to 0.036 in (0.87 to 0.91 mm)
Rear carrier-to-driving shell (8) .... 0.048 to 0.050 in (1.22 to 1.27 mm)

Governor pressure
20 to 21 mph	15 psi (103.4 kPa)
35 to 40 mph	40 psi (275.8 kPa)
52 to 57 mph	60 psi (413.7 kPa)

Shift speeds
Shift points (WOT)

1 – 2 upshift	35 to 45 mph
2 – 3 upshift	65 to 75 mph

Kickdown limit (WOT)

3 – 2 downshift	52 to 68 mph
3 – 1 downshift	24 to 34 mph

Converter stall speed
2200 to 2650 rpm

Torque specifications
	ft-lbs	(Nm)
Control rod adjusting locknut	9.4	(12.7)
Control arm-to-selector lever locknut	13 to 17	(18 to 24)
Transmission mounting bolts	22 to 30	(30 to 41)
Starter motor mounting bolts	15 to 22	(20 to 29)
Drive plate-to-torque converter bolts	25 to 30	(34 to 41)
Extension housing bolts	24	(32.3)
Transmission-to-rear crossmember bolts	50	(67.6)
Governor body-to-support bolt	8.3	(11.3)
Kickdown band adjusting screw		
With adapter	3.9 to 4.1	(5.4 to 5.6)
Without adapter	6.0	(8.1)
Kickdown band locknut	35	(47.0)
Kickdown lever shaft plug	12.5	(16.9)
Oil pan bolts	12.5	(16.9)
Oil pump housing bolts	14.6	(19.8)
Output shaft support bolt	12.5	(16.9)
Pressure test take-off plug	9.1	(12.4)
Reaction shaft support bolt	13.3	(18.0)
Reverse band adjusting screw	3.5	(4.6)
Reverse band locknut	30	(40.2)
Speedometer drive clamp screw	8.3	(11.3)
Valve body screw	3.0	(3.9)
Valve body mounting bolt	8.3	(11.3)

7 General information

The automatic transmission is conventional, in that it combines a torque converter and a fully automatic 3-speed gear system.

The torque converter is attached to the crankshaft through a flexible driving plate. Cooling of the converter is accomplished by circulating the transmission fluid through an oil-to-water type cooler, located in the lower tank of the radiator. The torque converter assembly is a sealed unit which cannot be disassembled.

The transmission fluid is filtered by an internal dacron-type filter attached to the lower side of the valve body assembly.

Due to the fact that the transmission receives lubrication only when the engine is running, it is a good practice to always tow a disabled vehicle with a suitable rear-end-supporting dolly or with the driveshaft removed.

8 Diagnosis – general

1   Automatic transmission malfunctions may be caused by 4 general conditions: poor engine performance, improper adjustments, hydraulic malfunctions and mechanical malfunctions. Diagnosis of these problems should always begin by checking the easily accessible variables: fluid level and condition, manual shift linkage adjustment and throttle linkage adjustment. Next, perform a road test to determine whether the problem has been corrected or that more diagnosis is necessary. If the problem persists after the preliminary tests and corrections are completed, additional diagnosis should be done by a dealer-authorized service department or a reputable automotive or transmission repair shop.

9 Fluid check

Refer to Chapter 1 for the procedure to follow when checking the automatic transmission fluid level.

10 Fluid and filter change

Fluid and filter changes are not normally required for average vehicle usage. Vehicles whose operation involves a great deal of stop-and-go driving, such as in heavy city traffic during hot weather (above 90°F), or vehicles used for commercial purposes, should have fluid and filter changes as a part of routine maintenance. Refer to Chapter 1 for the maintenance intervals and procedures to follow.

11 Throttle control linkage – adjustment

1   The throttle control linkage adjustment is very important to proper transmission operation. This adjustment positions a valve which controls shift speed, shift quality and part throttle downshift sensitivity. If the linkage is adjusted so that it is too short, early shifts and slippage between shifts may occur. If the linkage is adjusted so that it is too long, shifts may be delayed and part-throttle downshifts may be very erratic.

2   Start and run the engine until it reaches normal operating temperature. With the carburetor automatic choke disengaged from the fast idle cam, adjust the engine idle speed (by turning the speed adjusting screw) to the specified rpm. Turn off the engine.

3   Loosen the bolt so that rods B and C can slide back and forth easily.

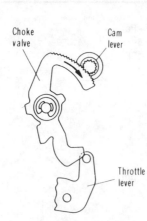

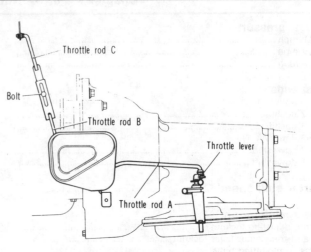

Fig. 7.19 Make sure the automatic choke is fully disengaged before making the throttle control linkage adjustment (Sec 11)

Fig. 7.20 Throttle rod adjustment (Sec 11)

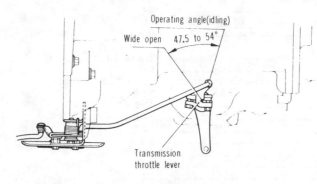

Fig. 7.21 The transmission throttle lever should move from idle to wide-open in a 47.5° to 54° arc (Sec 11)

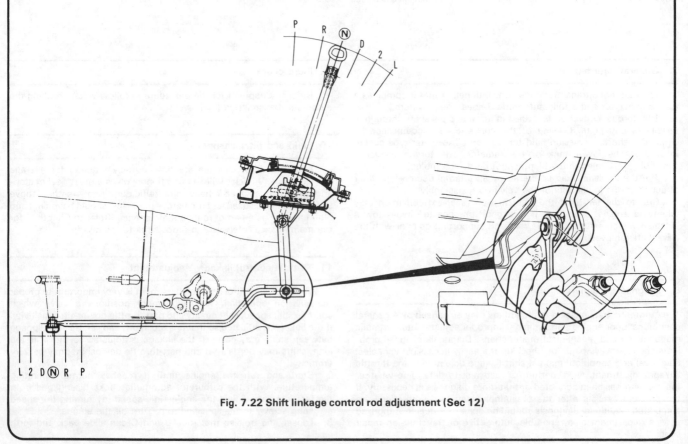

Fig. 7.22 Shift linkage control rod adjustment (Sec 12)

4   Gently push rod A all the way to the rear. Push rod C up so that the throttle is against the stop, then tighten the bolt so that rods B and C cannot move in relation to each other.

5   Open the throttle valve in the carburetor completely and observe the transmission throttle lever. It should move from the idle position to the wide open position in an arc of from 47.5 degrees to 54 degrees.

6   Make sure that when the throttle linkage is returned to the fully closed position (idle) the throttle lever on the transmission also returns to the idle position by the force of its return spring.

12 Shift linkage control rod – adjustment

1   The control rod is adjusted where it connects to the control arm.

2   Loosen the adjusting locknut on the control rod-to-control arm joint.

3   Place the gearshift control lever (on the left side of the transmission) in the neutral position. Place the selector lever (inside the vehicle) in the neutral position also.

4   At this point, the control rod adjustment is made automatically. Tighten the control rod-to-control arm adjusting locknut to the specified torque.

13 Removal and installation

1   Disconnect the negative battery cable from the battery.

2   Remove the air cleaner assembly by referring to Chapter 2, then disconnect the starter motor wiring and remove the starter. It is held in place by 2 bolts.

3   Place a drain pan under the transmission, then remove the fluid filler tube by pulling up on it.

4   Raise the vehicle and set it on jack stands.

5   Loosen the transmission oil pan mounting bolts (do not remove them completely) and allow the transmission fluid to drain into the drain pan. You may have to tap the pan with a soft-faced hammer to break the gasket seal. When the transmission fluid is finished draining, remove the oil pan from the transmission.

6   Remove the driveshaft by referring to Chapter 8.

7   Disconnect the speedometer cable and the exhaust pipe from the transmission.

8   Unhook the throttle rod from the throttle lever on the left side of the transmission.

9   Disconnect and plug the transmission oil cooler feed and return tubes and remove the linkage bellcrank, the control rod and the bellhousing cover from the transmission.

10   Mark the torque converter and drive plates so that they can be installed in the same position, then remove the torque converter attaching bolts. Use a wrench on the large bolt at the front of the crankshaft to rotate the engine clockwise so that all the bolts can be removed.

11   Securely support the rear of the engine with a jack or other suitable device.

12   Carefully support the transmission on a portable jack, then remove the rear engine support bracket.

13   Remove all the bolts attaching the transmission bellhousing to the engine.

14   Slowly withdraw the transmission from the engine by moving the jack toward the rear of the vehicle. Be very careful not to let the torque converter fall.

15   Carefully lower the jack and move the transmission out from under the vehicle. To remove the torque converter, slide it out of the transmission bellhousing.

16   Installation is basically the reverse of removal. Be sure to line up the marks on the torque converter and drive plate and do not forget to fill the transmission to the proper level with the recommended fluid (see the *Recommended lubricants and fluids section* at the front of the book).

14 Disassembly and repair

1   Due to the complexity of the clutches and the hydraulic control system, and because of the special tools and expertise required to perform an automatic transmission overhaul, it should not be undertaken by the home mechanic.

2   If the transmission requires major repair work, it should be left to an authorized dealer service department or a reputable automotive or transmission repair shop specializing in this type of work.

Chapter 8 Driveline

Refer to Chapter 13 for specifications and information related to 1981 thru 1988 models

Contents

Specifications

Clutch

Clutch pedal free play	
1979 models	0.8 to 1.0 in (20 to 25 mm)
1980 models	0.8 to 1.4 in (20 to 35 mm)
Clutch cable adjusting wheel-to-insulator clearance	0.12 to 0.16 in (3 to 4 mm)
Clutch pedal distance (A)	
U-engine	0.9 in (22 mm)
W-engine	0.8 in (20 mm)
Clutch pedal height	
U-engine	6.5 in (166 mm)
W-engine	6.9 in (176 mm)
Clutch pedal stroke	
U-engine	5.5 in (140 mm)
W-engine	5.9 in (150 mm)
Clutch disc rivet sink	0.012 in (0.3 mm) minimum

Driveshaft

U-joint journal end play	0 to 0.001 in (0 to 0.03 mm)
Snap-ring thicknesses	
MA 180905 (no color-code)	0.050 ± 0.0006 in (1.28 ± 0.015 mm)
MA 180906 (yellow)	0.516 ± 0.0006 in (1.31 ± 0.015 mm)
MA 180907 (blue)	0.0528 ± 0.0006 in (1.34 ± 0.015 mm)
MA 180908 (purple)	0.0539 ± 0.0006 in (1.37 ± 0.015 mm)
Driveshaft runout	0.020 in (0.5 mm) maximum
Driveshaft imbalance	0.18 oz (5.0 g) maximum

Rear Axle

Standard rear wheel bearing case-to-axle housing clearance	0.002 to 0.008 in (0.05 to 0.20 mm)

Wheel bearing preload adjusting shim thicknesses

MB 092491	0.002 in (0.05 mm)
MB 092492	0.004 in (0.10 mm)
MB 092493	0.0079 in (0.20 mm)
MB 092494	0.0118 in (0.30 mm)
MB 092495	0.0197 in (0.50 mm)
MB 092496	0.0394 in (1.00 mm)
MB 092497	0.0591 in (1.50 mm)
MB 092498	0.0787 in (2.00 mm)
Axle shaft axial play	0.002 to 0.008 in (0.05 to 0.20 mm)
Side gear-to-axle shaft spline clearance	0.0021 to 0.0067 in (0.054 to 0.171 mm)
Spyder gear-to-spyder shaft clearance	0 to 0.0025 in (0 to 0.063 mm)

Drive pinion height-adjusting shim thicknesses

MB 092160	0.0543 in (1.38 mm)
MB 092161	0.0555 in (1.41 mm)
MB 092162	0.0567 in (1.44 mm)
MB 092163	0.0579 in (1.47 mm)
MB 092164	0.0591 in (1.50 mm)
MB 092165	0.0603 in (1.53 mm)
MB 092166	0.0614 in (1.56 mm)
MB 092167	0.0626 in (1.59 mm)
MB 092168	0.0638 in (1.62 mm)
MB 092169	0.0650 in (1.65 mm)
MB 092170	0.0118 in (0.30 mm)

Pinion shaft bearing preload adjusting shim thicknesses

MB 092130	0.0118 in (0.30 mm)
MB 092131	0.0787 in (2.00 mm)
MB 092132	0.0799 in (2.03 mm)
MB 092133	0.0811 in (2.06 mm)
MB 092134	0.0823 in (2.09 mm)
MB 092135	0.0835 in (2.12 mm)
MB 092136	0.0846 in (2.15 mm)
MB 092137	0.0858 in (2.18 mm)
MB 092138	0.0870 in (2.21 mm)
MB 092139	0.0882 in (2.24 mm)
MB 092140	0.0894 in (2.27 mm)
MB 092141	0.0906 in (2.30 mm)
MB 092142	0.0917 in (2.33 mm)

Pinion spacer lengths

MB 092346 (no color-code)	2.2311 + 0 in (56.67 + 0 mm) − 0.0016 − 0.14
MB 092347 (white)	2.2445 + 0 in (57.01 + 0 mm) − 0.0016 − 0.14

Backlash between differential spyder gear and side gear	0.002 to 0.005 in (0.051 to 0.127 mm)

Side gear thrust spacer thicknesses

MB 092034	0.0315 + 0.0031 in (0.8 + 0.08 mm) − 0.0067 − 0.17
MB 092035	0.0315 + 0.0071 in (0.8 + 0.18 mm) − 0.0106 − 0.27
MB 092036	0.0315 + 0 in (0.8 + 0 mm) − 0.0028 − 0.07

Backlash between ring and pinion gear	0.005 to 0.007 in (0.13 to 0.18 mm)
Ring gear runout	Less than 0.002 in (0.05 mm)

Torque specifications

	ft-lb	(Nm)

Clutch

	ft-lb	(Nm)
Clutch cover bolts	11 to 15	(15 to 21)

Driveshaft

	ft-lb	(Nm)
Center bearing bracket nuts	22 to 29	(29 to 39)
Flange yoke bolts		
1979 models	22 to 25	(30 to 34)
1980 models	33 to 39	(45 to 53)
Center yoke nut	116 to 159	(157 to 216)

Rear axle

	ft-lb	(Nm)
Rear wheel bearing case-to-rear axle housing attaching nuts	36 to 43	(49 to 59)
Rear axle housing drain plug	43 to 50	(59 to 69)
Rear axle housing filler plug	29 to 43	(39 to 59)

Differential end yoke-to-pinion shaft nut		
1979 models	120 to 160	(160 to 210)
1980 models	137 to 180	(186 to 245)
Drive pinion bearing preload		
Without seal in place	6 to 9	(0.7 to 1.0)
With seal in place	9 to 11	(1.0 to 1.2)
Ring gear mounting bolts	58 to 65	(78 to 88)
Differential carrier cap bolts	40 to 47	(54 to 64)
Lock plate bolts	11 to 16	(15 to 22)
Differential carrier assembly-to-axle housing nuts	18 to 22	(25 to 30)

1 General description

The clutch in the Dodge D-50 is conventional in design and is composed of a single clutch disc and a Belleville-type diaphragm spring pressure assembly. Due to the fact that access to the clutch components is difficult and time consuming, the clutch disc, clutch cover (pressure plate) assembly and release bearing should be carefully inspected or replaced whenever either the engine or the transmission is removed.

Power is transmitted from the transmission to the rear axle by a 2-piece driveshaft. Universal joints are located at the front, rear and center bearing to alllow for vertical movement of the rear axle and slight movement of the engine/transmission unit. A slip-joint is used to allow for fore-and-aft movement of the drivetrain.

The rear axle assembly is also conventional in design, utilizing a separable differential carrier, hypoid final drive gears and semi-floating rear axles.

Most rear-end component problems reveal themselves in the form of some sort of noise. The noise may be caused by gears (in the differential carrier assembly) or bearings (in the differential and the outer ends of the rear axle housing).

Gear noise is usually a high-pitched whine, which may be more pronounced at certain speeds or when the vehicle is under load.

Bearing noise is generally a lower-pitched, steady growl. It tends to get louder when accelerating under load. Swerving the vehicle from side-to-side on a flat, level road may help to pinpoint faulty wheel bearings. This practice throws additional side loads on the bearings, which should increase any noise coming from them. A bad bearing could show up in the differential assembly, although bearing failure in this area is much less likely than in the wheel bearings.

Although a differential overhaul section is included in this Chapter, major repair work on the differential (and other rear-end components) requires many special tools and a high degree of expertise, and therefore should not be attempted by the home mechanic. Should major repairs be necessary, we recommend that they be performed by a dealer-authorized service department or a reputable repair shop.

2 Universal joints – inspecting on the vehicle

1   Universal joint problems are usually caused by worn or damaged needle bearings. These problems are revealed as vibration in the driveline or clunking noises when the clutch is engaged (or the transmission is put in 'Drive'). In extreme cases they are caused by lack of lubrication. If this happens you will hear metallic squeaks and, ultimately, grinding and shrieking sounds as the bearings are destroyed.

2   It is easy to check the needle bearings for wear and damage with the driveshaft in position on the vehicle. To check the rear universal joint, turn the driveshaft with one hand and hold the rear axle flange or wheel with the other. Any movement between the two is an indication of considerable wear. The front universal joint can be checked by holding the front driveshaft with one hand and the sleeve yoke in the transmission with the other. Any movement here indicates the need for universal joint repair. The center universal joint can be checked by holding the rear driveshaft in one hand and the front driveshaft in the other. If there is movement or play here, the center universal joint is worn or damaged. Lifting up on either driveshaft will also indicate whether there is play in the universal joints.

3   If they are worn or damaged, the universal joints will have to be disassembled and the bearings replaced as described in Section 5. Read over the procedure carefully before beginning the disassembly of the universal joints.

3 Driveshaft – removal and installation

1   Raise the vehicle and set it on jack stands. Drain the transmission lubricant into a suitable container.

2   Make a mark across the driveshaft flange yoke and the differential end yoke (where they come together) so that the driveshaft can be reinstalled in the exact same position (photo).

3   Remove the 4 nuts, bolts and lock washers that attach the driveshaft to the differential assembly.

4   Remove the 2 nuts attaching the center bearing assembly to the frame crossmember (photo).

5   Carefully lift up on the center bearing (photo), release the rear of the driveshaft from the differential (photo) and slide the driveshaft to the rear, out of the transmission housing. Be very careful not to damage the seal in the end of the transmission housing.

6   Refer to Section 5 for driveshaft inspection and repair procedures.

7   Before installing the driveshaft, thoroughly clean the outside surface of the sleeve yoke and apply a coat of multi-purpose grease to it. Also, check the inside of the sleeve yoke to make sure there is no foreign material present.

8   Carefully insert the sleeve yoke into the transmission housing, lining up the splines inside the sleeve yoke with the splines on the transmission output shaft (photo). Fit the driveshaft into place and install the bolts (photo), lock washers and nuts that attach it to the differential (be sure to line up the marks on the flange yoke and the end yoke). Tighten the nuts to the specified torque (photo).

9   Install the center bearing mount nuts and tighten the securely.

10   Fill the transmission to the proper level with the recommended lubricant (see the *Recommended Lubricants and Fluids* Section at the front of the book).

11   Lower the vehicle to the ground and test drive it.

4 Pinion oil seal – replacement

1   It is not uncommon for the pinion shaft oil seal to fail, which results in the leakage of differential gear lubricant past the seal and onto the driveshaft flange yoke. This seal is quite easily replaced without removing or disassembling the differential.

3.2 Make a mark across the driveshaft flange yoke and the differential end yoke before disassembly

2 Raise the vehicle and set it on jack stands.

3 Remove the drain and fill plugs from the rear axle housing and allow the differential lubricant to drain into a suitable container. When the draining is complete, loosely install the drain plugs.

4 Separate the driveshaft from the differential end yoke by referring to Section 3. Be sure to tie the end of the driveshaft up, out of the way.

5 Set the parking brake, to keep the rear wheels from turning, and remove the large nut and washer from the end of the pinion gear shaft.

6 Pull off the differential end yoke, using a gear puller. Carefully pry off the dust cover and the oil seal will be visible.

7 After noting what the visible side of the oil seal looks like, carefully pry it out of the differential with a screwdriver or a pry bar. Be careful not to damage the splines on the pinion shaft.

8 Clean the seal mounting area, the outside diameter of the new seal and the pinion shaft with a clean rag.

9 Lubricate the new seal lip with molybdenum disulfide grease and carefully install it in position in the differential. Tap it into place with a hammer and a block of hard wood or other suitable tool. Work around the entire circumference of the seal, a little at a time, with the hammer and block of wood, until the seal is properly seated. Work slowly, and do not damage the rubber lip of the seal.

10 Install the dust cover on the differential.

11 Clean the sealing lip contact surface of the differential end yoke. Apply a thin coat of molybdenum disulfide grease and carefully install it onto the end of the pinion shaft. You will have to rotate the end yoke slightly, to line up the splines in the yoke and on the shaft.

12 Use a soft-faced hammer to tap the yoke into place, then install the large washer and a new self-locking nut on the end of the pinion shaft.

13 Disengage the parking brake and snug up the nut as you let the flange rotate. This will help to seat the pinion shaft bearings properly as the nut is tightened.

14 Tighten the nut to the specified torque while holding the wheel to keep the pinion shaft from turning. This torque figure is very important, as it determines the pre-load on the pinion shaft bearings.

15 Fasten the rear of the driveshaft to the differential end yoke by referring to Section 3.

16 Tighten the drain plug in the rear axle housing to the specified torque and fill the housing to the proper level with the recommended gear lubricant (see the *Recommended Lubricants and Fluids* Section at the front of the book). Install the filler plug and tighten it to the specified torque.

17 Lower the vehicle to the ground. Test drive it and check around the differential end yoke for evidence of leakage.

5 Driveshaft/universal joints – disassembly, inspection and reassembly

1 It is a good idea to dismantle the center universal joint first so that the driveshaft can be broken into two pieces, which makes it easier to handle and work on.

2 Support the universal joint in a vise equipped with soft jaws and remove the snap rings from the universal joint yokes. It is recommended that each snap ring and yoke be marked so that the snap rings can be returned to the same position during reassembly.

3 To remove the bearings from the yokes, you will need 2 sockets. One should be large enough to fit into the yoke where the snap rings were installed and the other should have an inside diameter just large enough for the bearings to fit into when they are forced out of the yoke.

4 Mount the universal joint in a vise with the large socket on one side of the yoke and the small socket on the other side, pushing against the bearing. Carefully tighten the vise until the bearing is pushed out of the yoke and into the large socket. If it cannot be pushed all the way out, remove the universal joint from the vise and use a pair of pliers to finish removing the bearing.

5 Reverse the sockets and push out the bearing on the other side of the yoke. This time, the small socket will be pushing against the cross-shaped universal joint journal end.

6 Before pressing out the two remaining bearings, mark the universal joint journal (the cross) so it can be installed in the same position during reassembly.

7 The two remaining universal joints can be disassembled following the same procedure. Be sure to mark all components for each universal joint so that they can be kept together and reassembled in the proper position.

8 Remove the center bearing from the front driveshaft by referring to Section 6.

9 Clean the driveshaft and universal joint components with solvent and dry them thoroughly.

10 Inspect each of the driveshafts for cracks and damage. If possible, check the driveshaft run-out with a dial indicator. Replace both shafts if any defects are found in either one. Never replace only one of the shafts.

11 Check the universal joint journals (the crosses) for scoring, needle roller impressions, rust and pitting. Replace them if any of the above conditions exist.

12 Check the sleeve yoke splines for wear and damage.

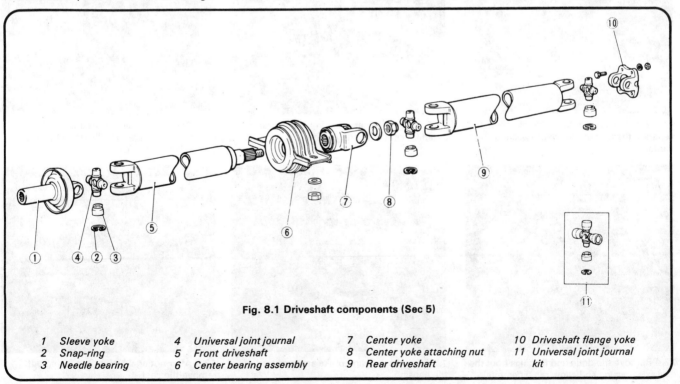

Fig. 8.1 Driveshaft components (Sec 5)

1 *Sleeve yoke*	4 *Universal joint journal*	7 *Center yoke*	10 *Driveshaft flange yoke*
2 *Snap-ring*	5 *Front driveshaft*	8 *Center yoke attaching nut*	11 *Universal joint journal*
3 *Needle bearing*	6 *Center bearing assembly*	9 *Rear driveshaft*	*kit*

3.4 Remove the 2 nuts attaching the center bearing assembly to the frame

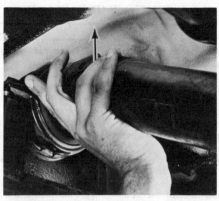
3.5a Lift up on the center bearing to remove the driveshaft

3.5b Disengage the driveshaft from the differential

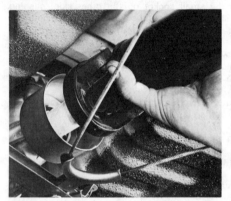
3.8a Carefully insert the sleeve yoke into the transmission housing

3.8b Install the bolts, lockwashers and nuts that hold the driveshaft to the differential end yoke

3.8c Tighten the nuts to the specified torque

11.2 Pull forward on the spring clips and separate them from the release bearing carrier

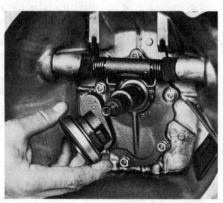
11.3 Slide the release bearing and carrier assembly off the bearing carrier

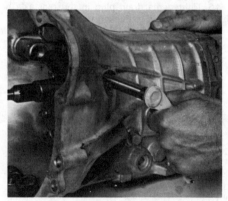
11.4 Remove the clutch control lever/shaft from the transmission bellhousing by twisting and pulling on the lever

12.4 Remove the drain and fill plugs from the rear axle housing and allow the differential lubricant to drain into a suitable container

12.7 Pull the axle and brake assembly out of the housing

12.9 After noting which side is facing out, remove the seal

13 When reassembling the universal joints, replace all needle bearings and dust seals with new ones.

14 Before reassembly, pack each grease cavity in the universal joint journals with a small amount of grease. Also, apply a thin coat of grease to the new needle bearing rollers and the roller contact areas on the universal joint journals.

15 Apply a thin coat of grease to the dust seal lips and install the bearings and universal joint journals into the yoke using the vise and sockets that were used to remove the old bearings. Work slowly and be very careful not to damage the bearings as they are being pressed into the yokes.

16 Once the bearings are in place and properly seated, install the snap-rings and check the snap-ring-to-bearing clearance (or universal joint journal end play) with a feeler gauge. This is done with both snap-rings in place and the bearings and journal pressed toward one side of the yoke. Measure the clearance at the opposite side of the yoke. If the clearance is greater than specified, install a snap-ring of a different thickness and recheck the clearance. Repeat the procedure until the correct clearance is obtained. If possible, use snap-rings of the same thickness on each side of the yoke so that driveshaft balance is not affected. A list of available snap-ring thicknesses is included in the Specifications Section at the front of this Chapter.

17 Install the center bearing as described in Section 6 and assemble the center U-joint.

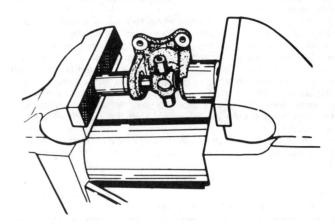

Fig. 8.2 The bearings can be removed from the U-joints with a vise and 2 appropriate size sockets (Sec 5)

---

6 Center bearing – disassembly, inspection and reassembly

1 Check for the presence of mating marks on the driveshafts and center yoke. If they are not visible, make some new ones to ensure correct reassembly of the driveshafts and center yoke.

2 Refer to Section 5 and disassemble the center universal joint so that the driveshaft can be separated into two pieces.

3 Support the driveshaft in a vise equipped wtih soft jaws and remove the center yoke attaching nut and the washer.

4 Pull the center yoke off and pry the center bearing bracket loose (be careful not to damage the rubber mount). The bearing bracket cannot be disassembled.

5 Using a suitable bearing puller, remove the center bearing from the shaft.

6 Clean the bearing parts and the yoke with solvent and dry them thoroughly.

7 Rotate the bearing and check for noise, excessive play and roughness. Replace the bearing if any defects are noted.

8 Check the center bearing bracket and mounting rubber for deterioration and damage. Replace as necessary.

9 Before installing the center bearing, fill the bearing grease cavity with multi-purpose grease.

10 Slip the bearing onto the shaft and fit the bracket to the bearing. The bracket mounting rubber should fit into the bearing groove around its entire circumference.

11 Align the mating marks on the shaft and the center yoke and slip the yoke into place on the shaft. Install the washer and a new nut and tighten the nut ot the specified torque. Since the nuts are the self-locking type, the old ones should not be reused.

12 Assemble the center universal joint as described in Section 5. Be sure to align the mating marks on the shafts and yoke.

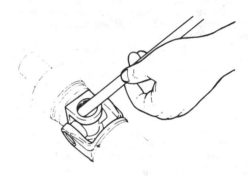

Fig. 8.3 The snap-ring-to-bearing clearance (U-joint journal end play) is checked with a feeler gauge (Sec 5)

---

7 Clutch pedal – adjustment

1 Correct clutch pedal adjustment is very important for proper clutch operation and to ensure normal clutch service life.

2 The clutch pedal adjustments affect the pedal height, the pedal stroke and the pedal free play. Correct clutch pedal height is important because it ensures complete clutch engagement and prevents slippage and overheating, which will lead to clutch failure. The pedal stroke indicates whether or not the clutch disengages properly (when the pedal is depressed) and provides for smooth, trouble-free gear shifts. Clutch pedal free play (the distance the pedal moves before the clutch release bearing contacts the clutch diaphragm spring) is necessary to prevent undue wear of the clutch release mechanism components.

3 To adjust the clutch pedal, loosen the adjusting bolt jam nut (on the pedal support member) and turn the bolt until the pedal height is as specified. Tighten the jam nut so that the adjusting bolt cannot turn. Measure distance A as shown in Figure 8.7 and compare it to the

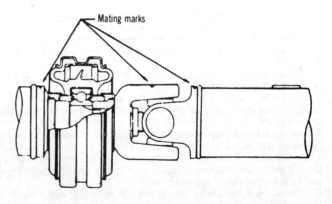

Fig. 8.4 The driveshafts and center yoke should have mating (alignment) marks stamped into them (Sec 6)

specifications. (When the pedal height is correct, distance A should also be correct).

4   Set the clutch cable adjusting wheel-to-insulator clearance (inside the engine compartment) to the specified amount by pulling out slightly on the cable housing and turning the adjusting wheel.

5   Check to make sure that the clutch pedal free play is as specified. (Slowly depress the pedal until the resistance offered by the clutch release mechanism is felt, then measure how far the pedal has moved). The clutch cable may stretch during normal operation, so the correct adjusting wheel-to-insulator clearance may not ensure correct pedal free play. Always make the adjustment so that the specified free play is present.

6   Check the clutch pedal stroke and compare it to the specifications. The transmission should shift smoothly and quietly with the pedal fully depressed.

8   Clutch cable – removal and installation

1   Pull out slightly on the clutch cable housing (inside the engine compartment) and loosen the adjusting wheel.

2   Loosen the jam nut on the clutch pedal adjusting bolt and back out the adjusting bolt.

3   Unhook the cable from the clutch pedal hook and pull the cable through the firewall from the engine compartment side.

4   Raise the front of the vehicle and set it on jack stands. Block the rear tires and set the parking brake to keep the vehicle from rolling. Remove the cotter key in the end of the clutch control lever. Push forward on the lever and unhook the clutch cable. Slide the rubber boot off the end of the cable and release the cable from its mount on the transmission bellhousing.

5   Before installing the new cable, apply a small amount of engine oil or other suitable lubricant between the cable and the cable housing.

6   Slip the lower end of the cable into position on the transmission bellhousing and slide the rubber boot over the end of the cable.

7   Push forward on the clutch control lever and hook the end of the clutch cable over the lever. Remember to install the cotter key in the end of the lever.

8   Lower the vehicle to the ground and insert the upper end of the cable through the firewall and into the driver's compartment. Loosen the adjusting wheel as far as possible and hook the end of the cable onto the clutch pedal hook.

9   Adjust the clutch pedal height, the clutch pedal stroke and pedal free play by referring to the appropriate section.

10 After the cable has been installed, make sure that the isolating pad touches the rear side of the left engine mount insulator.

9   Clutch pedal – removal and installation

Since the clutch pedal and brake pedal must be removed from the vehicle as a unit, refer to Chapter 9, *Brake pedal – removal and installation* for the proper procedure to follow when removal of the clutch pedal is necessary.

10   Clutch – removal, inspection and installation

1   Separate the transmission from the engine as described in Chapter 2.

2   Mark the clutch cover assembly and flywheel so that they can be reassembled in the same position.

3   Install a clutch alignment tool to support the clutch cover assembly and clutch disc (so they do not fall when the attaching bolts are removed).

4   Remove the 6 bolts attaching the clutch cover assembly to the flywheel. Loosen them one turn at a time each, in a diagonal or crisscross pattern, until they are loose enough to be removed by hand.

5   Lift the clutch cover assembly and the clutch disc off the flywheel and remove the clutch alignment tool.

6   Check the metal parts of the clutch disc for cracks and distortion. Check carefully for broken springs. Slip the clutch disc onto the transmission input shaft and check for excessive play in the direction of rotation between the splines of the clutch disc hub and the input shaft. Inspect the clutch disc friction lining for cracks, burned spots and

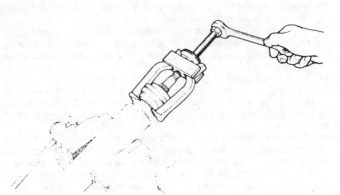
Fig. 8.5 Removing the center bearing from the shaft (Sec 6)

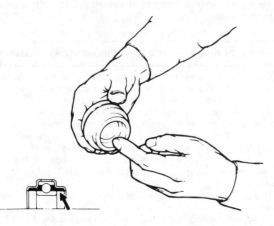
Fig. 8.6 Before installing the center bearing, fill the grease cavity with multi-purpose grease (Sec 6)

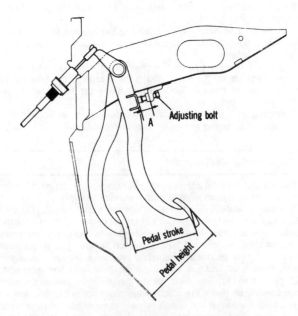
Fig. 8.7 Clutch pedal adjustment (Sec 7)

oil stains. If oil is present on the clutch components, the engine rear oil seal or the transmission front oil seal, or both, may be defective and require replacement. Minor oil stains may be removed with lacquer thinner or a similar solvent. Look for broken or loose rivets. Measure the clutch disc rivet sink (the distance from the top of the friction material to the rivet head) and compare it to the specifications. Replace any defective parts with new ones.

7   Inspect the clutch cover assembly for excessive finger wear, loose strap rivets and cracks. Check the pressure plate for scoring, burn marks and ridges. Shake the clutch cover assembly and listen for noise caused by a loose pivot ring. If any noise is heard, the pivot ring is excessively worn and the clutch cover assembly must be replaced.

8   Look for scoring, burn marks and deep ridges on the flywheel. If any of these problems exist, or if the surface is highly polished, remove the flywheel as described in Chapter 2 and have it resurfaced and balanced at a reputable automotive machine shop. Check the pilot bearing in the center hub of the flywheel. Make sure that it turns smoothly and quietly. If the transmission input shaft contact surface is worn or damaged, replace the bearing.

9   Disassemble and check the release bearing and clutch release mechanism as described in Section 11.

10   Hold the clutch disc and clutch cover assembly in place on the flywheel and loosely install the 6 attaching bolts (be sure to line up the marks on the flywheel and clutch cover). The manufacturer's stamped mark on the clutch disc must face away from the flywheel when the clutch is assembled.

11   Install the clutch disc alignment tool through the clutch disc and into the pilot bearing in the flywheel hub. This tool will center the clutch disc properly.

12   Tighten the 6 clutch attaching bolts to the specified torque. Use a crisscross pattern and tighten the bolts one turn each at a time, so that the clutch cover assembly is drawn down onto the flywheel evenly.

13   Remove the clutch disc alignment tool.

14   Install the transmission onto the engine as described in Chapter 7.

11 Release bearing/clutch release mechanism – disassembly, inspection and reassembly

1   Refer to Chapter 2 for the procedure to follow when separating the transmission from the engine.

2   Pull forward on the spring clips retaining the bearing carrier and separate them from the release bearing carrier (photo).

3   Slide the release bearing and carrier assembly off the bearing carrier (photo).

4   Using a $\frac{3}{16}$ in pin punch, drive out the 2 pins attaching the clutch shift arm to the control lever shaft. Remove the clutch control lever/shaft assembly, the return springs, the felt packings and the clutch shift arm from the transmission bellhousing by twisting and pulling on the lever (photo).

5   Wipe the release bearing clean. Do not clean it in solvent, since it is packed with grease and permanently sealed. Make sure that the bearing rotates smoothly and quietly. Check the face of the bearing

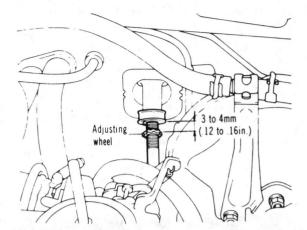

Fig. 8.8 Clutch cable adjusting wheel-to-insulator clearance (Sec 7)

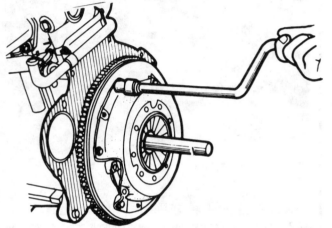

Fig. 8.9 Remove the 6 bolts attaching the clutch cover assembly to the flywheel (Sec 10)

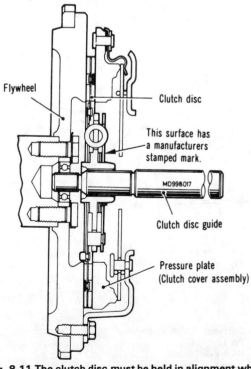

Fig. 8.11 The clutch disc must be held in alignment while installing the clutch cover assembly (Sec 10)

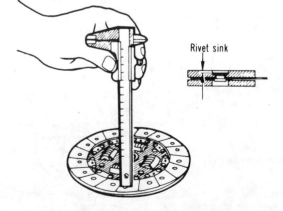

Fig. 8.10 Measure the clutch disc rivet sink with a calipers of a depth micrometer (Sec 10)

that contacts the diaphragm's ring fingers for excessive wear. Replace the bearing is any defects are found.

6 Clean the remaining parts with solvent and dry them thoroughly. Clean the inside of the transmission bellhousing.

7 Check the release bearing carrier for wear and damage. Inspect the clutch shift arm contact faces, the shift arm bore and the shaft assembly and bushings for wear. Replace any defective parts. Wipe clean the control lever shaft bushings in the transmission bellhousing and apply a thin coat of grease to them. Slide the control lever/shaft assembly into place with the felt packings, the return springs and the clutch shift arm installed in the proper order.

8 Engage the return spring in the clutch shift arm and install the pins that attach the arm to the control lever shaft. Make sure that the slots in the spring pins are at right angles to the control lever shaft axis. Apply a few drops of engine oil to each felt packing.

9 Slide the release bearing and carrier assembly into position and install the spring clips. Make sure they are properly engaged in the clutch shift arm and the release bearing carrier.

12 Axle shaft – removal and installation

1 The rear axle shafts must be removed to replace leaking seals, defective wheel bearings and, obviously, broken axle shafts. Removal of the differential assembly for repair also necessitates removal of the axle shafts. Since special tools are required to properly disassemble and reassemble the rear bearing housings, it is recommended that servicing of the rear wheel bearings be left to the dealer service department or a reputable repair shop.

2 Various shims, seals and O-rings are required to properly re-

12.22 The axle shaft axial play can be accurately checked with a dial indicator

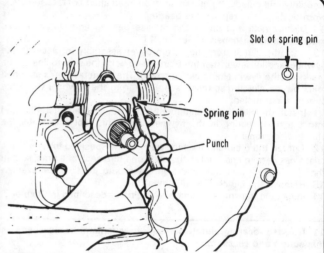

Fig. 8.12 Drive out the 2 pins attaching the shift arm to the shaft (Sec 11)

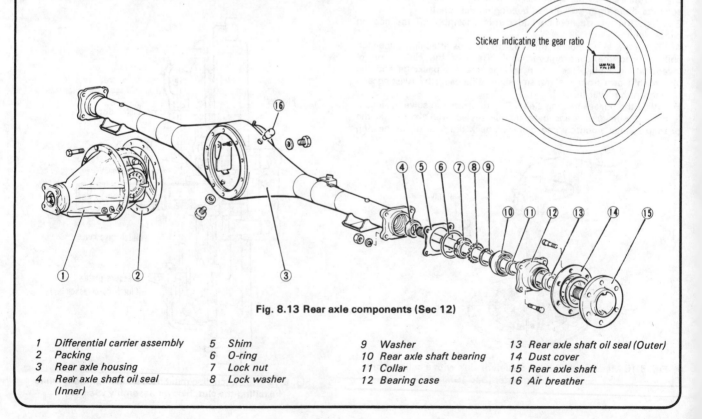

Fig. 8.13 Rear axle components (Sec 12)

1	Differential carrier assembly	5	Shim
2	Packing	6	O-ring
3	Rear axle housing	7	Lock nut
4	Rear axle shaft oil seal (Inner)	8	Lock washer
9	Washer	13	Rear axle shaft oil seal (Outer)
10	Rear axle shaft bearing	14	Dust cover
11	Collar	15	Rear axle shaft
12	Bearing case	16	Air breather

assemble and install the axle shafts, so be sure to read through the entire procedure before beginning the job to make sure that you have all the necessary parts.

3   Raise the vehicle and set it on jack stands. Remove the rear wheels.

4   Remove the drain and fill plugs from the rear axle housing (photo) and allow the differential lubricant to drain into a suitable container. When the draining is complete, reinstall the plugs loosely.

5   Remove the brake drum from the end of the axle and the metal brake line from the wheel cylinder by referring to Chapter 9. The brakes do not have to be disassembled to remove the axles.

6   Remove the parking brake cables from the vehicle as described in Chapter 9. Do not disconnect the cables from the levers in the rear brake assemblies. If only one axle shaft is being removed, remove only the cable on the side of the vehicle that the axle shaft is being removed from. If both axle shafts are being removed, both parking brake cables must also be removed.

7   Remove the 4 nuts and lock washers attaching the bearing case and brake backing plate to the axle housing and withdraw the axle, the bearing case, the brake backing plate and brake assembly from the axle housing (photo). A slide hammer-type axle puller may be required to dislodge the bearing housing from the axle housing. Do not pry between the two flanges, as damage to the gasket sealing surfaces will result. Support the axle shaft as it is removed from the axle housing to prevent damage to the oil seal in the end of the axle housing.

8   Remove the O-ring and shim (or shims) from the rear axle housing flange. Retain the shims for reassembly.

9   Inspect the oil seal inside the rear axle housing. If it is worn or damaged, or if there is any evidence of leakage, replace the seal. After noting which side of the seal is showing, pry or pull it out of the housing with a screwdriver or a slide hammer-type seal puller (photo).

10   Thoroughly clean the seal mounting area, and install a new seal (with the rubber side facing out) using a hammer and a block of wood or other suitable tool. Tap the seal carefully into place around its entire circumference and make sure it is properly seated in the axle housing.

11   At this point, the axle shaft assembly should be taken to a dealer service department or a reputable repair shop if the outer oil seal or wheel bearing has to be replaced.

12   Inspect the axle shaft splines where the shaft mates with the differential inside the axle housing. If these splines are damaged or worn, the axle shaft should be replaced. Check the oil seal lip contact

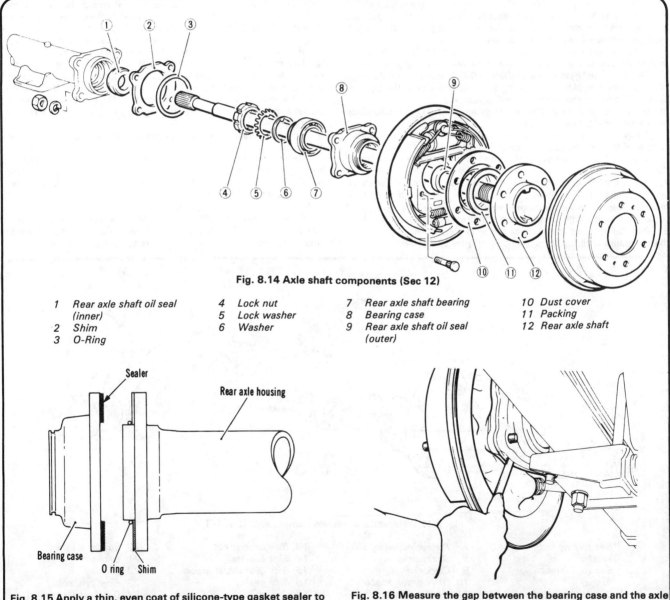

Fig. 8.14 Axle shaft components (Sec 12)

1	Rear axle shaft oil seal (inner)	4	Lock nut
2	Shim	5	Lock washer
3	O-Ring	6	Washer

7	Rear axle shaft bearing	10	Dust cover
8	Bearing case	11	Packing
9	Rear axle shaft oil seal (outer)	12	Rear axle shaft

Fig. 8.15 Apply a thin, even coat of silicone-type gasket sealer to the mating surface of the bearing case (Sec 12)

Fig. 8.16 Measure the gap between the bearing case and the axle housing with a feeler gauge (Sec 12)

area of the shaft for wear and cracks. If any defects are noted, replace the shaft.

13 Before beginning the assembly procedure, remove all old gasket sealer and any rust from the mating surfaces of the bearing case and the axle housing. Also, thoroughly pack the bearing case and axle housing end with high-temperature wheel bearing grease and lubricate the lip of the oil seal in the axle housing.

14 If both axle shafts have been removed, the left-side shaft should be installed first during reassembly.

15 Install a 0.040 in (1.0 mm) shim and a new O-ring into place on the left end of the axle housing.

16 Apply a thin, even coat of silicone-type gasket sealer to the mating surface of the bearing case and carefully install the left-side axle/brake assembly into the rear axle housing. (Do not damage the oil seal in the process). It may be necessary to turn the axle slightly to engage its inner splines with the differential. You may have to tap gently on the axle hub with a soft-faced hammer to seat the bearing case in the end of the axle housing.

17 Install the 4 lock washers and nuts attaching the bearing case and brake backing plate to the axle housing. Tighten the nuts to the specified torque.

18 Install the right-side axle into the housing without a shim or O-ring in place, and temporarily tighten the attaching nuts to a torque of 0.4 ft-lb (0.6 Nm). When the axle is installed in this manner, a gap will exist between the bearing case and the axle housing end flange, which must be measured with a feeler gauge.

19 Separate the axle shaft from the housing and select a shim with a thickness equal to the gap measured in the previous step. Also, select a shim with a thickness of from 0.020 to 0.079 in (0.05 to 0.20 mm). A list of available preload adjusting shims is included in the Specifications Section at the front of this Chapter.

20 Install the previously selected shims and a new O-ring into place on the end of the axle housing.

21 Apply a thin, even coat of silicone-type gasket sealer to the mating surface of the bearing case and carefully install the axle assembly into the housing. Install the lock washers and nuts and tighten the nuts to the specified torque.

22 Using a dial indicator, check the axial play of the axle shaft by pulling out and pushing in on the axle shaft hub (photo). If the play is more or less than specified, remove the right-side axle again and replace the shims with shims that are thicker or thinner, as required.

23 Reinstall the axle and recheck the axial play. If necessary, repeat the procedure until the correct amount of play is obtained.

24 Install the parking brake cables, hook up the brake lines and install the brake drums by referring to Chapter 9. Also, bleed the brakes at the rear wheel cylinder as described in Chapter 9.

25 Tighten the rear axle housing drain plug to the specified torque and fill the housing to the proper level with the recommended gear lubricant (see the *Recommended lubricants and fluids* Section at the front of the book). Install the filler plug and tighten it to the specified torque.

26 Install the wheels, lower the vehicle to the ground and test drive it. Check for leaks where the wheel bearing case attach to the rear axle housing.

13 Differential assembly – removal and installation

1 Raise the vehicle and set it on jack stands. Remove the rear wheels.

2 Remove the drain and fill plugs from the rear axle housing and allow the differential lubricant to drain into a suitable container. Reinstall the plugs loosely.

3 Make a mark across the driveshaft flange yoke and the differential end yoke (where they come together) so the driveshaft can be reinstalled in exactly the same position. Remove the 4 nuts, lock washers and bolts that attach the driveshaft to the differential. Pull the driveshaft loose from the differential and tie the end of it up out of the way so that the differential carrier assembly can be removed.

4 Remove the axle shafts as described in Section 12.

5 Remove the nuts and lock washers attaching the differential carrier assembly to the rear axle housing (photo). Tap the carrier with a soft-faced hammer, to break the gasket seal, and lift the carrier assembly out of the axle housing (photo). Do not pry between the carrier and the axle housing, as damage to the gasket sealing surfaces will result.

6 Scrape all traces of the old gasket and gasket sealer from the rear axle housing.

7 Before installing the differential carrier assembly into the rear axle housing, pack molybdenum disulfide grease into the ring gear teeth.

8 Apply an even coat of silicone-type gasket sealer to both sides of a new gasket and install the gasket into place on the rear axle housing with the tab to the right (photo).

9 Carefully install the differential carrier assembly into place on the rear axle housing. Install the lock washers and nuts and tighten the nuts to the specified torque, using a crisscross pattern (photo).

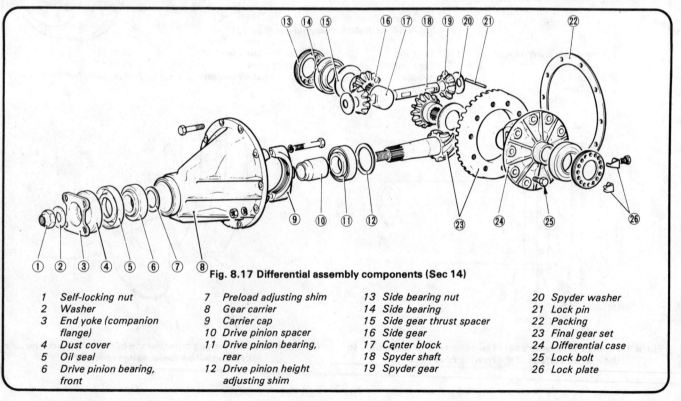

Fig. 8.17 Differential assembly components (Sec 14)

1	Self-locking nut	7	Preload adjusting shim	13	Side bearing nut	20	Spyder washer
2	Washer	8	Gear carrier	14	Side bearing	21	Lock pin
3	End yoke (companion flange)	9	Carrier cap	15	Side gear thrust spacer	22	Packing
4	Dust cover	10	Drive pinion spacer	16	Side gear	23	Final gear set
5	Oil seal	11	Drive pinion bearing, rear	17	Center block	24	Differential case
6	Drive pinion bearing, front	12	Drive pinion height adjusting shim	18	Spyder shaft	25	Lock bolt
				19	Spyder gear	26	Lock plate

13.5a Remove the nuts attaching the differential carrier assembly to the rear axle housing

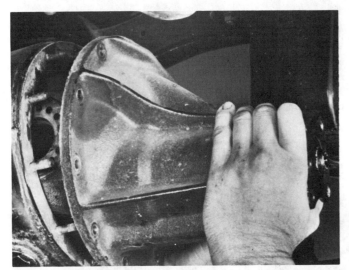

13.5b Carefully pull the differential carrier assembly off the axle housing

10 Fit the end of the driveshaft into place on the differential assembly. Be sure to line up the marks on the driveshaft flange yoke and the differential end yoke. Install the 4 bolts, lock washers and nuts and tighten the nut to the specified torque.

11 Install the axle shafts by referring to Section 12. Don't forget to fill the rear axle housing to the proper level with the recommended gear lubricant.

12 Install the wheels and lower the vehicle to the ground.

14 Differential assembly – overhaul

1   Problems in the differential cannot be accurately diagnosed or repaired without removing the differential from the rear axle housing.

2   As was mentioned before, major repair work on the differential is best left to a dealer-authorized service department or a reputable repair shop. The home mechanic can remove the differential, check for obvious problems, have the repair work done and then install it back in the vehicle.

3   If an overhaul is to be performed, be sure to read through the entire overhaul procedure before beginning. Also, check for availability of parts and arrange to borrow or rent any special tools that are required.

4   Remove the differential assembly from the vehicle by referring to Section 13.

5   Prior to disassembly of the differential, clean the exposed components with new, clean solvent and dry them thoroughly.

6   Check the ring gear and the drive pinion teeth for abnormal wear, scoring, pitting, cracks and other damage. A gear with damaged or broken teeth obviously must be replaced.

7   Check for correct gear tooth contact as follows: Apply a thin coat of white lead (or its equivalent) to both the drive and coast side of each of the ring gear teeth. Turn the ring gear through about 2 or 3 revolutions, then check the patterns on the gear teeth. Correct tooth contact will be indicated by a pattern of 60% to 80% contact on the drive side of the teeth (starting at the center and progressing toward the toe end) and a pattern of 40% to 60% on the coast side of the teeth, toward the toe end.

8   If the gears are not worn or damaged, the tooth contact can be adjusted by replacing the shims in the differential assembly, which moves the drive pinion and ring gear in relationship to each other. If correct tooth contact cannot be obtained by adjusting the gears, then excessive wear has occurred and both gears must be replaced. *Never replace only one gear.*

9   Remove the lock plate bolts and the lock plates from the carrier caps (photo).

10 Loosen the 4 carrier cap bolts (there are two on each cap) (photo). You may have to mount the carrier assembly in a vise equipped with soft jaws to facilitate disassembly. The carrier caps should be marked,

13.8 The tab on the gasket must face to the right

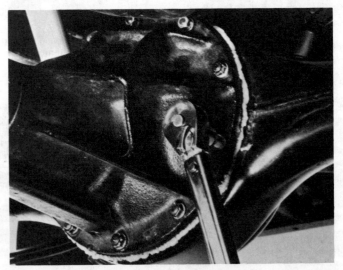

13.9 Tighten the mounting nuts to the specified torque

14.9 Remove the lock plate bolts and lock plates from the carrier caps

14.10a Loosen the 4 carrier cap bolts

14.10b The carrier caps should be marked so they can be properly mated during reassembly

14.11 Remove the side bearing nuts

14.12 Lift off the carrier caps and bolts

14.13 Carefully lift out the gear case assembly

14.14 Using a bearing puller, remove the side bearings (do not pull on the outer bearing race)

14.15 Loosen the ring gear mounting bolts $\frac{1}{4}$ turn at a time and remove the gear

14.16a Drive out the spyder shaft lock pin from the ring gear back side

14.16b Pull out the spyder shaft

14.16c Remove the center lock, the spyder gears and the washers

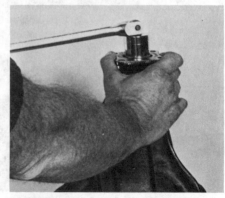

14.17 Loosen and remove the locknut and large washer at the end of the drive pinion shaft

14.18a Remove the end yoke from the differential pinion shaft with a gear puller

14.18b Drive out the pinion shaft with a soft-faced hammer

14.19a Remove the preload adjusting shim

14.19b Remove the drive pinion spacer

14.22 Remove the drive pinion oil seal from the differential case

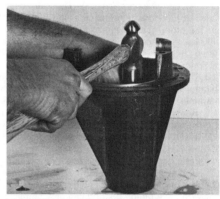

14.23a Drive the front bearing outer race out of the differential case

14.23b Drive the rear bearing outer race out of the differential case

14.44 Check the spyder gear-to-side gear backlash with a dial indicator

14.53 Check the backlash between the ring and pinion gears

14.55a Tighten the carrier cap bolts to the specified torque

14.55b Tighten the lock plate bolts to the specified torque

14.56 Check the ring gear runout (on the back side of the gear) with a dial indicator

so they do not get mixed up during reassembly (photo). If they are not marked, use a punch or scribe to mark them before disassembly.

11 Remove the side bearing nuts (photo).

12 Remove the carrier cap bolts completely and lift off the carrier caps (photo).

13 Lift out the differential gear case assembly, taking care not to drop the side bearing outer races (photo).

14 Using special tools numbered C-293-PA, C-4570 and MB990723 or an approved bearing puller, remove both differential side bearings (photo) (retain the bearings and any shims for reassembly). Lay the parts out on a clean surface in the order of disassembly.

15 Loosen the ring gear mounting bolts (photo) $\frac{1}{4}$ of a turn at a time in a crisscross pattern and dismount the ring gear. Again, it will probably be necessary to mount the differential gear assembly in a vise equipped with soft jaws to facilitate disassembly.

16 Drive out the spyder shaft lock pin from the ring gear back side (photo) and pull out the shaft, the center block, the spyder gears and the spyder washers (photo). The side gears and side gear thrust spacers can now be removed also. Lay the parts out on a clean surface in the order of disassembly.

17 Loosen and remove the locknut and large washer on the end of the drive pinion shaft (photo). You will have to hold the end yoke in a vise to keep the pinion shaft from turning.

18 Using a gear puller, remove the end yoke from the differential drive pinion shaft (photo). Drive out the pinion shaft using a soft-faced hammer (photo).

19 Remove the preload adjusting shim and the drive pinion spacer from the drive pinion shaft (photos).

20 Pull the rear drive pinion bearing using special tools numbered C-293-PA and C-293-36, or an approved bearing puller. Do not use a common gear puller, as damage to the bearing rollers will result.

21 Remove the drive pinion height adjusting shim.

22 Pry the drive pinion oil seal out of the differential case (photo). The forward drive pinion bearing can now be removed from the differential case.

23 Using a drift punch, remove the front and rear drive pinion bearing outer races (photo) (the differential case has grooves cast into it so that a drift punch can be placed directly on the bearing outer races). Lay the parts out on a clean surface in the order of disassembly.

24 Clean all the disassembled parts with solvent and dry them thoroughly.

25 Check all bearing races and rollers for cracks, pits and evidence of heat or seizure. Check bearing cages for deformation and cracks. Replace any defective bearings.

26 Install the differential side gears onto their respective axle shafts and check for play with a dial indicator on the spline pitch circle.

27 Check the spyder gear shaft and gear contact areas for evidence of heating or seizure. Check the differential spyder gear-to-spyder gear shaft clearance. Replace any part that is worn or damaged.

28 Assemble the pinion height gauge components (special tool number MB990819), and install the height gauge into the gear carrier.

29 Apply a thin coat of grease to the yoke side of the washer, then install the nut and tighten it to the drive pinion bearing preload (without the seal in place) torque with an appropriate torque wrench. This torque figure is only valid without the oil seal in place in the gear carrier.

30 Attach special tool number MB990552 to the gear carrier at the side bearing seats. Install the end cap and tighten the cap bolts to the specified torque.

31 Using feeler gauges, check the clearance between the two special tools.

32 Select a shim with a thickness equivalent to the clearance. A list of available drive pinion height adjusting shims is included in the Specifications Section.

33 If the clearance is more than 0.0650 in (1.65 mm), select one 0.0118 in (0.3 mm) thick shim and one other shim to produce a total shim thickness equal to the clearance.

34 If the drive gear set (the ring gear and drive pinion) is being replaced, install new drive pinion height adjusting shims of the same thickness as the shims that were removed during disassembly.

35 Remove the special tools from the gear carrier.

36 Install the selected shims or shims between the drive pinion gear and the rear bearing inner race. Using special tool number MB990802, press the bearing onto the drive pinion shaft.

37 Install the drive pinion shaft, the rear bearing, the pinion spacer and the front bearing into the gear carrier. Slide the differential end

yoke into place on the pinion shaft and install the large washer and nut. Tighten the nut to the specified torque.

38 Check the drive pinion bearing preload (the amount of torque required to start the drive pinion shaft turning) with an appropriate torque wrench and compare it to the specifications.

39 If the preload is not the same as the specifications, disassemble the drive pinion shaft, install a different thickness preload adjusting shim, reassemble the shaft and recheck the bearing preload. A list of available preload adjusting shims is included in the Specifications Section. Different length pinion spacers are also available and may be used in conjunction with the different shims to obtain the proper preload.

40 After completing the drive pinion bearing preload adjustment, remove the nut and washer from the end of the drive pinion shaft and install a new pinion seal by referring to Section 4.

41 Install the thrust spacers and side gears into the differential case.

42 Lay the spyder gear washers in position on the spyder gears. The washers have a lip on the inside diameter which must properly line up with the hole in the gear.

43 Mesh the spyder gears with the side gears exactly 180° apart and rotate them into position in the differential case.

44 Install the spyder gear shaft and check the spyder gear-to-side gear backlash with a dial indicator (photo). If the backlash is excessive, select a side gear thrust spacer of the proper thickness, install it and recheck the backlash. Backlash on the right and left side should be equal. A list of available side gear thrust spacers is included in the Specifications Section.

45 Disassemble the above parts, lubricate them with molybdenum dilsulfide grease, and reassemble them.

46 Place the center block into position. Install the spyder gear shaft and align the lock pin holes. Carefully drive the lock pin into position in the differential case and stake the differential case around the lock pin hole so that the pin will not back out.

47 Clean the ring-gear mounting bolts with a wire brush and the threaded holes in the ring-gear with the appropriate size tap.

48 Apply 'Lock-tite 271', or an equivalent adhesive, to the bolt threads and install the ring-gear onto the differential case. Tighten the

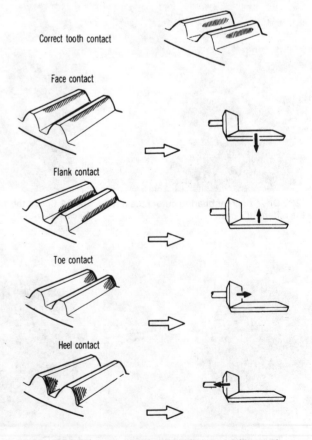

Correct tooth contact

Face contact

Flank contact

Toe contact

Heel contact

Fig. 8.18 Ring gear teeth contact patterns (Sec 14)

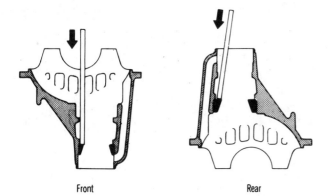

Fig. 8.19 Removing the drive pinion bearing outer races from the differential case (Sec 14)

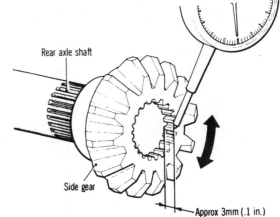

Fig. 8.20 The differential side gear-to-axle shaft spline clearance can be checked with a dial indicator (Sec 14)

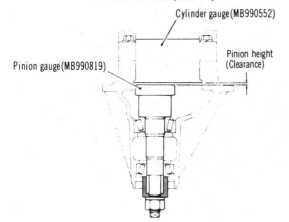

Fig. 8.21 Special tools are required to check the pinion height (clearance) (Sec 14)

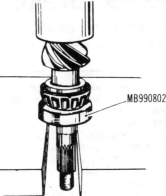

Fig. 8.22 The drive pinion rear bearing must be pressed onto the drive pinion shaft (Sec 14)

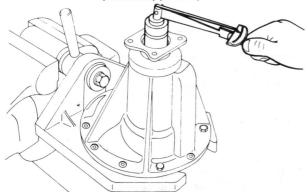

Fig. 8.23 Measuring the drive pinion bearing preload with a torque wrench (Sec 14)

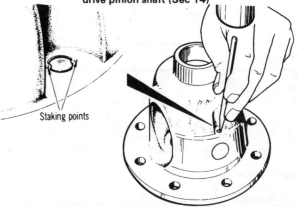

Fig. 8.24 Stake the differential case around the lock pin hole so that the pin will not back out (Sec 14)

bolts to the specified torque, following a crisscross pattern. Set the assembly aside for approximately one-half to one hour to allow the adhesive to harden properly.

49 Press on the differential side bearings.

50 Slip the outer races into place and install the differential gear assembly into the differential case. Lay the caps in place by lining up the mating marks on the right-hand cap. Install the cap bolts and tighten them finger-tight.

51 Carefully thread the side bearing nuts into position and, using special tool number MB990201, or an equivalent homemade tool, tighten the left-hand nut until all backlash between the ring and pinion gears is removed.

52 Loosen the left-hand nut $\frac{1}{16}$ of a turn (the distance between two of the holes) tighten the right-hand bearing nut to the specified torque.

53 Using a dial indicator, check the backlash between the ring and the pinion gears (photo). If the lash is less than specified, loosen the left-hand bearing nut $\frac{1}{16}$ of a turn and tighten the right-hand bearing nut the same amount. Recheck the backlash. If it is greater than specified,

loosen the right-hand bearing nut $\frac{1}{16}$ of a turn and tighten the left-hand bearing nut the same amount. Again, recheck the lash. Continue the operation until the basklash is within the specifications.

54 Next, tighten each bearing nut $\frac{1}{32}$ of a turn ($\frac{1}{2}$ the distance between holes) to preload the bearings properly.

55 Tighten the carrier cap bolts to the specified torque (photo) and recheck the pinion and ring-gear backlash. Install the lock plates on the bearing caps and tighten the bolts to the specified torque (photo).

56 Using a dial indicator, check the ring gear run-out on the back side of the ring gear (photo). If the run-out is greater than specified, change the ring gear location relative to the differential case and recheck the run-out. If it is still greater than specified, disassemble the ring gear and check the run-out of the ring gear mounting surface on the differential case. If it is more than specified, replace the ring gear case. If it is within the specifications, replace the ring gear with a new one.

57 Pack the ring gear teeth with molybdenum disulfide grease and install the differential assembly into the rear axle housing by referring to Section 13.

Chapter 9 Brake system

Refer to Chapter 13 for specifications and information related to 1981 thru 1988 models

Contents

Specifications

Brake pedal

Brake pedal play	0.4 to 0.6 in (10 to 15 mm)
Lateral play between brake/clutch pedals	0.120 in (3 mm)
Depressed pedal-to-floorboard clearance	1 in (26 mm) or more
Brake pedal height (distance between top of pedal and floorboard)	6.5 in (166 mm)

Master cylinder

Inside diameter	0.8748 to 0.8768 in (22.220 to 22.272 mm)
Piston diameter	0.8719 to 0.8732 in (22.147 to 22.180 mm)
Cylinder/piston clearance	0.0016 to 0.0049 in (0.040 to 0.125 mm)
Piston-to-power brake pushrod clearance	0 to 0.03 in (0 to 0.75 mm)

Disc brake

Pad thickness (standard)	0.41 in (10.5 mm)
Pad thickness (wear limit)	0.040 in (1.0 mm)
Brake disc thickness	0.79 in (20.0 mm)
Brake disc runout	Less than 0.006 in (0.15 mm)

Drum brake

Lining thickness (standard)	0.213 in (5.4 mm)
Lining thickness (wear limit)	0.040 in (1.0 mm)
Wheel cylinder bore	0.750 to 0.752 in (19.050 to 19.102 mm)
Piston diameter	0.7479 to 0.7492 in (18.997 to 19.030 mm)
Wheel cylinder/piston clearance	0.0008 to 0.0041 in (0.020 to 0.105 mm)
Brake drum I.D.	9.5 to 9.579 in (241.3 to 243.3 mm)
Drum/lining clearance	0.010 to 0.016 in (0.25 to 0.40 mm)
Adjusting cable length	10.020 ± .006 in (254.5 ± 0.15 mm)
Primary (green) brake shoe return spring free length	4.35 in (110.5 mm)
Secondary (grey) brake shoe return spring free length	4.23 in (107.5 mm)

Torque specifications

	ft-lb	(Nm)
Master cylinder check valve cap	18 to 25	(24 to 34)
Master cylinder check valve case	29 to 36	(39 to 49)
Piston stop	1.1 to 2.2	(1.5 to 3.0)
Wheel cylinder bleeder screws	5 to 7	(7 to 9)
Disc brake caliper assembly bolts	51 to 65	(69 to 88)
Brake disc-to-hub nuts		
1979 models	25 to 29	(34 to 39)
1980 models	34 to 38	(46 to 51)
Wheel cylinder attaching bolts	13 to 15	(18 to 20)
Power brake booster attaching nuts	6 to 9	(8 to 12)

1   General description

The Chrysler mini-truck is equipped with sliding caliper-type disc brakes at the front and drum brakes at the rear. Driver effort is assisted by a vacuum-operated power servo unit.

The system is a dual line type wth a dual master cylinder and separate hydraulic systems for the front and rear wheels. In the event of a brake line or seal failure, half the braking system will still operate.

2   Disc brake pads — inspection

1   Refer to Chapter 1 for disc brake checking procedures.

3   Disc brake pads – replacement

1   Raise the front of the vehicle and set it on jack stands. Block the rear tires and set the parking brake to keep the vehicle from rolling. Remove the wheels. It is a good idea to disassemble only one brake at a time so that the other brake can be used as a guide if difficulties are encountered during reassembly.

2   Remove the spigot pins from the stopper plugs (photo). Each caliper has two stopper plugs and each stopper plug has two spigot pins.

3   Pull out the stopper plugs and pad support plates from the caliper body (photo). Move the caliper assembly diagonally up and down to separate it from the caliper support bracket (the upper caliper bracket

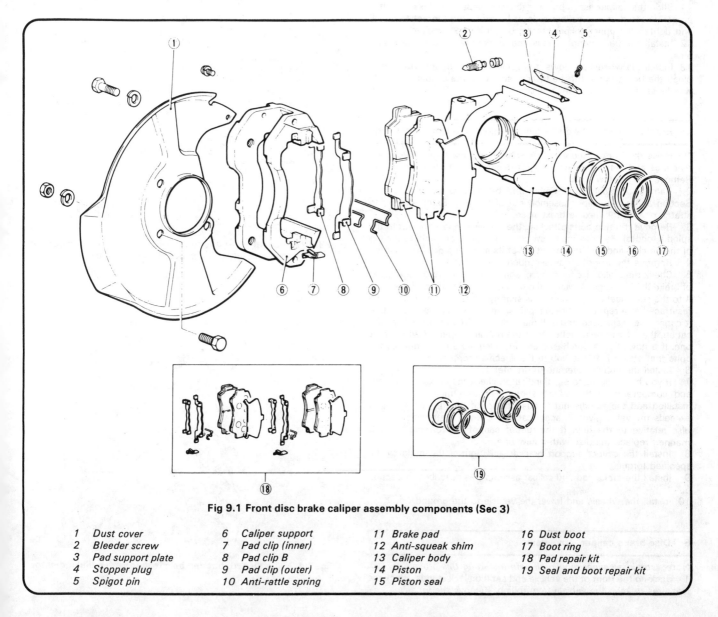

Fig 9.1 Front disc brake caliper assembly components (Sec 3)

1	*Dust cover*	*6*	*Caliper support*
2	*Bleeder screw*	*7*	*Pad clip (inner)*
3	*Pad support plate*	*8*	*Pad clip B*
4	*Stopper plug*	*9*	*Pad clip (outer)*
5	*Spigot pin*	*10*	*Anti-rattle spring*

11	*Brake pad*	*16*	*Dust boot*
12	*Anti-squeak shim*	*17*	*Boot ring*
13	*Caliper body*	*18*	*Pad repair kit*
14	*Piston*	*19*	*Seal and boot repair kit*
15	*Piston seal*		

bolt should be removed if it interferes with the metal brake line during caliper removal). Tie the caliper out of the way.

4   Remove the pads from the caliper support bracket. Separate the anti-squeal shim from the outer pad (photo). Remove the inner and outer pad clips and the pad clips labeled 'B' from the caliper support bracket (Fig. 9.2).

5   The pads in each caliper must be replaced as a set and the pads on both front wheels must be replaced during the same servicing. Never replace the pads on one wheel only.

6   Before installing the new brake pads, check the brake disc as described in Section 4. Also check the caliper assembly around the piston for signs of brake fluid leakage. If leakage is evident, refer to Section 5 for caliper repair procedures.

7   Check the stopper plugs, the pad support plates, the anti-rattle spring, and the pad clips for damage. Replace any defective parts.

8   Install the inner and outer pad clips and the pad clips labeled 'B' into position on the caliper support bracket (Fig. 9.2).

9   Slip the new brake pads into place. Make sure the anti-squeal shim is installed on the outer pad (photo).

10 Wipe clean the exposed part of the piston in the caliper assembly and, using a hammer handle, push the piston into its bore so that the caliper assembly will fit over the new pads. If the piston does not want to slide in, loosen the bleeder screw and push again. The piston should slide in easily. Be sure to bleed the system as described in Section 11 if you have to loosen the bleeder screw. Apply 2 very thin layers of grease to the sliding portion of the caliper assembly.

11 Slide the caliper assembly over the new pads and make sure it is properly seated on the caliper support bracket. Don't forget to install and tighten the upper caliper bracket bolt if it was removed.

12 Install the pad support plates, the stopper plugs and the spigot pins.

13 Install the wheels and lower the vehicle to the ground. Be sure to bleed the brake system if the bleeder screw on the caliper assembly was loosened. Test drive the vehicle.

---

4   Front hub and brake disc – removal, inspection and installation

1   Raise the front of the vehicle and set it on jack stands. Block the rear tires and set the parking brake to keep the vehicle from rolling. Remove the front wheels.

2   Remove the caliper assembly and brake pads as described in Section 3. Tie the caliper assembly out of the way. Be careful not to stretch or kink the flexible brake hose.

3   Remove the two bolts attaching the caliper support bracket to the spindle (photo). Remove the screw attaching the dust shield to the top of the bracket and lift the bracket out of its mounting position (photo).

4   Remove the front hub as described in Chapter 1.

5   Check the brake disc for scoring, abnormal wear, cracks, and signs of brake fluid leakage. Measure the thickness of the disc and compare it to the specifications. If the disc is slightly worn or scored, it can be resurfaced at a reputable brake repair shop. If it is worn so badly that it cannot be resurfaced and still meet the required thickness specification, then it can be unbolted from the hub and replaced with a new one. If a new disc is purchased and installed, be sure to tighten the bolts that attach it to the hub to the specified torque.

6   Install the hub by referring to Chapter 1.

7   If you have access to a dial indicator, check the brake disc runout and compare it to the specifications. The hub must be properly installed and the spindle nut torqued to specifications. If the runout exceeds the value given in specifications, change the position of the disc relative to the hub. If the runout cannot be corrected in this manner, replace the disc with a new one.

8   Install the caliper support bracket and tighten the bolts to the specified torque.

9   Install the brake pad and caliper assembly as described in Section 3.

10 Install the wheels and lower the vehicle to the ground.

---

5   Disc brake caliper – overhaul

Note: *Obtain a caliper rebuild kit before starting this procedure.*

1   Jack up the front of the vehicle and set it on jack stands. Block the rear tires to keep the vehicle from rolling. Remove the wheels.

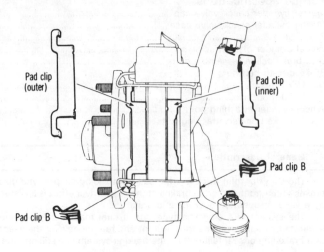

Fig. 9.2 Pad clip installation (Sec 3)

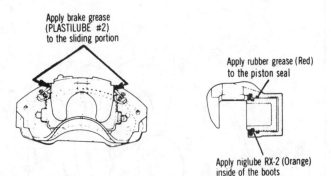

Fig. 9.3 The caliper must be properly lubricated when the pads are replaced and when the caliper is overhauled (Sec 3)

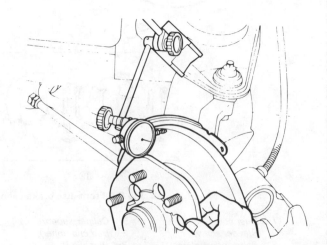

Fig. 9.4 Brake disc runout can be checked with a dial indicator

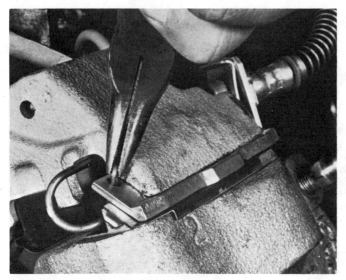

3.2 Pull the spigot pins out of the stopper plugs

3.3a Remove the stopper plugs from the caliper

3.3b Remove the pad support plate from the caliper

3.3c Carefully tie the caliper out of the way with a piece of wire

3.4 Remove the pads and separate the anti-squeal shim from the outer pad

3.9 Slip the new pads into place (make sure the anti-squeal shim is installed on the outer pad)

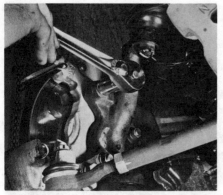

4.3a Remove the 2 bolts attaching the caliper support bracket to the wheel spindle

4.3b Lift the caliper out of its mounting position

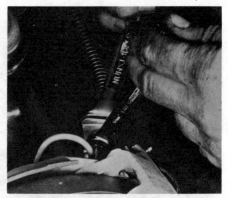

5.2a Use 2 wrenches to loosen the fitting which attaches the metal brake line to the flexible brake hose

5.2b Pull out the spring clip holding the flexible hose to the bracket

5.5a Remove the boot retaining snap-ring

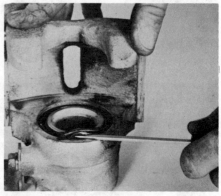

5.5b Remove the dust boot

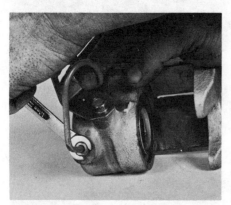

5.6 Loosen the fitting and remove the metal brake line from the caliper body

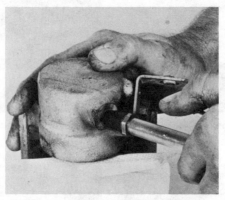

5.7 Air pressure blown into the metal brake line fitting hole can be used to remove the piston

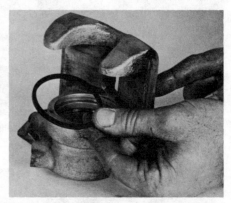

5.8 Remove the seal from the caliper bore (do not use a metal tool for this procedure)

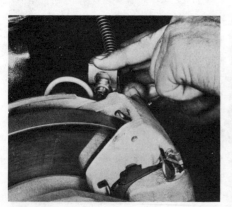

5.18 Install the spring clip that attaches the flexible hose to the bracket

7.2 The brake drum can be removed by screwing a bolt into each of the 2 threaded holes

7.3a Disengage the rear return spring from the pivot

7.3b Remove the forward spring

7.4a Disengage the adjusting cable from the pivot

7.4b Remove the rear brake return spring and cable guide

7.6 Spread the parking brake lever pivot retaining clip and remove the clip and wavy washer

7.14 Inspect the backing plate for grooves worn by the brake shoes

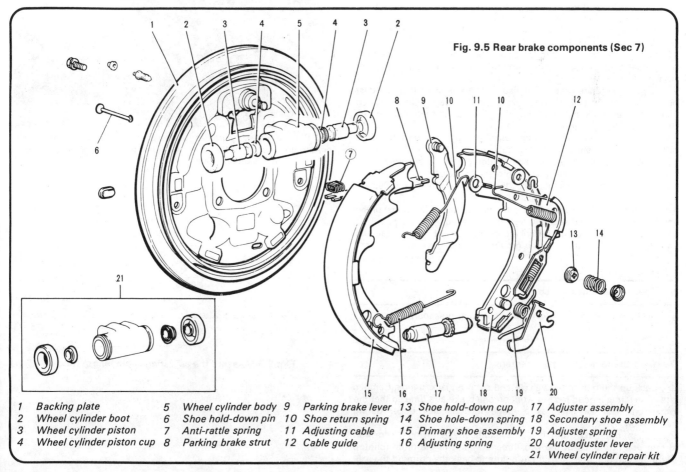

Fig. 9.5 Rear brake components (Sec 7)

1	Backing plate	5	Wheel cylinder body	9	Parking brake lever	13	Shoe hold-down cup	17	Adjuster assembly
2	Wheel cylinder boot	6	Shoe hold-down pin	10	Shoe return spring	14	Shoe hole-down spring	18	Secondary shoe assembly
3	Wheel cylinder piston	7	Anti-rattle spring	11	Adjusting cable	15	Primary shoe assembly	19	Adjuster spring
4	Wheel cylinder piston cup	8	Parking brake strut	12	Cable guide	16	Adjusting spring	20	Autoadjuster lever
								21	Wheel cylinder repair kit

2   Loosen the fitting which attaches the metal brake line to the flexible brake hose at the caliper bracket (photo). Pull out the spring clip holding the flexible hose to the bracket (photo) and disconnect the metal line from the flexible hose. Place a container under the fitting to catch any brake fluid that may drip. Plug the flexible hose to keep out dirt and other contaminants.

3   Remove the caliper assembly as described in Section 4.

4   You must have a clean place to work, clean rags, a caliper rebuild kit for each caliper, a container of brake fluid and some alcohol to perform the caliper overhaul.

5   Remove the pad support plates from the caliper assembly if you have not already done so. Next, remove the boot retaining snap ring and the dust boot from around the piston (photos).

6   Loosen the fitting and remove the metal brake line from the caliper body (photo).

7   The piston must now be removed from the caliper body. This can be achieved in one of three ways, depending upon the degree of difficulty. Make sure the caliper cavity is well cushioned with rags to prevent damage to the piston or bore. Also, do not pry on the piston with metal tools.

   (a)   First, try dislodging the piston by tapping the caliper with a wood block, or by jolting the caliper against two wood blocks.

   (b)   If the above procedure does not work, temporarily re-connect the caliper to the brake fluid line. Have an assistant depress the brake pedal. The fluid pressure should force the piston out.

   (c)   If compressed air is available, sometimes this air pressure can be used to move the piston. Blow the air into the brake line fitting hole (photo).

8   Remove the seal in the caliper bore with a plastic or wooden probe. Do not use a metal probe, as you may scratch or gouge the bore surface (photo).

9   Carefully clean the entire caliper and the piston with alcohol or clean brake fluid. Do not, under any circumstances, use a petroleum-base cleaning solvent. Dry the parts thoroughly and make sure none of the fluid passages are clogged or dirty.

10 Inspect the piston and caliper bore for signs of wear, scoring, pitting or rust. Replace any defective parts.

11 Lubricate the new piston seal with the red grease included in the rebuild kit and install the seal in the caliper bore.

12 Apply clean brake fluid to the caliper bore inside the seal and the piston. Carefully slide the piston into the caliper bore. Do not pinch or twist the seal.

13 Apply the orange grease supplied with the rebuild kit to the dust boot groove in the caliper body. Install the dust boot with the raised inner ring facing the piston. Make sure it is properly seated and install the boot retaining snap ring.

14 Wipe off any grease or brake fluid that may have gotten on the outside of the piston, dust boot or caliper.

15 Install the metal brake line and tighten the fitting securely.

16 Install the pad support plates onto the caliper.

17 Install the caliper assembly onto the vehicle by referring to Section 4.

18 Connect the metal brake line to the flexible brake hose. Install the spring clip (photo) and securely tighten the fitting.

19 Bleed the system as described in Section 11 and install the wheels. Lower the vehicle to the ground and test drive it.

6   Rear brake shoes – inspection

1   Refer to Chapter 1 for rear brake checking procedures.

7   Rear brake shoes – replacement

1   Jack up the rear of the vehicle and set it on jack stands. Remove the wheel. It is a good idea to work on one brake at a time so that the other one can be used as a guide if difficulties occur during reassembly.

2   Pull off the brake drum. If you have difficulty removing it, screw an 8 mm bolt into each of the two threaded holes in the drum (photo). Tighten each bolt one-half turn at a time to back the drum off the axle

7.15 Measure the free length of the brake shoe return springs

7.17 Place the parking brake strut into position with the spring on the forward end (note that the struts will be stamped 'R' for the right side and 'L' for the left side of the vehicle)

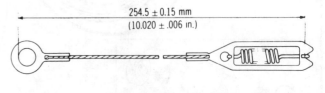

254.5 ± 0.15 mm
(10.020 ± .006 in.)

Fig. 9.6 Measure the adjusting cable length (Sec 7)

flange. Take a long, close look at the relationship between the parts before disassembling the brake.

3   Disengage the brake return springs from the pivot and remove the forward spring (photos).

4   Disengage the adjusting cable from the pivot (photo) and remove the rear brake return spring and cable guide (photo).

5   Disengage the adjusting cable from the auto-adjuster lever.

6   Spread the parking brake lever pivot retaining clip and remove the clip and wavy washer from the pivot (photo).

7   Remove the brake shoe hold-down cups, springs and pins.

8   Remove the front brake shoe by disengaging it from the adjusting spring and adjuster.

9   Separate the parking brake lever from the rear brake shoe and slide out the parking brake strut and spring.

10 Remove the auto adjuster lever from the rear brake shoe.

11 Check the brake return springs for cracks and other damage. Check the auto adjuster lever and the adjusting latch for wear and damage. Make sure the star wheel can be screwed into and out of the adjuster. Clean the star wheel threads and lubricate them with high-temperature grease if any resistance is felt. Measure the adjusting cable length and compare it to the specifications.

12 Check the wheel cylinders for signs of brake fluid leakage. Refer to Sections 9 and 10 if they need repair.

13 Check the drum inside diameter and compare it to the specifications. Inspect it for cracks, scoring, out of roundness and oil stains. Replace the drum or have it turned at a reputable brake service shop if any defects are noted.

14 Inspect the backing plate ledges for grooves (photo). If the grooves are not too deep, they can be removed by filing or sanding the backing plate. If the grooves are too deep, the backing plate must be replaced or the brake shoes will hang up in the grooves.

15 Check the free length of the primary (green) and secondary (grey) brake shoe return springs (photo) and compare them to the specifications. Replace any springs that are stretched with new ones.

16 Install the auto adjuster spring and lever onto the rear brake shoe.

17 Place the parking brake strut into position with the spring on the forward end (photo). Note that the parking brake struts will be stamped 'R' for the right side of the vehicle and 'L' for the left side of the vehicle.

18 Install the parking brake lever into the hole at the top of the rear brake shoe. Slip the wavy washer and retaining clip onto the pivot.

19 Install the auto adjuster assembly and spring into position between the lower ends of the brake shoes. Make sure that the auto adjuster mechanism is properly installed or it will not operate.

20 Lubricate the backing plate shoe contact points with the recommended lubricant (Fig. 9.7) and place the brake shoes into position on the backing plate, making sure they are properly aligned with the wheel cylinder. Do not damage the wheel cylinder boots. Engage the parking brake lever properly.

21 Install the brake shoe hold-down pins, springs and cups.

22 Hook the adjusting cable into the hole on the auto adjuster lever. Place the cable guide into position on the rear brake shoe and insert the shoe end of the return spring into the hole in the shoe.

23 Lift up on the end of the auto adjuster lever and place the adjusting cable eyelet over the brake shoe pivot at the top of the backing plate.

24 Place the end of the rear return spring over the pivot, then install the forward return spring.

25 Double-check to make sure all the springs and cables are properly installed. Operate the auto-adjuster mechanism by pulling the adjusting cable toward the edge of the backing plate. The adjusting lever should ratchet over the adjusting wheel and engage the next tooth when the cable is pulled.

26 Install the brake drum, adjust the brakes as described in Section 8, install the wheels and lower the vehicle to the ground.

8   Rear brake shoes – adjustment

1   The rear brake shoe lining-to-drum clearance is automatically adjusted when the brake pedal is depressed during normal vehicle operation. When the brakes are disassembled for servicing, or if the adjuster becomes corroded or gets damaged and fails to function, the shoe clearance can be adjusted manually.

2   When the brakes are being reassembled after servicing, turn the brake adjuster star wheel by hand until the brake drum will just slip

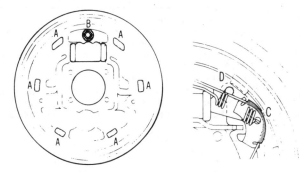

Fig. 9.7 Apply a thin layer of brake system grease to the backing plate shoe contact points (Sec 7)

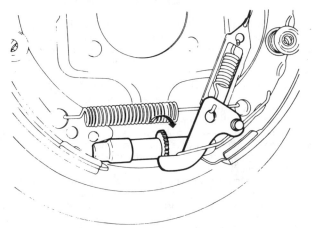

Fig. 9.8 The brake shoes are adjusted by turning the star wheel (Sec 8)

over the shoes and into position. The correct clearance will be automatically established as the vehicle is driven.

3   If the automatic adjuster fails to function, the shoe clearance can be temporarily adjusted so that the vehicle can be driven until the brake can be disassembled and the adjuster repaired or replaced.

4   Remove the rubber plug from the back side of the brake backing plate and turn the brake adjuster star wheel (with a brake adjusting tool or a screwdriver) in the direction opposite the arrow (see Figure 9.8) until the brake shoes just come into contact with the drum. Turn the rear wheel by hand, as the star wheel is being adjusted, and listen for a scraping sound which indicates that the shoes are touching the drum.

5   Using another screwdriver, push the adjusting lever clear of the star wheel and turn the wheel in the direction indicated by the arrow until the shoe just barely clears the drum.

6   Replace the rubber plug in the back of the brake backing plate.

7   The brake should be disassembled, and the adjuster mechanism repaired, as soon as possible (refer to Section 7).

9   Rear wheel cylinder – removal and installation

1   Remove the brake shoes as described in Section 7.

2   Disconnect the brake line from the wheel cylinder by loosening the fitting (photo).

3   Remove the two bolts which attach the wheel cylinder to the backing plate (photo) and lift out the wheel cylinder.

4   To install the wheel cylinder, slip it into position on the backing plate and connect the brake line to the wheel cylinder. Tighten the brake line fitting with your fingers to make sure the threads are properly engaged. Do not tighten it with a wrench at this point. Install the 2 wheel cylinder mounting bolts and tighten them to the specified torque. Now tighten the brake line fitting securely.

5   Install the brake shoes as described in Section 7.

6   Bleed the system by referring to Section 11, and inspect carefully for fluid leakage.

10 Rear wheel cylinder – overhaul

1   You must have a clean place to work, clean rags, a wheel cylinder rebuild kit, a container of brake fluid and some alcohol to perform the wheel cylinder overhaul.

2   Remove the wheel cylinder as described in Section 9.

3   Remove the bleeder screw from the cylinder body (photo).

4   Remove the dust boots and pistons from the cylinder body (photo). Separate the dust boots from the pistons, noting how they are installed.

5   Remove the rubber piston cups from the pistons, taking care that the pistons are not scratched or gouged in the process.

6   Check the wheel cylinder bore for wear, scoring, pitting and rust. If the bore is worn, pitted, scored or rusted, it can be honed slightly to restore it to reusable condition. Be sure to use the appropriate size hone. If a hone is not available, or if the damage is slight, polish the bore with crocus cloth.

7   Carefully clean the wheel cylinder body and the pistons with alcohol or clean brake fluid. Do not, under any circumstances, use a petroleum-base cleaning solvent. Dry the parts thoroughly with a lint-free rag or compressed air and make sure that none of the fluid passages are clogged or dirty.

8   Measure the piston outside diameter (photo) and compare it to the specifications. If the pistons are smaller than the specified diameter, replace them. Measure the cylinder bore diameter and compare it to the specifications. If it is larger than the specified diameter, the wheel cylinder must be replaced. Subtract the piston diameter from the cylinder bore diameter to obtain the piston-to-bore clearance. If the clearance is greater than specified, the pistons and wheel cylinder must be replaced.

9   Install the new piston cups onto the pistons. The widest outside diameter of the cup must be installed as shown (photo).

10   Apply the orange grease supplied with the rebuild kit to the dust boot grooves on the pistons and wheel cylinder body (photos).

11   Install the new dust boots onto the pistons as shown (photo).

12   Lightly lubricate the wheel cylinder bore, the pistons and piston cups with clean brake fluid. Slip the pistons into the cylinder bore (photo). Be careful not to pinch or twist the piston cups as the pistons are inserted into the bore. Fit the outer edges of the dust boots into the grooves on the cylinder body.

13   Wipe off any grease or brake fluid that may have gotten on the outside surfaces of the wheel cylinder body or the dust boots.

14   Install the bleeder screw into the wheel cylinder body.

15   Install the wheel cylinder onto the vehicle by referring to Section 9.

11 Brake system – bleeding

1   If the brake system has air in it, operation of the brake pedal will be spongy and imprecise. Air can enter the brake system whenever any part of the system is dismantled or if the fluid level in the master cylinder reservoir runs low. Air can also leak into the system through a fault too slight to allow fluid to leak out. In this case, it indicates that a general overhaul of the brake system is required.

2   To bleed the brakes, you will need an assistant to pump the brake pedal, a supply of new brake fluid, an empty glass jar, a plastic or vinyl tube which will fit over the bleeder nipple, and a wrench for the bleeder screw.

3   There are five locations at which the brake system is bled: the master cylinder; the front brake caliper assemblies; and the rear brake wheel cylinders.

4   Check the fluid level at the master cylinder reservoir. Add fluid, if necessary, to bring the level up to the full mark. Use only the recommended brake fluid, and do not mix different types. Never use fluid from a container that has been standing uncapped. You will have to check the fluid level in the master cylinder reservoir often during the bleeding procedure. If the level drops too far, air will enter the system through the master cylinder.

5   Raise the vehicle and set it securely on jack stands.

6   Remove the bleeder screw cap from the wheel cylinder or caliper assembly that is being bled. If more than one wheel must be bled, start with the one farthest from the master cylinder.

7   Attach one end of the clear plastic or vinyl tube to the bleeder screw nipple and place the other end in the glass or plastic jar submerged in a small amount of clean brake fluid.

8   Loosen the bleeder screw slightly, then tighten it to the point where it is snug yet easily loosened.

9   Have the assistant pump the brake pedal several times and hold it in the fully depressed position.

10   With pressure on the brake pedal, open the bleeder screw approximately one-half turn. As the brake fluid is flowing through the tube and into the jar, tighten the bleeder screw. Again, pump the brake pedal, hold it in the fully depressed position, and loosen the bleeder screw momentarily. Do not allow the brake pedal to be released with the bleeder screw in the open position.

11   Repeat the procedure until no air bubbles are visible in the brake fluid flowing through the tube. Be sure to check the brake fluid level in the master cylinder reservoir while performing the bleeding operation.

12   Fully tighten the bleeder screw, remove the plastic or vinyl tube and install the bleeder screw cap.

13   Follow the same procedure to bleed the other wheel cylinder or caliper assemblies.

14   To bleed the master cylinder, have the assistant pump and hold the brake pedal. Momentarily loosen the brake line fittings, one at a time, where they attach to the master cylinder. Any air in the master cylinder will escape when the fittings are loosened. Brake fluid will damage painted surfaces, so use paper towels or rags to cover and protect the areas around the master cylinder.

15   Check the brake fluid level in the master cylinder to make sure it is adequate, then test drive the vehicle and check for proper brake operation.

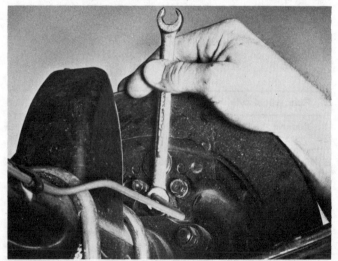

9.2 Loosen the fitting and disconnect the brake line from the wheel cylinder

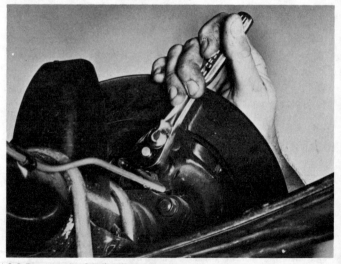

9.3 Remove the 2 bolts that attach the wheel cylinder to the backing plate

12 Master cylinder – removal and installation

1 Remove the air cleaner assembly by referring to Chapter 4.

2 Place a clean rag around and under the master cylinder so that any spilled brake fluid does not get on the painted surfaces of the body or frame. Slide back the hose clamps and disconnect the two hoses leading from the brake fluid reservoir to the top of the master cylinder (photos). Use a bolt or other suitable object to plug the hoses so that brake fluid does not leak out of them.

3 Loosen the fitting and remove the rear brake line from the master cylinder (photo). Loosen the through-bolt attaching the front brake line adapter to the master cylinder (photo). Be careful not to lose the two soft metal washers on the bolt. Note their positions so that the washers can be installed properly upon reassembly.

4 Slide back the hose clamp and remove the power brake vacuum hose from the booster fitting (photo). Remove the nut attaching the vacuum hose bracket to the master cylinder booster assembly (photo). Reinstall the nut onto the stud after removing the bracket.

5 Remove the 2 nuts and lock washers holding the master cylinder to the vacuum booster (photo) and withdraw the master cylinder straight ahead and out of the vehicle. Be careful not to spill any of the brake fluid onto painted surfaces.

6 Check for fluid leakage at the rear of the master cylinder. If there is evidence of fluid leakage, the master cylinder should be overhauled or replaced with a rebuilt unit. If the master cylinder requires overhaul, refer to Section 13. If for some reason you cannot or do not want to overhaul the master cylinder, a rebuilt unit may be purchased from your dealer or a reputable auto parts store and installed on the vehicle.

7 If a master cylinder other than the original is being installed, such as a commercially rebuilt unit, check the clearance between the back of the piston and the power brake pushrod. Using a depth micrometer, or vernier calipers, measure the distance from the piston to the master cylinder mounting flange. Next, measure the distance from the end of the power brake pushrod to the surface on the booster assembly that the master cylinder mounting flange is in contact with when installed. Subtract the two measurements to get the clearance. If the clearance is more or less than specified, turn the adjusting screw on the end of

10.3 Remove the bleeder screw from the wheel cylinder body

10.4 Remove the dust boots and pistons from the wheel cylinder

10.8 Measure the outside diameter of the pistons

10.9 Install the new piston cups onto the pistons

10.10a Apply the orange grease supplied with the rebuild kit to the dust boot grooves on the pistons

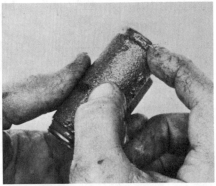

10.10b Apply the orange grease supplied with the rebuild kit to the dust boot grooves on the wheel cylinder

10.11 Install the dust boots onto the pistons

10.12 Lubricate the pistons and wheel cylinder bore with clean brake fluid, then carefully slip the pistons into the bore

12.2a Slide back the hose clamps and ...

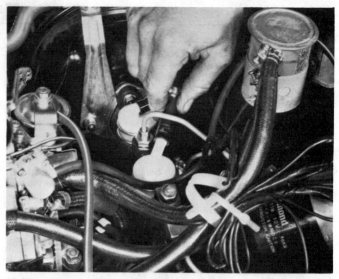

12.2b ... disconnect the 2 hoses leading from the brake fluid reservoir to the top of the master cylinder

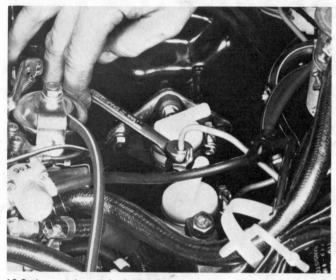

12.3a Loosen the rear brake line fitting

12.3b Loosen the through-bolt attaching the front brake line adapter to the master cylinder

12.4a Remove the power brake vacuum hose from the booster fitting

12.4b Remove the nut attaching the vacuum hose bracket to the master cylinder booster assembly

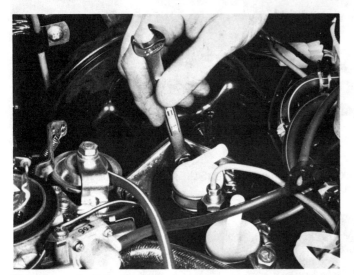

12.5 Remove the 2 master cylinder mounting nuts

the power brake pushrod until the clearance is within the specified limit. Be sure to lock the jam nut on the adjusting screw when the adjustment is completed.

8   Hold the master cylinder in place and loosely install the brake lines to the master cylinder. Don't forget to install the soft washers on the through-bolt that attaches the front brake line. If the washers are not installed properly, leakage will result.

9   Install the 2 lock washers and nuts that attach the master cylinder to the vacuum booster assembly. Tighten them securely.
10   Hold the power brake vacuum hose bracket in place and install the lock washer and nut that attached it to the vacuum booster assembly. Tighten the nut securely.
11   Tighten both brake line fittings securely.
12   Attach the power brake vacuum hose to the fitting on the vacuum booster assembly and slide the hose clamp into place.
13   Slip the two hoses from the brake fluid reservoir into place on the chamber caps. Install the hose clamps.
14   After installation of the master cylinder, the system must be bled as described in Section 11.

13 Master cylinder – overhaul

1   You must have a clean place to work, clean rags, a master cylinder rebuild kit, a container of clean brake fluid and some alcohol to perform the master cylinder overhaul.
2   Remove the master cylinder as described in Section 12.
3   Loosen and remove the clamps holding the chamber covers to the master cylinder (photo). It is a good idea to somehow mark the position of the spigots before removing the chamber covers (so they can be reinstalled with the spigots facing the same direction). Pry off the chamber covers. Be very careful when removing the covers; they are made of plastic and may be brittle.
4   Remove the check valve gap, the rear line seat, the check valve and the check valve spring from the rear brake line mounting hole (photos). Note the order in which they are removed to ensure proper reassembly. Next, remove the valve case, the washer, the check valve and the check valve spring from the front brake line mounting hole (photos). Again, note the order in which they are removed to ensure proper reassembly.

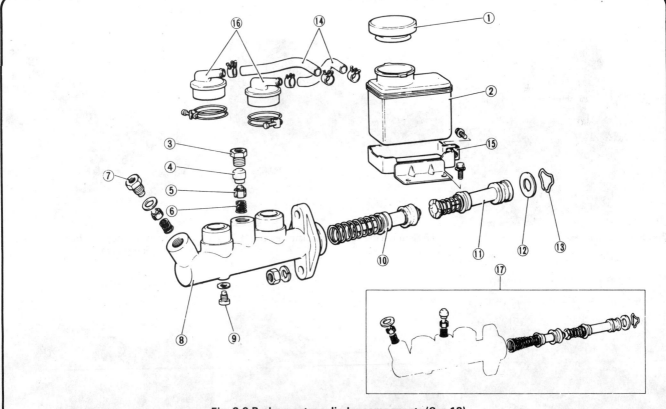

Fig. 9.9 Brake master cylinder components (Sec 13)

1 Reservoir cap	5 Check valve	9 Piston stopper	13 Stopper ring
2 Fluid reservoir	6 Check valve spring	10 Secondary piston assembly	14 Reservoir hose
3 Check valve cap	7 Valve case	11 Primary piston assembly	15 Bracket
4 Rear line seat	8 Master cylinder	12 Piston stopper	16 Chamber cover
			17 Master cylinder kit

13.3 Loosen and remove the clamps holding the chamber covers to the master cylinder

13.4a Remove the check valve cap from the rear brake line mounting hole

13.4b Lift out the rear line seat

13.4c The check valve

13.4d The check valve spring

13.4e Remove the valve case from the front brake line mounting hole

13.4f Remove the washer

13.5 Remove the secondary piston stop and O-ring

13.6a Remove the stop ring from the rear of the master cylinder bore

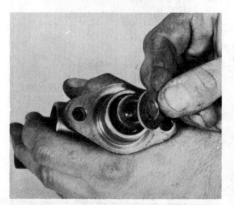

13.6b Remove the piston stop from the rear of the master cylinder bore

13.6c Carefully remove the primary piston assembly from the master cylinder bore

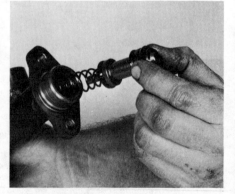

13.6d Carefully remove the secondary piston assembly from the master cylinder bore

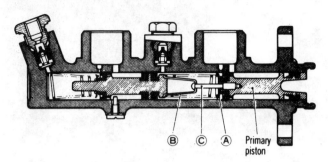

Fig. 9.10 Cross-sectional view of brake master cylinder (Sec 13)

5　Remove the secondary piston stop and O-ring from the bottom of the master cylinder (photo).
6　Remove the stop ring and piston stop from the rear of the master cylinder bore (photos). Slide out the primary and secondary piston assemblies (photos). Do not disassemble the primary piston assembly, as the distance between the spring seat (A) and the spring retainer (B) is factory set by screw (C) and must not be disturbed (see Fig. 9.10).
7　Check the master cylinder bore for wear, scoring, pitting and rust. If it is scored, pitted or worn, it can be honed slightly to restore it to usable condition. Check the piston contact surfaces for scoring and wear.
8　Clean the master cylinder, piston assemblies and all other parts with alcohol or clean brake fluid. Do not, under any circumstances, use a petroleum-base solvent. Dry the parts thoroughly and make sure that none of the fluid passages in the cylinder body are clogged or dirty.
9　Measure the master cylinder bore diameter with inside micrometers and compare it to the specifications. If it is larger than the specified diameter, the master cylinder must be replaced. Measure the outside diameter of the pistons and compare to the specifications. If they are smaller than the specified diameters, the pistons must be replaced. Subtract the piston diameter from the bore diameter to obtain the piston-to-bore clearance. If the clearance is greater than specified, the pistons and master cylinder body must be replaced.
10　Check the primary and secondary piston return springs for loss of tension and damage. If they are defective, the entire piston assembly must be replaced. It is a good practice, and highly recommended, that the piston assemblies be replaced whenever the master cylinder needs any type of repair work done on it.
11　Lightly lubricate the cylinder bore, the piston assemblies and the piston cups with clean brake fluid. Insert the new secondary piston assembly, followed by the primary piston assembly, into the cylinder bore. Be careful not to pinch or twist the piston cups in the process. Lay the piston stop in position and install the stop ring in the end of the cylinder bore. Install the piston stop and O-ring into the bottom of the cylinder.
12　Install the check valve spring, the check valve, the rear line seat and the check valve cap into the rear brake line mounting hole. Install the check valve spring, the check valve, the washer and the valve case into the front brake line mounting hole. Use the exploded view drawing (Fig. 9.9) to make sure they are installed in the proper order.
13　Install the chamber covers and clamps. Make sure the spigots are facing in the same direction as they were before removal.
14　Install the master cylinder in the vehicle by referring to Section 12. Bleed the brake system as described in Section 11.

14　Parking brake – adjustment

1　Raise the vehicle and set it on jack stands.
2　Adjust the parking brake turnbuckle until the stroke of the parking brake pullrod is as specified.
3　Check to see that the parking brake balancer is nearly parallel with the center line of the vehicle.
4　Check the parking brake lever-to-crossmember clearance and compare it to the specifications.
5　Release the parking brake and make sure that the rear cable is not taut. Readjust if necessary. The rear wheels should turn without any brake resistance.
6　Lower the vehicle to the ground.

15　Parking brake warning light switch – adjustment

1　Adjust the parking brake by referring to Section 14.
2　Loosen the two clamp-screws attaching the parking brake light switch to the pullrod bracket.
3　Move the switch until the brake warning light goes out when the pullrod is released and comes on when the pullrod is engaged on the first notch.
4　Tighten the clamp screws.

16　Parking brake cables – removal and installation

1　Raise the vehicle and set it on jack stands. Make sure the parking brake is fully released.
2　Disassemble the rear brakes and remove the ends of the parking brake cables from the parking brake levers by referring to Section 7.
3　Separate the parking brake cable at the turnbuckle. Hold the left-side end with a wrench. Loosen the jam nut at the turnbuckle and unscrew the left-side cable end from the turnbuckle (photo).
4　Remove the cotter key, washer and pin from the parking brake balancer. Remove the balancer (photo) and separate it from the right-side cable. Reinstall the balancer without the cable so the parts do not get misplaced.
5　Loosen and remove the 4 cable housing clamps (there are 3 on the frame and 1 on the rear spring) that attach each cable to the vehicle (photo).
6　Slip the cables and housings out of the rear backing plates by compressing the retaining clips with pliers. The right-side cable is the longer of the two. Apply a thin coat of all-purpose grease to the sections of the cables that are enclosed by the cable housings.
7　To install the cables, slip the ends through the rear brake backing plates and hook them to the parking brake levers. Make sure the cable housings are properly seated in the backing plates. Reassemble the brakes as described in Section 7.
8　Loosely attach the cable housing clamps, thread the right-side cable through the balancer, and install the balancer to the parking brake lever.
9　Join the right- and left-side cables at the turnbuckle.
10　Tighten the 4 cable housing clamps that attach each cable to the vehicle. Be sure to install the heat protector on the right side cable housing front mount.
11　Adjust the parking brake as described in Section 14.
12　Lower the vehicle to the ground.

17　Power brakes – checking

1　Slide back the hose clamp and remove the power brake side vacuum hose from the check valve. Place your thumb over the open end of the hose.
2　Have an assistant start the engine (keep clear of moving engine parts).
3　A vacuum should be produced and maintained. If no vacuum is felt, the check valve is probably defective and must be replaced with a new one. When installing a new check valve, make sure the arrow on the valve body points toward the engine (Fig. 9.14).
4　Check the vacuum hose leading to the check valve for cracks and leaks. Replace it if any are found.
5　Shut off the engine, reconnect the vacuum hose and slide the hose clamp into place.

18　Power brake booster – removal and installation

1　Remove the master cylinder by referring to Section 12.
2　Remove the cotter key and washer from the pin connecting the power brake pushrod to the brake pedal. Pull the pin out.
3　Remove the 4 nuts and lock-washers attaching the power brake booster to the brake pedal support. The power brake booster assembly can now be withdrawn from its mounting postion.
4　When installing the power brake booster, apply a silicone-type gasket sealer to the sealing surfaces of the booster assembly and the vehicle firewall.
5　Slip the power brake booster assembly into place and install the

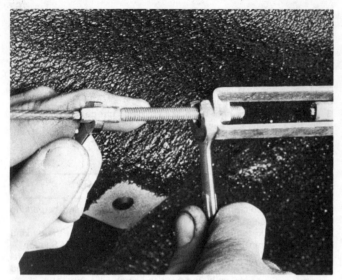

16.3 Loosen the turnbuckle jam nut and unscrew the cable end from the turnbuckle

16.4 Removing the balancer

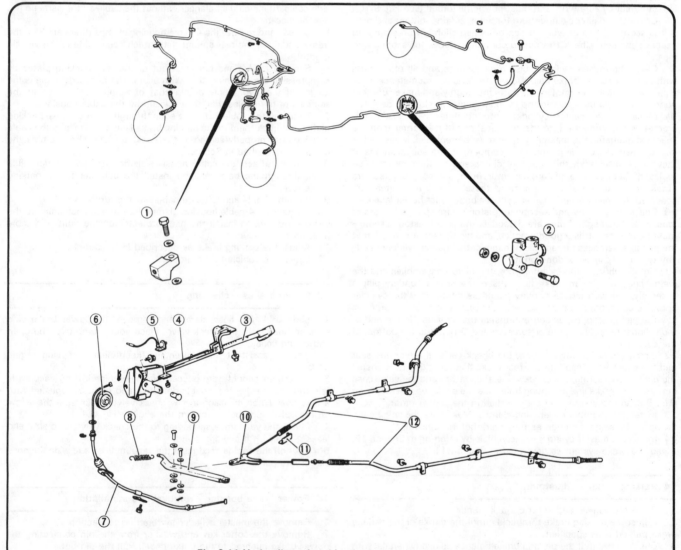

Fig. 9.11 Hydraulic and parking brake system components
(Sec 15)

1 Connector	4 Pull rod support tube	7 Front cable	10 Balancer
2 Blend proportioning valve	5 Parking brake switch	8 Return spring	11 Heat protector
3 Pull rod	6 Cable guide roller	9 Parking brake lever	12 Rear cable

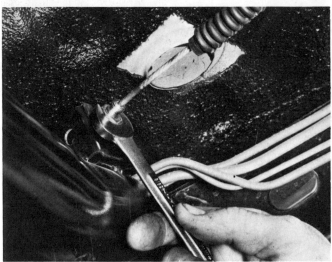

16.5 Loosening the front cable housing clamp

Fig. 9.12 Parking brake warning light switch adjusting screws (Sec 15)

nuts and lock washers that attach it to the brake pedal support. Tighten the nuts to the specified torque.

6   Attach the power brake pushrod to the brake pedal. Make sure that the cotter key is installed in the pin. Adjust the brake pedal as described in Section 22.

7   Install the master cylinder by referring to Section 12.

19 Power brake booster – overhaul

1   If the power brake booster is malfunctioning, perform a check valve test as described in Section 17 before replacing the power brake booster assembly.

2   Power brake units must not be disassembled for any reason. If the power brake unit is not operating properly, obtain a new or rebuilt unit and install it in the vehicle by referring to Section 18.

20 Blend proportioning valve – general description

1   Due to the fact that disc brakes are non-self-energizing, they require more hydraulic pressure than a drum brake to function properly. Also, drum brakes are normally fitted to the rear of a vehicle and thus require less hydraulic pressure to get the job done since most of the vehicle's weight is transferred to the front during braking.

2   If the hydraulic pressure were the same to the front and rear brakes, the rear drum brakes would be locked up almost every time the brakes were applied hard. The blend proportioning valve (BPV) allows only a portion or percentage of the front brake hydraulic pressure to be applied to the rear brakes, which provides for smoother, more controlled stops.

21 Blend proportioning valve – removal and installation

1   The blend proportioning valve (BPV) is located on the left frame rail near the front of the fuel tank. If removal of the BPV becomes necessary, refer to Chapter 4 and remove the fuel tank first.

2   After the fuel tank has been removed, disconnect the 2 brake line fittings from the BPV. Remove the 2 bolts, along with the nuts and lock washers, attaching the BPV to the frame.

3   Never disassemble the BPV in an attempt to repair it. If the BPV is malfunctioning, replace it with a new unit.

4   Hold the new BPV in position and install the 2 bolts that attach it to the frame. Tighten the nuts securely.

5   Connect the brake lines to the BPV and bleed the system as described in Section 11.

6   Install the fuel tank by referring to Chapter 4.

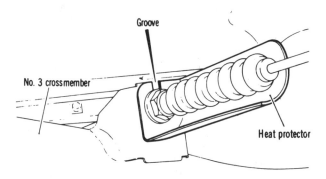

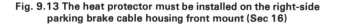

Fig. 9.13 The heat protector must be installed on the right-side parking brake cable housing front mount (Sec 16)

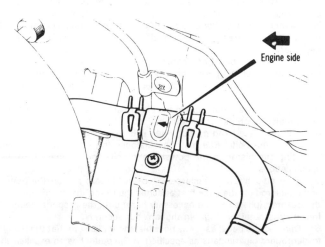

Fig. 9.14 When installing the power brake check valve, make sure the arrow on the valve body points toward the engine (Sec 17)

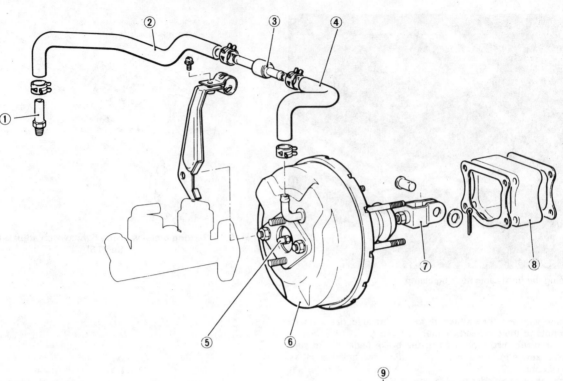

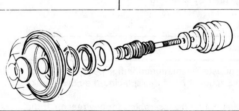

Fig. 9.15 Power brake components (Sec 18)

1	Fitting	3	Check valve	5	Push rod	7	Yoke
2	Vacuum hose	4	Vacuum hose	6	Power brake (booster assembly)	8	Booster spacer
						9	Brake booster repair kit

22 Brake pedal – adjustments

1   Pedal height and free play are the only adjustments that may be required. Brake pedal height, or the distance from the floorboard to the pedal (distance A in Fig. 9.16), should only need adjusting if the brake light switch is replaced or adjusted. If and when the brake pedal height is changed, the free play should also be checked and adjusted as necessary.

2   To adjust the pedal height, unplug the electrical connector in the wiring harness coming from the brake light switch. Loosen the jam nut and turn the brake light switch body until the specified pedal height is obtained.

3   Tighten the jam nut, plug in the electrical connector and check the brake lights for proper operation (they should come on when the brake pedal is depressed and go out when it is released).

4   Check the pedal free play (the distance the pedal travels before actuating the piston in the power brake unit) and compare it to the specifications.

5   If an adjustment is necessary, loosen the jam nut on the power brake pushrod (at the yoke that attaches the rod to the pedal) and turn the pushrod (pliers may be necessary here) until the proper amount of free play is obtained. Tighten the jam nut securely.

6   Depress the pedal as far as possible and make sure that the pedal-to-floorboard clearance is as specified. If the pedal has an excessively long stroke, check the master cylinder piston-to-power brake pushrod clearance (see Section 12) and the brake shoe lining-to-drum clearance.

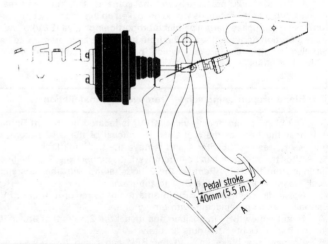

Fig. 9.16 Brake pedal adjustment (Sec 22)

23 Brake pedal – removal and installation

1   Remove the cotter key and washer from the pin connecting the power brake pushrod to the brake pedal. Pull out the pin.
2   If equipped with a manual transmission, back off the clutch adjusting wheel on the clutch cable (inside the engine compartment) and unhook the end of the clutch cable from the clutch cable hook on the pedal.
3   Remove the nuts, bolts and lock washers attaching the pedal support member to the firewall and dash, and lift out the brake pedal, the clutch pedal (if equipped) and the support member as an assembly.
4   Disengage the clutch return spring, remove the nut and washers on the end of the clutch pedal shaft and slip out the clutch pedal (if equipped). The clutch cable hook, the spacer and the spring washer will come off of the pedal shaft also.
5   Disengage the return spring from the brake pedal.
6   Remove the bolt holding the brake pedal pivot rod in place. Pull out the pivot rod and the brake pedal will slip out of the support member.
7   Check the bushings, pedal shafts and pads for wear and damage. Repair or replace any defective parts. Check the pedal(s) for distortion and repair or replace as necessary.
8   Apply a thin coat of grease to the pedal bushings and pivots. Hold the brake pedal in place and slip the brake pedal pivot rod into the support member and through the brake pedal. Install the pivot rod bolt.
9   Hook up the brake pedal return spring.
10   If equipped with manual transmission, slide the clutch pedal into place and install the spring washer, the spacer, the clutch cable hook and the washers and nut on the end of the clutch pedal shaft. Tighten the nut securely and hook up the clutch pedal return spring.
11   Check the lateral (side-to-side) play at the center of the foot pads on the clutch and brake pedals. If it is greater than the specified amount, replace the bushings with new ones.
12   Install the support member/pedal assembly into the vehicle and tighten all nuts and bolts securely.
13   Connect the power brake pushrod to the brake pedal and install the pin, the washer and the cotter key.
14   If applicable, apply a thin coat of grease to the clutch cable hook, hook up the clutch cable and adjust the clutch pedal height and free play by referring to Chapter 8.
15   Adjust the brake pedal height as described in Section 22.

24 Brake fluid – replacement

1   Because of the fact that the wheel cylinder and caliper assemblies must be removed to completely drain the brake hydraulic system, it is a good idea to time the brake fluid replacement maintenance interval so that it coincides with such operations as wheel cylinder overhaul and caliper overhaul.
2   Remove the caliper assemblies by referring to Section 5.
3   Remove the rear wheel cylinders by referring to Section 9.
4   Remove the master cylinder reservoir cap and pump the brake pedal slowly until all the brake fluid has been drained from the system. Catch the old fluid in suitable containers placed under each wheel.
5   Special brake system flushing fluids are available, but their use is not recommended, as problems will result if any trace of the flushing fluid is left in the system.
6   If the caliper assemblies and wheel cylinders are being rebuilt, do so now, then install them on the vehicle. If they are not being rebuilt, drain all the old brake fluid out of each one and install on the vehicle. Now is a good time to overhaul the master cylinder also.
7   Fill the master cylinder with clean, fresh brake fluid of the recommended type and bleed the brake system as described in Section 11.

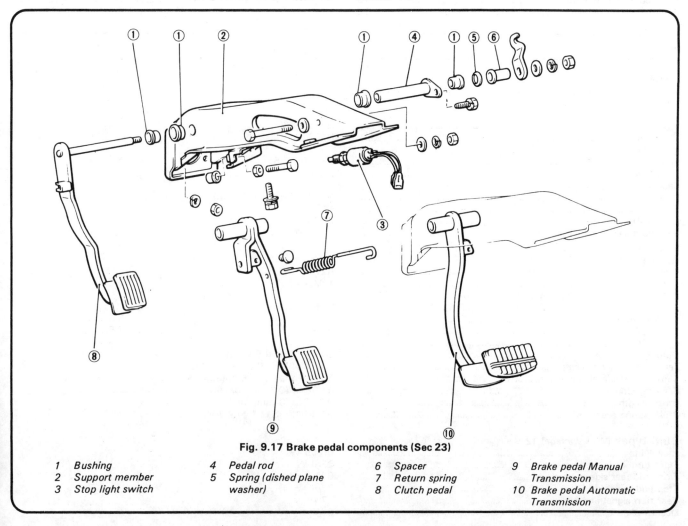

Fig. 9.17 Brake pedal components (Sec 23)

1	Bushing	4	Pedal rod	6	Spacer	9	Brake pedal Manual
2	Support member	5	Spring (dished plane	7	Return spring		Transmission
3	Stop light switch		washer)	8	Clutch pedal	10	Brake pedal Automatic
							Transmission

Chapter 10 Electrical system

Refer to Chapter 13 for specifications and information related to 1981 thru 1988 models

Contents

Specifications

Battery

Voltage	12 volt
Type	
U-engine	
USA	NT80 – S6
Canada	N50Z
W-engine	
USA	NX100 – S6
Canada	NS70
Capacity	
45 AH	NT80 – S6, NX100 – S6
60 AH	N50Z
65 AH	NS70
Specific gravity	1.200 or more

Alternator

Type	A2T16471
Output	12V – 45 A

Output current (indicated rpm is engine speed)

	Hot	Cold
585 rpm	16 A	18 A at 13.5 volts
1125 rpm	37 A	42 A at 13.5 volts
2250 rpm	44 A	44 A at 13.5 volts

Output voltage	14.4 ± .3 v at 68°F (20°C)
Temperature compensation	-0.1 v/50°F (10°C)
Slip ring outside diameter	No less than 1.268 in (32.2 mm)
Slip ring runout	0.008 in (0.2 mm) or less
Brush length	0.315 in (8 mm) minimum
Brush spring pressure	0.5 to 1.0 lb (2.1 to 4.2 N)

Bulb types (W = wattage) 12 V

Headlights	65/55 W
Front turn signal and parking	27/8 W
Front and rear side-marker	8 W
Stop and taillights	27/8 W
Rear turn signal and backup	27 W
License plate	8 W

Oil pressure indicator	3.4 W
Charging indicator	3.4 W
Seat belt warning	3.4 W
Parking brake indicator	3.4 W
High beam indicator	3.4 W
Turn signal indicator	3.4 W
Dome light	5 W
Cargo light	10 W
Meter lights	3.4 W
Combination gauge lights	3.4 W
Heater panel light	1.4 W
Wiper/washer switch light	1.4 W
Shift position light (automatic transmission only)	3.4 W

Fuel gauge

Winding resistance	55 Ω
Current	
Empty	46.7 mA
½	80.0 mA
Full	112.9 mA

Fuel gauge sending unit

Resistance	
Empty	110 ± 7 Ω
½	32.5 ± 4 Ω
Full	3.0 ± 2 Ω
Float travel	8.1 in (205.5 mm)

Voltmeter limiter range

	7.0 0.2 v

Coolant temperature gauge

Winding resistance	55 Ω
Current	
176°F (80°C)	53.7 mA
212°F (100°C)	73.0 mA

1 General information

The Chrysler mini-truck is equipped with a 12 volt negative-ground electrical system. Charging is handled by an engine driven alternator which has a built-in electronic voltage regulator.

2 Battery – checking

1 Certain precautions must be followed when checking or servicing the battery. Hydrogen gas, which is highly flammable, is always present in the battery cells so keep lighted tobacco or any other open flames away from the battery. The electrolyte inside the battery is actually dilute sulfuric acid, which can be hazardous to your skin and cause damage if splashed in the eyes. It will also ruin clothes and painted surfaces.

2 Check the battery case for cracks and evidence of leakage.

3 To check the electrolyte level in the battery, remove all vent caps. If the battery water level is low, add distilled water until the level is above the cell plates. There is an indicator in each cell to help you judge when enough water has been added. Do not overfill.

4 Periodically check the specific gravity of the electrolyte with a hydrometer. This is especially important during cold weather. If the reading is below the specification, the battery should be recharged.

5 Check the tightness of the battery terminals to ensure good electrical connections. The terminals can be cleaned with a stiff wire brush. Corrosion can be kept to a minimum by applying a layer of petroleum jelly or grease to the terminal and cable connectors after they are assembled.

6 Inspect the entire length of the battery cables for corrosion, cracks and frayed conductors.

7 Check that the rubber protector over the positive terminal is not torn or missing. It should completely cover the terminal.

8 Make sure that the battery is securely mounted.

9 The battery case and caps should be kept clean and dry. If corrosion is evident, clean the battery by referring to Section 3.

10 If the vehicle is not being used for an extended period, disconnect the battery cables and have it charged approximately every six weeks.

3 Battery – cleaning

1 Corrosion on the battery hold down components and inner fender panels can be removed by washing with a solution of water and baking soda. Once the area has been thoroughly cleaned, rinse it with clear water.

2 Corrosion on the battery case and terminals can also be removed with a solution of water and baking soda and a stiff brush. Be careful

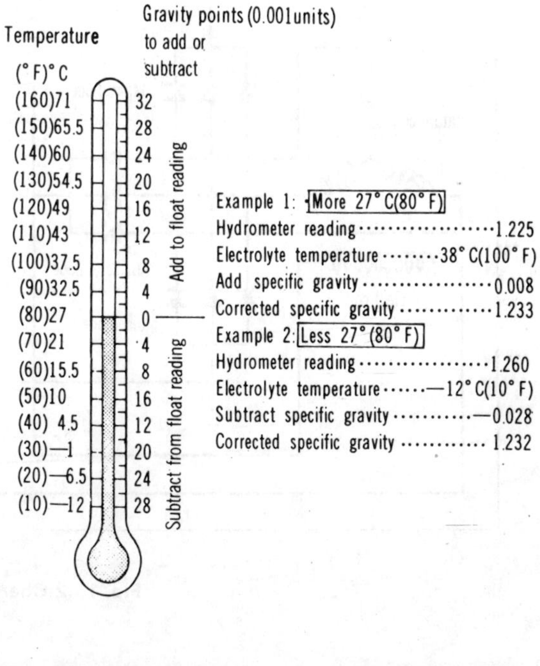

Fig. 10.1 Hydrometer reading temperature correction chart (Sec 2)

that none of the solution is splashed into your eyes or onto your skin (wear protective gloves). Do not allow any of the baking soda and water solution to get into the battery cell. Rinse the battery thoroughly once it is clean.

3   Metal parts of the vehicle which have been damaged by spilled battery acid should be painted with a zinc-based primer and paint. Do this only after the area has been thoroughly cleaned and dried.

4   Battery – charging

1   As was mentioned before, if the battery's specific gravity is below the specified amount, the battery must be recharged.

2   If the battery is to remain in the vehicle during charging, disconnect the cables from the battery to prevent damage to the electrical system.

3   When batteries are being charged, hydrogen gas, which is very explosive and flammable is produced. Do not smoke or allow an open flame near a charging or a recently charged battery. Also, do not plug in the battery charger until the connections have been made at the battery posts.

4   The average time necessary to charge a battery at the normal rate is from 12 to 16 hours (sometimes longer). Always charge the battery slowly. A quick charge or boost charge is hard on a battery and will shorten its life. Use a battery charger that is rated at no more than $3\frac{1}{2}$ amperes.

5   Remove all of the vent caps and cover the vent holes with a clean cloth to prevent the spattering of electrolyte. Hook the battery charger leads to the battery posts (positive to positive, negative to negative), then plug in the charger. Make sure it is set at 12 volts if it has a selector switch.

6   Watch the battery closely during charging to make sure that it does not overheat.

7   The battery can be considered fully charged when it is gassing freely and there is no increase in specific gravity during three successive readings taken at hourly intervals.

8   Overheating of the battery during charging at normal charging rates, excessive gassing and continual low specific gravity readings are an indication that the battery should be replaced with a new one.

5   Alternator – general description and precautions

1   The alternator develops current in the stationary windings and the rotor carries the field. The brushes, therefore, carry only a small current and should last a long time.

2   The most common indications of alternator problems are a low battery (which usually shows up when starting the engine), an overcharged battery (suspect this when the battery needs water frequently or when bulbs need frequent replacement), noise in the alternator (bad bearing) and faulty indicator light or ammeter operation.

3   The most important maintenance and adjustment procedure involving the alternator is belt tension. It should be checked frequently and the belt should be inspected for wear and damage at regular intervals. Further information on the drive belt can be found in Chapter 1.

4   When servicing the charging system, do not short across or ground any of the terminals on the alternator.

5   Never reverse the battery cables, even for an instant, as the reverse polarity current flow will damage the diodes in the alternator. Also, to prevent damage to the diodes, the alternator leads should be disconnected whenever arc welding is being done on the vehicle.

6   Overhaul of the alternator requires experience with electrical tools and test equipment and the need for replacement parts, which are sometimes difficult to obtain. Therefore, it may be in the best interests of the home mechanic to replace the alternator with a new or rebuilt unit if problems develop.

6   Alternator – testing on the vehicle

1   If the charging system is not working properly (indicated by the alternator warning light staying on or a battery that is constantly discharged or overcharged), the alternator output should be checked.

2   Connect a tachometer according to the manufacturer's instructions.

3   Make sure the ignition switch is off, then disconnect the cable from the positive terminal of the battery. Connect an ammeter

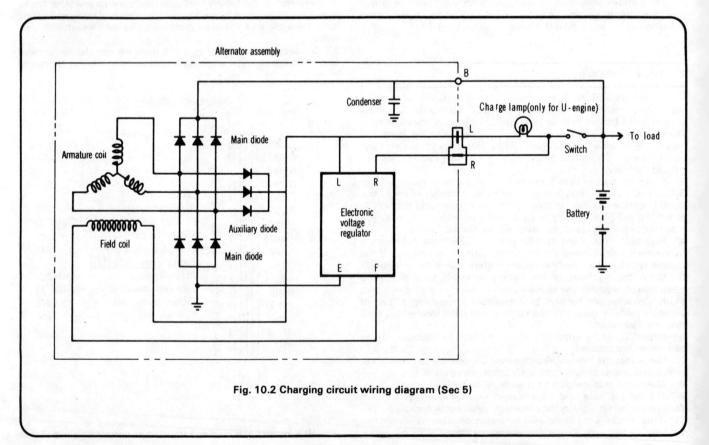

Fig. 10.2 Charging circuit wiring diagram (Sec 5)

between the cable and the positive battery terminal.

4 Connect a voltmeter between Terminal 'L' of the alternator and ground. Check to insure that the voltmeter reading is zero. If the pointer of the voltmeter deflects, which indicates voltage is present, a defective alternator or wiring should be suspected.

5 Turn the ignition switch to 'On' but do not start the engine. The voltmeter reading should be considerably lower than battery voltage. If the meter reading is nearly as high as battery voltage, a defective alternator is suspected.

6 Short across the ammeter terminals with a heavy jumper lead and start the engine, Make sure that when the engine is started, no starting current passes through the ammeter.

7 Remove the jumper lead across the ammeter terminals, increase the engine speed immediately to approximately 2000 to 3000 rpm and note the ammeter reading.

8 If the ammeter reading is 5 amps or less, take a voltmeter reading without changing the engine speed. This reading is the charging voltage. Compare it to the specifications. Since the electronic voltage regulator is a temperature compensated type, the charging voltage varies with temperature. Therefore, the temperature around the rear bracket of the alternator must be measured and the charging voltage corrected accordingly.

9 If the ammeter reading is more than 5 amps, continue to allow the battery to charge until the reading falls below 5 amps or replace the battery with a fullly charged one. An alternative method is to limit the charging current by connecting a $\frac{1}{4}$-ohm 25-watt resistor in series with the battery.

10 Turn the ignition switch off.

11 Disconnect the battery ground cable from the battery.

12 Disconnect the cable from terminal 'B' of the alternator and connect an ammeter between Terminal 'B' and the cable.

13 Connect a voltmeter between terminal 'B' (+) and ground (–).

14 Reconnect the battery ground cable to the battery. The voltmeter should indicate battery voltage.

15 Start the engine, turn on the headlights, accelerate the engine to the specified rpm and note the output current. Compare the results to the specifications.

7 Alternator – removal and installation

1 Before removing the alternator, make sure the ignition switch is off and disconnect the negative battery cable from the battery.

2 Remove the wire from Terminal 'B' and unplug the connector from the alternator.

3 Loesen the adjusting bolt and the pivot bolt nut, then remove the belt from the pulley.

4 Remove the adjusting bolt and nut and the pivot bolt nut, then pull out the pivot bolt and the alternator is free. Don't lose the thin washer that fits between the engine case and alternator front bracket.

5 When installing the alternator, hold it in position, align the holes in the alternator brackets and the engine case, then install the pivot bolt from the front. Make sure the thin washer is installed between alternator front bracket and the engine case.

6 Thread the nut onto the pivot bolt and install the adjusting bolt.

7 Place the belt on the pulley, adjust the tension, and tighten the pivot and adjusting bolts securely.

8 Plug in the connector and attach the wire to terminal 'B'.

9 Connect the negative battery cable to the battery.

8 Alternator – overhaul and testing

1 As previously mentioned, it may be advisable to simply replace the alternator with a new or rebuilt unit should a failure occur; however, the alternator can be disassembled and rebuilt if replacement parts are available.

2 Before beginning, read through this entire section to determine what tools and parts should be on hand.

3 Remove the three through-bolts and carefully insert a screwdriver between the front bracket and the stator. Carefully pry the front bracket/rotor assembly out of the rear bracket. Do not push the screwdriver into the alternator, as damage to the stator coil may result.

4 Carefully mount the rotor in a vice equipped with soft jaws and remove the pulley nut. Slip off the lock washer, the pulley, the fan, the

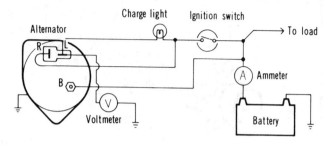

Fig. 10.3 Meter hookup for charging voltage test (Sec 6)

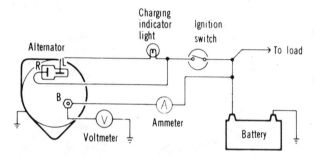

Fig. 10.4 Meter hookup for charging system output test (Sec 6)

spacer and the front seal. Next, slide the rotor out of the front bracket and remove the rear seal.

5 Unsolder the rectifier from the stator coil lead wires and remove the stator assembly. Make sure that the solder is removed quickly (in less than 5 seconds). If any of the diodes are overheated, they will be damaged. **Note:** *When only a brush or brush spring is being replaced, the job can be done without removing the stator.*

6 Remove the condenser from Terminal 'B'.

7 Unsolder plates 'B' and 'L' from the rectifier assembly. Again, work quickly and do not apply any more heat than is necessary.

8 Remove the mounting screw and Terminal 'B' bolt, then remove the electronic voltage regulator and brush holder. The regulator and brush holder cannot be separated from each other.

9 Remove the rectifier assembly. It is held in place with two screws. The brushes are removed as follows: with the brush holder assembly turned as shown in Figure 10.9, unsolder the pigtail of the brush. When the Terminals 'L' and 'B' of the rectifier assembly are bent, damage to the rectifier case can result. Therefore, Plates 'B' and 'L' should be gently bent only at the center.

10 Check the outside circumference of the slip rings for dirt and scratches. Clean and polish them with a strip of fine emery cloth. A badly roughened slip ring or a slip ring worn beyond the specifications must be replaced.

11 Check for continuity between the field coil and slip rings. If there is no continuity, the field coil is defective.

12 Check for continuity between the slip ring and shaft or core. If there is continuity, the coil or slip ring is faulty.

13 Check for continuity between the leads of the stator coil. If there is no continuity, the stator coil is defective.

14 Check for continuity between the stator coil leads and the stator core. If continuity exists, the stator is defective.

15 Check for continuity between the positive heat sink and stator coil

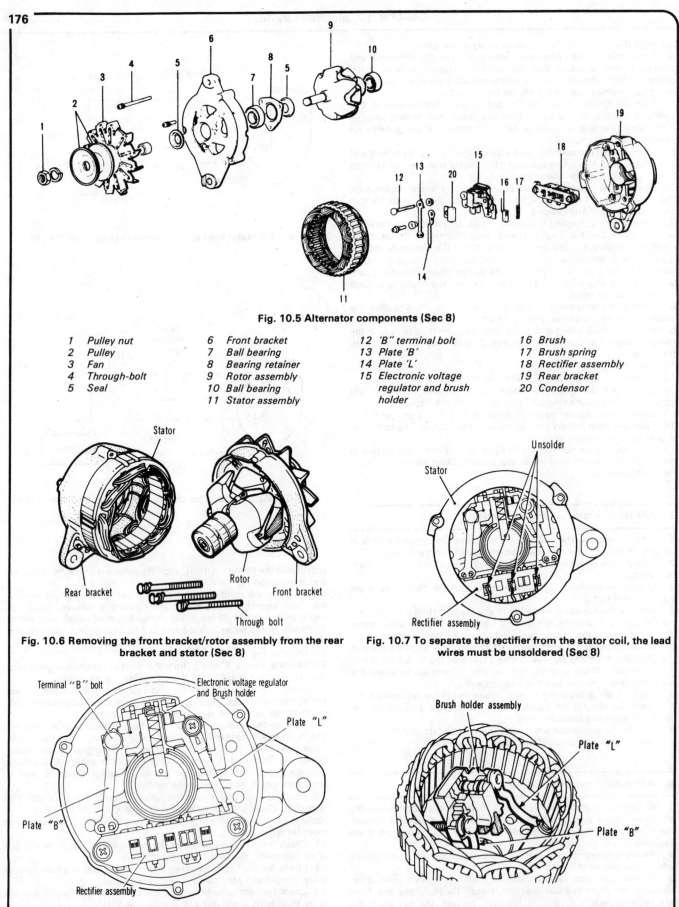

Fig. 10.5 Alternator components (Sec 8)

1	Pulley nut	6	Front bracket	12	'B" terminal bolt
2	Pulley	7	Ball bearing	13	Plate 'B'
3	Fan	8	Bearing retainer	14	Plate 'L'
4	Through-bolt	9	Rotor assembly	15	Electronic voltage
5	Seal	10	Ball bearing		regulator and brush
		11	Stator assembly		holder

16	Brush
17	Brush spring
18	Rectifier assembly
19	Rear bracket
20	Condensor

Fig. 10.6 Removing the front bracket/rotor assembly from the rear bracket and stator (Sec 8)

Fig. 10.7 To separate the rectifier from the stator coil, the lead wires must be unsoldered (Sec 8)

Fig. 10.8 Removing the regulator/rectifier assembly (Sec 8)

Fig. 10.9 Removing the brushes (Sec 8)

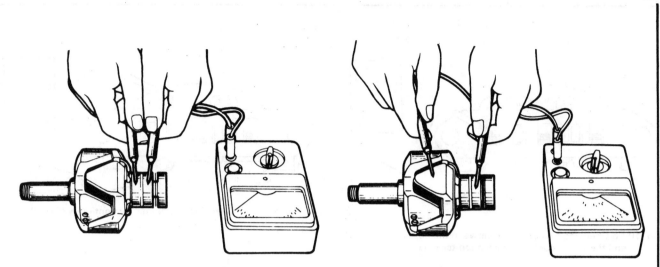

Fig. 10.10 Checking for continuity between the field coil and slip rings (Sec 8)

Fig. 10.11 Checking for continuity between the slip rings and core (Sec 8)

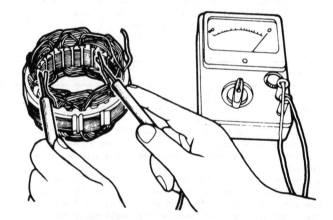

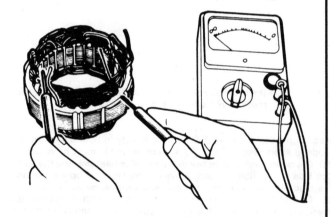

Fig. 10.12 Checking for continuity between the leads of the stator coil (Sec 8)

Fig. 10.13 Checking for continuity between the stator coil leads and the core (Sec 8)

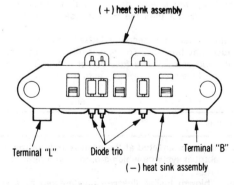

(+) heat sink assembly

Terminal "L"

Diode trio

Terminal "B"

(−) heat sink assembly

Fig. 10.14 Rectifier assembly (Sec 8)

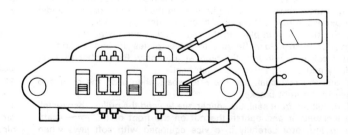

Fig. 10.15 Checking for continuity between the positive heat sink and stator coil lead connection terminal (Sec 8)

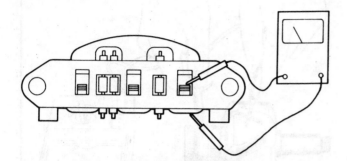

Fig. 10.16 Checking for continuity between the negative heat sink and the stator coil lead connection terminal (Sec 8)

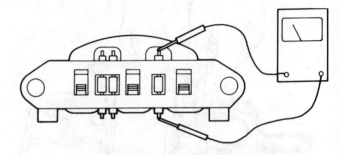

Fig. 10.17 Checking the diodes for continuity (Sec 8)

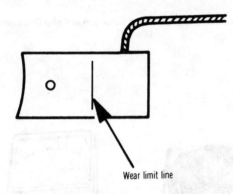

Wear limit line

Fig. 10.18 If the brushes are worn beyond the wear limit line, they must be replaced with new ones (Sec 8)

lead connection terminal. If there is continuity in both directions, the diode is short-circuited and the rectifier assembly must be replaced.
16 Check for continuity between the negative heat sink and the stator coil lead connection terminal. If there is continuity in both directions, the diode is short-circuited and the rectifier must be replaced.
17 Check the three diodes for continuity in both directions (by reversing the meter leads). If there is continuity or an open circuit in both directions, the diode is defective and the rectifier assembly must be replaced.
18 Measure the length of the brushes. If they are shorter than specified they must be replaced with new ones.
19 Check the brush spring pressure and make sure the brush moves smoothly in the brush holder.
20 Check the bearings for smooth operation. Replace them with new ones if noise or roughness is evident.
21 Install the rectifier assembly onto the rear bracket (do not over tighten the screws). Install the brushes in the brush holder and solder the pigtails in place. Work quickly and do not apply excessive heat.
22 Set the stator in place in the rear bracket and install the voltage regulator/brush holder. Be sure to solder plates 'B' and 'C' and the stator coil lead wires to the rectifier assembly. Remember to work quickly and do not apply too much heat.
23 Slip the rear seal over the rotor shaft, then slide the rotor into place in the front bracket.
24 Install the front seal, the spacer, the fan and the pulley, then install the lockwasher and tighten the nut on the front of the rotor shaft. Clamp the rotor carefully in a vice equipped with soft jaws when tightening the nut.
25 Push the brushes into the brush holder and insert a piece of wire to hold the brushes in place. After the rotor has been installed, pull out the wire.
26 Carefully slide the front bracket and rotor assembly into the bracket/stator assembly. Line up the bolt holes and install the three through-bolts. Tighten them evenly and securely.

9 Charging indicator light (U-engine only) – checking

1 If the indicator light goes off as the ignition switch is turned to the 'on' position, or if the light goes on as the engine is running, a shorted or open diode in the alternator or a shorted or open circuit in the electronic voltage regulator are the possible causes.
2 If the light dims but does not go out as the engine is running, check the ignition switch for excessive contact resistance and fuse No. 8 for proper contact with the fuse holder.

10 Fuse block

1 The fuse block is located on the left side of the vehicle under the dash and just forward of the door. It is easily accessible without removing any components.
2 If an electrical system or accessory fails to operate properly, your first check should be at the fuse block. A blown fuse can be readily identified since the thin wire inside the glass fuse will be melted or burned.
3 Replace the blown fuse only with one of the specified amperage. The fuse capacity and names of the main circuits are indicated on the fuse block cover. Do not be tempted to replace the fuse with one of a higher rating, as extensive damage to the electrical system (or fire) can result. If a fuse blows consistently, it is an indication that a problem exists in the system which should be traced and repaired as soon as possible.
4 Do not use a screwdriver or any other metal object to remove fuses, as damage to the system may occur. Plastic fuse pullers are available for this purpose. Also, do not install a wire, a piece of metal foil or any other object than the correct fuse, even for a temporary repair.
5 If the fuse holder itself becomes loose, it can heat up to a point where the fuse may burn out. To prevent this, check the fuse holders regularly for good contact. If a fuse holder is found to be defective, replace it or the fuse block assembly with a new one.

11 Fusible link

1 A fusible link is connected at the positive post of the batteries to protect the electrical systems which are not wired directly to the fuse block.
2 A melted (blown) fusible link can be detected by a swelling or discoloration of the insulation. If the fusible link is suspected, but does not appear discolored or swelled, check it for continuity. If no continuity exists, the fusible link is bad.
3 Replace the link with one of the same exact rating only after the cause of failure has been found and corrected. If a fusible link has melted, a current of 100 amps or more has been flowing through the

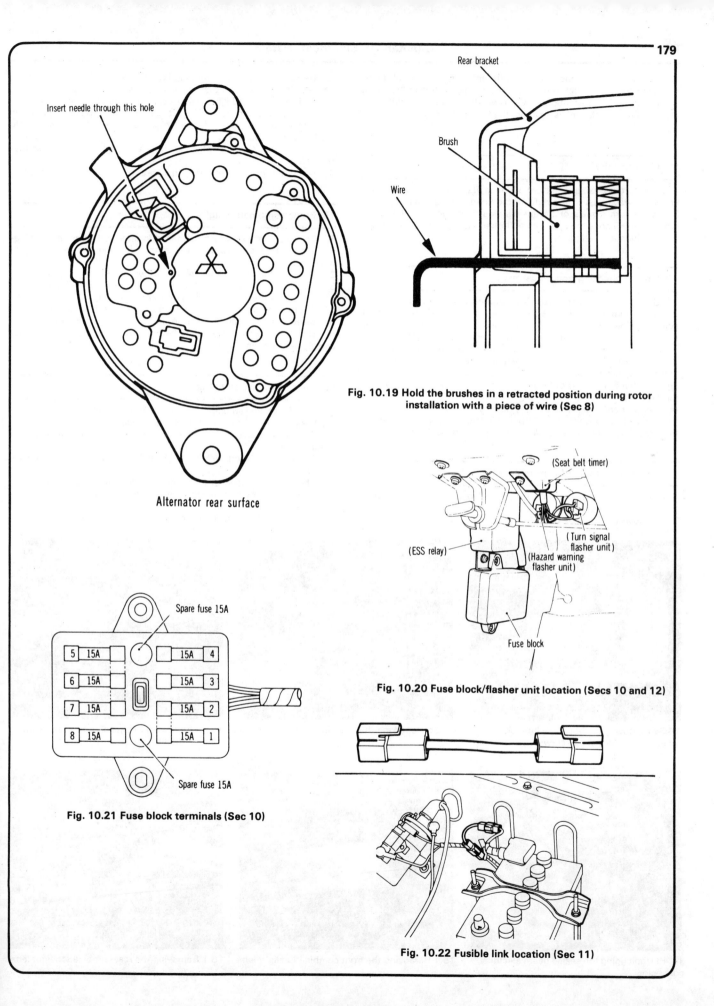

Insert needle through this hole

Alternator rear surface

Rear bracket

Brush

Wire

Fig. 10.19 Hold the brushes in a retracted position during rotor installation with a piece of wire (Sec 8)

(Seat belt timer)

(Turn signal flasher unit)

(ESS relay)

(Hazard warning flasher unit)

Fuse block

Fig. 10.20 Fuse block/flasher unit location (Secs 10 and 12)

Spare fuse 15A

5	15A			15A	4
6	15A			15A	3
7	15A			15A	2
8	15A			15A	1

Spare fuse 15A

Fig. 10.21 Fuse block terminals (Sec 10)

Fig. 10.22 Fusible link location (Sec 11)

circuit, so it is very important to locate and correct the fault before replacing the link. Check very carefully for a dead short in the wiring.

4   As as added precaution, never cover the fusible link with vinyl electrical tape. If the link is covered, the fact that it has blown may go unnoticed.

12 Flasher units

1   The turn signal and hazard warning flasher relays are located under the dash, just to the right of the hood release lever.

2   If the turn signals or hazard warning lights do not blink at the proper rate, remove the appropriate flasher relay and install a new one with an identical rating.

13 Horn – checking and adjustment

1   Sound the horn and adjust it by turning the adjusting screw.

2   If the horn does not sound, loosen the jam nut and slowly turn the adjusting screw 'up' until you hear a weak sound. From this point, turn the screw until the best tone is obtained (within a range of 180 degrees). Lock the screw in this position by tightening the jam nut.

3   If the horn makes a harsh, low sound or chokes, loosen the jam nut and slowly turn the adjusting screw toward 'up' until the best tone is obtained (within a range of 180 degrees). Lock the screw by tightening the jam nut.

4   If the horn makes a loud, vibrating, broken sound, turn the adjusting screw toward 'down' 20 to 30 degrees to a position where the best tone is obtained. Lock the screw in this position.

14 Headlight – sealed beam replacement

1   The lens, filament and reflector are sealed into a single unit which can be replaced as follows:

2   Remove the grille as described in Chapter 12.

3   Remove the 4 screws that hold the interior retaining ring in place (photos). Do not disturb the headlight adjusting screws.

4   Pull out the headlight sealed beam unit (photo) and unplug the electrical connector by pulling it straight out (photo). Plug the connector into the new sealed beam unit and place the new unit into the headlight mount.

5   Attach the interior retaining ring and tighten the 4 screws securely.

6   Install the grille by referring to Chapter 12.

15 Front combination lights

1   To replace a bulb which has failed in either of the front combination lights, first remove the two screws holding the lens in place (photo).

2   Remove the lens (do not tear or otherwise damage the gasket).

3   To remove the bulb, push it in and turn it counterclockwise. Be careful not to break the glass as you are removing the bulb.

4   Check the bulb socket for corrosion. Clean it if necessary.

5   Insert the new bulb (push it in and turn it clockwise to seat it).

6   Check for proper operation before replacing the lens. Do not overtighten the lens screws.

16 Rear combination lights

1   To replace a failed bulb in the rear combination lights, first remove the 6 screws that hold the lens in place (photo).

2   Carefully remove the lens (do not tear or otherwise damage the gasket).

3   Remove the failed bulb by pushing it in and turning it counterclockwise.

4   Check the bulb socket for corrosion. Clean it if necessary.

5   Insert the new bulb (push it in and turn it clockwise to seat it properly) (photo).

6   Check for proper operation before replacing the lens.

14.3a Removing the headlight interior retaining ring mounting screws

14.3b Removing the retaining ring

14.4a Removing the headlight sealed beam from its mount

14.4b Unplugging the sealed beam electrical connector

15.1 Removing the front combination light lens

16.1 Removing the rear combination light lens

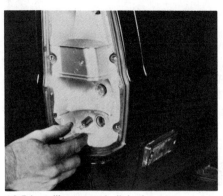

16.5 Installing a new bulb in the rear combination light

17.2 Removing the front side-marker light lens

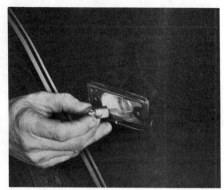

17.5 Installing a new bulb in the front side-marker light

7 When replacing the lens, be sure to install the long and short screws in the correct locations. Tighten them evenly, using a criss-cross pattern.

17 Front and rear side marker lights

1 To replace a bulb that has failed in one of the side marker lights, first remove the two screws attaching the lens to the body panel.
2 Carefully remove the lens (do not tear or otherwise damage the gasket) (photo).
3 To remove the bulb, push it in and turn it counterclockwise.
4 Check the bulb socket for corrosion. Clean it if necessary.
5 Insert the new bulb (push it in and turn it clockwise to seat it properly) (photo).
6 Check for proper operation before installing the lens. Do not overtighten the lens screws.

18 License plate light

1 To replace a failed bulb in the license plate light, first remove the two screws holding the light cover in place.
2 Carefully remove the cover and the glass (do not damage or lose the gasket).
3 To remove the bulb, push it in and turn it counterclockwise.
4 Check the bulb socket for corrosion. Clean it if necessary.
5 Insert the new bulb (push it in and turn it clockwise to seat it).
6 Check for proper operation before replacing the glass and cover.

19 Dome light activator switch – checking

1 At the rear of each door frame there is a plunger-type switch which activates the interior dome light whenever the door is opened.
2 Pull back the rubber boot and remove the screw from the switch housing.
3 Carefully pull the plunger assembly away from the door frame.
4 Make sure the wire is securely attached and check for corrosion on the switch contacts. Check to see if the switch closes properly and that the contacts touch.
5 Reinstall the switch and tighten the screws securely. Check for proper operation.

20 Heater fan switch – checking

1 Unplug the two electrical connectors leading from the switch to the fan motor.
2 Check for continuity between the terminals of the connector coming from the switch with the switch in the 'low', 'medium' and 'high' positions. Continuity should exist between the terminals labeled with a circle when the switch is in the indicated positions.

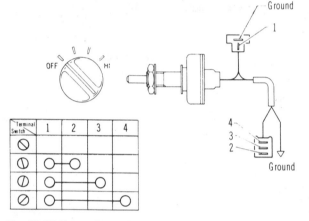

Fig. 10.23 Heater fan switch terminal arrangement (Sec 20)

21 Windshield wiper switch – checking

1 Place the ignition switch in the 'off' position and disconnect the wiper motor wiring harness connector leading from the wiper switch.
2 Check for continuity between the terminals of the connector with the switch in the 'off', 'low' and 'high' positions. Continuity should exist between the terminals labeled with a circle when the switch is in the indicated position.

22 Column switch – removal and installation

Refer to Chapter 11, *Steering wheel – removal and installation,* for column switch removal and installation procedures.

23 Column switch – checking

1 To check the column switch, an ohmmeter or continuity test light is required to check the continuity between the various terminals of the connector. If a defect in the switch is noted, it must be replaced as a single unit.
2 Unplug the column switch electrical connector at the base of the steering column.
3 Refer to the diagram in Figure 10.25 and check for continuity between the terminals of the connector with the switches in the various positions. Continuity should exist between the terminals labeled with a circlip when the switch is in the indicated position.

24 Ignition switch – checking

1 If you suspect that the ignition switch is malfunctioning, it can be checked as follows:
2 To perform this check of the ignition switch you will need an

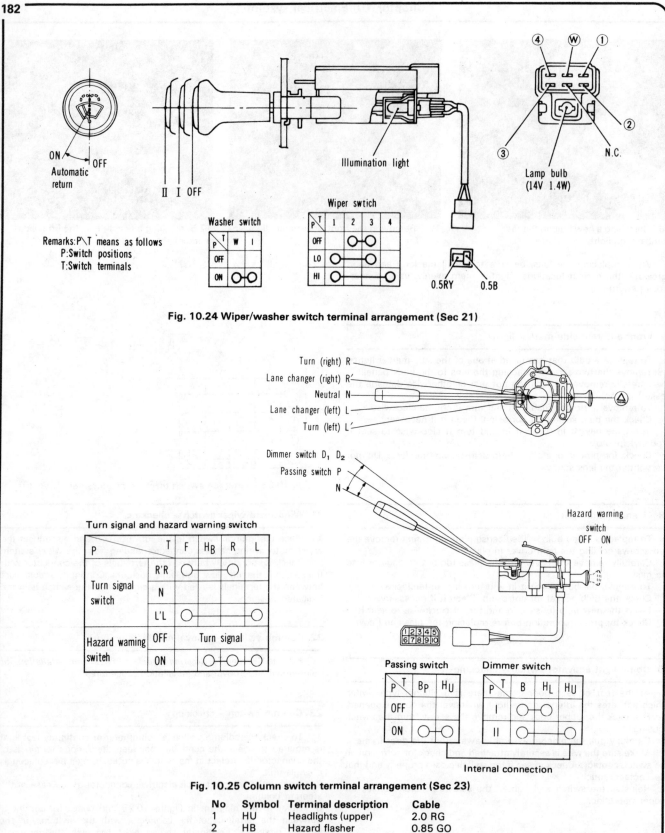

Remarks: P\T means as follows
P: Switch positions
T: Switch terminals

Washer switch

P\T	W	I
OFF		
ON	○—○	

Wiper swtich

P\T	1	2	3	4
OFF		○—○		
LO	○—	○—○		
HI	○—	—	○—	○

Fig. 10.24 Wiper/washer switch terminal arrangement (Sec 21)

Turn signal and hazard warning switch

P\T		F	HB	R	L
Turn signal switch	R'R	○—	—○		
	N				
	L'L	○—	—	—○	○
Hazard waming switch	OFF	Turn signal			
	ON	○—	○—	○	

Passing switch

P\T	BP	HU
OFF		
ON	○—	—○

Dimmer switch

P\T	B	HL	HU
I	○—	○	
II	○—	—	—○

Internal connection

Fig. 10.25 Column switch terminal arrangement (Sec 23)

No	Symbol	Terminal description	Cable
1	HU	Headlights (upper)	2.0 RG
2	HB	Hazard flasher	0.85 GO
3	B	Headlights battery	2.0 RL
4	L	Turn signal (left)	0.85 GL
5	BP	Passing battery	1.25 fR
6	R	Turn signal (right)	0.85 GY
7	HO	Horn	0.5 GB
8	F	Flasher	0.85 GR
9	BP	Passing	1.25 fR
10	HL	Headlights (lower)	2.0 RY

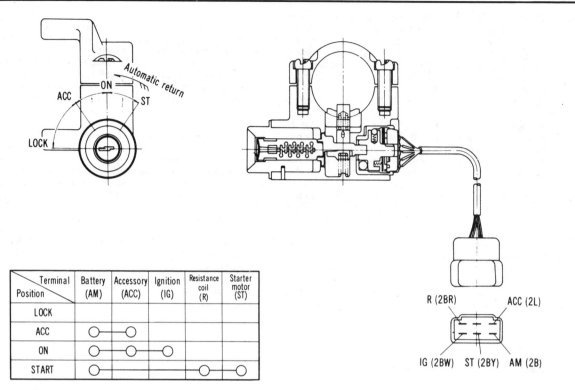

Terminal Position	Battery (AM)	Accessory (ACC)	Ignition (IG)	Resistance coil (R)	Starter motor (ST)
LOCK					
ACC	○——○				
ON	○——○——○				
START	○			○——○	

Fig. 10.26 Ignition switch terminal arrangement (Sec 24)

R (2BR)   ACC (2L)

IG (2BW)   ST (2BY)   AM (2B)

ohmmeter or a battery-powered circuit tester.

3   Unplug the ignition switch electrical connector at the base of the steering column.

4   Refer to the diagram in Figure 10.26 and check for continuity between the various terminals of the wiring connector (leading from the switch) with the switch in the lock, accessory, on and start positions. There should be continuity between the terminals that are labeled with a circle.

25 Fuel gauge – checking

1   Problems with the fuel gauge may occur in the sending unit (at the fuel tank), in the connecting wiring, in the constant-voltage limiter or in the fuel gauge itself.

2   Turn the ignition switch on but do not start the engine.

3   Wait approximately two minutes, then disconnect the wire at the fuel gauge sending unit on the fuel tank or the wire from the coolant temperature sending unit on the engine. (The coolant temperature sending unit is the more accessible of the two).

4   Connect a voltmeter positive lead to the wire and ground the voltmeter negative lead. If the voltmeter indicates a steady voltage of from 1 to 7 volts. the constant voltage limiter is operating properly. Proceed with the test.

5   Ground the wire that was disconnected from the sending unit in the previous test directly to the body or frame. Prolonged flow of current with the gauge grounded could cause problems, so carry out this check quickly. If the fuel gauge pointer indicates full, the fuel gauge is operating properly. If it does not indicate full, the gauge is probably defective.

6   To further check the fuel gauge, roll back the floor mat or carpet just to the right of the passenger seat. This will expose an electrical connector which can be separated by depressing the tab and pulling on the connector ends.

7   Measure the resistance between terminals 0.5Y and 0.5RL with an ohmmeter. A reading of 55 ohms indicates that the fuel gauge is in good condition.

8   If the resistance is extremely low (25 ohms or less), a shorted gauge coil is the possible cause. If it is high (150 ohms or more), the

gauge coil may be broken. In either case, replace the fuel gauge with a new one.

9   Make sure that the fuel tank is full and the vehicle is level before continuing this check.

10 Measure the resistance between the terminal 0.5Y and the body sheet metal (ground). The sending unit is probably good if the resistance for the highest fuel level is noted.

11 Completely drain the fuel into a suitable container by unscrewing the drain plug at the bottom of the tank. *Keep sparks and open flames away from the fuel tank when the gasoline is being drained.*

12 Repeat the measurement as described above. The sending unit is good if the resistance for the lowest fuel level is noted.

13 If the resistance measurements are not close to the specifications, the sending unit is probably defective and should be replaced with a new one. Since the fuel gauge sending unit is located on the fuel tank, which is difficult to remove, removal should not be done until the constant-voltage limiter, the fuel gauge, and the sending unit are thoroughly checked.

14 Refer to Chapter 4 for fuel tank removal and installation procedures.

15 If a new sending unit is installed, coat both sides of the gasket with a silicone-type gasket sealer to prevent leaks and be careful not to bend the float arm when installing the new sending unit.

16 After the sending unit is installed on the tank, ensure that it is properly grounded.

26 Coolant temperature gauge – checking

1   As with the fuel gauge, troubleshooting problems with the coolant temperature gauge is basically a process of elimination. The sending unit, the wiring, the constant voltage limiter, and the gauge must be checked systematically.

2   The voltage limiter serves both the coolant temperature gauge and the fuel gauge. The checking procedures are outlined in Section 25.

3   Disconnect the wire from the coolant temperature sending unit. Connect a 75-ohm resistor in series to the wire and ground the resistor. (Do not ground the wire directly). If the needle on the coolant temperature gauge registers as shown in Figure 10.31, the gauge is in satisfactory condition.

4   To check the gauge further, disconnect the negative battery cable from the battery and turn the ignition switch to 'on'.

5   Measure the resistance between the disconnected sending unit wire and the positive terminal of the ignition coil. This measurement is the coolant temperature gauge winding resistance. Compare the results to the specifications. If the resistance is much more or much less than specified, the gauge is probably faulty.

6   Drain the cooling system (see Chapter 3). Remove the sending unit from the engine block.

7   Suspend the sending unit and a thermometer in a container of water. Do not let the thermometer or the sending unit touch the bottom or sides of the container.

8   Slowly heat the water on a stove or hot plate until the thermometer indicates 176°F (80°C). At this point, measure the resistance of the sending unit by placing one lead of an ohmmeter on the terminal and the other lead on the sending unit body. Compare the results to the specifications. If the resistance was the same as that specified for a temperature of 176°F (80°C), the sending unit is good.

27 Oil pressure gauge – checking

1   Turn the ignition switch to 'on' but do not start the engine. Wait one or two minutes, then disconnect the wire from the oil pressure sending unit.

2   Connect a 14 volt 1.4W bulb in series with the wire and ground.

3   If the oil pressure gauge needle indicates as shown in Figure 10.34, the gauge is in good condition.

4   With the wire still disconnected, place one lead of an ohmmeter on the terminal of the sending unit and the other lead on the engine block. The ohmmeter should indicate a high resistance.

5   Start the engine; the resistance should decrease to 0.

28 Oil pressure indicator light switch (U-engine only) – checking

1   Vehicles equipped with the U-engine do not have an oil pressure gauge and sending unit. Instead, they have an indicator light that is on when oil pressure is low and off when it is above a predetermined level. The light is activated by a pressure switch.

2   The switch can be checked for proper operation as follows:

3   With the engine off, disconnect the wire from the switch.

4   Touch one lead of an ohmmeter or an electrical tester to the switch terminal and the other lead to the engine block. Continuity should exist.

5   Start the engine. If the switch is working properly, there should be no continuity after the engine is started.

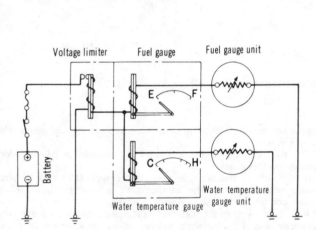

Fig. 10.27 Fuel and coolant temperature gauge circuit (Sec 25)

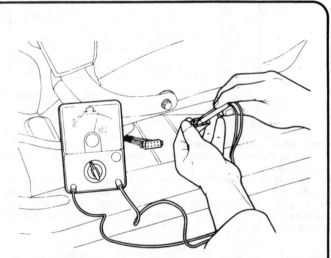

Fig. 10.28 Measuring the resistance of the fuel gauge meter coil (Sec 25)

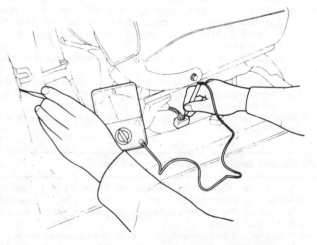

Fig. 10.29 Measuring the fuel level sending unit resistance (Sec 25)

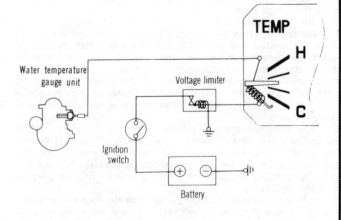

Fig. 10.30 Coolant temperature gauge circuit (Sec 26)

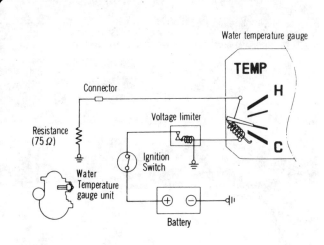

Fig. 10.31 Checking the coolant temperature gauge (Sec 26)

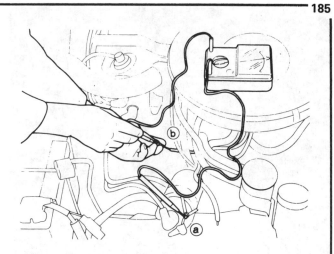

Fig. 10.32 Measuring the resistance between the disconnected coolant temperature sending unit wire and the positive (+) terminal of the coil (Sec 26)

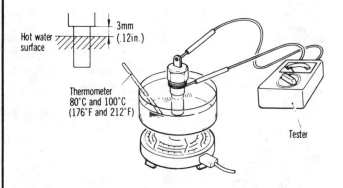

Fig. 10.33 Checking the resistance of the cooling temperature sending unit at the specified temperatures (Sec 26)

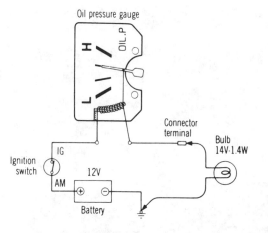

Fig. 10.34 Checking the oil pressure gauge (Sec 27)

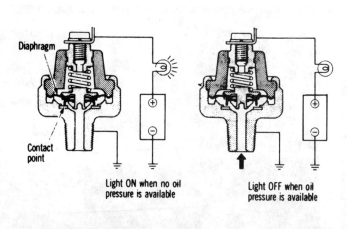

Fig. 10.35 Oil pressure indicator light switch operation (Sec 28)

Fig. 10.36 Checking the oil pressure switch for continuity (Sec 28)

29.3a Removing the nuts from the radio controls

29.3b Removing the radio trim plate

29.4 Removing the nut from the fan control

29.5a Removing the cluster rim mounting screws

29.5b Disconnecting the wiring harness

29.6 Removing the instrument cluster mounting screws

30.1 Removing the instrument cover mounting screws

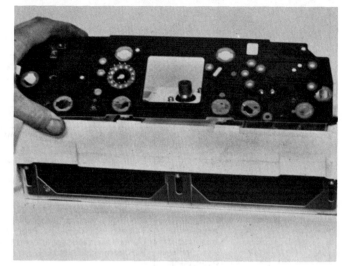

30.4 Lifting the printed circuit board off of the instrument cluster

29 Instrument cluster – removal and installation

1   It is necessary to remove the instrument cluster if any of the gauges or warning lights need servicing.
2   Disconnect the negative battery cable from the battery.
3   Slip off the radio knobs, remove the nuts on the studs (photo). Remove the radio trim plate (photo).
4   Pull off the heater fan control knob and the heater control lever ends. Remove the nut from the fan control stud (photo).
5   Remove the 4 screws from the cluster rim (photos) and lift it carefully out of place. Disconnect the wiring harness and the wire lead at the lower right corner of the rim (photo).
6   Remove the 4 screws from the cluster rim (photos) and lift it carefully out of place. Disconnect the wiring harness and the wire lead at the lower right corner of the rim (photo).
6   Remove the 4 screws attaching the instrument cluster to the dash (photo).
7   Unscrew the speedometer cable fitting and remove the cable from the back of the cluster. Disconnect the electrical wire from the buzzer.
8   Carefully pull out on the cluster until it is free of the dash, then disconnect the two electrical connectors at the rear of the cluster.
9   Installation is the reverse of removal.

30 Instrument cluster – disassembly and reassembly

1   Remove the 6 screws holding the clear plastic cover and the trim ring in place and lift them off (photo). Be careful not to damage or bend the instrument needles.
2   Turn the cluster over and remove the 5 nuts from the studs on the right side. Unscrew the buzzer mounting screw and remove the buzzer.
3   Remove the 9 bulb holders from the printed circuit board by turning them counterclockwise. Be very careful not to scratch or gouge the printed circuit board.
4   Remove the 8 self-tapping screws and the 6 machine screws. The machine screws have two different size threads, so be sure they are returned to the exact same locations they were removed from. Carefully lift the printed circuit board off the instrument cluster (photo).
5   The speedometer is held in position with two screws.
6   Reassembly is basically the reverse of disassembly.

31 Windshield wiper motor – removal and installation

1   Remove the battery cables (negative first, then positive) from the battery.
2   Unplug the electrical connector in the wiring harness leading from the wiper motor.

3   Remove the 3 bolts attaching the motor to the vehicle firewall.
4   Pull up on the wiper arm until the actuator arm joint is visible in the access hole, then pry the motor arm out of the actuator arm joint with a screwdriver.
5   Installation is the reverse of removal.

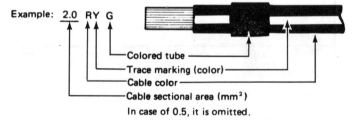

Example: 2.0 RY G

Colored tube
Trace marking (color)
Cable color
Cable sectional area (mm²)

In case of 0.5, it is omitted.

Fig. 10.37 Wiring color/size code

Nominal size (designated by sectional area in mm² of wire)	SAE gauge No.	Permissible current	
		Within engine compartment	Other areas
0.5	20	7A	13A
0.85	18	9A	17A
1.25	16	12A	22A
2.0	14	16A	30A
3.0	12	21A	40A
5.0	10	31A	54A

Symbol	Coloring	Connected circuit	System
B	Black	Grounding	
BW	Black/white	Ignition, Meter illumination and Washer motor	
BY	Black/yellow	Starter	Starting
BR	Black/red	Ignition	
W	White	Charging, E.S.S. relay, Tachometer and Ammeter	Charging
WB	White/black	Ammeter	
R	Red	Headlight, upper beam and Backup switch	
RW	Red/white	Headlight, lower beam	
RB	Red/black	Passing switch, Dome light and Seat belt warning	Lighting
RY	Red/yellow	Meter illumination, Wiper/washer switch ill. and Radio	
RL	Red/blue	Backup light	
G	Green	Stop light, Hazard flasher unit and Horn	
GW	Green/white	Tail light, Parking light, Front & rear side marker light and license plate light	
GR	Green/red	Dome light, Door switch and Lighting switch	
GY	Green/yellow	R.H. turn signal lights (front & rear) and indicator light	Signal
GB	Green/black	Horn	
GL	Green/blue	L.H. turn signal lights (front & rear) and indicator light	
Y	Yellow	Fuel gauge and Oil pressure gauge or light	
YR	Yellow/red	Water temp. gauge	Gauge
YB	Yellow/black	Seat belt warning light	and
YG	Yellow/green	Parking brake	indicator
YW	Yellow/white	Charging indicator light and Seat belt switch	
L	Blue	Wiper/washer switch, Alternator (S terminal) and Air-con relay (B) terminal	
LW	Blue/white	Radio, Cigarette lighter, Wiper motor and Heater switch	
LR	Blue/red	Heater fan switch and Oil pressure gauge	
LB	Blue/black	Heater switch and Air-con (B) terminal	Others
LY	Blue/yellow	Heater switch	
LO	Blue/orange	Wiper motor	

Fig. 10.38 Wiring color code key

Symbol	Part name	Location	Symbol	Part name	Location
CB–1	E.S.S. (Engine Speed Sensor) relay	Lower part of left side front pillar (Above the fuse block)	CE–3	Solenoid valve	Beside the ignition coil
CB–2	Parking brake lever switch	Above the guide roller for parking brake cable	CE–4	E.I.C. (Electronic Ignition Control) unit	Side of distributor body
CB–3	Seat belt switch	Inside of driver's seat belt buckle	CE–5	E.V.R. (Electronic Voltage Regulator)	Inside of the alternator
CB–4	Fuse block	Lower part of left side front pillar	CG–1	Body grounding point (Front)	Side of battery support
CB–5	Inhibitor switch	Inside of gearshift lever bracket	CG–2	Frame grounding point (Front)	Slide of left frame, engine compartment
CB–6	Backup light switch	Rear upper side of transmission	CG–3	Engine grounding point (Front)	Left side of cylinder block
CB–7	Stop light switch	Brake pedal support bracket	CG–4	Body grounding point (Cabin)	Fore of driver, under the Instrument panel
CB–8	Connector of front and frame	Under floor mat, right side of passenger's seat	CI–1	Air-con (B) terminal	One the wiring harness, side of left reinforcement
CB–9	Connector of frame and rear body wiring harness	Rear part of right side rear body frame	CI–2	Air-con relay (B) terminal	Along with the air-con (B) terminal
CB–10	Door switch L.H.	Lower part of left side rear pillar	CI–3	Seat belt warning timer	Left under side of instrument panel
CB–11	Door switch R.H.	Lower part of right side rear pillar	CI–4	Seat belt warning buzzer	Back side of combination meter case
CB–12	Fuel gauge unit	Left upper side of fuel tank	CI–5	Turn signal flasher unit	Fore of driver, under the instrument panel
CB–1	Wiper motor	Left side of front deck	CI–6	Hazard warning flasher unit	Along the turn signal flasher unit
CE–2	Washer motor	Lower side of washer liquid tank			

Fig. 10.39 Electrical system component location key

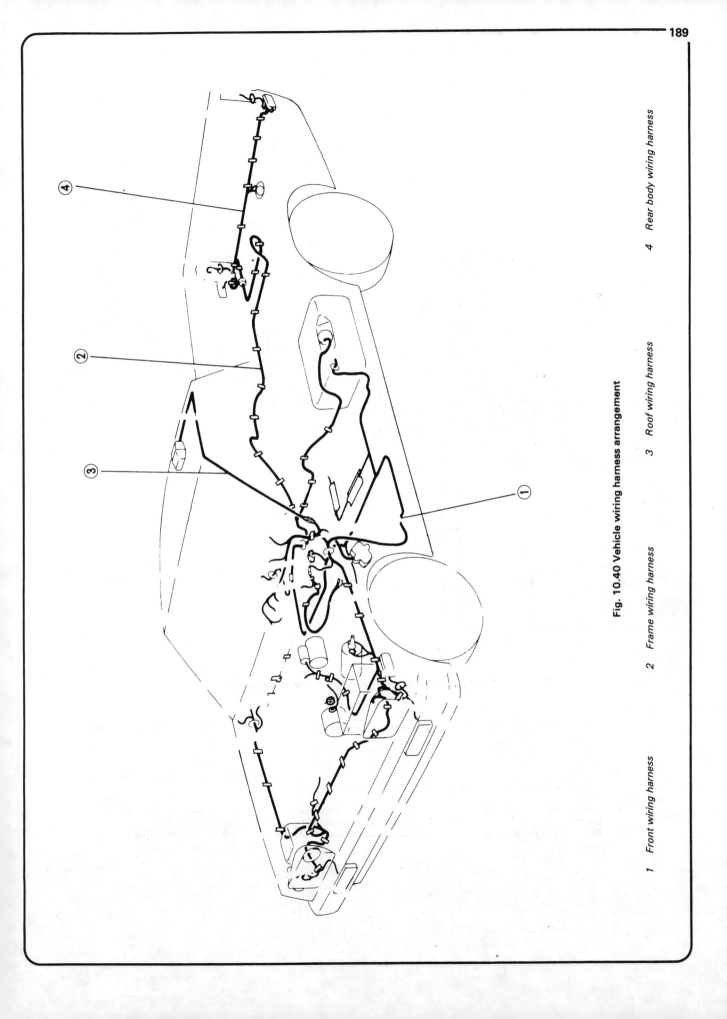

Fig. 10.40 Vehicle wiring harness arrangement

1   Front wiring harness

2   Frame wiring harness

3   Roof wiring harness

4   Rear body wiring harness

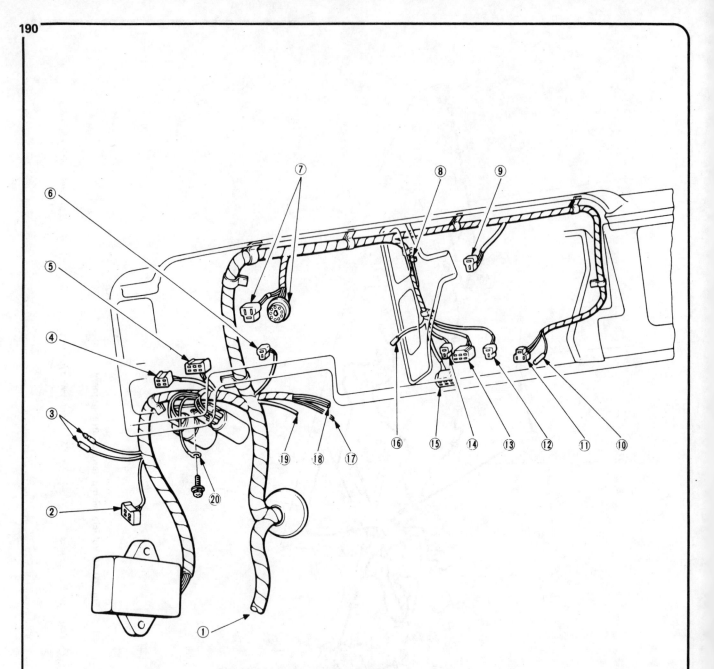

Fig. 10.41 Instrument panel wiring harness arrangement

1 To frame wiring harness
2 Connect with ESS relay
3 Connect with roof wiring harness
4 Connect with timer
5 Connect with lighting switch
6 Connect with belt warning buzzer
7 Connect with combination meter
8 Spare terminal for air conditioner
9 Connect with radio
10 Connect with cigarette lighter
11 Connect with heater panel light
12 Connect with wiper/washer switch illumination light (blue colored connector)
13 Connect with wiper/washer switch
14 Connect with heater fan switch
15 Connect with combination gauges
16 To parking brake switch
17 To stop light switch
18 To column switch
19 To ignition switch
20 Grounding point

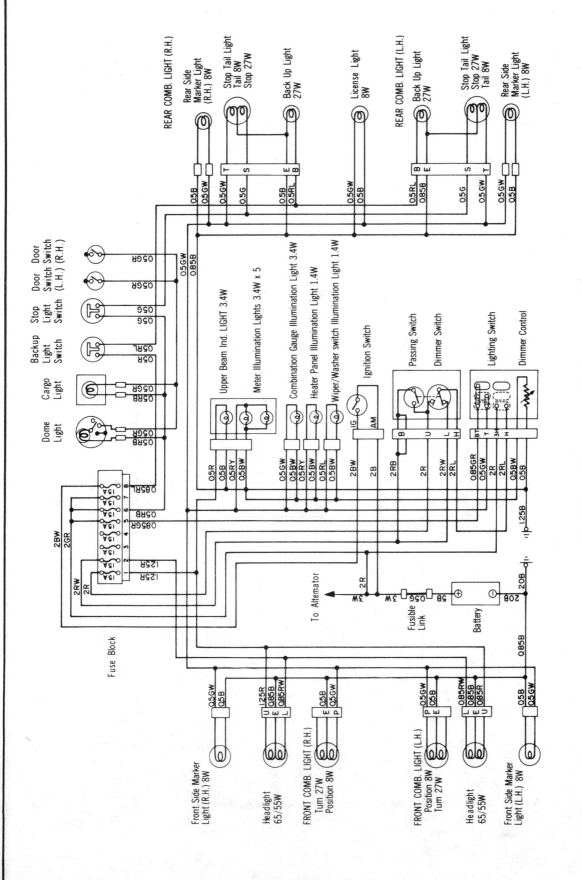

Fig. 10.42 Lighting system wiring diagram

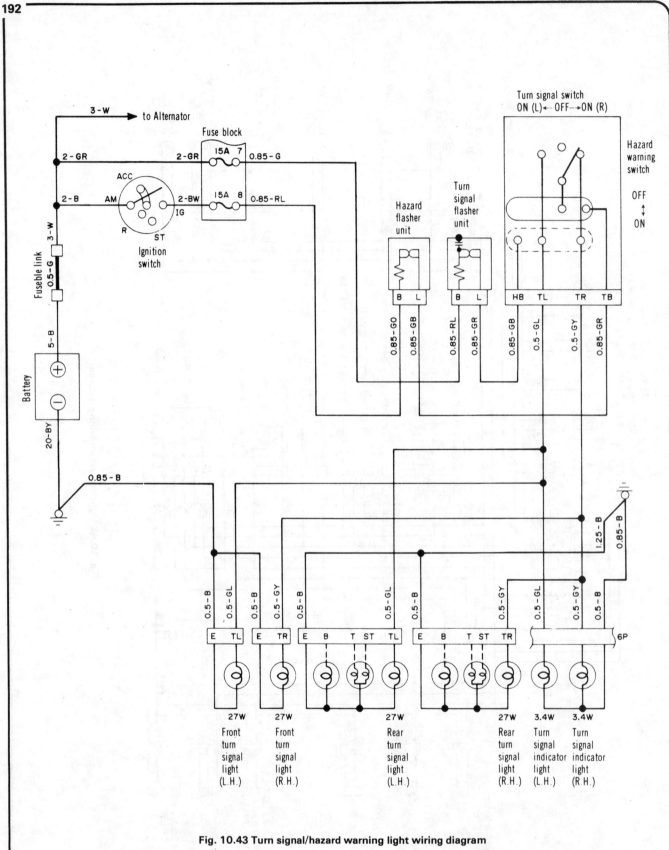

Fig. 10.43 Turn signal/hazard warning light wiring diagram

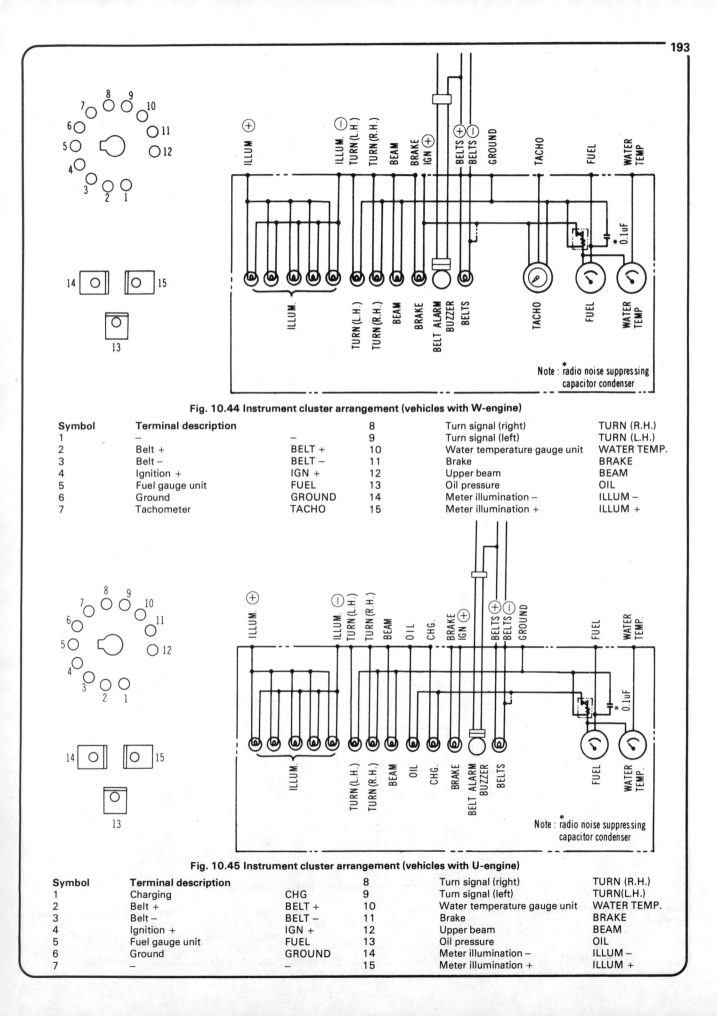

Fig. 10.44 Instrument cluster arrangement (vehicles with W-engine)

Symbol	Terminal description			Symbol	Terminal description	
1	–	–	8	Turn signal (right)	TURN (R.H.)
2	Belt +	BELT +	9	Turn signal (left)	TURN (L.H.)
3	Belt –	BELT –	10	Water temperature gauge unit	WATER TEMP.
4	Ignition +	IGN +	11	Brake	BRAKE
5	Fuel gauge unit	FUEL	12	Upper beam	BEAM
6	Ground	GROUND	13	Oil pressure	OIL
7	Tachometer	TACHO	14	Meter illumination –	ILLUM –
			15	Meter illumination +	ILLUM +

Fig. 10.45 Instrument cluster arrangement (vehicles with U-engine)

Symbol	Terminal description			Symbol	Terminal description	
1	Charging	CHG	8	Turn signal (right)	TURN (R.H.)
2	Belt +	BELT +	9	Turn signal (left)	TURN(L.H.)
3	Belt –	BELT –	10	Water temperature gauge unit	WATER TEMP.
4	Ignition +	IGN +	11	Brake	BRAKE
5	Fuel gauge unit	FUEL	12	Upper beam	BEAM
6	Ground	GROUND	13	Oil pressure	OIL
7	–	–	14	Meter illumination –	ILLUM –
			15	Meter illumination +	ILLUM +

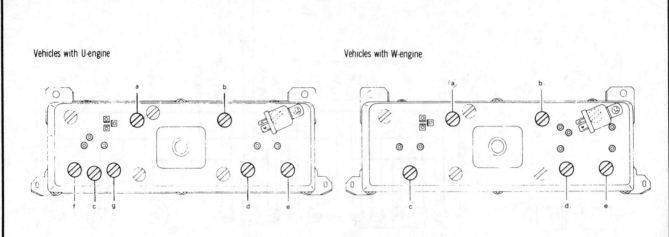

Vehicles with U-engine

Vehicles with W-engine

Fig. 10.46 Indicator light arrangement

a   *Turn signal indicator light R.H.*
b   *Turn signal indicator light L.H.*
c   *Seat belt warning light*

d   *Upper beam indicator light*
e   *Brake warning light*
f   *Oil pressure indicator light*
g   *Charging indicator light*

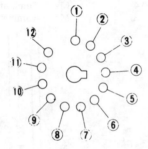

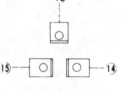

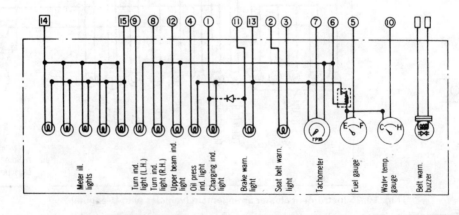

Fig. 10.47 Instrument cluster terminal arrangement (Sec 29)

Connection of 12-pole connector		Timer (No. 2 terminal)	8	Turn signal flasher line (r.h.)	**Connection of 3-pole connector**	
Terminal	3	Oil pressure switch	9	Turn signal flasher line (l.h.)	Terminal	
	4	Fuel gauge unit	10	Water temperature gauge unit	13	Fuse No. 8 (IG line)
	5	Earth (body as ground)	11	Parking brake switch	14	Lighting switch
1 Alternator (L terminal)	6	Ignition coil −	12	Headlight (upper beam)	15	Dimmer control
2 Fuse No. 6 (Battery line)	7					

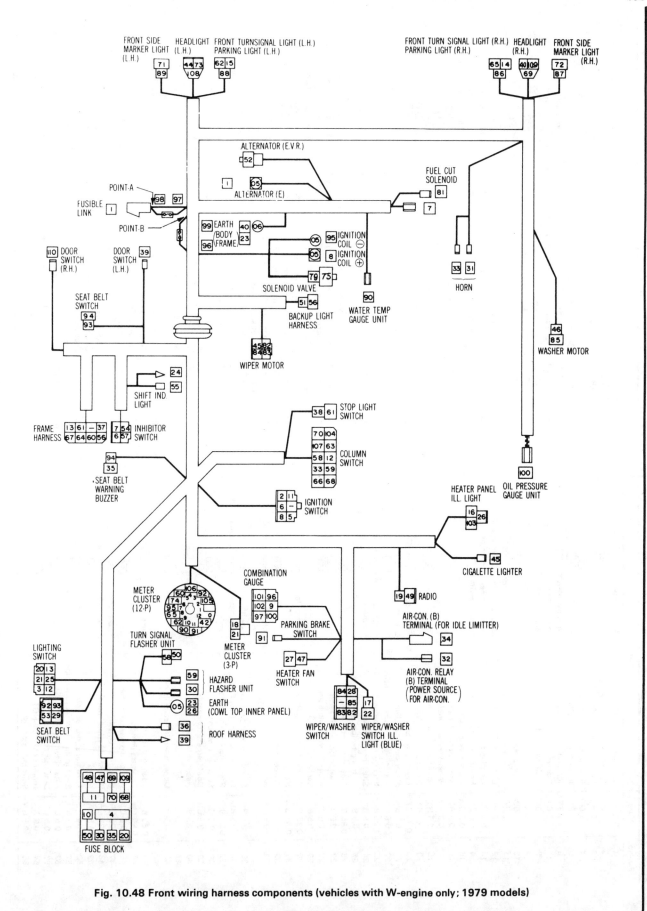

Fig. 10.48 Front wiring harness components (vehicles with W-engine only; 1979 models)

Front wiring harness component key (left half — Pin No. 1–55)

Pin No.	Wire	Circuit	Circuit
			Fusible link
1	3 W	Alternator [B]	[1]
2	2 B	Ignition switch [AM]	[1]
3	2 R	Light switch [BH]	[8]
4	2 GR	Fuse block [5'-6'-7']	
5	2 BR	Ignition switch [R]	Inhibitor switch [ST]
6	2 BY	Ignition switch [ST]	Inhibitor switch [ST]
7	2 BY	Starter motor	Ignition coil ⊕
8	2 BW	Ignition switch [IG]	Ignition switch [ACC] [8]
9			Column switch (Dimmer)
10	2 BW	Fuse block [8']	Frame harness connector [BH]
11	2 L	Fuse block [3'-4']	Lighting switch [T] [14]
12	2 RL	Lighting switch [H]	[13]
13	0.5 GW	Lighting switch [T]	[13]
14	0.5 GW	Front parking light (R.H.)	[13]
15	0.5 GW	Front parking light (L.H.)	[13]
16	0.5 RL	Heater panel ill. light	Fuse block [No. 5]
17	0.5 RY	Wiper/Washer switch ill. light	Lighting switch [BM] [21]
18	0.5 RY	Meter cluster ill. lights	
19	0.5 RY	Radio dial ill. light	
20	0.85 GR	Lighting switch [BT]	Earth (Cowl top inner panel) [23]
21	0.5 BW	Meter cluster ill. lights	[23]
22	0.5 BW	Wiper/Washer switch ill. light	[23]
23	1.25 B	Earth (Engine compartment)	Earth [23]
24	0.5 B	Shift indicator light	
25	0.5 B	Lighting switch [M]	
26	0.85 B	Cigarette lighter earth	
27	0.5 B	Heater fan switch earth	
28	0.5 B	Wiper/Washer switch earth	
29	0.5 B	Seat belt timer earth	
30	0.85 GL	Fuse block [No. 7]	Hazard flasher unit [47]
31	0.85 GL	Horn	[47]
32	0.5 L	Air-con relay (B)	Column switch (Horn switch)
33	0.5 GB	Horn	
34			
35	0.5 RB	Seat belt warning buzzer	Fuse block [No. 6] [23]
36	0.5 RB	Fuse block [No. 6]	[35]
37	0.85 R	Frame harness connector	Roof harness connector (Dome light) ⊙6 [40]
38	0.5 G	Stop light switch	Earth
39	0.5 GR	Roof harness connector	
40	0.85 B	Headlight (R.H.)	Door switch (L.H.) ⊙6 [109]
41			Earth [48] [47]
42	0.5 R	Upper beam indicator light	
43			Earth ⊙6 [40]
44	0.85 B	Headlight (L.H.)	
45	0.85 LW	Cigarette lighter	
46	0.5 L	Windshield washer motor	Fuse block [No. 3]
47	1.25 LR	Heater fan switch	Fuse block [No. 4]
48	1.25 LW	Windshield wiper motor	Fuse block [No. 8]
49	0.5 LW	Radio	[50]
50	0.85 RL	Turn signal flasher unit	[50]
51	0.5 R	Backup light harness connector	[50]
52	0.5 L	Alternator (E.V.R.) [S]	[50]
53	0.5 LR	Seat belt timer	
54	0.5 R	Inhibitor switch [IG]	
55	0.5 GW	Shift indicator light	

Front wiring harness component key (right half — Pin No. 56–110)

Pin No.	Wire	Circuit	Circuit
56	0.5 RL	Backup light harness connector	Frame harness connector [56]
57	0.5 RL	Inhibitor switch [L]	Column switch (Turn signal sw.)
58	0.85 GR	Turn signal flasher unit	Column switch (Hazard sw.)
59	0.85 G	Meter cluster (Fuel gauge)	Frame harness connector
60	0.5 Y	Stop light switch	Frame harness connector
61	0.5 G	Turn signal indicator light (L.H.)	Front turn signal light (L.H.) [62]
62	0.5 GL	Column switch (Turn signal sw.)	[62]
63	0.5 GL	Frame harness connector	
64	0.5 GL	Turn signal indicator light (R.H.)	Front turn signal light (R.H.) [65]
65	0.5 GY	Column switch (Turn signal sw.)	[65]
66	0.5 GY	Frame harness connector	
67	0.5 GY	Fuse block [1']	Column switch (Dimmer sw.) [HU]
68	2 R	Fuse block [No. 1]	Headlight (R.H.) [40]
69	0.85 RW	Fuse block [2']	[40]
70	2 RW	Front side marker light (L.H.)	Column switch (Dimmer sw.) [HL]
71	0.5 B	Front side marker light (R.H.)	Earth ⊙6 [40]
72	0.5 B	Headlight (L.H.) [Upper beam]	Earth ⊙6 [40]
73	0.85 R	Meter cluster earth	Earth ⊙5 [26]
74	0.5 B		
75			
76			
77			
78			
79	0.5 YW	Charging indicator light	Alternator (E.V.R.) [L]
80		Fuel cut solenoid valve	[8]
81	2 BW	Wiper/Washer switch [H]	
82	0.5 LB	Wiper/Washer switch [L]	
83	0.5 LO	Wiper/Washer switch [AS]	
84	0.5 L	Wiper/Washer switch [Washer]	Windshield wiper motor [H]
85	0.5 BW	Front turn signal light (R.H.)	Windshield wiper motor [L]
86	0.5 B	Front side marker light (R.H.)	Windshield wiper motor [AS]
87	0.5 GW	Front turn signal light (L.H.)	Windshield washer motor
88	0.5 B	Front side marker light (L.H.)	Earth ⊙6 [40] [15]
89	0.5 GW	Meter cluster (Water temp. gauge)	Earth ⊙6 [40] [15]
90	0.5 YR	Parking brake ind. light	
91	0.5 YG	Seat belt indicator light	Water temp. gauge unit
92	0.5 YB	Seat belt timer	Parking brake switch
93	0.5 RB	Seat belt warning buzzer	Seat belt timer
94	0.5 YW	Solenoid valve	Seat belt switch
95	0.5 BW	Solenoid valve	Seat belt switch
96	0.5 L	Engine speed sensor relay	Engine speed sensor relay
97	0.5 B	Engine speed sensor relay	Earth ⊙5 [50] [23]
98	0.5 W	Solenoid valve	Meter cluster connector [52]
99	0.5 L	Oil press. indicator light	Oil pressure switch [2]
100	0.85 Y	Air conditioner	[95]
101	2 LB		
102		Heater panel ill. light	[22]
103	0.5 BW	Column switch (Passing sw.)	[3]
104	2 RB	Seat belt ind. light	[35]
105	0.5 RL	Meter cluster power source [IG]	[50]
106	2 RB	Column switch (Passing sw.)	[3]
107		Headlight (L.H.) [Lower beam]	
108	0.85 RW	Headlight (R.H.) [Upper beam]	[69]
109	1.25 R	Door switch	Fuse block [No. 1]
110	0.5 GR		[39]

Fig. 10.49 Front wiring harness component key (vehicles with W-engine only; 1979 models)

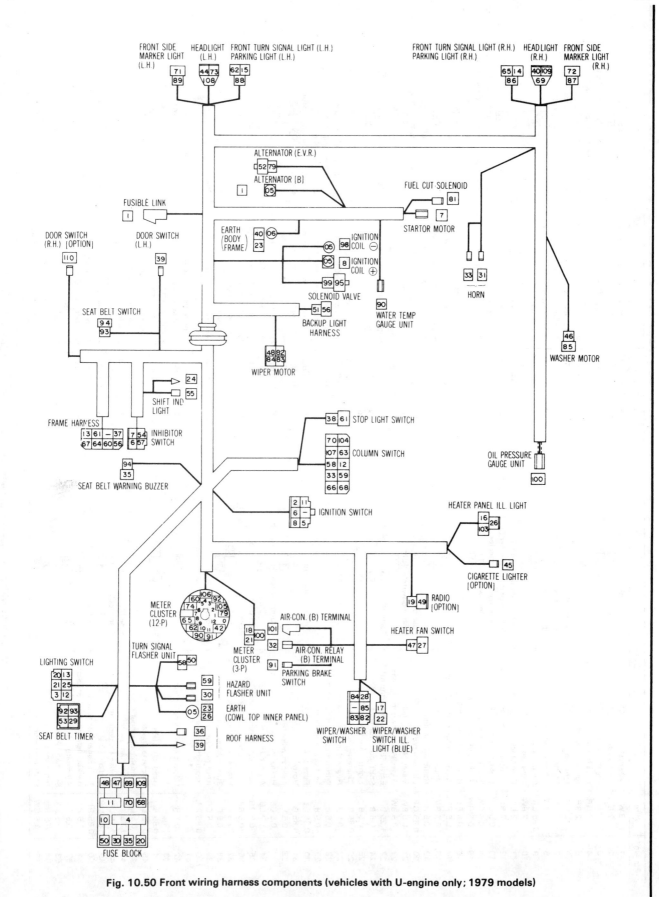

Fig. 10.50 Front wiring harness components (vehicles with U-engine only; 1979 models)

Left table (Pins 1–55)

Pin No.	Wire	Circuit	Circuit
1	3 W	Alternator [B]	Fusible link [1]
2	2 B	Ignition switch [AM]	[1]
3	2 R	Light switch [BH]	[3]
4	2 GR	Fuse block [5'-6'-7']	[8]
5	2 BR	Ignition switch [R]	
6	2 BY	Ignition switch [ST]	Inhibitor switch [ST]
7	2 BY	Starter motor	Inhibitor switch [ST]
8	2 BW	Ignition switch [IG]	Ignition coil ⊕ [8]
9	0.85 LR	Oil press. gauge	
10	2 BW	Fuse block [8']	Ignition switch [ACC] [8]
11	2 L	Fuse block [3'-4']	
12	2 RL	Lighting switch [H]	Column switch (Dimmer SW.) [BH]
13	0.5 GW	Lighting switch [T]	Frame harness connector [3]
14	0.5 GW	Front parking light (R.H.)	Lighting switch [14]
15	0.5 GW	Front parking light (L.H.)	Lighting switch [13]
16	0.5 RL	Heater panel ill. light	[13]
17	0.5 RY	Wiper/Washer switch ill. light	[13]
18	0.5 RY	Meter cluster ill. lights	[13]
19	0.5 RY	Radio dial ill. light	
20	0.85 BW	Lighting switch [BT]	Fuse block [No. 5] [21]
21	0.5 BW	Meter cluster ill. lights	Lighting switch [BM]
22	0.5 BW	Wiper/Washer switch ill. light	
23	1.25 B	Earth (Engine compartment)	Earth (Cowl top inner panel) [23]
24	0.5 B	Shift indicator light	[23]
25	0.5 B	Lighting switch [M]	[23]
26	0.85 B	Cigarette lighter earth	Earth (5) [23]
27	0.5 B	Heater fan switch earth	(5) [23]
28	0.5 B	Wiper/Washer switch earth	(5) [23]
29	0.5 B	Seat belt timer earth	(5)
30	0.85 GL	Fuse block [No. 7]	(5)
31	0.85 G	Horn	(5)
32	0.5 L	Air-con. relay (B)	Hazard flasher unit [47]
33	0.5 GB	Horn	[47]
34	2 LB	Air conditioner	Column switch (Horn switch) [2]
35	0.5 RB	Seat belt warning buzzer	Roof harness connector (Dome light)
36	0.5 RB	Fuse block [No. 6]	Fuse block [No. 6] [23]
37	0.85 R	Frame harness connector	Earth [35]
38	0.5 G	Stop light switch	Door switch (L.H.) (6) [40]
39	0.5 GR	Roof harness connector	Earth (6)
40	0.85 B	Headlight (R.H.)	[109]
41			
42	0.5 R	Upper beam indicator light	Earth (6) [48] [47]
43			
44	0.85 B	Headlight (L.H.)	
45	0.85 LW	Cigarette lighter	
46	0.5 L	Windshield washer motor	
47	1.25 LR	Heater fan switch	Fuse block [No. 3] [50]
48	1.25 LW	Windshield wiper motor	Fuse block [No. 4] [50]
49	0.5 LW	Radio	
50	0.85 RL	Backup light harness connector	Fuse block [No. 8] [50]
51	0.5 R	Alternator (E.V.R.) [S]	[50]
52	0.5 L	Seat belt timer	[50]
53	0.5 LR	Inhibitor switch [IG]	[50]
54	0.5 R	Seat belt timer	[50]
55	0.5 GW	Inhibitor switch [IG]	

Right table (Pins 56–110)

Pin No.	Wire	Circuit	Circuit
56	0.5 RL	Backup light harness connector	Frame harness connector [56]
57	0.5 RL	Inhibitor switch [L]	
58	0.85 GR	Turn signal flasher unit	Column switch (Turn signal sw.)
59	0.85 G	Hazard flasher unit	Column switch (Hazard sw.)
60	0.5 Y	Meter cluster (Fuel gauge)	Frame harness connector
61	0.5 G	Stop light switch	
62	0.5 GL	Turn signal indicator light (L.H.)	Front turn signal light (L.H.) [62]
63	0.5 GL	Column switch (Turn signal sw.)	[62]
64	0.5 GL	Frame harness connector	
65	0.5 GY	Turn signal indicator light (R.H.)	Front turn signal light (R.H.) [65]
66	0.5 GY	Column switch (Turn signal sw.)	[65]
67	0.5 GY	Frame harness connector	
68	2 R	Fuse block [1']	
69	0.85 RW	Fuse block [No. 1]	Column switch (Dimmer sw.) [HU]
70	2 RW	Fuse block [2']	Headlight (R.H.) [Lower beam]
71	0.5 B	Front side marker light (L.H.)	Column switch (Dimmer sw.) [HL]
72	0.5 B	Front side marker light (R.H.)	Earth (6) [40]
73	0.85 R	Headlight (L.H.) [Upper beam]	Earth (6) [40]
74	0.5 B	Meter cluster earth	
75	0.5 BW	Solenoid valve	Earth (5) [109]
76	0.5 L	Solenoid valve	Earth (5) [26]
77	0.5 B	Engine speed sensor relay	Engine speed sensor relay
78	0.5 W	Engine speed sensor relay	Earth (5) [50]
79	0.5 L	Solenoid valve	(5) [23]
80			Meter cluster connector [52]
81	2 BW	Fuel cut solenoid valve	
82	0.5 LB	Wiper/Washer switch [H]	
83	0.5 LO	Wiper/Washer switch [L]	
84	0.5 L	Wiper/Washer switch [AS]	
85	0.5 BW	Wiper/Washer switch [Washer]	
86	0.5 B	Front turn signal light (R.H.)	Windshield wiper motor [H]
87	0.5 GW	Front turn signal light (L.H.)	Windshield wiper motor [L]
88	0.5 B	Front side marker light (L.H.)	Windshield wiper motor [AS]
89	0.5 GW	Front side marker light (L.H.)	Windshield washer motor
90	0.5 YR	Meter cluster (Water temp. gauge)	Earth (6) [40]
91	0.5 YG	Parking brake ind. light	
92	0.5 YB	Seat belt indicator light	
93	0.5 RB	Seat belt timer	Water temp. gauge unit [8]
94	0.5 YW	Seat belt warning buzzer	Parking brake switch
95	0.5 W	Tachometer,	Seat belt timer [15]
96	1.25 W	Combination gauge (Ammeter)	Seat belt switch [40]
97	1.25 WB	Combination gauge (Ammeter)	Seat belt switch [15]
98	2 W	Shunt for ammeter fuse	Ignition coil ⊖
99	2 W	Shunt for ammeter fuse	Fuse for ammeter (5A) [1] point A
100	0.85 Y	Combination gauge (Oil press. gauge)	Fuse for ammeter (5A) [1] point B
101	0.5 GW	Combination gauge ill. light	
102	0.5 BW	Combination gauge ill. light	Oil pressure gauge unit [17]
103	0.5 BW	Heater panel ill. light	[22]
104	2 RB	Column switch (Passing sw.)	[22]
105	0.5 RB	Seat belt ind. light	[3]
106	0.5 RL	Meter cluster power source [IG]	[35]
107	2 RB	Column switch (Passing sw.)	[50]
108	0.85 RW	Headlight (L.H.) [Lower beam]	[3]
109	1.25 GR	Headlight (R.H.) [Upper beam]	[69]
110	0.5 GR	Door switch (R.H.)	Fuse block [No. 1] [39]

Fig. 10.51 Front wiring harness component key (vehicles with U-engine only; 1979 models)

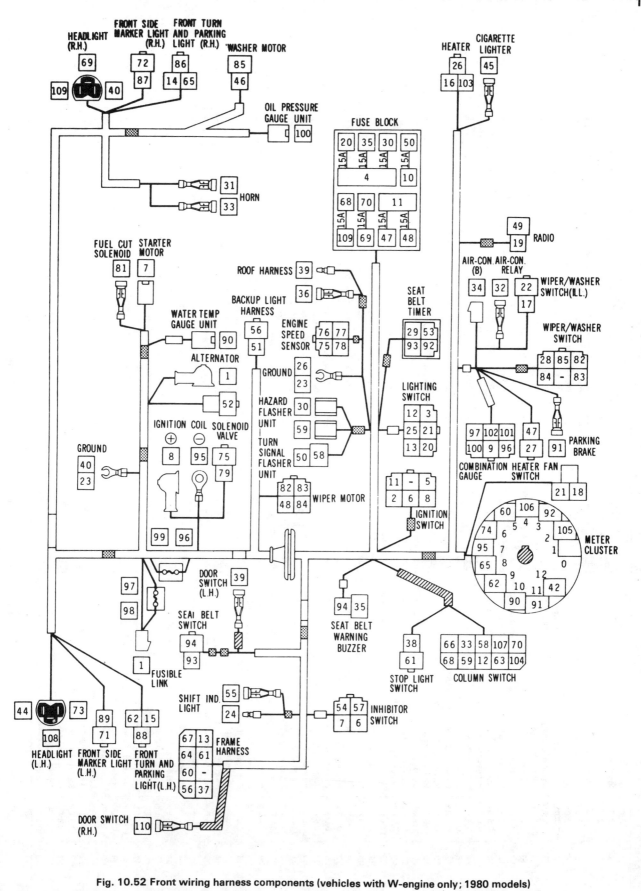

Fig. 10.52 Front wiring harness components (vehicles with W-engine only; 1980 models)

Pin No.	Wire	Circuit
1	3 W	Alternator
2	2 B	Ignition switch
3	2 R	Light switch
4	2 GR	Fuse block
5	2 BR	Ignition switch
6	2 BY	Ignition switch
7	2 BY	Starter motor
8	2 BW	Ignition switch
9	0.85 LR	Combination gauge
10	2 BW	Fuse block
11	2 L	Fuse block
12	2 RL	Lighting switch
13	0.5 GW	Front parking light (R.H.)
14	0.5 GW	Front parking light (L.H.)
15	0.5 GW	Heater panel ill. light (+)
16	0.5 RL	Wiper/Washer switch ill. light (+)
17	0.5 RY	Meter cluster ill. lights (+)
18	0.5 RY	Radio ill. light
19	0.5 RY	Radio ill. light
20	0.85 GR	Lighting switch
21	0.5 BW	Lighting switch
22	0.5 BW	Wiper/Washer switch ill. light (-)
23	1.25 B	Ground (Engine compartment)
24	0.5 B	Shift indicator light
25	0.5 B	Lighting switch
26	0.85 B	Cigarette lighter
27	0.5 B	Heater fan switch
28	0.5 B	Wiper/Washer switch
29	0.5 B	Seat belt timer
30	0.85 GL	Fuse block
31	0.85 G	Horn "B"
32	0.5 L	Air-con relay "B"
33	0.5 GB	Horn
34	2 LB	Air-con "B"
35	0.5 RB	Seat belt warning buzzer
36	0.5 RB	Roof harness (Dome light)
37	0.85 R	Frame harness
38	0.5 G	Stop light switch
39	0.5 GR	Roof harness (Dome light)
40	0.85 B	Ground
42	0.5 R	Upper beam indicator light (+)
44	0.85 B	Headlight (L.H.)
45	0.85 LW	Cigarette lighter
46	0.5 L	Windshield washer motor
47	1.25 LR	Heater fan switch
48	1.25 LW	Windshield wiper motor
49	0.5 LW	Radio
50	0.85 RL	Turn signal flasher unit
51	0.5 R	Backup light harness connector
52	0.5 L	Alternator (E.V.R.)
53	0.5 LR	Seat belt timer
54	0.5 R	Inhibitor switch
55	0.5 GW	Shift indicator light
56	0.5 RL	Backup light harness

Circuit (connector references):

Fusible link

- [1] point "B"
- [1]
- [3]
- [8]

Inhibitor switch

Inhibitor switch

Ignition coil (+) [50]
[8]

Ignition switch

Column switch (Dimmer)

Rear harness [13] [14] [13] [13] [13]

Fuse block [No. 5]

Meter cluster ill. light [21] (-)

Ground (Cowl top inner panel) [37]

[23]

Ground [26] [26]

Hazard flasher unit [47]

Column switch (Horn switch) [2]

Fuse block [35] [23] [35]

Door switch (L.H.) [48]

Headlight (R.H.)

Fuse block [50] [50] [50] [50]

Rear harness (Back)

Pin No.	Wire	Circuit
57	0.5 RL	Inhibitor switch
58	0.85 GR	Turn signal flasher unit
59	0.85 G	Hazard flasher unit
60	0.5 Y	Meter cluster (Fuel gauge)
61	0.5 G	Stop light switch
62	0.5 GL	Turn signal indicator light (L.H.)
63	0.5 GL	Column switch (Turn signal sw.)
64	0.5 GL	Rear harness
65	0.5 GY	Turn signal indicator light (R.H.)
66	0.5 GY	Column switch (Turn signal sw.)
67	0.5 GY	Rear harness
68	2 R	Fuse block
69	0.85 RW	Fuse block
70	2 RW	Fuse block
71	0.5 B	Front side marker light (L.H.)
72	0.5 B	Front side marker light (R.H.)
73	0.85 R	Headlight (L.H.) [Upper beam]
74	0.5 B	Meter cluster
75	0.5 BW	Solenoid valve
76	0.5 L	Engine speed sensor
77	0.5 B	Ground (E.S. sensor relay)
78	0.5 W	E.S. sensor relay
79	0.5 L	Charging indicator light
81	2 BW	Fuel cut solenoid valve
82	0.5 LB	Wiper/Washer switch
83	0.5 LO	Wiper/Washer switch
84	0.5 L	Wiper/Washer switch
85	0.5 BW	Wiper/Washer motor
86	0.5 B	Front turn signal light (R.H.)
87	0.5 GW	Front side marker light (R.H.)
88	0.5 B	Front turn signal light (L.H.)
89	0.5 GW	Front side marker light (L.H.)
90	0.5 YR	Water temp. gauge unit
91	0.5 YG	Parking brake switch
92	0.5 YB	Seat belt timer
93	0.5 RB	Seat belt timer
94	0.5 YW	Seat belt warning buzzer
95	0.5 W	Ignition coil
96	1.25 W	Fuse holder
97	1.25 WB	Fuse holder
98	2 W	Fuse holder
99	0.5 L	Fuse holder
100	0.85 Y	Oil press. indicator light
101	0.56 W	Metercluster ill. light
102	0.5 BW	Meter cluster ill. light
103	0.5 BW	Heater panel ill. light
104	2 RB	Column switch (Passing sw.)
105	0.5 RB	Seat belt ind. light (+)
106	0.5 RL	Meter cluster power source
107	2 RB	Column switch
108	0.85 RW	Headlight (L.H.) [Lower beam]
109	1.25 R	Headlight (R.H.) [Upper beam]
110	0.5 GR	Door switch (R.H.)

Circuit (connector references):

Column switch [56]

Column switch

Rear harness (Fuel gauge unit)

Rear harness (Stop)

Front turn signal light (L.H.) [62]

Rear harness [62]

Front turn signal light (R.H.) [65]

Column switch (Dimmer) [65]

Headlight (R.H.) [Lower beam]

Column switch (Dimmer sw.) [40] [40] [109]

Meter cluster [26]

E.S. Sensor relay [8]

Windshield wiper motor [50]

Windshield wiper motor [23]

Windshield wiper motor [95]

Windshield washer motor [52] [8]

Meter cluster (Water temp. gauge) [40]

Parking brake ind. light [15]

Seat belt indicator light [40]

Seat belt switch [15]

Meter cluster (Tachometer)

Combination gauge (Alternator) [35]

Combination gauge (Battery) [50] [104] [69]

[1] point "A"
[1] point "B"

Oil pressure unit [17] [22] [22] [3]

Fuse block [39]

Fig. 10.53 Front wiring harness component key (vehicles with W-engine only: 1980 models)

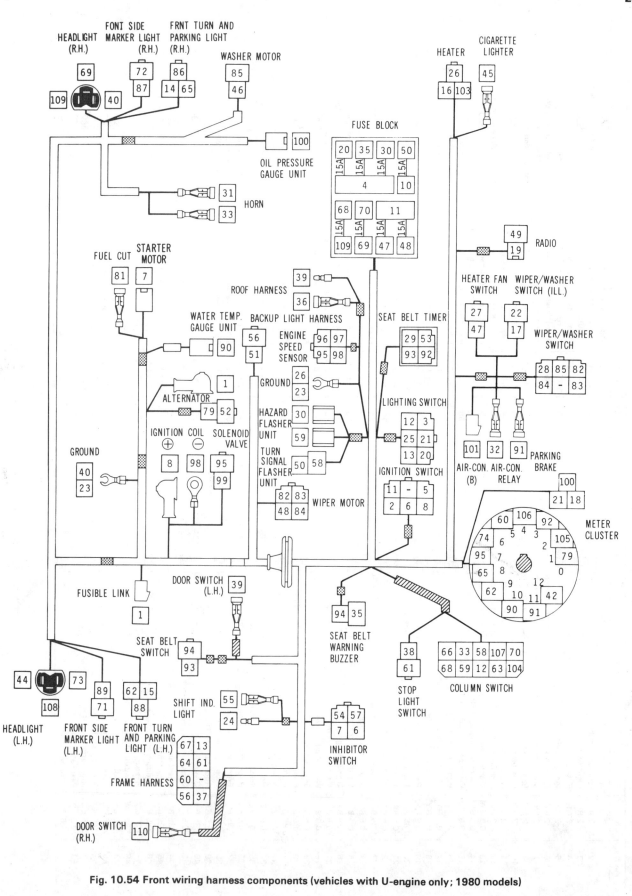

Fig. 10.54 Front wiring harness components (vehicles with U-engine only; 1980 models)

Left-hand table (Pin No. 1–54):

Pin No.	Wire	Circuit	Circuit (to)
1	3 W	Alternator	Fusible link [1]
2	2 B	Ignition switch	[1]
3	2 R	Light switch	[3]
4	2 GR	Fuse block	[8]
5	2 BR	Ignition switch	
6	2 BY	Ignition switch	Inhibitor switch
7	2 BY	Starter motor	Inhibitor switch
8	2 BW	Ignition switch	Ignition coil ⊕ [8]
10	2 BW	Ignition switch	
11	2 L	Fuse block	Ignition switch
12	2 RL	Lighting switch	Column switch (Dimmer SW.)
13	0.5 GW	Lighting switch	Rear harness [13]
14	0.5 GW	Front parking light (R.H.)	[14]
15	0.5 GW	Front parking light (L.H.)	[13]
16	0.5 RL	Heater panel ill. light ⊕	[13]
17	0.5 RY	Wiper/Washer switch ill. light ⊕	[13]
18	0.5 RY	Meter cluster ill. lights ⊕	[13]
19	0.5 RY	Radio dial ill. light	
20	0.85 GR	Lighting switch	Fuse block
21	0.5 BW	Lighting switch	Meter cluster ill. light ⊖ [21]
22	0.5 BW	Wiper/Washer switch ill. light ⊖	⊖
23	1.25 B	Ground (Engine compartment)	Ground (Cowl top inner panel) [37]
24	0.5 B	Shift indicator light	[23]
25	0.5 B	Lighting switch	Ground
26	0.85 B	Cigarette lighter	[26]
27	0.5 B	Heater fan switch	[26]
28	0.5 B	Wiper/Washer switch	[26]
29	0.5 B	Seat belt timer	
30	0.85 GL	Fuse block	Hazard flasher unit [47]
31	0.85 G	Horn	[47]
32	0.5 L	Air-con.relay	Column switch (Horn switch)
33	0.5 GB	Horn	
35	0.5 RB	Seat belt warning buzzer	Fuse block [35]
36	0.5 RB	Roof harness (Dome light)	[23]
37	0.85 B	Frame harness	[35]
38	0.5 G	Stop light switch	
39	0.5 GR	Roof harness (Dome light)	Door switch [48]
40	0.85 B	Ground	Headlight (R.H.) [109]
42	0.5 R	Upper beam indicator light ⊕	[40]
44	0.85 B	Headlight (L.H.)	[48]
45	0.85 LW	Cigarette lighter	[47]
46	0.5 L	Windshield washer motor	
47	1.25 LR	Heater fan switch	Fuse block [50]
48	1.25 LW	Windshield wiper motor	[50]
49	0.5 LW	Radio	
50	0.85 RL	Turn signal flasher unit	Fuse block [50]
51	0.5 R	Backup light harness	[50]
52	0.5 L	Alternator (E.V.R.)	
53	0.5 LR	Seat belt timer	
54	0.5 R	Inhibitor switch	

Right-hand table (Pin No. 55–110):

Pin No.	Wire	Circuit	Circuit (to)
55	0.5 GW	Shift indicator light	Rear harness (Back up light) [50]
56	0.5 RL	Backup light harness	[56]
57	0.85 GR	Inhibitor switch	Column switch
58	0.85 G	Turn signal flasher unit	Column switch
59	0.5 Y	Hazard flasher unit	Meter cluster (Fuel gauge)
60	0.5 G	Rear harness (Fuel gauge)	Stop light switch
61	0.5 G	Rear harness (Stop)	
62	0.5 GL	Turn signal indicator light (L.H.)	Front turn signal light (L.H.) [62]
63	0.5 GL	Column switch(Turn signal sw., L.H.)	[62]
64	0.5 GL	Rear harness (Fuel gauge)	
65	0.5 GY	Turn signal indicator light (R.H.)	Front turn signal light (R.H.) [65]
66	0.5 GY	Column switch(Turn signal sw.R.H.)	[65]
67	2 R	Rear harness (Turn signal, R.H.)	
68	0.85 RW	Fuse block	Column switch [HU]
69	2 RW	Fuse block	Headlight (R.H.) [40] [Lower beam]
70	0.5 B	Fuse block	Column switch [HL]
71	0.5 B	Front side marker light (L.H.)	[40]
72	0.5 R	Front side marker light (R.H.)	[109]
73	0.85 R	Headlight (L.H.) [Upper beam]	[26]
74	0.5 B	Meter cluster	Meter cluster (CHG)
79	0.5 YW	Alternator (E.V.R.)	[8]
81	2 BW	Wiper/Washer switch	Windshield wiper motor
82	0.5 LB	Wiper/Washer switch	Windshield wiper motor
83	0.5 LO	Wiper/Washer switch	Windshield wiper motor
84	0.5 L	Wiper/Washer switch [Washer]	Windshield washer motor
85	0.5 BW	Front turn signal light (R.H.)	[40]
86	0.5 B	Front turn signal light(L.H.)	[15]
87	0.5 GW	Front side marker light (R.H.)	[40]
88	0.5 B	Front side marker light (L.H.)	[15]
89	0.5 GW	Water temp. gauge unit	Meter cluster (Water temp. gauge) [50]
90	0.5 YR	Parking brake switch	Parking brake ind. light [23]
91	0.5 YG	Seat belt timer	Seat belt indicator light
92	0.5 YB	Seat belt switch	Seat belt timer
93	0.5 RB	Seat belt warning buzzer	Seat belt switch
94	0.5 YW	Solenoid valve	E.S. Sensor relay [50]
95	0.5 BW	E.S. sensor relay	
96	1.25 L	Ground (E.S. sensor relay)	
97	1.25 WB	Solenoid valve	Ignition coil ⊕ [50] — point A
98	2 W	Oil pressure gauge switch	Combination gauge (Oil press.) [52] — point B
99	2 L	Cooler	[2]
100	0.85 Y	Heater panel ill. light ⊖	[22]
101	0.5 LB	Column switch (Passing sw.)	[3]
103	0.5 BW	Seat belt ind. light	[35]
104	2 RB	Meter cluster power source	[104]
105	0.5 RB	Column switch (Passing sw.)	[69]
106	0.5 RL	Headlight (L.H.) [Lower beam]	
107	2 RB	Headlight (R.H.) [Upper beam]	
108	0.85 RW	Door switch (R.H.)	
109	1.25 R		Fuse block [39]
110	0.5 GR		

Fig. 10.55 Front wiring harness component key (vehicles with U-engine only: 1980 models)

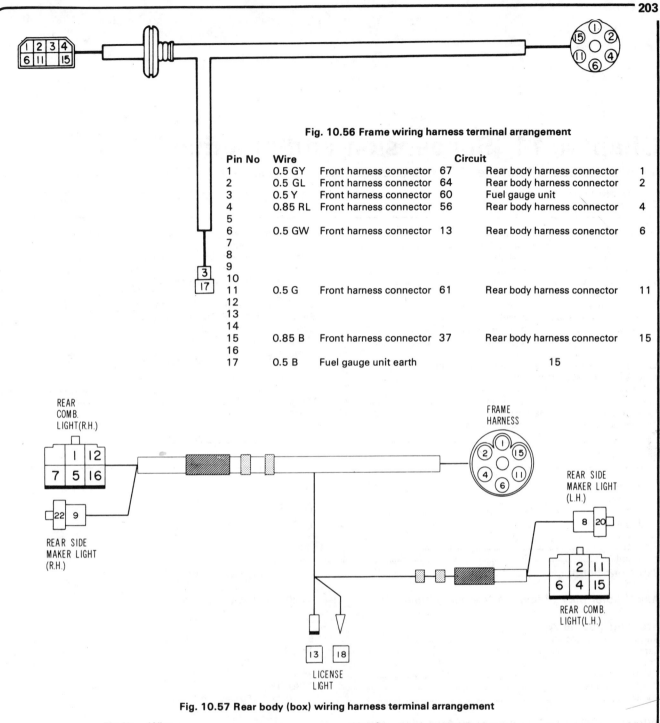

Fig. 10.56 Frame wiring harness terminal arrangement

Pin No	Wire	Circuit			
1	0.5 GY	Front harness connector	67	Rear body harness connector	1
2	0.5 GL	Front harness connector	64	Rear body harness connector	2
3	0.5 Y	Front harness connector	60	Fuel gauge unit	
4	0.85 RL	Front harness connector	56	Rear body harness connector	4
5					
6	0.5 GW	Front harness connector	13	Rear body harness conenctor	6
7					
8					
9					
10					
11	0.5 G	Front harness connector	61	Rear body harness connector	11
12					
13					
14					
15	0.85 B	Front harness connector	37	Rear body harness connector	15
16					
17	0.5 B	Fuel gauge unit earth		15	

Fig. 10.57 Rear body (box) wiring harness terminal arrangement

Pin No	Wire	Circuit	
1	0.5 GY	Frame harness	Turn signal flasher light (r.h.)
2	0.5 GL	Frame harness	Turn signal flasher light (l.h.)
4	0.5 RL	Frame harness	Backup light (l.h.)
5	0.5 RL	Backup light (r.h.)	4
6	0.5 GW	Frame harness	Tail (Stop/Tail) light (l.h.)
7	0.5 GW	Tail (Stop/Tail) light (r.h.)	6
8	0.5 GW	Rear side marker light (r.h.)	6
9	0.5 GW	Rear side marker light (l.h.)	7
11	0.5 G	Frame harness	Stop (Stop/Tail) light (l.h.)
12	0.5 G	Stop (Stop/Tail) light (r.h.)	11
13	0.5 GW	License plate light	6
15	0.85 B	Frame harness	Rear combination light ground (l.h.)
16	0.5 B	Rear combination light ground (r.h.)	15
18	0.5 B	License plate light earth	15
20	0.5 B	Rear side marker light ground (l.h.)	15
22	0.5 B	Rear side marker light ground (r.h.)	16

Chapter 11 Suspension and steering

Refer to Chapter 13 for specifications and information related to 1981 thru 1988 models

Contents

Specifications

Front coil spring

Standard free length

Left	11.850 in (301 mm)
Right	11.457 in (291 mm)

Color-code

Left	Green
Right	Pink

Strut bar bend .... 0.120 in or less (3 mm or less)

Axial/radial play of lower suspension balljoints .... 0.020 in or less (0.5 mm or less)

Steering geometry

Steering axis inclination .... 8°
Camber .... 1° 30'
Caster

1979 models	3° 1°
1980 models	2°30' 1°

Toe-in .... 0.080 to 0.350 in (2 to 9 mm)

Wheel spindle bearing contact surface diameters

1979 models

Inner	1.3743 to 1.3748 in (34.907 to 34.920 mm)
Outer	0.8430 to 0.8435 in (21.412 to 21.425 mm)

1980 models

Inner	1.3746 to 1.3751 in (34.915 to 34.928 mm)
Outer	0.8433 to 0.8438 in (21.420 to 21.433 mm)

Relay rod-to-Pitman arm clearance .... 0.15 to 0.17 in (3.7 to 4.3 mm)

Relay rod-to-idler arm clearance .... 0.15 to 0.17 in (3.7 to 4.3 mm)

Installed distance from threaded end of strut bar to rear face of jam nut .... 3.8 in (96 mm)

Installed distance from threaded end of stabilizer bar link bolt to top face of nut .... 0.87 to 0.94 in (22 to 24 mm)

Power steering system

Steering wheel free play	
Standard	Within 1 in (25 mm)
Limit	2 in (50 mm)
Clearance between slider and socket	0.020 to 0.021 in (0.50 to 0.55 mm)
Maximum backlash between groove of rack piston and balls	0.008 in (0.2 mm)
Cross-shaft axial (end) play	0 to 0.002 in (0 to 0.05 mm)
Range of cross-shaft adjusting plates:	
MB 076596	0.077 in (1.95 mm)
MB 076196	0.079 in (2.00 mm)
MB 076597	0.081 in (2.05 mm)
MB 076598	0.083 in (2.10 mm)
MB 076599	0.085 in (2.15 mm)
Input worm shaft preload torque	0.18 to 0.47 ft-lb (0.25 to 0.65 Nm)
Distance from rack piston to last ball (reassembly)	0.5 in (13 mm)
Total starting torque of input worm shaft (neutral)	0.36 to 0.65 ft-lb (0.5 to 0.9 Nm)
Clearance between center of bolt hole in gearbox and Pitman arm	0.77 in (19.5 mm)
Belt tension (at center)	$\frac{1}{4}$ to $\frac{3}{8}$ in (7 to 10 mm) deflection
Oil pump pressure (unit-type reservoir only)	
Valve closed	1066 to 1210 psi (7335 to 8336 kPa)
Valve open	142 psi or less (981 kPa or less)

Manual steering system

Steering wheel free play	
Standard	Within 1 in (25 mm)
Limit	2 in (50 mm)
Cross-shaft-to-bushing clearance	0.0004 to 0.0020 in (0.010 to 0.052 mm)
Standard end cover shim	0.020 in (0.5 mm)
Mainshaft preload (without cross-shaft)	3.0 to 4.8 in-lb (0.34 to 0.54 Nm)
Range of mainshaft adjusting shim	
MB 005890	0.0020 in (0.05 mm)
MB 005891	0.0024 in (0.06 mm)
MB 005892	0.0030 in (0.07 mm)
MB 005893	0.0040 in (0.10 mm)
MB 005894	0.0080 in (0.20 mm)
MB 005895	0.0120 in (0.30 mm)
MB 005896	0.0200 in (0.50 mm)
Cross-shaft axial (end) play	0 to 0.002 in (0 to 0.05 mm)
Range of cross-shaft adjusting shims	
MA 180202	0.077 in (1.95 mm)
MA 180203	0.079 in (2.00 mm)
MA 180204	0.081 in (2.05 mm)
MA 180205	0.083 in (2.10 mm)
Backlash between cross-shaft gear and mainshaft rack	0 to 0.002 in (0 to 0.05 mm)
Mainshaft preload (reassembly)	5.7 to 7.4 in-lb (0.64 to 0.83 Nm)

Wheels

With 'U' engine	5J-14 x 40
With 'W' engine	6JJ-14 x 27
Run-out limit	
Axial	0.060 in (1.5 mm)
Radial	0.060 in (1.5 mm)
Maximum projection of wheel weights from wheel edge	0.120 in (3.0 mm)

Tires

With 'U'-engine	6.00 x 14 6PR	
With 'W'-engine	185 SR14	
Inflation pressures (psi)	'U'-engine	'W'-engine
No cargo		
Front	26	22
Rear	26	22
Full cargo		
Front	26	22
Rear	46	32
Tire run-out limit (axial)	0.120 in (3.0 mm)	

Torque specifications

	ft-lb	(Nm)
Spindle arm bolts/nuts	40 to 54	(54 to 74)
Final tightening of pivot bushings	181 to 253	(245 to 343)
Lower ball joint-to-lower arm bolts	22 to 30	(29 to 41)
Upper arm shaft-to-crossmember bolts	40 to 54	(54 to 74)
Lower arm shaft-to-crossmember bolt	6 to 9	(8 to 12)
Lower arm shaft nut	40 to 54	(54 to 74)
Wheel spindle-to-upper balljoint bolts	43 to 65	(59 to 88)

Wheel spindle-to-lower balljoint bolts	87 to 130	(118 to 177)
Shock absorber-to-crossmember nuts	9 to 13	(12 to 18)
Shock absorber-to-lower arm bolts	6 to 9	(8 to 12)
Strut bar-to-lower arm bolts	51 to 61	(69 to 83)
Strut bar-to-frame nut	54 to 61	(74 to 83)
Strut bar bracket bolts	25 to 33	(34 to 44)
Stabilizer-to-lower arm bolt	18 to 25	(25 to 34)
Stabilizer bar bracket bolts	6 to 9	(8 to 12)
Steering angle adjusting bolt jam nut	14	(20)
Relay rod-to-Pitman arm nut	25 to 33	(34 to 44)
Tie-rod-to-wheel spindle nut	25 to 33	(34 to 44)
Tie-rod-to-relay rod nut	25 to 33	(34 to 44)
Tie-rod end jam nut	36 to 40	(49 to 54)
Idler arm-to-bracket nut	29 to 43	(39 to 59)
Idler arm bracket mounting bolts	25 to 29	(34 to 39)
Idler arm-to-relay rod nut	25 to 33	(34 to 44)
Rear spring U-bolt attaching nuts	47 to 54	(64 to 74)
Shackle pin nuts	22 to 33	(29 to 44)
Rear shock absorber nuts	13 to 18	(18 to 25)
Wheel lug nuts	51 to 58	(69 to 78)
Rear spring pin-to-hanger bracket bolt	10 to 14	(14 to 20)
Rear spring pin-to-hanger bracket nut	22 to 33	(29 to 44)
Power steering system		
Column clamp mounting bolt	3.6 to 5.8	(5 to 8)
Top cover	0.72 to 1.01	(1.0 to 1.4)
Valve housing nut	130 to 166	(176 to 225)
Circulator holder clamp bolt	2.5 to 3.3	(3.5 to 4.4)
Side cover bolts	33 to 40	(44 to 54)
Valve housing bolts	33 to 40	(44 to 54)
Pitman arm-to-gearbox shaft nut	94 to 109	(127 to 147)
Gearbox mounting nuts	40 to 47	(54 to 64)
Manual steering system		
Steering shaft clamp bolt	11 to 15	(15 to 20)
Steering wheel locknut	25 to 33	(34 to 44)
Gearbox end cover bolts	11 to 14	(15 to 20)
Gearbox upper cover bolts	11 to 14	(15 to 20)
Gearbox mounting nuts	25 to 29	(34 to 39)
Pitman arm-to-gearbox shaft nut	94 to 109	(127 to 147)

1   General information

The Chrysler mini-truck is equipped with a conventional wishbone-type independent front suspension with coil springs over double-acting shock absorbers. A stabilizer bar, which minimizes body roll during cornering, and strut bars attached to each lower control arm, which counteract longitudinal loads, complete the front suspension. The rear suspension is also conventional, with semi-elliptical leaf springs and double-acting shock absorbers.

The steering system employs a variable-ratio steering gearbox and tilt-type steering wheel which actuate a steering linkage consisting of a Pitman arm, an idler arm, tie-rods and a relay rod.

The front hubs are conventional, and use tapered roller bearings. The rear hubs are the semi-floating type. Chapter 8 contains additional information necessary for service and repair of the rear hubs.

2   Suspension – general checks

1   The suspension system should normally require little maintenance, except in cases where damage has occurred due to an accident. It should, however, be checked from time to time for signs of wear which will result in a loss of precision handling and ride comfort.
2   Ensure that the suspension components, particularly the springs and rubber bushings, have not sagged or worn out. Park the vehicle on a level surface and visually check to see that it sits level. Compare it with the photographs to see whether it has markedly sagged. This normally will occur only after many miles and will usually appear more on the driver's side of the vehicle.
3   Check the shock absorbers, as these are the parts of the suspension system likely to wear out first. If there is any evidence of fluid leakage, they will definitely need replacing. Bounce the vehicle up and down vigorously; it should feel stiff, and well damped by the shock absorbers. As soon as the bouncing is stopped, the vehicle should stop moving up and down. Do not replace shock absorbers as single units.

Replace them in pairs unless a failure has occurred at low mileage.

3   Steering and front suspension components – checking

1   Raise the front of the vehicle and set it on jack stands. Block the rear tires and set the parking brake to keep the vehicle from rolling.
2   Visually check the strut rods, the stabilizer bar, the springs, the shock absorbers, the control arms, the tie-rods, the relay rod and the Pitman and idler arms for any obvious problems such as cracks, bends, and deformation. Check the rubber bushings, bumpers and dust covers for cracks and deterioration. If the bushings appear to be 'squished out' of their mounts, they should be replaced.

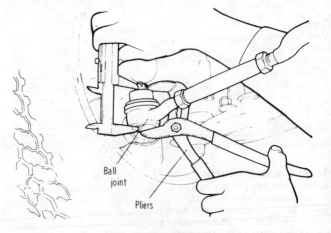

Fig. 11.1 Checking steering balljoint deflection (Sec 3)

3.4 Checking the upper control arm balljoint for wear

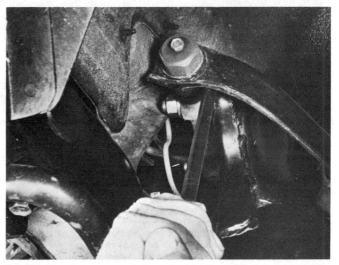

3.5 Checking the upper control arm bushing for wear

3.6 Checking the lower control arm balljoint for wear

3.7 Checking the lower control arm bushings for wear

3   Place a jack under the lower control arm and raise the suspension until the rubber rebound stop on the upper control arm is no longer touching the spring tower. Do not raise it too much, as you do not want to lift the vehicle off the jack stands.
4   To check the upper control arm balljoint, slip a large screwdriver or pry bar between the upper control arm and the wheel spindle (where the balljoint stud passes through it) and pry up on the control arm (photo).There should be no noticeable play in the balljoint.
5   Check the upper control arm pivot bushings by prying from side-to-side at the front and rear of the control arm, where the bushings are attached (photo). Any noticeable movement here would indicate that new control arm pivot bushings are needed.
6   Check the lower control arm balljoint the same way the upper balljoint was checked. Slip a large screwdriver or pry bar between the lower control arm and the wheel spindle and pry down on the control arm (photo). There will be some play noted at this point; if it is greater than $\frac{1}{32}$ in, the balljoint should be replaced. If you have a dial indicator set available for checking the balljoints, make sure the play is within the limits given in the Specifications Section. Since special tools, which are not generally available to the home mechanic, are required to remove and replace the suspension balljoints, we recommend that the job be done by a reputable front-end alignment and repair shop.
7   Using a large screwdriver or pry bar, check for side-to-side movement of the lower control arm at its pivot point (photo). Any noticeable movement here would indicate that new pivot bushings are in order.
8   Check for play in the balljoints at the tie-rod ends, the Pitman arm and the idler arm. Grasp the balljoint with a pliers as shown, and compress it completely. If it deflects more than $\frac{1}{16}$ in, it must be replaced. If you are using a precision measuring tool, such as a vernier or dial calipers to measure balljoint play, make sure it is within the limits given in the Specifications Section. You will have to replace the entire Pitman arm or idler arm if their balljoints are worn.
9   Check the steering wheel play.
10 On vehicles with manual steering, place the steering wheel in the straight-ahead position, slowly turn it from side to side, note the amount of free play and compare it to the specifications. If an adjustment is necessary, place the steering wheel in the straight-ahead position and loosen the adjusting screw jam nut on the steering gearbox. Turn the adjusting screw in or out, as required, until the free play is within the specified limit. It is important to note that the adjusting screw should not be tightened too much, as steering effort and recovery will be adversely affected. Hold the adjusting screw with a screwdriver and tighten the jam nut securely. When the adjustment is complete, make sure the steering wheel turns lightly and smoothly. If the free play cannot be reduced until it is within the specified limit, the steering gearbox will have to be repaired or replaced.
11 On vehicles with power steering, the engine must be running at approximately 1000 rpm when the steering wheel free play is measured (after this check, be sure to return the engine to the correct idle speed). Place the steering wheel in the straight-ahead position, slowly turn it from side to side, note the amount of free play and

compare it to the specifications. (Do not confuse the free play with the power ON range). The power steering wheel free play is adjusted in the exact same manner as the manual steering free play. (Shut the engine off before making the adjustment). If the adjusting screw is tightened too much, the result will be increased steering effort and poor recovery.

12 Lower the vehicle to the ground.

13 On vehicles equipped with power steering, the steering wheel recovery should be checked while driving. Make both gradual and sharp turns, in both directions, while checking for differences in steering effort and recovery of the wheel. There should be no differences between right and left-hand turns. While driving at approximately 30 mph, turn the steering wheel 90° in either direction and let the wheel go. If it returns 60° or more, the system is operating properly.

4 Tires

1 Tires are extremely important from a safety standpoint. The tread should be checked periodically to see that the tires have not worn excessively, a condition which can be dangerous, especially in wet weather.

2 To equalize wear and add life to a set of tires, it is recommended that they be rotated periodically. When rotating, check for signs of abnormal wear and foreign objects in the tread or sidewalls (refer to Chapter 1, *Routine Maintenance)*

3 Proper tire inflation is essential for maximum life of the tread and for proper handling and braking. Read through the appropriate Section in the beginning of this manual for more information on tire inflation.

4 Tires that are wearing in an abnormal way are an indication that their inflation is incorrect or the front-end components are not adjusted properly. Take the vehicle to a reputable front-end alignment and repair shop to correct the situation.

5 Wheels

1 Wheels can be damaged by an impact with a curb or other solid object. If the wheels are bent, the result is a hazardous condition which must be corrected. To check the wheels, raise the vehicle and set it on jack stands. Visually inspect the wheel for obvious signs of damage such as cracks and deformation. A dial indicator mounted so that the indicator stem touches the wheel at (A), as shown in Figure 11.2, will indicate axial run-out of the wheel (when the wheel is rotated by hand). If the dial indicator is mounted so that the stem contacts the wheel at (B), it will indicate radial run-out of the wheel. Moving the dial indicator again, so that the stem contacts the tire at (C), will reveal the axial run-out of the tire. The run-out measurements should not exceed the limits listed in the Specifications Section.

2 Tire and wheel balance is very important to the overall handling, braking and ride performance of a vehicle. Whenever a tire is disassembled for repair or replacement, the tire and wheel assembly should be balanced before being installed on the vehicle. The extreme outside edge of any balance weight installed on the wheels should not project more than the specified amount from the wheel edge. Also, no more than one balance weight should be installed on each side of a wheel.

3 Wheels should be periodically cleaned, especially on the inside, where mud and road salts accumulate and eventually cause rust and, ultimately, wheel failure.

6 Wheel alignment

Note: *Since wheel alignment and testing equipment is generally out of the reach of the home mechanic, this section is intended only to familiarize the reader with the basic terms used and procedures followed during a typical wheel alignment job. In the event that your vehicle needs a wheel alignment check or adjustment, we recommend that the work be done by a reputable front-end alignment and repair shop.*

1 The three basic adjustments made when aligning a vehicle's front end are toe-in, caster and camber.

2 Toe-in is the amount the front wheels are angled in relationship to

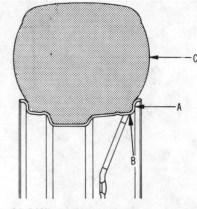

Fig. 11.2 Wheel runout checking points (Sec 5)

the centerline of the vehicle. For example, in a vehicle with zero toe-in, the distance measured between the front edges of the wheels is the same as the distance measured between the rear edges of the wheels. The wheels are running parallel with the centerline of the vehicle. On the Chrysler Mini truck the distance between the front edges of the wheels should be 0.080 to 0.350 in less than the distance between the rear edges of the wheels (0.040 to 0.175 in for each wheel). Toe-in is adjusted by lengthening or shortening the tie-rods. Incorrect toe-in will cause tires to wear improperly by making them 'scrub' against the road surface.

3 Camber and caster are the angles at which the wheel and suspension upright are inclined to the vertical. Camber is the angle of the wheel in the lateral (side-to-side) plane, while caster is the angle of the wheel and upright in the longitudinal (fore-and-aft) plane. Camber angle affects the amount of tire tread which contacts the road and compensates for change in the suspension geometry when the vehicle is travelling around curves or over an undulating surface. Caster angle affects the self-centering action of the steering, which governs straight-line stability.

4 Caster angle, which is always adjusted first, is changed by moving the upper control arm pivot shaft forward or backward in the pivot bushings. The correct caster angle for the 1979 Chrysler Mini truck is 3° ± 1°, while the 1980 model requires a caster angle of 2°30' ± 1°. Camber angle is adjusted by moving the upper control arm pivot shaft from side to side on its mount by inserting shims of varying thicknesses between the shaft and the frame crossmember. Standard camber angle is 1° ± 30'.

7 Front shock absorber – removal and installation

1 Raise the front of the vehicle and set it on jack stands. Block the rear tires and set the parking brake to keep the vehicle from rolling. Remove the front wheels.

2 Remove the two bolts that hold the bottom of the shock absorber in place on the lower control arm (photo).

3 While supporting the bottom of the shock, loosen and remove the jam nut and the retaining nut at the top of the shock (photo). The very top of the shock strut has 2 flats which can be gripped with a wrench to keep the strut from turning as the retaining nut is loosened. Slip the large washers and the rubber bushing off the strut. Note how they are positioned so you can install the new ones properly.

4 Pull the shock out of its mount from the bottom.

5 Extend the strut of the new shock absorber as far as possible and install the inner large washer and rubber bushing using the old shock as a guide. Slip the new shock into position, making sure that the strut fits into the mounting hole at the top of the shock mount. Install the 2 bottom shock mounting bolts finger-tight.

6 Install the outer rubber bushing and large washers onto the shock strut and thread the retaining nut into place. Be careful not to push the shock strut down through the mounting hole.

7 Tighten the upper retaining nut and the lower mount bolts. Thread the jam nut onto the shock strut and tighten it securely.

8 Install the wheels and lower the vehicle to the ground.

7.2 Removing the bottom shock absorber mounting bolts

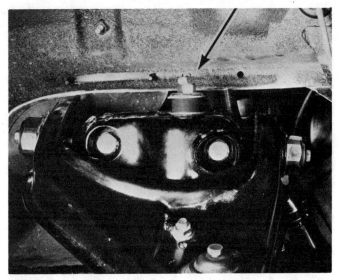

7.3 Loosen the jam nut and the retaining nut at the top of the shock strut

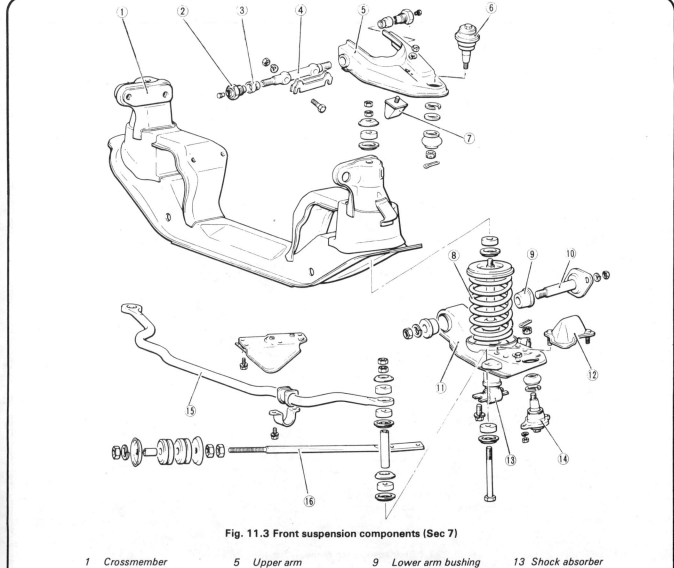

Fig. 11.3 Front suspension components (Sec 7)

1	Crossmember	5	Upper arm	9	Lower arm bushing	13	Shock absorber
2	Pivot bushing	6	Upper ball joint	10	Lower arm shaft	14	Lower ball joint
3	Dust seal	7	Rebound stopper	11	Lower arm	15	Stabilizer
4	Upper arm shaft	8	Front coil spring	12	Bump stopper	16	Strut bar

8.2 Removing the lower shock mount nut (rear shock absorber)

8 Rear shock absorber – removal and installation

1   Raise the rear of the vehicle and set it on jack stands. Block the front wheels to keep the vehicle from rolling.
2   Remove the upper and lower shock mount nuts and washers (photo).
3   Slip the shock absorber off the mounts and remove the large washers. Note how the washers are installed. Also, note which end of the shock is up.
4   Slip the new shock absorber into place after installing the large washers. Make sure that it is installed with the proper end up.
5   Slide the outside washers into place and thread the nuts onto the shock mounting studs. Tighten the nuts to the specified torque.
6   Lower the vehicle to the ground and test drive it.

9 Front hub – removal, inspection and installation

Since the front hub must be removed to service the front wheel bearings, refer to Chapter 1 for the removal and installation procedures.

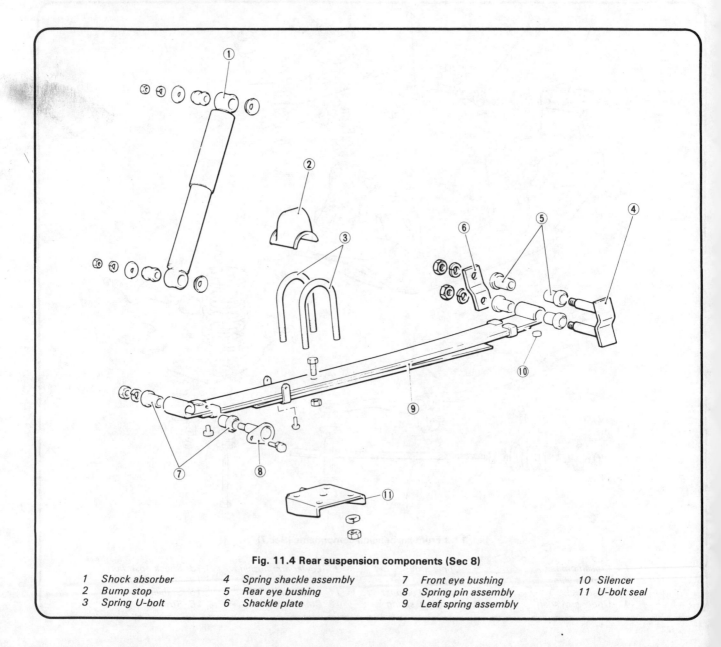

Fig. 11.4 Rear suspension components (Sec 8)

1 Shock absorber	4 Spring shackle assembly	7 Front eye bushing	10 Silencer
2 Bump stop	5 Rear eye bushing	8 Spring pin assembly	11 U-bolt seal
3 Spring U-bolt	6 Shackle plate	9 Leaf spring assembly	

11.2 Removing the stabilizer bar link bolts from the lower control arm

12.2 Removing the nut from the front of the strut bar

10 Front wheel bearings – repacking

Refer to Chapter 1, *Tune-up and routine maintenance,* for the procedure to follow when repacking front wheel bearings.

11 Stabilizer bar – removal and installation

1   Raise the front of the vehicle and set it on jack stands. Block the rear tires and set the parking brake to keep the vehicle from rolling.
2   Remove the stabilizer bar link bolts from the lower control arms (photo).
3   Refer to Section 12 and remove the strut bars.
4   Remove the bolts that attach the stabilizer bar bushings and the strut bar brackets to the frame crossmember. Support the stabilizer bar so that it will not fall when the last of the bolts is removed.
5   Lift out the stabilizer bar and brackets, then remove the brackets from the bar.
6   Place the stabilizer bar on a level surface and check it for

deformation. Check the stabilizer bar bushings for cracks and deformation.
7   Assemble the bushings and brackets on the stabilizer bar, then hold the bar in place on the vehicle and install the bolts that hold the brackets to the frame. Adjust the stabilizer bar from side to side until the distance from each end of the bar to the frame rails is equal. Tighten the bracket bolts to the specified torque.
8   When installing the ends of the stabilizer bar to the lower control arms, tighten the first nut on the link bolts to make the distance (A) from the top of the bolt to the face of the nut as specified. Hold the first nut with a wrench and tighten the top nut to the specified torque.
9   Refer to Section 12 and install the strut bars.
10 It is recommended that the front-end alignment be checked after the removal and installation of the strut bars and/or stabilizer bar.

12 Strut bar – removal and installation

1   Raise the front of the vehicle and set it on jack stands. Block the rear tires and set the parking brake to keep the vehicle from rolling.

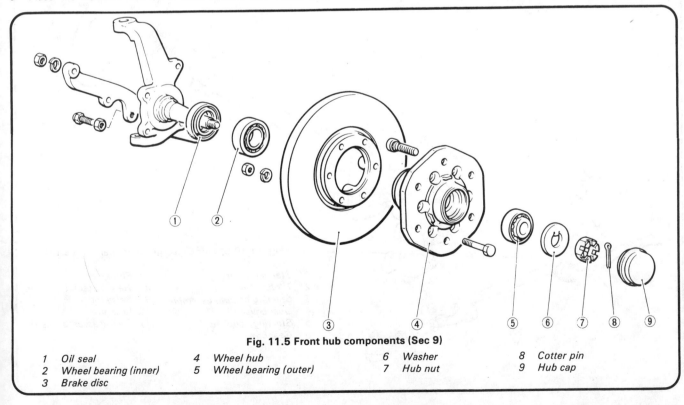

Fig. 11.5 Front hub components (Sec 9)

1	Oil seal	4	Wheel hub	6	Washer	8	Cotter pin
2	Wheel bearing (inner)	5	Wheel bearing (outer)	7	Hub nut	9	Hub cap
3	Brake disc				

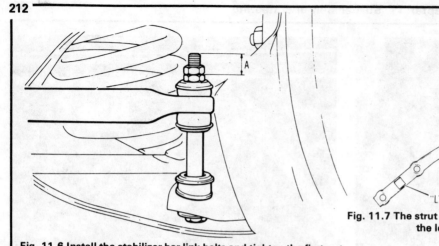

Fig. 11.6 Install the stabilizer bar link bolts and tighten the first nut so that the distance (A) is as specified (Sec 11)

Fig. 11.7 The strut bar stamped with an 'L' must be installed on the left side of the vehicle (Sec 12)

"L" mark

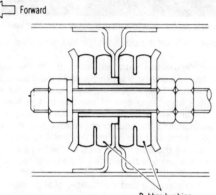

Forward

Rubber bushing

Fig. 11.8 Correct strut bar bushing installation (Sec 12)

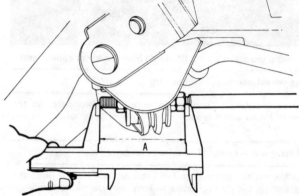

Fig. 11.9 When installing the strut bars, make sure distance (A) is as specified (Sec 12)

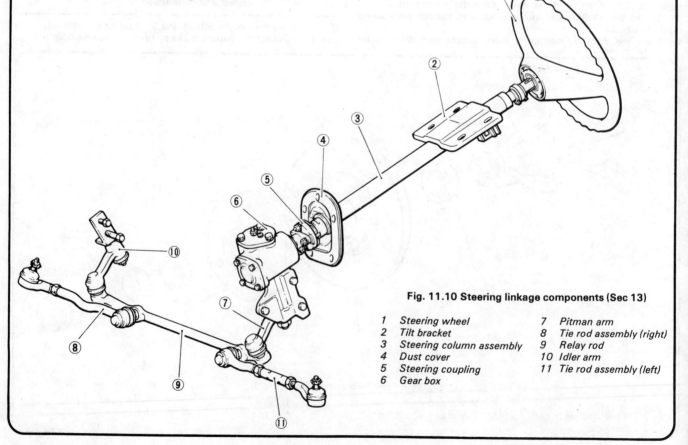

Fig. 11.10 Steering linkage components (Sec 13)

1 Steering wheel
2 Tilt bracket
3 Steering column assembly
4 Dust cover
5 Steering coupling
6 Gear box
7 Pitman arm
8 Tie rod assembly (right)
9 Relay rod
10 Idler arm
11 Tie rod assembly (left)

13.2 Loosening the tie-rod end jam nut

13.3 Loosening the tie-rod locknut

2   Remove the large nut and lock washer from the front end of the strut bar (photo). Loosen and remove the 2 nuts, then drive out the 2 bolts holding the strut bar to the lower control arm. The strut bar may spring back, so be careful when removing the bolts.
3   Push up on the rear of the strut bar to clear the control arm, then move the strut bar to the rear and out of the front frame bracket. As this is done, note how the rubber bushings and large washers are installed on the front of the strut bar.
4   Check the threaded end of the strut bar and the control arm mounting area for cracks and bends. Roll the straight portion of the bar on a flat surface and check for bend. Inspect all rubber bushings for cracks or damage and replace as necessary.
5   When installing the strut bars, observe the following items: the strut bar stamped with an 'L' must be installed on the left-hand side of the vehicle. The front and rear halves of each strut bar bushing have a definite shape. Install the bushing with the raised center area on the front side, with the raised area facing to the rear. When installing the strut bars to the brackets, set the standard distance (A) between the end of the strut bar and the face of the nut to specifications. Tighten the end nuts to the specified torque after the vehicle is lowered to the ground.
6   Attach the strut bar to the lower control arm and tighten the nuts to the specified torque.
7   Lower the vehicle to the ground and tighten the strut bar end nut to the specified torque.
8   It is recommended that the front-end alignment be checked after the removal and installation of the strut bars.

13 Tie-rods – removal and installation

1   Raise the front of the vehicle and set it on jack stands. Block the rear tires and set the parking brake to keep the vehicle from rolling. Remove the front wheel(s).
2   Loosen the tie-rod end jam nuts (photo).
3   Disconnect the tie-rod from the steering knuckle using a puller. To do this, remove the cotter pin from the end of the balljoint stud and loosen the locknut until it is at the end of the stud, covering the last few threads (photo). Pry the dust cover down and slip the jaws of the puller (a gear puller should work fine) between the tie-rod and the steering knuckle. Tighten the puller bolt against the stud until the tie-rod breaks loose from its mount. You may have to tap the end of the puller bolt with a hammer to jar the tie-rod loose.
4   Disconnect the tie-rod from the relay rod using the same method.
5   Remove the tie-rod from under the vehicle. Be careful not to disturb the tie-rod-to-tie-rod end relationship.
6   Measure the tie-rod overall length, count the number of threads exposed beyond the nuts on the tie-rod ends and note the relative position of the ends in relation to the rod.
7   To remove the tie-rod ends, simply unscrew them from the rod.
8   Check the tie-rod for bends, cracks and other damage. Replace it if any defects are found.

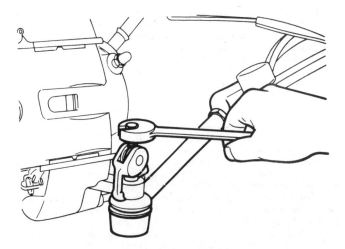

Fig. 11.11 Disconnecting the tie-rod from the steering knuckle with a puller (Sec 13)

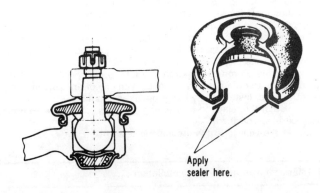

Apply sealer here.

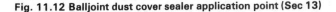

Fig. 11.12 Balljoint dust cover sealer application point (Sec 13)

14.2 Loosening the tie-rod-to-relay rod locknut

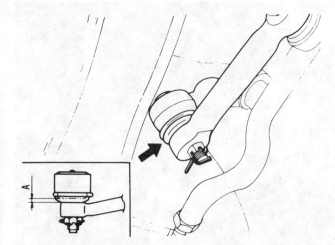

Fig. 11.13 Checking relay rod-to-idler arm/Pitman arm clearance
(Sec 14)

9   Thread the new tie-rod ends into the rod until the measured distances and the relationships of the tie-rod ends to the rod are achieved. With the tie-rod assembly mounted in a vise, tighten the jam nuts securely.

10   Install a new dust cover, using a sealer between the cover and tie-rod end, and connect the tie-rod to the relay rod and the steering knuckle. Tighten the locknuts to the specified torque, aligning the cotter pin holes in the studs with one of the slots in their respective nuts. Install a new cotter pin in each nut.

11   Install the wheel(s) and lower the vehicle to the ground.

12   Whenever a tie-rod end is replaced, front-end alignment should be checked for proper toe-in at a front-end alignment and repair shop.

14   Relay rod – removal and installation

1   Raise the front of the vehicle and set it on jack stands. Block the rear tires and set the parking brake to keep the vehicle from rolling.

2   Disconnect the relay rod from both tie-rods, the Pitman arm and the idler arm using a puller. To do this, remove the cotter pin and loosen the locknut until it is at the end of the stud, covering the threads (photo). Pry back the dust cover and slip the jaws of the puller (a gear puller should work fine) between the relay rod and the tie-rod/Pitman arm/idler arm. Tighten the bolt of the puller until it is tight against the stud and tap the head of the puller bolt with a hammer until the connection breaks loose. If it doesn't seem to be working, increase the puller pressure by tightening the bolt one-quarter turn and strike the head with the hammer again.

3   Remove the relay rod from under the vehicle and check it for cracks, deformation or other damage. If the holes in the relay rod have been enlarged due to wear, it must be replaced.

4   Position the relay rod under the vehicle and loosely install each of the 4 locknuts. Do not tighten any of them until all joints are in place.

5   Tighten the idler arm to relay rod locknut and the Pitman arm to relay rod locknut to the specified torque, aligning the cotter pin hole in the stud with one of the slots in the nut. Install a new cotter pin.

6   Tighten the tie-rod-to-relay rod locknuts to the specified torque, aligning the cotter pin holes in the studs with one of the slots in their respective nuts. Install a new cotter pin in each nut.

7   Check that the relay rod-to-idler arm and relay rod-to-Pitman arm clearance is as specified.

8   Lower the vehicle to the ground and test drive it.

15   Idler arm – removal and installation

1   Raise the front of the vehicle and set it on jack stands. Block the rear tires and set the parking brake to keep the vehicle from rolling.

2   Disconnect the idler arm from the relay rod. To do this, remove the cotter pin and loosen the locknut until it is at the end of the stud, covering the last few threads. Pry back the dust cover and slip the jaws

of a puller (a gear puller should work fine) between the relay rod end and the idler arm. Tighten the bolt of the puller until it is tight against the stud and tap the head of the puller bolt with a hammer until the connection breaks loose. If it doesn't seem to be working, increase the pressure of the puller by tightening the bolt one-quarter turn and strike the bolt head with the hammer again.

3   Remove the 2 bolts attaching the idler arm support bracket to the frame rail and lift out the idler arm assembly.

4   To disassemble the idler arm, place the assembly in a vise and remove the self-locking nut on the end of the idler arm shaft. Slip the washer and idler arm off the shaft and separate the bushings from the idler arm.

5   Check the bushings, the shaft and the idler arm for signs of wear or damage. If the balljoint at the end of the idler arm is loose or shows signs of wear or damage, the idler arm/balljoint should be replaced as a unit.

6   Apply lithium-based grease to the bushings and install them in the idler arm. Apply grease to the idler arm shaft and slip the idler arm over the shaft. The idler arm is installed properly when the threaded end of the idler arm shaft and the balljoint stud point in the same direction.

7   Slip the washer over the end of the idler arm shaft with its knurled surface facing the bushing. Install a new self-locking nut on the end of the idler arm shaft and tighten it to the specified torque.

8   Fasten the support bracket to the frame rail and tighten the 2 attaching bolts to the specified torque.

9   Connect the idler arm to the relay rod and tighten the locknut to the specified torque, aligning the cotter pin hole in the stud with one of the slots in the nut. Install a new cotter pin.

10   Check that the relay rod-to-idler arm clearance is as specified.

11   Lower the vehicle to the ground and test drive it.

16   Pitman arm – removal and installation

1   Raise the front of the vehicle and set it on jack stands. Block the rear tires and set the parking brake to keep the vehicle from rolling.

2   Disconnect the Pitman arm from the relay rod. To do this, remove the cotter pin and loosen the locknut until it is at the end of the stud, covering the last few threads. Pry back the dust cover and slip the jaws of a puller (a gear puller should work fine) between the relay rod end and the Pitman arm. Tighten the bolt of the puller until it is tight against the stud and tap the head of the puller bolt with a hammer until the connection breaks loose. If it doesn't seem to be working, increase the puller pressure by tightening the bolt $\frac{1}{4}$ turn and strike the bolt head with the hammer again.

3   At the other end of the Pitman arm, loosen the large nut that attaches the Pitman arm to the steering gear box cross-shaft. Back off the nut until it is at the end of the shaft, covering the last few threads.

4   Since this large locknut is installed with a considerable amount of torque, it may be necessary to use a large puller to remove the Pitman arm from the cross-shaft. The gear puller used for the other steering joints may not have enough force to break this connection.

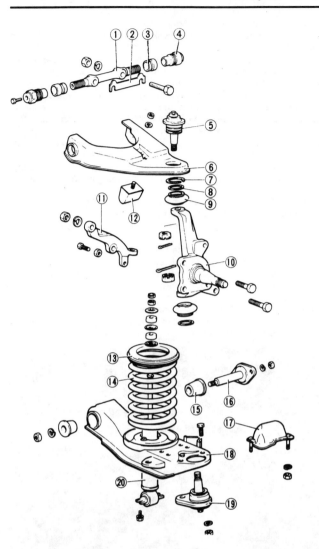

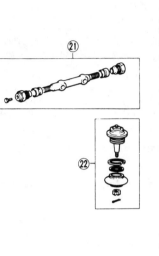

Fig. 11.14 Control arm components (Sec 17)

1   Upper arm shaft
2   Camber adjusting shim
3   Dust seal
4   Pivot bushing
5   Upper ball joint
6   Upper arm
7   Snap ring
8   Ring
9   Dust cover
10   Knuckle
11   Knuckle arm
12   Rebound stopper
13   Spring seat
14   Front coil spring
15   Lower arm bushing
16   Lower arm shaft
17   Bump stopper
18   Lower arm
19   Lower ball joint
20   Shock absorber
21   Upper arm bush and shaft kit
22   Upper ball joint kit
23   Lower ball joint kit

5   With the puller fork, or jaws, behind the Pitman arm and the puller
bolt tightened against the end of the cross-shaft, strike the end of the
puller bolt with a hammer to break the Pitman arm free from the cross-
shaft. It may be necessary to continue tightening and striking the bolt
to free the Pitman arm.
6   Remove the Pitrman arm from the shaft and check it for
deformation, cracks or other damage. If the balljoint at the end of the
Pitman arm is loose or shows signs of wear or damage, the Pitman
arm/balljoint should be replaced as a unit.
7   Slide the Pitman arm onto the cross-shaft with the slit on the end
of the cross-shaft lined up with the marks on the outside of the Pitman
arm. Install the large lock washer and nut and tighten the nut to the
specified torque.
8   Connect the Pitman arm to the relay rod and tighten the locknut
to the specified torque, aligning the cotter pin hole in the stud with one
of the slots in the nut. Install a new cotter pin.
9   Check that the relay rod-to-Pitman arm clearance is as specified.
10   Lower the vehicle to the ground and test drive it.

17 Wheel spindle – removal and installation

1   Raise the front of the vehicle and set it on jack stands. Block the
rear tires and set the parking brake to keep the vehicle from rolling.
Remove the wheel(s).
2   Remove the disc brake caliper assembly and tie it out of the way.
Remove the disc brake caliper bracket (see Chapter 9).
3   Remove the hub and brake disc assembly (see Chapter 1).
4   Separate the stabilizer bar from the lower control arm as described
in Section 11. Remove the strut bar from the vehicle by referring to
Section 12.

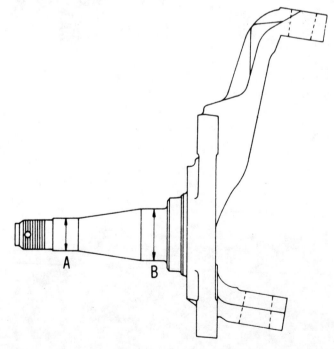

Fig. 11.15 Wheel spindle bearing contact surfaces (Sec 17)

5   Separate the tie-rod end from the steering knuckle as described in Section 13.
6   Remove the cotter pins from the upper and lower balljoint studs and loosen both nuts one full turn.
7   Remove the shock absorber as described in Section 7.
8   Using factory special tool No. MB9900792, or an equivalent home-made tool (photo), compress the front spring to the point that the rubber bumper on the upper control arm clears the spring tower by approximately ½ inch (photo). *Keep in mind that the spring, when compressed, is under a great deal of pressure. Be careful that nothing slips or moves.*
9   Install factory special tool No. C3564A, or its homemade equivalent (photo) between the upper and lower ball-joint studs. Using 2 wrenches, turn the 2 halves of the special tool so that the balljoints are forced apart (photo). A considerable amount of force will be required.
10   Using a soft-faced hammer, rap the spindle at the top and the bottom, where the balljoint studs pass through it, until the balljoints are jarred loose. You will hear a definite 'snap' when the balljoints are unseated (photo).
11   Remove the nuts from the upper and lower balljoint studs and slowly release the pressure on the spring until the spindle can be lifted off the studs.
12   If your vehicle has a steering knuckle that is bolted to the wheel spindle, remove the attaching bolts and separate them. Clean the steering knuckle and check it for cracks and other damage. Check the balljoint stud mounting hole for wear.
13   Clean the wheel spindle and check it for cracks, bends and wear at the bearing race contact areas. Using a micrometer or dial calipers, measure the wheel spindle bearing contact surface diameters and compare them to the specifications. If the measured diameters are less than specified, the spindle should be replaced.
14   If necessary, assemble the steering knuckle to the wheel spindle and tighten the attaching bolts to the specified torque.
15   Slip the wheel spindle over the balljoint studs, compress the spring, install the nuts on the balljoint studs and tighten them to the specified torque. Align the cotter pin holes in the studs with one of the slots in their respective nuts and install a new cotter pin in each nut. Make sure that the spring is compressed enough so that spring pressure does not interfere with the proper tightening of the balljoint stud nuts.
16   Carefully loosen the spring compressing tool and slide it out of the spring tower. Install the shock absorber as described in Section 7.
17   Join the tie-rod end to the steering knuckle as described in Section 13.
18   Attach the stabilizer bar to the lower control arm as described in Section 11. Install the strut bar by referring to Section 12.
19   Install the hub and brake disc assembly (see Chapter 1).
20   Install the disc brake caliper bracket and the disc brake caliper assembly (see Chapter 9).
21   Install the wheel(s) and lower the vehicle to the ground.
22   The front end should be checked for proper alignment at a front-end alignment and repair shop.

17.8a Homemade spring compressing tool components

17.8b Compressing the front spring

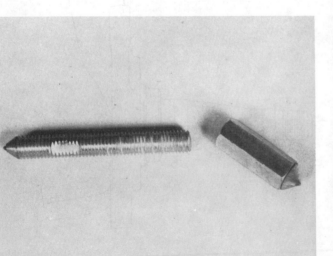

17.9a Homemade balljoint removal tool components

17.9b Forcing the balljoints apart

18 Front spring – removal and installation

1 Raise the front of the vehicle and set it on jack stands. Block the rear tires and set the parking brake to keep the vehicle from rolling. Remove the wheel(s).
2 Remove the wheel spindle as described in Section 17.
3 Once the wheel spindle has been lifted clear of the balljoint studs, slowly and carefully release the pressure on the spring by loosening the spring compressing tool.
4 While supporting the lower control arm and spring, withdraw the spring compressing tool. Remove the spring and spring seat from the spring tower. Note that the spring installed on the left side of the vehicle is color-coded green, while the spring installed on the right side is color-coded pink.
5 Install the spring, slip it into position, along with the spring seat, in the spring tower and rotate the lower control arm up until the spring is supported by it. Note: The spring must be installed with the closely spaced coils at the top and with widely spaced coils at the bottom.
6 Install the spring compressing tool and slowly compress the spring, making sure it is properly seated in the spring tower and the lower control arm groove.
7 Install the wheel spindle.
8 Install the wheel(s) and lower the vehicle to the ground.

17.10 Unseating the balljoints with a soft-faced hammer

19 Upper control arm – removal and installation

1 Raise the front of the vehicle and set it on jack stands. Block the rear tires and set the parking brake to keep the vehicle from rolling. Remove the wheel(s).
2 Disassemble the front suspension components and remove the spring as described in Section 18.
3 Remove the 2 bolts, lock washers and nuts that attach the upper control arm pivot shaft to the frame. Slip out the shim(s) from between the shaft and the frame, noting how they are installed (photo).
4 Slip the upper control arm and shaft assembly out of its mounting position (photo).
5 Refer to Section 20 for inspection and repair of the upper control arm and shaft assembly.
6 Slip the control arm and shaft assembly into position and install the bolts, lock washers and nuts that attach it to the frame. Be sure to install the shim(s) between the pivot shaft and the frame exactly as they were before removal. Tighten the nuts to the specified torque.
7 Assemble the front suspension components by referring to Section 18.
8 Install the wheels and lower the vehicle to the ground.
9 The front end should be checked for proper alignment at a front-end alignment and repair shop.

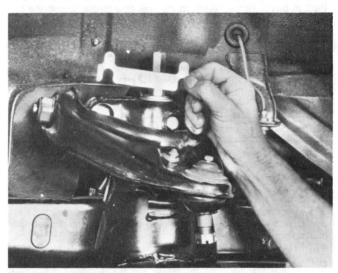

19.3 Removing the upper control arm shim

20 Upper control arm – inspection and rebuild

1 Remove the upper control arm and shaft assembly from the vehicle as described in Section 19.
2 Mount the upper control arm and shaft assembly in a vise, as shown, and remove the bushings from the shaft (photo). It will take a considerable amount of force to loosen the bushings.
3 Slide back the dust seals and free the control arm from the pivot shaft.
4 Check the upper arm shaft-to-pivot bushing play and the pivot bushing-to-upper arm play. Check the shaft and arm for bends, cracks and other damage. Check the rebound stopper and dust seals for cracks and deterioration. Replace any defective parts with new ones.
5 When replacing the pivot bushings, install the rubber dust covers, slip the upper arm over the shaft (photo) and install the pivot bushings by threading them onto the shaft and into the control arm simultaneously (photo). Be sure to grease the inner threads of the bushings before installation. The pivot bushings must be torqued to the exact values given in the torque specifications. Before installing the control arm and shaft assembly onto the vehicle, make sure that the shaft moves smoothly in the bushings.
6 Install the control arm and shaft assembly onto the vehicle by referring to Section 19.
7 Install the wheel(s) and lower the vehicle to the ground.
8 The front end should be checked for proper alignment at a front-end alignment and repair shop.

19.4 Removing the upper control arm from its mount

21 Lower control arm – removal and installation

1   Raise the front of the vehicle and set it on jack stands. Block the rear tires and set the parking brake to keep the vehicle from rolling. Remove the wheel(s).

2   Disassemble the front suspension components and remove the spring as described in Section 18.

3   Remove the nut and lock washer from the front of the lower control arm pivot shaft. Remove the 2 nuts and lock washers from the rear of the lower control arm pivot shaft (photo) and withdraw the shaft from the bushings (photo). It may be necessary to drive out the shaft with a hammer and punch.

4   Slip the back rubber bushing out of the lower control arm through the crossmember and withdraw the lower control arm from the crossmember (photo).

5   Check the shaft and control arm for cracks, bends and wear. Check the bushings and the rubber bump stopper for cracks and deterioration. Replace any parts found to be defective.

6   Hold the control arm in position at the crossmember and insert the back rubber bushing into the control arm from the rear.

7   Slip the pivot shaft into the crossmember and through the control arm and bushings from the rear. You will have to drive the shaft into place using a soft-faced hammer.

8   Install the 2 lock washers and nuts that hold the rear of the pivot shaft in place. Tighten them to the specified torque. Install the lock washer and nut at the front of the pivot shaft and tighten it to the specified torque.

9   Assemble the front suspension components by referring to Section 18.

10   Install the wheel(s) and lower the vehicle to the ground.

11   The front end should be checked for proper alignment at a front-end alignment and repair shop.

22 Rear spring – removal and installation

1   Remove the shock absorber as described in Section 8. It is a good idea to remove and replace only one spring at a time so that the other spring can be used as a guide if difficulties are encountered during reassembly.

2   Remove the emergency brake cable holder from the bracket on the bottom spring leaf (photo).

3   Raise the rear axle housing slightly with a jack and support it on jack stands.

4   Remove the U-bolt nuts (photo), U-bolt seat, U-bolts and bump stop.

5   Remove the nut from the inside and the bolt from the outside (photo) of the forward spring pin assembly and push it out of the front spring perch. If it will not slide out easily, use a soft-faced hammer to tap it out. Once the pin is removed, disengage the spring from the perch.

6   Remove the nuts and washers on the inside of the shackle assembly at the rear spring mount (photo). Pull off the shackle plate and remove the shackle assembly. Remove the rubber bushings from the spring and mount. (Do not mix them up).

7   Disassemble and inspect the rear spring by referring to Section 23.

8   To install the spring, make sure the rubber bushings are in place, then slip it into position in the front spring perch and install the spring pin. Install the bolt on the outside and the washer and nut on the inside of the spring pin. Do not tighten them completely at this point.

9   Slip the rubber bushings into the rear spring mount and the eye at the rear of the spring. Install the shackle assembly, the shackle plate and the washers and nuts. The plate fits on the inside of the spring. Do not tighten the nuts completely at this point.

10   Hold the U-bolt seat in position (the spring bolt head fits into the center hole in the U-bolt seat), and install the bump stop, the U-bolts and the lock washers and nuts. Tighten the U-bolt nuts to the specified torque. Make sure that the same number of threads are visible beyond the nuts on each U-bolt.

11   Lower the vehicle to the ground and tighten the front spring pin and rear shackle assembly nuts/bolts to the specified torque.

12   Fasten the emergency brake cable holder to the bracket on the bottom spring leaf.

13   Install the shock absorber as described in Section 8.

23 Rear spring – disassembly, inspection and reassembly

1   Using a screwdriver or pry bar, pry open the spring leaf clamp bands.

2   Mark the front of each spring leaf and remove the clamp bolt that holds the spring leaves together.

3   Remove any rust and loose paint from the spring leaves with a wire brush. Check each spring leaf, clamp, rubber bushing and silencer (photo) for wear, cracks and permanent set. Check the bump stop for cracks and distortion. Replace any defective parts.

4   Apply a zinc chromate primer and new paint to each spring leaf. Use new silencers when reassembling.

5   Reassemble the spring leaves in the proper order with the marked ends forward. Line up the center bolt holes and compress the spring leaves together with a C-clamp. Install the center bolt and tighten it securely.

6   Using a large pliers, close the spring leaf clamp bands (photo).

24 Manual steering gearbox – removal and installation

1   Raise the front of the vehicle and set it on jack stands. Block the rear tires and set the parking brake to keep the vehicle from rolling.

2   Remove the clamp bolt connecting the steering shaft yoke to the steering gearbox mainshaft.

3   Disconnect the left tie-rod from the relay rod by referring to Section 13. Disconnect the Pitman arm from the relay rod as described in Section 14.

4   Remove the 3 nuts and bolts that attach the steering gearbox to the frame and remove the gearbox down and out from under the vehicle.

5   Refer to Section 25 for steering gearbox disassembly and repair procedures.

6   To install the gearbox, slip it into place from under the vehicle and insert the bolts that attach it to the frame. Thread on the nuts and tighten them to the specified torque.

7   Connect the Pitman arm and the left tie-rod to the relay rod.

8   Install the clamp bolt in the steering shaft yoke and tighten it to the specified torque.

9   Lower the vehicle to the ground and test drive it.

25 Manual steering gearbox – overhaul

1   Due to the complexity of the component and the special tools and skills required, it is not recommended that the average home mechanic attempt to rebuild a steering gearbox. It would be far more economical, in terms of time and money, to purchase a used, new or rebuilt unit to install in place of the faulty one.

2   Modern steering gearboxes are well-designed and trouble-free, so before concluding that your gearbox is in need of major repairs, check the other steering system components. Worn or damaged shock absorbers, worn or misaligned front-end components, unbalanced wheels, worn or loose wheel bearings and improper tire pressures can produce symptoms similar to those produced by a defective steering gearbox.

3   If an overhaul is to be performed, you will need certain special tools, a clean place to work and plenty of time and patience to do the job properly. Before disassembling the gearbox, make sure that you have available all of the seals, gaskets and internal parts required for the overhaul.

4   Remove the gearbox from the vehicle as described in Section 24 and drain the lubricant through the filler plug into a suitable container.

5   Support the gearbox assembly in a vise equipped with soft jaws. Using special tool No. CT-1106, remove the Pitman arm from the cross-shaft.

6   Using special tool No. CT-1108, check the main shaft starting torque (the torque required to start the main shaft to turn) and record it for future reference.

7   Loosen the locknut on the gearbox adjusting bolt and turn the bolt counterclockwise about $\frac{1}{4}$ of a turn. Remove the 3 bolts attaching the upper cover to the gear housing.

8   Remove the upper cover from the gear housing by sliding it to one side until the adjusting spacer clears the T-slot on the end of the cross-shaft. Remove the adjusting bolt and lock nut from the upper cover.

20.2 Removing the upper control arm bushings from the shaft

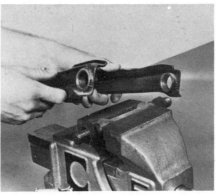

20.5a Installing the upper control arm on the shaft

20.5b Installing the upper control arm bushings

21.3a Removing the lower control arm pivot shaft retaining nuts

21.3b Withdrawing the lower control arm pivot shaft from the arm and suspension crossmember

21.4 Removing the rear bushing and the lower control arm

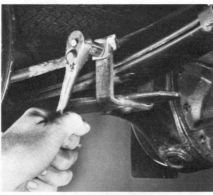

22.2 Removing the emergency brake cable holder from the lower spring leaf

22.4 Removing the nuts from the U-bolts

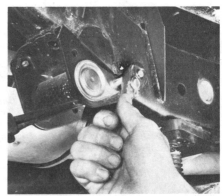

22.5 Removing the bolt from the forward spring pin

22.6 Removing the nuts from the inside of the shackle assembly

23.3 Checking the spring silencer

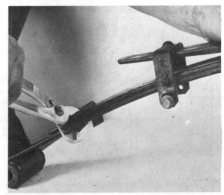

23.6 Closing the spring clamp bands with a pliers

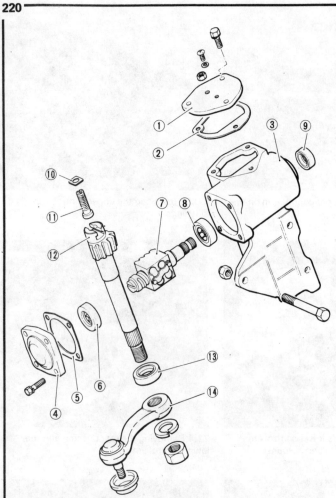

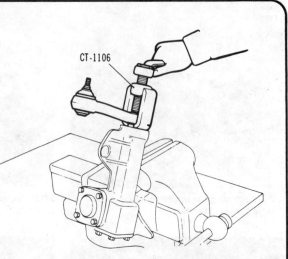

Fig. 11.17 Removing the Pitman arm from the cross-shaft (Sec 25)

Fig. 11.16 Manual steering gearbox components (Sec 25)

1 Gear housing upper cover	8 Mainshaft bearing
2 Packing	9 Mainshaft oil seal
3 Gear housing	10 Gear adjusting spacer
4 Gear housing end cover	11 Gear adjusting bolt
5 Mainshaft adjusting shim	12 Cross-shaft
6 Mainshaft bearing	13 Cross-shaft oil seal
7 Mainshaft assembly	14 Pitman arm

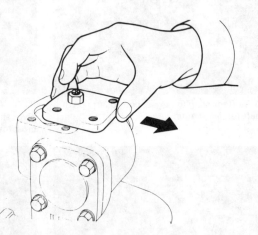

Fig. 11.18 Removing the upper cover from the gear housing (Sec 25)

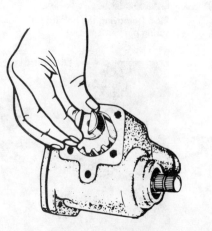

Fig. 11.19 Removing the cross-shaft from the gear housing (Sec 25)

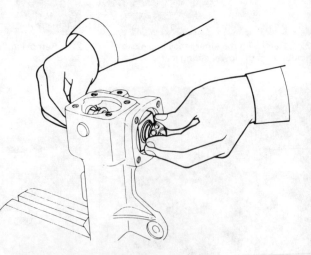

Fig. 11.20 Removing the mainshaft assembly from the gear housing (Sec 25)

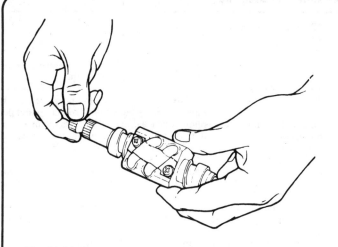
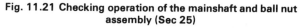

Fig. 11.21 Checking operation of the mainshaft and ball nut assembly (Sec 25)

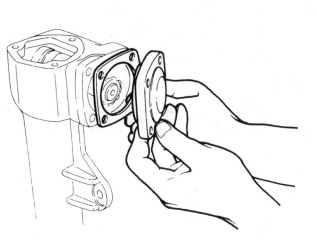

Fig. 11.22 Installing the gasket and end cover (Sec 25)

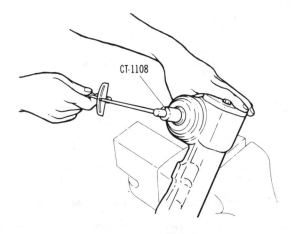

Fig. 11.23 Checking the mainshaft preload with a torque wrench (Sec 25)

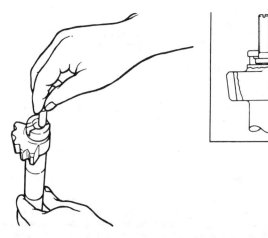

Fig. 11.24 Checking the adjusting bolt end play in the cross-shaft T-slot (Sec 25)

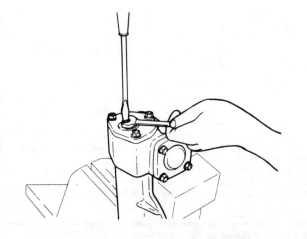

Fig. 11.25 Adjusting the backlash in the mainshaft (Sec 25)

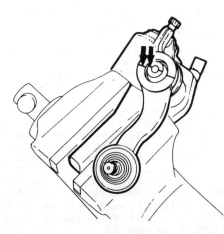

Fig. 11.26 Coupling the Pitman arm to the steering gearbox cross-shaft (Sec 25)

Lay the parts out on a clean surface in the order of disassembly.

9   Rotate the main shaft until the cross-shaft is in the neutral (center) position, then pull the cross-shaft out of the gear housing. Be careful not to damage the cross-shaft splines or the oil seal in the gear housing. Refer to Step 6 and measure the main shaft preload (starting torque) without the cross-shaft in place.

10   Remove the 4 bolts attaching the end cover to the gear housing. Remove the end cover, the gasket and the adjusting shim. Do not discard the shim, as it will be used during reassembly. Lay the parts out on a clean surface in the order of disassembly.

11   Carefully slide the main shaft and ball nut assembly, along with the bearings, out of the gear housing. Do not disassemble the main shaft and ball nut assembly.

12   Clean all of the parts with solvent and dry them thoroughly.

13   Measure the cross-shaft outside diameter and the gear housing bushing inside diameter. Subtract the two measurements to obtain the cross-shaft-to-bushing clearance. Compare it to the specifications. If it is more than specified, the cross-shaft and bushings must be replaced.

14   Pry out the oil seals from the gear housing and check the main shaft bearings in the gear housing and end cover for wear and pitting. Replace them if any damage is evident.

15   Check the operation of the main shaft and ball nut assembly by rotating the main shaft. (Do not move the ball nut completely to either end of the main shaft). Check for smooth operation and excessive end-to-end play in the main shaft. Replace the entire assembly if any defects are found.

16   Using a seal driver and hammer, install new oil seals into the gearbox and apply a thin coat of multi-purpose grease to their sealing lips.

17   While supporting the gear housing in a vise, insert the main shaft into the gear housing. Be careful not to damage the oil seal as the main shaft is passed through it.

18   Apply a thin coat of silicone-type gasket sealer to both sides of the end cover gasket and install the gasket, the shim and the end cover (in that order) to the gear housing. Install the 4 end cover bolts and tighten them to the specified torque.

19   Using special tool No. CT-1108, measure the main shaft preload (the torque required to start the main shaft to turn). If it is more or less than specified, adjust the preload by replacing the end cover shim with one that is either thicker or thinner.

20   Install the gear adjusting spacer onto the adjusting bolt and slide the bolt into the T-slot on the end of the cross-shaft. Using a dial calipers or a dial indicator, measure the axial (end) play between the adjusting bolt and the cross-shaft and compare it to the specifications. If the end play is not as specified, adjust it by replacing the gear adjusting spacer with one of a different thickness.

21   Lubricate the ball nut assembly and ball nut rack gear, the cross-shaft and the cross-shaft gear, then carefully insert the cross-shaft into the gear housing and mesh the cross-shaft gear with the ball nut rack gear. Be very careful not to damage the bushing or the oil seal in the gear housing.

22   Apply a thin coat of silicone-type gasket sealer to both sides of the upper cover gasket. Thread the adjusting bolt (with the adjusting spacer in place) into the upper cover, and assemble the upper cover and gasket to the gear housing by sliding the gear adjusting bolt into the T-slot on the end of the cross-shaft.

23   Install the three upper cover attaching bolts and tighten them to the specified torque. Loosely install the adjusting bolt locknut.

24   Adjust the backlash between the main shaft rack and the cross-shaft gear after rotating the main shaft carefully from lock to lock 2 or 3 times. Center the main shaft rack and turn the cross-shaft adjusting bolt in and out 2 or 3 times to properly mesh the gears. Next, slowly turn the adjusting bolt until the specified amount of backlash is obtained (with the main shaft centered) then tighten the adjusting bolt locknut.

25   After completing the reassembly operation, check the main shaft preload (the amount of torque required to start the main shaft to turn) using special tool No. CT-1108. If the preload exceeds the specifications, the upper cover or end cover may be installed wrong or the cross-shaft bushing may be damaged.

26   Fill the gear box to the proper level with the recommended gear lubricant and tighten the filler plug securely.

27   Slide the Pitman arm onto the cross-shaft with the slit on the end of the cross-shaft lined up with the marks on the outside of the Pitman arm. Install the large lock washer and nut and tighten the nut to the specified torque.

28   Install the steering gearbox into the vehicle by referring to Section 24.

26   Power steering hoses – removal and installation

1   Loosen and remove the fitting that attaches the pressure hose to the power steering pump (photo). Slide back the hose clamp and pull off the return hose at the pump. Place a drip pan or container under the pump to catch the fluid that will drain out when the hoses are disconnected. If your system has a remote-type reservoir, disconnect the return hose at the reservoir.

2   Loosen and remove the fittings that attach the hoses to the power steering gearbox. Place a drip pan or container under the gearbox to catch the fluid.

3   Plug the hoses at each end and the fittings on the pump/reservoir and steering gearbox to keep dirt and other contaminants out of the system.

4   Remove the clamp on the right wheel well (photo) and the two clamps on the firewall (photo) and lift out the hoses.

5   To install the hoses, hold them in position and fasten the clamps on the firewall and fenderwell. Connect the fittings to the steering gearbox and tighten them securely.

6   Connect the pressure hose fitting to the pump and tighten it securely.

7   Slip the return hose over the fitting on the reservoir and slide the hose clamp into place.

8   Add the appropriate fluid to the reservoir and bleed the system as described in Section 31.

9   Wipe off all fittings and hoses, as well as the pump and steering gearbox, and clean up any spilled fluid.

27   Power steering pump – removal and installation

1   Disconnect the wire lead from the oil pressure sending unit just above the power steering pump.

2   Loosen the fittings at the pressure and suction hoses and disconnect the hoses from the pump body. Plug the hoses to prevent the entry of dirt and other contaminants.

3   Loosen and remove the nut and lock washer attaching the pulley to the pump shaft.

4   Loosen the two pivot bolts at the bottom of the pump and the adjusting bolt at the top of the pump. Slip the pulley off the pump shaft and separate the pulley from the drive belt.

5   Remove the adjusting bolt and the pivot bolts and lift the pump out of its mounting bracket.

6   To install the pump, fit it into the mounting bracket and loosely install the pivot bolts and adjusting bolt. Do not tighten them completely.

7   Slip the pulley onto the pump shaft and loosely install the lock washer and nut on the end of the shaft.

8   Slip the drive belt onto the pulley (make sure it is also on the crankshaft pulley) and tighten the nut on the end of the pump shaft. Squeeze the belt together to keep the pulley from turning while the nut is tightened.

9   Adjust the belt tension by prying the pump body and the engine block with a pry bar or large screwdriver. When the belt has approximately $\frac{1}{4}$ to $\frac{3}{8}$ in of play at the center of its run, tighten the pivot and adjusting bolts securely.

10   Unplug and connect the hoses to the pump body. Do not mix them up. Tighten the fittings securely and make sure the hoses are not twisted or kinked.

11   Fill the reservoir with the specified fluid and bleed the system as described in Section 31.

12   Connect the wire lead to the oil pressure sending unit.

28   Power steering pump – overhaul

1   The home mechanic has two options available in the event that the power steering pump requires major repair work.

2   First, a rebuilt power steering pump can be purchased and installed by referring to Section 27.

3   Second, a power steering pump overhaul kit may be purchased

26.1 Removing the pressure hose fitting from the pump

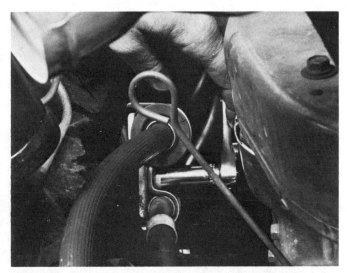

26.4a Removing the right wheel well power steering hose clamp bolt

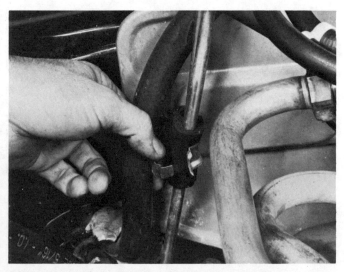

26.4b Unfastening the firewall power steering hose clamp

and the pump rebuilt following the instructions supplied with the kit. Due to the fact that a number of different pumps may be supplied as original equipment, we cannot cover pump overhaul in detail.

29 Power steering gearbox – removal and installation

1   Raise the front of the vehicle and set it on jack stands. Block the rear tires and set the parking brake to keep the vehicle from rolling.
2   Remove the clamp bolt attaching the steering shaft socket assembly to the power steering gearbox input shaft.
3   Disconnect the left tie-rod from the relay rod by referring to Section 13. Disconnect the Pitman arm from the relay rod as described in Section 14.
4   Place a container under the steering gearbox and remove the fittings that attach the power steering hoses to the steering gearbox. You may find it easier to work from the top of the vehicle when removing the hoses from the gearbox.
5   On vehicles equipped with manual transmissions, remove the starter motor by referring to Chapter 5.
6   On vehicles equipped with automatic transmissions, remove the throttle linkage and splash shield from the transmission.
7   Remove the 3 nuts and bolts that attach the steering gearbox to the frame and remove the gearbox down and out from under the vehicle.
8   Refer to Section 30 for power steering gearbox disassembly and repair procedures.
9   To install the gearbox, slip it into place from under the vehicle and insert the bolts that attach it to the frame. Thread on the nuts and tighten them to the specified torque.
10   Hook up the throttle linkage and splash shield or install the starter motor, as necessary.
11   Connect the power steering hoses to the gearbox and tighten the fittings securely.
12   Connect the Pitman arm and the left tie-rod to the relay rod.
13   Install the clamp bolt attaching the power steering shaft socket assembly to the power steering gearbox input shaft. Tighten it to the specified torque.
14   Bleed the system as described in Section 31, lower the vehicle to the ground and test drive it.

30 Power steering gearbox – overhaul

1   As with manual steering gearboxes, it is not recommended that the home mechanic attempt to disassemble or rebuild a power steering gearbox. The gearbox hydraulic components are carefully matched and fitted together at the factory, and unless you know exactly what you are doing, their operation could be adversely affected by taking them apart and putting them back together. If power steering gearbox problems occur, rather than attempting an overhaul, it is advisable to obtain a new or rebuilt unit to install in the vehicle.
2   Power steering pumps are probably the major source of problems encountered with power steering systems, so before deciding to replace or overhaul your power steering gearbox, check the pump and other system components carefully. Improper tire pressure, dragging brakes, faulty balljoints, damaged suspension components and mis-aligned front-end components can all cause symptoms for which you might at first suspect the steering gear. Again, be sure that the trouble in the system is in the power steering gearbox before rebuilding or replacing it.
3   If an overhaul is to be performed, you will need a clean place to work, a number of special tools, a container of power steering fluid of the appropriate type, some multi-purpose grease, and plenty of time and patience to do the job properly. Before disassembling the gearbox, make sure that you have available all of the internal parts required for the overhaul. A power steering gearbox seal kit, side cover O-ring, seal housing O-rings, seal housing seal ring, cross-shaft oil seal and top cover oil seal are the minimum parts that will be necessary.
4   Remove the gearbox from the vehicle as described in Section 29 and drain the fluid through the hose fitting holes into a suitable container.
5   Support the gearbox assembly in a vise equipped with soft jaws. Using special tool No. CT-1106, or a similar Pitman arm puller, remove the Pitman arm from the gearbox cross-shaft.

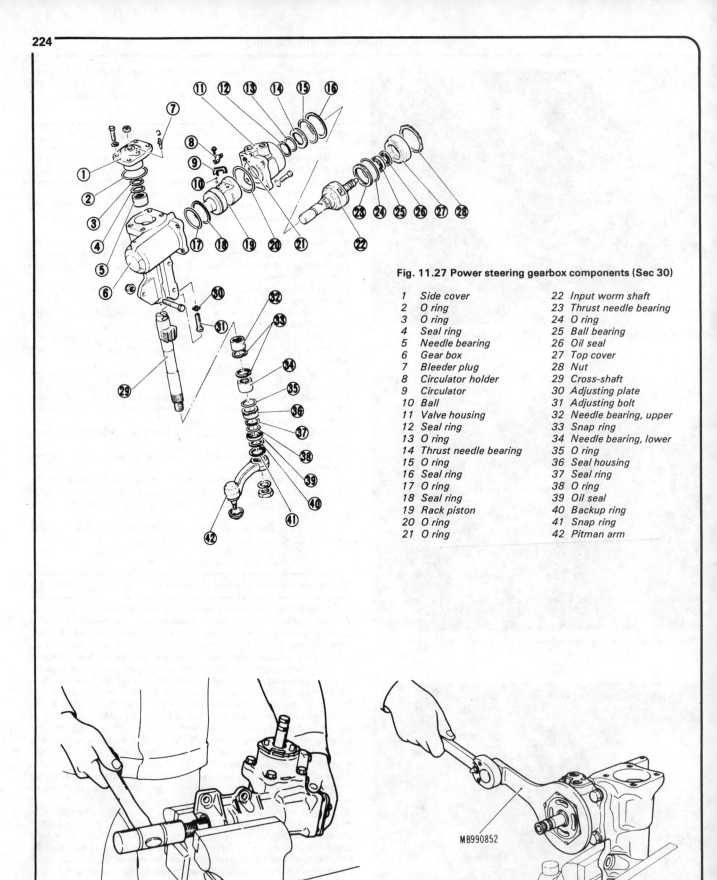

Fig. 11.27 Power steering gearbox components (Sec 30)

1	Side cover	22	Input worm shaft
2	O ring	23	Thrust needle bearing
3	O ring	24	O ring
4	Seal ring	25	Ball bearing
5	Needle bearing	26	Oil seal
6	Gear box	27	Top cover
7	Bleeder plug	28	Nut
8	Circulator holder	29	Cross-shaft
9	Circulator	30	Adjusting plate
10	Ball	31	Adjusting bolt
11	Valve housing	32	Needle bearing, upper
12	Seal ring	33	Snap ring
13	O ring	34	Needle bearing, lower
14	Thrust needle bearing	35	O ring
15	O ring	36	Seal housing
16	Seal ring	37	Seal ring
17	O ring	38	O ring
18	Seal ring	39	Oil seal
19	Rack piston	40	Backup ring
20	O ring	41	Snap ring
21	O ring	42	Pitman arm

Fig. 11.28 Separating the cross-shaft and side cover from the gearbox (Sec 30)

Fig. 11.29 Removing the valve housing nut (Sec 30)

MB990852

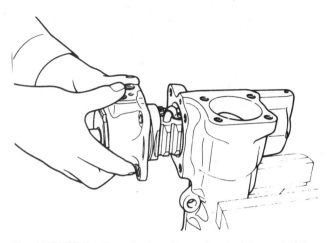

Fig. 11.30 Sliding the valve housing and rack piston out of the gearbox (Sec 30)

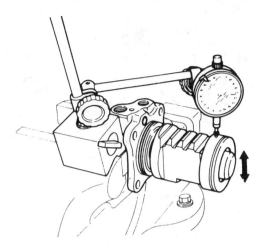

Fig. 11.31 Checking the backlash between the rack piston groove and circulator balls with a dial indicator setup (Sec 30)

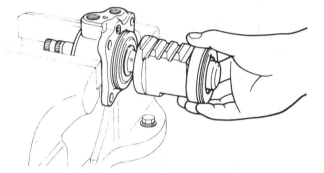

Fig. 11.32 Removing the rack piston from the ball screw unit (Sec 30)

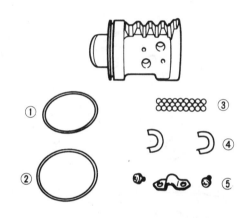

Fig. 11.33 Rack piston components (Sec 30)

1 O ring	4 Circulator
2 Seal ring	5 Circulator holder
3 Steel ball	

6   Remove the 4 bolts attaching the side cover the the gearbox. Loosen the adjusting bolt locknut and screw the adjusting bolt in 2 or 3 turns.

7   With the gear in the neutral position, tap the bottom of the cross-shaft with a soft-faced hammer. The cross-shaft and side cover will separate from the gearbox and can be pulled out through the top. Set the cross-shaft assembly aside.

8   Remove the valve housing nut using special tool No. MB9900852 or a similar large wrench.

9   Remove the valve housing bolts and slide the valve housing and rack piston out of the gearbox. Hold the rack piston with one hand so it does not rotate. Do not tilt the assembly down, as the rack piston will fall off and be damaged.

10 Remove the gearbox from the vise and carefully mount the valve housing in the vise. Mount a dial indicator as shown in Figure 11.31. Turn the rack piston clockwise until it is snug and zero the dial indicator. Check the backlash between the groove of the piston and the balls by moving the piston up and down. Turn the rack piston counterclockwise 2 full turns, zero the dial indicator and recheck the backlash. If it exceeds the specifications, the ball screw unit and rack piston must be replaced as an assembly.

11 Place a clean container under the assembly and carefully remove the rack piston from the ball screw unit by turning it counterclockwise. As it is being removed, the steel balls will drop out of the assembly and into the container. There should be a total of 26 balls in the assembly.

12 Remove the O-ring, the seal ring, the circulator, the circulator holder and any remaining steel balls from the rack piston. Note the relationship of the parts to each other as they are disassembled. Do not remove the end cap from the rack piston. Lay the parts out on a clean surface in the order of disassembly.

13 Turn the valve housing around in the vise and remove the top cover using special tool No. MB990853 or a similar pin-type spanner wrench.

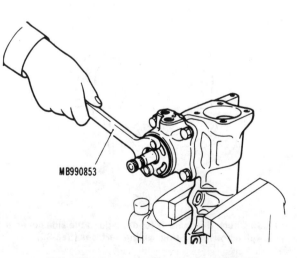

Fig. 11.34 Removing the top cover (Sec 30)

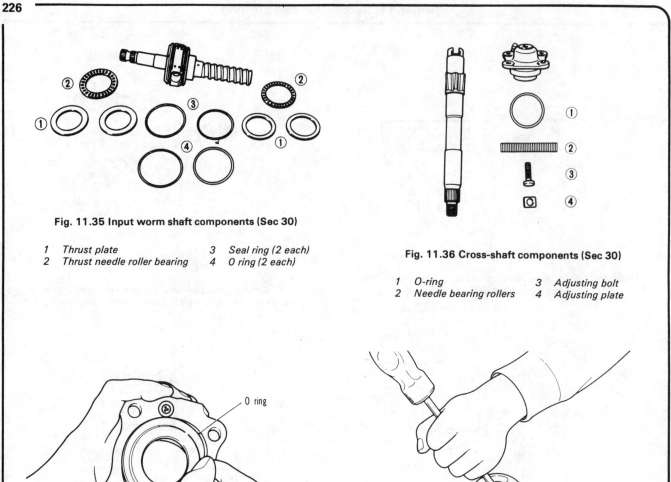

Fig. 11.35 Input worm shaft components (Sec 30)

1	Thrust plate	3	Seal ring (2 each)
2	Thrust needle roller bearing	4	O ring (2 each)

Fig. 11.36 Cross-shaft components (Sec 30)

1	O-ring	3	Adjusting bolt
2	Needle bearing rollers	4	Adjusting plate

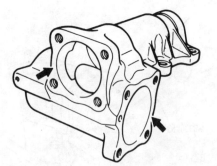

O ring

Fig. 11.37 Removing the O-ring and seal ring from the valve housing (Sec 30)

Fig. 11.38 Tapping out the valve housing ball bearing and oil seal (Sec 30)

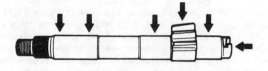

Fig. 11.40 Cross-shaft inspection points (Sec 30)

Fig. 11.39 Check the gearbox for damage to the side cover and valve housing O-ring sealing surfaces (Sec 30)

Fig. 11.41 Valve housing seal ring-to-housing contact surface (Sec 30)

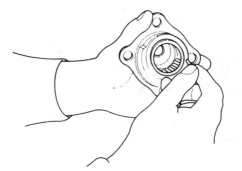

Fig. 11.42 Installing the needle bearing rollers in the side cover (Sec 30)

14 Carefully slide the top cover and input worm shaft out of the valve housing.

15 Remove the outer thrust plate, needle roller bearing, inner thrust plate, seal ring and O-ring from each end of the input worm shaft. Note the relationship of the parts to each other as they are removed. Lay the parts out on a clean surface in the order of disassembly. Do not disassemble the input worm shaft any further. Remove the valve housing from the vise and set it aside.

16 Next, screw the adjusting bolt into the side cover and separate the side cover from the cross-shaft by sliding the adjusting bolt and adjusting plate out of the T-slot on the end of the shaft. Be careful when handling the side cover, as the needle bearing rollers may fall out of place and be lost.

17 Carefully remove the O-ring, the needle bearing rollers (33 total), the adjusting bolt and locknut and the adjusting plate from the side cover. Do not remove the inner needle bearing seal unless there is evidence of fluid leakage on the outside of the side cover around the adjusting bolt. Do not remove the bleeder screw unless it is damaged. Lay the parts out on a clean surface in the order of disassembly.

18 Next, disassemble the valve housing. Remove the seal ring and the O-ring from the inside of the housing.

19 Tap out the ball-bearing and oil seal with a drift punch.

20 When disassembling the gearbox, remove only the lower snap ring, the back-up ring and the oil seal from the bottom of the gearbox body. Do not remove the needle bearings.

21 Before inspecting the disassembled gearbox parts, wash them in solvent and dry thoroughly. Do not mix them up during the cleaning process.

22 Inspect the needle bearings in the gearbox body. If they are damaged, the gearbox body must be replaced. Check the gearbox body for damage at the side cover O-ring sealing surface and the valve housing O-ring sealing surface. If damage is found, the gearbox body must be replaced.

23 Check the side cover needle bearings for damage. If any damage is found, the side cover must be replaced.

24 Inspect the cross-shaft for peeling and pitting on the needle bearing roller contact surfaces and for wear or damage on the gear teeth. Check the seal ring lip and oil seal lip for wear. Check for wear on the adjusting bolt shank and replace any worn or damaged parts.

25 Check the rack piston assembly for gear tooth damage, peeling or pitting in the grooves, uneven wear of the circulator rolling surface and broken or damaged balls. Replace any worn or damaged parts.

26 Inspect the input worm shaft assembly for pitting of the thrust needle bearing roller, peeling and pitting on the bearing contact surface of the thrust plate, peeling on the ball rolling surface of the worm shaft and damage to the input shaft oil seal contact surface. If the thrust bearing plate is defective, replace both as a set.

27 If free play is present at the pin fastening the torsion bar to the worm shaft and the pin fastening the torsion bar to the input shaft, replace the input worm shaft unit as as assembly.

28 Check the valve housing for damage to the seal ring-to-housing contact surface.

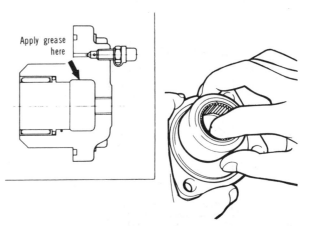

Fig. 11.43 Applying grease to the side cover cavity (Sec 30)

Apply grease here

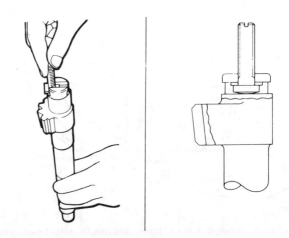

Fig. 11.44 Checking the adjusting bolt end play in the cross-shaft T-slot (Sec 30)

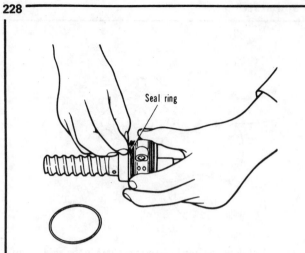

Fig. 11.45 Installing the O-ring and seal ring onto the ball end of the input worm shaft (Sec 30)

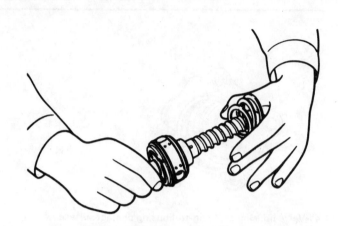

Fig. 11.46 Installing the thrust plates and needle roller bearing onto the ball end of the input worm shaft (Sec 30)

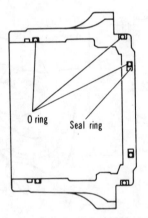

Fig. 11.47 Valve housing O-ring and seal ring locations (Sec 30)

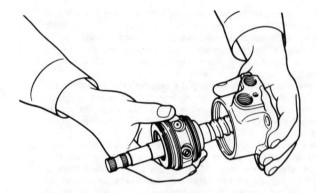

Fig. 11.48 Installing the input worm shaft in the valve housing (Sec 30)

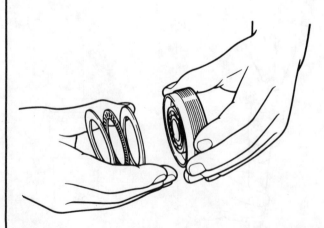

Fig. 11.49 Placing the thrust plates and needle roller bearing into the top cover (Sec 30)

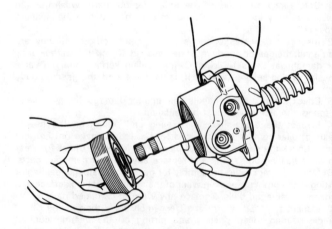

Fig. 11.50 Installing the top cover in the valve housing (Sec 30)

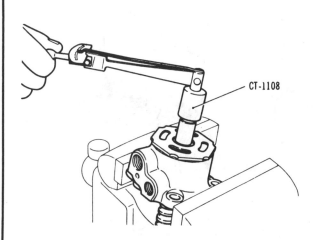

Fig. 11.51 Checking the input worm shaft preload with a torque wrench (Sec 30)

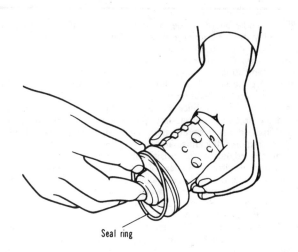

Fig. 11.52 Installing the seal ring in the rack piston groove (Sec 30)

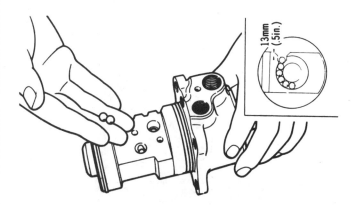

Fig. 11.53 Inserting the steel circulator balls (Sec 30)

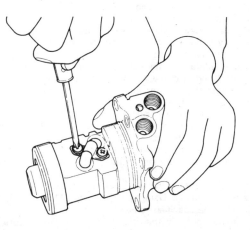

Fig. 11.54 Installing the circulator holder (Sec 30)

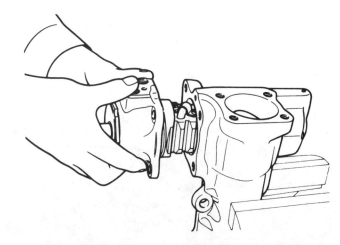

Fig. 11.55 Installing the valve housing/rack piston assembly in the gearbox housing (Sec 30)

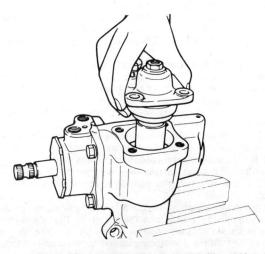

Fig. 11.56 Installing the cross-shaft (Sec 30)

29 Fill the needle bearing cage in the side cover with multi-purpose grease and lay the 33 bearing rollers in place. Apply a layer of grease to the cavity in the end of the side cover.

30 Install a new O-ring onto the side cover.

31 Slip the adjusting bolt through the adjusting plate (the chamfer on the adjusting plate should face the top of the T-slot), and install the adjusting bolt into the T-slot on the end of the cross-shaft. Using a dial calipers or dial indicator, check the axial (end) play between the cross-shaft and the adjusting bolt assembly and compare it to the specifications. If the end play is greater than specified, select a new adjusting plate of the required thickness and recheck the play.

32 Thread the adjusting bolt/cross-shaft assembly into place in the side cover from the inside. Be careful not to disturb the bearing rollers or damage the seal ring in the side cover. After the adjusting bolt has been threaded all the way into the side cover, install the locknut and tighten it temporarily. Set the assembly aside.

33 Remove the bearing and oil seal from the top cover with a drift punch. Install a new oil seal by tapping it into place with a seal driver and hammer. Check the ball-bearing for wear and damage, then tap it (or a new one) into place in the top cover. Do not hammer on the inner race of the bearing. Apply a thin coat of grease to the oil seal lip and set the top cover aside.

34 Using a seal driver and hammer, install a new oil seal into place in the bottom of the gearbox body. Install the back-up ring and the lower snap ring. Make sure the snap ring is properly seated in its groove.

35 When assembling the main components of the gearbox, be sure to apply a thin coat of the recommended power steering system fluid to all internal O-rings, seal rings, needle bearings and thrust plate. Also, always use new O-rings and seals during reassembly.

36 Install the O-ring, seal ring, inner thrust plate, needle roller bearing and outer thrust plate onto the ball end of the input worm shaft.

37 Install the O-rings and the seal ring into their grooves in the valve housing (compress the seal ring into a slight heart shape so it can be inserted into its groove).

38 Lubricate the O-rings and seal ring with power steering fluid and carefully slip the input worm shaft into place in the valve housing. Do not pinch or twist the O-rings.

39 Lay the outer thrust plate (the thinnest of the two thrust plates), the needle roller bearing and inner thrust plate in the top cover in that order.

40 Slip the top cover over the input shaft and thread it into the valve housing as far as it will go. Using special tool No. MB990853, tighten the top cover to the specified torque.

41 Turn the input shaft in the valve housing and make sure that it rotates smoothly, easily and quietly.

42 Using special tool No. MB990852, tighten the valve housing nut to the specified torque. The top cover must not rotate while the valve nut is tightened. Hold the cover, if necessary, to keep it from moving.

43 Check the input worm shaft preload starting torque (the torque required to start the input worm shaft to turn) with special tool No. CT-1108 and compare it to the preload specifications. If it is not within specifications, loosen the valve housing nut, change the the top cover position, reinstall the nut and recheck the starting torque.

44 Lubricate and install the O-ring and seal ring into the rack piston groove in that order.

45 Slide the rack piston onto the input worm shaft until it bottoms lightly on the shaft. Align the ball groove with the ball insertion hole by rotating the rack piston on the shaft. Insert 19 of the steel balls into the groove through the insertion hole. Be sure to hold the rack piston and shaft perfectly stationary while inserting the balls. If necessary, use a wooden or brass rod to gently push the balls into place.

46 After installing the last ball, measure the distance from the rack piston outer surface to the last ball and compare it to the specifications. If the clearance in greater than the specified amount, it is an indication that a ball has entered the wrong groove. Remove the rack piston (be sure to catch the balls in a container) and repeat the assembly procedure.

47 Grease the inside of the circulator with multi-purpose grease and insert the remaining 7 balls into the circulator. The grease will hold them in place. Install the circulator and holder in place on the rack piston and tighten the 2 attaching screws to the specified torque.

48 Mount the gearbox in a vise, and slide the valve housing/rack piston assembly into the gearbox. Be very careful not to twist or pinch the O-ring on the valve housing or the O-ring or seal ring on the rack piston.

49 Install the 4 valve housing bolts and tighten them to the specified

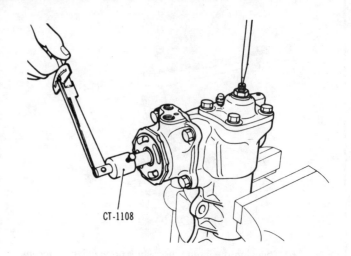

Fig. 11.57 Checking the input work shaft preload with a torque wrench (Sec 30)

Fig. 11.58 Connecting the Pitman arm to the cross-shaft (Sec 30)

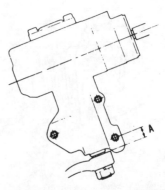

Fig. 11.59 The distance between the Pitman arm and the center of the first bolt hole must be as specified (Sec 30)

torque. After installation, move the rack piston to the neutral (center) position by rotating the input shaft.

50 Wrap a layer of vinyl tape around the splines on the end of the cross-shaft (to protect the O-rings and seals in the gearbox as the shaft is installed). Also, apply a thin coat of the recommended power steering fluid to the teeth and shaft of the cross-shaft and apply multi-purpose grease to the lower gearbox oil seal lip. Carefully slide the cross-shaft/side cover assembly into the gearbox. Do not rotate the side cover during installation, as damage to the O-ring may result. Install the 4 side cover bolts and tighten them to the specified torque.

51 Using special tool No. CT-1108, check the total starting torque of the input worm shaft (with the shaft in the neutral or center position) and compare it to the specifications. If it is greater than specified, repeat Steps 38, 39 and 40 and then recheck the total starting torque.

52 Recheck the large valve housing nut torque and then do one final check of the total starting torque of the input worm shaft.

53 Rotate the input worm shaft (so the rack piston moves through its entire stroke) and check for smooth operation.

54 Remove the vinyl tape from the splines and slide the Pitman arm onto the cross-shaft with the slit on the end of the cross-shaft lined up with the marks on the outside of the Pitman arm. Install the large lock washer and nut and tighten the nut to the specified torque.

55 Measure the distance between the Pitman arm and the center of the first bolt hole in the steering box, and compare it to the specifications.

56 Install the steering gearbox in the vehicle by referring to Section 29.

57 Bleed the system, as described in Section 31, then run the engine at 2000 rpm for 5 minutes and inspect the gearbox for fluid leaks.

32.3 Removing the steering wheel mounting nut

31 Power steering system – bleeding

1 Raise the front of the vehicle and set it on jack stands. Block the rear tires and set the parking brake to keep the vehicle from rolling.

2 You will need a container of clean power steering fluid of the recommended type, some rags, a piece of clear vinyl or plastic tubing, an empty glass or plastic jar and a wrench to fit the power steering gearbox bleeder screw.

3 Check the fluid level in the power steering fluid reservoir. It should be at the FULL mark. Recheck the fluid level periodically during the bleeding operation so that air does not enter the system through the reservoir.

4 Remove the rubber cap from the bleeder screw on the power steering gearbox. Connect one end of the clear plastic or vinyl tube to the bleeder screw and place the other end in a plastic or glass container about $\frac{1}{2}$ full of power steering fluid.

5 Start and idle the engine and turn the steering wheel fully from left to right at least 6 times.

6 With the engine idling, turn the steering wheel fully to the left. Momentarily open the bleeder screw and watch for air bubbles in the fluid escaping from the steering gearbox.

7 Turn the steering wheel fully from left to right at least 6 times.

8 Turn the steering wheel fully to the left and momentarily open the bleeder screw again.

9 Repeat the procedure until no air bubbles are visible in the fluid escaping from the steering box. Be sure to periodically check the fluid level in the reservoir during the bleeding operation.

10 Shut off the engine and remove the tube from the bleeder screw. Tighten the bleeder screw securely and install the rubber cap.

11 Any abrupt rise in the reservoir fluid level after the engine is shut off is a sign of incomplete bleeding, which will result in pump or flow control valve noise or pump failure.

12 Wipe up any fluid that may have spilled and wipe off the pump and steering gearbox. Lower the vehicle to the ground and test drive it.

32.4 Disconnecting the wire lead from the horn plate

32 Steering wheel – removal and installation

1 Disconnect the battery cables from the battery (negative first, then positive).

2 Carefully pry off the plastic horn button.

3 Make sure that the steering wheel is unlocked, then loosen and remove the nut and washer attaching the wheel to the steering shaft (photo).

32.5 Removing the horn plate

4   Disconnect the wire lead from the horn plate (photo) and feed it through the hole.

5   After noting how it is positioned, remove the horn plate (photo). It is held in place with 2 screws.

6   Mark the steering wheel and shaft so that they can be re-assembled in exactly the same position. Using an approved puller, remove the steering wheel (photo). *Do not hammer on the end of the puller bolt, as damage to the steering shaft may result.*

7   Installation is the reverse of removal. When installing the steering wheel, align the splines and carefully slide it onto the shaft. Do not bend or misalign the pins protruding from the front of the steering wheel hub. Tighten the steering wheel attaching nut to the specified torque. Be sure to align the tabs on the inside of the horn cover with the slots in the horn plate before snapping the cover in place.

33 Steering lock – removal and installation

1   Remove the steering wheel as described in Section 32. Move the steering column to its lowest position.

2   Remove the plastic cover surrounding the steering column (photo). It is held in place with 4 screws (the screws have 2 different types of threads, so don't mix them up).

3   Remove the 2 plastic ties holding the wiring to the steering column.

4   Unplug the 2 wiring connectors at the lower end of the column (photo).

5   Remove the 2 screws attaching the column switch assembly to the steering lock (photo) and lift the switch and backing plate off the column (note how the switch and backing plate are installed so they can be reassembled in the same way).

6   Remove the wiring harness from the ignition lock cylinder (photo) it is held in place with 1 screw).

7   To remove the lock from the steering column, cut a slot in the bolt heads with a hacksaw (photo) and remove the bolts with a large screwdriver.

8   When replacing the lock, new bolts and a new upper bracket will have to be purchased from a dealer and installed in place of the old ones.

9   Installation is the reverse of removal. When replacing the plastic steering column cover, make sure that the tabs on both sides are properly aligned. The machine screws are installed in the holes closest to the steering wheel, while the sheetmetal screws are installed in the lower holes.

10   Install the steering wheel, reconnect the battery cables (positive first, then negative) and check the horn, signal lights and emergency flasher lights for proper operation. Turn the wheel and make sure that the signal light cancel and check the steering lock for proper operation.

32.6 Removing the steering wheel

33.2 Removing the steering column cover mounting screws

33.4 Unplugging the wiring connectors at the base of the steering column

33.5 Removing the column switch mounting screws

33.6 Removing the ignition lock wiring harness mounting screw

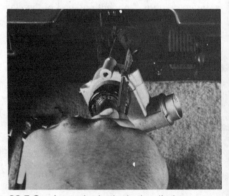

33.7 Sawing a slot in the lock cylinder mounting bolt

Chapter 12 Bodywork

Refer to Chapter 13 for specifications and information related to 1981 thru 1988 models

Contents

Specifications

Torque specifications

	ft-lb	(Nm)
Cab mounting bolts	20 to 23	(28 to 31)
Box mounting bolts	28 to 32	(39 to 43)
Hood latch cable locknut	2.5 to 2.9	(3.4 to 4)
Seat belt anchor bolts	17 minimum	(23 minimum)
Door hinge bolts	9.4 to 19	(13 to 26)

1 General information

1 The body and box are separate units made from steel stampings that are welded and bolted together. The frame is constructed of welded box-section rails and crossmembers.

2 The body and box are bolted to the frame and can be removed for repair or replacement.

2 Maintenance – body and frame

1 The condition of your vehicle's body is very important, as it is on this that the second hand value will mainly depend. It is much more difficult to repair a neglected or damaged body that it is to repair mechanical components. The hidden areas of the body, such as the fender wells, the frame, and the engine compartment, are equally important, although obviously not requiring as frequent attention as the rest of the body.

2 Once a year, or every 12 000 miles, it is a good idea to have the underside of the body and the frame steam cleaned. All traces of dirt and oil will be removed and the underside can then be inspected carefully for rust, damaged brake lines, frayed electrical wiring, damaged cables, and other problems. The front suspension components should be greased upon completion of this job.

3 At the same time, clean the engine and the engine compartment using either a steam cleaner or a water soluble degreaser.

4 The fender wells should be given particular attention, as undercoating can peel away and stones and dirt thrown up by the tires can cause the paint to chip and flake, allowing rust to set in. If rust is found, clean down to the bare metal and apply an antirust paint.

5 The body should be washed once a week (or when dirty). Thoroughly wet the vehicle to soften the dirt, then wash it down with a soft sponge and plenty of clean soapy water. If the surplus dirt is not washed off very carefully, it will in time wear down the paint.

6 Spots of tar or asphalt coating thrown from the road surfaces are best removed with a cloth soaked in solvent.

7 Once every six months, give the body and chrome trim a thorough wax job. If a chrome cleaner is used to remove rust on any of the vehicle's plated parts, remember that the cleaner also removes part of the chrome so use it sparingly.

3 Maintenance – upholstery and carpets

1 Every three months, remove the carpets or mats and thoroughly clean the interior of the vehicle (more frequently if necessary). Vacuum the upholstery and carpets to remove loose dirt and dust.

2 If the upholstery is soiled, apply an upholstery cleaner with a damp sponge and wipe it with a clean, dry cloth.

4   Body repair – minor damage

See color photo sequence on pages 238 and 239
Repair of minor scratches

If the scratch is very superficial, and does not penetrate to the metal of the body, repair is very simple. Lightly rub the area of the scratch with a fine rubbing compound to remove loose paint from the scratch and to clear the surrounding paint of wax buildup. Rinse the area with clean water.

Apply touch-up paint to the scratch, using a small brush. Continue to apply thin layers of paint until the surface of the paint in the scratch is level with the surrounding paint. Allow the new paint at least two weeks to harden, then blend it into the surrounding paint by rubbing with a very fine rubbing compound. Finally, apply a coat of wax to the scratch area.

Where the scratch has penetrated the paint and exposed the metal of the body, causing the metal to rust, a different repair technique is required. Remove any loose rust from the bottom of the scratch with a pocket knife, then apply rust inhibiting paint to prevent the formation of rust in the future. Using a rubber or nylon applicator, coat the scratched area with glaze type filler. If required, this filler can be mixed with thinner to provide a very thin paste, which is ideal for filling narrow scratches. Before the glaze filler in the scratch hardens, wrap a piece of smooth cotton cloth around the top of a finger. Dip the cloth in thinner and then quickly wipe it along the surface of the scratch. This will ensure that the surface of the filler is slightly hollowed. The scratch can now be painted over as described earlier in this section.

Repair of dents

When denting of the vehicle's body has taken place, the first task is to pull the dent out until the affected area nearly attains its original shape. There is little point in trying to restore the original shape completely as the metal in the damaged area will have stretched on impact and cannot be reshaped fully to its original contours. It is better to bring the level of the dent up to a point which is about $\frac{1}{8}$ in below the level of the surrounding metal. In cases where the dent is very shallow, it is not worth trying to pull it out at all.

If the underside of the dent is accessible, it can be hammered out gently from behind using a mallet with a wooden or plastic head. While doing this, hold a suitable block of wood firmly against the metal to absorb the hammer blows and thus prevent a large area of the metal from being stretched out.

If the dent is in a section of the body which has double layers, or some other factor making it inaccessible from behind, a different technique is in order. Drill several small holes through the metal inside the damaged area, particularly in the deeper sections. Screw long self-tapping screws into the holes just enough for them to get a good grip in the metal. Now the dent can be pulled out by pulling on the protruding head of the screws with a pair of locking pliers.

The next stage of repair is the removal of paint from the damaged area and from an inch or so of the surrounding 'sound' metal. This is accomplished most easily by using a wire brush or sanding disk in a drill motor, although it can be done just as effectively by hand with sandpaper. To complete the preparation for filling, score the surface of the bare metal with a screwdriver or the tang of a file (or drill small holes in the affected area). This will provide a very good grip for the filler material. To complete the repair, see the Section on filling and painting.

Repair of rust holes or gashes

Remove all paint from the affected area and from an inch or so of the surrounding 'sound' metal using a sanding disk or wire brush mounted in a drill motor. If these are not available, a few sheets of sandpaper will do the job just as effectively. With the paint removed, you will be able to determine the severity of the corrosion and therefore decide whether to replace the whole panel if possible, or repair the affected area. New body panels are not as expensive as most people think and it is often quicker to install a new panel than to attempt to repair large areas of rust.

Remove all trim pieces from the affected area (except those which will act as a guide to the original shape of the damaged body i.e. headlamp shells etc). Then, using metal snips or a hacksaw blade, remove all loose metal and any other metal that is badly affected by rust. Hammer the edges of the hole inwards to create a slight depression for the filler material.

Wire brush the affected area to remove the powdery rust from the surface of the metal. If the back of the rusted area is accessible, treat it with rust-inhibiting paint.

Before filling can be done it will be necessary to block the hole in some way. This can be accomplished with sheet metal riveted or screwed into place, or by stuffing the hole with wire mesh.

Once the hole is blocked off the affected area can be filled and painted (see the following section on filling and painting).

Filling and painting

Many types of body fillers are available, but generally speaking, body repair kits which contain filler paste and a tube of resin hardener are best suited for this type of repair work. A wide, flexible plastic or nylon applicator will be necessary for imparting a smooth and contoured finish to the surface of the filler material.

Mix up a small amount of filler on a clean piece of wood or cardboard (use the hardener sparingly). Follow the maker's instructions on the package, otherwise the filler will set incorrectly.

Using the applicator, apply the filler paste to the prepared area. Draw the applicator across the surface of the filler to achieve the desired contour and to level the filler surface. As soon as a contour that approximates the original one is achieved, stop working the paste. If you continue, the paste will begin to stick to the applicator. Continue to add thin layers of filler paste at 20-minute intervals until the level of the filler is just above the surrounding metal.

Once the filler has hardened the excess can be removed using a body file. From then on, progressively finer grades of sandpaper should be used, starting with a 180-grit paper and finishing with a 600-grit wet-or-dry paper. Always wrap the sandpaper around a flat rubber or wooden block, otherwise the surface of the filler will not be completely flat. During the sanding of the filler surface, the wet-or-dry paper should be periodically rinsed in water. This will ensure that a very smooth finish is produced in the final stage.

At this point, the repair area should be surrounded by a ring of bare metal, which in turn should be encircled by the finely feathered edge of the good paint. Rinse the repair area with clean water until all of the dust produced by the sand operation is gone.

Spray the entire area with a light coat of primer. This will reveal any imperfections in the surface of the filler. Repair these imperfections with fresh filler paste or glaze filler and once more smooth the surface with sandpaper. Repeat this spray-and-repair procedure until you are satisfied that the surface of the filler and the feathered edge of the paint are perfect. Rinse the area with clean water and allow it to dry completely.

The repair area is now ready for painting. Paint spraying must be carried out in a warm, dry, windless and dustfree atmosphere. These conditions can be created if you have access to a large indoor working area, but if you are forced to work in the open, you will have to pick the day very carefully. If you are working indoors, dousing the floor in the work area with water will help to settle the dust which would otherwise be in the air. If the repair area is confined to one body panel, mask off the surrounding panels. This will help to minimize the effects of a slight mismatch in paint color. Trim pieces such as chrome strips, door handles, etc., will also need to be masked off or removed. Use masking tape and several thicknesses of newspaper for the masking operations.

Before spraying, shake the paint can thoroughly, then spray a test area until the spray painting technique is mastered. Cover the repair area with a thick coat of primer. The thickness should be built up using several thin layers of primer rather than one thick one. Using 600-grit wet-or-dry sandpaper, rub down the surface of the primer until it is very smooth. While doing this, the work area should be thoroughly rinsed with water and the wet-or-dry sandpaper periodically rinsed as well. Allow the primer to dry before spraying additional coats.

Spray on the top coat, again building up the thickness by using several thin layers of paint. Begin spraying in the center of the repair area and then, using a circular motion, work out until the whole repair area and about two inches of the surrounding original paint is covered. Remove all masking material 10 to 15 minutes after spraying on the final coat of paint. Allow the new paint at least two weeks to harden, then using a very fine rubbing compound, blend the edges of the new paint into the existing paint. Finally, apply a coat of wax.

5   Body and frame repairs – major damage

1   Major damage must be repaired by an auto body/frame repair

shop with the necessary welding and hydraulic straightening equipment.

2　If the damage has been serious, it is vital that the frame be checked for correct alignment, as the handling of the vehicle will be affected. Other problems, such as excessive tire wear and wear in the transmission and steering may also occur.

6　Maintenance – hinges and locks

Once every 3000 miles, or every three months, the door and hood hinges and locks should be given a few drops of light oil or lock lubricant. The door striker plates can be given a thin coat of grease to reduce wear and ensure free movement.

7　Door trim panel – removal and installation

1　Pry out the plastic insert (photo) and remove the screws at the front and rear of the door pull (photo).

2　Remove the plastic backing in the door handle. It is held in place by one screw (photo).

3　Push in on the rubber spacer and release the clip on the window crank with a screwdriver. Pull off the crank and the plastic insert (photo).

4　Remove the four screws attaching the speaker to the door (if so equipped). Carefully pull out the speaker and disconnect the wiring connector (photo).

5　Insert a screwdriver between the door trim panel and the door (photo) and pop the retainers out of the door. Insert the screwdriver as close as possible to the retainers.

6　Remove the trim panel and carefully peel down the plastic moisture barrier.

7　Installation is the reverse of removal. Use tape to hold the moisture barrier in place while installing the trim panel. Install the window crank so that it faces the same direction as the one on the opposite door with the window fully closed.

8　Door glass regulator – removal, installation and adjustment

1　Remove the door trim panel and the window glass by referring to the appropriate sections.

2　Turn the window crank until the regulator is centered in the door.

3　Remove the six bolts attaching the regulator to the door (photo) and slip the regulator out through the large access hole (photo).

4　Inspect the regulator pinion and driven gear for wear and damage. Check the weather strip for damage and deterioration. Replace any worn or defective parts.

5　Apply a thin coat of multipurpose grease to all sliding and rotating parts of the regulator. Installation is basically the reverse of removal.

6　To adjust the regulator, raise the glass so that it fits into the track at the rear and top of the window properly, then tighten the regulator attaching bolts. Lower the window slowly and check to make sure it rides properly in the front track without binding. If not, loosen the front track adjusting bolts (photo) and move the track forward or backward, as necessary, then tighten the adjusting screw.

9　Door window glass – removal and installation

1　Remove the door trim panel by referring to Section 7. Set the window crank in place temporarily and lower the window until the door glass attaching screws are visible in the large access hole in the door panel.

2　Support the glass and remove the attaching screws (photo).

3　Carefully lower the glass to the bottom of the door and pry out the inner and outer glass weather strips with a screwdriver (photo). Tilt the glass at a 45° angle and carefully pull it up through the slot and out of the door.

4　Installation is basically the reverse of removal. Be sure to fit the weather strip in place before installing the glass in its mount. Tighten the glass attaching screws finger tight, close the window completely (to center the window in the regulator) and then tighten the screws securely.

7.1a Remove the plastic insert to expose the front door pull mounting screw

7.1b The door pull is attached to the door with two screws

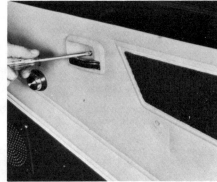
7.2 Removing the plastic escutcheon from the door handle

7.3 The window crank is held in place with a spring-type clip

7.4 Disconnect the electrical harness at the door speaker

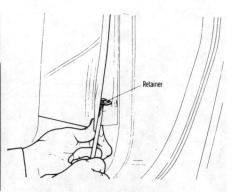
Fig. 12.1 Prying the door trim panel away from the door (Sec 7)

8.3a The door glass regulator is attached to the door panel with 6 bolts

8.3b The regulator can be slipped out through the large access hole

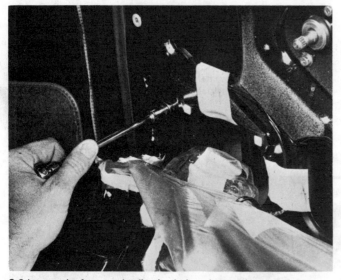

8.6 Loosen the front track adjusting bolt and move the track if the glass binds when it is lowered

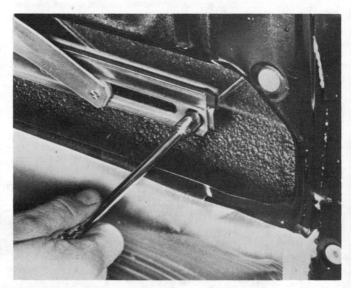

9.2 The glass is held in the regulator by two screws

9.3 Before removing the glass, carefully pry out the weatherstrips

Fig. 12.2 Removing the door window glass (Sec 9)

10 Door latch assembly – removal and installation

1 Remove the door trim panel as described in Section 7.
2 With the window all the way up (or removed) disconnect the cylinder lock activator rod at the lock lever.
3 Disconnect the inner door lock rod from the door latch lever.
4 Disconnect the door latch rod from the exterior door handle lever.
5 Remove the inner door handle rod from the door latch lever. It is held in place with a spring clip (photo).
6 Remove the four screws holding the latch assembly to the door. (It may be necessary to use a hand-held impact driver to loosen the screws). Then remove the latch assembly through the large access hole.
7 Check the latch mechanism for wear and damage. Make sure it operates smoothly. Apply a thin coat of multi-purpose grease to all moving parts.
8 Installation is basically the reverse of removal. Be sure to tighten the latch assembly mounting screws securely. After installation, check for proper operation of the interior door handle, the exterior door handle, the exterior lock and the interior lock.

11 Door interior handle – removal and installation

1 Remove the door trim panel by referring to Section 7.
2 Disengage the actuator rod from the door latch lever. It is held in place by a spring clip.
3 Remove the rear two screws and loosen the front screw (photo). Disengage the rod from the plastic clip and lift out the door handle assembly.
4 To install the handle, slip the rod into the door latch lever and install the three screws finger tight. Move the handle assembly forward or backwards, as necessary, until there is approximately $\frac{1}{4}$ in of free play in the handle, then tighten the mounting screws securely. Don't forget to install the clip and make sure that the foam rubber damper is in place on the rod.
5 Install the door trim panel by referring to Section 7.

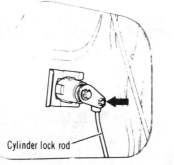

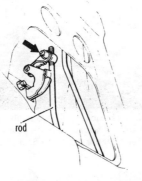

Fig. 12.3 Cylinder lock rod attachment fitting (Sec 10)

Fig. 12.4 Exterior handle/door latch rod attachment fitting (Sec 10)

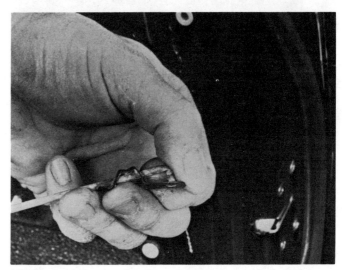

10.5 The inner door handle rod is attached to the latch lever with a spring clip

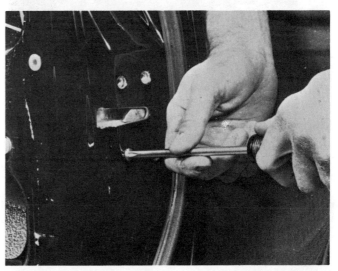

10.6 Remove the four screws holding the latch assembly to the door

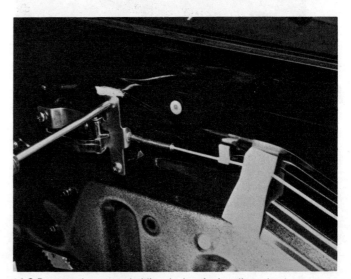

11.3 Remove the screws holding the interior handle to the door

This photo sequence illustrates the repair of a dent and damaged paintwork. The procedure for the repair of a hole is similar. Refer to the text for more complete instructions

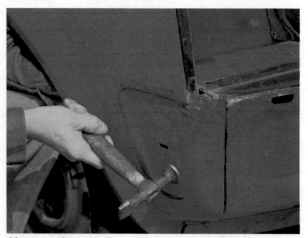

After removing any adjacent body trim, hammer the dent out. The damaged area should then be made slightly concave

Use coarse sandpaper or a sanding disc on a drill motor to remove all paint from the damaged area. Feather the sanded area into the edges of the surrounding paint, using progressively finer grades of sandpaper

The damaged area should be treated with rust remover prior to application of the body filler. In the case of a rust hole, all rusted sheet metal should be cut away

Carefully follow manufacturer's instructions when mixing the body filler so as to have the longest possible working time during application. Rust holes should be covered with fiberglass screen held in place with dabs of body filler prior to repair

Apply the filler with a flexible applicator in thin layers at 20 minute intervals. Use an applicator such as a wood spatula for confined areas. The filler should protrude slightly above the surrounding area

Shape the filler with a surform-type plane. Then, use water and progressively finer grades of sandpaper and a sanding block to wet-sand the area until it is smooth. Feather the edges of the repair area into the surrounding paint.

Use spray or brush applied primer to cover the entire repair area so that slight imperfections in the surface will be filled in. Prime at least one inch into the area surrounding the repair. Be careful of over-spray when using spray-type primer

Wet-sand the primer with fine (approximately 400 grade) sandpaper until the area is smooth to the touch and blended into the surrounding paint. Use filler paste on minor imperfections

After the filler paste has dried, use rubbing compound to ensure that the surface of the primer is smooth. Prior to painting, the surface should be wiped down with a tack rag or lint-free cloth soaked in lacquer thinner

Choose a dry, warm, breeze-free area in which to paint and make sure that adjacent areas are protected from over-spray. Shake the spray paint can thoroughly and apply the top coat to the repair area, building it up by applying several coats, working from the center

After allowing at least two weeks for the paint to harden, use fine rubbing compound to blend the area into the original paint. Wax can now be applied

12 Door exterior handle – removal and installation

1   Remove the door trim panel by referring to Section 7.
2   With the window all the way up (or removed) disconnect the exterior door handle rod from the lever on the handle (see Figure 4).
3   Remove the two bolts attaching the handle to the door (photo) and slip the handle out from the outside.
4   When installing the handle, turn the fitting on the end of the door handle rod until it can be pushed into the plastic bushing without changing the position of the handle. There should be approximately $\frac{1}{8}$ in of free play in the exterior handle. If necessary, disconnect and turn the fitting on the end of the door handle rod until the free play is correct, then snap the fitting back into place.

13 Door cylinder lock – removal and installation

1   Remove the door trim panel as described in Section 7.
2   With the window all the way up (or removed) disconnect the cylinder lock rod from the door latch lever (see Figure 12.3).
3   Remove the clip that holds the lock cylinder in place on the door by grasping it with pliers and pulling straight up (photo).
4   Slip the lock cylinder out of the door to the outside (photo).
5   When installing the lock cylinder, the lever should point to the rear of the vehicle and the key slots should be in the vertical position.

14 Windshield glass – removal

Note: *The windshield is bonded in place and requires special tools and sealant for proper removal and installation. This is a rather difficult, messy job and damage to the glass and the surrounding paint can occur if it is not done carefully. For these reasons, it is recommended that the job be left to the dealer service department or an auto glass shop.*
1   Remove the windshield wiper arms, the rearview mirror and the sun visors.
2   Using a screwdriver, push the upper molding joint to the right or left until the molding ends are visible. Insert the screwdriver into the gap between the molding ends. Pry the ends out of the rubber weather strip, then carefully pull the molding out of the weather strip by hand.
3   Working from inside the vehicle, slip the screwdriver between the weather strip and the body as shown in Fig. 12.9. Slide the screwdriver along the weather strip and push out on the glass. (It would be very helpful to have an assistant for this operation).
4   Pull the weather strip off of the glass and discard it; it should not be reused. If the glass is to be reused, be sure to scrape off all traces of the old sealant before installation.

15 Windshield glass – installation

1   Apply a bead of sealant to the bottom surface of the windshield glass groove in the new rubber weather strip.
2   Carefully fit the new weather strip in place on the windshield glass.
3   Lay a length of $\frac{1}{4}$ in cord in the body groove of the weather strip as shown in Fig. 12.11. The cord must be long enough so the ends overlap.
4   Coat the weather strip flange of the body with a soap-and-water solution, then place the windshield glass in position from the outside. The ends of the cord must be inside the vehicle.
5   Slowly pull on one end of the cord, keeping it at a right angle to the windshield, while an assistant pushes on the glass from the outside. Work from the ends towards the center of the windshield.
6   After the entire weather strip is in place, pull back the outside edge and remove the excess soap-and-water solution. Apply sealant between the weather strip and the body flange as shown in Fig. 12.13. Make sure the entire perimeter of the windshield is sealed or leaks could occur.
7   Coat the molding groove with a soap-and-water solution.
8   Using a screwdriver with a bent tip (see Fig. 12.14) spread the weather strip as shown in Fig. 12.15 and press the end of the molding in place.

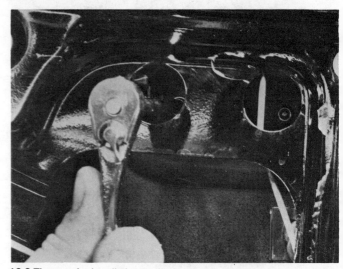

12.3 The exterior handle is attached to the door with two bolts that are accessible from the inside

13.3 The door cylinder lock is held in place with a spring clip

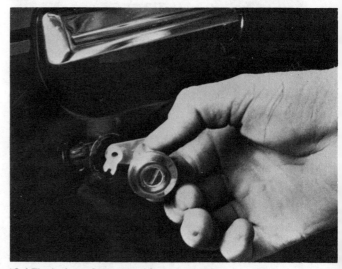

13.4 The lock can be removed from the outside

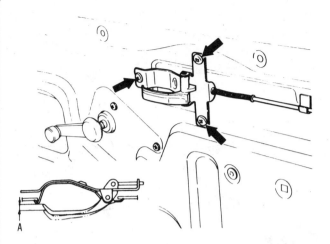

Fig. 12.5 Adjusting the free play of the interior handle (Sec 11)

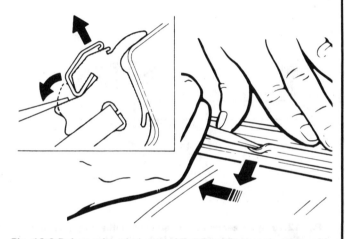

Fig. 12.6 Adjusting the free play of the exterior handle (Sec 12)

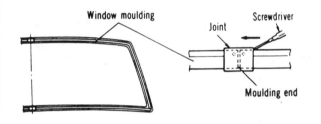

Fig. 12.7 Move the upper molding joint to expose the window molding ends (Sec 14)

Fig. 12.8 Release the window molding from the weatherstrip with a screwdriver (Sec 14)

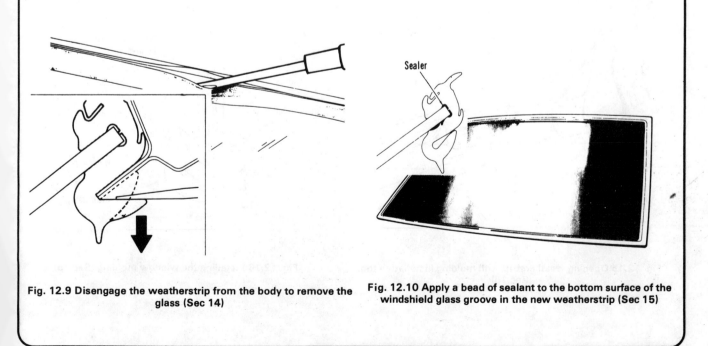

Fig. 12.9 Disengage the weatherstrip from the body to remove the glass (Sec 14)

Fig. 12.10 Apply a bead of sealant to the bottom surface of the windshield glass groove in the new weatherstrip (Sec 15)

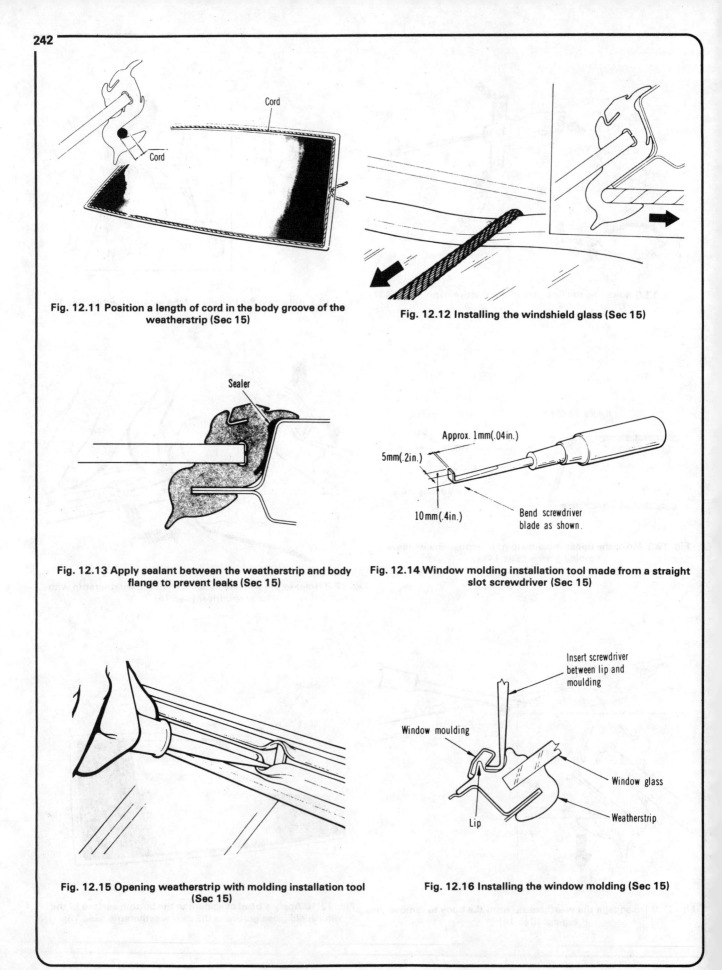

Fig. 12.11 Position a length of cord in the body groove of the weatherstrip (Sec 15)

Fig. 12.12 Installing the windshield glass (Sec 15)

Fig. 12.13 Apply sealant between the weatherstrip and body flange to prevent leaks (Sec 15)

Fig. 12.14 Window molding installation tool made from a straight slot screwdriver (Sec 15)

Fig. 12.15 Opening weatherstrip with molding installation tool (Sec 15)

Fig. 12.16 Installing the window molding (Sec 15)

9   Slide the screwdriver along the groove and press the molding firmly into place.

10 Carefully tap the molding joints into place by hand and wipe off any excess soap-and-water solution.

11 Install the windshield wiper arms, the rearview mirror and the sun visors.

16 Rear window glass – removal and installation

     To remove and install the rear window glass, refer to Sec 14, Windshield glass – removal and Sec 15, Windshield glass – installation. The procedures are identical.

17 Seat belts – removal and installation

1   Move the seat(s) as far forward as possible.

2   Remove the 2 anchor bolts attaching the seat belt to the cab floor and the 2 bolts attaching the shoulder harness to the rear door post. You will have to pry off the plastic cover before removing the upper shoulder harness anchor bolt.

3   Install the inside anchor plates or buckle side plates, depending on the type of vehicle, parallel with the center line of the body (see Fig. 12.17). Tighten the anchor bolts to the specified torque.

4   Make sure the belts are not twisted, then install the outside anchor plates so that the belt is directed upward at a 45° angle. Tighten the anchor bolts to the specified torque.

5   Make sure the shoulder harness belts are not twisted, then install the upper and lower mounting bolts and tighten them to the specified torque.

18 Hood – removal, installation, and adjustment

Note: *An assistant will be required to remove the hood.*

1   Prop open the hood and mark with paint (or scribe) the position of the hood hinge brackets. Place protective pads on the vehicle cowling so the hood will not damage the paint if it comes in contact with it.

2   Remove the four bolts attaching the hinge brackets to the hood (photo) and carefully lift the hood away from the vehicle. Remove the hood hook assembly. It is held in place by two bolts (photos).

3   When installing the hood, carefully hold it in place, using the previously scribed marks to align it, and install the four mounting bolts finger tight.

4   Very carefully close the hood and move it, if necessary, so that the gaps between the hood and fenders are equal. Raise the hood carefully (so it does not move on the hinge brackets) and tighten the four mounting bolts securely. Lower the hood and recheck the gaps.

5   Next, raise the hood and loosen the jam nuts on the four bumper screws at the front of the vehicle (photo). Screw the forward two bumper screws (the small ones) down as far as possible.

6   Lower the hood to see if the top of the hood is even with the top of the fenders. If not, raise the hood and screw the rear (large) bumper screws in or out to move the hood up or down, as necessary. Once the height is correctly adjusted, turn the two rear (large) bumper screws $\frac{1}{4}$ turn counter clockwise and tighten the jam nuts. Recheck the height one last time.

7   Using a light, check to see if the forward bumper screws are touching the bottom side of the hood. Raise the hood and screw them in or out until they do, then tighten the jam nuts.

8   Install the hood hook assembly and tighten the bolts finger tight (so the assembly will move when pushed but is not loose). Close the hood and engage the latch, then pull the hood release handle. Carefully disengage the safety hook, so as not to disturb the position of the hood lock assembly, and raise the hood. Tighten the mounting bolts securely.

9   Close the hood until it latches. It should latch properly when dropped from a height of 12 in. If excess pressure is required to engage the latch, or if the hood is loose after engaging the latch, adjust the length of the hood lock bolt. To do this, loosen the jam nut (photo) and turn the hood latch bolt in or out as necessary (photo) until the hood latches properly and is not loose. Don't forget to tighten the jam nut once the adjustment is complete.

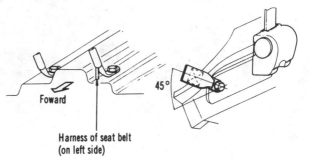

Harness of seat belt
(on left side)

Fig. 12.17 Install the outside seat belt anchor plate so that the belt is directed upward at a 45° angle (Sec 17)

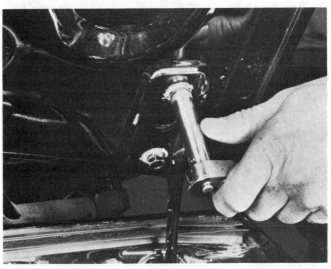

18.2a Removing the hood hinge bracket bolts

18.2b The hood hook assembly is held in place with two bolts

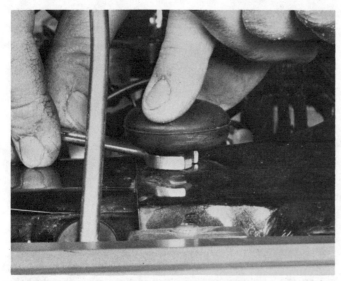

18.5 Before adjusting the bumper screws, the jam nuts must be loosened

18.9a Loosening the jam nut on the hood lock bolt

18.9b Adjust the hood lock bolt by turning it with a screwdriver

19.1a The grille is held in place with four screws along its top edge ...

19.1b ... and one screw at each bottom corner

20.4 The front bumper stays are held in place with a bolt that is accessible from the top

19 Grille – removal and installation

1   Remove the 8 screws holding the grille in position on the front of the vehicle (photos).
2   Pull the grille forward and away from the vehicle. Store it where it will not be damaged.
3   When installing the grille, be sure to center it in the opening before tightening the screws.

20 Front bumper – removal and installation

1   Disconnect the battery cables (negative first, then positive). Remove the battery hold-down and lift out the battery.
2   Disconnect the parking light wiring harness connectors located just behind the headlights. Trace the wires coming from the parking lights to make sure you disconnect the correct connector. The parking light wiring harnesses are held in place by plastic straps located just below the headlights; these straps will have to be cut. Pull the wiring harness out toward the front of the vehicle.
3   Remove the two screws attaching the rubber bumper ends to the fenders.
4   Remove the bolt and nut attaching each bumper stay to the frame rails (photo). The nuts do not have to be completely removed. Pull the bumper forward and away from the vehicle.
5   The bumper stays are attached to the bumper with two bolts each.
6   Installation is the reverse of removal.

21 Rear bumper – removal and installation

1   Raise the rear of the vehicle and set it on jack stands. Block the front tires to keep the vehicle from rolling.
2   An assistant will be required to remove the bumper.
3   Remove the two nuts and washers attaching each bumper stay to the frame (photo).
4   Support the bumper, pull out the two bolts in each bumper stay, and pull the bumper straight back off of the vehicle.
5   The bumper stays are attached to the bumper with two bolts each.
6   Installation is the reverse of removal. Be sure that the bumper is level before tightening the mounting bolts. Also, do not allow the bumper stay to touch the body. Leave approximately $\frac{1}{8}$ in clearance between them.

22 Tailgate – removal and installation

1   With the tailgate down, mark the hinge location with white paint (photo), or scribe along the hinge, then remove the hinge bolts (photo).
2   Support the tailgate and remove the shoulder bolts attaching the cables to the box (photo).
3   When installing the tailgate, be sure to line up the hinges before tightening the bolts. If this is not done, the tailgate will be out of alignment and may not close properly.

23 Tailgate latch – removal and installation

1   With the tailgate down, remove the access cover from the inside panel. It is held in place by 12 screws.
2   With the access cover removed (photo) the tailgate handle and latch pull rod are exposed.
3   Disconnect the pull rod from the latch by removing the spring clip and push out the rod. (Do not lose the spring clip). Remove the 3 latch mounting screws (photo). A hand-held impact driver may be required if they are difficult to loosen.
4   Lift off the latch shield, close the latch and push it out of its mount into the tailgate and remove it through the access hole. Check the latch components for excessive wear and damage (particularly the arm). Apply a thin coat of multi-purpose grease to the arm (where it contacts the latch body) and other moving parts, then check for smooth operation.
5   Install the latch in the closed position, then trip the actuating lever to open it before connecting the pull rod. Do not forget the spring clip.
6   After everything is installed and working properly, lay the access cover in place, install the screws and tighten them securely.

21.3 Remove the nuts attaching the rear bumper stays to the frame

22.1a Mark the tailgate hinge locations before removing the bolts

22.1b Removing the tailgate hinge bolts from the box

24 Tailgate handle – removal and installation

1   With the tailgate down, remove the access cover from the inside panel. It is held in place by 12 screws.
2   Pop the end of the bellcrank rod out of the plastic bushing in the handle.
3   Remove the 2 bolts attaching the handle to the tailgate and pull the handle through the tailgate toward the outside.
4   Check the handle for damage. It should pivot freely on its mount without binding.
5   When installing the handle, make sure the mounting bolts are tightened securely. Lubricate the pivot points with a small amount of engine oil.
6   There should be a small amount of free play in the handle. It can be adjusted by threading the fitting on the end of the bellcrank rod in or out, as required, before seating it in the plastic bushing in the handle.
7   After everything is installed and working properly, lay the access cover in place, install the screws and tighten them securely.

25 Cab – removal and installation

1   Removal of the cab requires the use of a hoist or crane.
2   Remove the hood by referring to Section 18.
3   Remove or disconnect the various cables, hoses, electrical wiring connectors, brackets, and controls shown in Fig. 12.18.
4   Remove the six cab mounting bolts and lift the cab off of the frame.
5   Installation is the reverse of removal. When installing the cab, set

it in place and assemble the mounting bolts, the rubber and metal spacers and washers as shown in Fig. 12.19. Be sure to tighten the mounting bolts to the specified torque.
6   Double check all the hoses, cables, electrical wiring connectors and controls for proper installation.

26 Box – removal and installation

1   Removal of the box requires the use of a heavy duty hoist or crane.
2   Disconnect the negative battery cable from the battery.
3   Remove the filler neck mud shield from the left rear wheel well. It is held in place with 3 bolts.
4   Remove the fuel tank filler cap, then loosen and slide back the hose clamps on the filler connecting hose (large) and the breathing hose (small) where they attach to the filler neck. Pull the hoses off the filler neck..
5   Remove the mud guards.
6   Remove the skirt panels and brackets shown in Fig. 12.20
7   Unplug the license plate, the tailgate and the fuel gauge electrical connectors, then remove the wiring harness from the box.
8   Remove the license plate bracket.
9   Remove the 8 mounting bolts and lift the box off of the frame.
10 Installation is the reverse of removal. Make sure the rubber pads are in place on the frame, then lay the box in position. If the rubber pads are deteriorated or cracked, replace them with new ones.
11 Install the mounting bolts and washers as shown in Fig. 12.21. Tighten the mounting bolt nuts to the specified torque.
12 When the installation is complete, connect the negative battery cable to the battery and check the taillights and license plate light for proper operation.

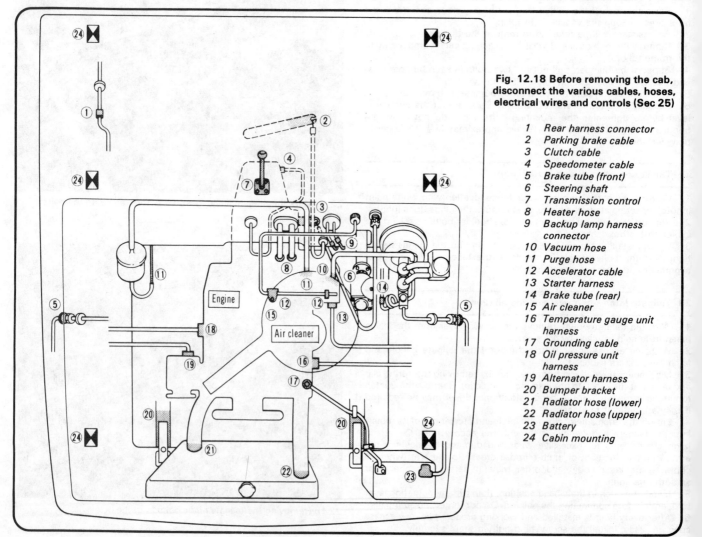

Fig. 12.18 Before removing the cab, disconnect the various cables, hoses, electrical wires and controls (Sec 25)

1   *Rear harness connector*
2   *Parking brake cable*
3   *Clutch cable*
4   *Speedometer cable*
5   *Brake tube (front)*
6   *Steering shaft*
7   *Transmission control*
8   *Heater hose*
9   *Backup lamp harness connector*
10 *Vacuum hose*
11 *Purge hose*
12 *Accelerator cable*
13 *Starter harness*
14 *Brake tube (rear)*
15 *Air cleaner*
16 *Temperature gauge unit harness*
17 *Grounding cable*
18 *Oil pressure unit harness*
19 *Alternator harness*
20 *Bumper bracket*
21 *Radiator hose (lower)*
22 *Radiator hose (upper)*
23 *Battery*
24 *Cabin mounting*

22.2 The tailgate cables are attached to the box with shoulder bolts

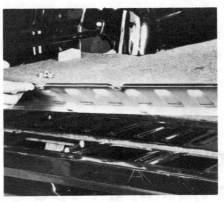

23.2 The tailgate access cover is removed to gain access to the latch and handle mechanism

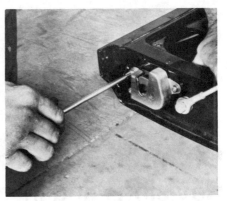

23.3 Removing the latch screws

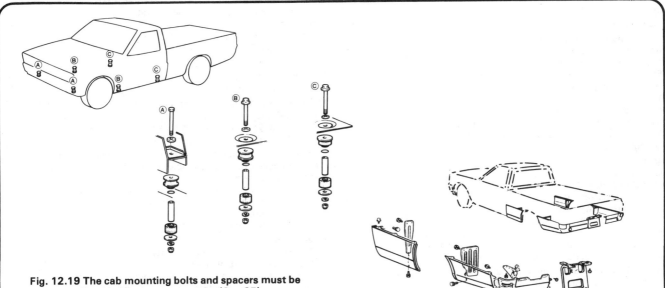

Fig. 12.19 The cab mounting bolts and spacers must be assembled in the proper order (Sec 25)

Fig. 12.20 The skirt panels must be removed before the box is lifted off the vehicle (Sec 26)

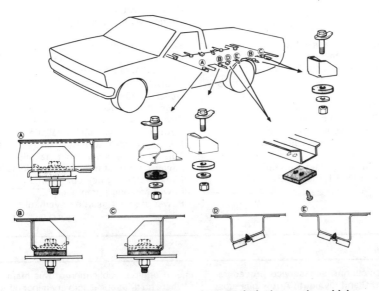

Fig. 12.21 The bolts and pads used to attach the box to the vehicle must be assembled in the proper order (Sec 26)

Chapter 13 Supplement:
Revisions and information on 1981 thru 1988 models

Contents

1 Introduction

This supplement contains specifications and service procedure changes that apply to all Dodge D-50 and Plymouth Arrow pick-ups produced from 1981 through 1988, as well as information related to Mitsubishi pick-ups produced from 1984 through 1988. Also included is information related to previous models that was not available at the time of original publication of this manual.

Where no differences (or very minor differences) exist between 1981 through 1988 models and earlier models, no information is given. In those instances, the original material included in Chapters 1 through 12 should be used.

2 Specifications

Note: *The specifications listed here include only the items which differ from those listed in Chapters 1 through 12. For information not specifically listed here, refer to the appropriate Chapter.*

Capacities

Fuel tank
  1981 models with W-engine and all 1982 models . . . . 18.0 US gal (15.0 Imp gal, 68.1 liters)
  1983 on
    rear wheel drive
      U-engine. . . . . 15.1 US gal (12.6 Imp gal, 57.2 liters)
      W-engine. . . . . 18.0 US gal (15.0 Imp gal, 68.1 liters)
    4WD (all) . . . . 18.0 US gal (15.0 Imp gal, 68.1 liters)
Engine oil — with filter change (1983 on)
  U-engine
    rear wheel drive . . . . 4.2 US qt (3.5 Imp qt, 4.0 liters)
    4WD . . . . 5.2 US qt (4.4 Imp qt, 5.0 liters)
  W-engine
    rear wheel drive . . . . 5.2 US qt (4.4 Imp qt, 5.0 liters)
    4WD . . . . 6.1 US qt (5.1 Imp qt, 5.8 liters)
Manual transmission oil (4WD models) . . . . 4.6 US pints (3.8 Imp pints, 2.2 liters)
Transfer case oil (4WD models) . . . . 4.6 US pints (3.8 Imp pints, 2.2 liters)
Rear axle lubricant (1983 on) . . . . 3.2 US pints (2.6 Imp pints, 1.5 liters)
Front axle lubricant (4WD models) . . . . 2.3 US pints (1.9 Imp pints, 1.1 liters)
Manual steering gearbox oil
  1983 and 1984 . . . . 0.38 US pints (0.32 Imp pints, 0.18 liters)
  1985 on . . . . 0.59 US pints (0.49 Imp pints, 0.28 liters)

Tune-up and routine maintenance

Jet valve clearance (1984 on). . . . . 0.010 in (0.25 mm)
Compression pressure (1986 on)
  standard . . . . 171 psi
  minimum
    U-engine . . . . 149 psi
    W-engine . . . . 156 psi
  maximum difference between cylinders . . . . 14 psi
Power steering belt deflection (1985 on)
  U-engine . . . . 1/4 to 11/32 in (6 to 9 mm)
  W-engine . . . . 23/64 to 15/32 in (9.5 to 12 mm)

Torque specifications

	Ft-lbs	Nm
Oil pan drain plug (1986 on).	26 to 32	35 to 44
Spark plugs (1981 on)	15 to 21	20 to 29
Transfer case drain and fill plugs.	22 to 25	30 to 34
Front axle		
inspection/fill plug	29 to 43	39 to 59
drain plug	43 to 50	59 to 68

Engine

Model designations
  U-engine (for USA) G63B
  U-engine (for Canada) 4G63
Displacement (U-engine — 1983 on) . . . . 121.9 ci (1997 cc)
Bore and stroke (U-engine — 1983 on) . . . . 3.35 x 3.46 in (85.0 x 88.0 mm)
Compression ratio (W-engine — 1985 on) 8.7:1
Standard cylinder bore (U-engine — 1983 on) . . . . 3.346 in (85.0 mm)
Silent shafts (U-engine — 1983 on)
  front journal OD
    right shaft . . . . 1.654 in (42.0 mm)
    left shaft . . . . 0.728 in (18.5 mm)
  rear journal OD . . . . 1.614 in (41 mm)
  left shaft front bearing oil clearance . . . . 0.0008 to 0.0020 in (0.02 to 0.05 mm)
Piston ring side clearance (1983 U-engine and 1984 W-engine)
  number 1 ring only . . . . 0.002 to 0.0035 in (0.05 to 0.09 mm)
Piston ring end gap
  1983 and 1984 U-engine
    number 2 ring . . . . 0.008 to 0.016 in (0.2 to 0.4 mm)
    oil ring side rail . . . . 0.008 to 0.020 in (0.2 to 0.5 mm)
  1985 on U-engine
    oil ring side rail only . . . . 0.008 to 0.028 in (0.2 to 0.7 mm)
  1983 W-engine
    number 1 ring . . . . 0.010 to 0.015 in (0.25 to 0.40 mm)
    oil ring side rail . . . . 0.012 to 0.024 in (0.3 to 0.6 mm)

Piston ring end gap (continued)
  1984 on W-engine
    number 1 ring . . . . 0.012 to 0.018 in (0.30 to 0.45 mm)
    number 2 ring . . . . 0.010 to 0.015 in (0.25 to 0.40 mm)
    oil ring side rail . . . . 0.012 to 0.024 in (0.3 to 0.6 mm)
Connecting rod bearing oil clearance
  1983 on U-engine . . . . 0.0008 to 0.0020 in (0.02 to 0.05 mm)
  1983 on W-engine . . . . 0.0008 to 0.0024 in (0.02 to 0.06 mm)
Main bearing oil clearance (1983 on) . . . . 0.0008 to 0.0020 in (0.02 to 0.05 mm)
Rod journal OD (1983 on U-engine) . . . . 1.772 in (45.0 mm)
Main bearing journal OD (1983 on U-engine) . . . . 2.244 in (57.0 mm)

Torque specifications

	Ft-lbs	Nm
1981 and 1982 only		
Rear insulator-to-crossmember	15 to 17	20 to 23
Rear insulator-to-transmission	29 to 36	40 to 49
Engine mount-to-block	11 to 14	15 to 19
Crossmember-to-frame	29 to 36	40 to 49
1981 on		
Driveplate bolts (A/T only)	94 to 101	128 to 137
1983 on (U-engine only)		
Camshaft sprocket bolt	59 to 72	79 to 98
Main bearing cap bolts	37 to 39	49 to 53
Oil pump sprocket nut	25 to 28	34 to 39
Silent Shaft sprocket bolt	25 to 28	34 to 39
Timing belt tensioner nut	16 to 21	22 to 29
Front case bolts	15 to 19	20 to 26
Engine support bracket bolts (RWD 10 mm only)	29 to 36	40 to 49
Oil pump cover bolt	11 to 13	15 to 17
1983 on (W-engine only)		
Engine support bracket bolts (RWD 10 mm only)	29 to 36	40 to 49
Chain guide B bolt		
upper	6 to 7	8 to 9
lower	11 to 15	15 to 21
Oil pump cover bolt	7 to 8	10 to 11

Cooling, heating and air conditioning

Radiator cap opening pressure
  1981 thru 1984 (U-engine w/ A/T, all W-engine) . . . . 10.7 to 14.9 psi (73.5 to 102.9 kPa)
  1985 on . . . . 11 to 15 psi (75 to 105 kPa)
Thermostat
  starts to open at . . . . 190°F (88°C)
  fully open at . . . . 212°F (100°C)
Drivebelt ID number (1981 and 1982 USA only) MD025826

Fuel and exhaust systems

Carburetor throttle bore size
  1981 and 1982 (U-engine — Canada only)
    primary . . . . 1.181 in (30 mm)
    secondary . . . . 1.260 in (32 mm)
  all others
    primary . . . . 1.260 in (32 mm)
    secondary . . . . 1.378 in (35 mm)

1981 models

Carburetor application   *Carburetor model*
Canada
  manual transmission 30-32DIDTA-132
  automatic transmission 30-32DIDTA-133
All others 30-32DIDTA
Main jet primary numbers
  U-engine
    California and Federal . . . . 107.5 (M/T) 108.8 (A/T)
    Canada 106.3
  W-engine
    California 115
    Federal 112.5
Main jet secondary numbers
  U-engine
    California and Federal 195
    Canada 190
  W-engine (all) 195

Pilot jet primary numbers
    U-engine
        California and Federal   55
        Canada   60
    W-engine (all) 57.5
Pilot jet secondary numbers
    U-engine
        California and Federal 72.5
        Canada   60
    W-engine (all) 72.5
Enrichment jet numbers
    U-engine (all)   40
    W-engine
        California   40
        Federal   50
Idle speed
    U-engine . . . .   750 ± 100 rpm
    W-engine . . . .   800 ± 100 rpm
Idle up speed
    U-engine . . . .   1000 ± 50 rpm
    W-engine . . . .   1050 ± 50 rpm

1982 models

Carburetor application   *Carburetor model*
U-engine
    Federal M/T (4-speed) 32-35DIDTA-78
    Federal M/T (5-speed) 32-35DIDTA-83
    California 32-35DIDTA-80
    Canada 32-35DIDTA
W-engine
    Federal (M/T) 32-35DIDTA-74
    Federal (A/T) 32-35DIDTA-75
    California (M/T) 32-35DIDTA-76
    California (A/T) 32-35DIDTA-77
Main jet primary numbers
    U-engine
        California 107.5
        Federal 106.3
    W-engine (all) . . . .   112.5 (M/T) 115 (A/T)
Main jet secondary numbers
    U-engine (all)   195
    W-engine (all)   195
Pilot jet primary numbers
    U-engine (all) 56.3
    W-engine (all) 62.5
Pilot jet secondary numbers
    U-engine (all) 52.5
    W-engine (all) 57.5
Enrichment jet numbers
    U-engine (all)   40
    W-engine (all) . . . .   45 (M/T) 40 (A/T)
Idle speed
    manual transmission
        4-speed . . . .   700 ± 100 rpm
        5-speed . . . .   750 ± 100 rpm
    automatic transmission . . . .   800 ± 100 rpm
Idle up speed . . . .   900 ± 50 rpm

1983 models

Carburetor application   *Carburetor model*
U-engine
    Federal (4-speed) 32-35DIDTA-117
    Federal (5-speed) 32-35DIDTA-121
    Federal (A/T) 32-35DIDTA-118
    California (M/T) 32-35DIDTA-115
    California (A/T) 32-35DIDTA-116
    Canada (M/T) 32-35DIDTA-144
    Canada (A/T) 32-35DIDTA-145
W-engine
    Federal (M/T) 32-35DIDTA-106
    Federal (A/T) 32-35DIDTA-107
    California (M/T) 32-35DIDTA-104
    California (A/T) 32-35DIDTA-105
    Canada (M/T) 32-35DIDTA-142
    Canada (A/T) 32-35DIDTA-143
Main jet primary numbers
    U-engine (all) 106.3
    W-engine (all) . . . .   113.8(M/T) 115(A/T)

1983 models (continued)

Main jet secondary numbers
  U-engine (all) 195
  W-engine (all) 195
Pilot jet primary numbers
  U-engine (all) 53.8
  W-engine
    California .... 65(M/T) 63.8(A/T)
    all others 63.8
Pilot jet secondary numbers
  U-engine (all) 52.5
  W-engine (all) 65
Enrichment jet numbers
  U-engine (all) 45
  W-engine
    California .... 50(M/T) 45(A/T)
    all others 45
Idle speed
  U-engine
    5-speed .... 700 ± 100 rpm
    Canada (all) .... 850 ± 50 rpm
    all others .... 750 ± 100 rpm
  W-engine
    manual transmission.......................... 750 ± 100 rpm
    automatic transmission....................... 800 ± 100 rpm
    Canada (all) .... 850 ± 50 rpm
Idle up speed .... 900 ± 50 rpm

1984 models

Carburetor application   *Carburetor model*
U-engine
  Federal (high altitude)
    4-speed 32-35DIDTA-165
    5-speed 32-35DIDTA-167
    automatic transmission....................... 32-35DIDTA-166
  Federal (4-speed) 32-35DIDTA-177
  Federal (5-speed) 32-35DIDTA-179
  Federal (A/T) 32-35DIDTA-178
  California (M/T) 32-35DIDTA-175
  California (A/T) 32-35DIDTA-176
  Canada (M/T) 32-35DIDTA-144
  Canada (A/T) 32-35DIDTA-145
W-engine
  Federal (high altitude)
    manual transmission.......................... 32-35DIDTA-168
    automatic transmission....................... 32-35DIDTA-169
  Federal (M/T) 32-35DIDTA-182
  Federal (A/T) 32-35DIDTA-183
  California (M/T) 32-35DIDTA-180
  California (A/T) 32-35DIDTA-181
  Canada (M/T) 32-35DIDTA-142
  Canada (A/T) 32-35DIDTA-143
Idle speed
  U-engine
    Federal
      5-speed .... 700 ± 100 rpm
      all others .... 750 ± 100 rpm
    California .... 750 ± 100 rpm
    Canada .... 850 ± 50 rpm
  W-engine
    Federal and California
      manual transmission........................ 750 ± 100 rpm
      automatic transmission..................... 800 ± 100 rpm
    Canada .... 850 ± 50 rpm
Idle up speed .... 850 to 900 rpm

1985 models

Carburetor application   *Carburetor model*
U-engine
  manual transmission 32-35DIDTF-205
  automatic transmission 32-35DIDTF-206
W-engine
  USA (M/T) 32-35DIDTF-207
  USA (A/T) 32-35DIDTF-208
  Canada (M/T) 32-35DIDTA-148
  Canada (A/T) 32-35DIDTA-149

Main jet primary numbers
  U-engine (all) 103.8
  W-engine
    USA 110
    Canada 115
Main jet secondary numbers
  U-engine (all) 185
  W-engine
    USA 200
    Canada .... 185(M/T) 190(A/T)
Pilot jet primary numbers
  U-engine (all) 55
  W-engine
    USA 62.5
    Canada 60
Pilot jet secondary numbers
  U-engine (all) 62.5
  W-engine
    USA 65
    Canada 60
Enrichment jet numbers
  U-engine (all) 100
  W-engine
    USA 100
    Canada .... 80 (M/T) 50 (A/T)
Fast idle opening (drill diameter)
  manual transmission .... 0.028 in (0.71 mm)
  automatic transmission .... 0.031 in (0.80 mm)
Idle speed
  U-engine .... 750 ± 100 rpm
  W-engine (manual transmission)
    Canada .... 750 ± 50 rpm
    all others .... 750 ± 100 rpm
  W-engine (automatic transmission)
    Canada .... 800 ± 50 rpm
    all others .... 800 ± 100 rpm
Idle up speed .... 850 to 900 rpm

1986 models

Carburetor application   *Carburetor model*
U-engine
  manual transmission 32-35DIDTF-205
  automatic transmission 32-35DIDTF-206
W-engine
  USA (M/T) 32-35DIDTF-207
  USA (A/T) 32-35DIDTF-208
  Canada (M/T) 32-35DIDTA-148
  Canada (A/T) 32-35DIDTA-149
Main jet primary numbers
  U-engine (all) 103.8
  W-engine
    USA 110
    Canada 115
Main jet secondary numbers
  U-engine (all) 185
  W-engine
    USA 200
    Canada .... 185(M/T) 190(A/T)
Pilot jet primary numbers
  U-engine (all) 55
  W-engine
    USA 62.5
    Canada 60
Pilot jet secondary numbers
  U-engine (all) 62.5
  W-engine
    USA 65
    Canada 60
Enrichment jet
  U-engine (all) 100
  W-engine
    USA 100
    Canada .... 80 (M/T) 50 (A/T)
Fast idle opening (drill diameter)
  U-engine with M/T .... 0.025 in (0.63 mm)
  W-engine with A/T .... 0.031 in (0.80 mm)

1986 models (continued)

Fast idle opening (drill diameter) (continued)

All others	0.028 in (0.71 mm)

Idle speed

U-engine	750 ± 100 rpm
W-engine (manual transmission)	
Canada	750 ± 50 rpm
all others	750 ± 100 rpm
W-engine (automatic transmission)	
Canada	800 ± 50 rpm
all others	800 ± 100 rpm
Idle up speed	850 to 900 rpm

1987 models

Carburetor application	*Carburetor model*
U-engine	
Federal M/T	32-35DIDEF-400
Federal A/T	32-35DIDEF-401
California M/T	32-35DIDEF-402
California A/T	32-35DIDEF-403
Canada M/T	32-35DIDEF-420
Canada A/T	32-35DIDEF-421
W-engine	
Federal M/T	32-35DIDEF-404
Federal A/T	32-35DIDEF-405
California M/T	32-35DIDEF-406
California A/T	32-35DIDEF-407
Canada M/T	32-35DIDEF-422
Canada A/T	32-35DIDEF-432
Main jet primary numbers	
U-engine	100
W-engine	107.5
Main jet secondary number (all)	190
Pilot jet primary numbers	
U-engine	47.5
W-engine	70
Pilot jet secondary number (all)	70
Enrichment jet	
U-engine	55
W-engine	65
Idle speed	
U-engine	750 rpm ± 100
W-engine	800 rpm ± 100

1988 models

Carburetor application	*Carburetor model*
U-engine	
Federal M/T	32-35DIDEF-400
Federal A/T	32-35DIDEF-401
California M/T	32-35DIDEF-402
California A/T	32-35DIDEF-403
Canada M/T	32-35DIDEF-420
Canada A/T	32-35DIDEF-421
W-engine	
Federal M/T	32-35DIDEF-429
Federal A/T	32-35DIDEF-430
California M/T	32-35DIDEF-435
California A/T	32-35DIDEF-436
Canada M/T	32-35DIDEF-437
Canada A/T	32-35DIDEF-438
Main jet primary numbers	
U-engine	100
W-engine	107.5
Main jet secondary number (all)	190
Pilot jet primary numbers	
U-engine	47.5
W-engine	55
Pilot jet secondary number (all)	70
Enrichment jet	
U-engine	55
W-engine	65
Idle speed	
U-engine	750 rpm ± 100
W-engine	800 rpm ± 100

Ignition and starting systems

U-engine distributor

1981 and 1982 model numbers
Federal M/T	T4T62079
Federal A/T	T4T62075
California	T4T62076
Canada	T4T60175
Centrifugal advance	0° @ 1200 rpm
	12° @ 2800 rpm
	20° @ 6000 rpm

Vacuum advance
Federal M/T	0° @ 2.36 in-Hg
	17° @ 5.91 in-Hg
	28° @ 9.45 in-Hg
Federal M/T	0° @ 3.15 in-Hg
	14.4° @ 9.84 in-Hg
	20° @ 14.17 in-Hg
California	0° @ 5.12 in-Hg
	7° @ 7.87 in-Hg
	15° @ 11.84 in-Hg
Canada	0° @ 3.15 in-Hg
	14.4° @ 9.84 in-Hg
	20° @ 14.17 in-Hg

1983 and 1984 model numbers
Federal 4-speed	T4T62186
Federal 5-speed	T4T63474
Federal A/T	T4T62180
California	T4T62185
Canada	T4T62172

Centrifugal advance
USA	0° @ 600 rpm
	6° @ 1400 rpm
	10° @ 3000 rpm
Canada	0° @ 500 rpm
	4.5° @ 1250 rpm
	7° @ 3000 rpm

Vacuum advance
Federal M/T	0° @ 2.36 in-Hg
	12° @ 7.87 in-Hg
	16° @ 11.02 in-Hg
California	0° @ 3.15 in-Hg
	10° @ 9.06 in-Hg
	11.5° @ 11.02 in-Hg
Canada	0° @ 3.15 in-Hg
	5.8° @ 9.84 in-Hg
	7.5° @ 11.81 in-Hg

1985 and 1986 model numbers
Federal M/T	100291-057
Federal A/T	100291-063
California M/T	100291-057
California A/T	100291-064

1987 model numbers
Federal M/T	MD112111
Federal A/T	MD110440
California M/T	MD110419
California A/T	MD110418

1988 model numbers
Federal M/T	MD110440
Federal A/T	MD125103
California M/T	MD110419
California A/T	MD110418

Centrifugal advance
1985	0° @ 1000 rpm
	12° @ 2800 rpm
	20° @ 6000 rpm
1986	0° @ 1000 rpm
	14° @ 2800 rpm
	23° @ 5000 rpm
1987 on	0° @ 1200 rpm
	12° @ 2800 rpm
	20 ° @ 6000 rpm

Vacuum advance
1985
Federal M/T	0° @ 5.12 in-Hg
	30° @ 11.81 in-Hg

Vacuum advance
  1985 (continued)
    Federal A/T .... 0° @ 5.12 in-Hg
                                                   23° @ 11.02 in-Hg
    California M/T .... 0° @ 5.12 in-Hg
                                                   30° @ 11.81 in-Hg
    California A/T .... 0° @ 3.15 in-Hg
                                                   20° @ 14.17 in-Hg
  1986
    Federal M/T .... 0° @ 3.15 in-Hg
                                                   23° @ 11.02 in-Hg
    Federal A/T .... 0° @ 2.36 in-Hg
                                                   32° @ 11.02 in-Hg
    California M/T .... 0° @ 3.15 in-Hg
                                                   23° @ 11.02 in-Hg
    California A/T .... 0° @ 3.15 in-Hg
                                                   20° @ 14.17 in-Hg
  1987
    California M/T .... 0° @ 3.15 in-Hg
                                                   12° @ 5.91 in-Hg
                                                   23° @ 11.03 in-Hg
    California A/T .... 0° @ 3.15 in-Hg
                                                   8° @ 5.91 in-Hg
                                                   20° @ 14.18 in-Hg
    Federal M/T .... 0° @ 2.36 in-Hg
                                                   12° @ 5.91 in-Hg
                                                   28° @ 11.82 in-Hg
    Federal A/T .... 0° @ 3.15 in-Hg
                                                   12° @ 5.91 in-Hg
                                                   23° @ 11.03 in-Hg
  1988
    California M/T .... 0° @ 3.15 in-Hg
                                                   12° @ 5.91 in-Hg
                                                   23° @ 11.03 in-Hg
    California A/T .... 0° @ 3.15 in-Hg
                                                   8° @ 5.91 in-Hg
                                                   20° @ 14.18 in-Hg
    Federal M/T .... 0° @ 3.15 in-Hg
                                                   12° @ 5.91 in-Hg
                                                   23° @ 11.03 in-Hg
    Federal A/T .... 0° @ 3.15 in-Hg
                                                   8° @ 5.91 in-Hg
                                                   20° @ 14.18 in-Hg
Pickup coil resistance (1981 thru 1984) .... 920 to 1120 ohms
Signal rotor air gap (1985 on) .... 0.031 in (0.8 mm)

W-engine distributor
1981 and 1982 model numbers
  Federal T4T62074
  California T4T62075
Vacuum advance
  Federal .... 0° @ 3.15 in-Hg
                                               12° @ 5.91 in-Hg
                                               23° @ 11.02 in-Hg
  California .... 0° @ 3.15 in-Hg
                                               14.4° @ 9.84 in-Hg
                                               20° @ 14.17 in-Hg
1983 and 1984 model numbers
  Federal T4T62074
  California (except below) and Canada T4T62075
  California w/4WD and M/T T4T62076
Centrifugal advance .... 0° @ 600 rpm
                                               5° @ 1400 rpm
                                               10° @ 3000 rpm
Vacuum advance
  Federal .... 0° @ 3.15 in-Hg
                                               10° @ 9.06 in-Hg
                                               11.5° @ 11.01 in-Hg
  California (except below) and Canada .... 0° @ 3.15 in-Hg
                                               7.2° @ 9.84 in-Hg
                                               10° @ 14.17 in-Hg
  California w/4WD and M/T .... 0° @ 5.12 in-Hg
                                               3.5° @ 7.87 in-Hg
                                               7.5° @ 11.81 in-Hg

1985 and 1986 model numbers
Federal	T3T61971
California (except below)	T3T61972
California w/4WD and A/T	T3T61973
Canada	T3T61973

Centrifugal advance
1985	0° @ 600 rpm
	7° @ 1900 rpm
	8.5° @ 2500 rpm
1986	0° @ 1200 rpm
	14° @ 3800 rpm
	17° @ 5000 rpm

Vacuum advance
1985
Federal	0° @ 5.12 in-Hg
	15° @ 11.81 in-Hg
California (except below)	0° @ 5.12 in-Hg
	11.5° @ 11.02 in-Hg
California w/4WD and A/T	0° @ 3.15 in-Hg
	10° @ 14.17 in-Hg
Canada	0° @ 3.15 in-Hg
	10° @ 14.17 in-Hg

1986
Federal	0° @ 5.12 in-Hg
	30° @ 11.81 in-Hg
California (except below)	0° @ 5.12 in-Hg
	23° @ 11.02 in-Hg
California w/4WD and A/T	0° @ 3.15 in-Hg
	20° @ 14.17 in-Hg
Canada	0° @ 3.15 in-Hg
	20° @ 14.17 in-Hg

1987 model numbers
All 2WD with HD suspension	T3T65472
Federal 4WD	T3T65472
Federal 2WD	T3T65473
California	T3T65572

Centrifugal advance (all)	0° @ 1600 rpm
	9° @ 2800 rpm
	19° @ 6000 rpm

Vacuum advance
All 2WD with HD suspension	0° @ 3.15 in-Hg
	12° @ 5.91 in-Hg
	23° @ 11.03 in-Hg
Federal 4WD	0° @ 3.15 in-Hg
	12° @ 5.91 in-Hg
	23° @ 11.03 in-Hg
Federal 2WD	0° @ 2.36 in-Hg
	12° @ 5.91 in-Hg
	28° @ 11.82 in-Hg
California	0° @ 3.15 in-Hg
	8° @ 5.91 in-Hg
	20° @ 14.18 in-Hg

1988 model numbers
Federal	T3T65476
California	T3T65572
Centrifugal advance	0° @ 1600 rpm
	9° @ 2800 rpm
	19° @ 6000 rpm
Vacuum advance	0° @ 3.15 in-Hg
	8° @ 5.91 in-Hg
	20° @ 14.18 in-Hg

Pickup coil resistance (1981 thru 1984)	920 to 1120 ohms
Signal rotor air gap (1985 on)	0.031 in (0.8 mm)

Ignition coil
1984	E-064
1986	
U-engine	E-064
W-engine	E-089
1987 on	F-100

Primary coil resistance
1983 thru 1985	1.04 to 1.27 ohms
1986	1.2 ohms
1987 on	1.1 to 1.3 ohms

Ignition coil (continued)

Secondary coil resistance

1983 thru 1985	7.10 to 9.60 K ohms
1986	
U-engine	13.7 K ohms
W-engine	17.0 K ohms
1987 on	22.1 to 29.9 K ohms

Spark plugs

1981 and 1982 (USA W-engine)	NGK BPR5ES-11
	NGK BP5ES-11
	NGK BUR5EA
1983 and 1984 (USA U-engine)	NGK BUR6EA-11
1985 and 1986 (USA W-engine)	NGK BUR6EA-11
1987 on	Nippon Denso W20EPR-S11
Gap (1985 and 1986 — Canada)	0.039 to 0.043 in (1.0 to 1.1 mm)

Starter motor

Commutator diameter (1983 on)

standard	
direct drive motor	1.524 in (38.7 mm)
reduction drive motor	1.260 in (32.0 mm)
service limit	
direct drive motor	1.484 in (37.7 mm)
reduction drive motor	1.220 in (31.0 mm)
Pinion shaft end play (reduction drive motor)	0.020 in (0.5 mm) or less

Emissions control systems

Dashpot adjustment (California M/T only)

engine set speed	2000 ± 100 rpm

Throttle opener idle up speed

1981 and 1983	
U-engine	1000 ± 50 rpm
W-engine	1050 ± 50 rpm
1982	900 ± 50 rpm

Manual transmission

Torque specifications	Ft-lbs	Nm
Transmission mounting bolts (1982 on)	31 to 40	42 to 54
Countershaft gear locknut	50 to 72	68.6 to 98.0

Automatic transmission

Band adjustments

kickdown	Backed off 3-1/2 turns from 4.3 Ft-lbs
low/reverse	Backed off 7 turns from 3.6 Ft-lbs

Transfer case

Rear bearing end play	0 to 0.004 in (0 to 0.1 mm)

Snap-ring and spacer thicknesses

input gear	
no color code	0.091 in (2.30 mm)
red	0.093 in (2.35 mm)
white	0.094 in (2.40 mm)
blue	0.096 in (2.45 mm)
green	0.098 in (2.50 mm)
high-low clutch hub	
no color code	0.084 in (2.14 mm)
yellow	0.087 in (2.21 mm)
white	0.090 in (2.28 mm)
blue	0.093 in (2.35 mm)
red	0.095 in (2.42 mm)
input gear bearing	
purple	0.106 in (2.70 mm)
pink	0.108 in (2.75 mm)
yellow	0.110 in (2.80 mm)
white	0.112 in (2.85 mm)
blue	0.114 in (2.90 mm)

output shaft bearing (spacer)
black	0.033 in (0.84 mm)
no color code	0.037 in (0.93 mm)
red	0.040 in (1.02 mm)
white	0.044 in (1.11 mm)
yellow	0.047 in (1.20 mm)
blue	0.051 in (1.29 mm)
green	0.054 in (1.38 mm)

Torque specifications

	Ft-lbs	Nm
Adapter-to-transfer case bolts/nuts	22 to 30	30 to 41
Chain/side cover bolts	22 to 30	30 to 41
Rear cover bolt	6 to 7	8 to 9.5
Select plug	22 to 25	30 to 34
Rear output shaft locknut	73 to 94	98 to 127
Seal plug	22 to 30	30 to 41
Cover bolt	11 to 15	15 to 21
Control housing bolt	7.5 to 9	10 to 12

Driveline (all models)

Front driveshaft runout (1981 W-engine only) .... 0.016 in (0.4 mm) TIR maximum

Torque specifications

	Ft-lbs	Nm
Driveshaft flange yoke bolts (1982 on)	36 to 43	49 to 59

Driveline (four wheel drive models)

Front hub turning force
1983	0.9 to 3.1 lbs (0.4 to 1.4 kg)
1984 on	1 to 4 lbs (5 to 18 Nm)
Brake (A) wear (automatic hub)	0.380 in (9.6 mm)
Return spring free length (automatic hub)	1.378 in (35 mm)
Shift spring free length (automatic hub)	1.181 in (30 mm)
Brake contact surface depth (1984 automatic hub)	0.470 to 0.480 in (11.7 to 12.3 mm)
Driveaxle axial play	0.008 to 0.020 in (0.2 to 0.5 mm)
Left driveaxle/inner shaft spline play (1983 and 1984)	0.020 in (0.5 mm) maximum
Front hub axial play (1985 on)	0.001 in (0.05 mm) or less

Torque specifications

	Ft-lbs	Nm
Free wheeling hub body assembly	37 to 43	50 to 58
Free wheeling hub cover assembly (manual hub only)	8 to 10	10 to 13
Right driveaxle-to-inner shaft	37 to 43	50 to 58
Drive gear-to-differential case	58 to 65	79 to 88
Companion flange self-locking nut	116 to 159	157 to 215
Carrier cap	40 to 47	54 to 63
Differential carrier-to-housing	58 to 72	79 to 98
Differential carrier-to-bracket		
1986 on	58 to 79	79 to 107
all others	58 to 72	79 to 98
Differential carrier-to-left differential bracket	58 to 72	79 to 98
Differential mounting bracket-to-frame	58 to 72	79 to 98
Housing-to-right differential bracket	58 to 72	79 to 98
Cover	11 to 15	15 to 21

Brake system

Parking brake pull rod stroke	16 to 17 notches
Master cylinder piston-to-power brake pushrod clearance	
1982 thru 1984	0.004 to 0.020 in (0.1 to 0.5 mm)
1985 on	0.016 to 0.030 in (0.4 to 0.8 mm)
Brake disc thickness limit	0.720 in (18.4 mm)
Drum brake (leading/trailing type — 1984 on 4WD models)	
lining thickness (standard)	0.180 in (4.6 mm)
lining thickness (wear limit)	0.040 in (1.0 mm)
wheel cylinder bore	0.813 to 0.815 in (20.640 to 20.692 mm)
piston diameter	0.811 to 0.812 in (20.587 to 20.620 mm)
wheel cylinder-to-piston clearance	
standard	0.0008 to 0.0041 in (0.020 to 0.105 mm)
wear limit	0.006 in (0.15 mm)
brake drum ID	
standard	10.0 in (254.0 mm)
wear limit	10.080 in (256.0 mm)
drum-to-lining clearance	0.010 to 0.016 in (0.25 to 0.40 mm)

Torque specifications

	Ft-lbs	Nm
Brake disc-to-hub nuts		
1982	36 to 44	49 to 59
1983 on		
four wheel drive........................	36 to 44	49 to 59
rear wheel drive	34 to 38	46 to 51
Caliper assembly bolts (1985 on — 4WD)	58 to 72	79 to 98
Caliper guide pins (1987 on	23 to 36	32 to 50

Electrical system

Battery type (1983)	
USA (U-engine — 4WD)	NT100-S6
Canada	
U-engine (rear wheel drive).....................	NS50
U-engine (four wheel drive)	NS70
W-engine	65D23R-MF
Battery type (1984)	
U-engine	
USA	NX100-S6(S)-LM*, NS70-LM**, or NX100-S6(S)-MF
Canada	NX100-S6(S)* or NS70-LM**
W-engine	
USA	NX120-7 or NX100-S6(S)-MF
Canada	NX120-7 or 65D23R-MF
Battery type (1985 on)	
USA	
manual transmission.......................	NX100-S6(S)-MF
automatic transmission	
U-engine	NX100-S6(S)-MF
W-engine	NX100-S6(S)-MF or NX120-7-MF
Canada	65D23R-MF
Battery capacity	
45 AH	NT100-S6, NX100-S6(S), NX100-S6(S)-LM, NX100-S6(S)-MF
60 AH	NS50
65 AH	NS70, NS70-LM, 65D23R-MF
80 AH	NX120-7
Alternator regulated voltage (1983 and 1984 only)	13.9 to 14.9 V at 68°F (20°C)
Bulb types (1983 on)	
Headlights (type I)...............................	50W
Headlights (type II)	40/60W

* *Rear wheel drive models*
** *Four wheel drive models*

Suspension and steering

Front spring free length (1983 on — U-engine)	11.457 in (291 mm)
Camber (1986 on 4WD only)	1°
Caster (4WD only)	
1983 thru 1985	2° ± 1°
1986 on	3°
Distance from threaded end of strut bar to front face of nut (1985 on)	2.90 in (74 mm)
Distance from threaded end of stabilizer bar link bolt to bottom face of nut (1984 only)	1.180 to 1.260 in (30 to 32 mm)
Tires (1982 on — U-engine)	6.00 x 14 6PR or 185SR14

Torque specifications

	Ft-lbs	Nm
Front suspension and steering		
Upper arm shaft-to-crossmember (1982 on)	73 to 86	99 to 117
Lower arm shaft-to-crossmember	40 to 54	54 to 73
Lower balljoint-to-lower arm (4WD)	40 to 54	53 to 73
Upper arm shaft-to-frame (4WD)	73 to 86	99 to 117
Lower arm shaft-to-frame (4WD)	102 to 115	138 to 156
Front suspension crossmember (4WD)	73 to 86	99 to 117
Front suspension crossmember-to-bracket (4WD)	22 to 30	30 to 41
Anchor bolt jam nut (4WD)	29 to 36	40 to 49
Rear suspension		
Spring U-bolt nuts	62 to 79	84 to 107
Spring pin/shackle pin nuts (1982 on)	33 to 43	45 to 58
Manual steering		
Tilt bracket mounting bolt (1981 and 1982)..........	6 to 9	8 to 12
Power steering		
Column clamp mounting bolt (1981 and 1982)	7 to 10	10 to 14
Steering wheel locknut	26 to 32	35 to 44
Idler arm bracket mounting bolts (4WD)	40 to 47	54 to 63
Gearbox mounting nuts/bolts (4WD)	40 to 47	54 to 63
Tie-rod end jam nut (4WD)	48 to 57	64 to 78

Bodywork

Torque specifications	Ft-lbs	Nm
Box mounting bolts	20 to 23	28 to 31
Seat belt anchor bolts		
1981 thru 1985	17 to 47	23 to 64
1986 on	25 to 39	34 to 53
Door hinge bolts (1986 on)...........................	12 to 18	17 to 25

---

3 Tune-up and routine maintenance

Routine maintenance intervals

The following maintenance procedures for later model vehicles are required in addition to the procedures outlined in Chapter 1. **Note:** *For routine maintenance procedures directly related to emissions control systems, refer to Section 8.*

Every 15,000 miles or 12 months — whichever comes first
Lubricate the upper control arm bushings (those with grease fittings)

Every 30,000 miles
Check the driveaxle boots for leaks and damage (4WD only)
Check the front axle (differential) oil level (4WD only)
Change the manual transmission/transfer case oil (severe use only)

Every 60,000 miles
Replace the timing belt with a new one (U-engine)

Severe use

If the vehicle is subjected to severe use conditions, as defined below, the following maintenance procedures must be performed more often (at shorter time/mileage intervals).

Severe use conditions include:
Driving in dust or off road
Towing a trailer
Extensive idling
Short trips in freezing temperatures
Driving in sandy or salty areas
Driving in heavy city traffic during hot weather more than
   50% of the time

Maintenance procedures:
Engine oil and filter change (every 3 months/3000 miles)
Air filter replacement (when dirty)
PCV system check/service (more frequently)
Disc brake pad inspection (more frequently)
Rear brake shoe inspection (more frequently)
Manual transmission/transfer case oil change (4WD models)
   (every 30,000 miles)
Upper control arm bushing lubrication (every 7500 miles)

Manual steering gearbox oil level check

1   To check the oil level on 1981 and later models, remove the breather plug and insert a thin screwdriver into the hole.
2   The oil level should be 1.40 inches (35 mm) below the upper face of the cover.

Front axle oil level check (4WD models)

3   The procedure for the front differential is the same as the one for the rear differential. Refer to Chapter 1.

Ignition timing adjustment

4   When checking and adjusting the ignition timing on 1984 models only, be sure to disconnect and plug the vacuum hoses attached to the distributor.

Valve clearance adjustment

5   It should be noted that 1985 and later models are equipped with automatic valve clearance lash adjusters on the intake and exhaust valves. The Jet valves are the only ones that require clearance checks/adjustments. Note also that the Jet valve clearance has been changed for all models from 1984 on.

Upper control arm bushing lubrication

6   On later models equipped with grease fittings on the upper control arm pivots, use a grease gun to lubricate the bushings at the recommended intervals. Stop injecting grease when it oozes out around the dust seal of the upper arm pivot shaft.

Driveaxle rubber boot check (4WD models)

7   If the driveaxle rubber boots are damaged or deteriorated, serious and costly damage can occur to the CV joints the boots are designed to protect. Therefore, the boots should be checked very carefully at the recommended intervals and whenever the vehicle is raised for servicing.
8   Raise the front of the vehicle and support it securely with jackstands.
9   Crawl under the vehicle and check the four driveaxle boots (two on each driveaxle) very carefully for cracks, tears, holes, deteriorated rubber and loose or missing clamps. If the boots are dirty, wipe them clean before beginning the inspection.
10 If damage or deterioration is evident, the boots must be replaced with new ones.

Manual transmission/transfer case oil change

11 On vehicles used under severe conditions (see Routine maintenance intervals), the manual transmission and transfer case oil must be changed at the recommended interval. Before proceeding, purchase enough of the specified oil to refill the transmission/transfer case.

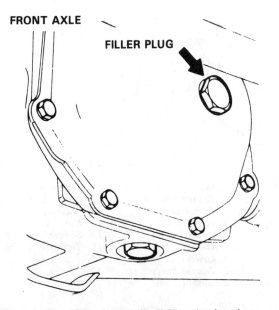

FRONT AXLE

FILLER PLUG

Fig. 13.1 Front axle oil filler plug location

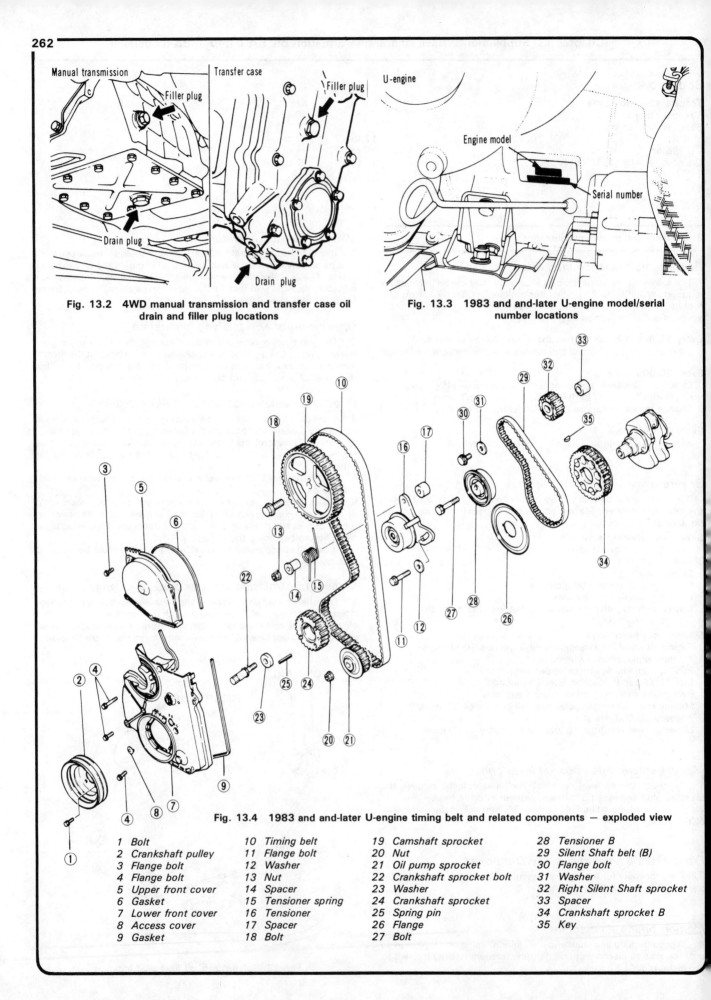

Fig. 13.2 4WD manual transmission and transfer case oil drain and filler plug locations

Fig. 13.3 1983 and and-later U-engine model/serial number locations

Fig. 13.4 1983 and and-later U-engine timing belt and related components — exploded view

1 Bolt	10 Timing belt	19 Camshaft sprocket	28 Tensioner B
2 Crankshaft pulley	11 Flange bolt	20 Nut	29 Silent Shaft belt (B)
3 Flange bolt	12 Washer	21 Oil pump sprocket	30 Flange bolt
4 Flange bolt	13 Nut	22 Crankshaft sprocket bolt	31 Washer
5 Upper front cover	14 Spacer	23 Washer	32 Right Silent Shaft sprocket
6 Gasket	15 Tensioner spring	24 Crankshaft sprocket	33 Spacer
7 Lower front cover	16 Tensioner	25 Spring pin	34 Crankshaft sprocket B
8 Access cover	17 Spacer	26 Flange	35 Key
9 Gasket	18 Bolt	27 Bolt	

12 The oil should be drained immediately after the vehicle has been driven. This will remove any contaminants better than if the oil were cold. Because of this, it may be a good idea to wear gloves while removing the drain plug.

13 After the vehicle has been driven to warm up the oil, raise it and place it on jackstands for access underneath. Make sure it is securely supported and as level as possible.

14 Move the necessary tools and a drain pan under the vehicle, being careful not to touch any hot exhaust or engine components. Place the drain pan under the appropriate component (transmission or transfer case) and remove the drain plug. Be careful not to burn yourself with the hot oil.

15 Allow the oil to drain completely, then reinstall the plug and tighten it securely. Next clean the area around the filler plug, then remove the plug.

16 Using a hand pump or squeeze bottle, fill the transmission/transfer case to the bottom of the filler hole with the recommended oil.

17 Reinstall the filler plug and tighten it securely, then lower the vehicle, test drive it and check for leaks around the plugs.

18 Pour the old oil into a sealable container and dispose of it at a service station or reclamation center.

U-engine timing belt replacement

19 Refer to Section 4 for this procedure.

---

4 Engine

General information

The engines used in later models are very nearly identical to the ones covered in Chapter 2. The major changes include the use of rubber belts instead of chains to drive the camshaft and Silent Shafts on U-engines from 1983 on and the addition of automatic valve lash adjusters on both U and W-engines in 1985 (intake and exhaust valves only). Minor changes are reflected in the Specifications at the front of this Chapter.

U-engine model/serial number locations

1 The engine model and serial numbers on 1983 and and-later U-engines are stamped into the right side of the engine block immediately above the oil dipstick.

Cylinder head removal

2 Follow the procedure in Chapter 2, or below, but note that on engines with automatic valve lash adjusters, you must install the special holders available from your dealer or tape the lash adjusters in place so they don't fall out when the rocker arm shaft assembly is removed.

3 On the U-engine with belt-driven camshaft only, follow the procedure in Chapter 2, but before positioning the number 1 piston at TDC on the compression stroke (Step 2), remove the upper timing belt front cover.

4 Turn the crankshaft until the marks on the cover and the camshaft sprocket are aligned. Mark the timing belt with a felt tip pen or a piece of chalk in line with the mark on the sprocket.

On-vehicle timing belt adjustment

5 If noise due to improper belt tension occurs, the belt tension can be adjusted. The right Silent Shaft belt adjustment is not included, since the front lower cover cannot be removed with the engine in the vehicle.

6 Remove the upper timing belt front cover, then carefully check the belt around its entire circumference for cracks and delamination.

7 Turn the crankshaft in a clockwise direction until the mark on the camshaft sprocket is aligned with the mark on the cylinder head or front cover. Do not turn the crankshaft counterclockwise or improper belt tension will result.

8 Continue turning the crankshaft very slowly until the second tooth past the timing mark is aligned with the mark on the cylinder head or cover as shown in the accompanying illustration.

9 Pry out the two access covers in the front of the timing belt cover.

10 Insert a socket through each cover and loosen the belt tensioner bolt and nut. **Caution:** *Loosen them only 180 to 200 degrees to avoid removing them completely and losing them inside the front cover.*

11 Insert a large screwdriver into the top of the timing belt cover and push the tensioner bracket to the right. This will free the tensioner and allow the large spring to automatically tension the belt the correct amount.

12 Tighten the tensioner mounting bolt first (bottom), then tighten the nut (top). If the nut is tightened first, improper belt tension will result.

13 Install the access covers and the timing belt upper front cover.

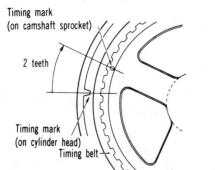

Fig. 13.5 Turn the crankshaft until the mark on the camshaft sprocket is two teeth past the mark on the head/cover when adjusting the belt in the vehicle

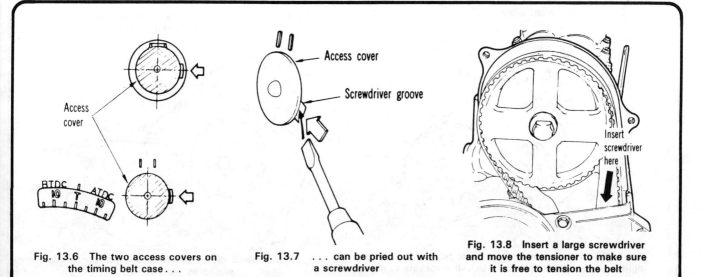

Fig. 13.6 The two access covers on the timing belt case...

Fig. 13.7 ...can be pried out with a screwdriver

Fig. 13.8 Insert a large screwdriver and move the tensioner to make sure it is free to tension the belt

Camshaft/Silent Shaft drivebelt removal, inspection and installation

Removal

14 It is assumed at this point that the engine has been removed from the vehicle and mounted on an engine stand. Remove the bolts and separate the crankshaft pulley from the sprocket.

15 Remove the upper and lower front timing belt covers, then remove the crankshaft sprocket mounting bolt. To keep the crankshaft from turning, hold the flywheel or install two flywheel mounting bolts in the rear crankshaft flange (180° apart) and wedge a large screwdriver between the bolts.

16 Loosen the belt tensioner nut and bolt, push the tensioner to the left and tighten the nut to prevent the tensioner from springing back.

17 After the tensioner has been released, slip the belt off the sprockets.

18 Remove the tensioner, the camshaft sprocket, the crankshaft sprockets and the flange and spacer.

19 Remove the plug from the bottom of the cylinder block on the left side. Insert a screwdriver through the opening to hold the Silent Shaft in position. **Note:** *The screwdriver should have a shank 0.3 in (8 mm) in diameter and it should be inserted into the hole at least 2.4 in (60 mm).*

20 Unscrew the nut securing the sprocket to the oil pump and detach the sprocket.

21 Loosen the mounting bolt for the right Silent Shaft sprocket until it can be turned by hand.

22 Remove the Silent Shaft belt tensioner "B" then separate the timing belt "B" from the sprockets as shown in the accompanying illustration.

23 Unscrew the bolt securing the right Silent Shaft sprocket. Remove the crankshaft sprocket "B" and the Silent Shaft sprocket and spacer.

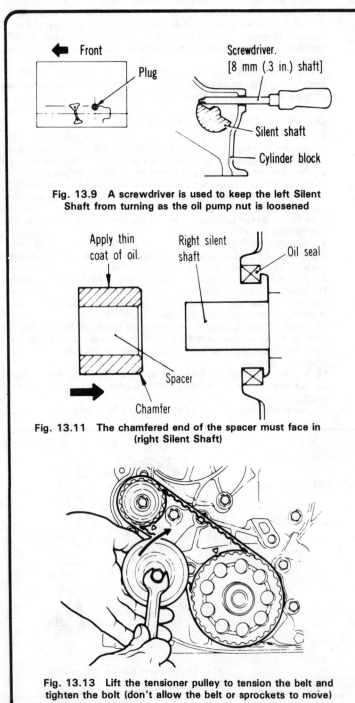

Fig. 13.9   A screwdriver is used to keep the left Silent Shaft from turning as the oil pump nut is loosened

Fig. 13.11   The chamfered end of the spacer must face in (right Silent Shaft)

Fig. 13.13   Lift the tensioner pulley to tension the belt and tighten the bolt (don't allow the belt or sprockets to move)

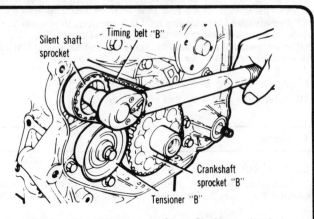

Fig. 13.10   Loosening the right Silent Shaft sprocket bolt

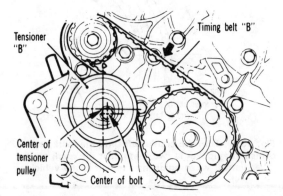

Fig. 13.12   Make sure the tensioner pulley is to the left of the bolt head

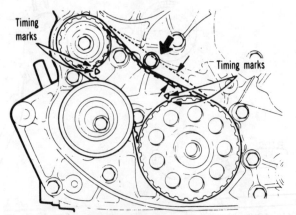

Fig. 13.14   Check the tension by pushing at the location shown by the arrows

Inspection

24 Check the belt carefully for oil and dirt deposits. Slight deposits can be removed with a shop towel. **Caution:** *Do not clean the belt with solvent.*

25 Whenever the belt is removed or the tension adjusted, check the belt for hardened or cracked back surface rubber, cracked or separated plies, worn, cracked or missing teeth and cracked or worn sides.

26 Check the sprockets and tensioner for cracks, damage and abnormal wear. The surfaces of the oil pump sprocket and camshaft spacer that contact the oil seals should also be checked for wear. Check the tensioner pulley for smooth operation. Replace any worn or damaged parts with new ones.

Installation

27 Apply oil to the outside surface of the spacer and slide it onto the right Silent Shaft with the chamfered end in. Position the Silent Shaft sprocket on the shaft, align the timing mark and temporarily tighten the mounting bolt.

28 Slide the crankshaft sprocket ''B'' onto the end of the crankshaft aligning the timing mark with the mark on the front case.

29 Place the timing belt ''B'' over the two sprockets. Be sure there is no slack in the belt on the tension side.

30 Install the tensioner pulley ''B'' with the center of the pulley to the left of the mounting bolt as shown in the accompanying illustration. The pulley flange must face the front of the engine. Lift on the pulley to tension the belt, then tighten the pulley bolt. Make sure the marks are aligned, then depress the tension side of the belt and see if it deflects 0.20 to 0.30 in (5 to 7 mm).

31 Align the timing mark on the oil pump with the mark on the engine. Install the oil pump sprocket and tighten the bolt to the specified torque.

32 Insert a screwdriver into the block as described in Step 19. If the screwdriver cannot be inserted at least 2.4 inches, turn the oil pump sprocket one complete revolution and realign the timing marks. Leave the screwdriver in position until the timing belt is installed.

33 Slip the spacer, the flange and the sprocket onto the crankshaft, then install the sprocket mounting bolt and tighten it to the specified torque. Make sure the lip on the flange is directed away from the timing belt as shown in the accompanying illustration. Turn the crankshaft until the flange notch is aligned with the pointer on the engine case.

34 Apply a thin coat of engine oil to the outside of the camshaft. Install the camshaft sprocket, tighten the bolt to the specified torque and align the timing marks on the sprocket and cover or cylinder head.

35 Install the tensioner spring, then install the tensioner and temporarily tighten the nut. The front end of the spring (bent at right angles) fits over the projection on the tensioner and the other end (straight) rests against the water pump body. Push the lower flange to the left, align the holes and install the bolt.

36 Push the tensioner to the left as far as possible and temporarily tighten the nut, then slip the timing belt onto the sprockets. The belt should be installed first on the crankshaft sprocket, then on the oil pump and camshaft sprockets. Check to make sure that the timing marks on the individual sprockets are properly aligned.

37 Temporarily install the crankshaft pulley to prevent misalignment of the belt as the crankshaft is turned, then loosen the tensioner mounting bolt and nut. The tensioner will be moved by the spring and will apply tension to the belt. Make sure the belt is completely meshed with each of the sprockets.

38 Tighten the tensioner mounting nut and bolt. Be sure to tighten the nut before tightening the bolt, or the tensioner may be turned and the belt given more tension than required.

39 Once again, check to ensure that the timing marks on all of the sprockets are properly aligned, then turn the crankshaft clockwise through a complete rotation. This will apply the proper tension to the timing belt. Make sure that the crankshaft is turned smoothly in a clockwise direction and do not push or shake the belt.

40 Loosen the tensioner mounting bolt and but. The trailing side of the belt will be tensioned. Then retighten them. Tighten the nut first, then tighten the bolt.

41 Check to ensure that when the center of the tension side of the belt and the under cover are held between the thumb and the forefinger the clearance between the belt and the cover is 0.550 in (14 mm). Repeat the adjustment procedure if necessary.

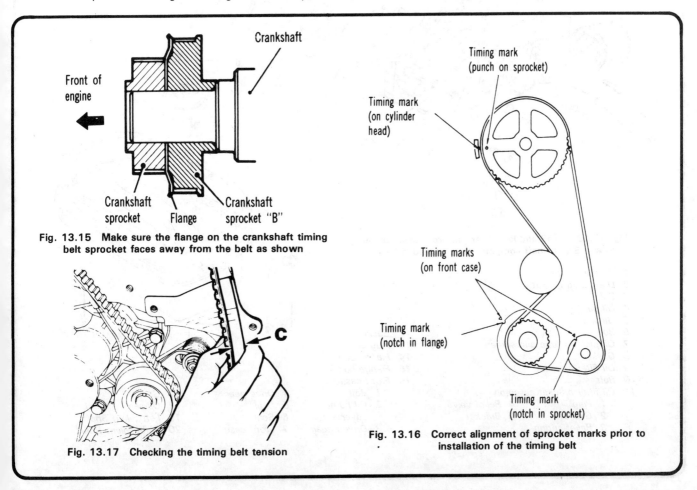

Fig. 13.15 Make sure the flange on the crankshaft timing belt sprocket faces away from the belt as shown

Fig. 13.17 Checking the timing belt tension

Fig. 13.16 Correct alignment of sprocket marks prior to installation of the timing belt

42 Remove the crankshaft pulley and install the upper and lower front timing belt covers.
43 Reinstall the crankshaft pulley and tighten the bolts.

Front case, oil pump and Silent Shaft removal and installation (U-engine with belt driven camshaft only)

44 It is assumed at this point that the engine has been removed from the vehicle. Remove the camshaft drivebelt and the Silent Shaft drivebelt as described above and make sure the oil pan has been removed.
45 Remove the bolts and detach the oil filter bracket assembly and the oil pick-up tube and screen.
46 Loosen the bolts in a criss-cross pattern, then remove them and carefully separate the front case and oil pump from the engine block. Do not pry on the case and do not damage the gasket sealing surfaces.

Be sure to mark the bolts and holes so they can be reinstalled correctly (they are different lengths and must not be mixed up).
47 The Silent Shafts can be removed after the front case has been detached.
48 Remove all traces of the old gasket(s) from the case and the engine block. be very careful not to nick or otherwise damage the cover gasket surface.
49 Clean the case with solvent, then check it for cracks and other damage and wear. The seals should be removed and new ones carefully driven into place with a section of pipe and a hammer.
50 The oil pump can be checked as described in Chapter 2.
51 Installation is the reverse of removal. Be sure to use a new gasket and do not damage the oil seal lips as the front case is positioned on the engine block. Tighten the bolts in a criss-cross pattern and work up to the final torque in three steps.

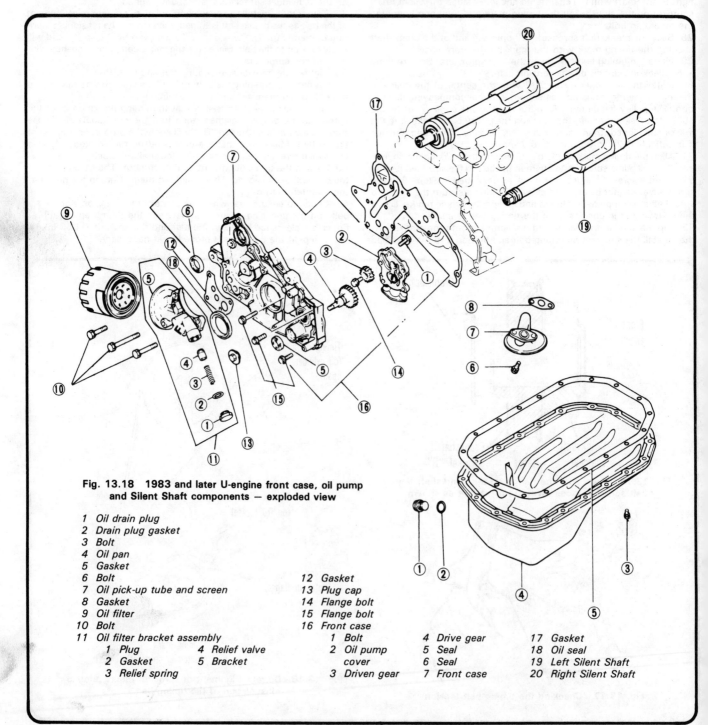

Fig. 13.18   1983 and later U-engine front case, oil pump and Silent Shaft components — exploded view

1   Oil drain plug
2   Drain plug gasket
3   Bolt
4   Oil pan
5   Gasket
6   Bolt
7   Oil pick-up tube and screen
8   Gasket
9   Oil filter
10 Bolt
11 Oil filter bracket assembly
    1   Plug
    2   Gasket
    3   Relief spring
    4   Relief valve
    5   Bracket

12 Gasket
13 Plug cap
14 Flange bolt
15 Flange bolt
16 Front case
    1   Bolt
    2   Oil pump cover
    3   Driven gear
    4   Drive gear
    5   Seal
    6   Seal
    7   Front case

17 Gasket
18 Oil seal
19 Left Silent Shaft
20 Right Silent Shaft

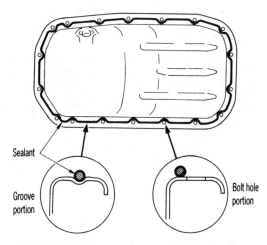

Fig. 13.19 Oil pan sealant application details

Oil pan removal and installation

52 On later model engines the oil pan gasket has been eliminated and RTV-type sealant is used in its place. Follow the procedure in Chapter 2, but apply the sealant to the oil pan as shown in the accompanying illustration. The bead must be approximately four millimeters in diameter to provide an adequate seal and the pan must be installed within 15 minutes of application of the sealant.

5 Cooling, heating and air conditioning

Water cut valve check and installation

1 A water cut valve is installed in the bypass hose attached to the intake manifold on 1986 and later models. It prevents warm coolant from flowing back to the carburetor when the key is in the Off position (which eliminates difficult restarts).
2 The valve should allow coolant to pass in the direction indicated by the arrow in the accompanying illustration (compressed air can be used to see if the valve opens or not).
3 If the valve is removed for any reason or replaced with a new one, make sure the arrow points toward the fitting as shown.

6 Fuel and exhaust systems

General information

The fuel system on later model vehicles is essentially the same as the system covered in Chapter 4. Minor changes were, of course, made to the carburetor over the years to keep pace with emissions and driveability requirements. A rather complex electronic feedback carburetor is used on 1985 and later models (more information on the FBC is included in the Section on Emissions control systems). **Warning:** *Gasoline is extremely flammable, so extra precautions must be taken when working on any part of the fuel system. Do not smoke or allow open flames or bare light bulbs near the work area. Also, do not work in a garage if a natural gas-type appliance with a pilot light is present (such as a water heater).*

Fuel filter replacement

1 In addition to the in-line filter, 1982 and later models are also equipped with an in-tank filter that may require servicing. Although it will not normally have to be replaced, it may become clogged and require cleaning.
2 To gain access to the filter, simply remove the drain plug from the fuel tank (make sure the tank is empty when this is done). Clean the filter and replace the plug (make sure the pickup tube in the tank is directed into the filter).
3 If the filter is damaged or cannot be cleaned, replace it with a new one by levering it out of the plug. Press the new filter into place until the claws snap into the locking holes in the drain plug.

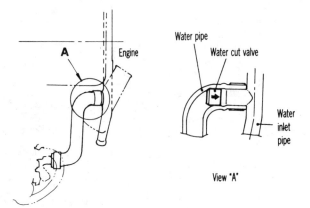

Fig. 13.20 Make sure the water cut valve is installed with the arrow pointing away from the intake manifold

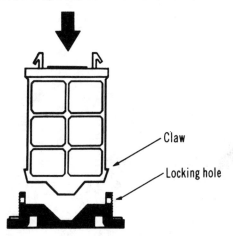

Fig. 13.21 Align the claws with the locking holes when replacing the in-tank fuel filter

4 Make sure the packing material on the drain plug is in good condition and tighten the plug securely.

Fuel pump removal and installation

5 The fuel pump installed on 1983 and later U-engines is actuated by a pushrod that may fall out when the pump is detached from the engine. Make sure the pushrod is in place when installing the pump.

Carburetor removal

6 Follow the procedure in Chapter 4, but note the following important points:
  a) On all models, drain enough coolant from the radiator to lower the level below the intake manifold.
  b) On 1985 and later models, be sure to disconnect the wires from the solenoid valves, the TPS and the ISC.

Carburetor disassembly, inspection and reassembly
1981 thru 1984
7 The procedure for carburetors installed on 1981 through 1984 models is essentially the same as described in Chapter 4, but be aware that detail changes made during the years may slightly affect the disassembly and reassembly sequence. Also, when checking the float level on 1984 models, measure the distance from the bottom of the float to the gasket surface of the float chamber (it should be 0.787 ± 0.394 inches (20 ± 1 mm).
1985 and later
Note: *Do not remove the choke and throttle valves from the shafts.*
8 Remove the coolant hose, the throttle return spring and the damper spring.
9 On USA models, grind off the heads on the choke cover screws with a hand grinder, then remove the cover.

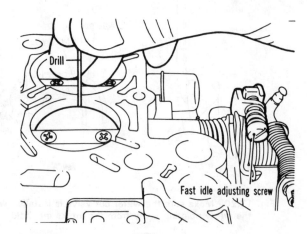

Fig. 13.22 Checking the fast idle opening with a drill bit
(1985 and later)

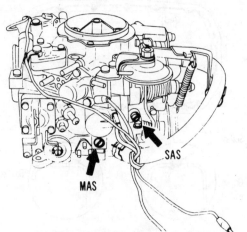
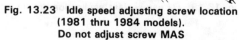

Fig. 13.23 Idle speed adjusting screw location
(1981 thru 1984 models).
Do not adjust screw MAS

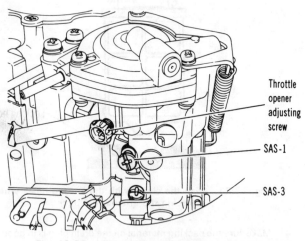

Fig. 13.24 Idle speed adjusting screw locations
(1985 and later models)

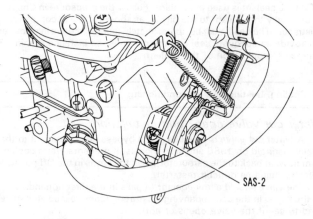

Fig. 13.25 Do not touch screw number 2 — it is factory
pre-set (1985 and later models)

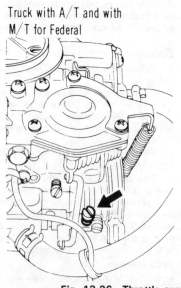

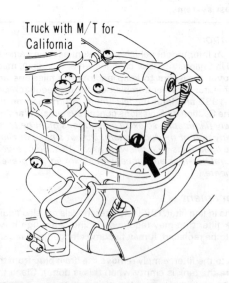

Fig. 13.26 Throttle opener adjusting screw location
(1981 thru 1983 models)

10 On USA models, remove the throttle position sensor (TPS).

11 Separate the throttle opener/dashpot rod from the free lever and the float chamber cover, then remove the throttle opener/dashpot.

12 On USA models, unplug the wiring harness connectors, then remove the three solenoid valves from the float chamber cover by unscrewing them.

13 Refer to Steps 8 and 9 in Section 12 of Chapter 4 (USA models only).

14 Remove the vacuum hose from the depression chamber and the throttle body fitting.

15 Remove the screws and detach the choke breaker cover.

16 Detach the rod from the secondary throttle lever, then remove the depression chamber.

17 Detach the accelerator pump rod from the throttle lever.

18 Remove the snap-ring from the choke rod, then disconnect the rod from the choke lever.

19 Refer to Step 22 in Section 12 of Chapter 4 for the remainder of the disassembly procedure.

20 The components removed in Steps 8 through 18 above can be reinstalled by reversing the procedure.

21 Check the float level as described above for 1984 models (Step 7). If adjustment is necessary, add or remove shims from under the inlet needle seat (Chapter 4, Section 12, Step 43).

22 The fast idle opening can be checked by inserting the specified size drill bit between the throttle valve and the bore wall (the carburetor must be at 73°F for at least one hour before making the check). Adjust the opening by turning the fast idle adjusting screw.

Idle speed and mixture adjustment

23 Due to the need for special equipment and expertise required to ensure compliance with emissions regulations, the fuel/air mixture must be adjusted by a dealer service department or a repair shop. The idle speed can be adjusted as follows (refer to Steps 3 and 4 in Section 14 of Chapter 4 before proceeding).

24 Start the engine and allow it to run until it reaches normal operating temperature, then drive it at speeds greater than 30 mph for at least five minutes (as an alternative, race the engine at 2000 to 3000 rpm for a minimum of five seconds).

25 Allow the engine to return to idle and leave it for two minutes.

26 Check the idle speed and compare it to the Specifications or the vehicle Emission Control Information label under the hood.

27 If adjustment is required, turn the idle speed adjusting screw (SAS in the accompanying illustration) until the idle speed is correct. Do not attempt to adjust screw MAS. **Caution:** *On 1984 and later models, do not touch idle speed adjusting screw number two (SAS-2). It is preset at the factory and if disturbed will affect the throttle opener and dashpot adjustment.*

28 On vehicles equipped with air conditioning, an idle up adjustment can also be made.

29 On 1981 models, lift the throttle opener lever by hand until it stops, then check the idle-up speed. If adjustment is required, turn the throttle opener adjusting screw as shown in the accompanying illustration until the specified speed is obtained.

30 On 1982 and 1984 and later models, switch the air conditioner on and check the idle-up speed. If adjustment is necessary, turn the throttle opener adjusting screw.

31 On 1983 models, make sure the air conditioner is off, then disconnect the vacuum hose from the throttle opener fitting. Connect a hand vacuum pump to the fitting and apply a vacuum (500 mm-Hg) to the throttle opener.

32 Check the idle-up speed. If it is not as specified, turn the throttle opener adjusting screw as required.

---

7 Ignition and starting systems

General information

Later model vehicles are equipped with ignition and starting systems which differ from earlier models only in certain details that do not appreciably affect maintenance and service procedures. Therefore, the material in Chapter 5 can be used in most cases. Note that 1986 and later models may be equipped with either Mitsubishi or Nippon-Denso distributors.

Secondary ignition test

1 This check has been changed slightly for later models.

1981 and 1982

2 On these models, disconnect the secondary coil wire from the distributor cap and hold the end about 1/4 inch from the engine block.

3 Turn the ignition switch on. Remove the distributor cap and turn the rotor in the normal direction of rotation until it stops, then return it to its original position. As this is done, a spark should occur between the coil wire and engine block.

4 If no spark occurs, the IC igniter or ignition coil may be bad (before replacing them, have the ignition system checked by a dealer service department).

1983

5 Repeat the check described in Steps 2 through 4 above.

6 If no spark is produced, remove the distributor cap and rotor and move a screwdriver in and out of the gap between one of the stator poles and the signal rotor projection as shown in the accompanying illustration.

7 If no spark is produced, refer to Step 4 above.

1984 and later

8 Disconnect the coil wire from the distributor cap and hold the end about 1/4 inch from the engine block.

9 Remove the distributor cap and turn the engine over by hand until the signal rotor is positioned as shown in the accompanying illustration (the projections must be clear of the pick-up coil).

10 Turn the ignition switch on and move the tip of a screwdriver in and out of the gap between the pick-up coil and the signal rotor as shown.

11 If no spark is produced, refer to Step 4 above.

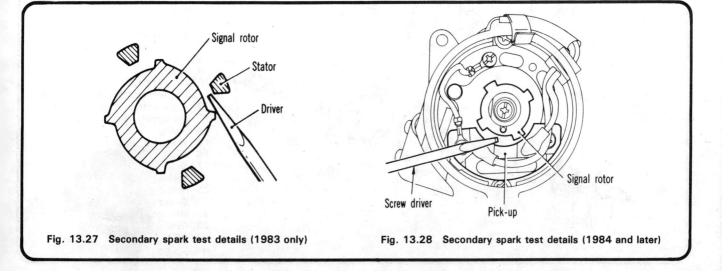

Fig. 13.27 Secondary spark test details (1983 only)   **Fig. 13.28 Secondary spark test details (1984 and later)**

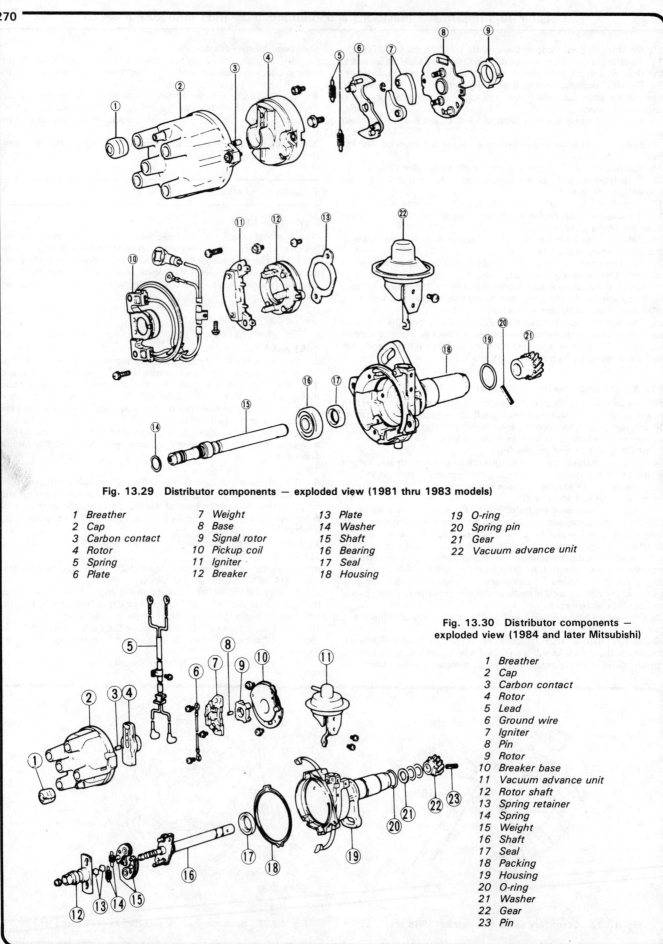

Fig. 13.29 Distributor components — exploded view (1981 thru 1983 models)

1 Breather	7 Weight	13 Plate	19 O-ring
2 Cap	8 Base	14 Washer	20 Spring pin
3 Carbon contact	9 Signal rotor	15 Shaft	21 Gear
4 Rotor	10 Pickup coil	16 Bearing	22 Vacuum advance unit
5 Spring	11 Igniter	17 Seal	
6 Plate	12 Breaker	18 Housing	

Fig. 13.30 Distributor components — exploded view (1984 and later Mitsubishi)

1 Breather
2 Cap
3 Carbon contact
4 Rotor
5 Lead
6 Ground wire
7 Igniter
8 Pin
9 Rotor
10 Breaker base
11 Vacuum advance unit
12 Rotor shaft
13 Spring retainer
14 Spring
15 Weight
16 Shaft
17 Seal
18 Packing
19 Housing
20 O-ring
21 Washer
22 Gear
23 Pin

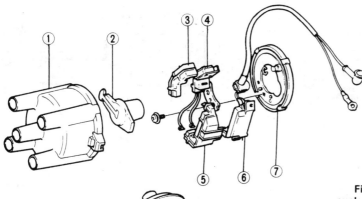

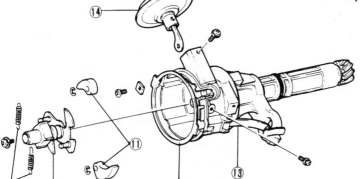

Fig. 13.31 Distributor components —
exploded view (1986 and later Nippon-Denso)

1 Cap
2 Rotor
3 Cover
4 Signal generator
5 Cover
6 Igniter
7 Breaker plate
8 Cap
9 Spring
10 Signal rotor shaft
11 Weight
12 Packing
13 Housing
14 Vacuum advance unit

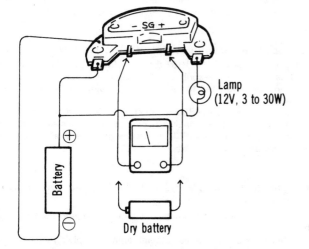

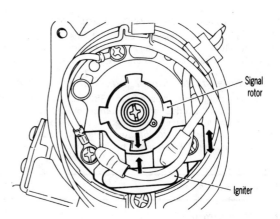

Fig. 13.32 Igniter check details (1981 thru 1983 models)   Fig. 13.33 Adjusting the air gap (1984 and later models)

Distributor disassembly, inspection and reassembly

12 Follow the procedure in Chapter 5, but note that later model distributors differ in certain details. Refer to the accompanying exploded view illustrations if problems are encountered.

13 On 1984 and later models (Mitsubishi distributor only), be sure to mark the relationship between the drive gear and distributor shaft before driving out the roll pin.

14 The igniter (control unit) on 1981 through 1983 models can be checked as follows. Connect jumper wires from the battery and a 12-volt test light to the igniter terminals as shown in the accompanying illustration.

15 Connect an ohmmeter or small dry cell to the remaining terminals

as shown (this will apply a small signal voltage to the igniter).

16 If the test light glows when the signal is applied and goes out when it is removed, the igniter is apparently working properly. If not, it is defective. **Note:** *Even if the test results are as specified, the igniter may be defective.*

17 When reassembling the distributor, be sure to align the mating marks on the gear and shaft before installing the roll pin (all years).

18 On 1984 and later models the air gap between the signal rotor and pick-up coil must be adjusted after the distributor is reassembled. Insert a brass feeler gauge between the rotor projection and the pick-up coil to check the gap. If adjustment is required, loosen the screws and move the igniter as required.

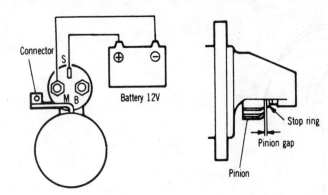

Fig. 13.34   Pinion gap check lead hook-up (1983 and later direct drive motor)

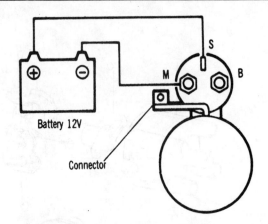

Fig. 13.35   Pull-in check lead hook-up (1983 and later)

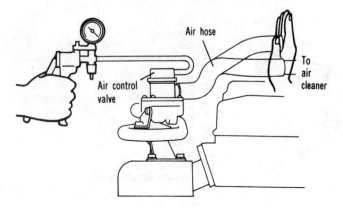

Fig. 13.36   Checking the air control valve diaphragm

Direct drive starter motor overhaul and testing

19 Follow the procedure in Chapter 5, but refer to the new accompanying illustrations when performing the magnetic switch pull-in coil test and the pinion gap check on 1983 and later models.

Reduction drive starter motor overhaul and testing

20 The reduction drive starters used from 1983 on may differ slightly in certain details from the reduction drive starter covered in Chapter 5, but the disassembly and reassembly procedure will not be appreciably affected. Note that the new illustrations for the direct drive starter motor tests mentioned in Step 19 also apply to the reduction drive motor.

8   Emissions control systems

General information

Several additional emissions control systems, including a deceleration spark advance system, a high altitude compensation system, a throttle opener and an electronic feedback carburetor system (1985 and later) have been used on later model vehicles. The existing systems have also been changed slightly to keep pace with more stringent emissions regulations.

Emissions control systems maintenance intervals

In order to ensure control of emissions and acceptable engine performance, the various emission control systems/components should be checked/serviced at the following intervals (in addition to the items outlined in Chapter 6).

Every 15,000 miles or 12 months
Perform the initial check of the throttle position system

Every 30,000 miles
Clean the carburetor choke mechanism and linkage with solvent

Every 50,000 miles
Replace the EGR valve with a new one
Disassemble and clean the sub-EGR valve
Replace the oxygen sensor with a new one (1985 and later)

Every 5 years or 50,000 miles
Check the secondary air supply system (1985 and later)
Check the throttle position system
Replace the vacuum control system solenoid valve/thermo valve air filters (1985 and later — USA)
Check the fasteners on the carburetor to make sure they are tight (1985 and later — USA)

Evaporation control system (ECS) general description

A carbon element, designed to store fuel vapors generated in the carburetor while the engine is off, is installed in the air cleaner on 1982 USA models. No routine maintenance is required, but if the element appears to be clogged or dirty, replace it with a new one.

Secondary air supply system (SAS) general description

The system installed on 1981 through 1984 models is basically the same as the system described in Chapter 6, with an additional reed valve and air pipe used to direct air to a point below the catalytic converter.

The system used on 1985 and later models is somewhat more complex, since it utilizes a secondary air control valve and a solenoid valve, which is controlled by the ECU, to control the flow of air through the reed valve and into the exhaust manifold.

Secondary air supply system (SAS) checking (1985 and later)

1   Refer to Section 12 in Chapter 5 and follow the procedure described there.
2   Check the air control valve diaphragm by applying vacuum with a hand pump (attach the pump to the valve fitting with a section of rubber hose) as shown in the accompanying illustration. The pump gauge needle should remain stable with a vacuum of 500 mm-Hg applied.
3   Start the engine and allow it to idle, then apply a vacuum of 110 mm-Hg or more to the air control valve with the hand pump.
4   Disconnect the hose from the air cleaner and place your hand over the open end of the hose. Suction should be felt.

Dashpot adjustment

5   This adjustment now applies to all Canadian and California models with a manual transmission from 1981 through 1984 and all models for 1985 and later, regardless of transmission type or destination.
6   Follow the procedure in Chapter 5 (Section 19), but disregard Steps 5 and 6. Refer to the accompanying illustrations for the adjusting screw location on later models.

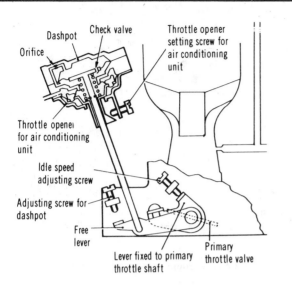

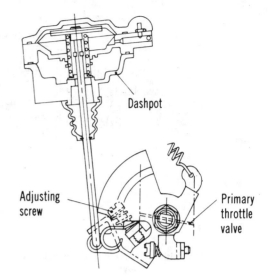

Fig. 13.37 Dashpot adjustment screw location
(1981 and later — USA models)

Fig. 13.38 Dashpot adjustment screw location
(1985 and later — Canada)

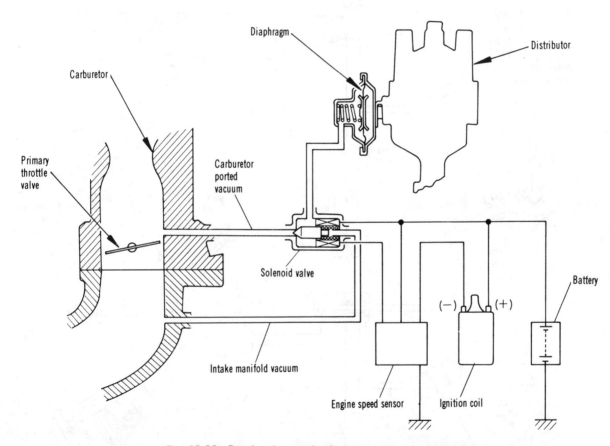

Fig. 13.39 Deceleration spark advance system component layout

Exhaust gas recirculation system (EGR) general description

Although the EGR systems used on later models differ from the system described in Chapter 6 in certain details, the system checks and component removal and installation procedures are unchanged.

Deceleration spark advance system (1981 and 1982)

7   In order to decrease HC emissions emitted during deceleration, ignition timing on these models is advanced by the deceleration spark advance system (ignition timing is normally controlled by ported vacuum and engine speed).

8   The system consists of a solenoid valve, an engine speed sensor and various hoses and wires.

9   During deceleration, ignition timing is advanced by intake manifold vacuum, which acts on the distributor advance unit through the solenoid valve. However, when the speed sensor detects engine speeds at or below a specified level, the vacuum acting on the distributor advance unit is changed to carburetor ported vacuum by the solenoid valve (in order to maintain smooth engine operation).

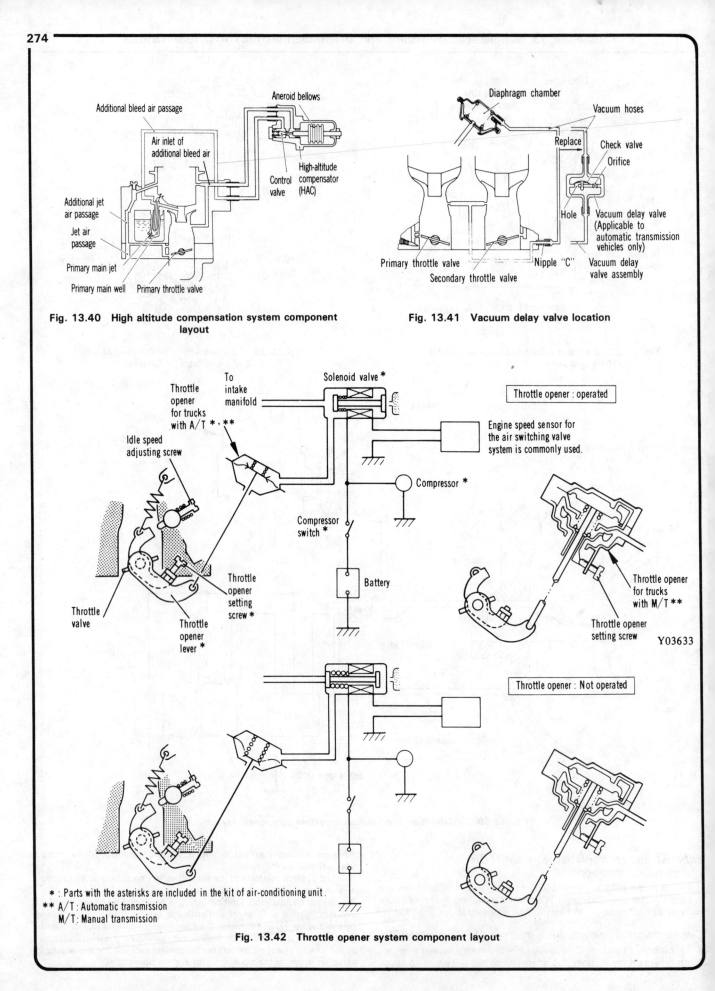

Additional bleed air passage

Air inlet of additional bleed air

Aneroid bellows

Control valve

High-altitude compensator (HAC)

Additional jet air passage

Jet air passage

Primary main jet

Primary main well

Primary throttle valve

Fig. 13.40 High altitude compensation system component layout

Diaphragm chamber

Vacuum hoses

Replace

Check valve

Orifice

Hole

Vacuum delay valve (Applicable to automatic transmission vehicles only)

Primary throttle valve

Secondary throttle valve

Nipple "C"

Vacuum delay valve assembly

Fig. 13.41 Vacuum delay valve location

Throttle opener for trucks with A/T *, **

Idle speed adjusting screw

To intake manifold

Solenoid valve *

Throttle opener : operated

Engine speed sensor for the air switching valve system is commonly used.

Compressor *

Compressor switch *

Battery

Throttle opener setting screw *

Throttle valve

Throttle opener lever *

Throttle opener for trucks with M/T **

Throttle opener setting screw

Y03633

Throttle opener : Not operated

* : Parts with the asterisks are included in the kit of air-conditioning unit.
** A/T : Automatic transmission
M/T : Manual transmission

Fig. 13.42 Throttle opener system component layout

10 Maintenance of the system consists of checking the vacuum hoses for cracks, leaks and secure connections and the wires for damage and secure connections.

11 Operation of the solenoid valve can be verified by applying battery voltage directly to the valve terminals with jumper wires. The advance unit on the distributor can be checked as described in Chapter 5.

High altitude compensation system

12 This system is installed on later model vehicles in order to maintain the appropriate fuel/air mixture at high altitudes. The system affects the primary metering system in the carburetor to alter the fuel/air mixture.

13 A small cylindrical bellows mounted on the fender well, along with several rubber hoses, are the only components of the system.

14 Maintenance consists of checking the hoses for cracks and other damage as well as secure connections.

Vacuum delay valve (1983 and 1984)

15 Vehicles with an automatic transmission are equipped with a vacuum delay valve, which delays the opening of the secondary throttle valve and reduces CO and HC emissions during acceleration.

16 Periodically check the vacuum hoses for cracks, leaks and correct installation. The delay valve itself should be open when a vacuum is applied to one end and restricted when vacuum is applied to the other end.

Throttle opener

17 This system is installed on all vehicles with air conditioning. It consists of a throttle opener assembly, a solenoid valve, an engine speed

sensor and the compressor switch for the air conditioner.

18 The throttle opener opens the throttle slightly when the air conditioning system is turned on (which prevents stalling and increased emissions due to the increased engine load).

19 The throttle opener adjustment is part of the idle speed adjustment procedure (see Section 6).

20 Maintenance consists of checking the vacuum hoses and wires for damage and correct installation and making sure the linkage is not binding in any way.

Feedback carburetor (FBC) system

General description

The fuel/air mixture delivered by the carburetor used on 1985 and later models is controlled by solenoid valves, which are activated by the ECU (electronic control unit). The ECU receives signals from several sensors, including the exhaust gas oxygen sensor, coolant temperature sensor, engine speed sensor, throttle position sensor, vacuum switch and intake air temperature sensor. Depending on the input from the various sensors, the ECU cycles the solenoid valves on the carburetor to regulate the fuel/air mixture to obtain the lowest emissions levels possible while maintaining an acceptable level of driveability.

The fuel inlet, primary metering, secondary metering, accelerator pump and choke systems are essentially the same as in a conventional carburetor. The jet (air) mixture, enrichment and fuel cut-off systems are electronically controlled.

The jet mixture solenoid, which is controlled by the ECU, is used to enrich the mixture if the exhaust gas oxygen sensor detects a lean condition. As the mixture is restored to optimum, the jet mixture solenoid responds appropriately.

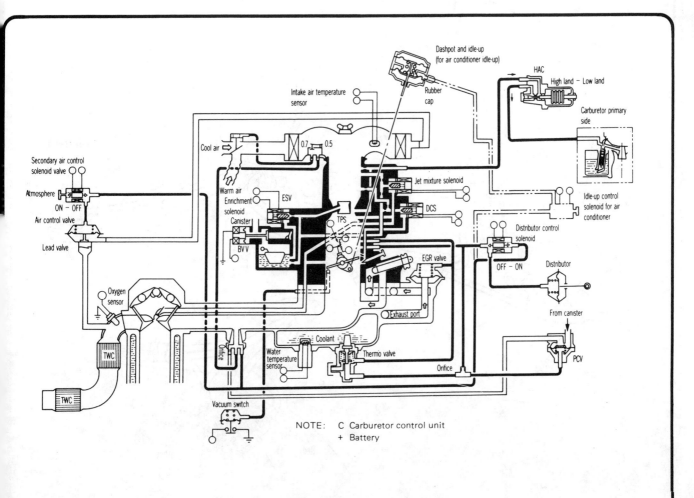

Fig. 13.43 Feedback carburetor system schematic

The enrichment system solenoid is activated in response to increased demand for rich fuel/air mixtures, such as during heavy acceleration or engine loads, cold start and warm-up operation. It provides additional fuel for the main metering system.

The fuel cut-off system deceleration solenoid cuts off fuel flow when the ignition key is turned off to prevent engine run-on (dieseling). Under certain deceleration conditions, the solenoid valve reduces fuel flow to decrease HC emissions and improve fuel economy.

Since the feedback carburetor is rather complex, major troubleshooting and testing of the system should be left to a dealer service department. However, the do-it-yourselfer can perform many of the maintenance checks and testing procedures without special equipment. Symptoms of a problem in the FBC include hard starting or failure to start, unstable idle and poor driveability. If a problem occurs, be sure to check the ignition system and engine mechanical condition before assuming that the FBC is at fault.

Throttle position system check

21 Remove the air cleaner from the engine and check the throttle position sensor plunger operation. Operate the throttle lever and see if the plunger follows the cam mounted on the throttle shaft.
22 Check the sensor body and plunger for damage and cracks.

23 Check the throttle sensor mounting screws to make sure they are tight (do not move the sensor or the fuel/air mixture will be adversely affected).
24 The sensor can be adjusted, but it should be done by a dealer service department (a digital voltmeter is required).

Solenoid valve/thermo valve air filter replacement

25 If the filters on the thermo valve and solenoid valve are clogged, driveability problems will result.
26 The thermo valve has a cap which fits over the filter. If the cap is removed by pulling out on it, the filter can be removed and a new one installed.
27 The solenoid valve filter is a one piece assembly which can be pulled off the valve and replaced with a new one.

Carburetor fastener check

28 To avoid mixture control problems resulting from air and fuel leaks, the carburetor fasteners must be checked and tightened at the recommended intervals.
29 Remove the air cleaner assembly and use a wrench, socket or screwdriver to check the tightness of the carburetor-to-intake manifold bolts, the float chamber cover screws and the accelerator pump mounting screws (see accompanying illustration).

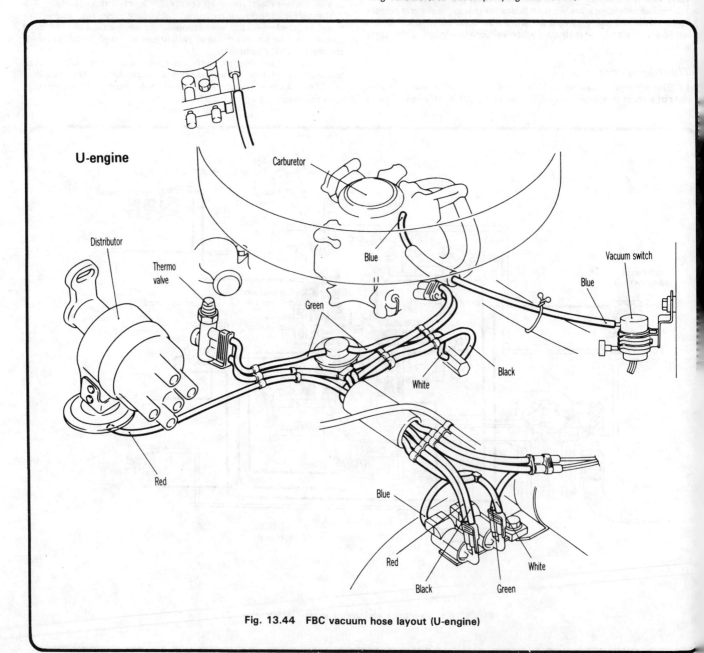

Fig. 13.44   FBC vacuum hose layout (U-engine)

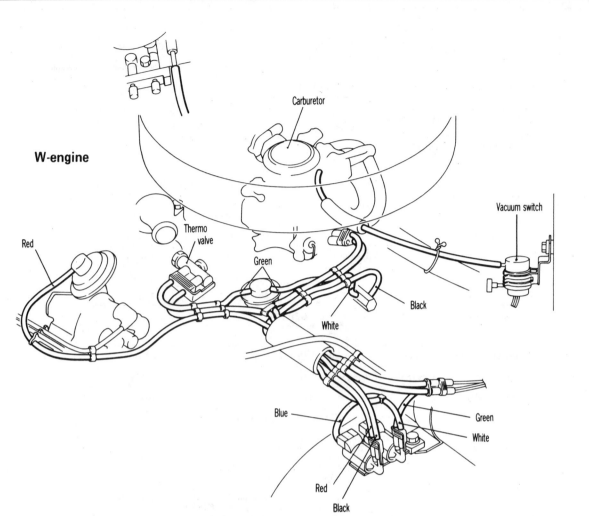

W-engine

Carburetor

Thermo valve

Vacuum switch

Red

Green

Black

White

Blue

Green

White

Red

Black

Fig. 13.45   FBC vacuum hose layout (W-engine)

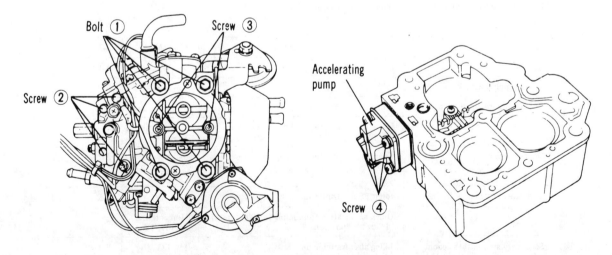

Bolt ① Screw ③

Screw ②

Accelerating pump

Screw ④

Fig. 13.46   The carburetor fasteners must be checked to make sure they are tight or air/fuel leaks will occur

Check item	Condition		Check meter reading when normal	Terminal number of computer
Power supply	Ignition switch OFF → ON		11–13V	A-7
Distributor advance vacuum exchange solenoid valve	Idling		0–1V	B-7
	2000 rpm		13–15V	
Throttle position sensor (TPS)	Ignition switch OFF → ON	Accelerator closed	0.2–1.5V	A-13
		Accelerator wide opened	5V	
Coolant temperature sensor	Ignition switch OFF → ON	20°C (68°F)	2.4–2.6V	A-12
		40°C (104°F)	1.4–1.6V	
		80°C (176°F)	0.5–0.7V	
Intake air temperature sensor	Ignition switch OFF → ON	20°C (68°F)	2.4–2.6V	A-4
		40°C (104°F)	1.4–1.6V	
		80°C (176°F)	0.5–0.7V	
Vacuum switch	Ignition switch OFF → ON		9–11V	A-5
	Idling		0–1V	
Idle up control solenoid valve	Ignition switch OFF → ON		0–0.6V	B-3
Enrichment solenoid valve (ESV)	Ignition switch OFF → ON		11–13V	B-5
A/C cut relay	Ignition switch and A/C switch OFF → ON	Accelerator closed	0–0.6V	B-6
		Accelerator wide opened	11–15V	
Power supply for sensor	Ignition switch OFF → ON		4–5.5V	A-3
Secondary air control solenoid valve	Ignition switch OFF → ON	Coolant temp. 30–40°C (86–104°F)	0–0.6V	B-4
		Coolant temp. Less than 30°C (86°F) or more than 40°C (104°F)	11–13V	

Check item	Condition		Check meter reading when normal	Terminal number of computer
Jet mixture solenoid valve (JSV)	Ignition switch OFF → ON		11–13V	B-1
	Idling		2–10V	
Idle up control solenoid valve	2000 rpm with A/C switch ON		13–15V	B-3
Ignition pulse	Idling		5–7V	A-10
Power supply for back-up	Idling		13–15V	A-9
Deceleration solenoid valve (DSV)	Idling		0–0.6V	B-2
	Quick deceleration from 4000 rpm to idling with "P" or "N" position		Momentarily 13–15V	
Oxygen sensor	Keep 1300 rpm after warming up		0–1V ↕ Flashing 2.7V	A-1
Enrichment solenoid valve (ESV)	Idling after warming up		12–15V	B-5
	Quick acceleration from idling to 4000 rpm with "P" or "N" position		Momentarily approx. 5V	
Secondary air control solenoid valve	Idling after warming up		11–13V	B-4
	Quick deceleration from 2000 rpm to idling with "P" or "N" position		Momentarily 0–0.6V	

Fig. 13.47 FBC control unit voltage check table

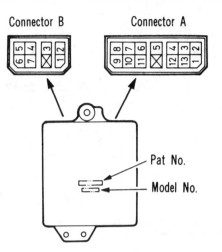

Fig. 13.48   FBC control unit connector terminal locations

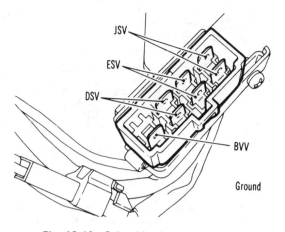

Fig. 13.49   Solenoid valve terminal locations

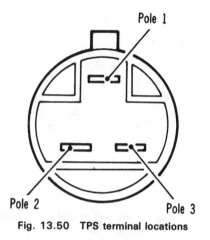

Fig. 13.50   TPS terminal locations

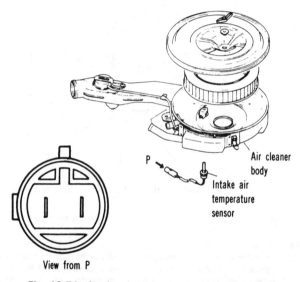

View from P

Fig. 13.51   Intake air temperature sensor location

System check (ECU input/output signals)

30 The FBC system can be checked with a voltmeter by referring to the accompanying terminal identification illustration and chart. The component is listed in the left column and the desired voltmeter reading is indicated in the second column from the right. Attach one voltmeter lead to the computer terminal indicated and the other lead to a good ground when making the check. Be sure to observe the conditions indicated in the chart.

Throttle opener check (A/C only)

31 Check the vacuum hoses and throttle opener control solenoid harness for correct installation.

32 Disconnect the vacuum hose from the fitting on the throttle opener and attach a hand-type vacuum pump to the fitting with a length of hose.

33 Start and run the engine at idle, then apply a vacuum of 11.8 in-Hg (300 mm-Hg) minimum with the pump. The engine speed should increase. If it doesn't, replace the throttle opener with a new one.

Throttle opener solenoid valve check

34 With the ignition switch off, disconnect the wires from the throttle opener solenoid valve.

35 Using an ohmmeter, check the resistance between the solenoid valve terminals (it should be approximately 40 ohms).

Solenoid valve check

36 With the ignition switch off, disconnect the wire harness from the solenoid valve.

37 Using an ohmmeter, check the resistance between the deceleration (DSV), enrichment (ESV) and jet mixture (JSV) solenoid valve terminals (see accompanying illustration). It should be 49.7 ohms.

38 Check the resistance between the bowl vent valve (BVV) terminal and ground. It should be 80 ohms.

39 If a valve is defective, it must be unscrewed from the carburetor and replaced with a new one.

Throttle position sensor check

40 Unplug the throttle position sensor connector and check the resistance between terminals 2 and 3 (see accompanying illustration) with an ohmmeter. When the throttle is closed, it should be approximately 1.2 K ohms.

41 As the throttle is opened, the resistance should increase smoothly until it is approximately 4.9 K ohms when the throttle is wide open.

42 If the sensor is defective, it should be replaced with a new one and adjusted by a dealer service department.

Intake air temperature sensor check

43 The intake air temperature sensor is mounted on the bottom of the air cleaner housing as shown in the accompanying illustration. Unplug the wiring harness connector and check the resistance between the sensor terminals.

44 It should be 2.45 K ohms at 68 °F. If it is considerably larger or smaller than specified, the sensor is open or short circuited and should be replaced with a new one.

Coolant temperature sensor check

45 If some means of monitoring the coolant temperature is available, the sensor can be checked in place by measuring the resistance between the sensor terminal and sensor body with an ohmmeter.

46 At 68 °F, the resistance should be 2.45 K ohms. At 176 °F (coolant temperature), the resistance should be 296 ohms.

47 If the coolant temperature cannot be monitored closely, drain the cooling system (Chapter 1), remove the sensor and heat the end in a pan of water to the specified temperatures, then take the resistance readings. If this is done, make sure the sensor body is at least 1/8 inch away from the water surface.

Fig. 13.52   The change shifter must be tilted to the left on 4-speed transmissions to separate the transfer case

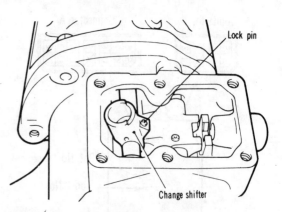

Fig. 13.53   On 5-speed transmissions, drive out the lock pin before attempting to separate the transfer case

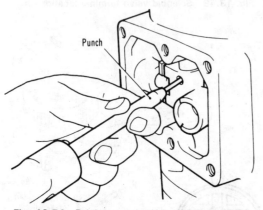

Fig. 13.54   Driving out the H-L shift fork spring pin

48 When reinstalling the sensor, use sealant on the threads and tighten it to 21 ft-lbs (30 Nm).

Vacuum switch check

49 The vacuum switch is mounted on the right side of the firewall.
50 Unplug the wiring harness connector and attach the leads of an ohmmeter or self-powered test light to the switch terminals. No continuity should be indicated.
51 Disconnect the vacuum hose from the switch fitting and attach a hand held vacuum pump to the fitting with a section of hose.
52 Apply a vacuum of 10.2 in-Hg (260 mm-Hg) or more and make sure continuity is indicated. Release the vacuum and verify that continuity is interrupted.
53 If the switch fails the check, replace it with a new one.

---

9   Manual transmission (4WD models only)

Removal and installation

The procedure in Chapter 7 is essentially correct for all vehicles, but note that on four wheel drive models the 4WD indicator switch harness must be unplugged and the bolts for the transfer case mounting bracket must be removed (detach the plate first). Also, be sure to support the rear of the engine with a jack or jackstand before separating the transmission from the engine (place a block of wood between the jack and the oil pan to prevent damage).

---

10   Automatic transmission

General information

1987 and later models use a 4-speed automatic transmission, model number AW372 for 2WD models and model number KM148 for 4WD models. The transmissions are essentially the same with the exception of a different tailshaft housing and the addition of a transfer case on the KM148 model.

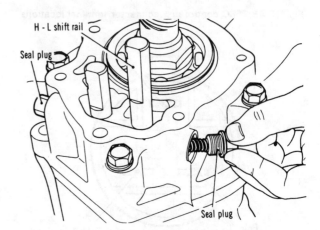

Fig. 13.55   Removing the seal plug to gain access to the springs and balls

The removal and installation procedures given in Chapter 7 Part B remain essentially correct for this transmission. No external band adjustments are possible.

Due to the complexity of the transmission and the special tools and expertise required to overhaul the transmission, the work should be done by a dealer service department or transmission repair shop.

---

11   Transfer case (4WD models only)

Removal and installation

1 The transfer case is removed as part of the transmission removal (see Sections 9 and 10).

Disassembly, inspection and reassembly

Note: *Since the transfer case overhaul requires special tools and expertise normally beyond the scope of the do-it-yourselfer, it may be a good idea to install a new or rebuilt unit rather than go to the trouble of attempting to overhaul a transfer case that is damaged or worn out.*

2 Once the transmission/transfer case assembly has been removed from the vehicle, proceed as follows.
3 Remove the back-up light switch from the lower right side of the adapter and take out the steel ball (M/T only).
4 Remove the plug from the right side of the transfer case and take out the select spring and the steel plunger.
5 If not already done, remove the bolts and detach the control lever assembly.
6 Remove the plug from the top of the adapter and take out the neutral return plunger and spring (4-speed M/T only).
7 Remove the plugs from the top of the adapter and take out the

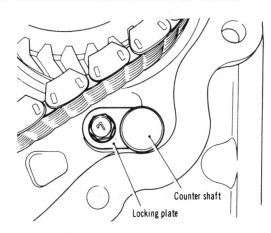

Fig. 13.56 Remove the bolt and locking plate to release the countershaft

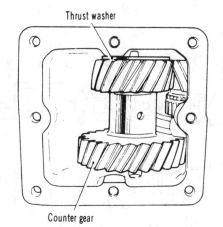

Fig. 13.57 Don't lose the thrust washer as the counter gear is removed

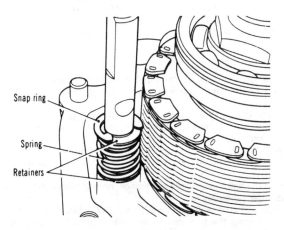

Fig. 13.58 The snap-ring, spring and retainers must be removed from the 2-4WD shift rail

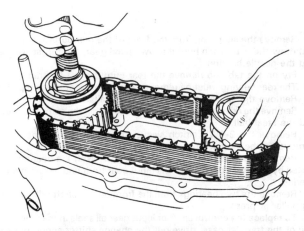

Fig. 13.59 The output shafts and chain are removed as an assembly

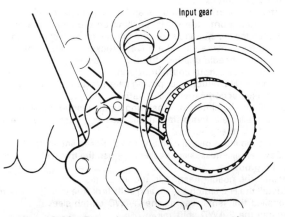

Fig. 13.60 Removing the input gear snap-ring

resistance spring, steel ball, neutral return springs and the plungers (5-speed M/T only).

8   Remove the transfer case adapter-to-transmission bolts (4-speed M/T and A/T only).

9   With the change shifter tilted to the left, remove the control finger from the shift lug groove and take out the shifter case assembly (4-speed M/T only).

10 Drive out the change shifter lock pin with a pin punch and hammer (5-speed M/T only).

11 Remove the four bolts and two nuts holding the transfer case to the adapter (5-speed M/T only).

12 Separate the transfer case from the adapter (5-speed M/T) and remove the change shifter from the control shaft.

Disassembly

13 Unscrew the 4WD switches and take out the steel balls.

14 Remove the speedometer sleeve clamp and sleeve assembly.

15 Remove the bolts and detach the rear cover, gasket and wave spring.

16 Remove the cover, gasket and wave spring.

17 Drive out the H-L shift fork spring pin with a pin punch and hammer.

18 Remove the seal plugs and take out the two poppet springs and balls (a magnet may be helpful here).

19 Pull out the H-L shift rail from the rear.

20 Take out the interlock plunger and remove the snap-ring from the rear bearing of the rear output shaft.

21 Remove the chain cover, the oil guide and the side cover.

22 Remove the bolt and locking plate, then pull out the countershaft.

23 Take out the counter gear, the two thrust washers, the two needle bearings and the spacer through the side cover opening.

24 Remove the snap-ring (E-clip), spring retainers and spring from the 2-4WD shift rail.

25 Remove the front and rear output shafts and the chain from the case as an assembly.

26 Withdraw the 2-4WD shift rail.

27 Remove the H-L shift fork and the clutch sleeve.

28 Remove the needle bearing from the input gear.

29 After removing the large snap-ring, withdraw the input gear assembly.

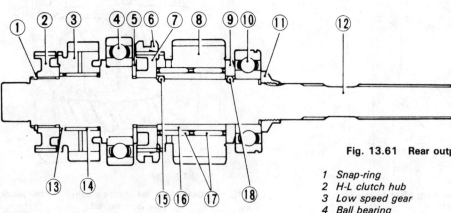

Fig. 13.61   Rear output shaft components

1 Snap-ring	10 Ball bearing
2 H-L clutch hub	11 Locknut
3 Low speed gear	12 Rear output shaft
4 Ball bearing	13 Thrust washer
5 Stop plate	14 Needle bearing
6 2-4WD clutch sleeve	15 Steel ball
7 2-4WD clutch hub	16 Sleeve
8 Drive sprocket	17 Needle bearings
9 Sprocket spacer	18 Steel ball

30   Remove the snap-ring from the front of the rear output shaft and withdraw the H-L clutch hub, the low speed gear, the thrust washer and the needle bearing.

31   Pry up the tab and remove the rear output shaft locknut.

32   The rear bearing must be removed with a press or bearing puller.

33   Remove the sprocket spacer and steel balls.

34   Remove the drive sprocket, the needle bearings, the sprocket sleeve and the steel ball.

35   Remove the 2-4WD clutch sleeve, the hub and the stop plate. Remove the bearing with a puller or press.

36   Remove the snap-ring from the input gear. With the bearing supported by the press base, push the input gear front end to remove the bearing.

37   Remove the two bearings from the front output shaft with a bearing puller or press.

38   To replace the control shaft or input gear oil seals in the front portion of the transfer case, drive out the change shifter spring pin and separate the case from the adapter.

Inspection

39   Wash all parts with clean solvent. Make sure that all old oil, dirt and metal particles are removed. Dry all of the parts with compressed air and lay them out for inspection.

40   Check all gear teeth for evidence of excessive wear and damage. Check all gear splines for burrs, nicks, wear and damage. Minor nicks and scratches can be removed with an oilstone, but replace any part showing significant wear or damage.

41   Inspect all snap-rings and thrust washers and replace any that are worn, distorted or damaged.

42   Inspect the cases for cracks, distortion and stripped bolt hole threads.

43   Inspect all needle, roller and ball bearings and check the shafts for wear and damage.

Reassembly

44   During reassembly, replace all gaskets, oil seals and spring pins (roll pins) with new ones. Apply sealant to all gaskets and plug threads before installation. Lubricate all sliding and rotating parts with gear oil before reassembly.

45   Press new control shaft, input gear and front output shaft oil seals into place in the case (use a hammer and block of wood or a large socket and apply pressure evenly to the outer circumference of the seal only). After installation, apply grease to the seal lips.

46   Assemble the transfer case and adapter with a new gasket placed between them. Be sure to install the change shifter over the control shaft before tightening the bolts and nuts (if this is not done, the change shifter cannot be installed). **Caution:** *When inserting the control shaft through the oil seal, do not damage the seal. If the spring pin hole in the shaft is burred, file the burrs away before inserting the shaft through the seal.*

47   Press the bearing onto the input gear, pushing on the inner race only. After installation, make sure the bearing rotates smoothly and quietly.

48   Fit a snap-ring over the front end of the input gear. Snap-rings are available in five different thicknesses — use the thickest one that will fit in the groove.

49   Press the two ball bearings onto the front output shaft, pushing on the inner race only. After installation, make sure they rotate smoothly and quietly.

50   Press the ball bearing onto the rear of the rear output shaft, pushing on the inner race only.

51   Mount the stop plate and install the 2-4WD clutch hub and sleeve. When mounting the hub and sleeve, pay close attention to the installed direction (see accompanying illustration).

52   Mount the steel ball (for sprocket sleeve positioning) on the rear output shaft and install the sprocket sleeve.

53   Install the two needle bearings over the sprocket sleeve and install the drive sprocket.

54   After installing the steel balls and sprocket spacer, press the remaining bearing onto the shaft, pushing on the inner race only.

55   Tighten the locknut and stake the tab into place with a punch. After the nut is tight, make sure the drive sprocket rotates freely.

56   Install the needle bearing, the thrust washer and the low speed gear on the rear output shaft front end.

57   Install the H-L clutch hub, paying careful attention to the installed direction (see accompanying illustration).

58   Install the H-L clutch hub snap-ring on the rear output shaft. Snap-rings are available in five different thicknesses — use the thickest one that will fit in the groove.

59   Insert the input gear assembly into the case and install the snap-ring. Several thicknesses are available — use the thickest one that will fit in the groove.

60   Install the needle bearing in the input gear.

61   Install the H-L clutch sleeve and shift fork (the clutch sleeve must be installed the same way as the 2-4WD clutch sleeve).

62   Install the 2-4WD shift rail.

63   Engage the chain in the front and rear output shaft sprockets, then assemble the 2-4WD clutch sleeve and shift fork and install the assembly over the shift rail. At the same time, slip the chain and output shafts into place.

64   Install the spring and retainers on the shift rail and attach the snap-ring.

65   Insert the needle bearings and the spacer into the countergear and install the assembly in the case. Install one thrust washer at each end of the countergear.

66   Insert the countershaft and install the locking plate and bolt.

67   Install the side cover and gasket and the oil guide.

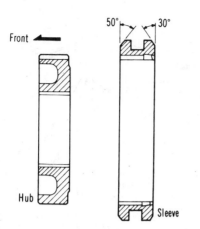

Fig. 13.62 Correct installation of the 2-4WD clutch hub and sleeve

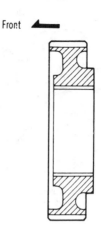

Fig. 13.63 Correct installation of the H-L clutch hub

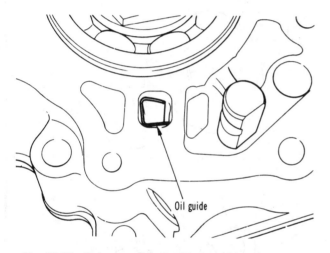

Fig. 13.64 Make sure the oil guide is positioned as shown before installing the chain cover

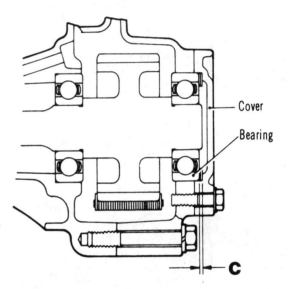

Fig. 13.65 The bearing-to-cover clearance (C) must be as specified

68 Install the chain cover and gasket. Make sure the oil guide end fits into the chain cover opening as shown in the accompanying illustration.
69 Fit the snap-ring in the groove of the rear output shaft rear bearing.
70 Insert the interlock plunger.
71 Insert the H-L shift rail and pass it through the H-L shift fork. If the 2-4WD shift fork is not in the 4WD position, the H-L shift rail will be blocked as it is inserted.
72 Insert the poppet balls and springs (small end toward the ball) and install the seal plugs.
73 With the H-L shift fork and rail holes aligned, install the spring pin with a hammer and punch. Make sure the spring pin slit is aligned with the centerline of the rail.
74 Mount the spacer on the rear end of the rear output shaft bearing and install the rear cover and gasket. Use a spacer that will produce rear bearing outer race end play of 0 to 0.004 inches (0 to 0.1 mm).
75 Position the wave spring on the rear end of the front output shaft rear bearing and install the cover and gasket. If the rear bearing-to-cover clearance as shown in the accompanying illustration exceeds 0.079 inch (2 mm), use a spacer that will reduce it to that amount or less.
76 Insert the speedometer sleeve assembly into the rear cover. Align the mating mark on the sleeve with the mark on the case corresponding to the number of teeth on the driven gear of the speedometer as shown in the accompanying illustration.
77 Install the sleeve clamp and tighten the bolt.
78 Insert the steel balls, then thread the 4WD switches into the case.

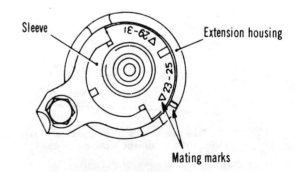

Fig. 13.66 Make sure the mark for the number corresponding to the teeth on the speedometer driven gear is aligned with the case mark

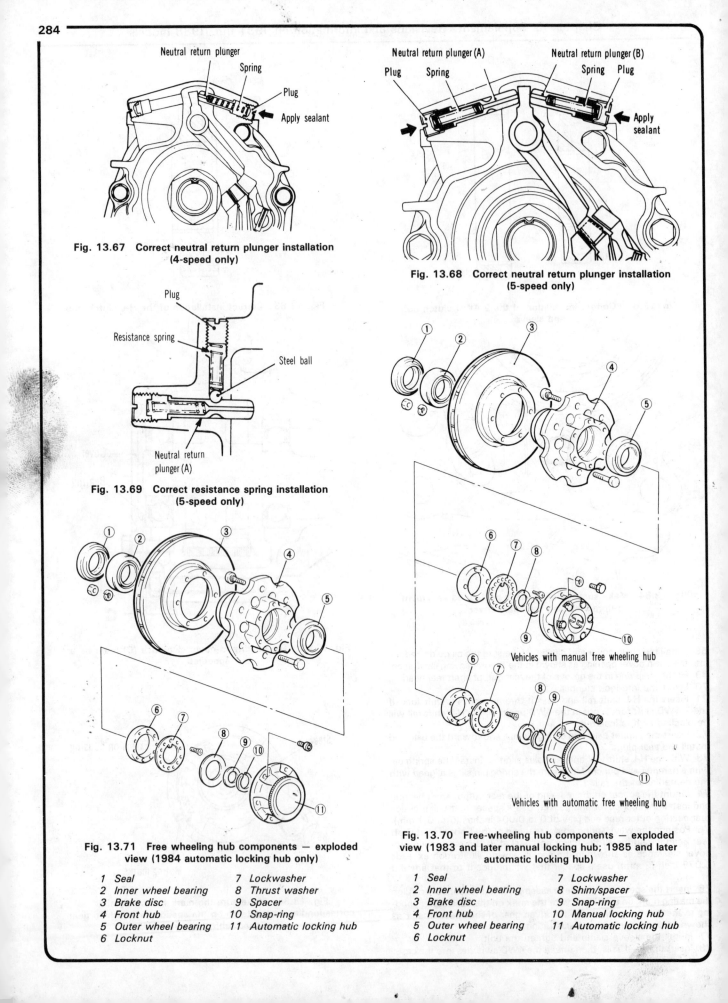

Fig. 13.67 Correct neutral return plunger installation (4-speed only)

Fig. 13.68 Correct neutral return plunger installation (5-speed only)

Fig. 13.69 Correct resistance spring installation (5-speed only)

Vehicles with manual free wheeling hub

Vehicles with automatic free wheeling hub

Fig. 13.70 Free-wheeling hub components — exploded view (1983 and later manual locking hub; 1985 and later automatic locking hub)

Fig. 13.71 Free wheeling hub components — exploded view (1984 automatic locking hub only)

1 Seal	7 Lockwasher
2 Inner wheel bearing	8 Thrust washer
3 Brake disc	9 Spacer
4 Front hub	10 Snap-ring
5 Outer wheel bearing	11 Automatic locking hub
6 Locknut	

1 Seal	7 Lockwasher
2 Inner wheel bearing	8 Shim/spacer
3 Brake disc	9 Snap-ring
4 Front hub	10 Manual locking hub
5 Outer wheel bearing	11 Automatic locking hub
6 Locknut	

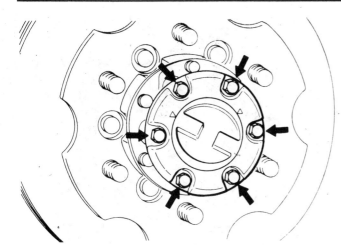

Fig. 13.72 On manual locking hubs, the cover is held in place with several bolts (arrows)

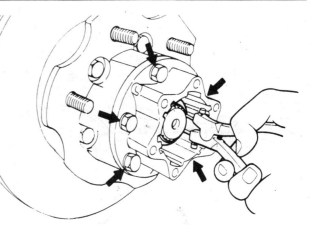

Fig. 13.73 Remove the snap-ring on manual locking hubs

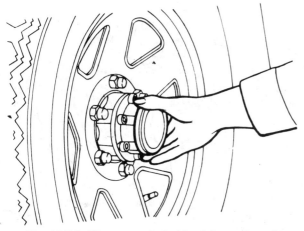

Fig. 13.74 The automatic locking hub cover can be unscrewed

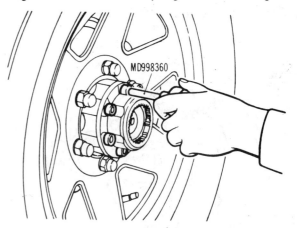

Fig. 13.75 A special tool is needed to unscrew the hub mounting bolts

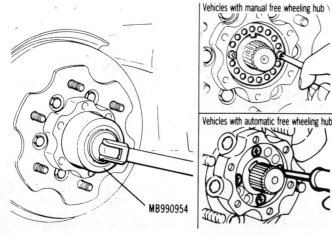
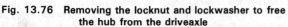

Fig. 13.76 Removing the locknut and lockwasher to free the hub from the driveaxle

79 Attach the transfer case to the transmission by reversing the procedure in Steps 2 through 12. Be sure to install the neutral return plungers and springs in the holes on the top of the adapter as shown in the accompanying illustration. Tighten the plugs until they are flush with the top of the adapter, then apply a sealant to prevent loosening. On 5-speed transmission equipped models, install the steel ball, spring and plug as shown in the accompanying illustration.

12 Driveline (4WD models only)

Front hub and bearing removal, inspection and installation

Note: *Special tools and a great deal of care are required to remove and install the hub on four wheel drive models, so be sure to read through the entire procedure before beginning work. It may be a good idea to leave the job to a dealer service department or repair shop.*

Removal
1   Raise the front of the vehicle and support it securely on jackstands.
2   Refer to Chapter 9 and remove the brake caliper/pad assembly. Do not disconnect the hose from the caliper and do not allow the caliper to hang by the hose — support it with a section of stiff wire so there is no strain on the hose.
3   On manual free wheeling hub models, turn the control handle to the *Free* position and remove the hub cover (it is held in place with several bolts). Remove the snap-ring from the end of the driveaxle with a snap-ring pliers, then remove the bolts and separate the free wheeling hub assembly from the wheel hub by pulling it straight out.
4   On automatic free wheeling hub models, unscrew the free wheeling hub cover (if it cannot be done by hand, wrap a rag around it and use an oil filter wrench to loosen it). Remove the O-ring from the hub cover, then remove the snap-ring and spacer/shim from the end of the driveaxle. Loosen and remove the bolts (a special tool is needed for this), then detach the free wheeling hub from the wheel hub by pulling straight out on it.
5   On all models, remove the screws and detach the lockwasher from the hub.
6   Using the special socket (available from your dealer) and a breaker bar, remove the locknut.
7   Carefully remove the hub from the spindle (don't drop the outer bearing).

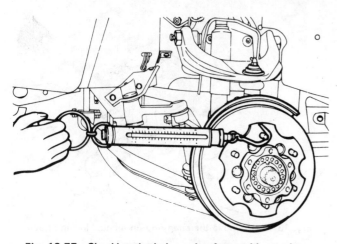

Fig. 13.77   Checking the hub turning force with a spring scale

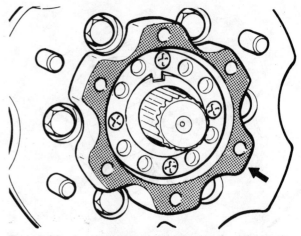

Fig. 13.78   Apply sealant to the shaded area of the hub mating surfaces

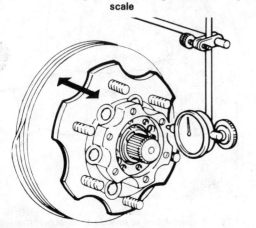

Fig. 13.79   Checking the hub axial play with a dial indicator

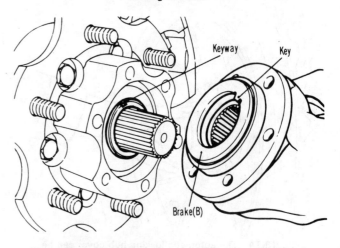

Fig. 13.80   Make sure the key and keyway are aligned when installing the automatic locking hub

Inspection

8   Free wheeling hub disassembly, inspection and reassembly is covered later in this Section. Refer to Chapter 1 for wheel bearing, hub and seal servicing procedures (Steps 6 through 14 in Section 21). If the brake disc and hub must be separated, be sure to mark them to ensure that they are reassembled in their original relationship. Tighten the nuts to the specified torque in a criss-cross pattern and be sure to check the disc runout after the hub is reinstalled (see Chapter 9).

Installation

9   Slide the hub into place on the wheel spindle (be careful not to damage the seal), then install the outer wheel bearing and adjust the bearing preload as follows.
10   Using the special tool and a torque wrench, tighten the locknut to 94 to 145 ft-lbs (130 to 200 Nm) while turning the hub by hand.
11   Loosen the locknut to relieve the pressure on the bearing, then retighten it to 18 ft-lbs (25 Nm).
12   On 1983 Chrysler vehicles (manual free wheeling hub), back the nut off 30 degrees, then install the lockwasher. If the holes in the lockwasher and locknut do not line up, loosen the locknut (20 degrees maximum). Attach a spring scale to one of the wheel nut studs and pull on the scale to see how much force is required to turn the hub. It should take 1 to 4 pounds of force. If it doesn't, repeat the locknut tightening procedure. Apply grease to the inner surfaces of the free wheeling hub assembly and coat the mating surfaces of the hubs with semi-drying gasket sealant, then install the free wheeling hub and tighten the bolts in a criss-cross pattern. Check the axial play of the driveaxle and make sure it is within the specified range (see the drive-axle installation procedure below), then install the hub cover assembly with the control handle and clutch in the *Free* position. Tighten the bolts in a criss-cross pattern.
13   On all 1984 vehicles, loosen the locknut about 30 to 40 degrees, then check the force required to turn the hub as described in Step 12

(it should be 1 to 4 pounds). Install the lockwasher. On vehicles with automatic free wheeling hubs, adjust the brake contact surface depth by adding or removing shims.
14   On all 1985 and later vehicles, loosen the locknut about 30 to 40 degrees, then check the force required to turn the hub as described in Step 12 (it should be 1 to 4 pounds). Check the axial play of the wheel hub as well as shown in the accompanying illustration, then install the lockwasher. If the holes in the lockwasher and locknut do not line up, loosen the locknut slightly (40 degrees maximum).
15   On all 1984 and later vehicles, install the free wheeling hub assembly.
16   On vehicles with a manual hub, apply grease to the inner surfaces of the free wheeling hub assembly and coat the mating surfaces of the hubs with semi-drying gasket sealant, then install the free wheeling hub and tighten the bolts in a criss-cross pattern. On 1984 models only, check the axial play of the driveaxle and make sure it is within the specified range (see the driveaxle installation procedure below). On all models, install the hub cover assembly with the control handle and clutch in the *Free* position. Tighten the bolts in a criss-cross pattern.
17   On 1984 vehicles with an automatic hub, apply semi-drying gasket sealant to the hub mating surfaces, then align the key of brake B with the slot in the spindle as shown in the accompanying illustration and install the hub assembly. Make sure the free wheeling hub and the wheel hub make contact when light pressure is applied to the free wheeling hub (if they don't, turn the hub as required). Install the mounting bolts and tighten them in a criss-cross pattern. Install the shim/spacer and snap-ring on the end of the driveaxle. Recheck the hub turning force and compare it to the figure obtained before the free wheeling hub was installed. The difference should be less than 3.1 pounds — if it isn't, the free wheeling hub is probably installed incorrectly (remove

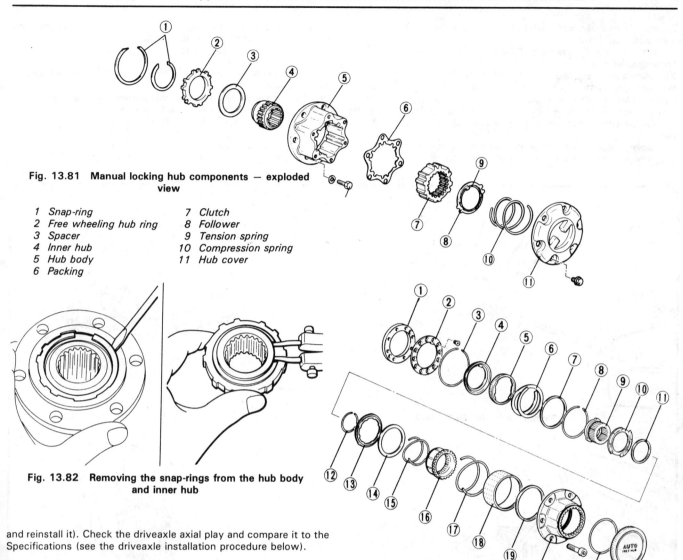

Fig. 13.81   Manual locking hub components — exploded view

1   Snap-ring
2   Free wheeling hub ring
3   Spacer
4   Inner hub
5   Hub body
6   Packing

7   Clutch
8   Follower
9   Tension spring
10   Compression spring
11   Hub cover

Fig. 13.82   Removing the snap-rings from the hub body and inner hub

Fig. 13.83   Automatic locking hub components — exploded view

1   Locknut
2   Lockwasher
3   Housing C-ring
4   Brake B
5   Brake A
6   Brake spring
7   Housing snap-ring
8   Retainer B C-ring
9   Drive gear
10   Retainer A
11   Drive gear snap-ring
12   Slide gear C-ring

13   Cam
14   Spring holder
15   Shift spring
16   Slide gear
17   Return spring
18   Retainer B
19   Thrust washer (retainer bearing — 85/86)
20   Hub body
21   O-ring
22   Hub cover

and reinstall it). Check the driveaxle axial play and compare it to the Specifications (see the driveaxle installation procedure below).

18   On 1985 and later vehicles with an automatic hub, recheck the hub turning force with a spring scale, then align the key of brake B with the slot in the spindle and install the hub assembly. Make sure the free wheeling hub and the wheel hub make contact when light pressure is applied to the free wheeling hub (if they don't, turn the hub as required). Install the mounting bolts and tighten them in a criss-cross pattern, then install the shim and snap-ring on the end of the driveaxle. Recheck the hub turning force and compare it to the figure obtained before the free wheeling hub was installed. The difference should be less than 3 pounds — if it isn't, the free wheeling hub is either assembled or installed incorrectly (remove and reinstall it and/or disassemble and reassemble it). Remove the free wheeling hub and apply semi-drying gasket sealant to the hub mating surfaces, then reinstall it and tighten the bolts in a criss-cross pattern.
19   On all 1984 and later vehicles with an automatic hub, apply grease to the cover O-ring and attach it to the cover. Install the cover and tighten it securely.
20   On all models, reinstall the brake caliper and wheel and lower the vehicle to the ground.

Free wheeling hub disassembly, inspection and reassembly

Manual locking hub
21   Using a screwdriver, remove the snap-ring and inner hub from the hub body.
22   Remove the inner hub snap-ring with snap-ring pliers.
23   Check for wear and evidence of seizure on the free wheeling hub ring, the inner hub, the hub body and the clutch.
24   Check the gasket for damage and look for deterioration of the springs.

25   Reassembly is the reverse of disassembly. Be sure to coat the entire periphery of the free wheeling hub ring, the inner hub and clutch and the inside of the hub body with NLGI grade 2 multi-purpose grease.
Automatic locking hub
Note: *Special tools and a great deal of care are required to disassemble the automatic locking hub, so be sure to read through the entire procedure before beginning work. It may be a good idea to leave the job to a dealer service department or repair shop.*

26 Push in on brake B and carefully remove the housing C-ring with a small screwdriver.
27 Lift out brake A, brake B and the brake spring, then remove the housing snap-ring.
28 Using a press and special tool number MB990811, compress the drive gear and remove the retainer B C-ring. **Note:** *Place a piece of cloth under the hub housing and make sure the press force does not exceed 441 pounds. Since the return spring relaxes approximately 1.570 inches, the press stroke must be greater to allow the spring to be released.*
29 Slowly reduce the pressure until the spring is fully relaxed. Make sure that retainer A does not hang up on retainer B.

30 Remove retainer B, the return spring, the slide gear assembly and the drive gear assembly from the hub body.
31 Remove the drive gear snap-ring and discard it. Use a new one during reassembly.
32 Push in on the cam and remove the slide gear C-ring while the spring is compressed.
33 Check the drive gear and slide gear splines for wear and damage. Check the cam portion of retainer A as well.
34 Check the cam for wear and damage.
35 Check the slide gear and body teeth, as well as the retainer B and body contact surfaces, for wear and damage.
36 Check the brakes for wear. Assemble brake A and B, then measure

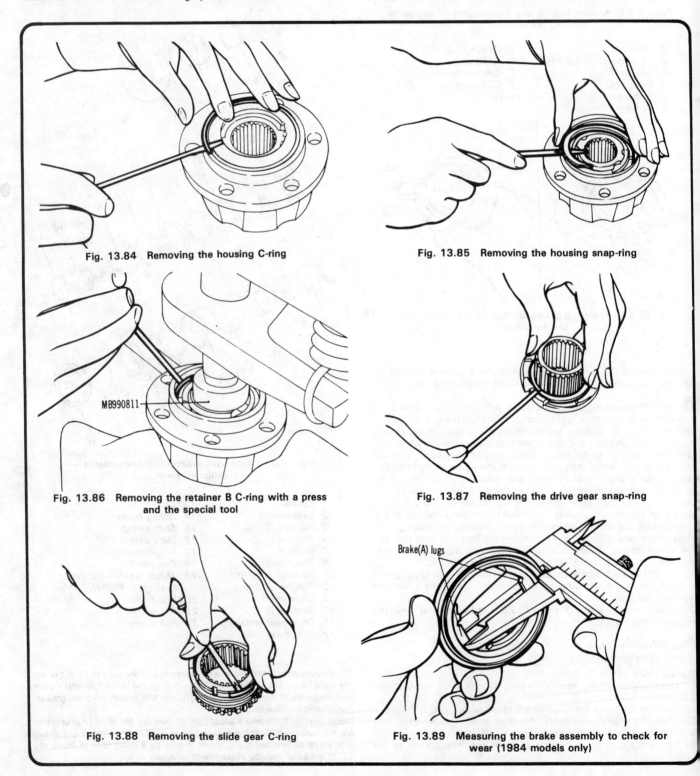

Fig. 13.84   Removing the housing C-ring

Fig. 13.85   Removing the housing snap-ring

Fig. 13.86   Removing the retainer B C-ring with a press and the special tool

Fig. 13.87   Removing the drive gear snap-ring

Fig. 13.88   Removing the slide gear C-ring

Fig. 13.89   Measuring the brake assembly to check for wear (1984 models only)

the combined thickness with a dial or vernier caliper. On 1984 models, position the caliper across the brake assembly at the lugs (A) to equalize the thickness of each side as the measurement is taken. On 1985 and later models, measure each side separately. If the measured value is less than the specified limit, replace the brakes as a set.

37 Check for deterioration of the return spring by measuring from the outer extremity of each end coil as shown in the accompanying illustration. Check the shift spring in the same manner. Replace any spring that is shorter than the specified limit.

38 Reassembly is the reverse of disassembly. Be sure to apply NLGI grade 2 multi-purpose grease to the contact surfaces of all components, especially the slide gear. Pack grease into the grooves of brake B and retainer B. Install the return spring with the smaller diameter coil facing the spring seat.

Driveaxle removal and installation
Removal

39 Raise the front of the vehicle and support it securely with jackstands, then remove the wheels and the brake caliper assemblies (see Chapter 9). Do not disconnect the hoses from the calipers and do not allow the calipers to hang by the hoses — suspend them with pieces of stiff wire so there is no strain on the hoses.

40 Detach the free wheeling hub cover assemblies and remove the snap-rings from the end of the driveaxles. Manual hub covers are held in place with several bolts, while automatic hub covers can be unscrewed from the hub.

41 Remove each steering knuckle and front hub assembly as a unit (see Section 14).

42 Grasp the inner and outer joints and pull the left driveaxle out of the differential. Be careful not to damage the differential oil seal with the driveaxle inner splines as it is removed.

43 Use a jack to raise the right lower suspension arm, then remove the nuts and detach the shock absorber from the upper mount. **Caution:** *Do not lower the jack until after the shock absorber has been reattached.*

44 Remove the nuts and bolts that attach the right driveaxle flange to the inner shaft, then carefully pull out the driveaxle. Remove the circlip from the inner end of the left driveaxle and replace it with a new one.

Installation

45 Attach the right driveaxle to the inner shaft flange, install the bolts and nuts and tighten them to the specified torque.

46 Attach the right shock absorber to the upper mount bracket and tighten the nuts. Make sure the shaft protrudes the specified amount (see Section 14).

47 Install the left driveaxle in the differential and seat it by tapping on the outer end with a soft-face hammer.

48 Install each steering knuckle and hub assembly and attach the balljoints, then adjust the driveaxle play as follows.

49 Install the snap-ring on the end of the driveaxle, but do not install the spacer/shim.

50 Mount a dial indicator on the front hub or brake disc and position the stem of the dial indicator against the end of the driveaxle as shown in the accompanying illustration.

51 Move the driveaxle in and out and note the reading on the indicator. This is the axial (end) play. **Note:** *On vehicles with automatic locking hubs, turn the driveaxle in both directions until resistance is felt (this is the center of the turning stroke), then check the driveaxle play with the dial indicator.*

52 If the axial play is not as specified, select a shim/spacer from the sizes available that will produce the correct play.

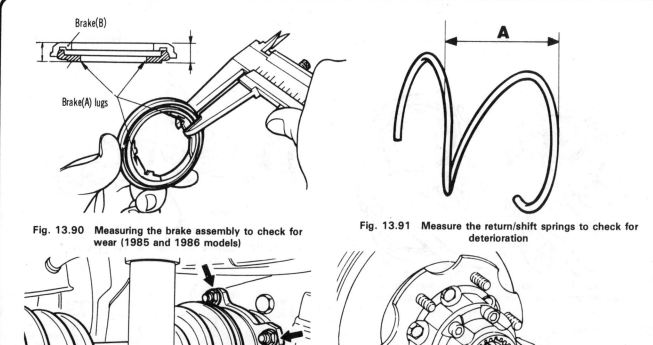

Fig. 13.90 Measuring the brake assembly to check for wear (1985 and 1986 models)

Fig. 13.91 Measure the return/shift springs to check for deterioration

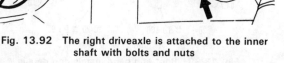

Fig. 13.92 The right driveaxle is attached to the inner shaft with bolts and nuts

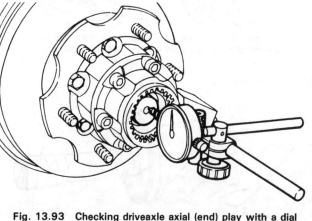

Fig. 13.93 Checking driveaxle axial (end) play with a dial indicator

Driveaxle disassembly, inspection and reassembly

Note: *Obtain a new rubber boot kit for each joint on the driveaxle before beginning disassembly. Do not disassemble the Birfield joints — if they are worn or damaged, new driveaxles are in order.*

53 Remove the boot bands by prying up the ends with a screwdriver or by cutting them off (new bands must be used during reassembly).

54 Use a screwdriver to remove the large circlip from the DOJ outer race.

55 Pull the driveaxle out of the DOJ outer race and wipe away as much of the grease as possible.

56 Push the balls in the DOJ cage up with a screwdriver and remove them.

57 Separate the cage from the inner race by turning it 30 degrees and sliding it down the driveaxle.

58 Remove the snap-ring from the driveaxle with snap-ring pliers, then pull off the inner race and slide the cage off the shaft.

59 Remove the circlip and the boots from the driveaxle. Wrap tape around the splines on the DOJ end of the shaft so the boots are not damaged by the splines.

60 Remove the dust covers with a large screwdriver.

61 Clean all of the components with solvent, then check the dust covers for damage and wear. Look for water, rust, foreign material and damage in the Birfield joints.

62 Inspect the driveaxle shafts for distortion and worn splines. Check all circlips for distortion and cracks.

63 Check the rubber boots for damage and cracks. **Note:** *Since the axles have been disassembled, it would be a very good idea to replace the boots with new ones, even if they appear to be in good condition.*

64 Check the cage, inner race, outer race and balls of each DOJ joint for wear and damage.

65 Drive new dust covers onto the joints with a section of pipe and a hammer. For Birfield joints, the pipe must be 2.710 inches in outside diameter with a 0.090 inch wall thickness. For DOJ joints, the pipe must be 2.240 inches in outside diameter with a wall thickness of 0.240 inch.

66 Wrap tape around the driveaxle splines, then install the new boots

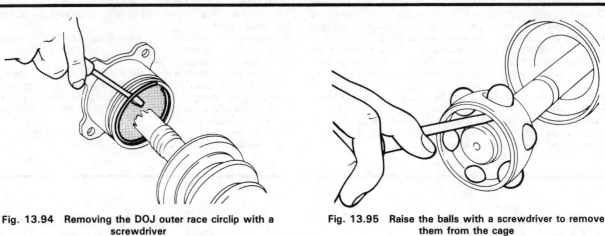

Fig. 13.94   Removing the DOJ outer race circlip with a screwdriver

Fig. 13.95   Raise the balls with a screwdriver to remove them from the cage

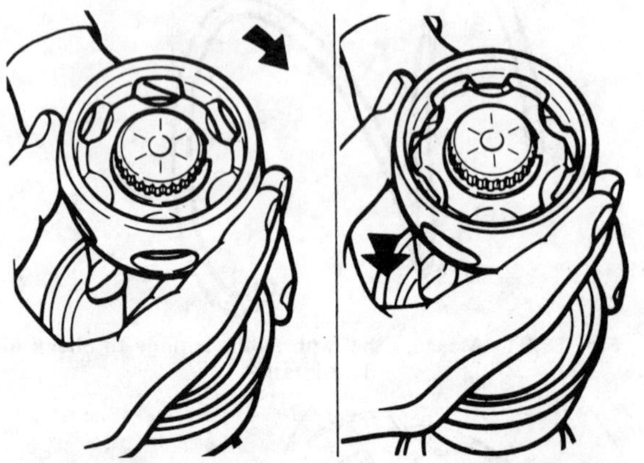

Fig. 13.96   Turn the cage 30 degrees to disengage it from the inner race and slide it down the driveaxle shaft

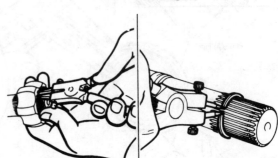

Fig. 13.97   Remove the snap-ring, the inner race and the circlip from the shaft

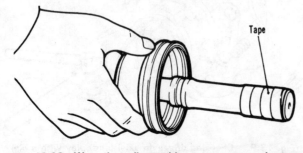

Fig. 13.98   Wrap the splines with tape to prevent damage to the boot as it is removed

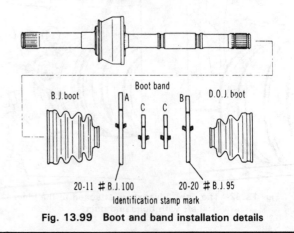

Fig. 13.99   Boot and band installation details

and bands on the shaft. The Birfield and DOJ boots are different sizes and shapes, so make sure they are correctly positioned on the shaft.
67 Slip the DOJ cage onto the shaft, smaller diameter first. Install the circlip and make sure it is seated in the shaft groove, then install the inner race and snap-ring. Make sure the snap-ring is seated in the groove.
68 Apply the specified grease (included with the boot kit) to the DOJ inner race and cage. Slip the cage into place on the inner race and turn it 30 degrees to align the ball races, then install the balls and lubricate them with the grease.
69 Pack the DOJ outer race with 1.8 to 2.8 ounces of the specified grease, then slide it onto the driveaxle while aligning the balls and races.
70 Pack an additional 1.8 to 2.8 ounces of grease into the outer race, behind the inner race and cage, then install the circlip (make sure it is seated in the groove).
71 Slip the boot over the outer race and install the band clamp (follow the directions in the boot kit). Position the other end of the boot as shown in the accompanying illustration and install the clamp band.
72 Pack the grease supplied with the boot kit into the Birfield joint to replace the grease that was wiped off, then install the boot (the clamping instructions are supplied with the boot kit).
73 Repeat the procedure for the remaining driveaxle.

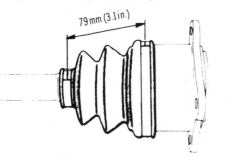

Fig. 13.100 The DOJ boot must be positioned as shown when the band clamps are installed

Front differential assembly removal and installation

74 Refer to Chapter 1 and drain the front axle oil.
75 Remove the driveaxles and pull the inner shaft out of the right side tube (a slide hammer-type puller with a flange adapter may be required

to remove the inner shaft from the differential).
76 Refer to Chapter 8 and detach the driveshaft from the front differential.
77 Support the differential with a jack.
78 Remove the left differential mounting bracket and the bolt holding the right bracket to the frame.
79 Remove the front crossmember-to-frame bolts and carefully lower the differential and crossmember as a unit.
80 Remove the bolt and detach the differential from the crossmember.
81 Installation is the reverse of removal. Be sure to tighten the bolts/nuts to the specified torque and refill the differential with the recommended gear oil (Chapter 1).

Front differential assembly overhaul

Due to the need for special tools and expertise, overhaul of the differential should not be attempted by the do-it-yourselfer. If major repairs are necessary, have them done by a dealer service department or repair shop or replace the differential with a new or rebuilt unit.

Driveshaft removal and installation

1987 and later models are equipped with one-piece driveshafts on all standard body 2WD models and both standard and long bodies with 4WD. Only the 2WD long body models continue to use the two-piece driveshaft with center bearing shown in Chapter 8.
Removal, U-joint replacement and installation remain essentially the same. However, there is no need to unbolt and disassemble the center bearing and U-joint on one-piece driveshaft models.

---

13 Brake system

Master cylinder removal and installation

1 The master cylinder on 1987 and later vehicles has mounting bolts in a horizontal plane for attachment to the power brake booster, as opposed to the earlier vertical mounting. When purchasing a new or rebuilt master cylinder, be sure to obtain one with the proper mounting bolt alignment.
2 1987 and later model master cylinders have a new connector block between the master cylinder and the front and rear brake lines, as shown in the accompanying illustration. Master cylinder removal,

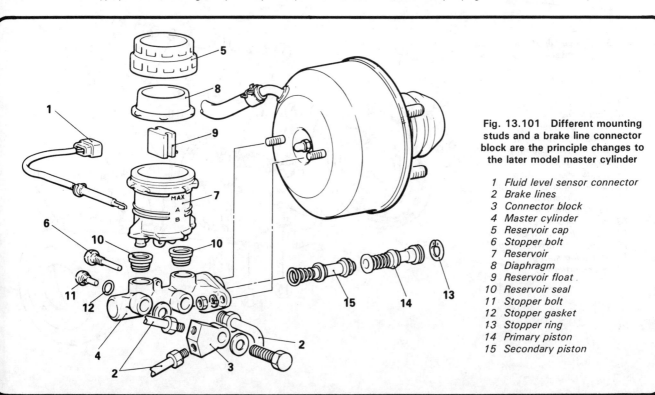

Fig. 13.101 Different mounting studs and a brake line connector block are the principle changes to the later model master cylinder

1 Fluid level sensor connector
2 Brake lines
3 Connector block
4 Master cylinder
5 Reservoir cap
6 Stopper bolt
7 Reservoir
8 Diaphragm
9 Reservoir float
10 Reservoir seal
11 Stopper bolt
12 Stopper gasket
13 Stopper ring
14 Primary piston
15 Secondary piston

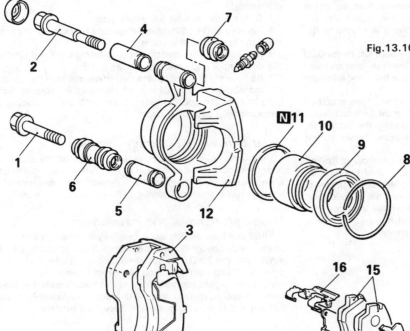

Fig.13.102 1987 and later models have a slightly redesigned front caliper assembly

1 Lock pin bolt
2 Guide pin bolt
3 Caliper support
4 Guide pin sleeve
5 Lock pin sleeve
6 Lock pin boot
7 Guide pin boot
8 Boot ring
9 Piston boot
10 Piston
11 Piston seal
12 Caliper body
13 Inner shim
14 Outer shim
15 Disc pad
16 Pad clip

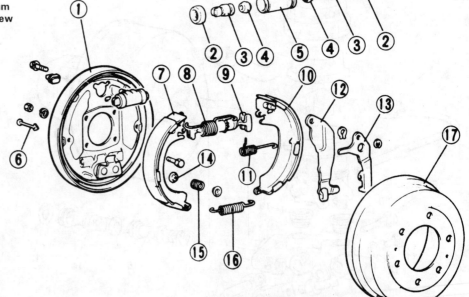

Fig. 13.103 Leading/trailing drum brake components — exploded view

1 Backing plate
2 Boot
3 Piston
4 Piston cup
5 Wheel cylinder
6 Shoe hold-down pin
7 Brake shoe assembly
8 Return spring
9 Adjuster
10 Shoe and lever assembly
11 Adjusting spring
12 Parking brake lever
13 Auto-adjuster lever
14 Shoe hold-down cup
15 Shoe hold-down spring
16 Retaining spring
17 Brake drum

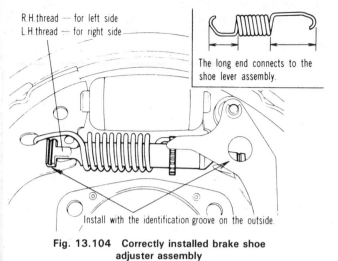

Fig. 13.104   Correctly installed brake shoe adjuster assembly

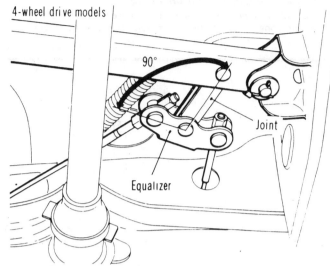

Fig. 13.105   On four wheel drive models, the equalizer and joint on the parking brake assembly must be at right angles to each other as the parking brake adjustment is made

rebuilding and installation procedures remain the same as given in Chapter 9.

Disc brake pad replacement

3   A redesigned front brake caliper is used on 1987 and later models. The primary design change affects the caliper guide pins, as shown in the accompanying illustration.
4   Pad replacement and caliper overhaul procedures remain essentially the same as those given in Chapter 9.

Rear brake shoe replacement (leading/trailing drum brakes)

5   The procedure for duo-servo drum brakes in Chapter 9 can be followed if the following points are noted. Refer to the accompanying exploded view illustration of the leading/trailing brake.
6   To release the shoe assembly, unhook the return spring, retaining spring and hold-down pins.
7   Attach the brake shoe adjuster and return spring to the shoes before installing them on the backing plate. Refer to the accompanying illustration for adjuster installation details.

Rear brake shoe adjustment (leading/trailing drum brakes)

8   After the shoes are reinstalled, turn the adjuster wheel until the outside diameter of the brake shoes is 9.960 to 9.970 inches (253.1 to 253.4 mm).
9   Once the wheels are reinstalled and the truck is driveable, drive

it in reverse and apply the brake pedal several times until the pedal stroke is firm and constant.

Parking brake adjustment (4WD only)

10   The parking brake on four wheel drive models does not have a turn-buckle in the cable. Instead, the nuts on the equalizer end of the cables must be turned. Make sure the equalizer is maintained at a 90 degree angle to the joint as the nuts are tightened. The rest of the procedure in Chapter 9 is correct as is.

Brake pedal adjustments

11   On later models, the brake pedal height is adjusted by turning the pushrod after loosening the jam nut. The brake light switch must not force the brake pedal down (make sure there is 0.020 to 0.030 inch (0.5 to 1.0 mm) of clearance between the pedal and the body of the switch).

---

14   Electrical system

Battery checking

1   Some later model vehicles are equipped with maintenance free batteries, which do not require the addition of water or periodic maintenance.
2   To determine the battery state of charge, look at the test indicator on top of the battery and compare what it looks like to the key printed on the battery.
3   In most cases, if the test indicator is blue, the battery is fully charged. If it is white, charging is required (stop charging when the blue dot appears).

Alternator removal and installation

4   Follow the procedure in Chapter 10, but note that on later models, the clearance between the front leg of the alternator and the timing chain case must be checked.
5   If the clearance is greater than 0.008 inch (0.2 mm), install spacers 0.0078 inch (0.198 mm) thick to bring the clearance into the specified range.

Alternator overhaul and testing

6   Since special tools and expertise are required to overhaul the alternator, and internal parts are often not available, if an alternator is defective it should be replaced with a new or factory rebuilt unit.

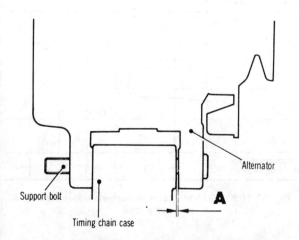

Fig. 13.106   When installing the alternator, make sure the clearance A is as specified or shims must be added to the bolt

Windshield wiper switch checking

7   Follow the procedure in Chapter 10, but use the new accompanying illustrations to locate the switch terminals and determine the continuity.

Column switch checking

8   Follow the procedure in Chapter 10, but use the new accompanying illustrations to locate the switch terminals and determine the continuity.

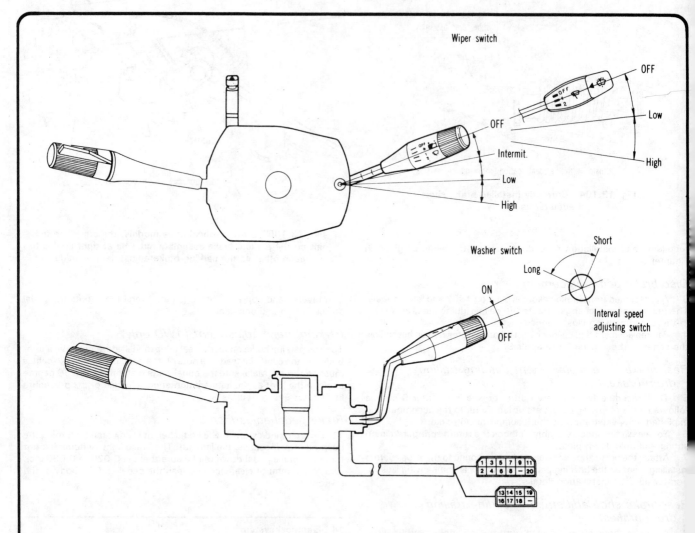

Fig. 13.107   Windshield wiper switch terminal locations (1983 and later models)

● Continuity table

Terminal / Lever position	18	16	15	14	17	13	19
OFF	o—		—o	o—		—o	
★	o—		—o	o——	—o		
				o--	- - - -	--o	
1	o—			—o			
				o--	- - - -	--o	
2		o—		—o			
				o--	- - - -	--o	
Intermittent time adjusting switch					o—WWW—o		

Fig. 13.108   1983 windshield wiper switch continuity table

● Continuity table

Terminal / Lever position	18	16	15	14	17	13	19
OFF	o—		—o	o--	- - -	--o	
★	o—		—o	o——	—o		
				o--	- - - -	--o	
1	o—			—o			
				o--	- - - -	--o	
2		o—		—o			
				o--	- - - -	--o	
Intermittent time adjusting switch					o—WWW—o		

Fig. 13.109   1984 and later windshield wiper switch continuity table

NOTE: Dashed lines indicate washer switch operation.

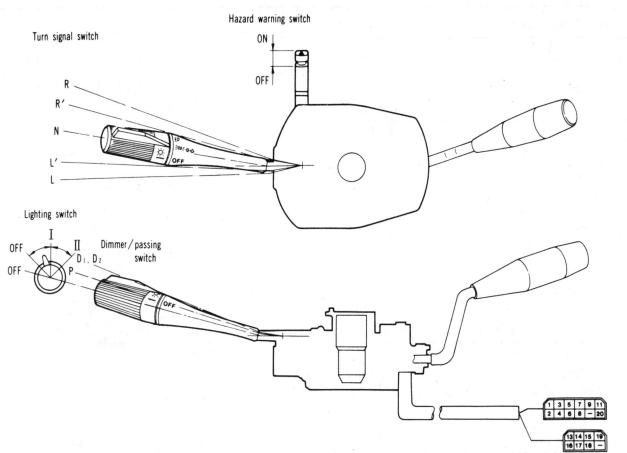

Fig. 13.110 Light switch position and terminal locations (top — 1983 and later; bottom — 1983 only)

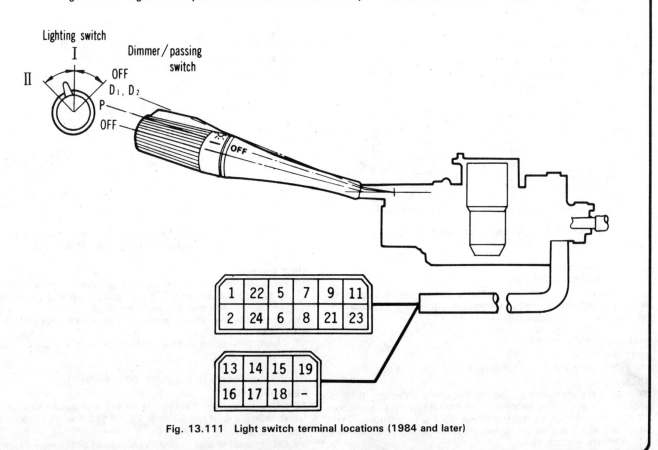

Fig. 13.111 Light switch terminal locations (1984 and later)

(a) Lighting switch

Lever position \ Terminal	1	2	9
OFF			
I	O————————O (1–9)		
II	O——O (1–2)		O (9)

NOTE: O——O indicates that there is continuity between the points.

(b) Dimmer and passing switch

Lever position \ Terminal	14	7	8	2
D₁	O——O (14–7)			
D₂	O————O (14–8)			
P	O————O——O (14–8–2)			

(c) Turn signal and hazard warning switch

Lever position		Terminal 3	5	6	4
OFF	L	O——O (3–5)			
	N				
	R	O————————O (3–6)			
ON	L·N·R		O——O——O (5–6–4)		

Fig. 13.112 Light switch continuity table
(top/middle — 1983 and later; bottom — 1983 only)

Continuity table

Position	Key	Terminal 1	2	3	4	5	Key reminder switch 6	7
LOCK	Removed						O——O	
ACC	Installed	O——O					O——O	
ON		O——O——O					O——O	
START		O			O——O——O		O——O	

NOTE
O—O indicates that there is continuity between the terminals.

Fig. 13.115 Ignition switch continuity table
(1984 and later)

Hazard switch	Turn signal switch	Terminal 24	6	5	22	23	21
OFF	L	O		O	O——O		
	N				O——O		
	R	O——O			O——O		
ON	L·N·R	O——O——O			O		O

Fig. 13.113 Light switch continuity table
(1984 and later)

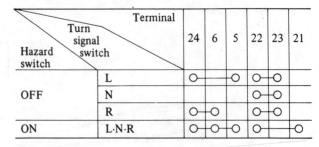

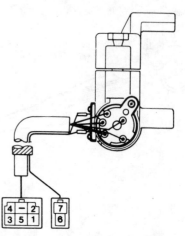

Fig. 13.114 Ignition switch terminal locations
(1984 and later)

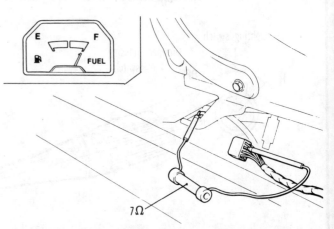

7Ω

Fig. 13.116 Hook a 7 ohm resistor in series as shown when checking the fuel gauge on 1985 models

Ignition switch checking

9 Follow the procedure in Chapter 10, but use the new accompanying illustrations to locate the switch terminals and determine the continuity for 1984 and later models.

Fuel gauge checking

1981 thru 1984
10 Follow the procedure in Chapter 10.

1985
11 Follow the procedure in Chapter 10 (Steps 1 through 4), then unplug the frame wiring harness to front wiring harness connector.
12 Connect a 7 ohm resistor and jumper leads to the yellow wire terminal (0.5 Y) of the front wiring harness and a good ground. The fuel gauge should indicate Full.
13 Follow the procedure in Chapter 10 from Step 6 on.

1986 and later
14 Unplug the frame wiring harness to front wiring harness connector.
15 Hook a 12-volt/3.4-watt test light and jumper leads to the front harness connector terminal 2 and a good ground.
16 Turn on the ignition switch and see if the light flashes and the fuel gauge needle fluctuates.
17 Check the sending unit by referring to the procedure in Chapter 10 (Steps 11 on).

Coolant temperature gauge checking

1981 thru 1985
18 Follow the procedure in Chapter 10, but note that the resistor mentioned in Step 3 must be 104 ohms for all 1982 through 1985 models.

1986 and later
19 Disconnect the wire from the sending unit on the engine and connect a 12-volt/3.4-watt test light to the connector and a good engine

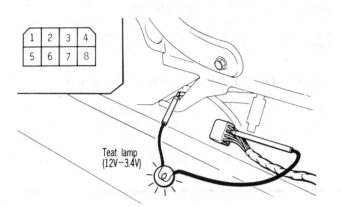

Fig. 13.117   Use a test light hooked up as shown to make a quick check of the 1986 and later model fuel gauge

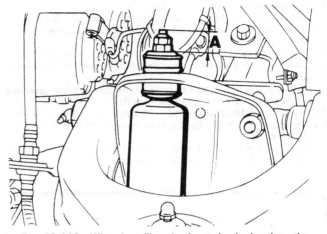

Fig. 13.118   When installing the front shock absorber, the distance A must be as specified in the text (1983 and 1984 models only)

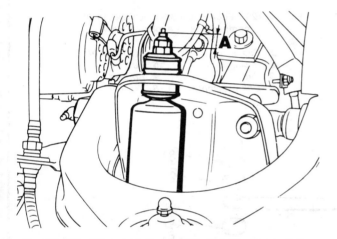

Fig. 13.119   When installing the front shock absorber, the distance A must be as specified in the text (1985 and later models)

ground.
20   Turn the ignition switch on and make sure the test light flashes and the gauge needle fluctuates.

Oil pressure gauge checking
1981 thru 1985
21   Follow the procedure in Chapter 10.
1986 and later
22   Disconnect the wire from the sending unit on the engine and connect a 12-volt/3.4-watt test light to the connector and a good engine ground.
23   Turn the ignition switch on and make sure the test light flashes and the gauge needle fluctuates.

Wiring diagrams
Wiring diagrams for 1981 and later models are included at the end of this supplement. Due to space limitations, not all diagrams for each year are included. However, they are a representative sampling.

---

15   Suspension and steering

General information
The suspension system used on rear wheel drive models has remained virtually unchanged during the entire lifespan of these vehicles.

The front suspension system used on four wheel drive vehicles is obviously different to accommodate the front wheel drive components. Instead of springs, torsion bars are utilized and the strut bars are eliminated. The stabilizer bar mounting arrangement is different and the wheel spindles are designed to allow for the installation of the driveaxles.
The rear suspension system on four wheel drive models is the same as the rear suspension on rear wheel drive models.

Front shock absorber removal and installation (4WD only)
1   Follow the procedure in Chapter 11, but note that the upper shock mounting nut must be tightened until the shock strut protrudes 0.810 inch (20.5 mm) on 1983 and 1984 models. On 1985 models it must protrude 0.490 inch (12.5 mm) and on 1986 and later models 0.300 inch (7.5 mm).
2   On 1983 and 1984 models the measurement is taken from the lower face of the nut, while on 1985 and later models it is taken from the upper face of the nut (see accompanying illustrations).
3   After the nut has been tightened to produce the specified strut protrusion, install and tighten the jam nut.

Stabilizer bar removal and installation
Rear wheel drive
4   Follow the procedure in Chapter 11, but note that the distance A mentioned in Step 8 is measured differently on 1984 models.
5   Instead of measuring from the top face of the nut, measure from the bottom face. The distance should be 1.180 to 1.260 inches (30 to 32 mm).

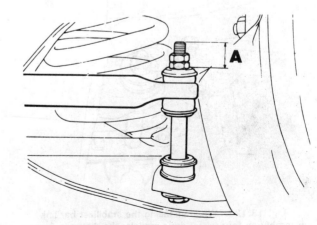

Fig. 13.120   When installing the stabilizer bar on rear wheel drive vehicles, the distance A must be as specified in the text (1984 models only)

Four wheel drive

6 Remove the stabilizer bar-to-link assembly nuts/bolts, followed by the stabilizer bar-to-lower arm nuts/bolts and detach the bar from the vehicle.

7 The link assemblies can be removed by unscrewing the nuts.

8 Check the bar, the bushings and the link assemblies for cracks and deformation.

9 Installation is the reverse of removal. Tighten the link assembly and stabilizer bar-to-lower arm nuts as follows.

10 On 1983 and 1984 models, tighten the nuts until the distance from the *Top* of each bolt to the *Bottom* of each nut is 0.630 to 0.710 inch (16 to 18 mm).

11 On 1985 and later models, it should be 0.240 to 0.310 inch (6 to 8 mm), measured from the *Top* of the bolt to the *Top* of the nut.

Strut bar removal and installation

12 Follow the procedure in Chapter 11, but note that distance A mentioned in Step 5 is measured from the end of the strut bar to the front face of the first nut on 1985 and later models. It should be 2.9 inches (74 mm).

Steering knuckle/wheel spindle removal and installation (4WD only)

13 Refer to Chapter 11 and follow the procedure in Steps 1 through 7 of Section 17. The hub removal procedure is covered in Section 11 of this Chapter. Leave the stabilizer bar and torsion bar in place.

14 Using special tools MB990635 and C-3894-A, separate the upper and lower suspension balljoints from the steering knuckle assembly

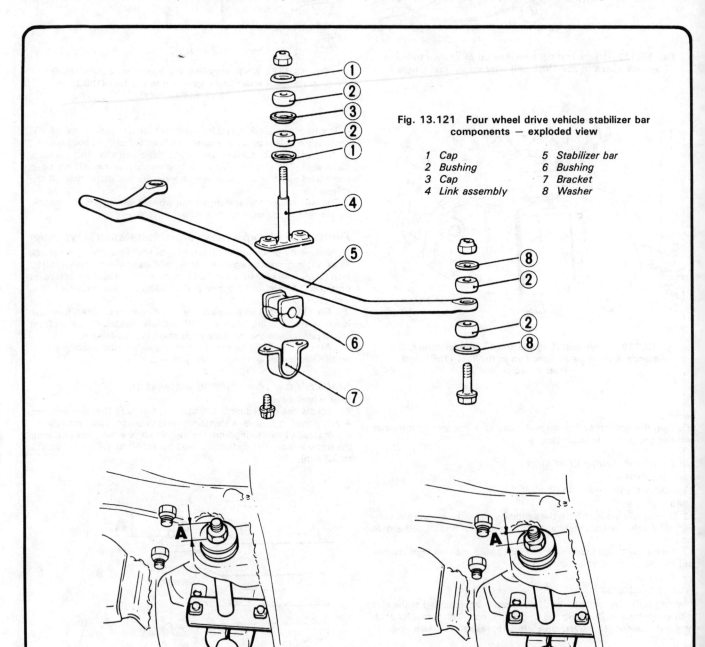

Fig. 13.121 Four wheel drive vehicle stabilizer bar components — exploded view

1	Cap	5	Stabilizer bar
2	Bushing	6	Bushing
3	Cap	7	Bracket
4	Link assembly	8	Washer

Fig. 13.122 When installing the stabilizer bar link assembly on four wheel drive models, the distance A must be as specified in the text (1983 and 1984 models only)

Fig. 13.123 When installing the stabilizer bar link assembly on four wheel drive models, the distance A must be as specified in the text (1985 and later models)

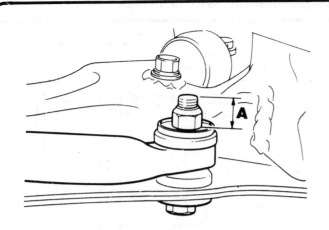

Fig. 13.124 When installing the stabilizer bar on four wheel drive models, the distance A must be as specified in the text (1983 and 1984 models only)

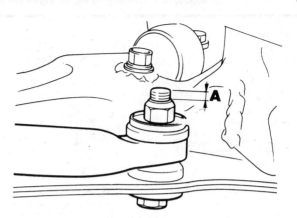

Fig. 13.125 When installing the stabilizer bar on four wheel drive models, the distance A must be as specified in the text (1985 and later models)

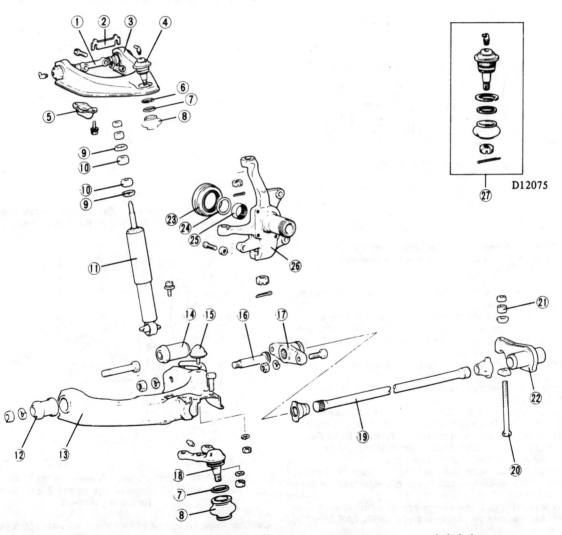

D12075

Fig. 13.126 Four wheel drive vehicle front suspension components — exploded view

1	Upper arm shaft	7	Ring	12	Bushing B	17	Anchor arm B	22	Anchor arm assembly
2	Camber shim	8	Dust cover	13	Lower arm	18	Balljoint	23	Seal
3	Upper arm	9	Cap	14	Bushing A	19	Torsion bar	24	Spacer
4	Balljoint	10	Bushing	15	Bump stop	20	Anchor bolt	25	Needle bearing
5	Rebound stop	11	Shock absorber	16	Lower arm shaft	21	Adjusting nut	26	Knuckle/wheel spindle
6	Snap-ring							27	Balljoint kit

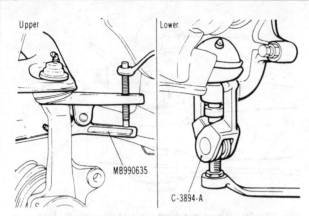

Fig. 13.127 The suspension balljoints are installed in a tapered hole and require special tools to separate them from the steering knuckle

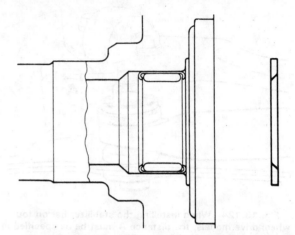

Fig. 13.128 The spacer must be installed in the bore before the seal is driven into place (make sure the small diameter of the hole is facing in, towards the bearing)

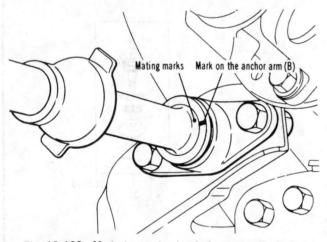

Fig. 13.129 Mark the torsion bar before removing it, but DO NOT scratch it or make a mark with a centerpunch

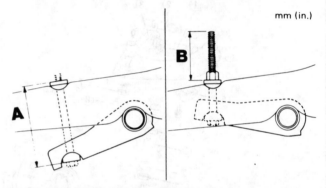

Fig. 13.130 Make sure the adjusting bolt measurements A and B are as specified in the text as the torsion bar is installed

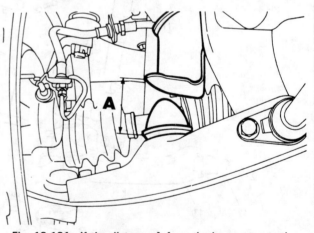

Fig. 13.131 If the distance A from the bump stop to the bracket is not as specified, the torsion bars may require further adjustment

(see the accompanying illustration). Tap on the knuckle around the balljoint studs to loosen them.

15 Once the balljoint studs have been released from the tapered holes in the knuckle, remove the nuts completely and carefully detach the knuckle from the suspension arms and the driveaxle. Do not damage the driveaxle boots in the process.

16 Pry out the oil seal and take out the spacer to gain access to the needle bearing in the rear of the driveaxle bore.

17 If the needle bearing is worn or damaged, carefully drive it out from the front of the spindle.

18 Apply grease (MOPAR 2525035 or equivalent) to the rollers in the new bearing, then carefully press or drive it into the knuckle bore until the end of the bearing is flush with the end of the bore. **Note:** *Do not drive the bearing in too far. Use a hammer and a section of pipe with an outside diameter that matches the bearing.*

19 Install the spacer with the small diameter hole face against the bearing, then apply grease (MOPAR 2525035 or equivalent) to the outer face of the spacer.

20 Carefully press or drive a new oil seal into place, then pack grease inside the seal and lubricate the seal lip with grease (MOPAR 2525035 or equivalent).

21 Installation of the knuckle is the reverse of removal. Be sure to tighten the balljoint nuts to the specified torque and install new cotter pins.

Torsion bar removal and installation (4WD only)

22 Raise the front of the vehicle and support it securely on jackstands, then remove the wheel and the brake caliper assembly (Chapter 9).

23 Remove the anchor arm dust covers.

24 Mark the torsion bar directly opposite the mark on the anchor arm.

Caution: *Do not punch or scratch the torsion bar — use paint to make the mark.*

25 Loosen the jam nut and adjusting nut at the anchor arm assembly until the torsion bar can be slipped out of the anchor arms.

26 To reinstall the torsion bar, apply grease to the torsion bar and anchor arm splines, the adjusting bolt threads and the inside of the dust boots.

27 If both bars have been removed, the right torsion bar can be distinguished from the left by checking the end of the bar. Look for an L or an R stamped into the end of each bar (R is right, L is left).

28 Position the marked end of the bar into anchor arm B with the

mating marks aligned (if a new bar is installed, align the white spline with the mark on the anchor arm).

29 With the rebound stop on the upper arm in contact with the frame and the distance from the underside of the adjusting bolt head to the bottom face of the nut 5.520 to 5.820 inches (140 to 148 mm) on the left side and 5.320 to 5.620 inches (135 to 143 mm) on the right side, assemble the torsion bar and the rear anchor arm.

30 Tighten the adjusting nut until the distance from the adjusting nut bottom face to the top of the bolt is 3.0 inches (76.5 mm) on the left side and 2.70 inches (68 mm) on the right side. **Note:** *On 1983 and 1984 vehicles with a U-engine, the left side distance must be 2.80 inches (72 mm).*

31 Reinstall the hub, wheel and brake caliper, then lower the vehicle and measure the distance from the bump stop to the bracket with the vehicle unloaded.

32 It should be 2.80 inches (71 mm). If not, tighten the adjusting nut on the anchor arm until the distance is as specified. **Note:** *If the anchor bolt protrusions exceed 3.50 inches (90 mm) on the left side and 3.30 inches (85 mm) on the right side, check the torsion bars, the anchor arms, the lower arms and the crossmember for damage and deformation. If no damage is evident, the torsion bar(s) will have to be removed and reinstalled with the splines moved one notch in the anchor arm.*

Lower control arm removal and installation (4WD only)

33 Follow the procedure in Chapter 11, but note that the lower arms on four wheel drive vehicles are attached at two pivot points. After removing the large nuts, the pivot bolts can be driven out to detach the arm from the frame.

Manual steering gearbox overhaul

34 Due to the need for special tools, equipment and expertise, the steering gearbox should not be disassembled by the home mechanic. If a gearbox failure occurs, replace it with a new or factory rebuilt unit.

Power steering pump overhaul

35 Due to the need for special tools, equipment and expertise, the power steering pump should not be disassembled by the home mechanic. If a pump failure occurs, replace it with a new or factory rebuilt unit.

Power steering gearbox overhaul

36 Due to the need for special tools, equipment and expertise, the steering gearbox should not be disassembled by the home mechanic. If a gearbox failure occurs, replace it with a new or factory rebuilt unit.

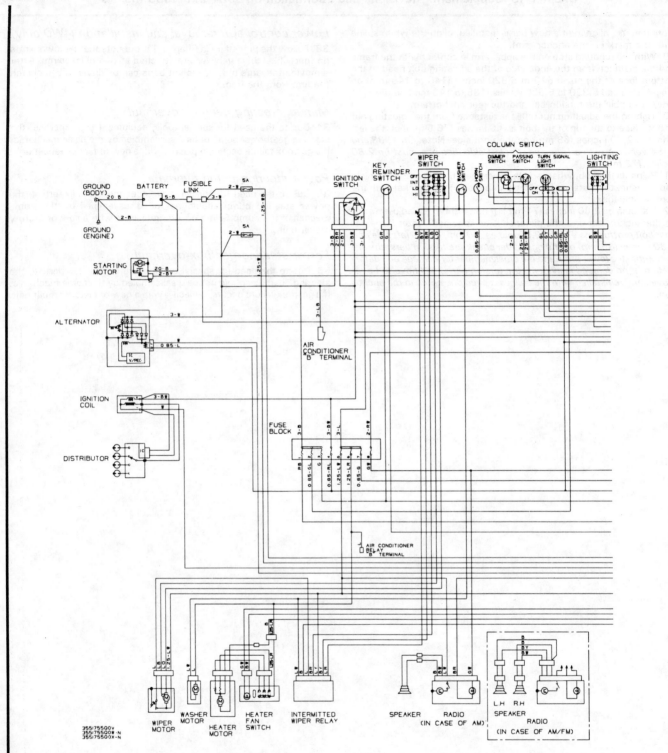

Fig. 13.132 Wiring diagram — 1983 and later models (1 of 3)

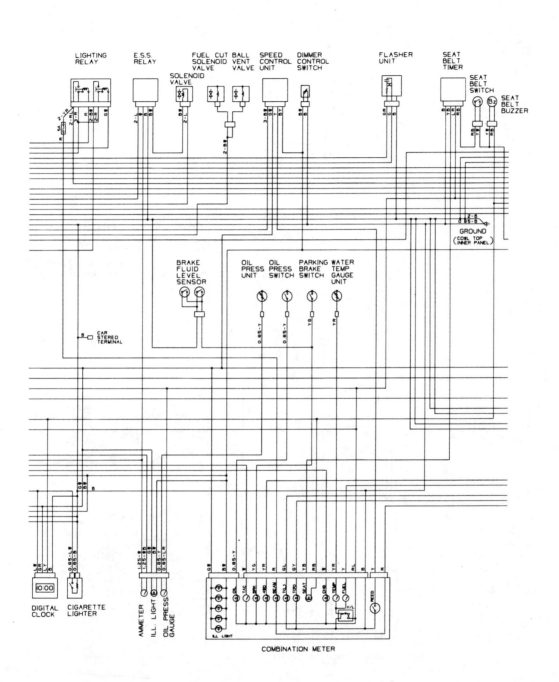

Fig. 13.133 Wiring diagram — 1983 and later models (2 of 3)

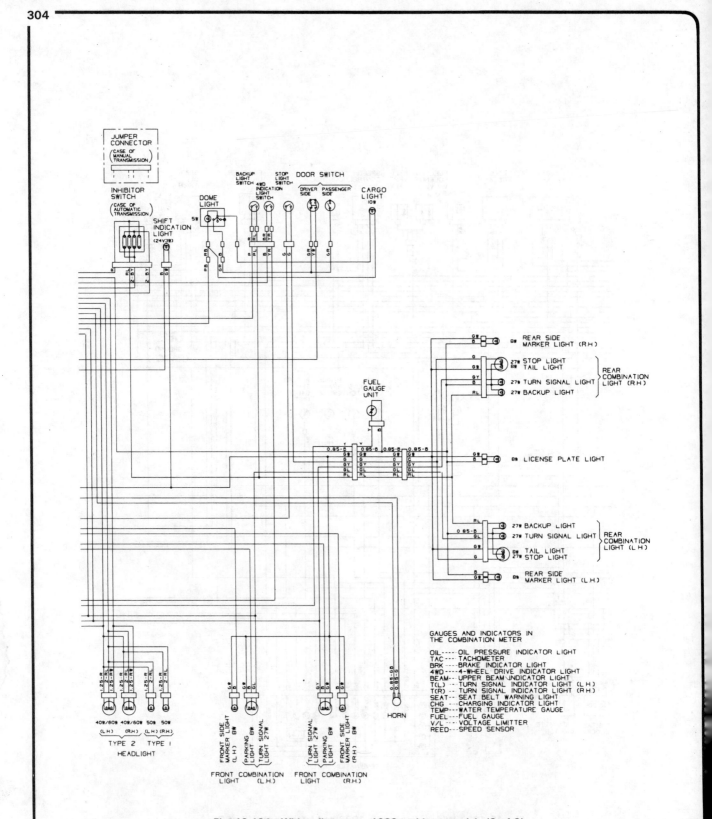

Fig. 13.134 Wiring diagram — 1983 and later models (3 of 3)

Conversion factors

Length (distance)
Inches (in)	X	25.4	= Millimetres (mm)	X	0.0394 = Inches (in)
Feet (ft)	X	0.305	= Metres (m)	X	3.281 = Feet (ft)
Miles	X	1.609	= Kilometres (km)	X	0.621 = Miles

Volume (capacity)
Cubic inches (cu in; in^3)	X	16.387	= Cubic centimetres (cc; cm^3)	X	0.061 = Cubic inches (cu in; in^3)
Imperial pints (Imp pt)	X	0.568	= Litres (l)	X	1.76 = Imperial pints (Imp pt)
Imperial quarts (Imp qt)	X	1.137	= Litres (l)	X	0.88 = Imperial quarts (Imp qt)
Imperial quarts (Imp qt)	X	1.201	= US quarts (US qt)	X	0.833 = Imperial quarts (Imp qt)
US quarts (US qt)	X	0.946	= Litres (l)	X	1.057 = US quarts (US qt)
Imperial gallons (Imp gal)	X	4.546	= Litres (l)	X	0.22 = Imperial gallons (Imp gal)
Imperial gallons (Imp gal)	X	1.201	= US gallons (US gal)	X	0.833 = Imperial gallons (Imp gal)
US gallons (US gal)	X	3.785	= Litres (l)	X	0.264 = US gallons (US gal)

Mass (weight)
Ounces (oz)	X	28.35	= Grams (g)	X	0.035 = Ounces (oz)
Pounds (lb)	X	0.454	= Kilograms (kg)	X	2.205 = Pounds (lb)

Force
Ounces-force (ozf; oz)	X	0.278	= Newtons (N)	X	3.6 = Ounces-force (ozf; oz)
Pounds-force (lbf; lb)	X	4.448	= Newtons (N)	X	0.225 = Pounds-force (lbf; lb)
Newtons (N)	X	0.1	= Kilograms-force (kgf; kg)	X	9.81 = Newtons (N)

Pressure
Pounds-force per square inch (psi; lbf/in^2; lb/in^2)	X	0.070	= Kilograms-force per square centimetre (kgf/cm^2; kg/cm^2)	X	14.223 = Pounds-force per square inch (psi; lbf/in^2; lb/in^2)
Pounds-force per square inch (psi; lbf/in^2; lb/in^2)	X	0.068	= Atmospheres (atm)	X	14.696 = Pounds-force per square inch (psi; lbf/in^2; lb/in^2)
Pounds-force per square inch (psi; lbf/in^2; lb/in^2)	X	0.069	= Bars	X	14.5 = Pounds-force per square inch (psi; lbf/in^2; lb/in^2)
Pounds-force per square inch (psi; lbf/in^2; lb/in^2)	X	6.895	= Kilopascals (kPa)	X	0.145 = Pounds-force per square inch (psi; lbf/in^2; lb/in^2)
Kilopascals (kPa)	X	0.01	= Kilograms-force per square centimetre (kgf/cm^2; kg/cm^2)	X	98.1 = Kilopascals (kPa)

Torque (moment of force)
Pounds-force inches (lbf in; lb in)	X	1.152	= Kilograms-force centimetre (kgf cm; kg cm)	X	0.868 = Pounds-force inches (lbf in; lb in)
Pounds-force inches (lbf in; lb in)	X	0.113	= Newton metres (Nm)	X	8.85 = Pounds-force inches (lbf in; lb in)
Pounds-force inches (lbf in; lb in)	X	0.083	= Pounds-force feet (lbf ft; lb ft)	X	12 = Pounds-force inches (lbf in; lb in)
Pounds-force feet (lbf ft; lb ft)	X	0.138	= Kilograms-force metres (kgf m; kg m)	X	7.233 = Pounds-force feet (lbf ft; lb ft)
Pounds-force feet (lbf ft; lb ft)	X	1.356	= Newton metres (Nm)	X	0.738 = Pounds-force feet (lbf ft; lb ft)
Newton metres (Nm)	X	0.102	= Kilograms-force metres (kgf m; kg m)	X	9.804 = Newton metres (Nm)

Power
Horsepower (hp)	X	745.7	= Watts (W)	X	0.0013 = Horsepower (hp)

Velocity (speed)
Miles per hour (miles/hr; mph)	X	1.609	= Kilometres per hour (km/hr; kph)	X	0.621 = Miles per hour (miles/hr; mph)

Fuel consumption*
Miles per gallon, Imperial (mpg)	X	0.354	= Kilometres per litre (km/l)	X	2.825 = Miles per gallon, Imperial (mpg)
Miles per gallon, US (mpg)	X	0.425	= Kilometres per litre (km/l)	X	2.352 = Miles per gallon, US (mpg)

Temperature
Degrees Fahrenheit = (°C x 1.8) + 32   Degrees Celsius (Degrees Centigrade; °C) = (°F - 32) x 0.56

It is common practice to convert from miles per gallon (mpg) to litres/100 kilometres (l/100km), where mpg (Imperial) x l/100 km = 282 and mpg (US) x l/100 km = 235

Index

NOTE: New manuals are added to this list on a periodic basis. If you do not see a listing for your vehicle, consult your local Haynes dealer for the latest product information.

ALFA ROMEO
531 Alfa Romeo Sedan & Coupe '73 thru '80

AMC
Jeep CJ — see JEEP (412)
694 Mid-size models, Concord, Hornet, Gremlin & Spirit '70 thru '83
*934 (Renault) Alliance & Encore all models '83 thru '85

AUDI
162 100 all models '69 thru '77
615 4000 all models '80 thru '87
428 5000 all models '77 thru '83
*1117 5000 all models '84 thru '86
207 Fox all models '73 thru '79

AUSTIN
049 Healey 100/6 & 3000 Roadster '56 thru '68
Healey Sprite — see MG Midget Roadster (265)

BLMC
260 1100, 1300 & Austin America '62 thru '74
527 Mini all models '59 thru '69
*646 Mini all models '69 thru '87

BMW
276 320i all 4 cyl models '75 thru '83
*632 528i & 530i all models '75 thru '80
240 1500 thru 2002 all models except Turbo '59 thru '77
348 2500, 2800, 3.0 & Bavaria all models '69 thru '76

BUICK
Century front-wheel drive — see GENERAL MOTORS A-Cars (829)
*627 Mid-size all rear-drive Regal & Century models with V6, V8 and Turbo '74 thru '87
Skyhawk — see GENERAL MOTORS J-Cars (766)
552 Skylark all X-car models '80 thru '85

CADILLAC
Cimarron — see GENERAL MOTORS J-Cars (766)

CAPRI
296 2000 MK I Coupe all models '71 thru '75
283 2300 MK II Coupe all models '74 thru '78
205 2600 & 2800 V6 Coupe all models '71 thru '75
375 2800 Mk II V6 Coupe all models '75 thru '78
Mercury in-line engines — see FORD Mustang (654)
Mercury V6 and V8 engines — see FORD Mustang (558)

CHEVROLET
554 Camaro V8 all models '70 thru '81
*866 Camaro all models '82 thru '87
Cavalier — see GENERAL MOTORS J-Cars (766)
Celebrity — see GENERAL MOTORS A-Cars (829)
*625 Chevelle, Malibu & El Camino all V6 & V8 models '69 thru '86
449 Chevette & Pontiac T1000 all models '76 thru '87
550 Citation all models '80 thru '85
274 Corvette all V8 models '68 thru '82
*1336 Corvette all models '84 thru '87
*704 Full-size Sedans Caprice, Impala, Biscayne, Bel Air & Wagons, all V6 & V8 models '69 thru '86
319 Luv Pick-up all 2WD & 4WD models '72 thru '82
*626 Monte Carlo all V6, V8 & Turbo models '70 thru '86
241 Nova all V8 models '69 thru '79
420 Pick-ups — Chevrolet & GMC, all V8 & in-line 6 cyl 2WD & 4WD models '67 thru '87
*831 S-10 & GMC S-15 Pick-ups all models '82 thru '87
*345 Vans — Chevrolet & GMC, V8 & in-line 6 cyl models '68 thru '85
208 Vega all models except Cosworth '70 thru '77

CHRYSLER
*1337 Chrysler & Plymouth Mid-size front wheel drive '82 thru '86
K-Cars — see DODGE Aries/Plymouth Reliant (723)
Laser — see DODGE Daytona & Chrysler Laser (1140)

DATSUN
402 200SX all models '77 thru '79
*647 200SX all models '80 thru '83
228 B-210 all models '73 thru '78
525 210 all models '79 thru '82

206 240Z, 260Z & 280Z Coupe & 2 + 2 '70 thru '78
563 280ZX Coupe & 2 + 2 '79 thru '83
300ZX — see NISSAN (1137)
679 310 all models '78 thru '82
123 510 & PL521 Pick-up '68 thru '73
430 510 all models '78 thru '81
372 610 all models '72 thru '76
277 620 Series Pick-up all models '73 thru '79
235 710 all models '73 thru '77
*771 720 Series Pick-up all models (including 4WD) '80 thru '85
*376 810/Maxima all gasoline models '77 thru '84
124 1200 all models '70 thru '73
368 F10 all models '76 thru '79
Pulsar — see NISSAN (876)
Sentra — see NISSAN (982)
Stanza — see NISSAN (981)

DODGE
*723 Aries & Plymouth Reliant all models '81 thru '86
*1231 Caravan & Plymouth Voyager Mini-Vans all models '84 thru '86
699 Challenger & Plymouth Sapporo all models '78 thru '83
236 Colt all models '71 thru '77
419 Colt (rear-wheel drive) all models '77 thru '80
610 Colt & Plymouth Champ (front-wheel drive) all models '78 thru '87
*556 D50 & Plymouth Arrow Pick-ups '79 thru '86
234 Dart & Plymouth Valiant all 6 cyl models '67 thru '76
*1140 Daytona & Chrysler Laser all models '84 thru '86
*545 Omni & Plymouth Horizon all models '78 thru '84
*912 Pick-ups all full-size models '74 thru '86
*349 Vans — Dodge & Plymouth V8 & 6 cyl models '71 thru '86

FIAT
080 124 Sedan & Wagon all ohv & dohc models '66 thru '75
094 124 Sport Coupe & Spider '68 thru '78
087 128 all models '72 thru '79
310 131 & Brava all models '75 thru '81
038 850 Sedan, Coupe & Spider '64 thru '74
479 Strada all models '79 thru '82
*273 X1/9 all models '74 thru '80

FORD
788 Bronco and Pick-ups '73 thru '79
*880 Bronco and Pick-ups '80 thru '86
295 Cortina MK III 1600 & 2000 ohc '70 thru '76
268 Courier Pick-up all models '72 thru '82
*789 Escort & Mercury Lynx all models '81 thru '87
560 Fairmont & Mercury Zephyr all in-line & V8 models '78 thru '83
334 Fiesta all models '77 thru '80
359 Granada & Mercury Monarch all in-line, 6 cyl & V8 models '75 thru '80
*754 Ford & Mercury Full-size, FORD: LTD ('75 thru '82); Custom 500; Country Squire; Crown Victoria MERCURY: Marquis ('75 thru '82); Gran Marquis; Colony Park, all V8 models '75 thru '84
773 Ford & Mercury Mid-size, FORD: Torino; Gran Torino; Elite; Ranchero; LTD II; LTD ('83 thru '84); Thunderbird ('75 thru '82); MERCURY: Montego; Comet; Marquis ('83 thru '86); Cougar ('75 thru '82); LINCOLN: Versailles, all 4 cyl, in-line 6 cyl, V6 & V8 models '75 thru '80
*654 Mustang & Mercury Capri all in-line models & Turbo '79 thru '87
*558 Mustang & Mercury Capri all V6 & V8 models '79 thru '87
*1418 Tempo & Mercury Topaz all gasoline models '84 thru '87
357 Mustang V8 all models '65 thru '73
231 Mustang II all 4 cyl, V6 & V8 models '74 thru '78
204 Pinto all models '70 thru '74
649 Pinto & Mercury Bobcat '75 thru '80
*1026 Ranger & Bronco II all gasoline models '83 thru '86
*344 Vans all V8 Econoline models '69 thru '86

GENERAL MOTORS
*829 A-Cars — Chevrolet Celebrity, Buick Century, Pontiac 6000 & Oldsmobile Cutlass Ciera all models '82 thru 87
*766 J-Cars — Chevrolet Cavalier, Pontiac J-2000, Oldsmobile Firenza, Buick Skyhawk & Cadillac Cimarron all models '82 thru '87

GMC
Vans & Pick-ups — see CHEVROLET (420, 831, 345)

HONDA
138 360, 600 & Z Coupe all models '67 thru '75
351 Accord CVCC all models '76 thru '83
*1221 Accord all models '84 thru '85
160 Civic 1200 all models '73 thru '79
633 Civic 1300 & 1500 CVCC all models '80 thru '83
297 Civic 1500 CVCC all models '75 thru '79
*1227 Civic all models except 16-valve CRX & 4 WD Wagon '84 thru '86
*601 Prelude CVCC all models '79 thru '82

JAGUAR
098 MK I & II, 240 & 340 Sedans '55 thru '69
*242 XJ6 all 6 cyl models '68 thru '86
*478 XJ12 & XJS all 12 cyl models '72 thru '85
140 XK-E 3.8 & 4.2 all 6 cyl models '61 thru '72

JEEP
412 CJ all models '49 thru '86

LADA
*413 1200, 1300, 1500 & 1600 all models including Riva '74 thru '86

LANCIA
533 Lancia Beta Sedan, Coupe & HPE all models '76 thru '80

LAND ROVER
314 Series II, IIA, & III all 4 cyl gasoline models '58 thru '86
529 Diesel models '58 thru '80

MAZDA
648 626 Sedan & Coupe (rear-wheel drive) all models '79 thru '82
*1082 626 (front-wheel drive) all gas models '83 thru '87
*267 B1600, B1800 & B2000 Pick-ups '72 thru '84
370 GLC Hatchback (rear-wheel drive) all models '77 thru '83
757 GLC (front-wheel drive) all models '81 thru '85
109 RX2 all models '71 thru '75
096 RX3 all models '72 thru '76
460 RX-7 all models '79 thru '85

MERCEDES-BENZ
346 230, 250 & 280 Sedan, Coupe & Roadster all 6 cyl sohc models '68 thru '72
983 280 123 Series all gasoline models '77 thru '81
698 350 & 450 Sedan, Coupe & Roadster all models '71 thru '80
697 Diesel 123 Series 200D, 220D, 240D, 240TD, 300D, 300CD, 300TD, 4- & 5-cyl incl. Turbo '76 thru '85

MERCURY
See FORD listing

MG
475 MGA all models '56 thru '62
111 MGB Roadster & GT Coupe all models '62 thru '80
265 MG Midget & Austin Healey Sprite Roadster '58 thru '80

MITSUBISHI
Pick-up — see Dodge D-50 (556)

MORRIS
074 (Austin) Marina 1.8 all models '71 thru '75
024 Minor 1000 sedan & wagon '56 thru '71

NISSAN
*1137 300ZX all models '84 thru '86
*876 Pulsar all models '83 thru '86
*982 Sentra all models '82 thru '86
*981 Stanza all models '82 thru '86

OLDSMOBILE
*658 Cutlass all standard gasoline V6 & V8 models '74 thru '87
Cutlass Ciera — see GENERAL MOTORS A-Cars (829)
Firenza — see GENERAL MOTORS J-Cars (766)
Omega — see PONTIAC Phoenix & Omega (551)

OPEL
157 (Buick) Manta Coupe 1900 all models '70 thru '74

PEUGEOT
161 504 all gasoline models '68 thru '79
663 504 all diesel models '74 thru '83

PLYMOUTH
425 Arrow all models '76 thru '80
For other Plymouth models see DODGE listing

PONTIAC
T1000 — see CHEVROLET Chevette (449)
J-2000 — see GENERAL MOTORS J-Cars (766)

6000 — see GENERAL MOTORS A-Cars (829)
*1232 Fiero all models '84 thru '87
555 Firebird all V8 models except Turbo '70 thru '81
*867 Firebird all models '82 thru '87
551 Phoenix & Oldsmobile Omega all X-car models '80 thru '84

PORSCHE
*264 911 all Coupe & Targa models except Turbo '65 thru '85
239 914 all 4 cyl models '69 thru '76
397 924 all models including Turbo '76 thru '82
*1027 944 all models including Turbo '83 thru '86

RENAULT
141 5 Le Car all models '76 thru '83
079 8 & 10 all models with 58.4 cu in engines '62 thru '72
097 12 Saloon & Estate all models 1289 cc engines '70 thru '80
768 15 & 17 all models '73 thru '79
081 16 all models 89.7 cu in & 95.5 cu in engines '65 thru '72
598 18i & Sportwagon all models '81 thru '86
Alliance & Encore — see AMC (934)
984 Fuego all models '82 thru '85

ROVER
085 3500 & 3500S Sedan 215 cu in engines '68 thru '76
*365 3500 SDI V8 all models '76 thru '84

SAAB
198 95 & 96 V4 all models '66 thru '75
247 99 all models including Turbo '69 thru '80
*980 900 all models including Turbo '79 thru '85

SUBARU
237 1100, 1300, 1400 & 1600 all models '71 thru '79
*681 1600 & 1800 2WD & 4WD all models '80 thru '86

TOYOTA
150 Carina Sedan all models '71 thru '74
229 Celica ST, GT & liftback all models '71 thru '78
437 Celica all models '78 thru '81
*935 Celica all models except front-wheel drive and Supra '82 thru '85
680 Celica Supra all models '79 thru '81
1139 Celica Supra all models '82 thru '86
201 Corolla 1100, 1200 & 1600 all models '67 thru '74
361 Corolla all models '75 thru '79
*961 Corolla all models (rear wheel drive) '80 thru '82
*1025 Corolla all models (front wheel drive) 1984
*636 Corolla Tercel all models '80 thru '82
230 Corona & MK II all 4 cyl sohc models '69 thru '74
360 Corona all models '74 thru '82
*532 Cressida all models '78 thru '82
313 Land Cruiser all models '68 thru '82
200 MK II all 6 cyl models '72 thru '76
*1339 MR2 all models '85 thru '87
304 Pick-up all models '69 thru '78
*656 Pick-up all models '79 thru '85
787 Starlet all models '81 thru '84

TRIUMPH
112 GT6 & Vitesse all models '62 thru '74
113 Spitfire all models '62 thru '81
028 TR2, 3, 3A, 4 & 4A Roadsters '52 thru '67
031 TR250 & TR6 Roadsters '67 thru '76
322 TR7 all models '75 thru '81

VW
091 411 & 412 all 103 cu in models '68 thru '73
036 Bug 1200 all models '54 thru '66
039 Bug 1300 & 1500 '65 thru '70
159 Bug 1600 all basic, sport & super (curved windshield) models '70 thru '74
110 Bug 1600 Super all models (flat windshield) '70 thru '72
238 Dasher all gasoline models '74 thru '81
*884 Rabbit, Jetta, Scirocco, & Pick-up all gasoline models '74 thru '84 & Convertible '80 thru '85
451 Rabbit, Jetta & Pick-up all diesel models '77 thru '84
082 Transporter 1600 all models '68 thru '79
226 Transporter 1700, 1800 & 2000 all models '72 thru '79
084 Type 3 1500 & 1600 all models '63 thru '73
*1029 Vanagon all air-cooled models '80 thru '83

VOLVO
203 120, 130 Series & 1800 Sports '61 thru '73
129 140 Series all models '66 thru '74
244 164 all models '68 thru '75
*270 240 Series all models '74 thru '86
400 260 Series all models '75 thru '84

Over 100 Haynes motorcycle manuals also available

ABCDE FGHIJ KLMNO PQRST

* Listings shown with an asterisk (*) indicate model coverage as of this printing. These titles will be periodically updated to include later model years — consult your Haynes dealer for more information.

Haynes Publications Inc., P.O. Box 978, Newbury Park, CA 91320 • (818) 889-5400 • (805) 498-6703